Berlin-Brandenburgische Akademie der Wissenschaften

Texte und Untersuchungen
zur Geschichte der altchristlichen Literatur

Archiv für die Ausgabe der Griechischen Christlichen Schriftsteller
der ersten Jahrhunderte

(TU)

Begründet von
O. von Gebhardt und A. von Harnack
herausgegeben von
Christoph Markschies

Band 158

Das Evangelium nach Petrus

Text, Kontexte, Intertexte

Herausgegeben von

Thomas J. Kraus und Tobias Nicklas

Walter de Gruyter · Berlin · New York

Herausgegeben im Auftrag der Berlin-Brandenburgischen Akademie der Wissenschaften
von Christoph Markschies

∞ Gedruckt auf säurefreiem Papier,
das die US-ANSI-Norm über Haltbarkeit erfüllt.

ISBN 978-3-11-019313-8

Bibliografische Information Der Deutschen Bibliothek

Die Deutsche Bibliothek verzeichnet diese Publikation in der Deutschen Nationalbibliografie;
detaillierte bibliografische Daten sind im Internet über http://dnb.ddb.de abrufbar.

ISSN 0082-3589

Vorwort

Der vorliegende Band legt die Ergebnisse des zweiten Teils eines Projekts zu petrinischen Apokryphen vor, das bereits im Jahr 2001 seinen Anfang nahm. Herrn Prof. Dr. Christoph Markschies ist nicht nur dafür zu danken, dass er den vorliegenden Band in die Reihe *Texte und Untersuchungen zur Geschichte der altchristlichen Literatur* der Berlin-Brandenburgischen Akademie der Wissenschaften aufnahm, sondern dass er uns bereits vor Jahren die Möglichkeit gab, unsere damals noch recht vagen Ideen für ein Projekt zu Petrusevangelium und Petrusapokalypse zu verwirklichen. So erschien im Jahr 2004 in der Reihe *Die Griechischen christliche Schriftsteller der ersten Jahrhunderte* eine Neuedition der beiden genannten Texte. Der nun vorliegende Sammelband zum Petrusevangelium diskutiert die Entscheidungen der Edition weiter und stellt inhaltliche Fragen nach dem Verständnis dieses faszinierenden Apokryphons. Wir danken allen Autorinnen und Autoren des vorliegenden Bandes für ihre Bereitschaft zur Mitwirkung und (manchmal kontroversen) Diskussion, die das Interesse am Text hoffentlich weiter beleben wird.

Die Fertigstellung eines Buches hat aber natürlich auch ihre technische Seite. Herrn Dr. Albrecht Döhnert vom Verlag Walter de Gruyter ist für sein professionelles und dabei überaus freundliches, unermüdliches Engagement und seine kompetenten Hilfeleistungen zu danken. Auf mehrfache Weise hat sich auch Frau Dr. Michaela Hallermayer, Regensburg, um den vorliegenden Band verdient gemacht: Mit ihrem textkritisch geschulten Auge hat sie noch so manchen Fehler im Manuskript entdeckt, mit großer Geduld hat sie die Register erstellt. Dafür sei ihr herzlich gedankt.

Hilpoltstein und Nijmegen im März 2007
Thomas J. Kraus und Tobias Nicklas

Inhaltsverzeichnis

Das *Evangelium nach Petrus*: Text, Kontexte, Intertexte
Einführende Gedanken

von

THOMAS J. KRAUS UND TOBIAS NICKLAS

Im Winter 1886/87 förderte eine Grabungskampagne in einem Gräberfeld unweit des antiken, oberägyptischen Akhmîm (nach Plinius, *nat. hist.* 5.11.61 Panopolis) eine Sammelhandschrift zutage, die fortan als Akhmîm-Codex (P.Cair. 10759) firmierte. Von Urban Bouriant im Jahr 1892[1] publiziert, stießen die einzelnen Texte des Codex rasch auf reges Interesse. Während Bouriant selbst noch die neu entdeckten Abschnitte des griechischen Buches Henoch für den wohl spektakulärsten Teil des Fundes hielt, konzentrierte sich das Interesse mehr und mehr auf die beiden petrinischen Apokryphen, die der Sammel-Codex enthielt: Abschnitte, die aus guten Gründen der griechischen Offenbarung des Petrus zuzuordnen sind,[2] sowie ein Text, der aus der Perspektive des Petrus Passion und Auferstehung Jesu erzählt und deswegen als Teil desjenigen Petrusevangeliums identifiziert wurde, das *bis dato* nur durch patristische Hinweise und Verweise bekannt gewesen war.[3]

---

[1] Vgl. U. Bouriant, Fragments grecs du livre d'Énoch et de quelques écrits attribués à Saint Pierre, MMAF 9.1, Paris 1892, 93-147.

[2] Zur Problematik dieser Zuordnung vgl. allerdings T. Nicklas, Zwei petrinische Apokryphen im Akhmîm-Codex oder eines? Kritische Anmerkungen und Gedanken, in: Apocrypha 16, 2005, 75-96.

[3] Davon zeugen beispielhaft die zahlreichen Publikationen aus den Jahren 1892/93, wie etwa J.A. Robinson/M.R. James, The Gospel of Peter, and the Revelation of Peter. Two Lectures on the Newly Recovered Fragments Together with the Greek Texts, London 1892; A. Lods, L'Évangile et l'Apocalypse de Pierre avec texte grec du livre d'Henoch. Reproduction en héliogravure du manuscrit d'Énoch et des écrits attribués à Saint Pierre, MMAF 9.3, Paris 1893; O. von Gebhardt, Das Evangelium und die Apokalypse des Petrus. Die neuentdeckten Bruchstücke nach einer Photographie der Handschrift zu Gizeh in Lichtdruck herausgegeben, Leipzig 1893; A. Harnack, Bruchstücke des Evangeliums und der Apokalypse des Petrus, TU 9.2, Leipzig ²1893; H.B. Swete, The Apocryphal Gospel of Peter. The Greek Text of the Newly Discovered Fragment, London ²1893; idem, ΕΥΑΓΓΕΛΙΟΝ ΚΑΤΑ ΠΕΤΡΟΝ. The Akhmîm Fragment of the Apocryphal Gospel of Peter, London-New York 1893; H. von Schubert, Das Petrusevangelium. Synoptische Tabelle nebst Übersetzung und kritischem Apparat, Berlin 1893 = The Gospel of Peter. Synoptical Tables with Translation and Critical Apparatus, transl. J. MacPherson, Edinburgh 1893; J. Rendell Harris, A Popular Account of the Newly Recovered Gospel of St Peter, London 1893; T. Zahn, Das Evangelium des Petrus. Das kürzlich gefundene Fragment seines Textes, Erlangen-Leipzig 1893.

Nach einer ersten Phase intensiver Auseinandersetzung mit dem Text rückte das Petrusevangelium dann aber für lange Zeit eher in den Hintergrund des Forschungsinteresses. Wo man sich mit dem Text beschäftigte, drehte sich die Diskussion weitestgehend allein um die (sicherlich interessante) Frage nach seinem literarischen Verhältnis zu den kanonischen Evangelien. Erst die provokativen und kontrovers aufgenommenen Thesen von Helmut Koester und John Dominic Crossan zur Entstehung des Petrusevangeliums einerseits,[4] wie auch ein allgemein mehr und mehr erwachendes Interesse für apokryphe Texte andererseits[5] rückten das Petrusevangelium wieder stärker ins Zentrum der Diskussion: Manche Facette des Texts des Hauptzeugen des Petrusevangeliums (P.Cair. 10759) wurde in den vergangenen Jahren speziell beleuchtet. Zudem werden vor allem aufgrund von Initiativen Dieter Lührmanns weitere Handschriften als vermeintliche Textzeugen des Petrusevangeliums diskutiert.[6]

Im Jahr 2001 entschieden wir uns vor dem Hintergrund dieser beachtlichen Entwicklung für die Bearbeitung eines zweigeteilten Projekts:

1) In einer im Jahr 2004 erschienenen Sammeledition der als Textzeugen des Petrusevangeliums diskutierten griechischen Handschriften war es unser Ziel, die für die weitere wissenschaftliche Auseinandersetzung notwendige zuverlässige Textbasis zur Verfügung zu stellen und damit die wissenschaftliche Auseinandersetzung mit dem Petrusevangelium auf eine solide Basis zu stellen.[7]

2) Auf dem Hintergrund dieser Edition war es nun unser zweites Ziel, zumindest eine Reihe deutlich werdender Fragestellungen zur Interpretation und historischen Einordnung des Textes in einem zweiten Schritt zu

---

[4]   Vgl. besonders J.D. Crossan, The Cross That Spoke. The Origins of the Passion Narrative, San Francisco et al. 1988; H. Koester, Ancient Christian Gospels. Their History and Development, Philadelphia-London 1990, 216-240. Siehe auch den Beitrag von J.D. Crossan im vorliegenden Band.

[5]   Zum Paradigmenwechsel innerhalb der Erforschung christlicher Apokryphen in den vergangenen zwei Jahrzehnten vgl. T. Nicklas, »Écrits apocryphes chrétiens« Ein Sammelband als Spiegel eines weitreichenden Paradigmenwechsels in der Apokryphenforschung, VigChr 60, 2006 [im Druck].

[6]   D. Lührmann, POx 2979: EvPt 3-5 in einer Handschrift des 2./3. Jahrhunderts, ZNW 72, 1981, 216-226; idem, POx 4009: Ein neues Fragment des Petrusevangeliums?, NT 35, 1993, 390-410; idem, Fragmente apokryph gewordener Evangelien in griechischer und lateinischer Sprache, MThSt 59, Marburg 2000, 72-95.

[7]   Vgl. T.J. Kraus/T. Nicklas, Das Petrusevangelium und die Petrusapokalypse. Die griechischen Fragmente mit deutscher und englischer Übersetzung, GCS.NF 11, Neutestamentliche Apokryphen 1, Berlin-New York 2004, 7. Im Verlauf des 23. Internationalen Kongresses für Papyrologie der *Association Internationale de Papyrologues* (AIP) in Wien (22.-28.07.2001) kündigten wir noch die „Erstellung einer Motiv-Geschichte, letztlich der Verwendung von auch in PE anzutreffenden Motiven bei den Kirchenvätern in einer gesonderten Publikation" an. Vgl. T.J. Kraus/T. Nicklas, Entstehungsprozess einer kritischen Edition frühchristlicher Apokryphen. Das Beispiel ‚Petrusevangelium', PapCongr XXIII [im Druck], die durch die Integration von „Hinweise[n] auf ein PE in der antiken christlichen Literatur" in unserer Edition (siehe Inhaltsverzeichnis und 11-23) hinfällig wurde.

motivieren und anzugehen. Schnell wurde dabei klar, dass es sinnvoll wäre, die dafür notwendigen Spezialstudien auf eine breitere Basis zu stellen. Das Ergebnis dieser Überlegungen liegt in diesem Sammelband vor, der, wie wir hoffen, zumindest einige wichtige Aspekte des hochinteressanten apokryphen Textes „Petrusevangelium" zu beleuchten hilft.

Die strukturelle Ausrichtung und inhaltliche Gestaltung des Bandes richtet sich nach folgenden Vorüberlegungen.

1. Den Ausgangspunkt bildet ein Beitrag von Paul Foster, der derzeit selbst mit der Vorbereitung eines Kommentars zum Petrusevangelium beschäftigt ist, welcher in der neuen, von Christopher Tuckett und Andrew Gregory edierten Reihe *Oxford Early Christian Gospel Texts* erscheinen wird.[8] Foster legt nicht nur Aspekte der wissenschaftlichen Auseinandersetzung mit dem Petrusevangelium unmittelbar nach dem Fund des Akhmîm-Codex am Ende des 19. Jahrhunderts vor, er stellt auch die Frage, inwiefern die dabei entstandenen ersten Arbeiten die weitere Forschung am Text beeinflussten.

2. Die Edition des Jahres 2004 trifft auf zwei Ebenen Entscheidungen, deren nochmalige Diskussion uns wichtig erschien: Dieter Lührmann wird hier die Möglichkeit geboten, auf unsere Kritik an seinen Zuweisungen einiger Fragmente zum Petrusevangelium zu reagieren. In einem Appendix setzt er sich zudem mit einem Anfang 2006 erschienenen Aufsatz von Paul Foster auseinander, der, was die Zuweisung früher kleinerer Fragmente zum Petrusevangelium betrifft, noch skeptischer ist als wir.[9] Peter Van Minnen wiederum tritt als Papyrologe in Dialog mit unseren paläographischen Beschreibungen der Textzeugen; von diesem Ausgangspunkt stellt er weitergehende Fragen zur historischen Einordnung von Text und Textzeugen.

3. Mit der Sprache des im Akhmîm-Codex überlieferten Ausschnitts des Petrusevangeliums setzen sich die Beiträge von Thomas J. Kraus und Stanley E. Porter auseinander. Sie vertiefen damit auf zweierlei Ebenen die in der Edition von 2004 angeführten, auf Details der Übersetzung ausgerichteten philologischen Beobachtungen. Während Thomas J. Kraus Vorüberlegungen zu einer ausführlichen sprach- und stilanalytischen Untersuchung des Petrusevangeliums stellt und dabei in kritische Diskussion mit den bisher erschienenen Arbeiten von F. Weißengruber und J. Karavidopoulos tritt,[10] bietet Stanley E. Porter die bisher umfangreichste Untersuchung zur Syntax des Petrusevangeliums.

---

[8]   P. Foster, The Gospel of Peter, Oxford Early Christian Gospel Texts, Oxford 2007 [in Vorbereitung]. U.W. ist zudem auch ein Kommentar von B.D. Ehrman für die Reihe *Hermeneia* sowie ein einführender Band von M. Myllykoski für die *Stuttgarter Bibelstudien* in Vorbereitung – eine äußerst erfreuliche Entwicklung des Interesses an diesem apokryphen Text.

[9]   P. Foster, Are there any Early Fragments of the So-called Gospel of Peter?, NTS 52, 2006, 1-28.

[10]   J. Karavidopoulos, «Hapax legomena» et autres mots rares dans l'*Évangile Apocryphe de Pierre*, Apocrypha 8, 1977, 225-230; F. Weißengruber, Grammatische Untersuchungen zum Petrusevangelium, in: Das Petrusevangelium, SNTU.B 2, hg. von A. Fuchs, Freistadt 1978, 121-144; idem, Zur Datierung des Petrusevangeliums, ebd., 117-120.

4. Produktion wie Rezeption von Texten geschieht nie quasi im luftleeren Raum, Texte können nicht als vollkommen isolierte Größen quasi „insulär" erfasst werden, sie leben vielmehr aus ihren Kontexten[11] und Intertexten. Dabei kommen *grundsätzlich* zwei Paradigmata des Begriffes „Intertextualität" in Frage:

– Wo die Umstände der Produktion von Texten interessieren, wird nach den Beziehungen, die der Autor bzw. die Autoren des Textes mit dessen Produktion zu anderen Texten herstellte(n), gefragt. Die dabei deutlich werdenden literarischen Bezugnahmen können dazu beitragen, das Petrusevangelium als einen Teil (spät)antiker Literaturgeschichte einzuordnen.

– In vielen Fällen lässt sich nicht ohne Weiteres entscheiden, ob formale oder inhaltliche Gemeinsamkeiten von Texten auf tatsächliche, von Autoren, Redaktoren oder Tradenten gewollte Bezugnahmen zurückgehen. Auch diese Gemeinsamkeiten und Unterschiede können jedoch im Hinblick auf die Frage, welche Leseweisen ein Text zulässt, welche Möglichkeiten ihn zu verstehen es gibt, bedeutsam werden. In diesem Zusammenhang aber kann nicht mehr von einem diachron orientierten literaturgeschichtlichen Schema ausgegangen werden, der Text (oder nur einige seiner Motive, Charaktere oder Themen) wird in einem derartigen Paradigma dann eher in eine literarische „Landschaft" eingebettet.

Gerade das an zweiter Stelle genannte Intertextualitätsparadigma würde grundsätzlich erlauben, die literarische „Landschaft", in die sich das Petrusevangelium einbetten ließe, bis ins Unendliche, selbst bis in unsere Zeit hinein auszuweiten. Trotzdem erscheint es zumindest aus pragmatischen Gründen sinnvoll, das Spektrum der Untersuchung auf einige uns besonders wichtig erscheinende Bereiche einzuschränken:

4.1 Die intertextuellen Beziehungen zu biblischen, besonders neutestamentlichen Texten spielen in jedem Begriff von „Apokryphen" eine Rolle.[12] Auch wenn in diesem Bereich sicherlich schon viel geleistet worden ist, erschien es lohnend, noch einmal Beobachtungen zum intertextuellen Verhältnis zwischen Petrusevangelium und biblischen Texten anzustellen: Thomas Hieke argumentiert in seinem Beitrag von einem bewusst textzentriert-leserorientierten Paradigma aus. Er überlegt dabei, welche Rolle alttestamentliche Texte für eine angemessene Interpretation des Petrusevangeliums spielen können.

Die Frage nach dem literarischen Verhältnis zwischen Petrusevangelium und den kanonischen Evangelien ist sicherlich die in den letzten Jahren am meisten kontrovers diskutierte. Deswegen widmen sich ihr drei Studien, die gleichwohl auf verschiedenen Ebenen argumentieren: John Dominic Crossan schlägt noch einmal die Annahme vor, eine Quelle des Petrusevangeliums,

---

[11] Dabei sei berücksichtigt, dass auch historische Kontexte, in denen Texte entstanden sind, uns wiederum nur über Texte zugänglich werden.

[12] Hierzu auch die Gedanken bei T. Nicklas, Semiotik – Intertextualität – Apokryphität: Eine Annäherung an den Begriff „christlicher Apokryphen", Apocrypha 17, 2006 [im Druck].

Cross Gospel genannt, sei nicht nur älter als die kanonischen Texte, sondern habe diesen als Vorlage gedient. In diesem Zusammenhang geht Crossan auch kritisch auf andere „klassische" Lösungsversuche der Frage ein – genannt werden explizit F. Neirynck, R.E. Brown und H. Koester. Demgegenüber diskutiert Alan Kirk in Fortführung von Theorien Jan Assmanns zu einem „kulturellen Gedächtnis" Möglichkeiten, die über rein literarisch argumentierende Paradigmata hinausgehen. Judith Hartenstein wiederum wirft die Frage auf, welche Rolle das Petrusevangelium innerhalb der Geschichte der Gattung „Evangelium" spielt. In ihrer Argumentation, die auch das so genannte „Unbekannte Berliner Evangelium" mit einbezieht, stellt Hartenstein eine Brücke zu den Beiträgen der folgenden Gruppe her.

4.2 Natürlich muss der Kreis möglicher Intertexte weiter gefasst werden als nur die Texte der christlichen Bibel allein. Vor allem geht es auch um die Frage, auf welche Texte das Petrusevangelium möglicherweise gewirkt hat und welche Texte parallele oder vergleichbare Ideen zum Ausdruck bringen. Bewusst wird diesem Abschnitt ein sehr grundlegender Beitrag von Martin Meiser vorangestellt, der – die Übersichten von J. Denker u.a. weiterführend[13] – nicht nur mögliche Spuren der altkirchlichen Rezeption des Petrusevangeliums zusammenstellt, sondern sich auch mit der Frage auseinandersetzt, warum dieser Text offensichtlich so wenige greifbare Spuren hinterlassen hat. Nicht nur für die Frage nach der Datierung des Petrusevangeliums, sondern auch für das Problem seiner Profilierung sind Parallelen zu einigen Autoren des 2. Jahrhunderts von großer Bedeutung: Katharina Greschat wirft deswegen noch einmal die alte, gleichwohl nicht gelöste Frage nach dem Verhältnis zwischen Justin und dem Petrusevangelium auf, während Thomas R. Karmann Othmar Perlers These, die Paschahomilie des Melito von Sardes weise deutliche Spuren einer Kenntnis des Petrusevangeliums auf,[14] kritisch unter die Lupe nimmt. F. Stanley Jones findet Parallelen zwischen dem Petrusevangelium und der in den Pseudoclementinischen Rekognitionen 1,27-71 erkennbaren judenchristlichen Quelle, während István Czachesz das literarische Zueinander von Petrusevangelium und apokryphen Apostelakten untersucht. Tobias Nicklas schließlich erkennt zwar Parallelen zwischen den Passionstraditionen im Petrusevangelium und denen im VIII. Buch der Sibyllinischen Orakel – der genauere Vergleich aber weise weniger auf literarische Abhängigkeit beider Texte hin, sondern lasse deren literarisches wie theologisches Eigenprofil deutlich werden.

5. Die letzte Gruppe von Artikeln schließlich beschäftigt sich mit entscheidenden Themen des Petrusevangeliums und ihrer Funktion für das Verständnis des Textes. Joseph Verheydens grundlegender Beitrag stellt die

---

[13] Vgl. J. Denker, Die theologiegeschichtliche Stellung des Petrusevangeliums: Ein Beitrag zur Frühgeschichte des Doketismus, EHS XXIII.36, Bern-Frankfurt/Main 1975.

[14] Vgl. O. Perler, L'Évangile de Pierre et Méliton de Sardes, RB 71, 1964, 584-590. Wiederabgedruckt in: idem, Sapientia et Caritas. Gesammelte Aufsätze zum 90. Geburtstag (Par. 29), hg. v. D. Van Damme/O. Wermelinger/F. Nuvolone, Freiburg/Schw. 1990, 331-337.

Frage nach der Funktion und dem Eigenprofil des Textes. Er argumentiert, dass das Petrusevangelium als die popularisierende Neufassung einer Erzählung zu verstehen sei, die dem anvisierten Leserkreis bereits in anderen Versionen bekannt war. Dem Autor sei es nicht darauf angekommen, eine besonders durchdachte theologische Botschaft zu erzählen. Er habe die Geschichte von Passion und Auferstehung vielmehr in einer Weise wiedergegeben, die weniger an theologischer Lehre denn daran interessiert gewesen sei, die Denkwelt seiner Leser mit ihren Vorstellungen und Vorurteilen zu befriedigen. Während die Christologie des Petrusevangeliums vor allem in der älteren Literatur aufgrund des Urteils von Serapion von Antiochien (bei Eusebius von Caesarea, *h.e.* 6,21,1-6) als doketisch bezeichnet wurde, haben sich in den letzten Jahrzehnten mehr und mehr andere Vorstellungen durchgesetzt.[15] Matti Myllykoskis Beitrag beschreibt die Christologie des Petrusevangeliums – auch in Auseinandersetzung mit Ideen von P.M. Head oder J.W. McCant[16] – als adoptianistisch. Heike Omerzu wiederum zeigt, dass das Vorurteil, das Petrusevangelium verurteile einseitig die „Juden" und stelle die Römer in hellstem Licht dar, nicht zutrifft. Die Autorin macht vielmehr deutlich, welch differenziertes Bild des Pilatus der Text zeichnet. Der Band schließt mit einem Beitrag, für den Todd Penner und Caroline Vander Stichele gemeinsam verantwortlich zeichnen: Sie stellen die Frage nach den sozialen und kulturellen Ideologien, die möglicherweise hinter der Produktion des uns erhaltenen Petrusevangeliums standen. Dabei gehen sie einen sehr eigenen Weg – sie untersuchen, in welcher Weise im Text „Körper" dargestellt werden und inwiefern sich in diesen Darstellungen Ideologie „materialisiert".

Fazit

H.-J. Klauck hat einmal den Satz formuliert: „Das Verstehen eines Textes gelangt erst zu seinem Ziel, wenn der ganze Zirkel seiner Kontexte abgeschritten ist."[17] Der Weg wissenschaftlicher Exegese, dem Verstehen von wichtigen Texten näher zu kommen, kann vielleicht schon deswegen nie ganz abgeschlossen sein, weil uns große Teile des Mosaiks antiker und spätantiker Kontexte heute fehlen. Hinzu kommt ein weiteres Problem: Zu den Kontexten, die mit dem Verstehen von Texten zusammenhängen, gehören auch die sich ändernden „Kontexte", in denen Ausleger verschiedener Zeiten Texte inter-

---

[15] Eine wichtige Rolle dabei spielte auch der Aufsatz von N. Brox, „Doketismus" – eine Problemanzeige, ZKG 95, 1984, 301-314, in dem die Verwendung des Begriffs „Doketismus" auf eine neue wissenschaftliche Basis gestellt wurde.

[16] P.M. Head, On the Christology of the Gospel of Peter, VigChr 46, 1992, 209-224; J.W. McCant, The Gospel of Peter, Docetism Reconsidered, NTS 30, 1984, 258-273.

[17] H.-J. Klauck, Herrenmahl und hellenistischer Kult, NTA 15, Münster 1982, 4.

pretieren bzw. in denen sie versuchen, dem Text angemessene Leseweisen vorzuschlagen. Auch wissenschaftliche Exegese wird diese Kontexte nie ganz ausblenden können (und wollen). So kann der vorliegende Band sicherlich keine abschließenden Antworten auf die Fragen, die das Petrusevangelium uns stellt, bieten – wir hoffen aber, dass die hier vorgelegten Ansichten und Einsichten wichtige Impulse für die weitere Beschäftigung mit einem derart interessanten christlich-antiken Text wie dem apokryphen Petrusevangelium bieten.

The Discovery and Initial Reaction to the So-called Gospel of Peter

by

PAUL FOSTER

1. Introduction

French imperial aspirations at the end of the eighteenth century were envisioned on such a scale that the geographical boundaries of Europe proved to be too confining a limit. Like the Romans before them, the French forces under the leadership of Napoleon turned their sights southward to the ancient and exotic land of Egypt. Thus French aggression was re-directed from consideration of an invasion across the channel, or the possibility of an expedition in support of the Irish rebellions. Instead, in May 1798, 35 000 military personnel were embarked at Toulon in preparation for an invasion of Egypt.[1] The objectives were not solely military. This is demonstrated by the fact that the French contingent included a corps of approximately 175 scholars, including archaeologists, as well as a large library containing a copy of virtually every book available in France on Egypt.[2] Events moved quickly. *En route* Malta was captured, the fleet landed at Alexandria in July and that city and Cairo were soon taken.[3] This initial rapid success proved to be short lived. The French fleet was destroyed at Aboukir bay, in the battle of the Nile.[4] Crawley's assessment of the outcome finds no fault with Napoleon or his admirals. He states, 'neither Napoleon nor his admirals can be blamed for this

---

[1] G. Bruun, The Balance of Power during the War Years, 1793-1814, in: The New Cambridge Modern History 9. War and Peace in an Age of Upheaval 1793-1830, ed. by C.W. Crawley, Cambridge 1965, 250-274, esp. 256.

[2] See: http://www.touregypt.net/featurestories/travel3.htm (24th February, 2005).

[3] C.W. Crawley, The Near East and the Ottoman Empire, 1798-1830, in: The New Cambridge Modern History 9. War and Peace in an Age of Upheaval 1793-1830, ed. by idem, Cambridge 1965, 525-550, esp. 530.

[4] For an assessment of the impact of the Battle of the Nile on the French Naval forces see N.A.M. Rodger, The Command of the Oceans. A Naval History of Britain, 1649-1815, London 2004, 459-460. For a detailed account of the battle and Nelson's leadership see G. Bennett, Nelson the Commander, London ²2002 (1972), 119-141. See also E. Vincent, Nelson. Love and Fame, Yale 2003, 259-273.

defeat, which was due to the ill-preparation state of the navy and to the initial luck and the bold genius of Nelson.'[5]

French aggression galvanised the previously disparate forces of Russia, England and Turkey into a coalition aimed at protecting their respective interests in the Levant. Significantly, '[t]he destruction of the fleet at Abuqir meant isolation from France and from any hope of reinforcement.'[6] Under such conditions French occupation of Egypt was destined to be short-lived, at least in the immediate future, but interest in that ancient African culture and its antiquities had been whetted and the French would return both for trade and scientific purposes when a more stable political climate dominated the European powers.

Four decades later, Egypt was again to become the corridor in which European political posturing would be played out. During the Near Eastern Crisis of 1839-40, there was a marked shift in the alignment of political powers. France sided with Mehemet Ali and his bid for independence from the Ottoman empire. British, Russian, Austrian and Prussian forces aligned with the Turks under the leadership of Sultan Mahmud.[7] Although settlement was reached through negotiation, the French had solidified their popularity in Egypt through this initial backing of Mehemet Ali. This typified the growing relationship between France and Egypt, which was only in part checked by the British occupation in Egypt in 1882. Thus, as Crawley astutely observes,

> The influence of France in the Levant, though often politically unpredictable, was strong and constant in sentiment and culture, based in Egypt on the impress of Napoleon and everywhere else on more traditional links. The French influence in these fields remained stronger on the whole than the British influence; yet it was far less radically different from the British than was that of Russia.[8]

It was towards the end of this period of French political favoured status that the *Mission archéologique française au Caire* was established. This *Mission* was founded in 1881 by the French Government as a school of archaeology, but also for the purpose of research and publication of the findings from excavations.[9] Although the British occupation of Egypt limited the political relationship between Cairo and Paris, the French maintained a significant presence. The

---

5   Crawley, The Near East and the Ottoman Empire, 1798-1830, 531.

6   D. Dykstra, The French Occupation of Egypt, 1798-1801, in: The Cambridge History of Egypt 2. Modern Egypt. From 1517 to the End of the Twentieth Century, ed. by M.W. Daly, Cambridge 1998, 113-138, esp. 122.

7   G. Craig, The System of Alliances and the Balance of Power, in: The New Cambridge Modern History 10. The Zenith of European Power 1830-1870, ed. by J.T.P. Bury, Cambridge 1960, 246-273, esp. 254-258.

8   C.W. Crawley, The Mediterranean, in: The New Cambridge Modern History 10. The Zenith of European Power 1830-1870, ed. by J.T.P. Bury, Cambridge 1960, 416-441, esp. 430.

9   The *Mission archéologique française au Caire* 'was re-organized in 1901 on a lavish scale under the title *Institut français d'archéologie orientale du Caire*, and domiciled with printing-press and library in a fine building near the museum.' See: http://encyclopedia.jrank.org/AUD_BAI/AUTHORITILS.html (24th February, 2005).

Mission archéologique française au Caire continued its scientific studies of the artefactual and literary remains of ancient Egyptian civilisations. The fruits of the *Mission's* findings were made accessible to the scholarly world through its own publication series known as *Mémoires publié par les membres de la Mission archéologique française au Caire*. The first part of the first *tome*, which contained miscellaneous articles on Egyptian, Coptic and Arabic archaeology and antiquities, appeared under the direction of Gaston Maspero in 1884, with the fourth and final part of the first *tome* being published in 1889.[10]

2. The Publication of the *Editio Princeps* of the Gospel of Peter

It has often been suggested that the editor of the *editio princeps* of the Gospel of Peter failed to realise the significance of the first text contained in the codex discovered in the grave in Akhmîm. This conclusion is based upon the five to six year gap between discovery during the winter season dig of 1886-87 and the publication of a transcription of the codex in 1892. Rendell Harris is perhaps the most fulsome exponent of this point of view. He states,

> It is curious that the publication of this great discovery should have been so long delayed; the documents seem to have been found as far back as the winter of 1886-87, and there was certainly no need for five years' delay. But the reason of it is not far to seek. The French scholars, with some noble exceptions, are no longer interested in Biblical and Patristic criticism; and it is evident that they did not, at first, realise what they had found.[11]

Harris, however, was not alone in this view. Robinson, describing the discovery of the Gospel of Peter by the French Archaeological Mission at Cairo refers to 'its somewhat tardy publication.'[12] This perspective is best resisted for a number of reasons. First, this suggestion is made by those with an interest in the area of New Testament studies or Christian origins rather than recognizing that the interests of the members of the *Mission archéologique française* was broader, encompassing all aspects of the material and literary cultures of Ancient Egypt. Second, even among the four texts contained in the Akhmîm codex, Bouriant appears to have considered the fragments of *1 Enoch* to be the most significant find. In part this was due to more extensive nature of the two fragments of *1 Enoch*, but this was not the only consideration. As Bouriant states,

---

[10]   G. Maspero, ed., Mémoires publiés par les membres de la Mission archéologique française au Caire, tome 1, 4 vols. pp. 787 + plates, Paris 1884-1889.

[11]   J. Rendell Harris, A Popular Account of the Newly Recovered Gospel of St Peter, London 1893, 17-18.

[12]   J.A. Robinson/M.R. James, The Gospel according to Peter, and the Revelation of Peter. Two Lectures on the Newly Recovered Fragments together with the Greek Texts, London 1892, 15.

Les petits fragments que je viens de mentionner (Évangile et Apocalypse de Saint-Pierre, Évangile canonique) seront publiés en temps et lieu. L'importance de livre d'Énoch dont le texte grec n'est connu que par de courts passages reportés dans Cédrénus et le Syncelle, est telle que je me suis décidé à commencer par lui la publication du manuscrit.[13]

Third, the wealth of material was a constraint to the speed at which individual items were published and this problem was not only experienced in relation to the codex discovered at Akhmîm.[14] Fourth, in the *editio princeps* the first text is cautiously identified by Bouriant as possibly being the Gospel of Peter. Although one cannot be certain when during the period 1886-87 to 1892 this identification was made, or by whom, there is no reason to suspect that there was either delay or hesitation on the part of Bouriant in recognizing the text as potentially being an exemplar of the Gospel of Peter, which hitherto had only been known by title or references in various Patristic witnesses. Fifth, Bouriant concludes his comments by supplying place and date details 'Le Caire, novembre 1891.'[15] This, perhaps, slightly reduces the perceived gap between discovery and preparation of the initial publication of the text. During this period Bouriant was involved with further winter season digs and publications.[16] Thus the gap between discovery and publication should not be taken as a failure on the part of the editors to perceive the potential significance of the text.

The circumstances surrounding the discovery of the codex are related in extremely compressed form in the *editio princeps*. The winter season dig of 1886-87 was conducted under the leadership of Eugene Grébaut. This dig resulted in the finding of not one, but two ancient manuscripts. The other manuscript, published by Baillet in the same volume of *Mémoires publié par les membres de la Mission archéologique française au Caire*, contained problems of an arithmetical and geometrical nature.[17] The remainder of the first part of tome

---

[13]   U. Bouriant, Fragments du texte grec du livre d'Énoch et de quelques écrits attribués à saint Pierre, in: Mémoires publiés par les membres de la Mission archéologique française au Caire 9.1, Paris 1892, 94.

[14]   Publication under the series title *Mémoires publiés par les membres de la Mission archéologique française au Caire* continued until the appearance of tome 19 part 1 in 1894. After this the series and *Mission archéologique française au Caire* changed their names. The series became known as *Mémoires publiés par les membres de l'Institut français d'archéologie orientale du Caire*, and the next volume was published as number 52 in that series. This was to remove confusion between volume and part numbers. *L'Institut français d'archéologie orientale* continues to publish volumes in this series under the abbreviation *MIFAO*. According to their website the most recent volume in this series was published in 2002. See http://www.ifao.egnet.net/.

[15]   Bouriant, Fragments du texte grec du livre d'Énoch et de quelques écrits attribués à saint Pierre, 147.

[16]   This is demonstrated by looking at his contributions to other volumes in the series *Mémoires publiés par les membres de la Mission archéologique française au Caire* especially for the period 1892-1894. During this period Bouriant contributed at least half a dozen articles to various volumes in this series.

[17]   J. Baillet, Le papyrus mathématique d' Akhmîm, in: Mémoires publiés par les membres de la Mission archéologique française au Caire 9.1, Paris 1892, 1-90.

nine was devoted to the publication of what Bouriant describes as '[c]e dernier manuscrit' and occupied pages 93-147.[18] Thus, if order of presentation is of significance, not only did Bouriant consider the text of *1 Enoch* of greater significance than that of the other three fragmentary texts,[19] but the placement of the mathematical manuscript before the codex edited by Bouriant may indicate that this was considered to be the more spectacular find. Bouriant used two independent indicators to date the codex. The first of these was based upon a palaeographical analysis of the four texts contained in the codex. On this basis he concluded that 'Seules, les particularités qu'on relève dans l'écriture ou dans la langue elle-même, peuvent nous mettre sur la voie, et montrent que le manuscrit n'est pas antérieur au VIIIe siècle ni postérieur au XIIe.'[20] In conjunction with this eighth to twelfth century date range, Bouriant marshals the location of discovery to corroborate this dating. He notes that the Christian cemetery at Akhmîm located upon a hill serves as a datum for determining the period of interment of the corpses. The graves range in date between the fifth and fifteenth centuries with the earliest being found at the foot of the hill that at its summit attains a height of 700 metres. The location of the grave containing the codex is described by Bouriant in the following manner: 'Le tombeau du propriétaire du manuscrit se trouve à environ 200 métres de la colline dans la direction nord-est.'[21] While Bouriant acknowledges that this method cannot give an exact dating, nonetheless, he sees this as aligning with the dating suggested by palaeographical analysis.

Bouriant's introductory comments to both the Gospel and Apocalypse of Peter are far briefer than those given for the fragments of *1 Enoch*. He draws a comparison between the Gospel of Peter and *1 Enoch* noting that both share a cursive style of handwriting, but the former has the more correct orthography.[22] He makes the following two further observations in his description. 'Le premier d'entre eux nous présente un récit de la Passion du Christ qui, comme nous l'apprend la dernière phrase, forme un épisode détaché de l'évangile apocryphe de saint Pierre … Cet évangile n'a jusqu'à présent, à ma connaissance au moins, été signalé nulle part.'[23] Thus, the initial

---

[18] Bouriant, Fragments du texte grec du livre d'Énoch et de quelques écrits attribués à saint Pierre, 93.

[19] This may be further suggested by the observation that the heading Bouriant gives to his publication on page 93 is 'Fragments du texte grec du livre d'Énoch', an abbreviated form of the description provided at the beginning of the volume. Moreover, this heading is used as a header on the odd numbered pages including those where the other three documents are discussed.

[20] Bouriant, Fragments du texte grec du livre d'Énoch et de quelques écrits attribués à saint Pierre, 93.

[21] Bouriant, Fragments du texte grec du livre d'Énoch et de quelques écrits attribués à saint Pierre, 93.

[22] Bouriant, Fragments du texte grec du livre d'Énoch et de quelques écrits attribués à saint Pierre, 137.

[23] Bouriant, Fragments du texte grec du livre d'Énoch et de quelques écrits attribués à saint Pierre, 137.

publication of this text contemplated no other possibility than identifying the first fragment as being a detached episode from the previously non-extant apocryphal Gospel of Peter. This point of view, introduced by Bouriant, has been virtually unrivalled in subsequent scholarship.

3. The Reception of the Gospel of Peter in England

The text of the so-called Gospel of Peter is first referenced in England on the 17th of November 1892. Robinson and James give the following account in the preface to their volume. 'The Lecture on the "Gospel according to Peter" was given in the Hall of Christ's College on the 20th of November, three days after the text was first seen in Cambridge, in response to a general desire for information as to the new discovery.'[24] Although not with the same degree of specificity, this is corroborated by the opening comment in Swete's text: 'At the end of November, 1892, shortly after the appearance of M. Bouriant's *editio princeps* …'.[25] Thus in England, Cambridge was the centre of dissemination of the text known as the Gospel of Peter. Besides the works of Robinson and Swete, a third scholar from that University was active in publishing a work treating the recent discovery of the text from Akhmîm. As its title suggests Rendell Harris provided a popular account of the discovery and significance of the text with an accompanying English language translation, but no Greek text.[26]

i. Henry Barclay Swete

Swete was the most prolific among the Cambridge trio in his work upon this text. He produced three works dealing exclusively with the Gospel of Peter, each of which was an expansion on its predecessor. The first appeared towards the end of 1892: this was an edition of the Greek text 'published', apparently privately, for use by his students.[27] Copies of this initial work are not available in the Copyright Libraries of the United Kingdom, or in the collection of Swete's private papers maintained at Gonville and Caius, where he was a Fellow.[28] This pamphlet was reprinted in early 1893, incorporating a number of corrections to the text. As Swete describes the pamphlet,

---

[24] Robinson/James, The Gospel according to Peter, and the Revelation of Peter, 7.

[25] H.B. Swete, The Akhmîm Fragment of the Apocryphal Gospel of St Peter, London 1893, v.

[26] J. Rendell Harris, A Popular Account of the Newly Recovered Gospel of St Peter, London 1893.

[27] In his preface to *The Akhmîm Fragment of the Apocryphal Gospel of St Peter*, Swete makes mention of this work. 'At the end of November 1892 … I published for the use of students a tentatively corrected text of the newly discovered fragment of the Petrine Gospel' (v).

[28] Thanks are to be expressed to the librarians of Gonville and Caius for searching through the archive and verifying that a copy of this work is not held in their collection.

This reprint was issued again in February, 1893, with some corrections obtained from the MS through the kindness of the late Professor Bensly, whose recent death has brought upon all studies of this kind a loss which is impossible to estimate.[29]

This pamphlet consists primarily of two parts: an introduction collecting Patristic references to a Gospel of Peter, and the Greek text of the first writing in the Akhmîm codex. It appeared under the title, *The Apocryphal Gospel of St. Peter, the Greek Text of the Newly Discovered Fragment*.[30]

The next contribution Swete made was to be his most enduring and comprehensive piece of scholarship on the Akhmîm fragment. His book length monograph, dated 'May 1893', consisted of thirty-eight pages of introductory material and thirty-four pages of textual analysis. The first section covered twelve issues under the following titles: (i) Petrine writings; (ii) Relation of the fragment to the Canonical Gospels; (iii) Use of a harmony; (iv) Chronology of the Passion; (v) Allusions to the Old Testament; (vi) References to the fragment in Church-writers; (vii) Comparison with other *apocrypha*; (viii) Doctrinal tendencies of the fragment; (ix) Literary character; (x) Place of origin and approximate date; (xi) Description of the MS.; and its probable age; (xii) Literature of the Petrine Gospel.[31] These introductory questions addressed by Swete became agenda setting for subsequent scholarship. Swete was in no doubt that the first text fragment discovered in the codex from Akhmîm was part of the text mentioned by the two Patristic authors he cites,[32] most notably Eusebius[33] but also a fleeting reference by Origin.[34] Swete asserted that '[t]here is no reason to doubt that the Akhmîm fragment was rightly assigned by M. Bouriant to the lost Gospel of Peter.'[35] Swete provides eight overlapping reasons for making such an identification, although not all can be said to be compelling. First, on internal evidence the text claims to be a personal account of Peter. Second, it appears to have been part of a complete gospel and not just a Passion account. Third, its tendency aligns with Serapion's account. Next Swete lists what he considers to be three docetic features; fourth, Jesus is addressed as ὁ κύριος or ὁ υἱὸς τοῦ θεοῦ; fifth, he is crucified without suffering pain; sixth, the resurrected body assumes supernatural proportions. Two further arguments are added. Seventh, the narrative is generally orthodox, which aligns with Serapion's initial assessment. Finally eighth, on internal evidence it should be dated to the second century.[36] Thus, although Swete

---

[29]   Swete, The Akhmîm Fragment of the Apocryphal Gospel of St Peter, v.

[30]   H.B. Swete, The Apocryphal Gospel of St. Peter, the Greek Text of the Newly Discovered Fragment, London 1893.

[31]   Swete, The Akhmîm Fragment of the Apocryphal Gospel of St Peter, see the table of contents, vii.

[32]   See the discussion in Swete, The Akhmîm Fragment of the Apocryphal Gospel of St Peter, ix-xii.

[33]   Eusebius, *h.e.* iii 3,1-3 and vi 12,1-6.

[34]   Origen, *comm. in Mt.* x 17.

[35]   Swete, The Akhmîm Fragment of the Apocryphal Gospel of St Peter, xii.

[36]   Swete, The Akhmîm Fragment of the Apocryphal Gospel of St Peter, xii-xiii.

acknowledges that Eusebius alone knows of six different texts that circulated in Peter's name,[37] this does not cause him to consider the possibility that more than one gospel-like text may have been associated with that apostolic figure. In part, this was due to the docetic features that Swete identified in the text. However, it might reasonably be asked whether these features would have been identified as particularly docetic if one were not already convinced of the identity of the text and thus sought to make it conform to Serapion's description.[38]

Swete's second section of his monograph consisted of three aspects: (i) an edition of the text with brief textual and exegetical notes under the passage to which they were referring;[39] (ii) an English translation of the text;[40] and (iii) two indices, referencing the Greek words in the fragment[41] and a subject index.[42] The brief notes often make highly significant and salient points, and this short treatment covering only twenty-four pages still remains the nearest approximation to a commentary on the text in the English language.

The appearance of Swete's monograph did not entirely signal the end of his work on the Gospel of Peter. More than a decade after the publication of his landmark volume, he presented 'a lecture to the ladies assembled for Biblical study at Newnham College, Cambridge, on 5th August, 1907.'[43] The lecture was subsequently published under the title 'The Gospels in the Second Century', in *The Interpreter* later in the same year. Although this article tends not to be referenced in the literature on the Gospel of Peter, Swete makes numerous references to the Akhmîm text. While some of these comments reiterate thoughts in his earlier printed works, he also provides a number of new reflections on the text. He sees the first document in the Akhmîm codex as an example of a type of Gospel which 'was directly antagonistic to the Gospels of the Church, although largely based upon them. Such was the docetic Gospel of Peter.'[44] Furthermore, and in contradistinction from Harnack,[45] Swete argued that the Akhmîm text was not directly dependent on the works of Justin Martyr. His statements about the relationship between Justin and the Gospel of Peter were couched in far more tentative terms in his earlier work.[46] Thus, while Swete's major work on the Akhmîm fragment was completed in 1893, less than six months after the text first appeared in Cambridge, he continued to

---

37 Swete, The Akhmîm Fragment of the Apocryphal Gospel of St Peter, ix.
38 Swete, The Akhmîm Fragment of the Apocryphal Gospel of St Peter, xxxvii-xliii.
39 Swete, The Akhmîm Fragment of the Apocryphal Gospel of St Peter, 1-24.
40 Swete, The Akhmîm Fragment of the Apocryphal Gospel of St Peter, 25-28.
41 Swete, The Akhmîm Fragment of the Apocryphal Gospel of St Peter, 29-32.
42 Swete, The Akhmîm Fragment of the Apocryphal Gospel of St Peter, 33-34.
43 H.B. Swete, The Gospels in the Second Century, The Interpreter 4, 1907, 138-155.
44 Swete, The Gospels in the Second Century, 139.
45 A. Harnack, Bruchstücke des Evangeliums und der Apokalypse des Petrus, TU 9.2, Leipzig 1893.
46 Swete, The Akhmîm Fragment of the Apocryphal Gospel of St Peter, xxxiii-xxxv.

interact with the text and publish fresh ideas about its relationship to the Canonical Gospels and the writings of Justin as late as 1907.

ii. J. Armitage Robinson

Perhaps the first public lecture to be given to the topic of the Gospel of Peter in England after the publication of Bouriant's *editio princeps* must be attributed to Armitage Robinson. Later as Dean of Westminster Abbey, Robinson was noted for his eccentricity and autocratic leadership.[47] However, his alacrity in publishing the text of this initial lecture is to be noted. The lecture given at Christ's College on the 20th of November 1892, just three days after the text was seen in Cambridge, was apparently followed only ten days later by the publication of a handsome hardback pocket sized edition of the lecture and the Greek text of the Gospel of Peter. The volume also encompassed a similar treatment of the second text in the Akhmîm codex, the Revelation of Peter. Robinson, in his preface dated the 1st of December 1892, expresses his gratitude to the production team at the University Press for their efficiency.

> For the rapidity with which this book has been published, without (we would fain believe) any consequent loss of accuracy in the printing, our thanks are due to the officers and workmen of the University Press.[48]

The preface also attests the death of F.J.A. Hort, the Lady Margaret's Reader in Divinity at the University of Cambridge. Hort's death occurred on the 30th of November 1892.[49] This chain of events establishes the speed at which the publication of the volume took place. Less than two weeks after the appearance of Bouriant's *editio princeps* Robinson and James had presented public lectures on the Gospel and Apocalypse of Peter respectively, sent their manuscripts to the University Publishers, received and checked the proofs, appended a short note in the preface referencing Hort's death, and had sent the proofs back to the press for printing. As the book appears with a publication date of 1892, it is to be assumed that the printing occurred equally rapidly, being completed at most within a month of the writing of the preface.

The treatment of the Gospel of Peter falls into a number of sections. Although not divided under separate heads, Robinson initially discussed introductory issues such as Eusebius' record of Serapion's reaction to the Gospel of Peter, and the nature of Doceticism.[50] The major component of the lecture consists of an English translation of the text, divided into fourteen

---

47 T. Beeson, The Deans. Cathedral Life, Yesterday, Today and Tomorrow, London 2004.
48 Robinson/James, The Gospel according to Peter, and the Revelation of Peter, 8.
49 Robinson/James comment that 'This little book was finally corrected for the press when we heard that he, whose latest message to us was permission to dedicate it to him, had gone to his rest.' See idem, The Gospel according to Peter, and the Revelation of Peter, 8.
50 Robinson/James, The Gospel according to Peter, and the Revelation of Peter, 13-16.

chapters, with brief comments following each chapter of text.[51] Two observations need to be made. First, although the English text is divided into fourteen chapters the numbering goes astray at the end, with the final two chapters both being numbered as 'thirteen'.[52] However, if one looks at the numbering system with the Greek text presented at the rear of the volume, the fourteen chapters are correctly numbered.[53] Second, Robinson's 'comments' are perhaps best described as observations on the text, rather than presenting detailed commentary or philological notes of the type offered by Swete. These observations appear to have two central functions: to draw attention to any intertextual links with canonical gospels, apocryphal texts, or Patristic writings; and, to highlight perceived docetic features in the text. In respect to this last point, Robinson felt that this was exemplified at a number of points. These included the common arguments that the references to 'He held his peace as having no pain' (G.Pet. 4,10) and the cry of dereliction transformed into a description of power leaving the crucified Christ are obvious examples of docetic doctrine. In relation to this second example Robinson argues,

> 'The power' then, so often emphasised in S. Luke's Gospel in connection with the person of our Lord, is here, by a strange perversion of our Lord's quotation from Ps. xxii. I, described as forsaking Him: the Divine Christ is 'taken up,' the Human Christ remains upon the Cross. ... We are thus confirmed in the belief that this was the Gospel, as Serapion tells us, of the *Docetae*.[54]

To this Robinson added one further observation not widely taken up by subsequent commentators. He notes that the Gospel of Peter omits the words 'I thirst' from the crucifixion narrative. Robinson states, 'If there is one word in the Canonical narratives of the Passion that is calculated to set our minds at rest on the question of whether our Blessed Lord truly felt the pain of Crucifixion, it is the word from the Cross, 'I thirst.'[55] Thus, this omitted detail is deemed highly significant in determining the docetic character of the text from Akhmîm, and this strengthens the equation that identifies this text with the Gospel of Peter depicted by Eusebius' narration of Serapion and his assessment of the Gospel in use at Rhossos. Obviously there is a certain circularity in this argument, and in many ways Robinson and his contemporaries found precisely that for which they were searching. This, however, is not to open the question of docetic tendencies in the Akhmîm text, rather it illustrates that for Robinson the 'discovery' of such tendencies was a primary task in his comments on the text.

In the final part of this published lecture Robinson drew together a number of conclusions. First, that the discovery, like many contemporary discoveries, resulted in a text which was not unknown, rather it had previously been non-

---

[51] This section of translation and commentary occupies pages 16-30.
[52] The two paragraphs numbered 'thirteen' are to be found on pages 28 and 29 respectively.
[53] The Greek text is presented on pages 83-88.
[54] Robinson/James, The Gospel according to Peter, and the Revelation of Peter, 21.
[55] Robinson/James, The Gospel according to Peter, and the Revelation of Peter, 20.

extant.[56] Second, the Gospel of Peter is an example of *Tendenzschriften*, whereby the perspectives of the canonical gospels are 'wilfully perverted and displaced' to advance docetic doctrines.[57] By contrast, one is able 'to return to the Four Gospels with a sense of relief at his escape from a stifling prison of prejudice into the transparent and the bracing atmosphere of pure simplicity and undesigning candour.'[58] It is fully apparent that Bauer's critique of the belief in a bedrock of orthodoxy which only subsequently was distorted by heresy needed to be heard.[59] Third, Robinson tentatively suggested that the dating of the Gospel of Peter 'may be nearer to the beginning than to the middle of the second century.'[60] Fourth, the author of the Gospel of Peter is acquainted with all four canonical accounts, but 'uses and misuses each in turn.'[61] It is striking to note the degree to which the rhetoric of these conclusions is shaped by a belief in the pristine, tendency-free nature of the canonical gospels. At every turn their superiority is asserted in comparison to their non-canonical counterpart from Akhmîm. The final contribution made by Robinson in this volume was an edition of the Greek text, with marginal references to parallels in the canonical gospels (and one reference to 1 Pet 3,19), along with a list of possible variant readings of the text at the foot of the page. It appears this list of variants was based on possible corrections to Bouriant's transcription, yet without reference to any images of the manuscript since this was not available in late 1892.

iii. J. Rendell Harris

Although the volume published by Harris is entitled *A Popular Account*[62] and contains no Greek text, it would be a mistake to underestimate his contribution to the early study of the text. Not only does his book contain important insights in its own right, but more significantly his textual work is evidenced by other scholars. In his preface Swete writes, 'To Mr J. Rendell Harris, Reader in Palaeography at Cambridge, I owe not only many valuable suggestions during the progress of my book, but much kind assistance in the final correction of the proofs.'[63] In a similar vein, at one point, Robinson explicitly acknowledges Harris' contribution in suggesting an emendation to the text.[64] Subsequently

---

56 Robinson/James, The Gospel according to Peter, and the Revelation of Peter, 30.
57 Robinson/James, The Gospel according to Peter, and the Revelation of Peter, 31.
58 Robinson/James, The Gospel according to Peter, and the Revelation of Peter, 32.
59 W. Bauer, Rechtgläubigkeit und Ketzerei im ältesten Christentum, Tübingen 1934.
60 Robinson/James, The Gospel according to Peter, and the Revelation of Peter, 32.
61 Robinson/James, The Gospel according to Peter, and the Revelation of Peter, 33.
62 The full title of the work is 'A Popular Account of the Newly Recovered Gospel of St Peter'.
63 Swete, The Akhmîm Fragment of the Apocryphal Gospel of St Peter, vi.
64 Robinson/James, The Gospel according to Peter, and the Revelation of Peter, 17 n. 1.

the emendation could be seen to be correct when images of the text became available.

However, Harris is best known for the volume that sought to make the contents of the first document in the Akhmîm codex accessible to a wider audience. Although the book has the appearance of being quite substantial, it should be noted that the paper is thick and that even on its ninety-seven pages of description, the margins are large and the space between lines is generous.[65] In fact the contents could have easily been contained in pamphlet instead of the impressive looking hardback edition produced by the publishers.

The book contains seven chapters of varying length and relevance to the Gospel of Peter. The first chapter describes a number of then recent manuscript discoveries as background to the find at Akhmîm. The next chapter then outlines the discovery by the French Archaeological Mission, and includes Harris' exasperated question, 'Is there any English Archaeological Mission in Egypt? and if not, why not?'[66] It seems to be the case that he is only aware of three texts in the codex, and has overlooked Bouriant's description of the 'actes de saint Julien' which is written in uncial script on the inside flyleaf pasted to the rear board of the codex.[67] Next, an introductory outline to Doceticism is provided in chapter three, with alleged tendencies of this 'heresy' in the Akhmîm text.[68] Then follows the English translation with marginal references to canonical passages.[69] Chapters five and six investigate respectively canonical[70] and non-canonical sources[71] behind the text. In relation to non-canonical texts, Harris discusses parallels between the Akhmîm text and the *Diatessaron* as well as the writings of Justin Martyr as a potential source. In relation to the *Diatessaron*, although acknowledging that further research is necessary, Harris leans towards the conclusion that Tatian's harmony is a source for the Gospel of Peter. The similarity between Justin and the Gospel of Peter is explained by Harris with greater certainty.

> I think the real explanation of these coincidences is that both Justin and Peter had a little text-book of fulfilled prophecies, to be used in discussions with Jews. These Old Testament prophecies were taken from a Greek version, which was not the Septuagint, but was probably the version of Aquila the Jew, or some distinctly Jewish version.[72]

---

[65] A quick count of a random selection of a number of pages indicates that full pages of typescript contain around 150 words. This is reduced for pages 43-56 where the translation of the text is presented with wider margins to accommodate an occasional reference to the canonical gospels.

[66] Harris, A Popular Account of the Newly Recovered Gospel of St Peter, 15.

[67] Bouriant, Fragments du texte grec du livre d'Énoch et de quelques écrits attribués à saint Pierre, 146.

[68] Harris, A Popular Account of the Newly Recovered Gospel of St Peter, 25-37.

[69] Harris, A Popular Account of the Newly Recovered Gospel of St Peter, 41-56.

[70] Harris, A Popular Account of the Newly Recovered Gospel of St Peter, 59-72.

[71] Harris, A Popular Account of the Newly Recovered Gospel of St Peter, 75-89.

[72] Harris, A Popular Account of the Newly Recovered Gospel of St Peter, 86.

Although Harris did not follow up on investigating these suggestions, the theory is a further development in the discussion surrounding the relationship between the writings of Justin and the first text in the Akhmîm codex. In his brief conclusion, Harris alludes to traces not only of Docetism in the Gospel of Peter, but also of Gnosticism and Marcionite teaching. Thus, according to Harris, the 'newly recovered Gospel of Peter' is tainted with heresy throughout its narrative, and reassuringly the four canonical gospels remain in the state of pristine purity first affirmed by Irenaeus.

4. French Scholarship after the *Editio Princeps*

Early French scholarship on the Gospel of Peter was not as prolific as that in England or Germany, but nonetheless it proved to be highly significant. Following the publication of the transcription of the text in the first part of the ninth volume of *Mémoires publiés par les membres de la Mission archéologique française au Caire*, the same body took the opportunity to publish a fresh transcription of the first two texts, the Gospel of Peter and the Apocalypse of Peter, along with heliographic images of these first two texts. Corrections were also listed for the text of the fragments of Enoch.

i. Adolph Lods

The work of re-transcribing the first text in the Akhmîm codex was undertaken by Lods, another member of the *Mission archéologique française au Caire*. He makes clear in his introduction that this was in no way to be seen as a criticism of the work undertaken by Bouriant. In fact Lods goes out of his way to laud the quality of work produced by his colleague. Not only does the tone appear fully sincere, but moreover, Lods describes the difficulties that faced Bouriant in his work. First, contrary to the suggestions levelled by both Robinson[73] and Harris,[74] Lods refutes any tardiness on the part of Bouriant. In fact he affirms the speed with which the task was brought to completion. He states, 'M. Bouriant reçut le manuscrit quelque temps après la découverte: il en reconnut aussitôt l'importance, le transcrivit rapidement, puis le rendit.'[75] Furthermore,

---

73 Robinson/James, The Gospel according to Peter, and the Revelation of Peter, 15.

74 Harris, A Popular Account of the Newly Recovered Gospel of St Peter, 17-18.

75 A. Lods, L'Évangile et l'Apocalypse de Pierre avec le texte grec du livre d'Hénoch. Text publié en facsimilé, par l'héliogravure d'après les photographies du manuscript de Gizéh, in: Mémoires publiés par les membres de la Mission archéologique française au Caire 9.3, Paris 1893, 217-231, 322-335. The page numbers are often cited as 217-235. This is fully understandable because page 322 follows page 231 without any intervening or lost material. The change to numbers in the three-hundred range is presumably due to an error in typesetting.

Lods describes the lack of opportunity that was afforded to Bouriant to compare his initial transcription with the manuscript, and later when the manuscript was available it appears that his own transcript was not. Bouriant's decision was to publish these texts rapidly rather than slow the process with time consuming proof-reading.

> Il ne le revit plus et, quand il se décida à le publier n'eut devant lui que sa première copie faite à la hâte. Quand plus tard, la manuscrit redevint accessible, il ne put qu'y vérifier quelques passages; il aurait dû sans doute différer encore la publication, mais il lui sembla que les retards avaient trop duré et il se décida d'autant plus aisément à donner sa copie qu'il espérait y joindre à bref délai les fac-similé du manuscrit. Ici encore les délais ont été plus longs qu'il ne s'y attendait pour des motifs sur lesquels il n'y a plus lieu de revenir.[76]

This passage perhaps gives a partial insight into the difficulties encountered by the *Mission archéologique française au Caire* as they attempted to prepare proofs of archaeological reports for printing in Paris. The problem was exacerbated by the large amount of artefactual and textual material that was being processed, along with the delays encountered in sending their reports to Paris for publication.

Despite these factors, there is little doubt that the transcription prepared by Lods was a significant improvement on that which appeared in the *editio princeps*. The transcription confirmed a number of emendations that had been proposed by both English and German scholars. What, however, aroused the attention of the scholarly world was not the improved transcription, but the appearance of images of the first two texts in the Akhmîm codex. The plates that appear at the rear of Lods work are heliographic images and not photographs in the modern sense. The term heliograph was originally given to the process invented by Niépce de St. Victor in 1826.[77] The process involves the formation of an engraving obtained by a process in which a specially prepared plate is acted on chemically by exposure to light. Although the process is not described in detail by Lods it was particularly suited to the imaging of static objects in an environment where the sunlight is brilliant and uninterrupted. Thus, taking the image of a manuscript in Egyptian sunlight was a particularly apt application of this technique. The process required perhaps some eight hours of bright sunlight to affix the image. These images circulated widely in other volumes besides that of Lods. Swete reproduced the recto and verso of leaf four, numbered as pages seven and eight respectively.[78] These served as frontispieces in Swete's volume. He acknowledges the generosity of the French publisher in allowing him to reproduce the two plates. 'Through the courtesy

---

[76]   Lods, L'Évangile et l'Apocalypse de Pierre avec le texte grec du livre d'Hénoch, 217.

[77]   The Columbia Electronic Encyclopedia contains the following description of Niépce and his invention. 'Niepce, Joseph Nicéphore, 1765–1833, French chemist who originated a process of photography. In 1826 he produced the first known photograph, which he called a heliograph, using bitumen of Judea (a form of asphalt) on a pewter plate.'

[78]   Swete, The Akhmîm Fragment of the Apocryphal Gospel of St Peter. See the two plates on unnumbered pages near the beginning of the volume.

of M. Leroux I am able to enrich my book with a specimen of this facsimile.'[79] Furthermore, Gebhardt[80] also reproduced the full set of heliographic images in his volume.

ii. Other French Contributions

Perhaps the work that was most comparable to that of Harris in attempting to make the text of the Gospel of Peter accessible to a wider audience in the French speaking world was that of Meunier.[81] It comprised a French translation with accompanying notes. In a similar vein, Sabatier discussed the relationship between the Akhmîm text and the canonical gospels.[82] Along with these volumes, French scholars produced a number of articles and notes of varying value. Most noteworthy were those of Lejay,[83] which appeared with a sample of the heliographic images, and Semeria.[84]

4. German Scholarship on the so-called Gospel of Peter

Early German scholarship was intense, varied and highly stimulating. A variety of questions were addressed and a number of figures helped to shape the debate within the German context in much the same fashion as was done by Swete in England. Issues surrounding the sources employed by the first text in the Akhmîm codex were paramount, as was the exploration of potential docetic features. However, following on from the publication of the heliographic images in Lods' volume, greater attention was paid to analysing the physical features of the manuscript. The debate and appearance of new scholarly works was made accessible to a wider audience within the pages of the *Theologische Literaturzeitung*.[85] In part, it is no surprise that this development was covered so thoroughly by the *Theologische Literaturzeitung* since one of its editors, Harnack, published the first German work on the Gospel and Apocalypse of Peter,[86] and his fellow editor wrote the review notices for volumes covering the topic including the book written by Harnack.[87]

---

79 Swete, The Akhmîm Fragment of the Apocryphal Gospel of St Peter, v.
80 O. von Gebhardt, Das Evangelium und die Apokalypse des Petrus. Die neuentdeckten Bruchstücke nach einer Photographie der Handschrift zu Gizéh in Lichtdruck herausgegeben, Leipzig 1893.
81 C. Meunier, L'Évangile selon saint Pierre, traduction française avec notes, Paris 1893.
82 A. Sabatier, L'Évangile de Pierre et les évangiles canoniques, Paris 1893.
83 P. Lejay, L'Évangile de Pierre, REG 1893, 59-84. 267-270.
84 J.B. Semeria, L'Évangile de Pierre, RB 1894, 522-560.
85 A. Harnack/E. Schürer, eds., ThLZ 1892, 609-614; 1893, 33-37.
86 A. Harnack, Bruchstücke des Evangeliums und der Apokalypse des Petrus, Sitzungsberichte der königl. Preussischen Akademie der Wissenschaften, Berlin 1892, 895-903. 949-965.
87 E. Schürer , ThLZ 1892, 612-614.

i. Adolf von Harnack

Building upon, and expanding his earlier articles in *Sitzungsberichte der königl. Preussischen Akademie der Wissenschaften*,[88] Harnack published[89] a short monograph, of the same title as the articles, describing both the Apocalypse and Gospel of Peter. Although the volume has a publication year of 1893, the preface is dated by Harnack as 'Berlin, den 15. Dec. 1892.'[90] This volume was the first German book to be published on the subject. In it Harnack developed the convention of dividing the text into sixty verses.[91] Although apart from Bouriant's *editio princeps* the only work cited by Harnack was the Robinson and James volume, he had nevertheless consulted numerous scholars concerning his own work. 'Für den Commentar verdanke ich dem Bischof von Durham, ferner den HH. Deissmann, Nestle, Wellhausen und den englischen Herausgebern einige Winke.'[92] Thus apart from fellow German scholars, it appears that by mid-December 1892, Harnack had managed to consult with Brooke Foss Westcott, the then Bishop of Durham concerning the new textual discoveries.

In his introduction Harnack drew attention to a number of unique features contained in the first text of the Akhmîm codex. Whereas Bouriant had drawn attention to the first person narrative in v. 60,[93] Harnack observed that Peter also spoke in the first person in v. 26,[94] and saw this as further reason to identify the text as the Gospel of Peter. After presentation of the Greek text and the accompanying German translation, Harnack devoted his attention to exploring intertextual links. After listing possible parallels he concludes, 'Ich habe oben bemerkt, unser Evangelium scheine auf den kanonischen Evangelien zu fussen und also jünger als diese zu sein.'[95] Thus, Harnack not only suggested that there is a literary relationship between the canonical gospels and the Akhmîm text, but he saw the Gospel of Peter as being later than, and dependent upon the canonical accounts. Apart from the canonical gospels, Harnack explored the parallels with the writing of Justin[96] and the

---

[88]   The two articles in "Sitzungsberichte der königl. Preussischen Akademie der Wissenschaften" appeared on the 3rd and 10th of November 1892.

[89]   A. Harnack, Bruchstücke des Evangeliums und der Apokalypse des Petrus, TU 9.2, Leipzig 1893.

[90]   Harnack, Bruchstücke des Evangeliums und der Apokalypse des Petrus, ii.

[91]   This can be seen in the Greek text presented on pages 8-12 and is also followed in the German translation on pages 12-16.

[92]   Harnack, Bruchstücke des Evangeliums und der Apokalypse des Petrus, ii.

[93]   Bouriant states, 'Le premier d'entre eux nous présent un récit de la Passion du Christ qui, comme nous l'apprend la dernière phrase, forme un épisode détaché de l'évangile apocryphe de saint Pierre.' Cf. Bouriant, Fragments du texte grec du livre d'Énoch et de quelques écrits attribués à saint Pierre, 137.

[94]   Harnack, Bruchstücke des Evangeliums und der Apokalypse des Petrus, 2.

[95]   Harnack, Bruchstücke des Evangeliums und der Apokalypse des Petrus, 32.

[96]   Harnack, Bruchstücke des Evangeliums und der Apokalypse des Petrus, 37-40.

Didascalia Apostolorum. In relation to latter, he argued that there is a clear case of literary dependency, but suggested that here the Gospel of Peter is acting as the source.[97] In addition to these texts Harnack also surveyed possible links between G.Pet. 36-40 and the form of Mark 16,4 preserved in Codex Bobbiensis;[98] the writings of Tatian;[99] and a number of weaker parallels.[100] Harnack's analysis is characterized by encyclopædic knowledge and close attention to detail. From the outset German scholarship approached the study of the Gospel of Peter with methodological sophistication and a clear focus on detailed analysis of source critical issues.

ii. Oscar von Gebhardt

Gebhardt's work was no less scholarly or meticulous than that of Harnack, but his emphasis was significantly different. With a preface dated 'Leipzig, den 13. Mai 1893',[101] the volume represented a detailed palaeographical and codicological study. His work was based on an analysis of the heliographic images presented by Lods,[102] and reproduced in his own volume.[103] He states, 'meine Lichtdrucktafeln für werthvoller zu halten, als die in den Memoires enthaltenen Heliogravüren.'[104] After the introductory discussion, Gebhardt gave a detailed description of the physical features of the codex and the use of *nomina sacra* as they occurred in the first text in the Akhmîm codex.[105] This was followed by a palaeographical analysis, which described the formation of the Greek letters in the text. Gebhardt drew attention both to consistent features as well as mentioning aberrant forms. As is fully apparent from the photographs published in the volume by Kraus and Nicklas, the scribe of the text did not possess particularly consistent or even legible handwriting.[106] Based on this analysis Gebhardt dated the first text in the Akhmîm codex to the ninth century. This dating aligned with the date proposed by Bouriant,[107] however, Gebhardt established a more secure basis for such a dating.

---

[97] See the extended discussion on pages 40-45.

[98] Harnack, Bruchstücke des Evangeliums und der Apokalypse des Petrus, 46.

[99] Harnack, Bruchstücke des Evangeliums und der Apokalypse des Petrus, 45-46.

[100] Harnack, Bruchstücke des Evangeliums und der Apokalypse des Petrus, 46-47.

[101] Gebhardt, Das Evangelium und die Apokalypse des Petrus, preface.

[102] Lods, L'Évangile et l'Apocalypse de Pierre avec le texte grec du livre d'Hénoch, plates.

[103] Gebhardt, Das Evangelium und die Apokalypse des Petrus, plates I-XX.

[104] Gebhardt, Das Evangelium und die Apokalypse des Petrus, 5.

[105] Gebhardt, Das Evangelium und die Apokalypse des Petrus, 7-10.

[106] See T.J. Kraus/T. Nicklas, Das Petrusevangelium and die Petrusapokalypse. Die griechischen Fragmente mit deutscher und englisher Übersetzung (GCS NS 11; Neutestamentliche Apokryphen 1), Berlin 2004, plates.

[107] Bouriant proposed a wider range of dates, eighth to twelfth century. See Bouriant, Fragments du texte grec du livre d'Énoch et de quelques écrits attribués à saint Pierre, 93.

Following this close analysis of the physical features of the text, Gebhardt discussed a number of possible variant readings at points where the text is uncertain.[108] Often this was due to the poor formation of letters by the scribe, although at some places the papyrus had become darkened, or there is a hole in the page. Gebhardt's work concluded with a presentation of the text, a bibliographical list of works published to that point, and reproduction of the heliographic images.[109] The strength of this volume lies in its unique study of the palaeographical and codicological aspects of the text. Such an analysis has not been undertaken again by later scholars to the same meticulous degree that Gebhardt focused on the physical features of the manuscript. While proposals have been made for an earlier dating of the text,[110] they fail to offer a study of palaeography, and thus seem to be based on less scientific grounds than the decisions presented by Gebhardt. It is for this reason that his contribution remains highly valuable, if unfortunately all too often neglected.

iii. A. Hilgenfeld

Another significant and early contribution to the discussion in Germany was undertaken by Hilgenfeld in two articles and a short note, all of which appeared in *Zeitschrift für Wissenschaftliche Theologie*, although subsequent works have failed to reference the short note.[111] In the first of these three articles Hilgenfeld presented the passage from Eusebius *h.e.* vi 12,3-5 (in Greek) outlining Serapion's reaction to the Gospel of Peter which was being used in Rhossos. Next he reproduced the Greek text of the first document contained in the Akhmîm codex. This was accompanied with a critical apparatus collating variants from four sources which are listed in the following form; 'B = Bouriant, C = Codex, D = Diels, H = Harnack.'[112] This list raises a number of questions. First it is not entirely clear what is meant by 'codex' since it is apparent in his final article that Lods' heliographs have only just become available to Hilgenfeld. Moreover, it appears that the emendations suggested by Diels had been gleaned from Harnack's work,[113] and that Diels did not publish these independently. As Hilgenfeld stated,

> Den Abdruck des Herrn U. Bouriant (Mem. Publ. par les membres de la Mission archéol. Française, T. IX, fasc. 1, 1892) hat A. Harnack (Sitzungsberichte der Kön.

---

[108]　Gebhardt, Das Evangelium und die Apokalypse des Petrus, 15-29.

[109]　See Gebhardt, Das Evangelium und die Apokalypse des Petrus, 30-41 and plates I-XX.

[110]　For a listing of various proposed dates see J. van Haelst, Catalogue des papyrus littéraires juifs et chrétiens, Paris 1976, 597, no. 598.

[111]　The three pieces are: A. Hilgenfeld, Das Petrus-Evangelium über Leiden und Auferstehung Jesu, ZWT 36.1, 1893, 439-454; idem, Zu dem Petrus-Evangelium, ZWT 36.2, 1893, 160; and idem, Das Petrus-Evangelium, ZWT 36.2, 1893, 220-267.

[112]　Hilgenfeld, Das Petrus-Evangelium über Leiden und Auferstehung Jesu, 440.

[113]　Harnack, Bruchstücke des Evangeliums und der Apokalypse des Petrus, i.

Preuss. Akademie der Wiss. zu Berlin vom 3. Nov. 1892), unterstützt von H. Diels, mehrfach verändert und, wie nicht anders zu erwarten war, auch berichtigt.[114]

Hilgenfeld's edition of the text with critical apparatus is then followed by brief observations and comments on the text.[115] These notes are primarily concerned with identifying parallels between the first document in the Akhmîm codex and the canonical gospels, although he does identify one extra-canonical parallel between G.Pet. 3,7 and Justin's *First Apology* (1,35).[116] The concluding paragraph re-asserts the case for seeing the document as originating in a second century context.[117]

The next contribution made by Hilgenfeld to the study of the Akhmîm text was a brief note in *ZWT*.[118] This note, however, further illustrates the works available to Hilgenfeld at the time of writing, for his ongoing textual work. Essentially the notice introduces a correction to the text of G.Pet. 2,5. Hilgenfeld's initial presentation of the text replicated an omission of the words καὶ παρέδωκεν αὐτὸν τῷ λαῷ πρὸ μιᾶς τῶν ἀζύμων τῆς ἑορτῆς αὐτῶν, initially omitted by Bouriant[119] and subsequently followed by Harnack.[120] As the note states, this correction had not been made by direct examination of the text, but through Robert Bensly's examination of the codex.[121] The same correction is made by Swete in his edition of the Akhmîm codex.[122] In his preface Swete also attributes this reading, and others, to the textual work of Bensly,

> This reprint was issued again in February 1893, with some corrections obtained from the MS. Through the kindness of the late Professor Bensly, whose recent death has brought upon all studies of this kind a loss which it is impossible to estimate.[123]

Bensly's death meant that he published no work on the Petrine gospel, but some of his textual observations have been preserved by others. Apart from this substantive correction, Hilgenfeld's note also records a smaller correction in v. 41.[124]

The third and final article that Hilgenfeld published on the Akhmîm text in *ZWT* reproduced and expanded upon his earlier work, as well as introducing a number of new features. The introduction acknowledged again Bensly's textual work undertaken while he was in Egypt, as well as mentioning the appearance of Lods' edition of the text with heliographic images.[125] As Hilgenfeld writes,

---

[114] Hilgenfeld, Das Petrus-Evangelium über Leiden und Auferstehung Jesu, 440.

[115] Hilgenfeld, Das Petrus-Evangelium über Leiden und Auferstehung Jesu, 444-452.

[116] Hilgenfeld, Das Petrus-Evangelium über Leiden und Auferstehung Jesu, 447.

[117] Hilgenfeld, Das Petrus-Evangelium über Leiden und Auferstehung Jesu, 452-454.

[118] Hilgenfeld, Zu dem Petrus-Evangelium, 160.

[119] Bouriant, Fragments du texte grec du livre d'Énoch et de quelques écrits attribués à saint Pierre, 137.

[120] Harnack, Bruchstücke des Evangeliums und der Apokalypse des Petrus, 9.

[121] Hilgenfeld, Zu dem Petrus-Evangelium, 160.

[122] Swete, The Akhmîm Fragment of the Apocryphal Gospel of St Peter, 3.

[123] Swete, The Akhmîm Fragment of the Apocryphal Gospel of St Peter, v.

[124] Hilgenfeld, Zu dem Petrus-Evangelium, 160.

[125] Hilgenfeld, Das Petrus-Evangelium, 220.

Am 29. März 1893 erhielt ich durch die Güte des Herrn Adolphe Lods in Paris dessen Schrift: L'Evangile et l'Apocalypse de Pierre publiés pour la 1ᵉ fois d'après les photographies du monument de Gizéh avec une appendice sur les rectifications à apporter au texte grec du livre d'Hénoch, Paris 1893.[126]

The appearance of these heliographic images enabled further corrections to the text, which were presented in this third article. However, prior to giving the text, Hilgenfeld discussed a far greater range of Patristic evidence to link the text with a second century dating.[127] Next the text is presented with a more extensive set of readings assembled from the works of various German and French editions of the text, with Harris being the only representative of English scholarship. The sources for the apparatus as listed are, 'B = Bouriant, Bl. = Blass, D = Diels, Gbh. = v. Gebhardt, Hn. = Harnack, Hr. = Harris, Hg. = Hilgenfeld (in dieser Zeitschrift XXXVI, 4), L = Lods, Z = Zahn.'[128] Although Hilgenfeld did not list 'C = Codex' in this list as he had done in his original list, the symbol still persists in his apparatus with no clarification of its meaning. The remaining two sections in the article explored, in detail, the connections between the Akhmîm text and the canonical gospels, as well as looking at other textual traditions that may have been known to the author of the Gospel of Peter.[129]

iv. Other Early German Contributions

While Harnack, Gebhardt and Hilgenfeld made early, diverse and significant contributions to the study of the text that was identified as the Gospel of Peter, these three scholars are only representative of the vibrant and voluminous work that was undertaken in the German context. Appearing slightly after the books of Harnack, Gebhardt and the first two of Hilgenfeld's articles, the work of Theodor Zahn also presented an edition of the Greek text with accompanying notes.[130] Another analysis of the relationship between the Akhmîm text and possible source material was provided by Hans von Schubert initially in German,[131] but also appearing later the same year in an English translation.[132] Schubert published, also in 1893, a fuller treatment of the text with translation and comments.[133] Alongside these works, a number of smaller

---

[126] Hilgenfeld, Das Petrus-Evangelium, 220-221.

[127] Hilgenfeld, Das Petrus-Evangelium, 221-233.

[128] Hilgenfeld, Das Petrus-Evangelium, 233.

[129] Hilgenfeld, Das Petrus-Evangelium, 239-267.

[130] T. Zahn, Das Evangelium des Petrus: Das kürzlich gefundene Fragment seines Textes, Berlin 1893.

[131] H. von Schubert, Das Petrusevangelium, synoptische Tabelle nebst Übersetzung und kritischem Apparat, Berlin 1893.

[132] H. von Schubert, The Gospel of St. Peter: Synoptical tables, with translations and critical apparatus, ET Rev. John MacPherson, Edinburgh 1893.

[133] H. von Schubert, Die Composition des pseudopetrinischen Evangelien-Fragments, Berlin 1893.

articles appeared, usually without an edition of the Greek text. What is fully apparent from even a brief survey of German scholarship at this stage is that it was characterized by great energy and diversity.

5. Conclusions

The voluminous early interest in the text identified as the Gospel of Peter surprisingly dissipated at a rate almost equivalent to its appearance. A trickle of articles continued to appear between 1894-1897,[134] but thereafter there was almost a total loss of interest in the text for approximately thirty years. In the interim period the text was referenced primarily in collections of apocryphal texts, but not on its own.[135] Then in the mid to late 1920's two scholars, to a limited extent, re-opened interest in the Gospel of Peter. First, Gardner-Smith published a two-part article that questioned the dependence of the Gospel of Peter upon the canonical gospel accounts.[136] Next, Leon Vaganay, published his magisterial commentary on the text, which still has no rival.[137] This brief flourish of interest again soon abated, with the next significant contribution coming forty years later with the appearance of the much briefer commentary by Mara in the *Sources Chrétiennes* series.[138] However, this handy-pocket edition was largely derivative upon the research and commentary of Vaganay.

In the last decade of the twentieth century there has been a revival of interest in the first text contained in the Akhmîm codex. In many ways this interest was sparked by J.D. Crossan in his book *The Cross that Spoke*.[139] His thesis was that the Gospel of Peter enshrined an earlier narrative, which he labelled *The Cross Gospel*, and that this source pre-dates the canonical Passion accounts. This theory captured the interest of certain sectors of the New Testament fraternity. Thus, Crossan's work proved to be a harbinger of ideas that are still being pursued by certain scholars in relation to the Gospel of Peter.[140] However, what is often lacking in such studies is an appreciation of

---

[134] Semeria, L'Évangile de Pierre, 522-560; A.C. McGifferd, The Gospel of Peter, Papers of the American Society of Church History 1894, 99-130; C. Bruston, De quelques texts difficiles de l'Évangile de Pierre, REG 1897, 58-65.

[135] E. Klostermann, Apocrypha I, Bonn 1921; M.R. James, The Apocryphal New Testament, Oxford 1924, 13-15. 90-92.

[136] P. Gardner-Smith, The Gospel of Peter, JThS 27, 1926, 255-271 and 401-407.

[137] L. Vaganay, L' Évangile de Pierre (ÉtB), Paris ²1930 (1929).

[138] M.G. Mara, Évangile de Pierre: Introduction, Texte Critique, Traduction, Commentaire et Index (SC 201), Paris 1973.

[139] J.D. Crossan, The Cross that Spoke. The Origins of the Passion Narrative, San Francisco 1988.

[140] A notable example of a scholar who has not only followed Crossan's hypothesis, but indeed has expanded its claims, is Paul Mirecki. He sees the first text contained in the Akhmîm codex, the Gospel of Peter, as itself pre-dating the synoptic gospels, rather than containing a source that antedates them. He states, 'The *Gospel of Peter* was a narrative gospel of the synoptic type which circulated in the mid-1st century under the authority of the name Peter.'(278). See P.A. Mirecki, 'Peter, Gospel of', The Anchor Bible Dictionary 5, New York 1992, 278-281.

the work that was undertaken as part of the initial reaction to the discovery of the codex. It is hoped that this discussion both points to the context of such research as well as highlighting some of the significant figures behind the early study, and the questions which were being asked of a text that had lain dormant as the precious keepsake of an unknown Egyptian Christian.

Die Überlieferung des apokryph gewordenen Petrusevangeliums

von

DIETER LÜHRMANN

I.

Irgendwann im Frühjahr 1975 schrieb ich bei Mk 15,43 an den Rand meiner Nestle-Studienausgabe: „POx 2949 (Bd. 41) → PtEv". Zur Vorbereitung einer Lehrveranstaltung über das Thomasevangelium hatte ich mir in der Bibliothek der Kirchlichen Hochschule Bethel die berühmten „Oxyrhynchus-Papyri" (POxy 1, 654 und 655) angeschaut, danach aber auch die übrigen Bände auf eventuelle weitere Fragmente durchgesehen. Der 41. Band war 1972 erschienen, und darin hatte R.A. Coles POxy 2949 als „Fragments of an Apocryphal Gospel (?)" veröffentlicht,[1] auch bereits auf eine mögliche Verbindung zum Petrusevangelium hingewiesen; nur dort nämlich wird wie hier Joseph von Arimathia als „Freund des Pilatus" bezeichnet, und das in einer Gerichtsverhandlung gegen Jesus unter Beteiligung des Herodes. Während einer Vorlesung zu den Passionsgeschichten, in die ich das Petrusevangelium einbezogen hatte, stolperte ich 1981 über diese meine Randnotiz und stellte fest, dass – wie ich damals und lange danach gemeint habe – niemand vor mir dieses neue Stück beachtet hatte.[2] Ich machte mich deshalb rasch an seine Bearbeitung, immer in der Angst, jemand anders könnte mir zuvorkommen, es als neues Fragment des Petrusevangeliums zu erweisen.

Mein Aufsatz erschien noch im selben Jahr,[3] und er hat bei kleinen Unterschieden in der Textrekonstruktion weitgehende Anerkennung gefunden, diesen Papyrus als Beleg dafür zu nehmen, dass der Inhalt des bis dahin allein bekannten Fragments des Petrusevangeliums (PCair 10759) sich in das

---

[1] R.A. Coles, 2949. Fragments of an Apocryphal Gospel (?), The Oxyrhynchus Papyri XLI, 1972, 15-16, mit Tafel II im Anhang (Faksimile in Originalmaßstab); Abbildung im Internet: http://www.csad.ox.uk/POxy/papyri/vol41/2949htm.

[2] Jetzt erst sehe ich, dass das nicht gilt für J. van Haelst, Catalogue des papyrus littéraires juifs et chrétiens, Paris 1976, dort 209 als Nr. 592, wohl aber weiterhin für K. Aland, Repertorium der griechischen christlichen Papyri I, PTS 18, 1976 (Vorwort vom 10.9.1974).

[3] POx 2949: EvPt 3-5 in einer Handschrift des 2./3. Jahrhunderts, ZNW 72, 1981, 216-226.

2. Jahrhundert zurückverfolgen lässt und nicht einen Text möglicherweise erst aus dem Mittelalter bietet.[4] Als ich im April 1984 anlässlich einer Konferenz in Oxford war, nutzte ich die Gelegenheit, mir im Ashmolean Museum diesen wie andere Papyri näher anzuschauen und eventuelle alternative Lesungen mit dem Erstherausgeber zu diskutieren. Darauf beruhen meine späteren leicht modifizierten Rekonstruktionen.[5]

Die Arbeit an meinem 1987 erschienenen Kommentar zum Markus-evangelium[6] machte mir das Fehlen einer Ausgabe der frühen apokryphen Evangelien auf neuestem Stand wieder einmal bewusst. Daher plante ich zusammen mit einem Kollegen, dem Patristiker Wolfgang Bienert, eine zweisprachige Edition, doch fand ein entsprechender Antrag auf Finanzierung von zwei Hilfskräften auf vier Jahre keine Gnade bei den Gutachtern der DFG. Im Rahmen eines solchen Projekts war eine systematische Durchsicht der Textfunde vorgesehen, die in den letzten Jahrzehnten in verschiedensten Zusammenhängen bekannt geworden sind. Sie hätte vermutlich noch einiges mehr erbringen können als schon die Einzelproben versprechen, bei denen es unter diesen Bedingungen bleiben musste.[7] Während ich mich nach einem Gastsemester in Yale als Vorsitzender des Fakultätentages hauptsächlich mit anderen Arten von Dokumenten beschäftigte, habe ich eine Reihe von Aufsätzen veröffentlicht zu immerhin ca. einem Dutzend Texten, die zwar bereits veröffentlicht, in der Apokryphenforschung aber noch gar nicht oder nur kaum rezipiert worden waren.[8] Als besonders ergiebig erwiesen sich die bis dahin – jedenfalls in dieser Hinsicht – wenig beachteten Kommentare von Didymus von Alexandrien aus den Tura-Papyri.[9] Auf sie hatte mich Wolfgang

---

4   Vgl. dazu zwei unterschiedliche Stufen der Bewertung durch W. Schneemelcher in ein und demselben Buch: NTApo[5] 81-82 („fraglich, ob es sich überhaupt um den Rest eines Evangeliums handelt") und 181 („daß man ... die Identifikation mit dem PE durch Lührmann für richtig halten wird"); eine ansprechende weiterführende Rekonstruktion hat M. Myllykoski vorgelegt: POx 2949 als Fragment des Petrusevangeliums, in: Verbum et calamus (FS T. Harviainen), hg. von H. Juusola/J. Laulainen/H. Palva, StOr 99, Helsinki 2004, 171-189.

5   Fragmente apokryph gewordener Evangelien in griechischer und lateinischer Sprache herausgegeben, übersetzt und eingeleitet in Zusammenarbeit mit E. Schlarb, MThSt 59, Marburg 2000, 85; Die apokryph gewordenen Evangelien. Studien zu neuen Texten und zu neuen Fragen, NT.S 112, Leiden-Boston 2004, 60-71.

6   Das Markusevangelium, HNT 3, Tübingen 1987.

7   Ein deutscher Rezensent, der nur zugestehen will, dass „das einschlägige Material jetzt (fast vollständig) in einer Sammlung greifbar ist, die auch die neueren Funde berücksichtigt" (ThLZ 126, 2001, 906), hätte vielleicht einen Satz auf die Hintergründe „dieser Berücksichtigung auch der neueren Funde" verwenden können. Er vermisst im Übrigen offenbar seinen Lieblingstext aus der lateinischen Origenes-Überlieferung; die aber wird wohl kaum noch jemand sonst für alt genug halten.

8   Diese Aufsätze sind in überarbeiteter Form eingegangen in den in Anm. 5 genannten Band „Die apokryph gewordenen Evangelien". Ein besonderer Dank gilt dabei Dr. Egbert Schlarb, der über lange Jahre, auch von Rumänien aus, meine Arbeit begleitet hat; ohne seine Beharrlichkeit wäre die ebenfalls in Anm. 5 genannte Ausgabe wohl kaum zustande gekommen.

9   Vgl. dazu B. Neuschäfer, Art. „Tura-Papyri", LACL[3] 701-702 (zur Abkürzung vgl. unten bei Anm. 49).

Bienert gestoßen,[10] und ich habe sie 1989/90 unter dieser Fragestellung systematisch Seite für Seite durchgesehen.[11]

Eine besondere Herausforderung bedeutete 1992 die Erstedition des POxy 4009 zusammen mit Peter J. Parsons. In Erinnerung an meinen früheren Besuch im Ashmolean Museum hatte ich nach dem Schicksal eines unveröffentlichten Papyrus gefragt, von dem damals die Rede gewesen war, und erhielt als Antwort das Angebot, selber an seiner Identifizierung und Rekonstruktion mitzuarbeiten.[12] Nachdem ich das freudig angenommen hatte, bekam ich hervorragende Fotos, verbunden auch schon mit einem Hinweis auf Mt 10,16b, freilich, wie sich herausstellte, in ungewohnter, da umgekehrter Fassung: „Seid aber ohne Falsch wie die Tauben und klug wie die Schlangen". Obwohl die Zeilen nur etwa zur Hälfte erhalten sind, gelang es, mit Hilfe von 2 Clem 5,2-4 und verwandten Stellen recht schnell, das „Recto" als Teil einer Rede Jesu zu rekonstruieren, die von einem Ich-Erzähler durch eine Gegenfrage unterbrochen wird. Für das „Verso" hingegen sehe ich auch weiterhin keine vergleichbare Möglichkeit, denn hier fehlt im erhaltenen Text jeglicher Anhaltspunkt lexikalischer oder grammatischer Art.[13]

Dieses neue Fragment habe ich dann im August des Jahres beim *Colloquium biblicum* in Leuven vorgestellt,[14] und eine ausführliche Interpretation erschien 1993.[15] Die Zuweisung zum Petrusevangelium beruht auf der Analogie zu dem großen Bruchstück aus dem Akhmîm-Codex, dass hier wie dort ein „Ich" als Erzähler auftritt und dass sich dahinter in beiden Fällen Petrus verbirgt, dort durch direkte Identifikation, hier über den Paralleltext 2 Clem 5,2-4, wo er als „dritte Person" spricht. Aus dieser Zuordnung ergäbe sich, dass das Petrusevangelium seinem Umfang nach nicht auf die Passions- und Ostergeschichte beschränkt zu denken ist,[16] sondern wie die synoptischen Evangelien eine Art Aussendungsrede enthalten hätte bzw. bei entsprechender anderer Einordnung dieses Fragments Gespräche mit Jesus nach seiner Auferstehung.[17]

Eine Durchsicht der sonstigen Petrusüberlieferungen unter der Frage vergleichbarer Beziehungen zum Petrusevangelium lenkte meinen Blick auf

---

[10] Vgl. in dem in Anm. 5 genannten Band 182-228, bes.183, Anm. 5.

[11] Eine „Nachlese" würde sich vermutlich lohnen, vielleicht auch für Fragen der Josephus- und der Philo-Überlieferung; vgl. auch die Dissertation von Thomas Holtmann: Die Magier vom Osten und der Stern, MThSt 87, Marburg 2005, zu der Fassung der „feindlichen" Magier mit Jes 8,14 als „Reflexionszitat".

[12] Die paläographische Arbeit dagegen stammt ganz von P.J. Parsons.

[13] Erstedition: D. Lührmann/P.J. Parsons, 4009. Gospel of Peter?, The Oxyrhynchus Papyri 60, 1994, 1-5; Abbildung im Internet: http://www.csad.ox.uk/POxy/papyri/vol60/4009htm.

[14] Ein neues Fragment des Petrusevangeliums, in: The Synoptic Gospels, hg. von C. Focant, BEThL 110, Leuven 1993, 579-581.

[15] POx 4009: Ein neues Fragment des Petrusevangeliums?, NT 35, 1993, 390-410.

[16] Vgl. seine Darstellung als Passionsevangelium bei H. Koester, Ancient Christian Gospels, Philadelphia 1990, 216-240.

[17] Vgl. H.-J. Klauck, Apokryphe Evangelien, Stuttgart 2002, 112.

PVindob Gr 2325, der unter dem Namen „Fajum-Fragment" schon lange die Evangelienforschung irritiert hatte.[18] Dass hier die Rekonstruktion eines Ich-Erzählers Petrus möglich sein kann, hat in diesem Fall weniger Beweiskraft als eine verblüffende inhaltliche Entsprechung zum Fragment des Akhmîm-Codex: Dort nämlich fehlt in der Botschaft des Jünglings im Grab (XIII 56)[19] jeder Verweis auf Galiläa ebenso wie hier, wo Jesus allein seine Verleugnung durch Petrus ankündigt, nicht aber auch eine Wiederbegegnung nach der Auferstehung.[20] Wenn auch der Plausibilitätsgrad geringer bleibt als im Fall von POxy 2949 und 4009, scheint mir eine Zuweisung von PVindob Gr 2325 zum Petrusevangelium vertretbar, zumal sie nicht eine zusätzliche Hypothese nach sich zieht.

Bei meinen Besuchen im Marburger Institut für Rechtsgeschichte und Papyrusforschung kamen mir zwei Bücher zur Kenntnis, die sich über die Interpretation des Petrusevangeliums hinaus als sehr hilfreich erwiesen. Ich hatte in meinen Veröffentlichungen für die Entstehung des Akhmîm-Codex immer wie in der Literatur üblich „8./9. Jahrhundert" angegeben, obwohl mir aus der Arbeit am Ersten Henoch-Buch bekannt war, dass dessen griechisches Fragment aus demselben Codex, dort zumeist „Gizeh-Fragment" genannt, üblicherweise auf das 5./6. Jahrhundert datiert wird.[21] Das hatten freilich bereits am Beginn des vorigen Jahrhunderts B.P. Grenfell und A.S. Hunt für den gesamten Codex angenommen.[22] Erst das neue Standardwerk zur Datierung handschriftlicher Überlieferung von G. Cavallo und H. Maehler[23] machte mir aber diese Zusammenhänge bewusst und führte mich dazu, in der Textausgabe von 2000 dies auch für das Petrusevangelium zu übernehmen, was sich angesichts einer so gewichtigen Referenzquelle nun auch in der Apokryphenforschung mehr und mehr durchsetzt.[24]

---

[18]   Erstveröffentlichung: G. Bickell, Ein Papyrusfragment eines nichtkanonischen Evangeliums, ZKTh 9, 1885, 498-504. 560.

[19]   „Warum seid ihr gekommen? Wen sucht ihr? Etwa jenen Gekreuzigten? Er ist auferstanden und weggegangen. Wenn ihr aber nicht glaubt, so beugt euch vor und seht den Platz, wo er lag, dass er nicht mehr da ist. Denn er ist auferstanden und dahin gegangen, woher er gesandt wurde."

[20]   Auf das Zitat von Sach 13,7 folgt in Mk 14,28/Mt 26,32 die Ankündigung Jesu, er werde nach Galiläa voranziehen, woran dann in Mt 28,7/Mk 18,7 erinnert wird. Bei Lk 24,6 hingegen gibt es nur eine pauschale Erinnerung an Jesu Verkündigung in Galiläa.

[21]   Vgl. C. Bonner, The Last Chapters of Enoch in Greek, StD 8, 1937, 4, unter Verweis auf F. Kenyon; M. Black, Apocalypsis Henochi graece, PVTG 3, 1970, 7-8; J.T. Milik, The Books of Enoch, Oxford 1976, 70.

[22]   Catalogue général des antiquités égyptiennes du Musée du Caire N° 10001-10869, 1903 (Ndr. Osnabrück 1972), 93.

[23]   Greek Bookhands of the Early Byzantine Period A.D. 300-800, BICS.S 47, 1987; zum Akhmîm-Codex 90: "near the end of the vi century".

[24]   Warum die Forschung zum Petrusevangelium so lange an der überholten Datierung festgehalten hat, ist schwer zu sagen. Vielleicht wegen des Vorurteils, dass Apokryphen eben spät sind?

Bei den Papyrologen lernte ich aber auch das Verzeichnis der Handschriften jüdischer und christlicher Provenienz von Joseph van Haelst kennen,[25] einschließlich seiner Weiterführung im „Archiv für Papyrusforschung" durch Kurt Treu[26] und – nach dessen Tod – Cornelia Römer.[27] Befremdlich wirkte dabei zunächst die Verwendung des Begriffs „Papyrus" in einem ganz weiten Sinne für Handschriftenfragmente generell,[28] hatte ich doch in neutestamentlichen Proseminaren immer und immer wieder die strikte Unterscheidung zwischen den Beschreibstoffen Papyrus und Pergament traktiert. Hier und allgemein in der Papyrologie aber wurde zusammengesehen, was zeitlich und sachlich zusammengehört.[29] Noch wichtiger war, dass ich unter Nr. 741 den Hinweis auf ein Ostrakon mit einem Bildnis des Evangelisten Petrus fand, datiert auf das 6./7. Jahrhundert und mit einer Inschrift auf der Rückseite. Es war bereits 1904 veröffentlicht[30] und ganz früh schon durch Adolf Deißmann in die Fachliteratur deutscher wie englischer Sprache eingebracht worden.[31] Obwohl aber das „Licht vom Osten" Generationen von Neutestamentlern geschienen hat, wurde m.W. dieser Hinweis auf das Petrusevangelium nirgends in der Apokryphenforschung aufgenommen.[32]

---

25 Vgl. Anm. 2; verwirrend sind freilich seine unterschiedlichen Angaben zur Datierung der Einzelteile des Akhmîm-Codex: 203 (1 Henoch Nr. 575: Ende 4. Jahrhundert), 212 und 219 (Petrusevangelium Nr. 598 bzw. Petrusapokalypse Nr. 617: 8./9., 8. oder 7./8. Jahrhundert unter Angabe verschiedener Autoritäten), 257 (Martyrium des Julian Nr. 707: 5./6. Jahrhundert).

26 APF 26, 1978, bis 37, 1991.

27 Seit APF 43, 1997.

28 „Il désigne aussi, comme il est d'usage en papyrologie, des textes écrits sur parchemin ..., ostracon, tablette de bois ou de plomb, papier, et même des graffiti", wie Anm. 2, 1.

29 Dementsprechend habe ich in die Tabelle 1 meiner Textausgabe (wie Anm. 5, 22) auch frühe Pergamenthandschriften aufgenommen; zu ergänzen ist dort: 0312, III/IV, Lk, so dass sich die Zahl am Ende der Lk-Spalte auf 8 erhöht.

30 P. Jouguet/G. Lefebvre, Deux ostraka de Thèbes, BCH 28, 1904, 201-209, hier 205-206, mit Fotographie der Bildseite pl. X; zusätzlich idem, Notes sur un ostrakon des Thèbes (Égypte), BCH 29, 1905, 104.

31 A. Deißmann, damals Neutestamentler in Heidelberg, hatte 1905 beim Freien Deutschen Hochstift in Frankfurt/M. – die Stadt besaß zu der Zeit noch keine Universität – einen „Lehrgang" gehalten, der in dessen Jahrbuch (1905, 80-95) dokumentiert ist: „Das Neue Testament und die Schriftdenkmäler der römischen Kaiserzeit". Die fünf Vorträge erschienen zunächst in englischer Übersetzung (von L.R.M. Strachan, seinerzeit Englischlektor an der Universität Heidelberg) unter dem Titel „The New Testament in the Light of Recent Discoveries" in der Zeitschrift Expository Times (18, 1906/07, 8-15. 57-63. 103-108. 202-211. 305-310), dann 1907 als das Buch: „New Light on the New Testament from Records of the Graeco-Roman Period" im selben Verlag (T. & T. Clark, Edinburgh). Erstmals 1908 in der deutschen Fassung dieses Buches erwähnt Deißmann das Petrus-Ostrakon: „Licht vom Osten" (Tübingen 1908, 30, wörtlich identisch dann: [2.3]1909, 31, und [4]1923, 43), danach dann auch in der englischen Ausgabe (übersetzt aus den jeweils aktuellen deutschen Auflagen weiterhin von Strachan, inzwischen German Lecturer in the University of Birmingham): „Light from the Ancient East" (nun im Verlag Hodder and Stoughton, London, 1910, 48, bzw. 1927, 57).

32 Ich verdanke Cornelia Römer die Kenntnis eines einzigen weiteren, von Deißmann offenbar unabhängigen Hinweises auf das Ostrakon: H. Leclercq, Art. „Ostraka", DACL 13/1, 1937, 70-

Ich besaß lange eine Fotokopie der Erstveröffentlichung des Ostrakons; erst in der letzten Phase der Arbeit an der Textausgabe stellte sich jedoch definitiv die Frage, wie mit diesem Stück zu verfahren sei. Es war im strengen Sinne kein „Fragment" des Petrusevangeliums, aber einschließlich seiner Votivinschrift doch ein bemerkenswerter Hinweis auf seine tatsächliche Benutzung, wie wir ihn für kein anderes apokryph gewordenes Evangelium kennen. Das rechtfertigt gegen allen Purismus seine Aufnahme in die Ausgabe.[33] Verbunden mit der neuen Datierung des Akhmîm-Codex auf etwa die gleiche Zeit ergaben sich zudem überraschende Aspekte hinsichtlich der Überlieferung des Petrusevangeliums zu so später Zeit noch, bevor der Ansturm der Araber in den Jahren 639-641 dem Christentum griechischer Sprache in Oberägypten das definitive Ende brachte. Dies habe ich zusätzlich in einem zusammenfassenden Aufsatz entwickelt,[34] der dann auch die Grundlage des Kapitels zum Petrusevangelium in der Gesamtdarstellung gebildet hat.[35]

Erstaunlich sind beim Petrusevangelium eigentlich nicht so sehr die frühen Zeugnisse des 2. bzw. 3. Jahrhunderts. Aus dieser Zeit gibt es mittlerweile nämlich eine ganze Reihe von Texten, die den apokryph oder den kanonisch gewordenen Evangelien zugerechnet werden können.[36] Am bekanntesten sind vermutlich einerseits der $\mathfrak{P}^{52}$ der neutestamentlichen Handschriftenliste (= PRyl 457) mit ein paar Zeilen aus dem Johannesevangelium, nach neuer Datierung wohl aus der Mitte des 2. Jahrhunderts stammend,[37] andererseits sein üblicherweise „PEgerton 2" (= PLondon Christ. 1) genannter und als „Fragments of an Unknown Gospel" eingeführter Konkurrent, nun ergänzt durch PKöln 255 und auf ca. 200 datiert,[38] damit aber immer noch eines der ältesten christlichen Zeugnisse.[39] Etwa ebenso alt sind beim Petrusevangelium POxy 2949 und POxy 4009 sowie PVindob Gr 2325, und die bei Euseb

---

112, hier 108. Bei Deißmann nachgesehen habe ich selber erst, nachdem Michael Wolter die – wie sich herausstellte – zutreffende Vermutung ausgesprochen hatte, da müsse doch „natürlich" etwas zu finden sein.

[33]   Wie Anm. 5, 74-75. 94-95.

[34]   Petrus als Evangelist – ein bemerkenswertes Ostrakon, NT 43, 2001, 348-367.

[35]   Wie Anm. 5, 55-104.

[36]   Vgl. S.E. Porter, Apocryphal Gospels and the Text of the New Testament before A. D. 200, in: The New Testament Text in Early Christianity, hg. von C.-B. Amphoux/J.K. Elliott, HTB 6, Prahins 2003, 235-259.

[37]   Erstveröffentlichung C.H. Roberts, An Unpublished Fragment of the Fourth Gospel in the John Rylands Library, Manchester 1935; zur neuen Datierung vgl. A. Schmidt, Zwei Anmerkungen zu P.Ryl. III 457, APF 35, 1989, 11-12.

[38]   Erstveröffentlichung: H.I. Bell/T.C. Skeat, Fragments from an Unknown Gospel, London 1935; idem, The New Gospel Fragments, London 1935; zur neuen Datierung vgl. M. Gronewald, Kölner Papyri 6, PapyCol 7, Opladen 1987, 137. Zur Geschichte der Erforschung vgl. S.R. Pickering, The Egerton Gospel and the New Testament Textual Criticism, in: The New Testament Text in Early Christianity, hg. von C.-B. Amphoux/J.K. Elliott, HTB 6, Prahins 2003, 215-234.

[39]   Vgl. in meiner Gesamtdarstellung (wie Anm. 5) 125-143.

überlieferte Auseinandersetzung des Bischofs Serapion von Antiochien mit diesem Evangelium fällt in dieselbe Zeit.[40]

Ab dem 4. Jahrhundert gibt es in griechischer Sprache zwar eine breite Überlieferung der kanonisch gewordenen Evangelien, nicht zuletzt als Teil der großen Codices ℵ, B, A, C, D. Für apokryph gewordene Evangelien hingegen kennen wir vergleichbare Gesamttexte allenfalls in koptischer Übersetzung. Vom Thomasevangelium[41] etwa ist eine griechische Fassung zwar ebenfalls aus ähnlich früher Zeit erhalten in den drei eingangs dieses Aufsatzes erwähnten „Oxyrhynchus-Papyri",[42] jedoch nur fragmentarisch, ganz dagegen die koptische im Codex II der Bibliothek von Nag Hammadi. Mit fortgeschrittenem Kanonbewusstsein wurden die Apokryphen überflüssig, wie Didymus von Alexandrien einen „alten rechtgläubigen" Bischof zitiert:

> Wenn (die Apokryphen) das gleiche sagen wie die öffentlich gebrauchten (Schriften), haben wir die öffentlich gebrauchten unwidersprochen und nehmen zu ihnen nicht die hinzu, die Widerspruch finden können. Wenn sie aber in Wirklichkeit nicht das gleiche wie die öffentlich gebrauchten sagen, halten wir sie für verwerflich. (EcclT I 8,8-11)

Dieses Urteil mag gelegentlich umgesetzt worden sein in planmäßige Vernichtung der Bücher, entscheidend war aber wohl eher, dass für benutzte Exemplare kein Ersatz mehr geschaffen wurde, so dass sie zerfielen und ihr Text auf die Dauer verloren ging. Auch der Akhmîm-Codex bietet ja nicht das Petrusevangelium als Ganzes, sondern nur einen mitten in einem Satz beginnenden und ebenso endenden Ausschnitt; und doch schien dieses Fragment offenbar so wertvoll, dass es wie ein liturgisches Buch ausgeschmückt wurde, und das Ostrakon beweist die gottesdienstliche Verehrung des Evangelisten und damit seines Evangeliums. Hier im erhaltenen Teil erscheint Petrus als Augenzeuge des Vorgangs der Auferstehung, und das mag den Wert dieses Bruchstücks ergeben haben in der Debatte um den Auferstehungsleib Christi, eines der dogmatischen Themen dieser späten Zeit. Die griechische Sprache derer, die in ihm lasen, weist auf diejenigen Ägypter, die an sich eher reichstreu und in diesem Sinne orthodox

---

[40] Vgl. seine Erwähnung bei Euseb, *h.e.* V 19,1; der eigentliche Brief: *h.e.* VI 12,2-6.

[41] Erstveröffentlichung: Faksimileausgabe von P. Labib, Coptic Gnostic Papyri in the Coptic Museum of Old Cairo I, Kairo 1956. 1959 folgten drei parallele Ausgaben mit gedrucktem koptischem Text und englischer, französischer bzw. deutscher Übersetzung, gemeinsam hg. von A. Guillaumont/H.-C. Puech/G. Quispel/W.C. Till und dem damals bereits verstorbenen Y. ʿAbd al Masîh; weitere Ausgabe mit koptischem Text: J. Leipoldt, Das Evangelium nach Thomas, TU 101, Leipzig 1967; H. Koester/B. Layton, The Gospel according to Thomas, in: Nag Hammadi Codex II.2-7, hg. von B. Layton, NHS 20, Leiden et al. 1989, 37-93; Appendix I Evangelium Thomae copticum, hg. von H.-G. Bethge, in: K. Aland, Synopsis quattuor evangeliorum, Stuttgart ab [15]1996, 517-546.

[42] Erstveröffentlichungen: B.P. Grenfell/A.S. Hunt, ΛΟΓΙΑ ΙΗΣΟΥ. Sayings of Our Lord, London 1897 (POxy 1); idem, New Sayings of Jesus and Fragment of a Lost Gospel, London 1897 (POxy 654 und 655). Erst 1882 war der erste Papyrus mit Text aus dem Neuen Testament selber, 𝔓[3], veröffentlicht worden, 1890 𝔓[14], 1892 𝔓[4], 1885 das „Fajum-Fragment" PVindob G 2325.

waren, weniger der Häresie verdächtig als die Koptisch sprechenden, aus deren Überlieferung wir sonst viel mehr an Apokryphen kennen.

II.

In der bisher biographisch angelegten Darstellung[43] zeigte sich, wie zufällig gelegentlich die Forschung gelenkt wird, ebenso, wie eng Forschung und Lehre ineinander gehen können, und schließlich, dass mich keineswegs eine Art Panpetrismus dazu gebracht hat, immer neu Fragmente des Petrus-evangeliums zu entdecken. Soweit es den Umfang angeht, entspricht meinen Ergebnissen nun die Ausgabe von Thomas J. Kraus und Tobias Nicklas – zumindest auf den ersten Blick. Auch sie nämlich bieten unter der Überschrift „Die griechischen Handschriften des so genannten Petrusevangeliums" die vier Fragmente PCair 10759, POxy 2949, POxy 4009 und PVindob G 2325 (25-68) und stellen vorher (20-23) ausführlich das Petrus-Ostrakon dar, wenn auch natürlich nicht als eine solche Handschrift (7).[44] Außerdem lehnen sie wie ich den Versuch von D.F. Wright ab, PEgerton 2 dem Petrusevangelium zuzurechnen (6),[45] und auch (ebd.) H.-M. Schenkes ziemlich haltlose Vermutung, bei den Fragmenten des Ende der 1990er Jahre bekannt gewordenen „unbekannten Berliner Evangeliums" (UBE = Gospel of the Savior = PBerol 22220) in koptischer Sprache[46] handle es sich um einen Teil des Petrusevangeliums. Um das behaupten zu können, hatte er einfach gegen den Wortlaut der Handschrift ein „ich" = Petrus eingesetzt, und zwar in einem ganz und gar maroden Textstück.[47]

---

[43]   Anmerkungsweise sei noch erwähnt, dass mich das Jesus-Seminar 1991 in Edmonton zum Ehrenmitglied auf Lebenszeit ernannt hat, was keineswegs zwangsläufig zum Ausschluss von kirchlichen Examina führte, wie gelegentlich für einen Göttinger Kollegen behauptet wird.

[44]   Das Petrusevangelium und die Petrusapokalypse. Die griechischen Fragmente mit deutscher und englischer Übersetzung, GCS.NF 11, Neutestamentliche Apokryphen 1, Berlin-New York 2004. Vgl. zum Folgenden auch meine Rezension dieser Ausgabe in ThR 70, 2005, 242-245, und in ZAC meine Erwiderung auf Kraus (vgl. Anm. 51): Das Petrusbildnis *van Haelst 741* – eine Replik.

[45]   The „Unknown Gospel" (Pap. Egerton 2) and the Gospel of Peter, GoPe 5, 1984, 207-232; Papyrus Egerton 2 (the Unknown Gospel) – Part of the Gospel of Peter?, SecCen 5, 1985-86, 129-150.

[46]   Erstveröffentlichung: C.W. Hedrick/P.A. Mirecki, Gospel of the Savior. A New Ancient Gospel, Santa Rosa/Ca 1999. Diese Edition ist angesichts der Kritik von Stephen Emmel und Peter Nagel weitgehend überholt: S. Emmel, The Recently Published Gospel of the Savior („Unbekanntes Berliner Evangelium"): Righting the Order of Pages and Events, HThR 95, 2002, 45-72; P. Nagel, „Gespräche Jesu mit seinen Jüngern vor der Auferstehung" – zur Herkunft und Datierung des „Unbekannten Berliner Evangeliums", ZNW 94, 2003, 215-257; trotz der Erwiderung von C.W. Hedrick, Caveats to a ‚Righted Order' of the *Gospel of the Savior*, HThR 96, 2003, 229-238.

[47]   Es handelt sich um p. 116,29-32 der ursprünglich verwendeten Zählung: H.-M. Schenke, Das sogenannte „Unbekannte Berliner Evangelium" (UBE), ZAC 2, 1998, 199-213, hier 205; vgl. zu der genannten Stelle S. Emmel (Anm. 46) 48, Anm. 17; P. Nagel (Anm. 46) 252, Anm. 31.

Es bleibt abzuwarten, ob bzw. wie sich diese Umfangsbestimmung in weiteren Ausgaben, in Lexikonartikeln und in allgemeinen Darstellungen durchsetzen wird. Hans-Josef Klauck z.B. referiert in seinem Buch „Apokryphe Evangelien" zum Petrusevangelium zwar im Wesentlichen nur das Hauptzeugnis PCair 10759, geht jedoch auch auf die beiden Oxyrhynchus-Papyri als Teile des Petrusevangeliums ein und erwähnt das Ostrakon.[48] Georg Röwekamp hat anders als in der ersten Auflage des Lexikons der antiken christlichen Literatur von 1998 in der dritten (2002) POxy 2949 und 4009 mitaufgenommen, freilich auch – mit Einschränkungen zwar – das „Unbekannte Berliner Evangelium".[49] Dem 2003 erschienenen allzu knappen RGG[4]-Artikel zum Petrusevangelium von Éric Junod hingegen ist nicht zu entnehmen, dass es vom Petrusevangelium außer PCair 10759 möglicherweise noch andere Handschriften geben könnte.[50]

Bei aller Übereinstimmung kann jedoch nicht übersehen werden, dass einem zweiten Blick nicht unerhebliche Differenzen auffallen werden. Vor allem hat Thomas J. Kraus den in der ZAC gewährten Raum genutzt, mich in drei ausführlichen Äußerungen einerseits so hoch zu loben, dass vor diesem Hintergrund die dann folgenden Einwände andererseits um so schwerer wiegen müssen,[51] und Tobias Nicklas hat sich ebenfalls, freilich sehr viel moderater, in ähnlicher Weise kritisch zu meinen Arbeiten geäußert.[52] Die dabei hervortretenden Unterschiede sollen im Folgenden thematisiert werden, denn sie führen, jedenfalls soweit es sich um sachliche handelt,[53] über Detailfragen hinaus zu grundsätzlichen Überlegungen.

Die von den beiden Herausgebern immer wieder, nicht nur in der zitierten Überschrift benutzte Formulierung „so[54] genanntes Petrusevangelium" z.B. soll wohl mit Recht darauf aufmerksam machen, dass sich diese Überschrift in keinem der in Frage kommenden Fragmente selber findet, sie ihnen –

---

[48] Stuttgart 2002, 110-118.

[49] LACL[3], 565-566 gegenüber LACL[1], 495.

[50] „Vom EvPetr ist ein bedeutendes Frgm. in griech. Sprache erhalten." Wer diesen Satz im Artikel „Petrusevangelium" (RGG[4] 6, 2003, 1182) liest, wird (ohne die angegebene Literatur zu kennen) nicht auf die Idee kommen, dass derselbe Autor in einer anderen Darstellung des Petrusevangeliums POxy 2949 und 4009 jedenfalls zur Kenntnis genommen hat: Évangile de Pierre, in: Écrits apocryphes chrétiens, hg. von F. Bovon/P. Geoltrain, Paris 1997, 239-254, bes. 243-244.

[51] T.J. Kraus, P.Vindob.G 2325, Das sogenannte Fayûm-Evangelium – Neuedition und kritische Rückschlüsse, ZAC 5, 2001, 197-212; Petrus und das Ostrakon *van Haelst* 741 – einige klärende Anmerkungen, ZAC 7, 2003, 203-212; ausführliche Rezension meiner in Anm. 5 genannten Textausgabe: ZAC 8, 2004, 128-137.

[52] Vgl. seine Aufsätze: Die „Juden" im Petrusevangelium (PCair 10759), NTS 47, 2001, 206-221; Erzähler und Charakter zugleich. Zur literarischen Funktion des „Petrus" in dem nach ihm benannten Evangelienfragment VigChr 55, 2001, 318-326; Ein „neutestamentliches Apokryphon"? Zum umstrittenen Kanonbezug des sog. „Petrusevangeliums", VigChr 56, 2002, 260-272.

[53] Um manche herablassend wirkende Töne ist es schade.

[54] Die ungewohnt wirkende Getrenntschreibunng (nicht „sogenanntes") ergibt sich aus der neuen deutschen Rechtschreibung.

angefangen mit Harnack – vielmehr erst von den modernen Herausgebern beigegeben worden ist. Vermutlich um das zu unterstreichen, haben beide jedoch auch mehrfach den Vorwurf wiederholt,[55] ich hätte in der Textausgabe den Titel εὐαγγέλιον κατὰ Πέτρον in die Wiedergabe des PCair 10759 hineingemogelt,[56] um dieses Fragment bzw. die Fragmente insgesamt eindeutiger als erlaubt dem Petrusevangelium zuweisen zu können. Nun war es in der Tat ein Ziel meiner Ausgabe, in Frage kommende Fragmente, vor allem natürlich zuvor unbekannte, soweit wie möglich als Teilstücke von apokryph gewordenen Evangelien zu identifizieren. Deren Zahl ist nicht unendlich, wenn auch zu keiner Zeit abgeschlossen; sie ergibt sich aus unserer immer noch einmal vermehrbaren Kenntnis von in alten Texten genannten Evangelien, erhaltenen oder verloren gegangenen.[57] Es bleibt jedoch immer ein Rest „nicht identifizierbarer Fragmente", sei es, weil ein entsprechendes Evangelium bisher unbekannt war wie z.B. im Falle von PEgerton 2, sei es auch nur, weil die erhaltenen Bruchstücke einen zu geringen Umfang haben oder zu wenige spezifische Charakteristika aufweisen.[58]

Nur in seltenen Fällen ergibt sich eine solche Identifikation über einen im jeweiligen Fragment selber erhaltenen Titel,[59] denn dessen Platz am Ende bzw. zu Beginn einer Handschrift war in besonderer Weise dem Verschleiß ausgesetzt. Häufiger ist es daher nötig, bei der Identifikation Erwägungen inhaltlicher Art anzustellen: Klassifizierung nach synoptischem oder johanneischem Typ, als erzählendes bzw. Spruchevangelium, besondere Charakteristika wie der in der ersten Person schreibende Autor beim Petrusevangelium u.a.m. Einen solchen Weg können Kraus und Nicklas für ihre Ausgabe jedoch nicht wählen, denn sie betonen für ihre Arbeit insgesamt programmatisch: „Diskussion und Interpretation des Inhalts des PE (= Petrusevangeliums, D.L.) bleiben dabei ausgeschlossen" (25)[60]. Ihrerseits lässt

---

[55]   Zuletzt in der Textausgabe (wie Anm. 44) 4, Anm. 11.

[56]   Allenfalls handelt es sich um ein Problem der graphischen Gestaltung in der Spalte der deutschen Übersetzung. Beim griechischen Text steht der Titel deutlich unter der abschließenden Flechtleiste der Handschrift. Dass ich ihn an dieser Stelle eingefügt habe, hat zwei gänzlich andere Gründe. Erstens standen Buchtitel in der Antike regelmäßig am Ende der jeweiligen Werke. Daran wollte ich erinnern wie zum andern daran, dass εὐαγγέλιον κατὰ Πέτρον und vergleichbare Titel anderer apokryph gewordener Evangelien breit belegt sind. In der Konstruktion entsprechen sie denen der kanonisch gewordenen Evangelien. Vor dieser Parallelität hat sich kein noch so orthodoxer Kirchenvater gescheut.

[57]   Üblicherweise werden als Orientierung benutzt die Aufzählung apokrypher Evangelien bei Origenes (*hom. in Lk* 1) oder die verschiedenen bekannten Verzeichnisse apokrypher Schriften.

[58]   Das ist anders für Fragmente von kanonisch gewordenen Evangelien, wo die vorhandenen Gesamttexte helfen. Dort können aber *variae lectiones* irritieren bei der Zuweisung zu dem einen oder dem anderen Evangelium.

[59]   So z.B. beim Maria- und beim Thomasevangelium, aber jeweils nur in der koptischen Überlieferung. Die folgenden Erwägungen gelten *cum grano salis* für antike Literatur aller Art.

[60]   Vgl. ebenso für die Petrusapokalypse: „Wiederum aber bleiben Diskussion und Interpretation des Textes weitgehend ausgenommen und den sich an die Edition hoffentlich anschließenden Abhandlungen vorbehalten." (101)

sich demnach inhaltlich die Zusammengehörigkeit der Fragmente – in welcher Zahl auch immer – zu dem einen Petrusevangelium allenfalls begründen, wenn es sich um Handschriften gleichen Inhalts handelt;[61] sonst ergibt sie sich einzig forschungsgeschichtlich dadurch, dass andere Forscher eines von ihnen wie die anderen „so genannt" haben. Damit bleibt die neue Ausgabe aber unnötig vage in der Begründung der Auswahl der aufgenommenen Fragmente und fördert möglicherweise geradezu das Beharren auf einem alten Stand der Forschung gegen die Einordnung von neuen Funden. So begrüßenswert an sich alle Vorsicht sein mag, darf sie doch inhaltliche Gesichtspunkte der Identifikation von Handschriften nicht *a priori* ausschließen.

Eine zweite Differenz ergibt sich aus einem unterschiedlichen Verständnis davon, was als „Textzeugnis" zu betrachten sei. Thomas J. Kraus und Tobias Nicklas unterscheiden in ihrer Ausgabe nur zwischen „Hinweisen in der antiken (christlichen) Literatur" einerseits und „griechischen Handschriften" andererseits; es fehlen die Übersetzungen und vor allem die Zitate in Fremdtexten. Beim Petrusevangelium scheint das zunächst nicht viel auszumachen, führt aber bei der Petrusapokalypse zum totalen Ausschluss des Hauptzeugen, der äthiopischen Überlieferung. Dort gibt es einen Gesamttext dieser Schrift, der eine sinnvolle Zuordnung der fragmentarischen Handschriften in griechischer Sprache ermöglicht.[62] Dass sich die Reste frühchristlicher Literatur auf mehrere Sprachen verteilen, ist ein bekanntes Problem und erleichtert ihre Bearbeitung nicht gerade, darf jedoch nicht überspielt werden durch Beschränkung auf die eine griechische Überlieferung.[63] Selbst die neuesten Nestle-Ausgaben führen unter den Textzeugen noch Übersetzungen an, die äthiopische eingeschlossen,[64] und das trotz der in jeder Hinsicht unvergleichbar hohen Zahl griechischer Handschriften des Neuen Testaments. Beim Petrusevangelium als einem nicht kanonisch gewordenen Evangelium sind zwar gerade die Spuren eines relativ späten Gebrauchs in griechischer Sprache auffällig; dennoch hätten die oft notierten Anklänge in Mk 16,3 der lateinischen Handschrift *k* sowie in Lk 23,48 *g¹* (und der Vetus Syra) oder auch die Beziehungen zu Turfan-Texten[65] der Erwähnung in einer Textausgabe wert sein können.

Zu den „Hinweisen" auf die Petrusapokalypse (87–99) gehören bei Thomas J. Kraus und Tobias Nicklas Kanonverzeichnisse und bloße Erwähnungen,

---

61 Beim Petrusevangelium also z.B. POxy 2949.

62 Vgl. dazu insgesamt J.N. Bremmer/I. Czachesz, Hg., The Apocalypse of Peter, Studies on Early Christian Apocrypha 7, Leuven 2003.

63 „Die vorliegende Edition möchte einen Überblick über die vorhandenen *griechischen* Handschriften dieses Werkes geben." (82; Hervorhebung D.L.) Diese Einschränkung auf die griechische Überlieferung galt nicht immer für GCS (trotz des Buchstabens G wie Griechisch).

64 Nestle-Aland²⁷, 30*.

65 Zu Anklängen an das Petrusevangelium in manichäischen Texten aus Turfan vgl. H.-Ch. Puech, NTApo³ I, 262 = NTApo⁵ I, 321; E. Morano, A Survey of the Extent Parthian Crucifixion Hymns, in: Studia Manichaica, hg. von R.R. Emmerich/W. Sundermann/P. Zieme, BABBW.S 4, Berlin 1999, 404–408.

jedoch überraschenderweise auch „Zitate". Sie gelten ihnen nicht als „Fragmente",[66] während die neuesten Nestle-Ausgaben als Textzeugen weiterhin nicht nur – wie erwähnt – Übersetzungen, sondern auch Kirchenväterzitate berücksichtigen,[67] ganz zu schweigen von den klassischen Werkausgaben der „Fragmente" der Vorsokratiker, der Stoiker oder der antiken Historiker, die überwiegend aus derartigen Zitaten bestehen. Für das Petrusevangelium finden sich, abgesehen allenfalls von den Turfan-Texten, solche Zitate nicht, und leider zitierte auch Bischof Serapion von Antiochien nicht aus dem Evangelium[68], jedenfalls so weit Eusebs Exzerpt reicht. Von anderen apokryph gewordenen Evangelien, dem Hebräerevangelium etwa, kennen wir jedoch überhaupt nur „Zitate". Sie bieten ihre eigenen Schwierigkeiten, denn im Umfang nicht anders als im Wortlaut können sie dem jeweiligen Kontext angepasst und dadurch verändert sein;[69] in der neutestamentlichen Exegese sind ähnliche Phänomene bekannt bei alttestamentlichen Zitaten wie in der lange Zeit überschätzten Herausarbeitung von Quellen aus literarischen Texten mittels der „Literarkritik". Aber auch Handschriften sind keineswegs frei von vergleichbaren Abweichungen; zudem zeigt die Überlieferung der christlichen Bibel einen relativ freien Umgang mit normativen Texten; die jüdische wie auch die spätere islamische wirken sehr viel stabiler.[70]

III.

Unsere Kenntnis antiker Literatur welcher Art auch immer, also auch die der kanonisch und der apokryph gewordenen Evangelien, verdankt sich drei grundsätzlich voneinander zu unterscheidenden Wegen. Einerseits gibt es die direkte Weitergabe der Texte von Generation zu Generation, wobei in bestimmten Abständen die Abschriften erneuert werden mussten, um Ersatz für verschlissene zu schaffen.[71] Voraussetzung dafür ist ein institutionelles

---

66   Für Kraus und Nicklas konzentriert sich alles auf die (griechischen) Handschriften der Petrusapokalypse; wie im ersten Teil für das Petrusevangelium heißt es: „Wiederum aber bleiben Diskussion und Interpretation des Textes weitgehend ausgenommen." (101) Neben den Akhmîm-Codex (101-120) treten nur zwei mit ihm sich überlappende Fragmente eines griechischen Pergamentcodex aus der zweiten Hälfte des 5. Jahrhunderts (122), die getrennt nach Wien und Oxford gekommen sind (121-130).

67   Vgl. das Verzeichnis Nestle-Aland[27], 33*-35*.

68   Vgl. Anm. 40.

69   Vgl. z.B. die beiden Fassungen desselben Zitats aus dem Evangelium der Ebionäer bei Epiphanius in meiner Textausgabe (wie Anm. 5), 35.

70   Da es bei den apokryph gewordenen Evangelien faktisch keine Parallelhandschriften gibt, kommt das textkritische Problem abweichender Lesarten selten in den Sinn; vgl. dazu in meinem Band (wie Anm. 5), 99.

71   In der Zeit des Buchdrucks entsprach dem in gewisser Weise der Nachdruck oder die Neuauflage. Mit den Kopiergeräten erst wurde es möglich, Druckausgaben antiker Texte in beliebiger Zahl zu reproduzieren, z.B. zur Verwendung in Lehrveranstaltungen, deren

Interesse an ihnen, etwa in der Kirche oder der Schule, für andere Textsorten auch im Rechtswesen oder der Medizin. Bei den apokryph gewordenen Evangelien ist diese Art kontinuierlicher Überlieferung abgebrochen, seit sich auf die eine oder andere Weise ein Kanonbewusstsein durchgesetzt hat.[72] Eine Ausnahme bildet nur scheinbar das „Protevangelium Jacobi", das bis heute eine große Verbreitung hat, da es in den Ostkirchen zu Marienfesten gelesen wird.[73] So genannt wurde es jedoch erst in westlichen Ausgaben seit dem 16. Jahrhundert; sein eigener Titel ist „Marias Geburt. Offenbarung des Jakobus", nicht der eines Evangeliums nach dem Muster εὐαγγέλιον κατὰ …[74].

Zweitens kann ein solcher Traditionsprozess Übersetzungen einschließen, mit oder ohne Verlust des Originals. Nachdem der weithin einheitliche griechische Sprachraum rund um das Mittelmeer sich seit dem 2. Jahrhundert mehr und mehr aufgelöst hatte, wurde christliche Überlieferung nicht nur ins Lateinische, sondern auch ins Koptische, ins Syrische und manch andere Sprache übertragen und weiterentwickelt.[75] Wo sich solch ein Vorgang im Vergleich zweier Sprachen kontrollieren lässt, zeigt sich freilich, dass nicht überall das Ideal wortgetreuer Übersetzung vorauszusetzen ist, das streng genommen wohl erst seit der Schulphilologie des 19. Jahrhunderts gilt.[76] Daher ergibt sich ein griechischer Originaltext z.B. für das Thomasevangelium nicht mittels einer direkten „Rückübersetzung" aus dem Koptischen der Bibliothek von Nag Hammadi; vielmehr bietet dieser auch inhaltlich eine Fassung erst des 4. Jahrhunderts gegenüber der griechischen der Oxyrhynchus-Papyri 654, 1 und 655.[77]

Das größte Interesse erregen schließlich drittens Handschriften aus archäologischen Funden, zumal wenn sie durch die Medien spektakulär aufbereitet ein „fünftes" oder ein „unbekanntes Evangelium" versprechen, wobei manches andere übersehen wird. Es kann dabei um neue Handschriften gehen,[78] in griechischer oder einer anderen Sprache, aber auch um Kirchenväter-Texte, in denen sich wie bei Didymus von Alexandrien Zitate

---

Thematik nun nicht länger auch davon abhängig sein musste, dass genügend Textausgaben vorhanden waren.

[72]   Vgl. oben am Ende von Absatz I.

[73]   Vgl. dazu in meiner Textausgabe (wie Anm. 5), 6-7; im lateinischen Bereich entspricht ihm die als Pseudo-Matthäus bezeichnete Schrift; vgl. insgesamt zu den „Kindheitsevangelien" die Ausgabe von G. Schneider, Apokryphe Kindheitsevangelien, FC 18, Freiburg et al. 1995.

[74]   Daher habe ich es auch nicht in die Ausgabe (vgl. Anm. 5, 7) aufgenommen.

[75]   Für weite Bereiche antiker Literatur ist als Träger später das Arabische wichtig; vgl. zu islamischen Agrapha Klauck (wie Anm. 17), 30-32.

[76]   Aber auch danach gibt es noch Beispiele genug, in denen Übersetzungen den Sinn des Textes ändern.

[77]   Vgl. das Kapitel zur griechischen Überlieferung des Thomasevangeliums in meinem Buch (wie Anm. 5) 144-181, und die dortige Kritik an derartigen „Rückübersetzungen".

[78]   Vgl. etwa die Chester-Beatty- und die Bodmer-Papyri für die kanonisch gewordenen Evangelien, für die apokryph gewordenen die bereits erwähnten und andere Beispiele.

finden.[79] Verglichen mit alldem ergibt sich für die Überlieferung des Petrusevangeliums ein geradezu untypisches Bild. Eine kontinuierliche Überlieferung findet sich zwar auch hier nicht, doch haben wir in griechischer Sprache neben alten Zeugnissen auch jüngere, wie sie eigentlich nicht zu erwarten sind für Zeiten eines längst entwickelten Kanonbewusstseins; andererseits finden sich jedoch kaum Spuren von Übersetzungen oder Zitierungen.

Wer an apokryph gewordenen Evangelien arbeitet, wird grundsätzlich mit allen der drei genannten Überlieferungswege zu rechnen haben und sich nicht einseitig auf einen von ihnen beschränken dürfen. Das aber scheint mir der Kern der Kontroverse mit Thomas J. Kraus zu sein, dass er als Textzeugnisse allein Handschriften akzeptieren will, als „wirkliche Realien" oder „Finger-abdrücke", wie er emphatisch reden kann.[80] Das zeigt sich schon in der Darstellung der Petrusapokalypse, für die nur die griechischen Handschriften PCair 10759, Bodl. MS Gr. th.f. [4] und PVindob G 39756 als Fragmente genommen werden, nicht der Gesamttext in äthiopischer Sprache und ebenso wenig Zitate bei Kirchenvätern. Es bestimmt aber vor allem seine Verteilung von Lob und Tadel in der Rezension meiner Textausgabe wie anderswo. Seine Zustimmung findet am ehesten, wer an der Erschließung neuer Handschriften arbeitet; sie sinkt schlagartig, sobald es um andere Gebiete geht, insbesondere bei Zitaten.

Damit legt er jedoch die Methodik der Apokryphenforschung einseitig fest auf die diplomatische Edition griechischer Handschriften und kann Zitate wie Übersetzungen lediglich als „Hinweise" einbeziehen. Um die Begrifflichkeit und das Instrumentarium der Papyrologie an sich braucht es gar nicht zum Streit zu kommen, denn sie hat es als eine eigene Wissenschaft zu tun mit der Herausgabe jener Riesenschätze, die in Museen und Instituten oder noch im Wüstensand verborgen auf ihre Veröffentlichung nach den Regeln der Kunst warten.[81] Innerhalb dieser Wissenschaft zeigen sich aber unterschiedliche Interessen, eher philologische lexikalischer und grammatikalischer Art im Studium der Sprache oder mehr literarischer Art in der Rekonstruktion von Werken antiker Autoren bzw. eher historische in der Bearbeitung von Dokumenten unter sozial- oder rechtsgeschichtlichen Gesichtspunkten; daraus ergeben sich auch unterschiedliche Verortungen innerhalb der Universitäten.

---

[79] Vgl. das Kapitel „Wer nicht gesündigt hat, hebe einen Stein auf und werfe ihn!" Neue Texte bei Didymus von Alexandrien, in meinem in Anm. 5 genannten Buch, 182-228.

[80] Vgl. in seiner Rezension (wie Anm. 51), 132. Es bleibt abzuwarten, in welcher Weise die Neuausgabe von NTApo durch C. Markschies „der Notwendigkeit einer strukturellen Aufteilung von direkten Realien und Zitaten Rechnung tragen" wird. Ich sehe für mich jedenfalls keinen Sinn darin, „zu überlegen, ob nicht die Kirchenväterzitate für sich ein weiteres Kapitel bilden sollten" (neben den identifizierbaren und den nicht identifizierbaren Fragmenten).

[81] Vgl. H.-A. Rupprecht, Kleine Einführung in die Papyruskunde, Darmstadt 1994.

Von all dem profitiert immer auch die neutestamentliche Exegese,[82] vor allem bei der Frage nach dem ursprünglichen Text, aber auch für die Wörterbücher zum Neuen Testament und in der Rekonstruktion von sozialen Vorgängen in den frühen Gemeinden.[83]

In meiner Textausgabe habe ich auf einen Aufsatz von Stanley E. Porter verwiesen,[84] der 1995 beim 21. Papyrologenkongress in Berlin nachdrücklich das Desiderat einer Ausgabe der griechischen Papyri mit apokryphen Evangelien herausgestellt „und bestimmte Anforderungen dafür genannt [hatte], die ich (D.L.) im folgenden auf[zu]nehme[n]" versprach, wobei ich meinte, kommentarlos den folgenden Satz anfügen zu können: „Eine Ausweitung auf Zitate bei Kirchenvätern bedarf keiner eigenen Begründung." (17) Porter selber hatte zunächst auf die seinerzeit noch kaum erfasste Zahl neuer Papyri solchen Inhalts hingewiesen, von denen ich freilich PBerol 11710 und PCair 10735 „als relativ späte und nicht sicher Evangelien zuzurechnende Texte" nicht aufgenommen habe,[85] dafür aber die Fragmente des Mariaevangeliums (POxy 3525 und PRyl 463) sowie PSI 1220bis, denn „wegen seines hohen Alters sollte dieser Papyrus vor dem Vergessen bewahrt bleiben." (178)[86] In einem Anhang habe ich zudem das umstrittene „geheime Markusevangelium" dargestellt, wobei ich wie schon in meinem Markus-Kommentar[87] meinte, dass mein eigenes Urteil darüber trotz aller Zurückhaltung deutlich sei.[88]

Ungewöhnlich ist jedoch, das Evangelium Marcions (56-61) und Tatians Diatessaron (102-105) in diesem Zusammenhang zu finden, denn sie gelten ja nicht als „apokryphe" Evangelien. Sie haben aber nachweislich in der Antike für weite Kreise kanonisches Ansehen genossen und sind erst durch massive Verdrängungsprozesse apokryph geworden; daher bilden sie vorzügliche Beispiele gerade für diese Kategorie.[89] Damit ergeben sich insgesamt andere

---

82   Freilich ist der Kontakt nicht immer so eng gewesen wie bei Deißmann (s. Anm. 31). Abzuwarten bleibt, was sich aus den verschiedenen Ankündigungen eines erneuerten Interesses an den Papyri ergeben wird.

83   Ein geradezu klassisches Feld ist die Interpretation des Philemonbriefs.

84   The Greek Apocryphal Papyri. The Need for a Critical Edition, in: Akten des 21. Internationalen Papyrologenkongresses Berlin 1995, APF.B 3, Berlin 1997, 795-803; vgl. meine Textausgabe (wie Anm. 5), 17.

85   Cornelia Römer vermisst in ihrer Rezension meiner Textausgabe (APF 47, 2001, 369) zudem PAberd 3 (= van Haelst Nr. 590), das ist aber ein recht später (6. Jahrhundert) und auch nicht eindeutig einem Evangelium zuzuordnender Text; vgl. zu diesem Ostrakon T. Nicklas, Fragmente christlicher Apokryphen und die Textgeschichte des Neuen Testaments, ZNW 96, 2005, 129-142, bes. 133.

86   Auch ein intensiver Vergleich mit den Testamenten der zwölf Patriarchen hat zu keinem Ergebnis geführt.

87   Wie Anm. 6, 2. 5.

88   Vgl. jetzt in meinem Sammelband (wie Anm. 5) 27-29. E. Rau, Das geheime Markusevangelium, Neukirchen-Vluyn 2003, dagegen hat der Echtheit den Vorzug gegeben.

89   Schwierig ist dabei die Auswahl der Texte. PDura 10 ist als Text des Diatessaron nach wie vor umstritten; für Marcion gibt es keine neuere Ausgabe. In beiden Fällen lassen sich in

Auswahlkriterien als für Stanley Porter. Mir ging es nicht um den papyrologischen Anteil der Apokryphenforschung, sondern um eine inhaltlich definierte Ausgabe von unterschiedlich überlieferten Fragmenten, seien es Handschriften, seien es Zitate. Doch würde es auch darüber wohl kaum einen Dissens geben müssen.[90]

Die vorliegenden Editionen schienen Stanley Porter aber nicht nur durch neue Funde überholt, sondern auch veraltet, sofern sie – von Ausnahmen abgesehen – lediglich aus vorhandenen Ausgaben kopierten[91] und nicht auf eigener Kollation von Handschriften beruhten; nötig sei das Studium der Originalhandschriften (795). Thomas Kraus hat dies aufgenommen und exemplarisch in einem Aufsatz das Fajum-Fragment (PVindob G 2325) noch einmal neu von seinem in Wien lagernden Original her dargestellt.[92] Prinzipiell ist dem natürlich zuzustimmen, wie ich meinerseits für das Studium des POxy 2949 bestätigen kann,[93] doch ergibt sich daraus eine Reihe von neuen Problemen. Nicht nur ist das Petrus-Ostrakon (van Haelst 741) ja verloren, wie sich nach langen, mühevollen Recherchen ergeben hatte,[94] sondern nun möglicherweise auch der Akhmîm-Codex (PCair 10759) selber,[95] so dass beim Hauptzeugen eine Überprüfung am Original in Alexandrien gar nicht mehr möglich ist.

Thomas Kraus und Tobias Nicklas verweisen deshalb auf „Qualitäts-fotografien", und deren Wiedergabe im Bildanhang der Textausgabe[96] zusammen mit den Abbildungen von POxy 2949, POxy 4009 und PVindob G 2325 für das Petrusevangelium sowie PBodl. MS Gr. th.f. [4] und PVindob G 39756 für die Petrusapokalypse macht insgesamt den Vorzug dieser Textausgabe aus. Doch müssen die Herausgeber damit zwangsläufig hinter den von ihnen selbst gesetzten Maßstäben einer Kontrolle am Original zurückbleiben. Merkwürdigerweise nennen sie auch nichts, woran sich die „Qualität" ihrer Fotos messen ließe, z.B. wann die in Kopenhagen gefundenen Negative von wem, wo, mit welchen Brennweiten, welcher Belichtung usw.

Lehrveranstaltungen mit der vorgelegten Textauswahl aber typische Züge der Evangelien-überlieferung aufzeigen.

[90] Vgl. auch die Umkehrung bei Römer in ihrer (papyrologischen) Rezension meiner Textausgabe: „Das Buch enthält neben den durch Zitate zu erschließenden Apokryphen auch papyrologische Zeugnisse" (wie Anm. 85, 369), oder H. Förster, der in seiner Rezension (Tyche 16, 2001, 309) meine beiden oben bei Anm. 84 zitierten Sätze positiv aufnimmt.

[91] Ein hübsches Beispiel für solche Traditionsketten bietet übrigens der verbreitete (auf Klostermann, Apocrypha I, KlT 3, Bonn 1908, 6, zurückgehende?) Druckfehler des Namens des römischen Hauptmanns Πετρώνιον statt Πετρώνιον in EvPetr VIII 31.

[92] Wie Anm. 51; vgl. in meinem Band (wie Anm. 5), 88-90.

[93] Vgl. oben bei Anm. 5.

[94] Vgl. in meinem in Anm.5 genannten Band, 93-96; Kraus und Nicklas (wie Anm. 44), 9.

[95] Vgl. Kraus und Nicklas (wie Anm. 44), 8.

[96] Wichtig ist hier der Hinweis auf Blattvertauschungen auf einem lose beiliegenden Zettel: „Im Bildteil ist P.Cair. 10759 f.6v fälschlicherweise als f.5r sowie P.Cair. 10759 f.5r als f.6v bezeichnet. Die korrekte Reihenfolge der richtig bezeichneten Fotos ist f.5r, f.5v, f.5r, f.6r und f.6v."

gemacht worden sind.[97] Die neuen Satztechniken ermöglichen viel mehr an gedruckten Fotos verglichen mit der Trennung zwischen (billigerem) Buchdruck und (teurer) Bildwiedergabe früherer Zeiten. Doch stehen inzwischen im Internet auf Dauer angelegte Abbildungen auch für Papyri zur Verfügung, so dass ein solcher „Bildanhang" fast schon wieder überholt wirkt.[98]

Schließlich fällt auf, dass bei Thomas Kraus und Tobias Nicklas von einer Überprüfung an „Originalfotos" nur im Zusammenhang mit den „Handschriften" die Rede ist, nie bei den „Hinweisen", die als Texte bzw. Zitate von Kirchenvätern doch ebenfalls auf kritischen Editionen, zum Teil in derselben GCS-Reihe, beruhen und daher denselben Kriterien unterliegen müssten.[99] Das mag übertrieben klingen, so hätte aber vielleicht das Problem von Justin, *dial.* 106,3, entschieden werden können, das sich eben nicht „aus dem überlieferten Text selbst" ergibt, wo vielmehr M. Marcovich in seiner Ausgabe eine Konjektur gegen den überlieferten Text anbringt,[100] um eine Aussage Justins anzugleichen an seine anderen.[101]

IV.

Für die Interpretation des Petrusevangeliums insgesamt ist noch nicht viel gewonnen. Über eine reine Passions- und Ostergeschichte, wie sie mit dem Akhmîm-Fragment, aber auch in POxy 2949 und PVindob G 2325 vorzuliegen scheinen konnte, führt POxy 4009 hinaus; der möglicherweise zeigt, dass das Petrusevangelium als ein umfangreicheres Werk zu denken ist, nicht auf diesen Bereich allein beschränkt.[102] Zudem spricht er dafür, dass jedenfalls das Matthäusevangelium als bekannt vorausgesetzt gewesen ist.[103] Der Verdacht, den Serapion in seinem Brief äußerte, hatte das Interesse der Forschung zwar

---

[97] Wie Anm. 44, 8.

[98] In meiner Textausgabe habe ich zwar 2000 noch auf derartige Hinweise verzichtet, von ihnen 2004 aber Gebrauch gemacht; vgl. zum Akhmîm-Codex im Internet C. Römer, Christliche Texte VII, 2004, 275-283, bes. 279, doch ließen sich diese Angaben nicht verifizieren (3. Februar 2005).

[99] Vgl. auch den relativ neuen Text Didymus, EcclT I 7,34-8,5 (so die übliche Zählung, nicht Eccl. 1,1-8).

[100] Vgl. Kraus und Nicklas (wie Anm. 44), 12: ἀπομνημονεύματα τῶν ἀποστόλων αὐτοῦ statt ἀπομνημονεύματα αὐτοῦ.

[101] So oder so ist jedoch nicht das Petrusevangelium gemeint. Das gilt auch für Didymus, JohT 10,20-21, wie bereits die Herausgeberin Bärbel Kramer betont hat (PTA 34, 1985, 91 A.5: gemeint ist Markus, der „Sohn" des Petrus, vgl. 1Petr 5,13): εἶχεν καὶ Πέτρος δό[σι]ν ἰδίου υ(ἱο)ῦ ἰδ[ι]α τέκ[ν]α, τοὺς [γεννηθέ]ντας ἐκ τοῦ [κατ '] αὐτ[ὸ]ν εὐαγγελίου, [τ]ὸν ἐν δίκῃ πάπ[π]ον χρηματίσαν[τα μι]μούμενα; dieser Text hätte mit demselben Recht wie Justins unter die „Hinweise" aufgenommen werden können.

[102] Vgl. Anm. 16.

[103] Vgl. oben bei Anm. 12 den Hinweis auf die Verkehrung von Mt 10,16b.

immer wieder auf die Frage des Doketismus gelenkt;[104] weder das Akhmîm-Fragment noch die neuen Texte weisen aber deutlich genug in diese Richtung.[105] Martin Dibelius hatte auf die starke Betonung alttestamentlicher Motive aufmerksam gemacht.[106] Doch auch für spätere Generationen noch bedeutete das mehr und mehr zum „Alten" werdende Testament eine Grundlage, ihre Geschichte zu verstehen; deshalb ergibt sich daraus nicht ein Indiz für ein hohes Alter des Petrusevangeliums. Nach einem ohne größere Resonanz gebliebenen Aufsatz von Nikolaus Walter[107] war es schließlich vor allem John D. Crossan, der literarkritisch aus dem Petrusevangelium ein ursprüngliches Kreuz-Evangelium gewinnen wollte, das unabhängig von aller sonstigen kanonisch oder apokryph gewordenen Jesusüberlieferung eine Größe eigener Art gewesen sein soll.[108]

Nach wie vor kennen wir weder den Anfang noch das Ende des Werkes, damit auch nicht seine Mitte; das macht – anders als z.B. beim Thomasevangelium – seine Interpretation so schwierig. Hier wie anderswo in der Evangelienforschung führen vielleicht neue Fragen weiter, z.B. nach der literarischen Gestaltung der erhaltenen Fragmente des Petrusevangeliums oder nach seiner Stellung in der Geschichte der Evangelienüberlieferung im 2. Jahrhundert. Vielleicht aber findet sich eines Tages noch der Gesamttext, und alle wundern sich darüber, was sie nicht einmal geahnt haben.

Postscriptum

Ende Januar 2006 erschien als Generalabrechnung mit meinen Arbeiten ein umfangreicher Aufsatz unter der negativ beantworteten Frage, ob es frühe Fragmente des so genannten Petrusevangelium gebe.[109] Allenfalls bleibe, so das

---

[104] Vgl. bei Anm. 40.

[105] Vgl. H. von Campenhausen, Die Entstehung der christlichen Bibel, BHTh 39, Tübingen 1968, 247, Anm. 8; anders J. Denker, Die theologiegeschichtliche Stellung des Petrusevangeliums, EHS XXIII/36, Frankfurt/Main et al. 1972, 93-125; auch J.W. McCant, The Gospel of Peter, Docetism Reconsidered, NTS 30, 1984, 258-273; R.E. Brown, The Death of the Messiah II, New York et al. 1994, 1337-1138; T.K. Heckel, Vom Evangelium des Markus zum viergestaltigen Evangelium, WUNT 120, Tübingen 1999, 290-291.

[106] Die alttestamentlichen Motive in der Leidensgeschichte des Petrus- und des Johannes-Evangeliums, in: idem, Botschaft und Geschichte I, Tübingen 1953, 221-247. Vgl. auch den Beitrag von Thomas Hieke im vorliegenden Band.

[107] Eine vormatthäische Schilderung der Auferstehung Jesu, NTS 19, 1972/73, 415-429, bes. 426-429.

[108] J.D. Crossan, The Cross that Spoke. The Origins of the Passion Narrative, San Francisco 1988 sowie den Beitrag von Crossan im vorliegenden Band. Vgl. zur Auseinandersetzung mit vorausgehenden Äußerungen Crossans R.E. Brown, The Gospel of Peter and Canonical Gospel Priority, NTS 33, 1987, 321-343.

[109] P. Foster, Are there any Early Fragments of the So-called *Gospel of Peter*?, NTS 52, 2006, 1-28. Die Herausgeber des vorliegenden Bandes haben mir freundlicherweise Gelegenheit zu einer schnellen Reaktion in Form eines knappen Postscriptums gegeben.

Ergebnis, der Akhmîm-Codex, aber der stamme erst aus der Zeit des 7. bis 9. Jahrhunderts.[110] Manches mag auf Missverständnissen des Autors beruhen.[111] Wie hätte ich denn z.B. behaupten können (22-23), εὐαγγελιστής werde seit dem 2. Jahrhundert primär nur noch im Sinne von „Autor eines Evangeliums" gebraucht? Anderes ist in dem vorliegenden Aufsatz bereits implizit gesagt.[112] Ich beschränke mich auf ein paar knappe Bemerkungen.

1. Sofern Papyri nicht durch in ihnen selbst enthaltene Angaben datiert werden können, geschieht das nach paläographischen Gesichtspunkten. Dabei gilt eine Toleranz von 50 Jahren,[113] denn wer schreibt, wird weitgehend ein Leben lang bestimmte einmal erlernte Eigenheiten des Stils beibehalten, ob die noch in Mode sind oder nicht. Angesichts der knappen Zeitspannen, um die es bei den hier in Frage kommenden Papyri geht, ist das bedauerlich, aber nicht zu ändern; die äußeren Kriterien zur Datierung relativieren sich dadurch jedoch nicht unerheblich und ertragen keineswegs eine weitere Reduktion (15).[114] Im derzeitigen papyrologischen Standardwerk von G. Cavallo und H. Maehler wird für den Akhmîm-Codex in diesem Sinne das Ende des 6. Jahrhunderts angegeben.[115]

2. Außer den für christliche Texte kennzeichnenden *nomina sacra* gibt es natürlich andere Abkürzungen, wie nicht zuletzt ⊓⊓⊓ in PVindob Gr 2325 Z. 5 zeigt. Daher erübrigen sich alle Einwände, es handle sich dabei nicht um ein *nomen sacrum* (21), wenn auch meine dementsprechende Äußerung missverständlich formuliert sein mag.[116] Für die Abkürzungen auf der Rückseite des Ostrakons (24-25) ist zusätzlich zu berücksichtigen, dass diese normalerweise verdeckt und gar nicht zum Lesen gedacht war; sie fasst als Votivinschrift lediglich in Worte, was die Vorderseite bedeutet.

3. Die Abbildung des Ostrakons auf Seite 23 stammt eindeutig aus meiner Textausgabe,[117] nicht, wie vorgegeben (22, Anm. 77), aus der Erstver-

---

[110] J. van Haelst gibt jedoch, gegen Fosters Behauptung (1-2, Anm. 2: „He sees the scribal hand being characteristic of the period from the seventh to the ninth centuries"), keine eigene Datierung, sondern referiert nur drei unterschiedliche Meinungen anderer Autoren (wie Anm. 2, 212): „VIIIᵉ-IXᵉ siècle (Omont, cité par M.A. Lods); VIIIᵉ siècle (von Gebhardt); VIIᵉ-VIIIᵉ siècle (Swete)" – kein Wort mehr.

[111] Ein Indiz dafür bilden die ungewöhnlich vielen Druckfehler in deutschsprachigem Text.

[112] Falsch z.B. ist es, POxy 2949 und 4009 in Oxford in der Bodleian Library zu lokalisieren (5, Anm. 17), auch wenn Foster dort studiert hat.

[113] „Mitte des 2. Jahrhunderts" z.B. bedeutet: zwischen ca. 125 und ca. 175.

[114] Die paläographische Bestimmung des POxy 4009 stammt im Übrigen, wie ich immer betont habe, von dem Oxforder Papyrologen P.J. Parsons, nicht von mir (15).

[115] Vgl. Anm. 23. Erstmals habe ich in der Textausgabe (wie Anm. 5, 72) auf dieses Werk hingewiesen.

[116] „... die beiden Punkte über π und τ, vergleichbar dem bei ‚nomina sacra' sonst gebräuchlichen Querstrich" (Evangelien, wie Anm. 5, 89); eindeutiger wäre ein Verzicht auf „sonst" gewesen. Dabei gibt er meine Meinung mit „a kind of *nomen sacrum*" (21) durchaus richtig wieder, wenn „kind of" deutschem „eine Art" entspricht, also nur Ähnlichkeit, nicht Gleichheit meint.

[117] Wie Anm. 5, 95. Die Idee, die Buchstaben (einschließlich des als Itazismus erkannten Jota rechts unten) und die (moderne) Ziffer 12 aus dem Ostrakon an den Rand zu übertragen, kam

öffentlichung, wofür der Autor und die Herausgeberin der Zeitschrift sich inzwischen entschuldigt haben.[118] Behandelt wird dieses Stück jedoch nicht als Bild, sondern rein literarisch als Text, und zwar im Anschluss an van Haelst als „liturgischer Text" (22).[119] Hingegen stellt es sich ikonographisch dar als Petrusikone mit einer rückseitigen Votivinschrift.[120] Dass es sich bei dem Abgebildeten nicht um einen beliebigen heiligen Missionar namens Petrus handelt, sondern um den aus dem Neuen Testament bekannten Apostel, zeigt der Kreuzstab in seiner linken Hand, wie ihn in seiner Nachfolge noch heute der römische Bischof statt eines Krummstabs führt.[121] Da andererseits für den Apostel εὐαγγελιστής ein zu geringer Rang wäre, bleibt nur der (vorgebliche) Autor des Petrusevangeliums.

4. Von der Rückseite besitzen wir kein Foto, sondern nur eine Zeichnung,[122] und die hat in allen Partien einen gleichmäßig schwarzen Druck im Unterschied zu den grauen Zwischentönen auf der Vorderseite. So ist die Buchstabenfolge ου zwar auf der Zeichnung deutlich (25) erkennbar, jedoch an einer Stelle, wo sich entsprechend der Vorderseite starke Abnutzungserscheinungen finden müssten. Vorsicht ist also geboten bei allen Rückschlüssen aus der Zeichnung.

5. In Fragen der Identifikation und Rekonstruktion von Fragmenten scheint der Autor davon auszugehen, dass Texte buchstäblich identisch sein müssen, um vergleichbar zu sein. Unter dieser Prämisse meint er jedenfalls, meine Überlegungen zu POxy 2949 und 4009 ad absurdum führen zu können. Wäre es so, gäbe es freilich keine Textkritik des Neuen Testaments oder anderer Werke. Dass z.B. das Wort von den Schlangen und den Tauben aus Mt 10,16b durch seine Umkehrung in POxy 4009 eine neue Pointe bekommt, entgeht ihm (17) dadurch ebenso wie die Schlüsselfunktion des allzu schnell abgetanen Textes 2 Clem 5,2-4 (18).

---

von mir, die technische Durchführung und die Verwendung von Buchstaben eines koptischen Zeichensatzes von Dr. Egbert Schlarb.

[118] Hat Foster die Erstveröffentlichung gar nicht gesehen? Irreführend ist im Übrigen unsere Verwendung des Buchstabens Chi (χ) unten rechts; besser wäre es gewesen, zwei sich kreuzende Linien (×) zu zeigen.

[119] Diese Klassifizierung stammt nicht aus der Erstveröffentlichung (wie Anm. 30), sondern von van Haelst, der so die m.E. richtigste Kennzeichnung als „mobilier liturgique" (= „liturgische Ausstattung"; H. Leclercq wie Anm. 32, 108) abwandelt.

[120] Vgl. dazu ausführlicher meinen demnächst erscheinendem Aufsatz: Das Petrusbildnis van Haelst 741 – eine Replik, ZAC 9 (2005).

[121] Für die Verbindung zwischen Petrus und Markus meint Foster (24, Anm. 82), mich auf den Markus-Kommentar meines früh verstorbenen Freundes Bob Guelich (Robert A. Guelich, Mark 1-8:26, WBC 34A, 1989, xxvi-xxix) hinweisen zu sollen. Mein eigener Kommentar (wie Anm. 6, 3-7) hätte es auch getan, denn beide sind aus einem gemeinsam geleiteten SNTS-Seminar in guter Zusammenarbeit entstanden (vgl. die jeweiligen Vorworte). Die Reihenfolge „Crossan and Lührmann" (10) grenzt hingegen an Infamie; Crossan hat sich 1988 auf meinen Aufsatz von 1981 berufen, nicht umgekehrt.

[122] Außer in der Erstedition (wie Anm. 30, 205) in meinem Buch (Evangelien, wie Anm. 5) 94.

Insgesamt kann die starke Rhetorik vor allem der Überleitungsstücke die großen und kleinen handwerklichen Fehler nicht verdecken, die den wissenschaftlichen Wert des Aufsatzes ganz erheblich in Frage stellen. Die im Aufsatztitel gestellte Frage ist für POxy 2949 m.E. auch weiterhin positiv zu beantworten. Für POxy 4009 hängt meiner Beobachtung nach vieles davon ab, sich beim Petrusevangelium von der Vorstellung eines reinen Passionsevangeliums zu trennen, wie sie jahrzehntelang vom Akhmîm-Codex genährt worden ist, noch dazu unter dem Primat der Formgeschichte. Für PVindob Gr 2325 schließlich habe ich immer betont, dass es sich bei der Zuordnung zum Petrusevangelium um eine Möglichkeit handelt; die aber sehe ich auch weiterhin.

The Akhmîm *Gospel of Peter*

by

PETER VAN MINNEN

In an earlier contribution,[1] I discussed the codex containing a fragment of the *Apocalypse of Peter* from a palaeographical, codicological and philological point of view. The same codex contains a fragment of the *Gospel of Peter* as well. I will summarize the basic insights from my earlier contribution here and attempt to draw implications for the interpretation of the *Gospel*.[2]

First, I will attempt a description of the codex. Without recourse to the original,[3] part of what I am going to say remains hypothetical. Second, I will consider briefly whether the fragment of the *Gospel of Peter* is an edited version of the original *Gospel*, known very imperfectly through a few testimonia.

When the fragment of the *Gospel of Peter* was published in 1892,[4] little attention was paid to the material aspects of the codex that contained it. This is quite understandable: the discovery of substantial fragments of the *Gospel* and the *Apocalypse of Peter* and of the first part of *1 Enoch* caused great excitement. Scholars focussed on the text and even more on the content of the *Gospel* and the *Apocalypse of Peter*. The circumstances of the find, the composition of the codex and the date of the manuscripts (plural) contained in it were very hard

---

[1] P. van Minnen, The Greek *Apocalypse of Peter*, in: The Apocalypse of Peter, Studies on Early Christian Apocrypha 7, ed. by J.N. Bremmer/I. Czachesz, Leuven 2003, 15-39.

[2] I will not discuss the other fragments on papyrus that have been claimed for the *Gospel of Peter* here, as none is decidedly from the *Gospel*. See the discussion in T.J. Kraus/T. Nicklas, Das Petrusevangelium und die Petrusapokalypse, GCS.NF 11. Neutestamentliche Apokryphen 1, Berlin-New York 2004, 55-68.

[3] From Kraus/Nicklas, Petrusevangelium, 8.

[4] U. Bouriant, Fragments grecs du livre d'Énoch, MMAF 9.1, Paris 1892, 91-147. Retouched plates (except pp. 11-12) were published by A. Lods, L'Évangile et l'Apocalypse de Pierre, MMAF 9.3, Paris 1893; photos of pp. 1-20 only by O. von Gebhardt, Das Evangelium und die Apokalypse des Petrus, Leipzig 1893, and Kraus/Nicklas, Petrusevangelium, whose foliation of the codex introduces unnecessary complications. Moreover, their foliation of the *Apocalypse* fragment is erratic (7r should be 10r, 8r should be 9v, 8r should be 9r, 9v should be 8v, 9r should be 8r, 10v should be 7v and 10r should be 7r), and the photos in their edition are not printed in the correct order. I will therefore stick to the traditional pagination of the two fragments, the second of which was bound upside down, thus pp. 1-12 and 20-13, with text appearing only on pp. 2-10 and 19-13. Kraus/Nicklas, Petrusevangelium, unfortunately do not give the pagination for the first manuscript (their f. 1v equals p. 2, their f. 2r equals p. 3, etc.). Lods also gives an image of the inside of the cover, but not of the outside.

to pin down.[5] Most recently, G. Cavallo and H. Maehler[6] redated most of the manuscripts to the late sixth century, and I have supported such a date (without, however, excluding a slightly later one) in my previous contribution.[7]

Here I have to repeat what I said about the circumstances of the find. The codex was found about 200 meters north-east from the top of the cemetery to the north-east of Akhmîm, ancient Panopolis in Upper Egypt.[8] This cemetery is a low ridge of over two kilometers in length and was used from the pre-dynastic period onwards. The tombs were dug in the surface and are generally not well preserved. In 1884, excavations started there without supervision. No reliable information on anything that was found exists today.

In my previous contribution,[9] I argued that the find was made in the central part of the cemetery. The antiquities' service had started from the north of the ridge and was working its way to the south, which it reached only in 1888. The first editor claims that the codex was found in the tomb of a monk. This seems no more than an inference from the content, not from indications in the tomb itself. The inference may be correct but is not an independent fact. Monks are not the only candidates for the ownership of early Christian texts in the Panopolis area. Any Greek-speaking inhabitant of Panopolis with a penchant for apocryphal literature may have been buried in the cemetery. It would have been natural to include a codex with his or her favorite texts in the tomb.

The construction of the codex was not satisfactorily discussed by the first editor, and I will repeat the reconstruction I proposed in my previous contribution.[10] The codex is made up of two small parchment manuscripts in a carefully written documentary hand (containing the fragments of the *Gospel* and the *Apocalypse of Peter*) and of the left-overs of two other parchment manuscripts in three different 'biblical majuscule' hands (containing the fragments of *1 Enoch* and the *Martyrdom of Julian of Anazarbus*). Although the first editor does not say anything about quires, I have attempted to reconstruct the codex physically with the help of paper, glue and common sense.[11]

---

5   For a brief statement see L. Vaganay, L'Évangile de Pierre, ÉtB, Paris 1930, 14-16.

6   G. Cavallo/H. Maehler, Greek Bookhands of the Early Byzantine Period, A.D. 300-800, London 1987, no. 41, illustrating three hands represented in the codex. They did not take the fourth hand that wrote the fragment of the *Martyrdom of Julian of Anazarbus* into consideration.

7   Van Minnen, Apocalypse of Peter, 20-21 (on the *Gospel* and the *Apocalypse of Peter*) and 23-24 (on *1 Enoch*).

8   See "Friedhof A" on the map in K.P. Kuhlmann, Materialien zur Archäologie und Geschichte des Raumes von Achmim, Mainz 1983, 53, Abb. 14, reproduced in Van Minnen, Apocalypse of Peter, 18.

9   Van Minnen, Apocalypse of Peter, 17.

10   Van Minnen, Apocalypse of Peter, 19-23.

11   I also availed myself of the photos made by the International Photographic Archive, digitally accessible at http://cpa.csad.ox.ac.uk/GP/GP.html and illustrated in Kraus/Nicklas, Petrus-evangelium.

The first manuscript containing a fragment of the *Gospel of Peter* consists of a binio of two bifolia or four leaves or eight pages to which a bifolium consisting of two leaves or four pages was added.[12] The first page contains an illustration, an ornamental cross. The second page is headed by a small cross to indicate the beginning of the text. The fragment of the *Gospel* occupies nine pages (pp. 2-10), which leaves the last two pages (pp. 11-12) blank. At the bottom of p. 10 we find an ornamental border with three small crosses to indicate the end of the text. The text ends abruptly in mid-sentence. This has usually been taken as an indication that the text was copied from a defective exemplar, just as the text of the *Apocalypse of Peter* contained in the next manuscript. But both texts begin with a proper sentence and the *Apocalypse* ends with one, so I do not think the inference is correct. I think that the fragments of the *Gospel* and the *Apocalypse of Peter* were considered complete in themselves, but that in the case of the *Gospel* there was no room left at the bottom of p. 10 to finish the fragment. It seems as if the scribe drew the ornamental border on that page first and that he or she[13] could not continue the text beyond it on the next page. Originally s/he used a binio, as in the case of the fragment of the *Apocalypse of Peter*, but towards the end of p. 8 s/he realized that s/he had to add more text. S/he must have calculated the length of the remainder and found that the text would occupy another two pages. S/he then added a bifolium of which s/he thought s/he could use only two pages, because s/he expected the other two pages to be folded before p. 1. But the binder[14] folded the other two pages after p. 10, so that p. 1 with the illustration remained up front. The scribe apparently could not foresee this, so s/he drew the ornamental border on p. 10, which s/he expected to be the last page. S/he continued to copy the text on p. 9. When s/he had almost reached the end on p. 10, s/he found that there was not enough room. S/he put as many words in the last line as possible, but s/he could not complete the sentence. Presumably there was not much text left to copy. The fragment of the *Gospel of Peter* s/he wanted to copy consisted of a selection from the larger text which started with a proper sentence and ended with one. This selection was not much longer than what we now have. I score an important point here, because the selection we have was made on purpose. The fragment of the *Apocalypse of Peter* also seems to be a selection rather than a left-over.[15]

The second manuscript is a binio consisting of two bifolia or four leaves or eight pages. It was bound upside down in the codex. The first page of the

---

[12]   The photos made by the International Photographic Archive show that pp. 9-12 are one bifolium.

[13]   That the scribe of the first two manuscripts contained in the codex may have been a woman should not be ruled out. The leftward slant rather supports it. I have therefore written 's/he' throughout when referring to the scribe of the fragments of the *Gospel* and the *Apocalypse of Peter*.

[14]   There seem to be small holes about 0,5 cm from the top and the bottom of the bifolium containing pp. 9-12, but without recourse to the original, this is no more than an impression.

[15]   As argued in Van Minnen, Apocalypse of Peter, passim.

second manuscript (p. 20) is left blank. No doubt it was intended for an illustration such as the one adorning the first page of the first manuscript, but this was never added. The second page of the second manuscript (p. 19) is headed by a small cross to indicate the beginning of the text just as in the first manuscript. The fragment of the *Apocalypse of Peter* occupies seven pages (pp. 19-13). On the seventh page (p. 14) the text is headed by another small cross. Something went wrong here, because the text ends only at the bottom of the eighth page (p. 13), where one might have rather expected the cross. There is no ornamental border there either, and the writing stops in the middle of the line. The last sentence is complete as it stands, and the letters in the last line are larger than in the rest of the text, indicating that it is the end.

The third quire is written in a different hand. It is a quaternio consisting of four bifolia or eight leaves or sixteen pages. The first leaf is missing now, but my reconstruction presupposes its one-time presence. It must have fallen out before the codex was deposited in the tomb. The text starts with a section of *1 Enoch* repeated from somewhat further on. Only on the third preserved page does chapter 1, verse 1 start without any indication that it does, right in the middle of a line. How much text preceded this quire originally we cannot tell, because yet another quire may have preceded. The mistake probably arose because the exemplar had skipped sections 20 and following and added them at the front. The scribe copied this addition supposing it was the beginning of the text, but then also copied it at its proper place where the exemplar had no doubt added a marginal note referring to the addition at the front.

The fourth quire is written in the same hand as the third. It is again a quaternio consisting of four bifolia or eight leaves or sixteen pages. The text continues that of the preceding quire.

The fifth quire is written in yet another hand. It is again a quaternio consisting of four bifolia or eight leaves or sixteen pages. The text continues that of the preceding quire, but breaks off at the end. This is indicated by a small symbol which fills the space at the end of the line. Clearly, the person who put the Akhmim codex together had only three quires of a larger codex with *1 Enoch* at his or her disposal. Codices with incomplete texts are quite common in late antiquity.

The last leaf of the codex was glued to the inside of the cover. Originally this may have been another quire, a quaternio consisting of four bifolia or eight leaves or sixteen pages. The text is from the *Martyrdom of Julian of Anazarbus*. The handwriting is the most literary in the codex and can be securely dated to the first half of the seventh century,[16] which could therefore be the *terminus post quem* for the composition of the codex, unless the last leaf was not original to the codex but added at a later date to strengthen the back cover.

The fragments of *1 Enoch* and the *Martyrdom of Julian of Anazarbus* appear to stem from the same scriptorium, because the format and layout of the pages is

---

[16]   See Van Minnen, Apocalypse of Peter, 23.

the same, and this incidentally lends support to my reconstruction of the quire containing the first fragment of *1 Enoch* as a quaternio. The scriptorium employed three different scribes or styles, but not necessarily all at the same time, as the last leaf could be somewhat later than the rest.

The codex was in part composed of left-overs. The three quires with *1 Enoch* and the leaf of the *Martyrdom of Julian of Anazarbus* are clearly incomplete and were certainly not written for the present codex. The first two manuscripts, however, although they do not give a complete text, were nevertheless regarded by their scribe as selections complete in themselves. They were written in one go and no doubt originally conceived as independent binios (in the first case a bifolium had to be added because the text was too long). Were the two manuscripts with the fragments of the *Gospel* and the *Apocalypse of Peter* specifically written for the codex or were they available before it was put together, just as the left-overs of *1 Enoch* and the *Martyrdom* had been? If the *Gospel* and *Apocalypse* manuscripts were written specifically for this codex, they were presumably copied from an exemplar in a different size, which did not fit the codex, and perhaps also on different material (papyrus). The exemplar may have contained both the *Gospel* and the *Apocalypse of Peter*, because the latter was edited to fit the former, as we will see. Yet the exemplar must have clearly distinguished the two texts, because they were not copied in one manuscript but in two. The *Apocalypse of Peter* was not incorporated into the *Gospel of Peter*, and the first two manuscripts in the Akhmim codex do not represent detached fragments of a single composite text either, but rather two selections regarded more or less complete in themselves.

The illustration on the first page of the first manuscript suggests that it was intended as the beginning of a book. The blank page on the first page of the second manuscript suggests that it too was meant for an illustration and as the beginning of yet another book. But in this case the intended illustration was never added, presumably because the second manuscript was incorporated into the codex immediately after the first manuscript. The two 'booklets' were made at the same time and by the same scribe and in the order in which they were supposed to be incorporated into the codex. The script is most careful at the beginning of the *Gospel of Peter*, but becomes less careful later on. The *Apocalypse* continues this less careful script, which shows that it was written immediately after the *Gospel* by the same scribe.

Whoever wrote the two 'booklets' transferred two older but related fragments onto parchment leaves in a size similar to that of the fragments of *1 Enoch* and the *Martyrdom of Julian of Anazarbus* with which they were to be joined in a codex. They were written on rather small and squarish leaves (about 12 x 15 cm), which are otherwise rare at such a late date.[17] This format must have been current in the scriptorium where the other manuscripts contained in

---

[17] A fifth-century parallel from Panopolis that comes to mind is the famous Berlin gnostic papyrus codex (inv. 8502).

the codex were written and was applied also to the first two manuscripts but without any ruling and in a documentary hand. It seems likely that the scribe of the fragments of the *Gospel* and the *Apocalypse of Peter* already owned the left-overs of the other manuscripts and adopted their format but not their script, presumably because s/he did not work in that scriptorium but operated more like an amateur, who could write a fairly regular documentary but not a literary hand. Whoever owned the codex did not mind the incomplete state of any of the manuscripts contained in it. The *Gospel* and the *Apocalypse of Peter* were incomplete, but they represented already edited chunks of the original texts. After the codex was put together, it may not have been used much. There are no certain signs of use in the texts themselves. The occasional correction seems original, i.e. made by the original scribe. The leaf of the *Martyrdom*, which was glued to the back cover, may, however, have been added at a later stage, and the above reconstruction of the third quire as a quaternio even implies that the first page fell out of the codex before it was deposited in the tomb in which it was found.

In late antiquity left-overs of several manuscripts were often put together in a bundle to create a new codex, or selections from various texts were made to create a composite manuscript. Both phenomena seem to be at work in the Akhmîm codex. The last three quires and the last leaf are clearly left-overs. The first two manuscripts are more or less complete as they stand, but their texts are selections of larger compositions. We may be tempted to look for a reason why the different parts were thus combined. A common denominator in the codex is Greek, and the combination of two apocalypses (that of Peter and *1 Enoch*) seems deliberate. The *Martyrdom of Julian of Anazarbus* may be connected with the *Gospel of Peter*, which records the trial of Christ just as much as it records the trial of Julian. The *Gospel* naturally joins the *Apocalypse of Peter*. The parallel between the Jews who condemned Jesus with whom the *Gospel* fragment opens and the false prophets with whom the *Apocalypse* fragment opens must also be deliberate.

What does this description tell us about the *Gospel of Peter*? If the text was copied from a defective exemplar, which was itself incomplete, there is no use speculating about the selection of this particular portion of the text. But if the selection was made already in the exemplar, as I have suggested, the choice itself becomes the subject of historical inquiry. Both the *Gospel* and the *Apocalypse of Peter* begin with a proper sentence, even if the sentences seem to refer back to something that originally preceded. The *Gospel* fragment ends abruptly, but this may well have been the result of a lack of space, as I have argued above. The *Apocalypse* fragment ends with a proper sentence. If the selection of these texts was made specifically for the two manuscripts, it would be one of the last creative acts in Greek on the part of Egyptian Christians. It is not impossible to identify Egyptian Christians literate in Greek at this late date, even in monasteries, but if they were not writing documents but creative works of literature, they would no longer do so in Greek. There may still have been pockets of Greek-speaking Origenists in Egypt, who may not have been unsympathetic towards this kind of early Christian literature, but even they would be preserving, not creating, such selections by this date. Presumably, therefore, the selection of the first two manuscripts in the codex was already made in the exemplar or earlier still, and this pushes its date back to a time when Greek was still in active use among Egyptian Christians.

Most intriguing is the fact that the first two manuscripts are related, not in the sense that they are detached fragments of the same book, but in that the selection of both texts together was a coordinated effort which resulted in a set of two texts transmitted together but kept separate. The scribe of the exemplar and the scribe of the first two manuscripts in the Akhmîm codex knew that they were dealing with two distinct texts, but the scribe of the exemplar (or an even earlier scribe) had edited the *Apocalypse* fragment to conform it to the *Gospel* fragment. Because we do not have another text of the *Gospel of Peter*, we cannot tell whether it was not also edited in the process. The opening sentence of the *Apocalypse of Peter*, for which there is no parallel in the Ethiopic text, was added when the selection was made and edited. 'Many of them will be pseudoprophets' cannot refer back to a previous portion of the text of the *Apocalypse*, because there is nothing in the Ethiopic to link it with. It should be read in light of the opening of the *Gospel* fragment. There the first sentence begins with a clear reference to the Jews. It is an anti-Jewish text and blames the Jews and king Herod while it leaves Pilate off the hook: 'Of the Jews no one washed his hands.' The reference to the Jews is echoed by the added opening of the *Apocalypse* fragment: 'Many of them will be pseudoprophets.' Here 'them' cannot refer to a group of people mentioned earlier in the *Apocalypse*, as we know from the Ethiopic. Because it was added when the selection was made, it must refer to a group of people the editor had in mind when editing the *Apocalypse of Peter*, which immediately follows the *Gospel*.

The fragment of the *Apocalypse of Peter* has become an anti-Jewish text to conform it to the anti-Jewish slant of the *Gospel* fragment. Originally, the *Gospel* may, but does not have to, have had an anti-Jewish slant. The original *Apocalypse* was in fact a Jewish-Christian text, as we can tell from the Ethiopic, but almost all Jewish-Christian traces of the original were deftly edited away in the version of the Greek text preserved in the Akhmîm codex. If the original *Gospel of Peter* was also a Jewish-Christian text (with Peter as the protagonist there is no reason why it could not have been such[18]), it may also have been deftly edited to become an anti-Jewish text. The only thing we can say is that this would have been done before the *Apocalypse of Peter* was edited, but not necessarily long before. In fact, the presence of a coordinated set of excerpts from both texts in the Akhmîm codex favors the possibility, if not the likelihood, that the anti-Jewish slant was put on both texts in one go.

---

[18] See J. Gnilka, Petrus und Rom. Das Petrusbild in den ersten zwei Jahrhunderten, Freiburg et al. 2002.

Maybe it is time to stop using the text of the *Gospel* fragment as it appears in the Akhmîm codex as if it reflected the original, early, character of the *Gospel of Peter*. The testimonia do not provide a clear indication of the nature of the *Gospel*, unless one presses the testimony of Theodoretus,[19] who says the 'Nazoraeans' (Jewish-Christians) used the *Gospel of Peter*. If the *Gospel* fragment was heavily edited, this would also explain why we cannot find much wrong with it. The docetic tendency found in the *Gospel* by Serapion of Antioch (bishop in 190-211)[20] has never been confirmed by a close reading of the Akhmîm text. Perhaps, Serapion was reading something substantially different from what we have today. Just as the *Apocalypse* fragment contained in the Akhmîm codex was made more orthodox in the process of changing its original Jewish-Christian character into an anti-Jewish slant,[21] the *Gospel* fragment in the same codex may have 'suffered' likewise in transmission. It is not my task here to consider the implications, for the study of gospel traditions and the wider world of early Christianity, of what seems to me a most attractive scenario.

---

[19]   See Kraus/Nicklas, Petrusevangelium, 18.
[20]   See Kraus/Nicklas, Petrusevangelium, 12-16.
[21]   On this see my remarks in Van Minnen, Apocalypse of Peter, 28-29.

„Die Sprache des Petrusevangeliums?"
Methodische Anmerkungen und Vorüberlegungen für eine Analyse von Sprache und Stil

von

THOMAS J. KRAUS

1. Die Problemsituation

Wann auch immer das apokryph gewordene[1] Petrusevangelium (fortan EvPetr) Gegenstand der wissenschaftlichen Diskussion wird, erfolgt die Konzentration auf dessen theologische Dimension, dessen Relation zu den kanonisch gewordenen Evangelien,[2] die Zuordnung und Interpretation von Textzeugen – seien sie Hinweise in der (spät)antiken christlichen Literatur oder auch konkrete Manuskripte[3] – bzw. auf Einleitungsfragen wie etwa Verfasserschaft, Datierung und Herkunftsort.[4] Anmerkungen zu Sprache, Stil und

---

[1] Der Begriff stammt von D. Lührmann (Fragmente apokryph gewordener Evangelien in griechischer und lateinischer Sprache. Unter Mitarbeit von E. Schlarb [MThSt 59], Marburg 2000) und ist „klarer Ausdruck scharfen Problembewußtseins" (vgl. meine Rezension in ZAC 8, 2004, 129-137, hier 131), denn solche Texte dürften zunächst in normalen Gebrauch gestanden haben und wurden erst im Zuge der Herausbildung des Kanons als „apokryph" diskutiert und eingestuft (hierzu Lührmann, Fragmente, 6-9).

[2] Weiteres diesbezüglich in diesem Band die Beiträge von J.D. Crossan sowie J. Verheyden.

[3] Zu beiderlei Art vgl. ausführlich die kritische Edition von T.J. Kraus/T. Nicklas, Hg., Das Petrusevangelium und die Petrusapokalypse. Die griechischen Fragmente mit deutscher und englischer Übersetzung, GCS.NF 11, Neutestamentliche Apokryphen 1, Berlin-New York 2004.

[4] Es ist beachtlich, dass in einigen Dissertationen zum EvPetr die Frage nach dem Verhältnis des Textes des EvPetr (wie im Akhmîm-Codex, *P.Cair.* 10759, erhalten) gerade zu den kanonischen Evangelien als wichtig erachtet wird, ohne dass letztlich dabei wirklich systematische philologische Erwägungen eine Rolle spielen. Vgl. vor allem B.A. Johnson, Empty Tomb Tradition in the Gospel of Peter (Ph.D. Diss., Harvard University, 1965), Ann Arbor 1966; J. Denker, Die theologiegeschichtliche Stellung des Petrusevangeliums. Ein Beitrag zur Frühgeschichte des Doketismus, EHS XXIII.36, Bern-Frankfurt/Main 1975, bes. 31-57; J.W. McCant, The Gospel of Peter: The Docetic Question Re-Examined (Ph.D. Diss., Emory University, 1978), Ann Arbor 1980, bes. 35-115; S.E. Schaeffer, The „Gospel of Peter", the Canonical Gospels, and Oral tradition (Ph.D. Diss., Union Theological Seminary, NY, 1991), Ann Arbor 1991. Immerhin geht Letztgenannte auf drei sprachliche Aspekte gesondert ein („rare words" und „late usage", „use of simple verbs" und die mögliche Verwendung des Optativs), verzweckt gleichzeitig aber ihre Beobachtungen für die Datierung des EvPetr (85-90).

Lexikon sind dann allenfalls Nebenprodukte, die im Laufe der Interpretation als nützlich erachtet werden.[5] Selbst die wenigen Ausnahmen hiervon beinhalten einige methodologische wie auch teilweise inhaltliche Probleme. Dennoch sind diese Arbeiten nicht nur erste Versuche und Orientierungshilfen für eine weiter führende Sprachanalyse des EvPetr, sie können vielmehr mit ihren enthaltenen wertvollen Beobachtungen für die Zukunft dann von großem Wert sein, wenn sie kritisch durchleuchtet und gegebenenfalls modifiziert werden.

Einige sprachliche Beobachtungen lieferte bereits M.R. James,[6] die jedoch im Kontext seiner Beschäftigung mit der Frage nach dem Verhältnis der beiden Texte des Akhmîm-Codex (*P.Cair.* 10759), die dann als Petrusevangelium und Petrusapokalypse (fortan: ApkPetr) bezeichnet werden, stehen und fast ausschließlich auf der Wortvergleichsebene ohne weitere Kommentierung verbleiben.[7] Wesentlicher für die gestellte Frage erscheinen mir insbesondere die Ausführungen von F. Weißengruber[8] zu Datierung und Grammatik des EvPetr sowie die knappe Studie von J. Karavidopoulos zu zwei *Hapax legomena* und weiteren seltenen Wörtern des EvPetr.[9] Auf beide wird unter 3. (Weißengruber) und 4. (Karavidopoulos) noch näher einzugehen sein, dann unter Einbeziehung der philologischen Notizen in der kritischen Edition des Textes, die ich zusammen mit T. Nicklas erstellt habe.[10]

Mit Recht wird der Mangel einer fehlenden systematischen Sprachanalyse des griechischen EvPetr (wie auch der griechischen ApkPetr) bemerkt und eine Behebung dessen gefordert.[11] Dieser Mangel kann mit der vorliegenden Studie nicht beseitigt werden. Allenfalls sind erste Beobachtungen möglich. Vielmehr sollen hier grundsätzliche methodische Vorüberlegungen erfolgen, mit Hilfe

---

5   In dieser Hinsicht noch mit den meisten Angaben L. Vaganay, L'Évangile de Pierre, ÉtB, Paris ²1930; weniger bereits bei M.G. Mara, Évangile de Pierre, SC 201, Paris 1973. Darüber hinaus finden sich philologische Beobachtungen in vielen Arbeiten, wobei diese Beobachtungen dann jeweils dem individuellen Untersuchungsgegenstand untergeordnet sind. Vgl. etwa J.W. McCant, The Gospel of Peter: The Docetic Question Re-Examined, Ann Arbor 1980; Schaeffer, The „Gospel of Peter".

6   M.R. James, A New Text of the Apocalypse of Peter, JThS 12, 1911, 36-64. 157. 362-383. 573-583, hier 579-580.

7   Entsprechend kritisch hierzu Vaganay, L'Évangile, 189. Eine Ausnahme mag ἡμεῖς οἱ δώδεκα μαθηταί (EvPetr XIV 49; ApkPetr 5) bilden. Hierzu und grundsätzlich über die Relation dieser beiden Texte des Codex die Studie von T. Nicklas, Zwei petrinische Apokryphen im Akhmîm-Codex oder eines?, Apocrypha 16, 2005, 75-96.

8   F. Weißengruber, Zur Datierung des Petrusevangeliums, 117-120, und idem, Grammatische Untersuchungen zum Petrusevangelium, 121-144, beide in: Das Petrusevangelium, SNTU.B 2, hg. von A. Fuchs, Linz 1978.

9   J. Karavidopoulos, «Hapax legomena» et autres mots rares dans l'*Évangile de Pierre*, Apocrypha 8, 1997, 225-230.

10 Kraus/Nicklas, Das Petrusevangelium und die Petrusapokalypse, 32-49. Allerdings sind diese Notizen als Verständnishilfen für die Übersetzungen sowie als Hervorhebungen von Auffälligkeiten sehr knapp angelegt.

11 So v.a. T. Nicklas, Zwei petrinische Apokryphen im Akhmîm-Codex. Allerdings muss im Vorfeld offen bleiben, ob eine systematische Sprachanalyse wirklich die Erwartungen erfüllen kann, die mancherorts auf sie gerichtet sind.

derer dann eine sprachliche Untersuchung des EvPetr *und* der (griechischen) ApkPetr erfolgen kann, die jedoch gleichzeitig als Regulativ für die Diskussion beider Texte dienen soll. Exemplarisch wird abschließend dann anhand der *Hapax legomena* aufgezeigt, wie ein erster, hier lexikalischer Schritt in die Richtung einer Sprachbeschreibung des EvPetr aussehen kann.

2. Methodische Vorabklärungen: Möglichkeiten und Grenzen einer sprachlichen Untersuchung

Zu (1): Welcher Text *des* EvPetr ist Grundlage der Diskussion?
Aus den Hinweisen in der (spät)antiken christlichen Literatur lässt sich leider nichts auf Umfang und Inhalt des EvPetr schließen, zumal immer auch mitbedacht sein will, dass unsicher bleibt, ob sich diese Hinweise wirklich auch auf *das* EvPetr beziehen. Denn *das* EvPetr, das hier in diesem Band diskutiert wird, ist nur bezeugt auf dem ersten Bogen des Akhmîm-Codex (*P.Cair.* 10759), der auf das Ende des 6. bzw. den Anfang des 7. Jahrhunderts zu datieren ist.[12]

Die zwei Papyrusfragmente von *P.Oxy.* XLI 2949 aus dem 2. bis 3. Jahrhundert, die schon R.A. Coles in seiner *Editio princeps* in die Nähe des EvPetr rückte und D. Lührmann[13] als Textzeugen (parallel zu EvPetr II 3-5) letztlich plausibel machte, bieten nur einige Wörter (in der Rekonstruktion von Lührmann einige Zeilen), so dass sie immerhin als Beleg dafür dienen können, dass *das* EvPetr – jener Text des Akhmîm-Codex (*P.Cair.* 10759) – in dieser Zeit in Ägypten zirkulierte. Eine Erweiterung des Textkorpus erlangt man dadurch aber ebenso wenig wie Rückschlüsse auf den Umfang, Inhalt und die ursprüngliche Textgestalt über das Erhaltene des Akhmîm-Codex hinaus.[14]

Kurzum: Es wird stets ein Text interpretiert, dessen umfangreichster und damit auch betrachteter Zeuge aus der Zeit des ausgehenden 6. bzw. des einsetzenden 7. Jahrhunderts stammt und der darüber hinaus sicher einen längeren Überlieferungs- und Rezeptionsprozess hinter sich hatte. Deshalb wird fortan unter EvPetr stets der entsprechende Text des ersten Bogens des

---

12 Vgl. G. Cavallo/H. Maehler, Greek Bookhands of the Early Byzantine Period, A.D. 300-800, BICS.S 47, London 1987, no. 41. Im Anschluss hieran P. van Minnen, The Greek *Apocalypse of Peter*, in: The Apocalypse of Peter, Studies on Early Christian Apocrypha 9, hg. von J. Bremmer/I. Czachesz, Leuven 2003, 15-39, hier 20-21; idem, The Akhmîm Gospel of Peter (in diesem Band); Kraus/Nicklas, Das Petrusevangelium und die Petrusapokalypse, 29.

13 So D. Lührmann, POx 2949: EvPt 3-5 in einer Handschrift des 2./3. Jahrhunderts, ZNW 72, 1981, 216-226; idem, Fragmente, 72. 84-85. Ferner Kraus/Nicklas, Das Petrusevangelium und die Petrusapokalypse, 55-58.

14 Zur Diskussion um weitere in die Diskussion eingebrachte Textzeugen des EvPetr vgl. Kraus/Nicklas, Das Petrusevangelium und die Petrusapokalypse, 5-7 (allgemein) sowie 59-63 (*P.Oxy.* LX 4009) und 65-68 (*P.Vindob.G* 2325).

Akhmîm-Codex (*P.Cair.* 10759) verstanden. Erstaunlicherweise wird in der Literatur hierauf nicht explizit hingewiesen.[15]

zu (2): Was kann eine linguistisch-lexikalisch orientierte Untersuchung
          überhaupt leisten?
Angesichts der Bezeugungslage sind die Möglichkeiten einer linguistisch-lexikalisch orientierten Untersuchung stark eingeschränkt. Ein sprachlicher Vergleich mit anderen Texten birgt das Problem, auf welche Zeit die Konzentration dann erfolgen soll. Sicherlich liegt die potentielle Abfassungszeit des EvPetr – meist Mitte des 2. Jahrhunderts – hier nahe. Methodisch allerdings ergibt sich dann ein Problem: Werden nicht mitunter Sprachgestalten miteinander verglichen, zwischen denen ein Zeitraum von eventuell mehreren Jahrhunderten liegt und auch dann ein zeitlicher Abstand verbleibt, wenn wiederum deren Handschriftenzeugen als Ausgangspunkt gewählt werden? Handelt es sich bei einem solchen Vorgehen nicht schon um eine bloße Verzweckung einer Untersuchung als Hilfe für die Datierung?

Zudem verhält es sich mit dem EvPetr in Form von *P.Cair.* 10759 anders als mit anderen Texten, deren Bezeugungslage deutlich umfangreicher und deren Datierung bereits anhand von Querverweisen wahrscheinlich gemacht werden kann.[16] Deshalb muss die sprachanalytische Arbeit an EvPetr noch mehr als sonst deskriptiv erfolgen, als Ausgangspunkt dient eben der Text von *P.Cair.* 10759 aus dem 6./7. Jahrhundert. Erst dann mögen einige Anhaltspunkte als Indizien in einem Argumentationsgebäude für Datierungsfragen, Mutmaßungen über Abfassungsort, Hypothesen über die Rezeptions- und Überlieferungsgeschichte (unter Einbeziehung von *P.Oxy.* XLI 2949) und vorsichtige Erwägungen über den Autor des EvPetr dienen können. Und erst dann lassen sich Vergleiche mit anderen Texten wirklich ohne ideologische bzw. konzeptionelle Vorbelastung durchführen.

zu (3): Was ist von einer linguistisch-lexikalisch orientierten Untersuchung für
          die Diskussion um das EvPetr zu erwarten und was nicht?
Wie ich an anderer Stelle bereits ausgeführt habe, kann eine linguistisch-lexikalisch orientierte Untersuchung nicht als eigenständiges Argument für konkrete Schlussfolgerungen fungieren, etwa hinsichtlich Ort, Zeit und Autorenschaft. Vielmehr muss eine deskriptiv ausgelegte Analyse einzig und allein den Text selbst in den Mittelpunkt stellen und kann so erst Indizien für

---

[15] Zumindest angedeutet bei T. Nicklas, Ein „neutestamentliches Apokryphon"? Zum
      umstrittenen Kanonbezug des sog. „Petrusevangeliums", VigChr 56, 2002, 260-272, hier 262-
      263 und *passim.*

[16] Hierzu T.J. Kraus, Sprache, Stil und historischer Ort des zweiten Petrusbriefes, WUNT 2.136,
      Tübingen 2001, bes. 31-32. 40-50. Auch wenn es sich bei 2Petr um eine pseudepigraphische und
      relativ kurze Schrift handelt, so ist die Ausgangssituation für eine Sprachanalyse doch
      signifikant besser: z.B. Konsens in der Forschung über Anfang und Ende; Bestand an
      Handschriften für die Rekonstruktion des Texts; Vorarbeiten im Bereich Sprache und Stil;
      Bezeichnung, damit Identifizierung des Texts als „2Petr".

Schlussfolgerungen liefern, die jedoch noch auf weiteren, aussagekräftigen Indizien fußen müssen, etwa hinsichtlich Datierung und Abfassungsort.[17]

Auch Rückschlüsse auf den Autor sind nur bedingt und wenn, dann unter Rückbezug auf den Inhalt des Texts, vorsichtig möglich. Was ist, wenn der Autor ursprünglich archaisiert, d.h. einem früheren Sprachduktus folgt als dem in seiner Zeit und Region üblichen? Wie lässt sich ein bestimmter Sprachduktus generell identifizieren? Inwiefern kann einem Schreiber (dann der entsprechenden Abschritte des Akhmîm-Codex) auch eigenständiges Modifizieren einer Textvorlage – bewusst oder unbewusst – zugerechnet bzw. zugetraut werden?

Was durchaus realistisch erscheint, ist ein Sprachvergleich zwischen EvPetr und ApkPetr, zumal beide Texte von *P.Cair.* 10759 vom selben Schreiber kopiert und damit die zu betrachtenden, vorliegenden Texte *de facto* zur selben Zeit geschrieben wurden, ungeachtet dessen, wann deren Vorlage oder potentielles Original verfasst worden waren. Hieraus ergeben sich möglicherweise durchaus Indizien, welche für die Klärung der Relation von EvPetr und ApkPetr (des Akhmîm-Codex) Ausschlag gebend sein könnten.

Eine deskriptive Analyse linguistischer und lexikalischer Art liefert jedoch grundlegende Beobachtungen, die als stete Mahnung zur Rückbindung aller Interpretation an den erhaltenen Text und als begleitende Indizien für weiterführende Argumentationen dienen können.

zu (4): Wie kann solch eine Untersuchung letztlich aussehen?
Muss eine Untersuchung jedes auch noch so diffuse Detail auf hunderten von Seiten sammeln, damit wirklich von einer angemessenen Sprachanalyse die Rede sein kann? Sicherlich ist es für die Leserschaft nur von Vorteil und aus Sicht einer Person, die eine Sprachanalyse über EvPetr anfertigt, nur redlich, wenn möglichst alle Beobachtungen ausführlich dargelegt werden.[18] Dennoch kann aus ökonomischen Gründen auch eine Konzentration auf wesentliche Beobachtungen erfolgen, wenngleich deren Auswahl den Grad an Subjektivität erhöht.

Die Ergebnisse der durchgeführten Analyse können getrost als Vademekum der ausführlichen Beschäftigung mit dem Text dienen, stellt sich doch grundsätzlich stets die Frage: Was muss der Leser/die Leserin alles wissen, um zu verstehen? oder im Kontext einer Sprachuntersuchung von EvPetr: Welche Details können überhaupt nur zu weiter führenden Rück- und Aufschlüssen führen?[19]

---

[17] Vgl. Kraus, Sprache, 411-414. Eine Datierung wird allenfalls durch mögliche Relationen zu anderen Texten erzielbar (mit Recht kritisch A.D. Baum, Rez. Kraus, Sprache, JETh 16, 2002, 270-271). Für 2Petr mussten aber konkrete Rückschlüsse auf Abfassungsort und Adressatenkreis aufgrund von sprachlichen Beobachtungen rein hypothetisch bleiben.

[18] Dieses waren meine Beweggründe für mein Vorgehen bei einer diesbezüglichen Untersuchung von 2Petr, die sich auf über 300 Seiten erstreckt. Vgl. Kraus, Sprache.

[19] Berechtigterweise angemahnt von T. Fornberg, Rez. Kraus, ThLZ 127, 2002, 1303-1305.

Deshalb gilt es auch die bereits vorliegenden Arbeiten bezüglich Sprache, Stil und Lexikon des EvPetr für weitere Analyseschritte dienstbar zu machen.

3. Methodische Anmerkungen und Vorschläge zur Nutzbarmachung der Arbeiten von F. Weißengruber

Wie schon oben angeführt, beschäftigt sich F. Weißengruber in zweierlei Hinsicht mit dem Text des EvPetr: (1) Einmal, um Licht in das Dunkel der Datierung des Texts zu bringen,[20] und (2) dann mit der Grammatik, um „die Eigentümlichkeiten des nachklassischen christlichen Sprachgebrauchs im einzelnen aufzuzeigen" und „eine Hilfe zum besseren Verständnis des vom klassischen Griechisch abweichenden Sprachgebrauchs dieser Schrift [zu] bieten."[21]

Bei (1) weist Weißengruber zu Recht die vorgebrachte Konjektur[22] von ἀποθάνοι des Manuskripts zu ἀποθάνῃ zurück und hält an dem Optativ fest. Seine Schlussfolgerungen aber, „[s]olange man vom NT ausgeht, wird der Optativ anstößig erscheinen"[23] und der Autor des EvPetr sei „von jener den Optativ wieder belebenden, literarischen Welle erfasst" worden, die auf den Attizisten beruhe,[24] bergen unterschiedliche Engführungen in sich. Erstens kann *das* Neue Testament nicht bedenkenlos als Richtschnur, damit als Kanon des Sprachempfindens gesetzt werden, handelt es sich eben nicht um ein einheitliches Ganzes.[25] Auch hier mag das Vorurteil, es handle sich letztlich doch um einen apokryph gewordenen Text, eine wichtige Rolle für die Einschätzung spielen. L. Vaganay, den Weißengruber als Autorität anführt, stellt zwei Möglichkeiten in Aussicht, indem er den Optativ als „construction usitée seulement dans le classique et la koine littéraire"[26] ausweist. Auch ein

---

[20] Vgl. Weißengruber, Zur Datierung, 119. Weißengruber versucht zu klären, ob dem Datierungsansatz von Vaganay, L'Évangile, 163, oder Mara, Évangile de Pierre, 215-218, Recht zu geben sei.

[21] Weißengruber, Grammatische Untersuchungen, 123.

[22] Ausgehend von O. von Gebhardt, Das Evangelium und die Apokalypse des Petrus. Die neuentdeckten Bruchstücke nach einer Photographie der Handschrift zu Gizeh in Lichtdruck herausgegeben, Leipzig 1893, auch v.a. Zahn, Harnack und Vaganay.

[23] Weißengruber, Zur Datierung, 119.

[24] Weißengruber, Zur Datierung, 120. Entsprechend im Ergebnis übernommen von Schaeffer, The „Gospel of Peter", 89-90, die zudem auch die bevorzugte Benutzung von einfachen Verben im Gegensatz zu *Composita* und generell den Stil des EvPetr („the evangelist's desire to emulate a classical literary style", 89) dem Einfluss der Attizisten zuschreibt.

[25] Dahin gehend auch meine Bemühungen um Klarstellungen in Kraus, Sprache, 44-50, in meinem „Exkurs: Biblisches und jüdisches Griechisch, Κοινή und Attisch". Das Auflösen dieser Aporie ist nach wie vor untrennbar mit dem Namen A. Deissmann verbunden.

[26] Vaganay, L'Évangile, 147.

Rekurs auf Belege in den Handschriften wie den (dokumentarischen) Papyri[27] hilft, das unvorsichtige Urteil zu relativieren:

(a) Wenn, wie Weißengruber ansetzt, der Autor des EvPetr wirklich „viele klassische Formen und manche klassische Vokabel anstelle der in der Koine gebräuchlichen"[28] verwendet, dann läge es doch auch nahe, dem Autor zuzutrauen, den Optativ aufgrund dieser Orientierung folgerichtig – womöglich archaisierend – zu gebrauchen, auch ohne deshalb einzig auf die Wiederbelebung durch die Attizisten zu rekurrieren,[29] was jedoch als Möglichkeit unbenommen bleibt.

(b) Eine auffällige grammatische Form in einer Handschrift des 6./7. Jahrhunderts lässt zunächst an den Schreiber selbst, seine Vorlage und erst dann an den ursprünglichen Text denken, zumal kein weiteres Manuskript über diese Lesart Aufschlüsse ermöglicht. Auch könnte, wie analog für Codex Sinaiticus (ℵ) Mk 12,2 mit ἵνα λάβοι denkbar, ebenso eine Optativform erst nach dem Wirken der Attizisten durch das Sprachempfinden eines Schreibers (oder Redaktors) Eingang gefunden haben.[30]

(c) In umgekehrter Blickrichtung, wenn die Form also erst im Laufe des Überlieferungs- und Rezeptionsprozesses Eingang in den Text des EvPetr (P.Cair. 10759) gefunden hat, sind dann keinerlei Rückschlüsse mehr auf die ursprüngliche Form hier erlaubt.

Bei (2) ist Weißengruber vorsichtiger und zeigt hohes Problembewusstsein, indem er von „der Handschrift" schreibt und die Kürze des Textes als Problem für weitere Aussagen wahrnimmt.[31] Sicherlich waren die Phänomene des Itazismus und der Assimilation schon vor Erscheinen von Weißengrubers Arbeit näher erforscht,[32] und es war auch damals nicht mehr angebracht, grundsätzlich von „einem Fehler des Abschreibers" zu reden. Auch ist es

---

[27] Vgl. die Beispiele für *Optativus obliquus* in Finalsätzen in E. Mayser, Grammatik der griechischen Papyri aus der Ptolemäerzeit mit Einschluß der gleichzeitigen Ostraka und der in Ägypten verfaßten Inschriften. II,1. Satzlehre. Analytischer Teil. Erste Hälfte, Berlin 1933, 238. 252-253; F. Blass/A. Debrunner, Grammatik des neutestamentlichen Griechisch, bearb. v. F. Rehkopf, Göttingen ¹⁷1990, § 386,4 (Anm. 5).

[28] Weißengruber, Zur Datierung, 120. Wiederum konform geht Schaeffer, The „Gospel of Peter", 87-89.

[29] Eine grundsätzliche Orientierung über den Optativ ist anzuraten, etwa anhand von E. Schwyzer, Griechische Grammatik 2. Syntax und syntaktische Stilistik, vervollst. u. hg. von A. Debrunner, HAW 2,1,2, München ⁵1988, 319-338, bes. 337-338 (über den Optativ in nachklassischer Zeit). Selbst in der attizistischen und nach-attizistischen Zeit ist nicht automatisch von einem „regelkonformen grammatischen Gebrauch" des Optativs auszugehen, wie Schwyzer für Prokop von Cäsarea konstatiert, vielmehr war schon bald die Verwirrung groß.

[30] Hinsichtlich attizistischer Tendenzen (Attizismen) im Neuen Testament sind vor allem G.D. Kilpatrick und J.K. Elliott zu nennen. Kritisch zu beiden (mit Literatur) G.H.R. Horsley, Koine or Atticism – a Misleading Dichotomy, NDIEC 5, 1989, 41-48.

[31] Weißengruber, Grammatische Untersuchungen, 125.

[32] Vgl. E. Mayser, Grammatik der griechischen Papyri aus der Ptolemäerzeit. Band I: Laut- und Wortlehre. 1. Teil: Einleitung und Lautlehre (Bearb. v. H. Scholl), Berlin ²1970; F.T. Gignac, A Grammar of the Greek Papyri of the Roman and Byzantine Periods. Vol. I: Phonology, TDSA 55, Mailand 1975.

unsinnig, über Fragen der Akzentsetzung zu spekulieren (für EvPetr II 5 ΑΔΕΛΦΕ), da das Manuskript nur Majuskeln[33] und keine Akzente aufweist. Entscheidender sind aber andere Beobachtungen, die der Autor zur Verfügung stellt: So sind seine Beschreibungen der Tempus-Formen ebenso wertvolle Daten wie auch die der „periphrastische[n] Tempusbildung" des EvPetr.[34]

Dennoch sollten diese Beobachtungen ebenso anhand weiterer Hilfsmittel[35] überprüft, gegebenenfalls modifiziert und ergänzt werden, wie dies auch hinsichtlich der Beschreibung des Artikel-Gebrauchs in EvPetr gilt. Hier – wie auch an anderer Stelle – muss die Frage erlaubt sein, was letztlich die Vergleichsgröße ist, genauer gesagt, ob wirklich ein grammatisches Regelwerk überhaupt und wenn ja in welchem Maße anzulegen ist. Letztlich muss hier eine systematische Untersuchung anhand der komplexen Funktionen des Artikels im Griechischen erfolgen (Substantivierung, Individualisierung – Generalisierung, Determination) sowie seine Verwendung im Syntagma (attributiv – prädikativ).[36] Analoges gilt auch für die Möglichkeiten der Negation im Griechischen, die dann mit den α-privativum-Bildungen auch in den Bereich der Wortbildungsparadigmata hineinreichen.[37]

Die wertvollen, deskriptiven Beobachtungen zu Präpositionen, Pronomina wie auch Verba/Tempora können wiederum den Grundstock zu weiterer Datenerhebung bilden, wobei möglicherweise insbesondere die Verwendung der *Verba infinita* (v.a. Infinitive und Partizipien) auf Stileigentümlichkeiten und ein gewisses literarisches Niveau (z.B. *Genetivus absolutus* in EvPetr I 1; V 39) hinweisen könnten.[38]

Letztlich wäre dann noch Weißengrubers „Zusammenfassung" zu modifizieren, in der er angenehm vorsichtig und schlüssig aus seinen Beobachtungen folgert. Allerdings sollte auch immer vorab geklärt sein, welcher Stilbegriff zugrunde gelegt wird,[39] soll eine Bewertung nicht dem Verdacht erliegen, dann doch ein Geschmacksurteil des Bewertenden selbst

---

[33] Zum Vorzug der Bezeichnung 'Majuskel' gegenüber 'Unziale' vgl. E.G. Turner, Greek Manuscripts of the Ancient World, ed. by P.J. Parsons, BICS.S 46, London ²1987, 1-4.

[34] Weißengruber, Grammatische Untersuchungen, 126-128. Zur Diskussion um παραλημφθῆναι in EvPetr I 2 aber nun Kraus/Nicklas, Das Petrusevangelium und die Petrusapokalypse, 32-33. Ferner auch Mara, Évangile de Pierre, *ad loc.*

[35] Für eine Auswahl der wichtigsten vgl. die Bibliographie in Kraus, Sprache, 419-423.

[36] Hierzu ausführlich T.J. Kraus, Der Artikel im Griechischen: Nutzen einer systematischen Beschäftigung anhand von ausgewählten Syntagmata (Hab 1,12; Jud 17; Joh 6,32), RB 107, 2000, 260-272; idem, Sprache, 54-86 (allgemein und dann hinsichtlich 2Petr). Dabei besagt die Nicht-Verwendung des Artikels nicht gleichzeitig automatisch, dass etwas dann nicht substantiviert oder determiniert ist. Dies kann auch ohne Artikel bereits Ausdruck finden. Entsprechend zu überarbeiten Weißengruber, Grammatische Untersuchungen, 128-131.

[37] Vgl. Kraus, Sprache, 196-204. 300-309 und idem, Grammatisches Problembewusstsein als Regulativ für angemessene Sprachbeurteilung – das Beispiel der griechischen Negation und 2 Petr, FilolNT 27-28, 2001, 87-99. Dies kann methodisch für die Erweiterung von Weißen-gruber, Grammatische Untersuchungen, 141-142, dienen.

[38] Diesbezüglich die grundsätzlichen Anmerkungen und der modellhafte Nachweis für 2Petr in Kraus, Sprache, 265-275 (u.ö. zu *Gen. abs.*; vgl. Sachregister auf S. 480).

[39] Hierzu meine Begriffsklärungen und methodischen Überlegungen in Kraus, Sprache, 27-44.

zu sein. Nur so ist man vor qualitativen Extremurteilen in beiderlei Richtung gefeit.[40]

4. So genannte *Hapax legomena* und „seltene Wörter" des EvPetr – die knappe Studie von Karavidopoulos

In einer kurzen Studie widmete sich J. Karavidopoulos im Jahr 1997 nicht nur zweier so genannter *Hapax legomena* (a), sondern auch noch einiger weiterer „seltener Wörter" (b) des EvPetr.[41] Leider fehlt eine Problematisierung des Phänomens *Hapax legomenon*, so dass nur erkennbar wird, in welchem Kontext diese Wörter jeweils „Einzelwörter" sind: (a) Die beiden Verben σταυρίσκω (EvPetr II 3) und σκελοκοπέω (EvPetr IV 14) sind *Hap. leg.* „dans toute la littérature grecque, aussi bien classique que chrétienne", (b) die weiteren „mots rares" sind solche, „qui ne se rencontrent pas dans le NT".[42] In Bezug auf die „seltenen Wörter" vermeidet Karavidopoulos die Bezeichnung *Hap. leg.*, verwendet diese nur für (a).

zu (a):
σταυρίσκω (EvPetr II 3)
Die singuläre Form σταυρίσκω überrascht angesichts der sonstigen Verwendung von σταυρόω (IV 10; XII 52; XIII 56) und σταυρός (IV 11; X 39.42). Die Bildung mit -ίσκω stellt hier morphologisch weder einen Fehler, noch ein Problem dar.[43] Grundsätzlich „ist hier an eine Neubildung zu denken",[44] findet sich sonst mit den üblichen Hilfsmitteln nirgends auch nur ein Beleg für diese Präsentien-Bildung.

Mit Recht lehnt auch Karavidopoulos nach einer Diskussion des Einzelwortes in seinem Vers-Kontext vorgeschlagene Konjekturen (zu einer Form von σταυρόω) ab, schließt jedoch direkt auf den Autor des EvPetr, der sich hier – obgleich sonst in diesem Vers der Terminologie der Evangelien – „à la manière des narrateurs populaires" der Alltagssprache bediene.[45] Erinnert aber sei an die methodische Prämisse, die ich oben unter 2. (1) ausführte: Die Form findet sich in einem Manuskript, das aus das 6./7. Jahrhundert stammt. Berücksichtigt man den Vers auf *P.Oxy.* XLI 2949 – leider ist eben genau dieses Verb oder eine Variante dessen nicht erhalten – so ist auch mit Modifikationen

---

[40] Berechtigterweise warnt Karavidopoulos, «Hapax legomena», 230, vor einer Überschätzung der literarischen Leistung des Autors von EvPetr, wie er sie bei Weißengruber, Grammatische Untersuchungen, 144 (ähnlich idem, Zur Datierung, 119-120), gegeben sieht.

[41] Vgl. Karavidopoulos, «Hapax legomena», 225-230. Von „rare words" schreibt auch Schaeffer, The „Gospel of Peter", 85-90, und listet diese auf.

[42] Karavidopoulos, «Hapax legomena», 226. 229.

[43] Zu -ίσκω vgl. E. Schwyzer, Griechische Grammatik 1: Allgemeiner Teil, Lautlehre, Wortbildung, Flexion, HAW 2,1,1, München ³1959, 707-710.

[44] Kraus/Nicklas, Das Petrusevangelium und die Petrusapokalypse, 33.

[45] Karavidopoulos, «Hapax legomena», 227.

im Laufe des Überlieferungsprozesses für jede Rekonstruktion zu rechnen, selbst wenn Schreibern durchaus Genauigkeit beim Kopiervorgang zugetraut werden muss. So könnte durchaus sein, dass der Schreiber die ungebräuchliche Form seiner Vorlage entnommen hat. Doch dann müsste konsequent gefragt werden, warum nur oder ausgerechnet dieser Schreiber diese Form übernommen habe, während ansonsten σταυρίσκω nicht mehr erhalten ist, also auch etwa später bei den Kirchenvätern nicht.

Eben deshalb erscheint plausibler, den Schreiber des Akhmîm-Codex selbst als möglichen Ursprung dieser Form in Erwägung zu ziehen. Dies hat den Vorteil, dass so die Frage, warum σταυρίσκω auch in der (spät)antiken christlichen Literatur nicht vorkommt, einfach zu beantworten ist: Die Form bildet erst der Schreiber selbst.[46]

σκελοκοπέω (EvPetr IV 14)

Das bildhafte Verb σκελοκοπέω (σκέλος „Schenkel", „Bein") ist ebenfalls sonst nirgends belegt, verwandtes σκελοκοπία nur in Glossen.[47] Hier gilt Analoges wie zu σταυρίσκω: Mit Karavidopoulos ist an eine spontane bzw. freie Neubildung zu denken, die merkwürdigerweise wiederum keine Spur in der späteren Literatur hinterlassen hat.[48] Natürlich ist auch ein potentieller Tradierungsprozess zwischen dem ursprünglichen Text des EvPetr und dem auf dem Akhmîm-Codex (*P.Cair.* 10759) erhaltenen zu rechnen. Konkret wird dies jedoch nicht, und so erscheint – selbst wenn diese Möglichkeit ähnliche Plausibilität genießt – wiederum ein Rückgriff auf den Schreiber und nicht auf den eigentlichen Autor des EvPetr einleuchtend, wodurch auch das Ausbleiben eines Gebrauchs der Bildung in der (spät)antiken christlichen Literatur erklärt wäre.[49]

---

[46] Veranschlagt werden könnte auch, dass diese Bildung als abnormes Gebilde empfunden worden war und deshalb nicht Aufnahme in die Sprachverwendung fand, war diese semantische Stelle doch schon mit σταυρόω und dessen Composita belegt. Allerdings lassen sich diesbezüglich in der (spät)antiken christlichen Literatur Gegenbeispiele finden, denkt man nur an die Psalmen-Kommentare einzelner Kirchenväter, wo sonst ungebräuchliche Bildungen sehr wohl Aufnahme fanden.

[47] Vgl. G. Goetz/G. Gundermann, Glossae latinograecae et graecolatinae, Corpus Glossariorum Latinorum 2, Leipzig 1888, 432-57.

[48] So Karavidopoulos, «Hapax legomena», 227; Kraus/Nicklas, Das Petrusevangelium und die Petrusapokalypse, 35. Zu σκελοκοπέω und seinem kontextuellen Hintergrund vgl. T. Hieke, Das Petrusevangelium vom Alten Testament her gelesen, „PE 14: Das Zerbrechen der Schenkel" (in diesem Band).

[49] Anders verhält es sich beispielsweise mit dem NT-*Hap. leg.* ἀλεκτρυών und dem biblischen *Hap. leg.* κοκκύζω auf *P.Vindob.G* 2325, dem so genannten Fayûm-Evangelium: Zwar hätten auch hier der Schreiber *oder* Autor des zugrunde liegenden Textes entsprechend der kanonisch gewordenen Evangelien in diesem Kontext scheinbar gebräuchlichere sprachliche Alternativen gehabt (ἀλέκτωρ und etwa φονέω), doch sind beide *Hap. leg.* durchaus gebräuchliche Wörter. Ausführlicher T.J. Kraus, P.Vindob.G 2325: Das sogenannte Fayûm-Evangelium – Neuedition und kritische Rückschlüsse, ZAC 5, 2001, 197-212, hier 207-208. 210.

zu (b):

Was für die beiden absoluten *Hapax legomena* auch methodisch problemlos und damit relativ einfach zu erstellen war – eine Hypothese über ihren Ursprung –, gestaltet sich hinsichtlich weiterer als „mots rares" eingestufter Wörter problematischer. Was Karavidopoulos unter *Hap. leg.* versteht, wird klar, ohne dass er es explizit zu entwickeln braucht: *Hap. leg.* sind für ihn jene Wörter, die nur einmal und ansonsten an keiner anderen Stelle im Griechischen vorkommen. Also sind für ihn jene Wörter des EvPetr nicht *Hap. leg.*, die außerhalb der griechischen Bibel (Septuaginta und Neues Testament) sehr wohl Verwendung fanden, wie λαχμός oder ὑπορθόω.

Dieses Verständnis von *Hap. leg.* fordert zu methodischen Überlegungen heraus. An anderer Stelle widmete ich mich ausführlich einer kritischen Auseinandersetzung mit den diffusen Definitionsversuchen für dieses Sprachphänomen,[50] um schließlich zu einer praxisorientierten Umschreibung zu gelangen: Ein *Hap. leg.* ist somit nur dahingehend ein Einzelwort, als es in einem Text durchaus mehrmals auftreten darf, jedoch dann in einem bestimmten sprachlichen Referenzrahmen sonst nicht vorkommt. Grundsätzlich besteht dieser Referenzrahmen aus allem verfügbaren (alt)griechischen Material, wird aber wiederum in einzelne Bereiche unterteilt. Einer dieser Bereiche ist beispielsweise die griechische Bibel, bestehend aus Septuaginta und dem Neuen Testament, selbst wenn dies eine künstliche Grenzziehung ist. Doch durch Aneinanderreihung vieler solcher Bereiche (z.B. noch Inschriften, Papyri, Kirchenväter) und der Berücksichtigung der jeweiligen Zeit ergeben sich Daten, aufgrund derer vorsichtig auf den Hintergrund des Autors bzw. Texts selbst geschlossen werden kann. Entsprechend mag ein biblisches *Hap. leg.* durchaus sonst in regem Gebrauch gestanden haben, wie etwa καθαρεύω (XI 46), weshalb mehr das Fehlen im biblischen Bereich überraschen mag als die Verwendung im EvPetr. Sonst kann man noch ein Einzelwort als NT-*Hap. leg.* bezeichnen. Stets ist aber mit einzubeziehen, ob nicht doch *simplex* oder *composita* in einem anderen Verwendungsbereich aufzufinden sind, wodurch dann beispielsweise der Gedanke einer möglichen Neu- oder Spontanbildung durch den Autor (hier auch der Schreiber; s.o.) bedenkenswert wird.

Demnach sind folgende Wörter *Hapax legomena* in dem einen oder anderen Sinn, hier also nur mehr biblisches *Hap. leg.* oder NT-*Hap. leg.*, da die beiden absoluten bereits abgehandelt sind:[51]

---

50 Vgl. T.J. Kraus, „Uneducated", „ignorant", or even „illiterate"? Aspects and Background for an Understanding of αγραμματοι (and ιδιωται) in Acts 4.13, NTS 45, 1999, 434-449, bes. 438-444; idem, Sprache, 313-353 (Problemanalyse; Umschreibung; Ausweis für 2Petr; Rückschlüsse)

51 Für eine erste Orientierung wurden folgende Hilfsmittel konsultiert: W. Bauer, Griechisch-deutsches Wörterbuch zu den Schriften des Neuen Testaments und der frühchristlichen Literatur, hg. v. K. Aland/B. Aland, Berlin-New York ⁶1988; F.W. Danker, A Greek-English Lexicon of the New Testament and other Early Christian Literature (Based on W. Bauer's *Wörterbuch*), Chicago-London ³2000; J. Lust/E. Eynikel/K. Hauspie, Greek-English Lexicon of the Septuagint, Stuttgart ²2003; H.G. Liddell/R. Scott, A Greek-English Lexicon. Rev. and augm. by H.S. Jones. With a revised supplement 1996, Oxford ⁹1940 [1996]. Ferner computergestützte

ἀγωνιάω (V 15)
NT: --; LXX: Esther 5,1; Dan 1,10; 2Makk 3,21 (dort wie in EvPetr mit μεγάλως);
Ferner: Josephus, ant. 9,32; Papyri; Profanliteratur oft. — Vgl. die Verwendung
von ἀγωνία (Lk 22,44; 2Makk 3,14.16; u.a.).

διανοέομαι (XI 44)
NT: -- (Lk 11,17 διανόημα; 12x διανοία); LXX: 57x; Ferner: Auch bei Josephus,
Philo, in Papyri und Profanliteratur oft.

εἴλλω, auch εἰλέω, εἰλέω, εἴλλω, εἴλω (VII 24)
NT: --; LXX: 4Kön 2,8; Jes 11,5 (Composita mit ἀν-, ἀπ-, ἐν-); Ferner:
Profanliteratur oft.

ἐπιχωρέω (IX 37)
NT: --; LXX: 2Makk 4,9; 12,13; Ferner: In Profanliteratur gebräuchlich (LSJ).

καθαρεύω (XI 46)
NT: --; LXX: --; Ferner: Philo; Josephus; Papyri; Profanliteratur häufig.

λαχμός (IV 12)
NT: --; LXX: --; Ferner: Justin, dial. 97,3; Scholien; selten.

μνημοσύνη (XII 54)
NT: --; LXX: --; Ferner: Vor allem literarisch gut gebräuchlich (u.a. auch als
Mutter der Musen).

ὀρθόω (IV 11)
NT: -- (Lk 13,13; Apg 15,16; Hebr 12,12 ἀνορθόω; Tit 1,5 ἐπιδιορθόω); LXX: 7x
(auch Composita); Ferner: Philo; insbes. in Profanliteratur häufig.

ὀφλισκάνω (XI 48)
NT: --; LXX: --; Ferner: Philo; Inschriften; Papyri; in Profanliteratur gebräuchlich.

τιτρώσκω (VII 26)
NT: --; LXX: 19x; Ferner: Philo; Josephus; in Profanliteratur häufig.

ὑπορθόω (X 39)
NT: -- (vgl. zu simplex ὀρθόω); LXX: --, doch Sym Ps 43,19 (vgl. zu simplex ὀρθόω;
Compositum mit κατα- in LXX vorhanden); Ferner: Schol.D Od. 8,66; Dositheus,
ars gramm. 76,1; selten.

φρουρά (IX 35)
NT: --; LXX: 12x; Ferner: Philo; Josephus; in Profanliteratur in gutem Gebrauch.

Hilfsmittel wie Bibleworks und die Duke Data Bank of Documentary Papyri (DDBDP;
http://scriptorium.lib.duke.edu/papyrus/texts/DDBDP.html; letzter Zugriff 23.01.2005).

ὠθέω (III 6)
NT: --; *LXX:* 7x (und div. *Composita*); *Ferner:* In allen Bereichen der Profanliteratur sehr häufig.

Diese Wörter sind auch bei Karavidopoulos aufgelistet, der jedoch

συσκέπτομαι (XI 43) — *NT:* --; *LXX:* --, doch Sym Ps 2,2; 30,14 (*simplex* und andere *Composita* in LXX vorhanden); *Ferner:* Justin, *dial.* 46,2; Herodian 1,17,1; Jamblichus, *protr.* 21,31

nicht berücksichtigt.[52] Dabei bietet er die Wörter unter Angabe ihres Verses in EvPetr und ihre Bedeutung in dessen Kontext. Entsprechend kann er auf weitere „mots rares" verweisen, da es ihm offensichtlich auch um einen Ausweis dieser seltenen Wörter nach semantischen Gesichtspunkten geht:

ἑταῖρος (VII 26)
NT: Mt 20,13; 22,12; 26,50; *LXX:* 28x; *Ferner:* In allen anderen Bereichen in gutem Gebrauch.

λίνον (XIV 60)
NT: Mt 12,20; Offb 15,6; *LXX:* 8x; *Ferner:* In allen Bereichen gut gebräuchlich (insbes. auch Inschriften und Papyri).

ὑπακοή (X 42)
NT: 15x (nur Röm; 2Kor; Phlm; Hebr; 1Petr); *LXX:* 2Kön 22,36; *Ferner:* Sehr häufig in allen Bereichen. – Vgl. auch ὑπακούω.

Allerdings muss die Frage erlaubt sein, ob nicht zuerst ein Verwendungsnachweis – selbst in der knappen und für weitere Rückschlüsse nicht ausreichenden Form wie oben – erfolgen sollte, bevor die Bedeutung eines solchen *Hap. leg.* bzw. besonderen Wortes in seinem Kontext erschlossen wird. Letztlich wird erst so ein Lexikon eines Textes erstellt, müssen Alternativbedeutungen anhand des Kontexts überprüft und letztlich die möglichen Interpretationswege erschlossen und schließlich auf eine Entscheidung hin kanalisiert werden.

Der Ausweis von auffälligen, nicht alltäglichen Wörtern ist jedoch ebenso wichtig wie eine Orientierung über die *Hap. leg.*, gerade wenn ein Text wie jener des EvPetr nur in einer Fassung vorliegt (zumindest in EvPetr II 3-5 in zwei, wenn man das Spärliche von *P.Oxy.* XLI 2949 mit einbezieht).[53]

---

52 Vgl. Karavidopoulos, «Hapax legomena», 229.
53 Vgl. methodisch Kraus, Sprache, 348-352.

Darüber hinaus wäre unter anderem noch festzuhalten:

χειραγωγέω[54] (X 39) — *NT:* Apg 9,8; 22,11; *LXX:* Ri 16,26 [A]; Tob 11,16 [S]; *Ferner:* Josephus, *ant.* 5,3,15; *UPZ* I 110,54-55; *BGU* VIII 1843,11; *CPJ* I 141,5 = *SB* VI 9564; Appian, *bell. civ.* 2,60 §248.

Selbstverständlich bedarf es auch der Strukturierung des Vokabulars in Wortfelder und Wortfamilien, wodurch man Aufschlüsse über die primäre thematische Orientierung der EvPetr erwarten kann, auch in welchem semantischen Duktus letztlich diese Thematiken dann erschlossen werden.[55]

Aber nochmals zurück zu den *Hapax legomena* des EvPetr (= *P.Cair.* 10759) und deren Relevanz für Urteile über Sprache und Stil des Autors (in geringerem Maße bei Details auch des Schreibers; s.o.): Wie bei einer Durchsicht des Datenmaterials, das im Einzelfall — vor allem bei besonders seltenen Wörtern wie λαχμός und ὑπορθόω — natürlich anhand von Referenzwerken noch umfangreicher ausfallen kann und muss, auffällt, besitzen nicht alle *Hap. leg.* die gleiche Qualität für Aussagen über das Vokabular, die thematische Orientierung wie auch den Sprachhintergrund des Autors: Ansonsten gebräuchliche Wörter wie καθαρεύω sind letztlich doch nichts so Spektakuläres wie etwa die überraschende Verwendung von ἑταῖρος („Gefährte"), wenn eben der Plural in EvPetr VII 26 diejenigen bezeichnet, mit denen der in XIV 60 als Simon Petrus identifizierte Ich-Erzähler trauert und sich versteckt hält, also die Apostel oder Jünger.

Auch helfen Verweise auf die bisherigen Qualitätsurteile über das Vokabular und einzelne Wörter des EvPetr ebenso wenig weiter wie bloße Feststellungen dieser Art. Beispielsweise muss mehr Sprachmaterial zu Rate gezogen werden als nur biblische und christliche Texte und bedarf es weiterer, etwa morphologischer wie etymologischer Überlegungen, um einen potentiellen liturgischen Stil in der Verwendung von κυριακή (EvPetr IX 35; 50) und ὑπακοή (X 42) wirklich zu erhärten. Vielmehr ist dann auch in die andere Richtung zu denken, eben ob sich nicht vielleicht erst aus dieser Verwendung in EvPetr sogar der mutmaßliche liturgische Stil erst entwickelt hat.[56]

In ähnlicher Weise vermag das abstrakte μνημοσύνη unauffällig erscheinen, sind doch gerade die Bildungen aus *μεν-, *μνα- (*μιμνήσκω)[57] beliebt und sollten für die christliche Literatur als nahe liegend gelten. Warum also trifft man μνημοσύνη nicht an, das ansonsten rege gebraucht wurde? Sollte dahinter womöglich die Namensbezeichnung der Mutter der Musen stecken, so dass ein frühchristlicher Autor normalerweise davon Abstand nahm, das Wort zu verwenden?

---

54 Hierzu T.J. Kraus, P.Vindob.G 35835 (vormals 26132A). Notizen über das Endgericht?, ZPE 141, 2002, 153.

55 Als Beispiel das Vorgehen bei Kraus, Sprache, 354-360.

56 Gegen die klare Einstufung bei Schaeffer, The „Gospel of Peter", 85-88. 90, die sich unter anderen auch beruft auf Vaganay, L'Évangile, 142.303; Mara, Évangile de Pierre, 190; Johnson, Empty Tomb, 278-279.

57 Näheres bei Kraus, Sprache, 355.

Da ὀρθόω als NT-*Hap. leg.* und das *Compositum* ὑπορθόω als biblisches *Hap. leg.* im Text des Akhmîm-Codex vorkommen, könnte man auch dem Autor, hier aber ebenso gut wieder einem Schreiber die eigenständige Bildung des *Compositums* zutrauen. Auf der jetzigen Datenbasis allerdings bleibt solch ein Schluss rein hypothetisch und lässt sich auch nicht weiter erhärten.

Gerade jene Wörter, vor denen ansonsten in der biblischen und frühchristlichen Literatur andere, semantisch ähnliche Wörter den Vorzug erhalten haben, verdienen besonderes Augenmerk, verweisen sie mitunter auf das Register und den Hintergrund des Autors selbst. Ebenso verhält es sich mit biblischen *Hap. leg.* wie ὀφλισκάνω, deren vorwiegender Verwendungsbereich erst noch näher ausfindig zu machen ist.

Schließlich sei – nur der Vollständigkeit halber – daran erinnert, dass grundsätzlich weder die Anzahl noch die Auffälligkeit von seltenen Wörtern und *Hapax legomena* in ihrer Signifikanz überschätzt werden darf. Als Beispiel kann der Vergleich des Texts des Akhmîm-Codex (*P.Cair.* 10759) mit dem Text der griechischen Petrusapokalypse dienen. Die gegenüber EvPetr deutlich höhere Zahl von *Hap. leg.* ist auch dadurch verursacht, dass die darin vorliegenden Themen und Motive in den kanonischen Texten des Neuen Testaments und der Septuaginta überhaupt nicht vorkommen. Verweise ergeben sich dann erst konsequent auf jüngere Texte wie die Apokalypse des Paulus, wenn dort dann auch die unterschiedlichen Dimensionen von Strafe in bildhafter Weise beschrieben werden und andererseits zudem Ausdrücke der Botanik Verwendung finden.[58] Das wird etwa für einen Sprach- und Stilvergleich von EvPetr und ApkPetr zu berücksichtigen sein.

Abschließend bleibt zu hoffen, dass diese methodischen Gedanken als Fingerzeige für eine philologische Untersuchung des Texts der EvPetr nützlich sein werden, dass ein angemessenes Problembewusstsein gleichzeitig immer auch Regulativ für die zu machenden Beobachtungen und Schlüsse aus diesen sein wird und dass dann der Text der EvPetr selbst als solcher eigenständig wahrgenommen und beurteilt wird, ganz gleich in welcher potentiellen Relation er letztlich zu den kanonisch gewordenen Evangelien des Neuen Testaments stehen mag.

Denn schließlich hat eine Person im 6./7. Jahrhundert das – schon apokryph gewordene[59] – EvPetr (und auch die ApkPetr, das Henochbuch, das Martyrium des Julian von Anazarbus) abgeschrieben, wurden verschiedene Texte von anderen Personen zusammen gebunden (*P.Cair.* 10759), hat wiederum jemand anders diese Kompilation dann einer Person als Grabbeigabe[60] mitgegeben.

---

58 Vgl. Kraus/Nicklas, Das Petrusevangelium und die Petrusapokalypse, 102.
59 Damit ist nicht automatisch gesagt, dass der Schreiber und diejenigen, welche die Texte zusammen gebunden, in das Grab gelegt und als Grabbeigabe erhalten haben, das EvPetr (und die anderen Texte von *P.Cair.* 10759) als apokryph angesehen haben. Zudem ist zu fragen, inwieweit der heute gebräuchliche Begriff „apokryph" überhaupt bzw. in eingeschränkter Bedeutung für die damalige Zeit angesetzt werden darf.
60 Es deutet nichts darauf hin, dass es sich bei dem Grab um das eines Mönches handeln muss (reine Vermutung des Erstherausgebers U. Bouriant), kommen doch auch Nicht-Kleriker und

Demnach hinterließen so konkrete Menschen auch Spuren, was allein schon Anlass sein sollte, nach diesen Personen, ihren Lebensbedingungen, ihrer Gedankenwelt, kurzum ihrem sozio-kulturellen Kontext zu fragen.

Frauen hier ebenso in Frage. Der Grabungsbefund jedenfalls stützt die Annahme eines Mönchsgrabs nicht. Vgl. van Minnen, The Greek *Apocalypse of Peter*, 18-19, analog idem, The Akhmîm *Gospel of Peter* (im vorliegenden Band); Kraus/Nicklas, Das Petrusevangelium und die Petrusapokalypse, 26-27.

The Greek of the Gospel of Peter:
Implications for Syntax and Discourse Study[1]

by

STANLEY E. PORTER

1. Introduction

Studies of the Greek of the Gospel of Peter have not been numerous.[2] There are, as one might expect, comments made in the commentaries on the Gospel of Peter, but these are not extensive and far from systematic. The commentary by Vaganay has a few pages on its language and style in a section on the literary problems of the Gospel of Peter.[3] These few pages begin from the assumption that 'notre évangile a été composé dans la langue de la koine'.[4] With this 'certain fact' in place, Vaganay analyzes the koine of the Gospel of Peter in terms of its vocabulary and its grammar. The section on vocabulary is concerned to show that the forms utilized, especially verbal forms, are common in the koine. The section on grammar treats both morphology and syntax. The morphology is seen to reveal Hellenistic influence, while the syntax is said to indicate constructions that are unknown in the classical language, but others that are characteristic of it. The section concludes with the statement that koine Greek was the original language of the Gospel of Peter, rather than it being a Semitic translation, even if there is a lack of style and elegance in the Greek.

---

1   I wish to thank my friends, Professor Dr. Tobias Nicklas and Dr. Thomas J. Kraus, for their invitation to contribute to this volume of essays on the Gospel of Peter, and their support of the work that it contains.
2   This is consistent with the lack of extended treatments of Hellenistic Greek as a whole. Works that address some of the issues of the language of the time, apart from the standard New Testament Greek grammars, include: H. Reinhold, De Graecitate Patrum apostolicorum Librorumque Apocryphorum Novi Testamenti Quaestiones Grammaticae, Dissertationes philologicae Halenses 14.4, Halle 1898; H. Ljungvik, Studien zur Sprache der Apokryphen Apostelgeschichten, Uppsala Universitets Arsskrift, Uppsala 1926; idem, Beiträge zur Syntax der spätgriechischen Volkssprache, Skrifter utgivna av. K. Humanistiska Vetenskaps-Samfundet i Uppsala 17.3, Uppsala-Leipzig 1932. None of these treats the Gospel of Peter, so far as I can determine.
3   L. Vaganay, L'Évangile de Pierre, ÉtB, Paris 1930, 141-147.
4   Vaganay, L'Évangile de Pierre, 141. M.G. Mara, Évangile de Pierre, SC 201, Paris 1973, 28-29, responds to this section in Vaganay, but does not discuss the grammar.

Even a number of what might be considered Semitisms are recognizably Greek. In a volume edited by Albert Fuchs, there are two further articles that treat the grammar of the Gospel of Peter, both by Franz Weißengruber.[5] In the first, on the dating of the book, Weißengruber analyzes whether the form found in 4.14 should be an optative or a subjunctive (ἀποθάνοι or ἀποθάνη).[6] The manuscript reads the optative, but many have disputed this, since in the koine the subjunctive is used in final clauses, rather than the optative found in classical dialects. Blass and Debrunner contend that there is no example in the New Testament of a final sentence with the optative.[7] On the basis of this, Weißengruber concludes that the Gospel must have been written not before the second century when there was a revival of usage of the optative. Weißengruber's second essay on grammatical investigations in the Gospel of Peter is much fuller. He takes as his starting point the discussion in Vaganay, but goes into much greater detail on a number of topics. These include, first, the sound-system. Here he treats similar sounding vowels, itacism assimilation and gemination. The second section, on morphology, treats substantives, pronouns and verbs. The section on the verbs, though the largest, is far from inclusive, since the particular features treated are the aorist stem, passive aorists, the perfect, periphrastics and augmentation. The section on syntax first treats the article, and then nouns, pronouns (reflexive, relative, and intensive), prepositions, verbs (tense, voice and mood), infinitive, participle, sentence linkage, concord, indirect speech, numerals, negation and word order – with a few select examples from each. Whereas in the area of phonology and morphology, the language of the Gospel of Peter, so Weißengruber concludes, is very regular and precise, in the area of syntax, he contends, there are numerous departures from the regular patterns of the time.[8]

These three studies provide enough information to show that there is still much room for further study of the Greek of the Gospel of Peter. First, there is no regular or complete study of the Gospel. The individual linguistic elements treated are not necessarily representative or even important, and they are not put in a larger context of the entire language system, whether it be of the Gospel of Peter or the koine as a whole. Secondly, discussion only goes as high as the clause, apart from occasional discussion of periodic style.[9] Much of the discussion is at the level of morphology. There is minimal discussion of

---

5   A. Fuchs, Das Petrusevangelium, SNTU B.2, Linz 1978, with F. Weißengruber, Zur Datierung
     des Petrusevangeliums, 117-120, and idem, Grammatische Untersuchungen zum Petrus-
     evangelium, 121-144.
6   The optative is the reading in the latest critical edition, by T.J. Kraus/T. Nicklas, Das
     Petrusevangelium und die Petrusapokalypse. Die griechischen Fragmente mit deutscher und
     englischer Übersetzung, GCS.NF 11, Neutestamentliche Apokryphen 1, Berlin-New York 2004.
7   F. Blass/A. Debrunner, A Greek Grammar of the New Testament and Other Early Christian
     Literature, trans. by R.W. Funk, Chicago 1961, par. 386.3; F. Blass/A. Debrunner, Grammatik
     des neutestamentlichen Griechisch, ed. by F. Rehkopf, Göttingen [17]1990, par. 386.4.
8   Weißengruber, Grammatische Untersuchungen, 143.
9   Weißengruber, Grammatische Untersuchungen, 139-140.

constituent structure at the lower levels, and the analysis at the clause level does not systematically treat clause structure or their relations. Levels beyond the clause are virtually entirely neglected. This would include more systematic discussion of the clause level, and how clauses are systematically related to each other at the level of the clause complex or sentence, or beyond. What is lacking is a sustained treatment of the language of the Gospel of Peter from the smallest level of meaningful structure up to a complete analysis of its discourse structure. Such a task, though desirable, is beyond the scope of a paper such as this. All that can be attempted here is a preliminary analysis that provides some of the data for further analysis.

In the remaining space of this paper, I wish to make some observations on the Greek grammar of the Gospel of Peter. The corpus is smaller than we would ideally like when we attempt to establish a textual corpus, and for that reason a study such as this would ideally fit within the kind of structured corpus of Hellenistic Greek texts such as is being created by the OpenText.org project.[10] This project is designed to gather a structured corpus of approximately 600,000 words of ancient Greek across a range of textual types to provide the foundation for making pertinent observations about Greek usage of the Hellenistic period. The richly annotated corpus is structured around a register-based model of discourse analysis, and annotates the text on the basis of linguistic levels, beginning with the word-group and moving to clause, clause complex, paragraph and then discourse. The type of analysis offered below is the kind of preliminary analysis necessary for incorporating the Gospel of Peter into such a corpus of materials.[11] I will first make some observations about word-group syntax, then move to clausal syntax, and then conclude with some discourse observations.

2. Word-Group Syntax of the Gospel of Peter

A number of observations may be made about word-group syntax in the Gospel of Peter.[12] I will concentrate on making some observations about the

---

[10] See M.B. O'Donnell, Designing and Compiling a Register-Balanced Corpus of Hellenistic Greek for the Purpose of Linguistic Description and Investigation, in: Diglossia and Other Topics in New Testament Linguistics, ed. by S.E. Porter, JSNT.S 193, Sheffield 2000, 255-297. The OpenText.org project can be found at www.opentext.org.

[11] Note that I say that this is a preliminary analysis. No doubt some if not many of the categorizations below are debatable (I am sure that I have also missed or mis-classified a number of examples because of the speed with which I have done the search). Nevertheless, this study provides a starting point for further study. For the text below, I essentially use the electronic form of the Gospel of Peter found on the web-site of Wieland Wilker, most recently corrected against the edition of Kraus and Nicklas, with some modifications.

[12] In analysis for the OpenText.org project, we have found that the word group is the smallest unit of meaningful structure. The categories for description are taken from S.E. Porter, Idioms of the Greek New Testament, BLG 2, Sheffield ²1994, 286-297, which is based upon the work in

normal patterns, and then treat a number of patterns that deviate from this norm. Overall, the word-group syntax fits that of Hellenistic Greek.

a. *Adjectival Modifiers.* The placement of adjectival modifiers in relation to the head-term of a word-group appears to reflect authorial preference. For example, authors of the Greek New Testament vary in their placement. Mark and Luke have the modifier following the head-term in approximately 75% of all instances (and thus preceding in 25%), while Paul has the modifier preceding in approximately 62% of the instances (and thus following in 38%).[13] Whereas one might be tempted to think that this alteration is influenced by literary form (narrative prefers the head-term preceding, while epistolary form prefers modifier preceding), this does not hold for the Gospel of Peter, and so tends to indicate that this choice is dictated by authorial choice.

In the Gospel of Peter, adjectival modifiers preceding or follow their head-term are not as frequent as one might expect. Those with the modifier following the head-term include the following: στεφανον ακανθινον (3.8); η γη πασα (6.21); φοβος μεγας (6.21); ωρα ενατη (6.21); τουτοις πασιν (7.27); ο λαος απας (8.28); λιθον μεγαν (8.32); ανθρωπος τις (11.44); στολην λαμπροτατην (13.55). Those with the modifier preceding the head-term include these examples: δυο κακουργους (4.10); πασαν την Ιουδαιαν (5.15); αυτης ωρας (5.20); ιδιον ταφον (6.24); ταυτα τα μεγιστα σημεια (8.28); τρεις ημερας (8.30); μεγαλη φωνη (9.35); δυο ανδρας (9.36); πολυ φεγγος (9.36); μεγιστην αμαρτιαν (11.48); τινα νεανισκον (13.55); τελευταια ημερα (14.58); πολλοι τινες (14.58); οι δωδεκα μαθηται (14.59). Thus approximately 60% of the instances have the modifier preceding the head-term, a ratio very similar to that found in the letters of Paul.[14]

b. *Demonstrative Pronouns.* In the Greek of the New Testament, the demonstrative pronoun as modifier overwhelmingly follows its head-term throughout the New Testament. It follows its head-term in approximately 85% of the instances in Paul and 78% of the instances in Luke. The same seems to be the case for the papyri, although Epictetus appears to have the reverse, with 70% of demonstratives preceding their head-term.[15]

The Gospel of Peter is limited in its use of the demonstrative pronoun. In four instances the demonstrative precedes the head-term: ταυτη τη τιμη (3.9); ουτος δε σωτηρ (4.13); ταυτα τα μεγιστα σημεια (8.28); εκεινη τη ημερα (12.52), while in three instances the demonstrative follows the head-term: των

S.E. Porter, Word Order and Clause Structure in New Testament Greek: An Unexplored Area of Greek Linguistics Using Philippians as a Test Case, FilolNT 6, 1993, 177-206.

[13] In Porter, Idioms of the Greek New Testament, I draw on the statistical work of M.E. Davison, New Testament Greek Word Order, Literary and Linguistic Computing 4, 1989, 19-28. He notes that Epictetus has the modifier preceding the head-term approximately 77% of the time, and following 23%.

[14] See Porter, Idioms of the Greek New Testament, 291 and n. 1 for discussion of other authors and research on this topic.

[15] See Porter, Idioms of the Greek New Testament, 291 and no. 2, citing work by E. Mayser, Grammatik der griechischen Papyri, II.2, Berlin 1934, 80, and Davison, New Testament Greek Word Order, 126.

κακουργων εκεινων (4.13); ο δε λιθος εκεινος (9.37); οι στρατιωται εκεινοι (10.38). This means that in roughly 57% of the instances the demonstrative precedes and 43% of the instances it follows the head-term. This is closest to the usage in Epictetus.

c. *Genitive Modifiers.* In the Greek of the New Testament, genitive modifiers in substantival word-groups generally follow the head-term of the group. This is the case in 96% of the instances in Paul and in 99% of the instances in Luke.[16] This same pattern holds for the Gospel of Peter as well. Thus, in the Gospel of Peter, we have the following instances of the genitive modifier following its head-term: των κριτων αυτου (1.1), ο φιλος Πειλατου και του κυριου (2.3), το σωμα του κυριου (2.3), της εορτης αυτων (3.5), τον υιον του θεου (3.6, 9), εξουσιαν αυτου (3.6), καθεδραν κρισεως (3.7), τις αυτων (3.8; 5.16), της κεφαλης του κυριου (3.8), τας σιαγονας αυτου (3.9), μεσον αυτων (4.10), ο βασιλευς του ισραηλ (4.11), εις δε τις των κακουργων (4.13), της κεφαλης αυτων (5.17), η δυναμις μου (5.19), το καταπετασμα του ναου της Ιερουσαλημ (5.20), των χειρων του κυριου (6.21), το σωμα αυτου (6.22), το τελος Ιερουσαλημ (7.25), των εταιρων μου (7.26), τω θανατω αυτου (8.28), τη θυρα του μνηματος (8.32), υιος ην θεου (11.45), του αιματος του υιου του θεου (11.46), χειρας του λαου των Ιουδαιων (11.48), μαθητρια του κυριου (12.50), τω μνηματι του κυριου (12.50), του μνηματος αυτου (12.52), ημερα των αζυμων (14.58), τους οικους αυτων (14.58), της εορτης παυσαμενης (14.58), οι δωδεκα μαθηται του κυριου (14.59), τον οικον αυτου (14.59), ο αδελφος μου (14.60). There are only four examples of the genitive modifier preceding its head-term: των δε Ιουδαιων ουδεις (1.1), αυτου το σωμα (2.4), αυτου ταις οψεσι (3.9), των μεν δυο την κεφαλην (10.40). This means that four of roughly 40 examples have the genitive modifier preceding the head-term in the word group. This means that roughly 90% of the instances in the Gospel of Peter have the genitive modifier preceding, very close to the percentages found in the New Testament, especially the writings of Paul.

There is much more that could be done with word group analysis in the Gospel of Peter. A complete analysis would want to analyze the structure of each group in terms of its modifiers, and the types of modifiers to be found. Such analysis would be necessary for inclusion of the Gospel of Peter in the OpenText.org annotated corpus of ancient texts. The results would allow for a more thorough analysis of the constituent structure of the word group. However, in the light of these three representative examples for which there is some comparative data, it appears that the Greek of the Gospel of Peter fits comfortably within the range of texts represented by the New Testament, as well as several other related authors.

---

[16] This seems to be the case in other literature as well, including Epictetus (63%) and the papyri (with estimates ranging from 65% to 90%). See Porter, Idioms of the Greek New Testament, 291 n. 3 for discussion.

3. Clausal Structure of the Gospel of Peter

Many different types of observations may be made about the clausal structure of the Gospel of Peter. I will concentrate on some of those that I think have particular interest, both in terms of the kind of annotation that is fundamental to the OpenText.org project, but also in terms of the kind of analysis that is useful for exegesis.

In an article that was published in 1993, and that formed the basis for some of the conclusions summarized in my *Idioms of the Greek New Testament*, I explored the clause structure of sample portions of the Greek of the New Testament.[17] The categories used in this discussion have become those used for clausal analysis in the OpenText.org project. The clausal constituents are the Subject, Predicator,[18] Complement and Adjunct. Contrary to the way that much sentence analysis and diagramming takes place in Greek study,[19] all of the constituents, and especially the Subject, do not have to be expressed as explicit elements in a given clause. In a complete analysis of clausal structure, the Adjunct must be included, but I have found that for determining basic clause structure, the three other elements are the most important. The Predicator is the fundamental element of the Greek clause, and its arguments – the elements as Subject and Complement that complete the Predicator – are the next most important elements to analyze to understand clausal structure, and hence function. Predicators may or not require a Complement, and there is no syntactical reason, only discourse factors, that necessitates an explicit Subject. As a result, the Predicator and Complement appear to be the most frequent elements, although the Adjunct also appears quite frequently. The Adjunct in Greek clausal syntax is not as significant, since so many elements, from a single particle such as an adverb to an entire embedded participial clause might be labeled an Adjunct in clausal syntax, and they can be placed at a wide variety of positions within the clause.

In the analysis below, I have taken all of the clausal units – which consist of any construction with a Predicator – and analyzed their syntax. I do not differentiate between primary, secondary and embedded clauses.[20] As a result, we can see that the clausal structure of the Gospel of Peter appears to be

---

[17] Porter, Word Order and Clause Structure, 186-203; Idioms of the Greek New Testament, 292-295.

[18] This term is changed from Predicate in previous discussion.

[19] As an example, see J.A. Brooks/C.L. Winbery, Syntax of New Testament Greek, Lanham/MD 1979, 139-147.

[20] Primary clauses are clauses that are free-standing and constitute the main line of the narrative or discourse. Secondary clauses are clauses that are off this main line and provide grammatically dependent supportive or developmental material. Embedded clauses are clauses, usually with participles and infinitives in their Predicator element, that are syntactically contained within a primary or secondary clause.

consistent with clausal syntax of Hellenistic Greek, so far as this can be determined.[21]

a. Predicator. There are approximately 90 examples of Predicator structure alone. Included here are clauses with a Predicator and no Complement or Subject (even if there are Adjuncts). Sometimes these are finite verbs of primary or secondary clauses, or participles or infinitives. This is the most common clausal structure in the Gospel of Peter. Since the Predicator is the fundamental element, it is not precise to simply say that the first element in a Greek clause is the fronted or emphatic element, since the first element may well be a required element, such as the Predicator usually is (the exception is verbless clauses). Examples include: ηλθεν προς τον Πειλατον (2.3); πεμψας προς Ηρωδην (2.4); γεγραπται γαρ εν τω νομω (2.5); πεφονευμενω (2.5); τρεχοντες (3.6); Δικαιως κρινε (3.7); εστωτες (3.9); διεμερισαντο (4.12); αγανακτησαντες επ αυτω (4.14); εκελευσαν (4.14); μη σκελοκοπηθη (4.14); βασανιζομενος (4.14); αποθανοι (4.14); και εθορυβουντο, και ηγωνιων (5.15); ετι εζη (5.15); πεφονευμενω (5.15); κερασαντες (5.16); εποτισαν (5.16); επεσαντο (5.18); ελουσε και ειλησε σινδονι και εισηγαγεν εις ιδιον ταφον (6.24); κοπτεσθαι (7.25); τετρωμενοι κατα διανοιαν εκρυβομεθα (7.26); εζητουμεθα γαρ υπ αυτων (7.26); θελοντες εμπρησαι (7.26); επι δε τουτοις πασιν ενηστευομεν (7.27); εκαθεζομεθα (7.27); πενθουντες και κλαιοντες νυκτος και ημερας εως του σαββατου (7.27); ηλθον προς Πειλατον (8.29); ελθοντες (8.30); εκ νεκρων ανεστη (8.30); εφυλαξαν (8.33); εσφραγισμενον (9.34); ανοιχθεντας ... και ... κατελθοντας εκειθε (9.36); ο βεβλημενος επι τη θυρα αφ εαυτου κυλισθεις (9.37); ιδοντες (10.38); φυλασσοντες (10.38); εξελθοντας απο του ταφου (10.39); χωρουσαν μεχρι του ουρανου (10.40); χειραγωγουμενου υπ αυτων (10.40); κοιμωμενοις (10.41); απελθειν (11.43); ανοιχθεντες (11.44); κατελθων και εισελθων εις το μνημα (11.44); αγωνιωντες μεγαλως (11.45); αποκριθεις (11.46); προσελθοντες (11.47); μη εμπεσειν εις χειρας του λαου των Ιουδαιων και λιθασθηναι (11.48); φοβουμενη δια τους Ιουδαιους (12.50); επειδη εφλεγοντο υπο της οργης (12.50); ποιειν (12.50); αποθνησκουσι (12.50); ηλθε επι το μνημειον (12.51); οπου ην τεθεις (12.51; periphrastic); εφοβουντο (12.52); εσταυρωθη (12.52); κλαυσαι και κοψασθαι (12.52); τεθεντα επι της θυρας του μνημειου (12.53); εισελθουσαι (12.53); οφειλομεναν (12.53); φοβουμεθα (12.54); μη δυναμεθα (12.54); κλαυσομεν και κοψομεθα (12.54); ελθωμεν εις τον οικον ημων (12.54); απελθουσαι (13.55); ηνεωγμενον (13.55); προσελθουσαι (13.55); παρεκυψαν εκει (13.55); καθεζομενον μεσω του ταφου ωραιον (13.55); τον σταυρωθεντα εκεινον (13.56; elliptical?); ανεστη και απηλθεν (13.56); πιστευετε (13.56); παρακυψατε (13.56); ενθα εκειτο (13.56); ουκ εστιν (13.56); ανεστη (13.56); απηλθεν εκει (13.56); οθεν απεσταλη (13.56); φοβηθεισαι (13.57); υποστρεφοντες εις τους οικους αυτων της εορτης παυσαμενης (14.58); λυπουμενος δια το συμβαν (14.59); συμβαν (14.59).

---

[21] I have usually listed each example separately with its own reference, except where the two elements appear close together (I have not been entirely consistent in this practice, however).

b. Predicator-Complement. The next most frequent clausal structure consists
of the Predicator-complement (in that order), with approximately 60 instances.
The Predicator is the heart of Greek syntax, but many verbs require a
complement (one place verbs, or verbs with a single argument). As noted
above, if the element is a syntactical requirement, then analytic weight cannot
be unduly given to exemplification of this element. It has sometimes been said
that the final position in the Greek clause is the place of second highest
emphasis. This is not the case in terms of the Complement, since when it is
expressed, it often follows the Predicator, and hence tends to be near the end of
the clause. Similarly, the Predicator in this clausal structure is not fronted.[22] A
number of the instances of the Predicator-Complement structure listed below
include Predicators such as participles and other verbs of speaking, and their
content clauses (often just the verb of speaking or the like is listed below).
Examples include: ειπων αυτοις οτι (1.2); ποιησαι αυτω (1.2); ειδως οτι (2.3); ητησε
το σωμα (2.3); παρεδωκεν αυτον τω λαω (2.5); λαβοντες τον κυριον (3.6); ελεγον (3.6);
συρωμεν τον υιον (3.6); εκαθισαν αυτον (3.7); λεγοντες (3.7); ενεγκων στεφανον
ακανθινον (3.8); ταυτη τη τιμη τιμησωμεν τον υιον του θεου (3.9); ηνεγκον δυο
κακουργους και εσταυρωσαν ανα μεσον αυτων τον κυριον (4.10); ωρθωσαν τον
σταυρον (4.11); επεγραψαν οτι (4.11); τεθεικοτες τα ενδυματα (4.12); λεγων (4.13);
γεγραπται αυτοις (5.15); ποτισατε αυτον χολην μετα οξους (5.16); επληρωσαν παντα
(5.17); ετελειωσαν κατα της κεφαλης αυτων τα αμαρτηματα (5.17); νομιζοντες οτι
(5.18); κατελειψας με (5.19); ειπων ανεληφθη (5.19); απεσπασαν τους ηλους απο των
χειρων του κυριου (6.21); εθηκαν αυτον επι της γης (6.21); δεδωκασι τω Ιωσηφ το
σωμα αυτου (6.23); θεασαμενος ην οσα (6.23); λαβων δε τον κυριον (6.24);
καλουμενον Κηπον Ιωσηφ (6.24); γνοντες οιον κακον εαυτοις εποιησαν (7.25); λεγειν
(7.25); θελοντες εμπρησαι (7.26); ακουσαντες οτι (8.28); λεγοντες οτι (8.28); ιδετε οτι
(8.28); δεομενοι αυτου (8.29); λεγοντες (8.29); παραδος ημιν στρατιωτας (8.30);
φυλαξωμεν το μνημα αυτου επι τρεις ημερας (8.30); ποιησωσιν ημιν κακα (8.30); ο δε
Πειλατος παραδεδωκεν αυτοις Πετρωνιον τον κεντυριωνα μετα στρατιωτων (8.31);
φυλασσειν τον ταφον (8.31); κυλισαντες λιθον μεγαν (8.32); επεχρισαν επτα
σφραγιδας (8.33); ιδωσι το μνημειον (9.34); ειδον ανοιχθεντας τους ουρανους και δυο
ανδρας κατελθοντας εκειθε πολυ φεγγος εχοντας και εγγισαντας τω ταφω (9.36);
εγγισαντας τω ταφω (9.36); παλιν ορωσιν ... τρεις ανδρας, και τους δυο και σταυρον
ακολουθουντα αυτοις, και των μεν δυο την κεφαλην (10.39-40); ακολουθουντα αυτοις
(10.39); υπερβαινουσαν τους ουρανους (10.40); λεγουσης (10.41); εκηρυξας τοις
κοιμωμενοις (10.41); ενφανισαι ταυτα τω Πειλατω (11.43); αφεντες τον ταφον ον
εφυλασσον (11.45); εξηγησαντο παντα απερ ειδον (11.45); λεγοντες (11.45);
παρεκαλουν (11.47); κελευσαι τω κεντυριωνι και τοις στρατιωταις μηδεν ειπειν
(11.47); οφλησαι μεγιστην αμαρτιαν εμπροσθεν του θεου (11.48); αγαπωμενοις αυταις
(12.50); λαβουσα μεθ εαυτης τας φιλας (12.51); ελεγον (12.52); εδυνηθημεν κλαυσαι
και κοψασθαι (12.52); νυν επι του μνηματος αυτου ποιησωμεν ταυτα (12.52);

---

[22]   The OpenText.org analysis of clause structure of the entire New Testament (recently
completed) indicates that the Predicator is the first element in clause structure for all clauses, as
well as for primary clauses, secondary clauses and embedded clauses.

παρακαθεσθωμεν αυτω (12.53); ποιησωμεν τα οφειλομεναν (12.53); καν επι της θυρας βαλωμεν α φερομεν (12.54); ευρον τον ταφον ηνεωγμενον (13.55); ορωσιν εκει τινα νεανισκον (13.55); περιβεβλημενον στολην λαμπροτατην (13.55); ιδετε τον τοπον (13.56); ην δε τελευταια ημερα των αζυμων (14.58; periphrastic).

I think that it is fair to say that any of the other examples of clause structure constitute marked word order in the Greek of the Gospel of Peter, especially when their frequency is compared to that of the two structures above.

c. Complement-Predicator. By contrast to the over 60 examples of Predicator-Complement structure above, there are only about 20 examples of Complement-Predicator structure. This alteration would indicate that the fronting of the Complement would tend to indicate a marked structure. One of the types of example to note, however, is the use of the relative clause, where, as is typical for Hellenistic Greek, the relative pronoun (as Complement) precedes the verb (as Predicator). However, a good example in which there are two examples, but in which the larger clausal unit has a fronted Complement (even if the relative clause has regular order for a relative clause) is 1.2 below. The following instances are found in the Gospel of Peter: οσα εκελευσα υμιν ... ποιησατε (1.2); εξουσιαν αυτου εσχηκοτες (3.6); πορφυραν αυτον περιεβαλον (3.7); μηδενα πονον εχων (4.10); λαχμον εβαλον επ αυτοις (4.12); α εποιησαμεν (4.13); αυτο θαψη (6.23); οσα αγαθα εποιησεν (6.23); ποσον δικαιος εστιν (8.28; verbs of being are difficult to categorize); σκηνην εκει πηξαντες (8.33); πολυ φεγγος εχοντας (9.36); α ειδον (10.39); τον ενα υπορθουντας (10.39); φωνης ηκουον εκ των ουρανων (10.41); ταυτα ιδοντες (11.45); ον εφυλασσον (11.45); απερ ειδον (11.45); μηδεν ειπειν (11.47); α ειδον (11.47); μηδεν ειπειν (11.49); α φερομεν (12.54); τι ηλθατε (13.56); τινα ζητειτε (13.56).

d. Subject-Predicator. The explicitly expressed Subject is not a syntactical necessity in the Greek clause. Instances where it is expressed are to be noted, since it performs a valuable discourse function, such as introducing new participants, shifting places, location or time, or selecting a particular element for direct comment. There are approximately 30 instances in the Gospel of Peter where the explicit Subject is placed before the Predicator. These include: ο Ηρωδης εφη (2.5); σαββατον επιφωσκει (2.5); ηλιον μη δυναι επι πεφονευμενω (2.5); τις αυτων ... εθηκεν (3.8); αυτος δε εσιωπα (4.10); ημεις δια τα κακα ... ουτω πεπονθαμεν (4.13); ο ηλιος εδυ (5.15); ηλιον μη δυναι επι πεφονευμενω (5.15); ο κυριος ανεβοησε (5.19); η γη πασα εσεισθη (6.21); φοβος μεγας εγενετο (6.21); ηλιος ελαμψε (6.22); εγω δε μετα των εταιρων μου ελυπουμην (7.26); ο λαος απας γογγυζει (8.28); τω θανατω αυτου ταυτα τα μεγιστα σημεια γεγονεν (8.28); μετα του κεντυριωνος και των στρατιωτων ομου παντες οι οντες εκει εθηκαν επι τη θυρα του μνηματος (8.32; note object from preceding participial clause); μεγαλη φωνη εγενετο εν τω ουρανω (9.35); ο δε λιθος εκεινος ... επεχωρησε παρα μερος (9.37); ο ταφος ηνοιγη (9.37); αμφοτεροι οι νεανισκοι εισηλθον (9.37); υπακοη ηκουετο απο του σταυρου οτι ναι (10.42); οι περι τον κεντυριωνα νυκτος εσπευσαν προς Πειλατον (11.45); αληθως υιος ην θεου (11.45); ορθρου δε της κυριακης Μαριαμ η Μαγδαληνη ... ουκ εποιησεν επι τω μνηματι του κυριου (12.50); τοτε αι γυναικες ... εφυγον

(13.57); πολλοι τινες εξηρχοντο (14.58); ημεις δε οι δωδεκα μαθηται του κυριου εκλαιομεν και ελυπουμεθα (14.59); εκαστος ... απηλλαγη εις τον οικον αυτου (14.59); εγω δε Σιμων Πετρος και Ανδρεας ο αδελφος μου ... απηλθαμεν εις την θαλασσαν (14.60); λαβοντες ημων τα λινα (14.60).

e. Predicator-Subject. The Predicator-Subject clausal structure is the next most frequent ordering of elements when the Subject is grammatically expressed. This pattern occurs nearly 25 times in the Gospel of Peter. These are the instances: ανεστη Πειλατος (1.1); κελευει Ηρωδης (1.2); παραλημφθηναι τον κυριον (1.2); ειστηκει δε εκει Ιωσηφ (2.3); περιηρχοντο δε πολλοι (5.18); αυτης ωρας διεραγη το καταπετασμα του ναου της Ιερουσαλημ εις δυο (5.20); ευρεθη ωρα ενατη (6.22); εχαρησαν δε οι Ιουδαιοι (6.23); ηγγισεν η κρισις και το τελος Ιερουσαλημ (7.25); συναχθεντες δε οι γραμματεις και φαρισαιοι και πρεσβυτεροι προς αλληλους (8.28; note no finite verb in this clause); εφοβηθησαν οι πρεσβυτεροι (8.29); συν αυτοις ηλθον πρεσβυτεροι και γραμματεις επι το μνημα (8.31); πρωιας δε επιφωσκοντος του σαββατου (9.34); ηλθεν οχλος απο Ιερουσαλημ και της περιχωρου (9.34); η επεφωσκεν η κυριακη (9.35); φυλασσοντων των στρατιωτων ανα δυο δυο κατα φρουραν (9.35); παρησαν γαρ και αυτοι (10.38); εξηγουμενων αυτων (10.39); ετι διανοουμενων αυτων (11.44); φαινονται παλιν ... οι ουρανοι και ανθρωπος τις (11.44); συμφερει γαρ ... ημιν οφλησαι (11.48; this impersonal verb could be analyzed otherwise); μεγας γαρ ην ο λιθος (12.54); ην συν ημιν Λευεις του Αλφαιου (14.60).

f. Subject-Predicator-Complement. When all three of the elements of clause structure are expressed, the most frequent pattern is Subject-Predicator-Complement in the Gospel of Peter. This syntactical ordering occurs approximately 20 times. The instances are as follows: ουδεις ενιψατο τας χειρας, ουδε Ηρωδης ουδε τις των κριτων αυτου (1.1; but note it is discontinuous in terms of the Subject); ο Πειλατος ... ητησεν αυτου το σωμα (2.4); ο Ηρωδης εφη (2.5); οι δε λαβοντες τον κυριον ωθουν αυτον (3.6); ετεροι ... ενεπτυον αυτου ταις οψεσι (3.9); ετεροι καλαμω ενυσσον αυτον (3.9); εις δε τις των κακουργων εκεινων ωνειδισεν αυτους (4.13); σκοτος κατεσχε πασαν την Ιουδαιαν (5.15); τις αυτων ειπεν (5.16); οι Ιουδαιοι και οι πρεσβυτεροι και οι ιερεις, γνοντες οιον κακον εαυτοις εποιησαν ηρξαντο κοπτεσθαι και λεγειν (7.25); ο λαος απας ... και κοπτεται τα στηθη (8.28); οι μαθηται αυτου κλεψωσιν αυτον (8.30); οι στρατιωται εκεινοι εξυπνισαν τον κεντυριωνα και τους πρεσβυτερους (10.38); ο Πειλατος εφη (11.46); εγω καθαρευω του αιματος του υιου του θεου (11.46); παντες εδεοντο αυτου (11.47); τις δε αποκυλισει ημιν και τον λιθον τον τεθεντα επι της θυρας του μνημειου (12.53); οστις εφη αυταις (13.55).

g. Subject-Complement-Predicator. This syntactical pattern, with the Complement preceding the Predicator but following the Subject, only occurs about six times in the Gospel of Peter: τις αυτον ητηκει, ημεις αυτον εθαπτομεν (2.5); αλλοι τας σιαγονας αυτου εραπισαν (3.9); τινες αυτον εμαστιζον (3.9); ουτος δε σωτηρ γενομενος των ανθρωπων τι ηδικησεν υμας (4.13); τις ημας ιδη (12.54).

h. Predicator-Subject-Complement. This pattern occurs four times in the Gospel of Peter. This is a pattern that places the Subject after the Predicate:

υπολαβη ο λαος οτι (8.30); συνεσκεπτοντο ουν αλληλοις εκεινοι απελθειν και ενφανισαι ταυτα τω Πειλατω (11.43; this pattern could be analyzed as Predicator-Complement-Subject-Complement); εκελευσεν ουν ο Πειλατος τω κεντυριωνι και τοις στρατιωταις (11.49); ιδωσιν αυτας οι Ιουδαιοι (12.52).

i. Complement-Subject-Predicator. This pattern occurs once in the Gospel of Peter: υμιν δε τουτο εδοξεν (11.46).

j. Complement-Predicator-Subject. This pattern occurs once in the Gospel of Peter: α ειωθεσαν ... αι γυναικες (12.50). The Complement-Predicate structure is to some extent motivated by its being a relative clause, but it is noteworthy how few relative clauses there are with an explicit Subject in this position.

k. Discontinuous Structure. There are a number of places where there are discontinuous syntactical patterns, that is, where an element may intervene within another element. I note some examples below (in most instances I have placed the example into a category above): των δε Ιουδαιων ουδεις ενιψατο τας χειρας, ουδε Ηρωδης ουδε τις των κριτων αυτου (1.1); σταυρισκειν αυτον μελλουσιν (2.3); συμφερει γαρ, φασιν, ημιν (11.48; see above); ημιν οφλησαι μεγιστην αμαρτιαν (11.48).

4. Paragraph Level Analysis of the Gospel of Peter

Previously I have treated two common types of clauses that appear in clause clusters or sentences. These are relative clauses and conditional clauses. One of the reasons that these clauses are important for study is that they are to a large extent predictable clause clusters within Greek, and so provide a suitable basis for comparison.

a. Relative Clauses. In the Greek of the New Testament, the relative clause follows its reference in over 80% of the instances. In Paul, this is true in approximately 93% of the instances and in Luke approximately 96%.[23] The same pattern holds for the Gospel of Peter as well. All of the examples of relative clauses with referents have the relative clause follow the antecedent. Examples include: τα κακα α εποιησαμεν (4.13); τη δε νυκτι η επεφωσκεν η κυριακη (9.35); αφεντες τον ταφον ον εφυλασσον (11.45); εξηγησαντο παντα απερ ειδον (11.45); μηδεν ειπειν α ειδον (11.47); επι τω μνηματι του κυριου α ειωθεσαν ποιειν αι γυναικες (12.50); τη ημερα η εσταυρωθη (12.52); τινα νεανισκον ... οστις εφη αυταις (13.55). There is at lest one instance where there is an unspecified referent for the pronoun: οσα εκελευσα υμιν ποιησαι αυτω, ποιησατε (1.2); and several instances where the relative clause is the object of another clause: θεασαμενος ην οσα αγαθα εποιησεν (6.23); εξηγουμενων αυτων α ειδον (10.39); βαλωμεν α φερομεν (12.54).

b. Conditional Clauses. Conditional clauses also usually have the protasis preceding the apodosis. In some ways this runs contrary to the linear nature of

---

23   Porter, *Idioms of the Greek New Testament*, 244. 292.

Greek, but it follows a logical order not unknown in Greek in the use of adverbial participles in embedded clauses preceding the verb of their main clause. All of the conditional clauses in the Gospel of Peter appear to have the protasis preceding the apodosis. The examples include: ει και μη τις αυτον ητηκει, ημεις αυτον εθαπτομεν (2.5); ει τω θανατω αυτου ταυτα τα μεγιστα σημεια γεγονεν, ιδετε οτι ποσον δικαιος εστιν (8.28); ει και μη εν εκεινη τη ημερα η εσταυρωθη εδυνηθημεν κλαυσαι και κοψασθαι (12.52); ει μη δυναμεθα, καν επι της θυρας βαλωμεν α φερομεν εις μνημοσυνην αυτου, κλαυσομεν και κοψομεθα (12.54); ει δε μη πιστευετε, παρακυψατε (13.56); ει και μη εν εκεινη τη ημερα η εσταυρωθη εδυνηθημεν κλαυσαι και κοψασθαι, και νυν επι του μνηματος αυτου ποιησωμεν ταυτα (12.52); ει μη δυναμεθα, καν επι της θυρας βαλωμεν α φερομεν εις μνημοσυνην αυτου, κλαυσομεν και κοψομεθα εως ελθωμεν εις τον οικον ημων (12.54); ει δε μη πιστευετε, παρακυψατε και ιδετε τον τοπον ενθα εκειτο (13.56).

5. Discourse Analysis of the Gospel of Peter

The above discussion of word-group, clausal structure and paragraph level analysis in the Gospel of Peter provides the basis for further and extended work beyond the level of the clause to take place. Discourse analysis (or textlinguistics) is concerned with studying the use of language in terms of how elements function at levels beyond the individual clause. Discourse analysis is thus concerned with larger patterns of usage, but it does not neglect how smaller units within the clause and even the word group function as well. However, the larger interpretative framework is units such as pericopes, pericope groups and even the entire discourse. I can only here make a few preliminary observations on the basis of the results found above.[24]

Section I.[25] The opening line of the Gospel of Peter, if it is indeed the opening line, begins with a number of noteworthy features that set the stage of the Gospel. One of the three instances of the genitive modifier preceding its head-term opens the section, των δε Ιουδαιων (1.), distancing the event from the Jews. This is reinforced by the essentially Subject-Predicator-Complement structure, but with a discontinuous continuation of the Subject: ουδεις ενιψατο τας χειρας, ουδε Ηρωδης ουδε τις των κριτων αυτου (1.1). For the next several verses, even though there are shifts in speakers and actors, there is a mitigating of the emphasis upon the agent. In the scene-setting genitive absolute, there is no explicit subject (μη βουληθεντων νιψασθαι; 1.1), and there is a tendency to place the Subject after the Predicator: ανεστη Πειλατος *(1.1)* και τοτε κελευει Ηρωδης ο βασιλευς ... (1.2). ειστηκει δε εκει Ιωσηφ ο φιλος Πειλατου και του κυριου (2.3), until Pilate chooses to take decisive action in terms of Herod. At

---

24 A complete discourse analysis – if there could be such a thing – would include much more than this.

25 I realize that the section and verse numbers are a modern convention, but it would be interesting to pursue the linguistic grounds for making such divisions.

this point both are brought forward with the Subject preceding the Predicator to create prominence:[26] και ο Πειλατος πεμψας προς Ηρωδην ητησεν αυτου το σωμα (2.4) και ο Ηρωδης εφη, αδελφε Πειλατε, ει και μη τις αυτον ητηκει, ημεις αυτον εθαπτομεν, επει και σαββατον επιφωσκει (2.5). Both use Subject-Predicator-Complement structure. That the issue of Jesus' body and who has control over it is the center of the dispute is made clear through a variety of factors. One is the use of the unusual word group structure in which the genitive modifier precedes the head-term when Pilate refers back to Jesus' body in 2.4 (αυτου το σωμα), and the other is the conditional structure used by Herod. The conditional, itself a marked clause complex has both the protasis and the apodosis using Subject-Complement-Predicator structure (τις αυτον ητηκει, ημεις αυτον εθαπτομεν), two of only about six instances in the entire Gospel of Peter. When the subject switches away from the discussion between Pilate and Herod in 3.6 to those who now have responsibility for crucifying Jesus, the new subject is introduced in a Predicate-Predicator-Complement structure (with the Subject itself an embedded clause with Predicate-Complement structure).

Section X. Much has been made of this section, because of the way that the three men and the cross emerge from the tomb.[27] However, the discourse structure does not draw its greatest attention to these features of the Gospel account. After an initial participle (Predicator structure), the shift in subject to the soldiers occurs by means of a Subject-Predicator-Complement structure: οι στρατιωται εκεινοι εξυπνισαν τον κεντυριωνα και τους πρεσβυτερους (10.38), a fairly frequent pattern to introduce a shift in agent. The subjects continue to be grammaticalized, but both of them in Predicator-Subject(-Complement) structure (παρησαν γαρ και αυτον … και εξηγουμενων αυτων α ειδον; 10.38-39). The vision is introduced with Predicator-Complement structure: ορωσιν … τρεις ανδρας και τους δυο … και σταυρον … και των μεν δυο την κεφαλην (10.39-40), even if the Complement is extended. It is only in terms of the internal structure of the vision that some attention is drawn to the components by way of the word-group structure. The structure of the individual word-groups of the Complement (though they do not use adjectival modifiers) follow the pattern of having the modifier precede the head-term in only one instance (εξελθοντας απο του ταφου τρεις ανδρας; the probably unmarked order with the least significant verbal tense-form), but the modifier following the head-term in four instances (και τους δυο τον ενα υπορθουντας και σταυρον ακολουθουντα αυτοις και των μεν δυο την κεφαλην χωρουσαν μεχρι του ουρανου του δε χειραγωγουμενου υπ αυτων υπερβαινουσαν τους ουρανους; the probably marked order with the marked

---

[26] On the notion of prominence, see S.E. Porter, Prominence: An Overview, in: Studying the Greek New Testament: Papers from the SBL Greek Language and Linguistics Section, ed. by S.E. Porter/M.B. O'Donnell (New Testament Monographs), Sheffield 2005.

[27] On the issue of a Cross Gospel, see J.H. Charlesworth/C.A. Evans, Jesus in the Agrapha and Apocryphal Gospels, in: Studying the Historical Jesus: Evaluations of the State of Current Research, ed. by B. Chilton/C.A. Evans, NTTS 19, Leiden 1994, 479-533, esp. 503-514. But see also Crossan's article in this volume.

present tense-form). Thus there is some emphasis upon the individual components of the vision, even if the vision itself is not central to the pericope. The center of the pericope is the words that were heard from the cross. The Gospel states that they heard a voice from the heavens, asking whether they had preached to those who were sleeping, and then a response is heard from the cross (Subject-Predicator), yes indeed: και υπακοη ηκουετο απο του σταυρου οτι ναι (10.42).[28]

6. Conclusion

This entirely preliminary study is designed to do several things. One is to re-introduce and begin again discussion of the grammar and syntax of the Gospel of Peter, using recent advances in linguistic analysis. My hand-searches can no doubt be improved upon in many ways, but they do show that even such a relatively short document as the Gospel of Peter provides useful linguistic data. By examining the Greek language in more detail, pertinent observations can be made regarding the nature of its use of the Greek language, and then suitable comparisons can be made with other bodies of literature of the time, including especially the Greek of the New Testament. A second goal of this study is to show the useful and productive relationship that can exist between what might be perceived to be more traditional syntactical analysis – such as study of the word-group and clausal structure – and larger questions of discourse composition and shape. One of the next frontiers for Greek linguistic study is to create useful and productive models that extend discussion beyond analysis of levels of language that stop at the clause or sentence, and to explore the nature of how entire discourses are composed and function. By drawing upon the useful data provided by the Gospel of Peter in terms of its word-group and clausal structure, I believe that we can begin to gain insights into the larger function of the Gospel of Peter as a whole and how it functioned in relation to other texts of the ancient world of its time.

---

[28]   Cf. J.D. Crossan, The Historical Jesus: The Life of a Mediterranean Jewish Peasant, New York 1992, 389, who believes that it is the holy ones who follow Jesus who respond. The use of the passive verb without specified causality perhaps is used to ensure that direct causality is not specified.

Das Petrusevangelium vom Alten Testament her gelesen

Gewinnbringende Lektüre eines nicht-kanonischen Textes vom christlichen Kanon her

von

THOMAS HIEKE

Textgrundlage und Fragestellungen

Die Textgrundlage der folgenden Untersuchung zum Petrusevangeliums (EvPetr) ist die neue Edition des Textes von T.J. Kraus und T. Nicklas.[1] Dabei wird nur derjenige Papyrus in Betracht gezogen, der den größten Textbestand überliefert, also P.Cair. 10759 (Akhmîm-Codex). Auf der Seite des Petrusevangeliums ist daher die Textgrundlage relativ eindeutig, weil nur ein vorhandener, konkret als Handschrift vorliegender Text verwendet wird.

Schwieriger gestaltet sich die Sache auf der Seite des intertextuellen Resonanzraumes, von dem her das EvPetr gelesen werden soll. Das Thema spricht sehr allgemein vom „Alten Testament", doch diese Aussage muss hinsichtlich der Textgrundlage präzisiert werden. Zunächst liegt es von der gemeinsamen Sprache her nahe, die griechische Bibel (für das „Alte Testament" die Septuaginta) heranzuziehen. Sie ist – wiederum rein pragmatisch gesehen – am einfachsten in der Ausgabe von Alfred Rahlfs zugänglich.[2] Es muss jedoch klar sein, dass diese beliebte Taschenausgabe („Codex Rahlfs") nicht unmittelbar das abbildet, was Leser der Antike – und eventuell auch der oder die Verfasser des EvPetr – an „Bibeltext" zur Verfügung hatten. Es geht hier aber nicht um die kaum mehr zu beantwortende Frage, welchen Text der „Bibel" – und ob überhaupt einen – der oder die *Autor(en)* oder die Erstleser des EvPetr vor sich hatten. In den folgenden Überlegungen muss die Textgeschichte weitgehend ausgeklammert bleiben. Dennoch ist es für eine leserorientierte intertextuelle Analyse unabdingbar, den

---

[1] T.J. Kraus/T. Nicklas, Das Petrusevangelium und die Petrusapokalypse. Die griechischen Fragmente mit deutscher und englischer Übersetzung, GCS.NF 11, Neutestamentliche Apokryphen 1, Berlin-New York 2004.

[2] A. Rahlfs, Hg., Septuaginta. Id est Vetus Testamentum graece iuxta LXX interpretes, 2 Bde., Stuttgart [8]1965.

vorausgesetzten Text zu spezifizieren. Damit auf der Seite des „Alten Testaments" ein ebenso konkreter Textbestand wie beim EvPetr in Form von P.Cair. 10759 vorliegt, erfolgt eine Beschränkung auf die Septuaginta-Ausgabe von Rahlfs.[3]

Mit der genannten Textgrundlage können bestimmte Fragen nicht behandelt werden: So wird hier nicht gefragt, welchen „alttestamentlichen" Text der oder die Autor(en) des EvPetr verwendeten[4] und was er/sie damit machen wollte/n. Sowohl die Intention der historischen Autoren als auch die Gedanken der Erstleser bleiben im Verborgenen; Rückschlüsse darauf sind vielleicht möglich, sind aber hypothetisch. Ferner wird nicht nach einer Geschichte der mit der Passion Jesu verbundenen alttestamentlichen Motive gefragt, etwa nach der Art, welches Motiv wo zum ersten Mal begegnet usw.[5]

Statt solcher textgenetischer Fragen wird auf einer leserorientierten und textzentrierten Ebene angesetzt: (1) Welche alttestamentlichen Texte werden bei der Lektüre des EvPetr möglicherweise angestoßen? Genauer: Was kann ein Leser, der die Rahlfs-Septuaginta kennt, im EvPetr entdecken? (2) Welchen Verständnisgewinn oder Verständniszuwachs erreicht man durch das Einspielen dieser alttestamentlichen Texte?

Dabei ist „der Leser" nicht ein empirischer (männlicher) Leser des 21. Jahrhunderts,[6] sondern der Versuch, eine im Text (des EvPetr) verankerte Textstrategie zu beschreiben. Der Leser ist ein Modellleser als aus dem Text selbst gewonnene Abstraktion, damit aber auch nur ein Vorschlag möglicher Lektüreweisen. Dieser Vorschlag erhebt weder den Anspruch, Intentionen der historischen Textproduzenten noch Gedankenvorgänge bei möglichen Erstlesern zu beschreiben. Ferner wird nicht der Anspruch auf Vollständigkeit erhoben. Spätere empirische Leserinnen und Leser, die besser mit der Septuaginta vertraut sind, können eventuell noch mehr Bezüge entdecken und auswerten. Insofern kann die Aufgabe nicht „abschließend" behandelt werden.

Die konkrete Vorgehensweise wird so aussehen, dass eine reflektierende Lektüre am Text des EvPetr entlang geht und den Befund beschreibt: Welche Elemente könnten intertextuelle Beziehungen zum Resonanzraum „Septuaginta" („Altes Testament") aufweisen? Die Lektüre bleibt aber nicht dabei stehen, die Bezüge zu notieren, sondern versucht auch eine Auswertung unter der Fragestellung, wie das Einspielen des „alttestamentlichen Hintergrundes"

---

[3]   Eine vertiefende Reflexion der Frage nach dem so genannten „Septuaginta-Kanon" findet sich in T. Hieke/T. Nicklas, „Die Worte der Prophetie dieses Buches". Offenbarung 22,6-21 als Schlussstein der christlichen Bibel Alten und Neuen Testaments gelesen, BThS 62, Neukirchen-Vluyn 2003, 113-124.

[4]   Die großen Schwierigkeiten dieser Frage reflektiert R.E. Brown, The Death of the Messiah. From Gethsemane to the Grave 2, ABRL, New York et al. 1993, 1340.

[5]   Eine solche Motivgeschichte will M. Dibelius, Die alttestamentlichen Motive in der Leidensgeschichte des Petrus- und des Johannes-Evangeliums, in: idem, Botschaft und Geschichte. Erster Band, Tübingen 1953 (Erstveröffentlichung 1918), entwickeln.

[6]   Daher erfolgt auch keine „inklusive" Sprachregelung mit Leser/in o.ä.

die Wahrnehmung des Untersuchungstextes „EvPetr" verändert. Abschließend werden die Beobachtungen systematisiert.[7]

Beschreibung des Befunds

EvPetr 1: Das Reinigen der Hände

EvPetr 1 zeigt deutlich, dass ein vorausgehender Text verloren ist, denn der „Einstieg" ist kein solcher, sondern setzt eine bestimmte Szene voraus. Ein Leser mit Kenntnis der kanonischen Evangelien denkt an Mt 27,24: Pilatus wäscht sich öffentlich die Hände und deklariert seine Unschuld (vgl. auch EvPetr 46).[8] Vom Unterlassen einer Waschung der Hände ist in den kanonischen Evangelien nicht die Rede. Vom AT her geraten folgende Stellen in den Blick: Ex 30,19-21; Dtn 21,6; Ps 26,6; Ps 73,13.

(1) Ex 30,19-21 überliefert die Vorschrift für Aaron und seine Söhne, also für alle Priester, sich vor der Ausübung des priesterlichen Dienstes Hände und Füße zu waschen. Es handelt sich um eine symbolische Waschung zur Heiligung der Priester, die in Kontakt mit den Dingen des Heiligtums kommen.[9] Die Waschung zur Heiligung ist nötig, damit die Grenze zwischen heilig und profan gewahrt bleibt. Daher liegt der Grund für diese Anordnung darin, „damit sie (die Priester) nicht sterben". Eine Unterlassung der Waschung hätte also verheerende Folgen, wäre ein Sakrileg, das entsprechende Konsequenzen hat. Trägt man dieses ferne Echo in EvPetr 1 ein, so erhält der Leser ein subtiles Warnsignal: Auch im EvPetr geht es um ein Sakrileg, das die „Juden" begehen; sie waschen sich die Hände nicht, und die Folgen werden schlimm sein.

(2) Dtn 21,6 regelt ein Ritual für den Umgang mit einem Ermordeten, der auf freiem Feld aufgefunden wird und dessen Mörder nicht gefasst werden kann. Bei diesem Ritual sollen sich die Ältesten der benachbarten Stadt unter anderem die Hände waschen – auch hier liegt ein Symbol dafür vor, dass das Blut des Ermordeten, also die Schuld an dieser Tat, nicht bei der nahen Stadt liegt, die Ältesten und die Einwohner der Stadt frei von Schuld sind (Dtn 21,7-8). Der Umkehrschluss heißt dann aber, dass bei Unterbleiben des Rituals und der Händewaschung das vergossene Blut eine entsprechende Schuld mit sich

---

[7] Die Methodik ähnelt damit der Vorgehensweise in Hieke/Nicklas, Worte der Prophetie. Diese Art des Herangehens hat sich insgesamt bewährt. Im genannten Werk findet sich auch eine ausführliche Reflexion und Begründung der Methodik, so dass sich hier weitere Ausführungen dazu erübrigen.

[8] Vgl. dazu J. Denker, Die theologiegeschichtliche Stellung des Petrusevangeliums. Ein Beitrag zur Frühgeschichte des Doketismus, EHS.T XXIII.36, Bern-Frankfurt am Main 1975, 58.

[9] Vgl. C. Dohmen, Exodus 19-40, HThKAT, Freiburg et al. 2004, 276-277.

bringt. Somit macht von Dtn 21,6 her das Unterlassen der Händewaschung in EvPetr 1 subtil deutlich, dass die Schuld am folgenden Geschehen – also die „Ermordung des Herrn"[10] – an den ungewaschenen Händen der „Juden", des Herodes und seiner Richter klebt.[11]

(3) Ps 26,6 und Ps 73,13 stellen das Waschen der Hände in Unschuld als symbolische Geste dar, die eine Distanzierung vom Tun der Frevler und Heuchler bezeichnet. Der Beter macht keine gemeinsame Sache mit denen, die Unrecht tun, vielmehr hält er sein Herz rein. Bringt man diesen Hintergrund in EvPetr 1 ein, erscheinen erneut die Juden, Herodes und seine Richter, in sehr schlechtem Licht.

Da das Petrusevangelium mit EvPetr 1 so unvermittelt einsetzt, steht das Unterlassen der Reinigung der Hände, das nicht aus den kanonischen Evangelien bekannt ist, zunächst als Rätsel da. Die Aktivierung von alttestamentlichen Hintergrundtexten, die das Waschen der Hände als symbolischen Akt darstellen, der letztlich einen Schutz vor tödlichen Konsequenzen bzw. die Deklaration der eigenen Unschuld bedeutet, eröffnet für den Leser eine Hintergrundbotschaft zwischen den Zeilen: „die Juden", Herodes und seine Richter, werden für das Folgende voll verantwortlich gemacht – das Blut des Gekreuzigten klebt an ihren Händen. Die Einbeziehung der Heiligen Schriften Israels offenbart die antijüdische Tendenz des EvPetr.

EvPetr 5 und 15: Der Umgang mit einem Ermordeten

Der einzige explizite Schriftbezug des EvPetr begegnet zweimal: In EvPetr 5 wie EvPetr 15 wird erwähnt, dass (im Gesetz) geschrieben steht, dass die Sonne nicht über einem Ermordeten untergehen solle. So ist dies *expressis verbis* jedoch in der Tora nicht zu finden.[12] Aller Wahrscheinlichkeit nach ist an Dtn 21,22-23 gedacht.[13]

Dtn 21,22-23 regelt jedoch die Vorgehensweise bei einer Hinrichtung. Das Aufhängen am Holze ist dabei nicht die Exekutionsweise, die selbst nicht mitgeteilt wird, sondern die abschreckende Zurschaustellung der Leiche, die jedoch aus Gründen der Reinheit des Landes nicht über Nacht erfolgen soll, also höchstens einen Tag lang dauern darf. Selbst ein „von Gott Verfluchter" hat dabei das Recht, noch am gleichen Tag bestattet zu werden.[14] In der

---

[10]   EvPetr 5; 15 sprechen deutlich von einem „Ermordeten", d.h. diese Wendungen machen deutlich, dass das EvPetr die Kreuzigung Jesu als Mord ansieht (s.u.).

[11]   Vgl. dazu auch H. Koester, Ancient Christian Gospels. Their History and Development, Philadelphia-London 1990, 221-222.

[12]   Vgl. Brown, Death, 1339.

[13]   Denker, Stellung, 60-61, spricht von einem besonderen Interesse des EvPetr an Dtn 21,22-23 im Gegensatz zu den kanonischen Evangelien, in denen diese Stelle keine Rolle spielt. Daraus zieht Denker den weit reichenden Schluss, das EvPetr habe von den kanonischen Evangelien keine Notiz genommen und nur das AT und die Gemeindetradition als Quellen.

[14]   Vgl. T. Hieke, Das Alte Testament und die Todesstrafe, Bib. 85, 2004, 349-374, hier 363.

jüdischen Tradition wird dieses Gebot durch einen *Qal wa-Chomer*-Schluss auf jede gestorbene Person ausgeweitet: Wenn dies für einen Kriminellen gilt, um wie viel mehr dann für andere (vgl. bSanh 46a.b).[15] Heißt es aber in Dtn 21,23 οὐκ ἐπικοιμηθήσεται τὸ σῶμα αὐτοῦ ἐπὶ τοῦ ξύλου, so wird in EvPetr 5; 15 daraus ἥλιον μὴ δῦναι ἐπὶ πεφονευμένῳ. Eine *wörtliche* Anspielung liegt also nicht vor, wohl aber eine sinngemäße Umformulierung, die vor allem zu EvPetr 15 (Finsternis als Sonnenuntergang) passt. In EvPetr 3-5 steht die Erwähnung des Bestattungsgebots noch am selben Tag im Kontext der Bestattungsbitte durch Josef, der aus den synoptischen Evangelien als „Josef aus Arimathäa" bekannt ist (Mt 27,57-61; Mk 15,42-47; Lk 23,50-56; Joh 19,38-42). Herodes erscheint hier als „gesetzesfürchtig", da er die Leiche auch dann begraben hätte, wenn Josef nicht darum gebeten hätte. In EvPetr 15 entsteht wegen der Dunkelheit am Mittag unter den Juden die Furcht, die Sonne sei bereits untergegangen, so dass die Gefahr entstünde, man könnte gegen das (umformulierte) Gebot aus Dtn 21,22-23 verstoßen.[16]

Der wichtigste Unterschied zwischen Dtn 21,22-23 und EvPetr 5; 15 besteht wohl darin, dass aus dem, der aufgrund eines Kapitalverbrechens hingerichtet wird (Dtn 21,22: ἐὰν δὲ γένηται ἔν τινι ἁμαρτία κρίμα θανάτου), im EvPetr ein „Ermordeter" (ἐπὶ πεφονευμένῳ) wird. Durch diese Abweichung vom alttestamentlichen Hintergrund wird der Leser gewahr, dass das EvPetr die Kreuzigung Jesu ziemlich unverblümt nicht als „Hinrichtung", sondern als Ermordung versteht. Dies gilt in jedem Fall, auch wenn umstritten ist, ob in EvPetr 5 der Schriftbezug noch Herodes-Rede sein soll oder bereits Kommentar.[17] Wenn der Satz noch zur Rede des Herodes gehört, dann gibt Herodes *expressis verbis* zu, dass es sich bei der Kreuzigung um eine Ermordung handelt. Der Terminus „Ermordeter" (πεφονευμένος) ruft u.a. den Satz aus den Zehn Geboten wach: „Du sollst nicht morden" (οὐ φονεύσεις; Ex 20,13; Dtn 5,18; Mt 5,21; 19,18; Röm 13,9).

Erneut dient der Bezug des EvPetr auf die Heilige Schrift Israels dazu, das Tun des Herodes als Verstoß gegen die Zehn Gebote und damit als große Sünde darzustellen. Um die Aufmerksamkeit dafür zu wecken, wird bei einem expliziten Verweis auf das im Gesetz Geschriebene ein an der angespielten Stelle nicht verwendetes Wort (φονεύω, „[er]morden"), das selbst wiederum die Zehn Gebote auf den Plan ruft, eingesetzt. Einem Leser, der die entsprechenden Verknüpfungen herstellt, drängt sich der antijüdische Schluss auf: Die Juden haben den Herrn ermordet.

---

[15] Vgl. W.G. Plaut, Die Tora in jüdischer Auslegung. Band V, Dewarim (Deuteronomium), Gütersloh 2004, 246.

[16] Vgl. M.G. Mara, Il Vangelo di Pietro, Bologna 2003, 68.

[17] Vgl. Kraus/Nicklas, Petrusevangelium, 33.

EvPetr 6: Das Laufen

Dass die Folterknechte den übernommenen Herrn „im Laufen" (τρέχοντες) stoßen, ist zwar plausibel vorstellbar, aber nicht mit diesem Verb in den kanonischen Evangelien bezeichnet. Auffälligerweise begegnet das Verb τρέχω an zwei alttestamentlichen Stellen in einem Kontext, der ein dramatisches Licht auf EvPetr 6 wirft: Spr 1,16; Jes 59,7.[18]

(1) Spr 1,16 ist Teil einer Warnung, sich nicht auf das Tun der Sünder (1,10: Gottlose, ἀσεβεῖς) einzulassen: οἱ γὰρ πόδες αὐτῶν εἰς κακίαν τρέχουσιν καὶ ταχινοὶ τοῦ ἐκχέαι αἶμα. Die Frevler stellen also dem Arglosen nach, scheuen das Blutvergießen nicht – doch am Ende wird sich das geplante Böse gegen sie selbst richten (Spr 1,18-19).

(2) Jes 59,1-21 liefert in einer Prophetenrede eine Begründung für das Ausbleiben des Heils: Die durchtriebenen Machenschaften und die Gewalttaten der Angesprochenen stehen als große Sünden zwischen ihnen und Gott. Jes 59,7 charakterisiert das sündhafte Tun: οἱ δὲ πόδες αὐτῶν ἐπὶ πονηρίαν τρέχουσιν ταχινοὶ ἐκχέαι αἶμα. Wie schon in Spr 1,16 zielt das „Laufen" auf ein Vergießen von unschuldigem Blut.[19]

Lässt sich der Leser von der Wendung τρέχοντες in EvPetr 6 dazu anleiten, Spr 1,16 und Jes 59,7 einzuspielen, so wird die *Bewertung* des Sachverhaltes durch das EvPetr überdeutlich: Die Folterknechte sind gottlose Frevler, die schnell bereit sind, unschuldiges Blut (nämlich das des Herrn) zu vergießen. Erneut zeigt sich die antijüdische Tendenz, denn aus EvPetr 1-6 ist zu schließen, dass es „das Volk" ist, das hier zu Werke geht (vgl. EvPetr 5: Herodes παρέδωκεν αὐτὸν τῷ λαῷ).

EvPetr 6 (und 9): Der Sohn Gottes

Der „Sohn Gottes" in EvPetr 6 und 9 ist zunächst ein christologischer Titel in Analogie zu den anderen Epitheta κύριος und βασιλεὺς τοῦ Ἰσραήλ, die abwechselnd im EvPetr auftreten (der Name „Jesus" fehlt auffälligerweise)[20]. Der Kontext der Gewaltanwendung und der Verspottung ruft jedoch auch einen deuterokanonischen alttestamentlichen Text auf den Plan: Weish 2,18-20.

In Weish 2 wird zunächst die Rede der Frevler (ἀσεβεῖς) berichtet, die aus der Kürze des Lebens das „Recht" zu hemmungslosem Genießen ableiten und sich gegen den Gerechten (δίκαιος) wenden: Ihrem Treiben ist dessen aufrichtige Gesinnung ein Dorn im Auge, daher wollen sie ihm Gewalt (bis zum Tod: 2,20) antun, um zu prüfen, ob der Gerechte wirklich „Sohn Gottes"

---

[18] Denker, Stellung, 65-66, verweist noch auf Ps 117,13 LXX: ὠσθεὶς ἀνετράπην τοῦ πεσεῖν καὶ ὁ κύριος ἀντελάβετό μου, wertet aber den notierten Bezug nicht interpretatorisch aus.

[19] Vgl. M.G. Mara, Évangile de Pierre, SC 201, Paris 1973, 89; eadem, Vangelo di Pietro, 46.

[20] Zur Christologie des EvPetr vgl. v.a. P.M. Head, On the Christology of the Gospel of Peter, VigChr 46, 1992, 209-224, sowie den Beitrag von M. Myllykoski im vorliegenden Band.

ist und von Gott gerettet wird (εἰ γάρ ἐστιν ὁ δίκαιος υἱὸς θεοῦ ἀντιλήμψεται αὐτοῦ καὶ ῥύσεται αὐτὸν ἐκ χειρὸς ἀνθεστηκότων; Weish 2,18). Die Analogie zur Verspottung des Herrn in EvPetr 6 und 9 ist unverkennbar.

Ist der Bezug zu Weish 2 einmal hergestellt, dann erinnert sich der Leser aber auch an die Beurteilung des Tuns der Frevler in Weish 2,21-24 (und in den folgenden Kapiteln des Weisheitsbuches). Die Frevler irren sich, sie gehören dem Tod, während die Gerechten auf Unvergänglichkeit und Gottes Lohn nach dem Tod hoffen dürfen. Diese Argumentationslinie konvergiert mit der weiteren Darstellung im EvPetr.

EvPetr 7: Richte gerecht!

Ein weiterer christologischer Titel nach dem „Sohn Gottes" ist der „König". Dazu gehört in der Passion Jesu ein ganzer Motivkomplex mit Purpurmantel, Krone und Unterwerfungsgesten. Ein besonderer Akzent des EvPetr ist das Sitzen des Verurteilten und Verspotteten auf dem Richterstuhl.[21] Von daher ist die Aufmerksamkeit auf die spöttische Aufforderung „Richte gerecht" (δικαίως κρῖνε) gelenkt. Sie begegnet wörtlich in Spr 31,9.

(1) Spr 31,9 ist der Abschluss der kurzen Spruchsammlung, die als „Worte an Lemuël, den König von Massa" überschrieben ist (Spr 31,1). Bei diesem Kompendium nichtisraelitischen Ursprungs handelt es sich um Ermahnungen für die rechte Ausübung der Königsherrschaft, in deren Mittelpunkt die Fürsorge für die Schwachen und Armen steht. Die Aufforderung am Ende lautet: ἄνοιγε σὸν στόμα καὶ κρῖνε δικαίως διάκρινε δὲ πένητα καὶ ἀσθενῆ. Dieses leuchtende altorientalische Königsideal steht damit in scharfem Kontrast zur Szenerie der Verspottung des Herrn im EvPetr. Welche Wirkung kann das beim Leser haben? Ein möglicher Effekt besteht sicher in der wachsenden Distanz zu den Verspottenden, denen offenbar nichts mehr heilig ist und die alle Werte pervertieren. Diese Tendenz wird sich in ihrem weiteren Tun fortsetzen (s.u.).

(2) Wachgerufen wird mit der Aufforderung „Richte gerecht" aber auch ein klassischer biblischer Topos:[22] das gerechte Gericht Gottes in eschatologischer Zeit. Beispiele dafür sind Ps 9,9; 96[95],13; 98[97],9. Dass Gott am Ende die Welt

---

21 Vgl. Mara, Vangelo di Pietro, 49. Dibelius, Motive, 224-227, sieht eine Beziehung zwischen EvPetr 7 und Jes 58,2 (αἰτοῦσίν με νῦν κρίσιν δικαίαν καὶ ἐγγίζειν θεῷ ἐπιθυμοῦσιν) – wohl aufgrund der wenigen gemeinsamen Worte –, entfaltet aber nicht, welcher Sinnzuwachs dadurch entsteht. Es wäre denkbar, hier ein weiteres Spottmotiv zu sehen, das mit einer antijüdischen Tendenz versehen ist, sei es in der einen Richtung, dass „die Juden" als Folterknechte mit dem Szenario auch das Prophetenwort verspotten, sei es in der anderen Richtung, dass sie im Sinne von Jes 58,2 in verfehlter Weise ein gerechtes Gericht erwarten. Jes 58 deckt auf, dass die Angesprochenen mit ihren Ansprüchen (Fasten, Buße) nicht durchkommen, weil sie in Wirklichkeit zahlreiche Sünden begehen. Man muss hier mehrfach um die Ecke denken, daher erscheint es eher problematisch, Jes 58,2 mit EvPetr 7 in Verbindung zu bringen. Vgl. auch Mara, Évangile de Pierre, 93.

22 Vgl. Mara, Évangile de Pierre, 93; eadem, Vangelo di Pietro, 48.

in Gerechtigkeit richten wird, könnte bei der Lektüre des EvPetr als hoffnungsvoller Grundton mitschwingen, der angesichts der Gewalt gegen den Herrn und Sohn Gottes, der Pervertierung der Werte und der augenscheinlichen Ohnmacht des Herrn gegen Verunsicherung angeht und signalisiert, dass am Ende doch die Gerechtigkeit siegen wird. Diese Gewissheit bringt auch eine weitere Analogie ein: Jer 11,18-23 erzählt von den Mordplänen gegen den Propheten Jeremia, die dieser mit Hilfe Gottes durchschaut. Der Prophet schildert sich als zutraulich wie ein Lamm, das zum Schlachten geführt wird, und berichtet von den Plänen seiner Gegner (ähnlich wie Weish 2). Zuversicht gewinnt Jeremia durch sein Vertrauen auf Gott: κύριε κρίνων δίκαια δοκιμάζων νεφροὺς καὶ καρδίας ἴδοιμι τὴν παρὰ σοῦ ἐκδίκησιν ἐξ αὐτῶν (Jer 11,20).[23]

(3) Das Richten in Gerechtigkeit ist auch die Aufgabe der in Jes 11,1-10 angekündigten messianischen Gestalt: κρινεῖ ταπεινῷ κρίσιν ... καὶ ἔσται δικαιοσύνη ἐζωσμένος τὴν ὀσφὺν αὐτοῦ (11,4-5). Als junger Trieb aus dem Baumstumpf Isais hat diese Figur königliche Züge, so dass die Verbindung zur Verspottung des „Königs Israels" in EvPetr 7-11 durchaus nahe liegt.

Die beiden letztgenannten Motive (2) und (3) sind Anti-Texte zur Erzähllogik des EvPetr, so dass sich für den Leser der Schluss aufdrängt, dass das Tun der Folterknechte „nicht schriftgemäß" bzw. gegen die Heilige Schrift gerichtet ist: Sie vergehen sich gegen Gott und seinen Gesalbten. Wer aber der Gerechtigkeit Gottes spottet, begeht ein Sakrileg. Damit bestätigt sich eine schon beobachtete Tendenz im EvPetr (s.o.).

EvPetr 7-8: König und Krone

Die Pervertierung des Königsmotivs setzt sich in EvPetr 8 fort, wenn die aus den synoptischen Evangelien bekannte Dornenkrone dem Herrn auf den Kopf gesetzt wird. Der Gegentext ist Ps 21[20],4: ὅτι προέφθασας αὐτὸν ἐν εὐλογίαις χρηστότητος ἔθηκας ἐπὶ τὴν κεφαλὴν αὐτοῦ στέφανον ἐκ λίθου τιμίου. Ursprünglich beschreibt dieser Königspsalm in liturgischer Feierlichkeit, wie JHWH den irdischen König mit Macht und Segen ausstattet.[24] Dazu gehört auch, dass JHWH die Feinde des Königs vernichtet und ihre bösen Pläne vereitelt (21[20],12). Genau das Gegenteil findet in EvPetr 7-8 statt, so dass erneut das Tun der Folterknechte als „schriftwidrig" erscheint.

---

[23] Vgl. Mara, Évangile de Pierre, 93.

[24] Für die nachexilische Zeit vgl. auch die Krönung des Hohenpriesters Jeschua in Sach 6,11: καὶ λήψῃ ἀργύριον καὶ χρυσίον καὶ ποιήσεις στεφάνους καὶ ἐπιθήσεις ἐπὶ τὴν κεφαλὴν Ἰησοῦ τοῦ Ιωσεδεκ τοῦ ἱερέως τοῦ μεγάλου.

EvPetr 9: Verspottung

Die weitere Verspottungsszenerie in EvPetr 9 ist aus den synoptischen Evangelien bekannt[25] und nimmt Anleihen bei den Gottesknechtsliedern des Jesajabuches. Zu EvPetr 9 ist v.a. Jes 50,6 einschlägig:[26] τὸν νῶτόν μου δέδωκα εἰς μάστιγας τὰς δὲ σιαγόνας μου εἰς ῥαπίσματα τὸ δὲ πρόσωπόν μου οὐκ ἀπέστρεψα ἀπὸ αἰσχύνης ἐμπτυσμάτων. Das Tun des Herrn entspricht damit ganz der Schrift und dem darin angekündigten Ergehen des Gottesknechtes. Auf dieser Linie liegen auch die weiteren, für die Darstellung der Passion Jesu typischen Analogien zum vierten Gottesknechtslied (v.a. Jes 53,4-12).

EvPetr 10: Er schwieg

Das Schweigen des Herrn in EvPetr 10 erinnert an die Widerstandslosigkeit des Gottesknechts in Jes 53,7. Diese Stelle dient in Apg 8,32-33 als Ausgangspunkt für die missionarische Predigt des Philippus an den Hofbeamten der Königin der Äthiopier.

Ist das vierte Gottesknechtslied als Hintergrundtext präsent, so ergibt sich eine Verbindung von den zwei mitgekreuzigten Übeltätern in EvPetr 10, die aus Lk 23,32 bekannt sind, zu Jes 53,9 in der hebräischen Fassung:[27] „Bei den Ruchlosen gab man ihm sein Grab, bei den Verbrechern seine Ruhestätte, obwohl er kein Unrecht getan hat und kein trügerisches Wort in seinem Mund war."[28]

EvPetr 11: Dieser ist der König Israels!

Der Kreuzestitulus lautet in den kanonischen Evangelien zwar „Das ist der König der Juden" (Mt 27,37; Mk 15,26; Lk 23,38; Joh 19,19), doch die Anrede als

---

[25] So findet sich z.B. das Anspucken in Verbindung mit dem Schlagen mit dem Rohr in Mt 27,30; Mk 15,19.

[26] Siehe dazu Dibelius, Motive, 240; ferner Koester, Ancient Christian Gospels, 224-226. Koester weist darauf hin, dass nur in EvPetr 9 alle drei Elemente aus Jes 50,6 (Schläge, Wangen und Spucken) rezipiert werden (vgl. auch Denker, Stellung, 62: Nähe zur LXX), während in den kanonischen Evangelien immer höchstens zwei dieser Elemente wörtlich auftauchen. Daher hält er diese Verspottungsszene (EvPetr 9) für älter als die entsprechenden Passagen in den kanonischen Evangelien. Zur Diskussion um die Frage der Priorität von EvPetr oder kanonischen Evangelien – die hier nicht zur Debatte steht – vgl. ferner u.a. Denker, Stellung, passim; J.D. Crossan, The Cross That Spoke. The Origins of the Passion Narrative, San Francisco et al. 1988, passim; R.E. Brown, The *Gospel of Peter* and Canonical Gospel Priority, NTS 33, 1987, 321-343; A. Kirk, The Johannine Jesus in the Gospel of Peter, in: Jesus in Johannine Tradition, ed. by R.T. Fortna/T. Thatcher, Louisville 2001, 313-321, bes. 319-321, sowie die Beiträge von J.D. Crossan, A. Kirk und J. Hartenstein im vorliegenden Band.

[27] Die LXX weicht hier deutlich ab: καὶ δώσω τοὺς πονηροὺς ἀντὶ τῆς ταφῆς αὐτοῦ καὶ τοὺς πλουσίους ἀντὶ τοῦ θανάτου αὐτοῦ ὅτι ἀνομίαν οὐκ ἐποίησεν οὐδὲ εὑρέθη δόλος ἐν τῷ στόματι αὐτοῦ.

[28] Vgl. Denker, Stellung, 68.

„König Israels" (vgl. EvPetr 7) begegnet auch in Mt 27,42; Mk 15,32. Wachgerufen werden damit die klassischen messianischen Texte, die einen eschatologischen Friedenskönig aus dem Geschlechte Davids ankündigen (Jes 9,1-6; 11,1-10). Wie die kanonischen Evangelien (vgl. z.B. Lk 1,32-33 mit Jes 9,5-6 oder Mt 4,14-16 mit Jes 8,23-9,1) identifiziert auch das EvPetr Jesus mit dieser messianischen Figur.

EvPetr 12: Das Verteilen der Kleider

Das Verteilen der Kleider eines Hingerichteten an die Henker war wohl eine gängige Praxis, die in den kanonischen Evangelien wie in EvPetr 12 mit Ps 22[21],19 in Verbindung gebracht wird: διεμερίσαντο τὰ ἱμάτιά μου ἑαυτοῖς καὶ ἐπὶ τὸν ἱματισμόν μου ἔβαλον κλῆρον. In EvPetr 12 werden dabei die ἱμάτια und der ἱματισμός mit τὰ ἐνδύματα zusammengefasst, und für κλῆρος steht das *Hapax legomenon* (LXX und NT) λαχμός.[29] Letztere Ersetzung könnte auf das Verb λαγχάνω in Joh 19,24 zurückzuführen sein. Wie bei Joh 19,23-24 sind in EvPetr 12 das Aufteilen der Kleider und das Werfen des Loses zwei verschiedene Vorgänge, anders als in den synoptischen Evangelien, in denen es eine Tätigkeit ist (Mt 27,35; Mk 15,24; Lk 23,34)[30]. Doch das Detail, dass der Leibrock (χιτών) *ein* Teil war und daher verlost werden sollte (Joh 19,23-24), wird in EvPetr 12 nicht aufgenommen. Ob mit ἔνδυμα in EvPetr 12 auf das leuchtend weiße Gewand des Engels bei der Auferstehungsszene in Mt 28,3 angespielt wird,[31] sei dahingestellt.

EvPetr 14: Das Zerbrechen der Schenkel

Dass das EvPetr das Evangelium nach Johannes voraussetzt, ist unbestritten. Von daher ist auch der christologische Motivkomplex des Pascha-Opfer-Lammes bekannt und die Äußerung in EvPetr 14 entsprechend zu verstehen (vgl. Joh 19,32-36). Die alttestamentlichen Stellen, die davon sprechen, dass dem Pascha-Lamm kein Knochen zerbrochen werden darf, sind Ex 12,46 und Num 9,12.

(1) Ex 12,46 und Num 9,12 formulieren gleich: ὀστοῦν οὐ συντρίψετε ἀπ' αὐτοῦ bzw. ὀστοῦν οὐ συντρίψουσιν ἀπ' αὐτοῦ. EvPetr 14 verwendet dagegen ein absolutes *Hapax legomenon*: μὴ σκελοκοπηθῇ.[32] Der Verweis auf ein Schriftwort, wie er in Joh 19,36 unternommen wird, unterbleibt hier. Stattdessen wird eine

---

[29]   Vgl. Kraus/Nicklas, Petrusevangelium, 35. Siehe dazu z.B. L. Vaganay, L'Évangile de Pierre, ÉtB, Paris ²1930, 239; J. Denker, Stellung, 68.

[30]   Vgl. Dibelius, Motive, 230.

[31]   So die Vermutung von Mara, Vangelo di Pietro, 61.

[32]   Nach Kraus/Nicklas, Petrusevangelium, 35, „womöglich eine (spontane) Neubildung". Vgl. auch den Artikel von T.J. Kraus im vorliegenden Band.

andere, weitaus „profanere" Deutung des Nicht-Zerbrechens der Gebeine
angegeben: „damit er unter Qualen sterbe". Damit bewegt sich EvPetr 14 nicht
wie Joh 19,36 auf der Ebene der schriftgemäßen Deutung des Todes Jesu,
sondern in der Realität des Kreuzigungstodes: Ein Zerbrechen der Unter-
schenkel bewirkte bei den Gekreuzigten, dass die Last des Körpers an den
Armen hing und ein schneller Erstickungstod eintrat. Unterblieb das
Zerbrechen, war der Tod umso länger und qualvoller. Zu beachten ist auch,
dass in Joh 19,32-36 das Zerbrechen der Gebeine unterbleibt, weil Jesus schon
tot ist, und insofern passt die Pascha-Opfer-Lamm-Motivik auch besser. Sie ist
dagegen in EvPetr 14 nur noch von ferne im Hintergrund – im Vordergrund
steht ein weiteres Detail eines grausamen Foltertodes. Der Schriftbezug zum
Pascha-Lamm wird in EvPetr 14 interpretatorisch nicht mehr verfolgt und
ausgewertet.

(2) Ps 34[33],21 ist ein Vertrauenselement, das den Schutz Gottes für den
Gerechten bekennend zum Ausdruck bringt. Der Gerechte muss zwar viel
leiden, doch allem wird JHWH ihn entreißen. Der Schutz wird konkret so
ausgedrückt: κύριος φυλάσσει πάντα τὰ ὀστᾶ αὐτῶν ἓν ἐξ αὐτῶν οὐ συντριβήσεται.
Die Verbindung aus Pascha-Lamm-Motivik und dem Bekenntnis, dass JHWH
für den leidenden Gerechten eintreten wird, liefert für Joh 19,32-36 einen
eindrucksvollen Hintergrund – in EvPetr 14 ist davon nichts mehr übrig, denn
durch das Unterbleiben des Zerbrechens der Gebeine wird das Leiden des
Gerechten[33] auch noch verlängert. Warum die subtile schriftgestützte Argumentation des Johannesevangeliums im EvPetr verlassen wurde, darüber lässt
sich nur spekulieren: Vielleicht wurde der Zusammenhang nicht mehr
durchschaut? Ein Leser, der die Bezüge des Johannesevangeliums zu Ex 12,46;
Num 9,12 und Ps 34[33],21 kennt, bleibt ratlos, denn der „intertextuelle
Spaziergang" läuft ins Leere. Was bleibt, ist die Grausamkeit des Foltertodes.[34]

EvPetr 15: Finsternis am Mittag

Das Passionsmotiv der Finsternis am Mittag hat eine Reihe von Analogien in
alttestamentlichen Gerichtstexten, die ein bezeichnendes Licht auf die Szenerie
in EvPetr 15 werfen. Im Einzelnen sind Am 8,9; Jer 15,9; Dtn 28,29; Jes 59,10
heranzuziehen.[35]

(1) Am 8,9 steht in der Gerichtsansage der vierten Vision des Amos. Auf
den Schuldaufweis, der die Ausbeutung der Armen drastisch schildert, folgt
die Beschreibung des Gottesgerichts: καὶ ἔσται ἐν ἐκείνη τῇ ἡμέρᾳ λέγει κύριος ὁ
θεός καὶ δύσεται ὁ ἥλιος μεσημβρίας καὶ συσκοτάσει ἐπὶ τῆς γῆς ἐν ἡμέρᾳ τὸ φῶς.
Zeigt die Finsternis am Mittag das Gericht an, so äußert es sich darin, dass alle

---

33 Eine andere (wenn auch weniger wahrscheinliche) Möglichkeit wäre, EvPetr 14 nicht auf „den
    Herrn", sondern auf den Übeltäter von EvPetr 13 zu beziehen, vgl. Denker, Stellung, 70.
34 Vgl. z.B. Kirk, Johannine Jesus, 317.
35 Vgl. Mara, Évangile de Pierre, 125-126.

Freude in Trauer umgewandelt wird. Diese Trauer wird sein ὡς πένθος ἀγαπητοῦ – also wie die Trauer um einen geliebten Menschen.

(2) In ähnlicher Weise ist in Jer 15,9 das Untergehen der Sonne am Mittag Zeichen abgrundtiefer Trauer. Der Kontext ist ein Trauerlied (als Gottesrede) über den Untergang Jerusalems. Symbol unendlichen Leids ist die Mutter, die sieben Söhne gebar, und jetzt ihre Seele aushaucht: ἐπέδυ ὁ ἥλιος αὐτῇ ἔτι μεσούσης τῆς ἡμέρας.[36]

(3) Dtn 28,28-29 ist Teil der großen Fluch- und Strafrede in der Tora, die die Strafsanktionen verkündet, die Israel ereilen werden, wenn es nicht auf die Stimme JHWHs, seines Gottes hört und die Gebote und Gesetze nicht einhält (Dtn 28,15). Eine dieser Sanktionen besteht darin, dass JHWH Israel mit Wahnsinn, Blindheit und Irresein schlägt: καὶ ἔσῃ ψηλαφῶν μεσημβρίας ὡσεὶ ψηλαφήσαι ὁ τυφλὸς ἐν τῷ σκότει.

(4) Jes 59,10 gehört zu jenem Abschnitt im Tritojesajabuch, der bereits angetippt wurde (EvPetr 6 – Jes 59,7) und die frevlerischen Machenschaften bestimmter Gruppen thematisiert, die dazu führen, dass Gottes Heil nicht verwirklicht wird. Ab 59,9 artikuliert eine Wir-Gruppe die Einsicht, dass aufgrund der Sünden der Frevelnden die Gerechtigkeit fern bleibt. Die Situation wird als Dunkelheit am Mittag metaphorisch ausgedrückt: (9) διὰ τοῦτο ἀπέστη ἡ κρίσις ἀπ' αὐτῶν καὶ οὐ μὴ καταλάβῃ αὐτοὺς δικαιοσύνη ὑπομεινάντων αὐτῶν φῶς ἐγένετο αὐτοῖς σκότος μείναντες αὐγὴν ἐν ἀωρίᾳ περιεπάτησαν (10) ψηλαφήσουσιν ὡς τυφλοὶ τοῖχον καὶ ὡς οὐχ ὑπαρχόντων ὀφθαλμῶν ψηλαφήσουσιν καὶ πεσοῦνται (vgl. EvPetr 18) ἐν μεσημβρίᾳ ὡς ἐν μεσονυκτίῳ ὡς ἀποθνήσκοντες στενάξουσιν.

Mit Jes 59,10 ist auch ein alttestamentlicher Bezugstext für EvPetr 18 gefunden.[37] Das Einspielen der genannten Texte lädt die Rede von der Finsternis am Mittag (EvPetr 15) und dem Hinfallen trotz der Leuchter (EvPetr 18) metaphorisch auf: Die Kreuzigung erscheint als Auftakt des göttlichen Gerichts, angezeigt durch die Finsternis am Mittag. Die Folge wird abgrund-tiefe Trauer sein – und von entsprechenden emotionalen Reaktionen sprechen auch EvPetr 15 und EvPetr 30. Die Finsternis am Mittag ist aber auch Anzeichen für gravierendes menschliches Fehlverhalten, für das Missachten der Weisung Gottes; sie ist die Folge der unheilvollen Pläne der Menschen und des Vergießens von unschuldigem Blut (Jes 59,7 in Verbindung mit Jes 59,10). Der alttestamentliche Hintergrund bewirkt damit eine eindeutig negative Qualifikation des Verhaltens der „Juden" durch das EvPetr: Sie handeln gegen die Weisung Gottes. In bitterer Ironie folgt darauf in EvPetr 15 die Befürchtung der „Juden", sie könnten gegen das Gesetz verstoßen, weil der Gekreuzigte ja noch lebt, die Sonne aber schon untergegangen sei – wo doch über einen „Ermordeten" (!) die Sonne nicht untergehen soll. Der Kontrast zwischen der durch die Finsternis am Mittag gekennzeichneten großen Sünde der

---

[36] Vgl. dazu Mara, Vangelo di Pietro, 66, mit Hinweisen auf Kirchenväterzitate in der Fußnote.
[37] Vgl. dazu Dibelius, Motive, 228.

Kreuzigung und der Befürchtung, gegen Dtn 21,22-23 zu verstoßen, ist kaum anders denn als antijüdische Polemik aufzufassen: „Die Juden" erscheinen als blind gegenüber ihren gravierenden Verstößen gegen die Weisung Gottes, die durch die Finsternis geradezu sichtbar vor Augen geführt werden.

EvPetr 16: Galle und Essig

Dass dem zu Kreuzigenden bzw. dem Gekreuzigten ein Mischgetränk angeboten wird, ist ein verbreitetes Motiv in den Passionserzählungen der Evangelien, ebenso der Bezug auf Ps 69[68],22. Der Befund ist vielfältig, daher ist eine Übersicht hilfreich:[38]

Ps 69[68],22: καὶ ἔδωκαν εἰς τὸ βρῶμά μου <u>χολὴν</u>
καὶ εἰς τὴν <u>δίψαν</u> μου <u>ἐπότισάν</u> με <u>ὄξος</u>

Mt 27,34: ἔδωκαν αὐτῷ πιεῖν οἶνον μετὰ <u>χολῆς</u> μεμιγμένον·
καὶ γευσάμενος οὐκ ἠθέλησεν πιεῖν.

Mk 15,23: καὶ ἐδίδουν αὐτῷ ἐσμυρνισμένον οἶνον· ὃς δὲ οὐκ ἔλαβεν

Mt 27,48: καὶ εὐθέως δραμὼν εἷς ἐξ αὐτῶν καὶ λαβὼν σπόγγον πλήσας τε
<u>ὄξους</u> καὶ περιθεὶς καλάμῳ <u>ἐπότιζεν</u> αὐτόν.

Mk 15,36: δραμὼν δέ τις [καὶ] γεμίσας σπόγγον <u>ὄξους</u> περιθεὶς καλάμῳ
<u>ἐπότιζεν</u> αὐτόν ...

Lk 23,36: ἐνέπαιξαν δὲ αὐτῷ καὶ οἱ στρατιῶται προσερχόμενοι, <u>ὄξος</u>
προσφέροντες αὐτῷ

Joh 19,28-30: Μετὰ τοῦτο εἰδὼς ὁ Ἰησοῦς ὅτι ἤδη πάντα τετέλεσται, ἵνα
τελειωθῇ ἡ γραφή, λέγει· <u>διψῶ.</u> [29] σκεῦος ἔκειτο <u>ὄξους</u> μεστόν·
σπόγγον οὖν μεστὸν <u>τοῦ ὄξους</u> ὑσσώπῳ περιθέντες προσήνεγκαν
αὐτοῦ τῷ στόματι [30] ὅτε οὖν ἔλαβεν <u>τὸ ὄξος</u> [ὁ] Ἰησοῦς εἶπεν·
τετέλεσται, καὶ κλίνας τὴν κεφαλὴν παρέδωκεν τὸ πνεῦμα

EvPetr 16-17: καί τις αὐτῶν εἶπεν ποτίσατε αὐτὸν <u>χολὴν</u> μετὰ <u>ὄξους</u> καὶ
κεράσαντες <u>ἐπότισαν</u> [17] καὶ ἐπλήρωσαν πάντα καὶ ἐτελείωσαν
κατὰ τῆς κεφαλῆς αὐτῶν τὰ ἁμαρτήματα.

Die Besonderheiten lassen sich jeweils knapp andeuten: Bei Mt und Mk begegnen *zwei* „Getränke". Im ersten Fall handelt es sich um ein betäubendes Getränk *vor* der Kreuzigung – Mt ersetzt vermutlich unter Rückbezug auf Ps 68,22 die Myrrhe des Mk durch Galle (χολή). Im zweiten Fall begegnet der Essig (ὄξος), das allen Stellen gemeinsame Element, das auf Ps 68,22 hinweist. Nur bei Joh wird der Bezug zum Psalm als Schrifthinweis ausdrücklich erwähnt bzw. sogar als „Erfüllung der Schrift" hingestellt. Doch bei Joh fehlt die Galle. Die

---

[38] Vgl. auch Koester, Ancient Christian Gospels, 229.

meisten Elemente aus Ps 68,22 hat EvPetr 16-17 übernommen, zeigt aber auch
die Kenntnis der kanonischen Evangelien: Aus dem Bikolon des Psalms (Essen
und Trinken) wird im EvPetr – wohl in Anlehnung an Mk 15,23/Mt 27,34 – ein
Mischgetränk aus Galle und Essig (vgl. auch Barn 7,3).[39]

Vom Kontext her ist das Mischgetränk in EvPetr 16 – wiederum in getreuer
Anlehnung an den Psalmtext – ein Akt der Verspottung, Folter und
Verfolgung,[40] vielleicht auch der direkten Ermordung, wenn man hinter dem
Mischgetränk einen Gifttrank vermutet.[41] Ps 69[68] ist als „Hilferuf eines
unschuldig Verfolgten" zu charakterisieren und passt somit sehr gut zur
Passion Jesu. Eine der Torturen, über die sich der Psalmist beklagt, ist die
(metaphorisch gemeinte) Speisung mit Gift (LXX: Galle) und die Tränkung mit
Essig, mithin die Verweigerung von genießbaren Lebensmitteln, die
Bedrohung der physischen Lebensgrundlage. Das EvPetr erreicht durch diesen
Schriftbezug erneut, die Bosheit der Folterknechte kräftig herauszustreichen.

EvPetr 17: Sie erfüllten alles … Sünden über ihrem Haupt

Die Wendung „sie erfüllten alles" im Kontext des Mischgetränks aus Galle und
Essig scheint in EvPetr 17 auf die Schrifthermeneutik von Joh 19,28-30
anzuspielen.[42] Dort ist das Dürsten und Trinken Jesu letzter Ausdruck der
vollkommenen Schrifterfüllung und -vollendung, und dies wird explizit so
formuliert. Nachdem Jesus auch das Dürsten aus den Klagepsalmen
nachempfunden hat und die Versorgung mit Anti-Lebensmitteln (Essig)
verkostet hat, ist in symbolischer Weise die äußerste Not, die die Heilige
Schrift (Altes Testament) kennt, vom Gekreuzigten eingeholt worden, der
Abstieg des Logos ins menschliche Fleisch ist an seinen tiefsten Punkt
gekommen, „es ist vollbracht". Mit dem eintretenden Tod ist der Aufstieg
„zum Vater" und die Verherrlichung in der Gesamtbewegung des
Johannesevangeliums eingeleitet.

Im EvPetr ist dies nur sehr verhalten angedeutet, wenn es überhaupt so
gemeint ist. EvPetr 17 fokussiert nicht das Werk des Herrn, sondern die Bosheit
und Sünde der Folterknechte, die durch ihr Tun das in den Psalmen
„prophezeite" Geschehen „erfüllen". Die Fortsetzung zeigt, dass der Vers am
(Über-)Maß der Sünden über ihrem Haupt interessiert ist.[43] Diese eingängig

---

[39]   Koester, Ancient Christian Gospels, 230, hält die Version in EvPetr 16-17 für die älteste Fassung
       dieser Schriftinterpretation von Ps 68,22 in den Passionsgeschichten. Dass die Argumentation
       auch genau umgekehrt verlaufen kann, zeigt z.B. Brown, Gospel of Peter, 327.
[40]   Vgl. u.a. Denker, Stellung, 71.
[41]   Vgl. Kirk, Johannine Jesus, 318.
[42]   Vgl. dazu Dibelius, Motive, 241.
[43]   Vgl. Denker, Stellung, 71: „Das AT ist damit nicht in erster Linie eine Weissagung auf Christus,
       sondern auf die Sünden der Juden hin." Denker sieht das EvPetr in einer urchristlichen
       Strömung, „die die Hinrichtung Jesu mit den Prophetenmorden vergleicht." Der Fall
       Jerusalems 70 n. Chr. wird dann als Strafe für die Ermordung Jesu verstanden (vgl. EvPetr 25).

klingende Wendung ruft bei näherem Hinsehen zwei alttestamentliche Kontexte auf den Plan: Esra 9,6 (1 Esd 8,72) und Lev 16,21.

(1) 1 Esd 8,72 gehört zur Einleitung des Bußgebetes Esras, nachdem er von den Mischehen erfahren hatte. Der Satz ist ein Bekenntnis, dass die Sünden übergroß geworden sind:

Esra 9,6: αἱ ἀνομίαι ἡμῶν ἐπληθύνθησαν ὑπὲρ κεφαλῆς ἡμῶν καὶ αἱ πλημμέλειαι ἡμῶν ἐμεγαλύνθησαν ἕως εἰς οὐρανόν

1 Esd 8,72: αἱ γὰρ ἁμαρτίαι ἡμῶν ἐπλεόνασαν ὑπὲρ τὰς κεφαλὰς ἡμῶν αἱ δὲ ἄγνοιαι ἡμῶν ὑπερήνεγκαν ἕως τοῦ οὐρανοῦ

In EvPetr 17 bleibt davon nur das Faktum, dass die Sünden auf dem Kopf sind, übrig – von einem Bekenntnis dieser Sünden ist nicht die Rede. Es ist in keiner Weise sicher, ob der Verfasser von EvPetr 17 auf Esra 9 verweisen wollte. Doch die Aktivierung dieser Verbindung durch einen Leser bewirkt, dass die Sünde derer, die den Herrn gekreuzigt haben, geradezu „historische" oder „kosmische" Dimensionen annimmt, wie auch das Bußgebet Esras die „Sünde" zu einem tiefgehenden Grundsatzproblem der Gottesbeziehung des Volkes macht.

(2) Lev 16,21 ist Teil des Rituals am Versöhnungstag (Jom Kippur):[44] καὶ ἐπιθήσει Ααρων τὰς χεῖρας αὐτοῦ ἐπὶ τὴν κεφαλὴν τοῦ χιμάρου τοῦ ζῶντος καὶ ἐξαγορεύσει ἐπ' αὐτοῦ πάσας τὰς ἀνομίας τῶν υἱῶν Ισραηλ καὶ πάσας τὰς ἀδικίας αὐτῶν καὶ πάσας τὰς ἁμαρτίας αὐτῶν καὶ ἐπιθήσει αὐτὰς ἐπὶ τὴν κεφαλὴν τοῦ χιμάρου τοῦ ζῶντος καὶ ἐξαποστελεῖ ἐν χειρὶ ἀνθρώπου ἑτοίμου εἰς τὴν ἔρημον. Durch das Handauflegen wird alle „Sünde" auf den Kopf des Bockes übertragen, der dann die „Sünde" in die Wüste trägt (und so vom Volk entfernt). Dieses Ritual symbolisiert Versöhnung und Sündenvergebung – es ist ein zentraler Inhalt der Tora (strukturell steht es in ihrem Zentrum) und der jüdischen Religion bis heute. Der dahinter stehende Gedanke ist ein wesentlicher Aspekt auch im Christentum. EvPetr 17 erscheint vor diesem Hintergrund als beängstigender Anti-Text: Die Sünden der Folterknechte bleiben auf ihrem eigenen Kopf! Für Vergebung und Versöhnung ist in der Logik des EvPetr an dieser Stelle wohl kein Platz mehr.

EvPetr 19: Du hast mich verlassen

Ps 22[21] ist bekanntermaßen *der* Passionspsalm schlechthin, v.a. Mt und Mk sind auf diesen Text hin ausgerichtet. Auch hier ist der Befund jedoch nicht unkompliziert, so dass sich eine Übersicht empfiehlt:

---

44 Jüdische Traditionen zum Ritual des Versöhnungstages, die in Mischna und Talmud bezeugt sind, listet Koester, Ancient Christian Gospels, 224-225, auf. Von diesen Beobachtungen aus zeigen sich interessante Verbindungslinien zu frühchristlichen apokryphen Texten (EvPetr, Barnabasbrief, Sibyllinische Orakel).

Ps 22,2 MT: אֵלִי אֵלִי לָמָה עֲזַבְתָּנִי

Ps 21,2 LXX: ὁ θεὸς ὁ θεός <u>μου</u> πρόσχες μοι ἵνα τί <u>ἐγκατέλιπές</u> <u>με</u>

Mt 27,46:   ηλι ηλι λεμα σαβαχθανι; τοῦτ᾽ ἔστιν·
               Θεέ <u>μου</u> θεέ <u>μου</u>, ἱνατί <u>με</u> <u>ἐγκατέλιπες</u>;

Mk 15,33:   ελωι ελωι λεμα σαβαχθανι; ὅ ἐστιν μεθερμηνευόμενον·
               ὁ θεός <u>μου</u> ὁ θεός <u>μου</u>, εἰς τί <u>ἐγκατέλιπές</u> <u>με</u>;

EvPetr 19:   καὶ ὁ κύριος ἀνεβόησε λέγων
               ἡ δύναμίς <u>μου</u> ἡ δύναμις <u>κατέλειψάς</u> <u>με</u> καὶ εἰπὼν ἀνελήφθη

Die auffällige Zufügung der LXX (πρόσχες μοι) begegnet in keiner der drei
Evangelienfassungen. Während ansonsten Mt und Mk recht nahe am
Psalmtext sind, entfernt sich EvPetr 19 signifikant durch die Auslassung der
Fragepartikel ἵνα τί und die Ersetzung von ὁ θεός <u>μου</u> durch ἡ δύναμίς <u>μου</u>. Ob
hier einfach eine Angleichung an Ps 22[21],16 (ἐξηράνθη ὡς ὄστρακον ἡ ἰσχύς
μου) vorliegt?[45] Dass ἡ δύναμις ein Äquivalent für „Gott" sein kann, zeigt z.B.
Mk 14,62/Mt 26,64.[46] In der Verhörszene bekennt sich Jesus als „Sohn Gottes"
und fährt fort: ἀπ᾽ ἄρτι ὄψεσθε τὸν υἱὸν τοῦ ἀνθρώπου καθήμενον ἐκ δεξιῶν <u>τῆς</u>
<u>δυνάμεως</u> καὶ ἐρχόμενον ἐπὶ τῶν νεφελῶν τοῦ οὐρανοῦ. Hier steht „Kraft, Macht"
stellvertretend für „Gott".

Ein ausschlaggebender Hinweis könnte die Umwandlung der klagenden
Frage in eine Feststellung in EvPetr 19 sein. Der Text hat kein Interesse daran,
auch nur den Anschein aufkommen zu lassen, *Gott* hätte den *Kyrios* verlassen.[47]
Daher ist die „Kraft" an dieser Stelle auch nicht ein Äquivalent für Gott,
sondern die Kraft des Herrn (Jesus),[48] die Wunderwerke bewirkt, wie sie so oft
im Neuen Testament beschrieben werden (z.B. Mk 6,2.14; 9,39; 13,26; Lk 1,35;
4,14.36; 5,17 [δύναμις κυρίου]; 6,19 u.ö.). Sie ist es auch, die bewirkt, dass der
Herr in EvPetr trotz der Schmerzen schweigen kann – und erst, wenn diese
Kraft ihn verlassen hat, kann er sterben: „La *dýnamis* del nostro testo potrebbe
essere la potenza divina che abita in lui e la cui presenza ha reso possibile il
silenzio del *Kýrios* in *EvPt* 10, e rende ora impossibile la sua morte. Solo
quando la *dýnamis* ha abbandonato Gesù, egli può morire."[49] Damit hätte das
EvPetr dem bekannten Psalmzitat eine ganz eigene Wendung gegeben, die auf
der Basis neutestamentlicher Texte eine plausible Deutung erlaubt, ohne
heterodox (z.B. doketisch) zu werden und ohne eine Gottverlassenheit des

---

[45] So vermutet es Dibelius, Motive, 242. Zu weiteren Deutungsmöglichkeiten vgl. Mara, Vangelo
di Pietro, 71.

[46] Vgl. Denker, Stellung, 74. 118; Head, Christology, 214.

[47] Ein ähnliches Interesse hat wohl Lk 23,46, da dort das Psalmzitat aus Mk durch einen anderen
Psalm (Ps 31[30],6) ersetzt ist. Vgl. dazu und zum Folgenden auch Vaganay, L'Évangile de
Pierre, 256; Mara, Évangile de Pierre, 135; Denker, Stellung, 119.

[48] Vgl. hierzu auch den Beitrag von M. Myllykoski im vorliegenden Band.

[49] Mara, Vangelo di Pietro, 71.

Kyrios zu unterstellen.[50] Der Schriftbezug zum Klagepsalm 22[21] wäre dann relativ wirkungslos, da es ja nicht um eine Klage geht und sich auch gleich die „Aufnahme" (also nicht ausdrücklich der Tod!) anschließt. Leiden und Klage (und damit auch der Psalm als solcher) werden gleichsam „übersprungen".

Als alternative Deutung wäre auch – unter Heranziehung der synoptischen Parallele Lk 23,46, die Ps 30[31],6 zitiert – eine Vorstellung denkbar, die annimmt, im Moment des Todes kehre der Geist des Menschen zum Himmel zurück. Dass die „Kraft" den Herrn verlassen habe, würde damit feststellen, dass der Geist Jesu zu Gott aufgestiegen ist („… in deine Hände lege ich meinen Geist").[51]

EvPetr 19: Er wurde aufgenommen

Im Moment des Sterbens des Herrn vermeidet das EvPetr einen direkten Ausdruck für Tod oder Sterben[52] und greift auf einen biblischen Terminus bzw. ein biblisches Motiv zurück: die Entrückung des Gerechten. Die „klassischen" Figuren dafür sind Henoch und Elija, und bei diesen beiden begegnen auch die zwei dafür herangezogenen griechischen Verben. Der Befund gestaltet sich wie folgt:

(1) Für *Henoch* wird in Gen 5,24 das Verb μετατίθημι (Aorist Aktiv, Subjekt: Gott) verwendet. Diese Stelle wird in Sir 44,16 (Passiv) und Hebr 11,5 (Passiv und Aktiv) aufgegriffen. An beiden Stellen geht es um die Vorbildlichkeit Henochs, im Hebräerbrief zugespitzt auf den „Glauben". In Weish 4,10 begegnet ebenfalls das Verb μετατίθημι im Passiv, doch die Aussage wird auf „den Gerechten" verallgemeinert: Kommt sein Ende auch früh, geht er doch in Gottes Ruhe ein. Seine Entrückung mitten aus den Sündern erfolgt vorzeitig, damit er, der von Gott Geliebte, nicht zur Sünde verführt werde.

(2) Das in EvPetr 19 auftretende Verb ἀναλαμβάνω (Passiv; *passivum divinum*) wird an der klassischen Stelle für *Elija* verwendet (4 Kön 2,9.10.11). Die Entrückung Elijas wird in 1 Makk 2,58 (Belohnung für Elijas leidenschaftlichen Eifer) und Sir 48,9 (Preisgedicht auf Elija) aufgegriffen. In Sir 49,14 steht das Verb bei Henoch (die großen Männer des Anfangs). Im Neuen Testament begegnet es bei der Himmelfahrtsszene im sekundären Markus-Schluss (Mk 16,19) sowie in Apg 1,2.11.22 (Himmelfahrt Jesu) und in 1 Tim 3,16 (in einer Art Glaubensbekenntnis).

Damit sind Terminus und Motiv so breit bezeugt, dass das EvPetr keine Schwierigkeiten hatte, eine geeignete Formulierung für das Ableben Jesu zu finden. Dabei siegt eindeutig der Schriftbezug bzw. die Glaubensaussage über die Erzähllogik. Das EvPetr parallelisiert „den Herrn" mit Henoch und Elija

---

50 Ähnlich Denker, Stellung, 74.
51 Die weitere Ausfaltung dieser dem gnostischen Denken nahe stehenden Vorstellung findet sich bei Mara, Vangelo di Pietro, 72-74.
52 Vgl. dazu u.a. Head, Christology, 214-215.

bzw. greift die Himmelfahrtsterminologie von Apg 1 auf. Und ähnlich wie im
Buch der Weisheit, wo der Begriff „sterben" für den Tod des Gerechten
tunlichst vermieden wird, wird dieser Terminus nicht für Jesus verwendet, da
das EvPetr – vielleicht noch stärker als die kanonischen Evangelien – aus der
Perspektive der Auferstehung bzw. einer bestimmten Christologie schreibt.
Aus dieser Glaubensposition heraus ist es angemessen, dass der Herr (direkt?)
aufgenommen wird – auch wenn das im Widerspruch zur Erzähllogik steht,
die erfordert, dass der Leichnam nach wie vor vorhanden ist (EvPetr 21; 23-24).
Eher unwahrscheinlich ist es vom Gesamtduktus des EvPetr her, dass an eine
Trennung in Leib („Leichnam") und Geist/Seele/Selbst („aufgenommen") zu
denken wäre, zumal am Ende eine Art „leibliche" Auferstehung geschildert
wird (EvPetr 39). Plausibler ist daher die Annahme, dass der Begriff der
Aufnahme an die geschilderte biblische Terminologie und Motivik anknüpfen
will und dabei die Erzähllogik hintanstellt.

EvPetr 20: Der Vorhang

Der griechische Begriff κατάπέτασμα, den das EvPetr für den Tempelvorhang
verwendet, steht in der Septuaginta beim Bau des Zeltheiligtums[53] als
Äquivalent für zwei verschiedene Dinge. Der Begriff übersetzt zunächst das
hebräische פָּרֹכֶת – ein vielleicht besser unübersetzt („Parochet") bleibender
Spezialbegriff für den „Vorhang" bei der „Platte" („Kapporet") auf der
Bundeslade (Ex 26,31ff), der zwischen dem Heiligen und dem Allerheiligsten
(ἀνὰ μέσον τοῦ ἁγίου καὶ ἀνὰ μέσον τοῦ ἁγίου τῶν ἁγίων; Ex 26,33) trennen soll.
Dabei gilt das Allerheiligste mit der Kapporet und der Bundeslade als der
Offenbarungsort Gottes (Lev 16,2). Zum Zweiten dient κατάπέτασμα als
Übersetzung für מָסָךְ, das ist der Vorhang am Zelteingang (Ex 26,37 u.ö.). Beim
irdischen Tempel begegnet die Parochet nur in 2 Chr 3,14 (einziger Beleg von
פָּרֹכֶת außerhalb der Tora), der Vorhang am Vorhof (der dem Zelteingang
entspricht) nur in 1 Kön 6,36 (nur LXX). Das heißt aber auch, dass sich
κατάπέτασμα primär auf die Verhältnisse des Zeltheiligtums bezieht und diese
Hintergrundtexte einbezogen werden müssen. Fasst man die Stellen
zusammen, so haben die Vorhänge trennende und verbergende Funktionen.

Gerade die Entsprechung zwischen κατάπέτασμα und פָּרֹכֶת, der Parochet, die
zwischen dem Heiligen und dem Allerheiligsten als Offenbarungsort Gottes
trennt, ist für die neutestamentliche Rede vom Zerreißen des Vorhangs (vgl.
Mt 27,51/Mk 15,38/Lk 23,45) besonders bezeichnend. Das Allerheiligste gilt als
der Offenbarungsort des heiligen Gottes, und nicht zu jeder Zeit hatte Aaron
als Priester ungefährdet Zutritt in dem Raum hinter dem Vorhang (vgl. Lev
16,2): In Lev 16 wird im Ritual des Versöhnungstags beschrieben, wie eine
Begegnung mit dem sich offenbarenden, versöhnenden Gott für den Menschen

---

[53]   Zu den folgenden Stellen aus dem Exodusbuch vgl. Dohmen, Exodus 19-40, passim.

Aaron (und seine Nachfolger) möglich ist, so dass der Mensch am Leben bleibt. Genau dieser Zusammenhang wird in Hebr 9 aufgegriffen und mit dem Opfer Christi verbunden – durch Christus, so der Anspruch des Hebräerbriefes, ist der unmittelbare Zugang zu Gott und Gottes Offenbarung „durch den Vorhang hindurch" möglich (vgl. Hebr 6,19; 9,2-3.12; 10,20). Was der Hebräerbrief durch ausgefeilte schriftgelehrte Argumentation deutlich macht, wird in den Passionserzählungen durch das Zerreißen des Tempelvorhangs „sinnenfällig" gemacht. Wer mit den Beschreibungen des Zeltheiligtums in Ex 26ff und mit dem Ritual des Versöhnungstags (Lev 16) vertraut ist, vermag den tieferen Sinn des zunächst rätselhaft erscheinenden Motivs zu entschlüsseln. Der Tod Jesu wird mit dem zeitgleichen Zerreißen des Vorhangs zu einer Theophanie oder Epiphanie, zu einer Gottesoffenbarung. Aus christlicher Sicht ist dies ein erhellender, ausdeutender Zug der Darstellung zur Untermauerung der eigenen Glaubensposition – zugleich aber liegen hier Potentiale für die Ab- oder Entwertung der jüdischen Gottesvorstellung bzw. des jüdischen Gottesdienstes. Die Grenze zwischen der (legitimen) Ausdeutung des Christusgeschehens mit Hilfe der Schrift (der Bibel Israels) und einer Enterbung des Judentums ist hier erreicht, wenn nicht schon überschritten. Für die schon mehrfach beobachtete antijüdische Tendenz des EvPetr ist das Element des zerreißenden Vorhangs ein weiterer Baustein.

EvPetr 25: Wehe unseren Sünden

Das EvPetr drückt unmissverständlich aus, dass die Kreuzigung des Herrn ein Übel war, das sich die Juden und die Ältesten und die Priester selbst angetan hatten. Die in EvPetr 25 geschilderte (zu) späte Einsicht wird in Anlehnung an einschlägige Jesaja-Stellen zum prophetischen Aufweis der Schuldigkeit des Volkes formuliert:

EvPetr 25:	οὐαὶ ταῖς ἁμαρτίαις ἡμῶν ἤγγισεν ἡ κρίσις καὶ τὸ τέλος Ἰερουσαλήμ
Jes 1,4:	οὐαὶ ἔθνος ἁμαρτωλὸν λαὸς πλήρης ἁμαρτιῶν σπέρμα πονηρὸν υἱοὶ ἄνομοι (vgl. auch Jes 5,18; Jes 30,1)
Jer 13,27:	οὐαί σοι Ιερουσαλημ ὅτι οὐκ ἐκαθαρίσθης ὀπίσω μου ἕως τίνος ἔτι

Der Trauergestus (κόπτεσθαι) könnte als eine Anspielung auf Sach 12,10-11 gewertet werden (vgl. auch Offb 1,7).[54] Damit würde dann die rätselhafte Gestalt des „Durchbohrten" christlich vereindeutigt werden.

---

[54]   Vgl. Mara, Évangile de Pierre, 152.

Die Einsicht „der Juden" bleibt aber im EvPetr weithin folgen- und wirkungslos, so dass die Vermutung nahe liegt, sie dient vornehmlich dazu, die prophetische Kritik am Volk und seinen Oberen sowie die prophetischen Gerichtsansagen pauschal einzuspielen und mit der Chiffre ἡ κρίσις καὶ τὸ τέλος Ἰερουσαλήμ an das Exil und die breite theologische Auseinandersetzung und Aufarbeitung in der Bibel Israels zu erinnern: Das Ereignis der Kreuzigung Jesu erhält damit allerhöchsten geschichtstheologischen Rang. Zu Lasten der „Juden" wird die Hinrichtung gleichgesetzt mit all den Verfehlungen, die zur Zerstörung Jerusalems und des Tempels sowie zum Exil geführt haben.

EvPetr 26-27: Trauer und verstörter Sinn; Fasten und Weinen

Wenn einmal die Parallelisierung zwischen dem Untergang Jerusalems 587 v. Chr. und dem Tod des Herrn auf der Agenda steht, dann ist es auch nicht mehr abwegig, hinter dem Fasten und Weinen der Jünger in EvPetr 27 ein alttestamentliches Vorbild zu sehen: Nehemia weint, trauert, fastet und betet angesichts des zerstörten Mauern Jerusalems (Neh 1,4).[55] Die Parallelisierung Nehemias, des Erbauers der nachexilischen Stadtmauer Jerusalems, mit Petrus, auf den Jesus seine Kirche baut (Mt 16,18), wird im EvPetr nicht weiter ausgeführt – ist das aber eine zu weit weg führende Spekulation?

Die Parallelisierung der Kreuzigung des Herrn und ihrer Begleiterscheinungen mit Ereignissen aus der Geschichte Israels ist ein charakteristischer Zug des EvPetr. Er zeigt sich auch in der Reaktion des Sprechers (Petrus) und seiner Gefährten in EvPetr 26: „Ich aber trauerte mit meinen Gefährten, und verstörten Sinnes hielten wir uns versteckt." Die Wendung „verstörten Sinnes" deutet hin auf die Trauer und Bestürzung über die Sorge des Hohenpriesters Onias III. (192-175 v. Chr.) anlässlich des Versuchs des seleukidischen Kanzlers Heliodor, den Jerusalemer Tempelschatz für die Staatskasse Seleukus' IV. Philopator zu konfiszieren: „Wer aber die Gestalt des Hohenpriesters sah, dem blutete das Herz (dem wurde der Sinn verstört). Wie er aussah und wie sein Gesicht sich verfärbt hatte, verriet seine innere Qual."[56]

EvPetr 26: ἐγὼ δὲ μετὰ τῶν ἑταίρων μου ἐλυπούμην καὶ <u>τετρωμένοι κατὰ διάνοιαν</u> ἐκρυβόμεθα

2 Makk 3,16: ἦν δὲ ὁρῶντα τὴν τοῦ ἀρχιερέως ἰδέαν <u>τιτρώσκεσθαι τὴν διάνοιαν</u> ἡ γὰρ ὄψις καὶ τὸ τῆς χρόας παρηλλαγμένον ἐνέφαινεν τὴν κατὰ ψυχὴν ἀγωνίαν

---

[55] Vgl. Mara, Vangelo di Pietro, 85.
[56] Vgl. Mara, Évangile de Pierre, 155-156.

Die Übereinstimmung könnte zufällig sein, doch der Bezug wird durch eine weitere Beobachtung unterstützt: Entscheidend für 2 Makk ist das Ergehen des Jerusalemer Tempels, dessen Wohl und Wehe eng mit der Torabefolgung bzw. den Sünden Israels verknüpft ist. Programmatisch formuliert 2 Makk 5,19-20: „Aber der Herr hat nicht das Volk erwählt wegen des Ortes, sondern den Ort wegen des Volkes. Deswegen litt auch der Ort mit unter den Unglücks- schlägen, die das Volk trafen, wie er später Anteil hatte an seinem Glück. Als der Allherrscher zürnte, lag der Ort verlassen da; als aber der große Herr sich wieder versöhnen ließ, wurde er in aller Pracht wiederhergestellt." Vom Tempel ist mehrfach im EvPetr die Rede, gerade in EvPetr 26. Die Zerstörung des Tempelvorhangs (EvPetr 20) und die Rede vom „verstörten Sinn" des Sprechers Petrus und seiner Gefährten, die an die Gefährdung des Tempels durch Heliodor in 2 Makk 3 erinnert (EvPetr 26), drängen somit in Anlehnung an die Grundaussage von 2 Makk 5,19-20 dem Leser unterschwellig erneut den Schluss auf, dass die Juden eine große Sünde begangen haben.[57]

EvPetr 30: Drei Tage

Die Rede von den drei Tagen, die das Grab bewacht werden soll, könnte als Anspielung auf Hos 6,2 gewertet werden: In der Erzähllogik des EvPetr wollen die Ältesten einen Diebstahl der Leiche verhindern, damit das Volk nicht eine Realisierung des Prophetenwortes „Nach zwei Tagen gibt er uns das Leben zurück, am dritten Tag richtet er uns wieder auf, und wir leben vor seinem Angesicht" annehmen kann. EvPetr 30 liegt hier ganz auf der Linie von Mt 27,64.

EvPetr 32-33: Ein großer Stein; Siegel

Die Verschließung und Versiegelung des Grabes in EvPetr 32-33, die auf Mt 27,60 (Stein) und 27,66 (Versiegelung) zurückgehen dürften, erinnern an Dan 6,18:[58] Um Daniel offiziell in der Löwengrube festzuhalten und Manipulationen an seiner Lage zu verhindern, wird der Eingang mit einem Stein verschlossen und mit den Siegeln des Königs und seiner Großen versiegelt.

Ein Leser, der die Danielgeschichte kennt und sich bei den Vorkehrungen in EvPetr 32-33 daran erinnert fühlt, wird die „richtige" Schlussfolgerung im Sinne des EvPetr ziehen: Auch in dieser vermeintlich aussichtslosen Lage kann

---

[57] Vgl. Mara, Évangile de Pierre, 156: „Cependant en *II Macc.* 3-5, le récit, non seulement nous montre la sainteté du Temple de Jérusalem, mais souligne que si quelque malheur s'abat sur le Temple, c'est à cause du péchés d'Israël. Ce n'est donc pas seulement la ressemblance de l'expression «blessé dans son cœur» qui rapproche *Ev.P.* de *II Macc.*, mais c'est aussi l'allusion à la destruction du Temple comme conséquence des péchés du Juifs."

[58] Vgl. u.a. Vaganay, L'Évangile de Pierre, 285.

Gottes heilvolles Wirken an seinem Gerechten nicht von menschlichen Maßnahmen verhindert werden.

Die Siebenzahl der Siegel ist weniger eine Anspielung an die sieben Augen Gottes nach Sach 3,9 und 4,10, sondern eher eine Parallele zu den sieben Siegeln in Offb 5,1, zumal auch in EvPetr 35 wie in Offb 5,2 eine „laute Stimme" zu hören ist.[59] Wie im EvPetr allein der Auferstandene die sieben Siegel von EvPetr 33 überwindet, ist es auch in Offb 5 das Lamm, der erhabene Christus, der die sieben Siegel des Buches öffnet.

EvPetr 48: Es ist besser für uns …

Die Ältesten, der Zenturio und seine Leute werden im EvPetr zu Auferstehungszeugen, wobei die römischen Soldaten sogar eine Art Glaubensbekenntnis ablegen (EvPetr 45). Die anderen „alle" (EvPetr 47: πάντες) – die jüdischen Autoritäten – bestürmen Pilatus, die Sache geheim zu halten. Ihre Argumentation läuft darauf hinaus, dass es besser für sie sei, vor Gott zu sündigen, als dem Volk in die Hände zu fallen.

(1) Diese Formulierung nimmt eine Anleihe in 2 Sam 24,14: Als Strafe für das verbotene Abhalten der Volkszählung wählt David die Pest mit der Begründung: „Wir wollen lieber dem Herrn in die Hände fallen, denn seine Barmherzigkeit ist groß; den Menschen aber möchte ich nicht in die Hände fallen." Der zweite Teil der Argumentation stimmt zwischen EvPetr 48 und 2 Sam 24,14 überein: Menschen in die Hände zu fallen, ist gefährlich. Doch während David ausdrücklich auf die Barmherzigkeit Gottes baut, ist davon in EvPetr 48 nicht die Rede – eher hat man den Eindruck, dass die jüdischen Autoritäten in ein schlechtes Licht gerückt werden, da sie sich vor menschlichen Racheakten mehr fürchten als vor Gott.

(2) Eine gegenteilige Argumentation vertritt Susanna in Dan 13,23: „Es ist besser für mich, es nicht zu tun und euch in die Hände zu fallen, als gegen den Herrn zu sündigen." So weigert sich Susanna, sich den Ältesten sexuell hinzugeben, und nimmt in Kauf, unschuldig verurteilt zu werden. In vorbildlicher Weise sieht sie es als schlimmer an, gegen Gott zu sündigen, als in die Hände eines ungerechten menschlichen Gerichts zu fallen. Aktiviert man als Leser die Susanna-Szene als Hintergrundtext zu EvPetr 48, drängt sich ein vernichtendes Urteil über das Fehlverhalten der jüdischen Autoritäten geradezu auf.

---

[59]   Vgl. Mara, Vangelo di Pietro, 91-92.

Schlussfolgerungen

In formaler Hinsicht ist festzuhalten, dass das EvPetr keine ausdrückliche Schriftauslegung betreibt. Bis auf eine Ausnahme begegnen keine expliziten Zitationsformeln oder wörtliche, als solche erkennbare Zitate.[60] Insofern ist auch nicht zu vermuten, dass in der Textstrategie eine bestimmte, gezielte Schrifthermeneutik, die bewusst reflektiert ist, aufscheint. Bei der Lektüre ist somit kein systematisch-gezielter Schriftbezug erkennbar, sondern es handelt sich eher um „ad-hoc"-Bezüge, deren Aktivierung in der Regel nicht zwingend erforderlich ist.

Bei der einen Stelle, die davon spricht, dass etwas im Gesetz geschrieben steht (EvPetr 5 und 15), erfolgt kein wörtliches Zitat, sondern eine kreative Umgestaltung, die den Bezugstext (Dtn 21,22-23) gerade noch erkennen lässt. Die Umgestaltung geht so weit, dass ein signifikantes Element der alttestamentlichen Stelle (dass es um eine Hinrichtung geht) durch ein anderes Wort ausgetauscht wird: EvPetr 5; 15 sprechen von einem „Ermordeten".

Die meisten anderen Anspielungen an alttestamentliche Stellen sind eher als „locker" zu bezeichnen, d.h. es ist nicht sicher erkennbar, ob eine literarische Abhängigkeit vorliegt und ob der Bezug – unter produktions-orientierter Fragestellung – intendiert ist.[61] Insofern können die beobachteten Phänomene ohnehin nur unter einer – rezeptionsorientierten – Lektüre- oder Leserperspektive ausgewertet werden. In vielen Fällen genügt auch eine intertextuelle Bezugnahme zu den kanonischen Evangelien, ein Rekurs auf das Alte Testament ist meist nicht zwingend in dem Sinne, dass der Text ohne Einspielung der Intertexte unverständlich wäre. Auf der anderen Seite führt jedoch eine „schriftkundige" Lektüre zu entsprechenden Sinnzuwächsen.

Insofern ist der Schriftbezug des EvPetr auf formaler Ebene anders zu beurteilen als etwa derjenige der Offenbarung des Johannes (Offb), um ein deutliches Extrembeispiel zu nennen. In Offb sind die Texte ohne alttestamentlichen Hintergrund bisweilen völlig undurchschaubar, banal oder sinnlos – der Text zwingt zur Lektüre biblischer Texte![62] Vergleichbares ist im EvPetr nicht zu finden.

Die inhaltlichen Implikationen, die die Aktivierung bestimmter Schriftbezüge mit sich bringen, lassen sich unter zwei Hauptpunkten systematisieren: eine antijüdische Tendenz und eine bestimmte Darstellung „des Herrn" („Christologie").

---

60   Vgl. auch Vaganay, L'Évangile de Pierre, 102.
61   Zuversichtlicher ist hier Denker, Stellung, 77, der sich sicher ist, dass der Verfasser des EvPetr die Hauptzüge seiner Passionsgeschichte im AT verankert sehen will. Freilich sagt auch Denker, dass die Grundtendenz dieser Rezeption des AT darin bestehe, in der Kreuzigung Jesu die Fortsetzung und den Höhepunkt der Unheilsgeschichte der Juden, von der das AT immer wieder spreche, zu sehen.
62   Vgl. beispielsweise zu Offb 22,6-21 Hieke/Nicklas, Die Worte der Prophetie, 57.

(1) Die antijüdische Tendenz ist in einer Vielzahl der Belege festzustellen.[63] Viele Schriftbezüge bewirken, dass die Folterknechte, die von den jüdischen Autoritäten nicht unterscheidbar sind, von ihrer eigenen Schrift her in einem sehr schlechten Licht dastehen. Sie erscheinen beispielsweise wie die Frevler in der Weisheitsliteratur, die hinter dem Gerechten her sind, um sein Blut zu vergießen. Denkt man hier ein Stück weiter und importiert man die drohenden Worte über das fatale Geschick der Frevler, so verstärkt sich die antijüdische Tendenz. Des Weiteren erscheinen die Folterknechte als diejenigen, die etwas tun, was schon die Propheten mehrfach verurteilt haben und was zum Untergang Jerusalems (Tempelzerstörung, Exil) geführt hat. Somit werden sowohl die prophetischen Gerichtsreden als auch die deuteronomistischen Vorstellungen über die theologische Bewältigung des Exils als Strafe für ein Verhalten, das Gottes Weisung zuwiderläuft, auf diejenigen appliziert, die den Herrn kreuzigen („ermorden"!). „Die Juden" erscheinen damit auch als Leute, die ihrer eigenen Schrift zuwider handeln – und genau die Sünden wieder begehen, die schon „im Alten Testament" zum Untergang geführt haben.

(2) „Der Herr" erscheint im EvPetr in der Rolle des Gottesknechtes von Deuterojesaja, als messianischer König (Jes 9; 11) und als leidender Gerechter, der am Ende nicht „stirbt", sondern „aufgenommen wird" (wie einst Henoch und Elija). Insofern besteht im EvPetr schon eine christologische Anknüpfung Jesu an alttestamentliche Vorstellungen. Der Blick auf die kanonischen Evangelien zeigt aber, dass sich diese Anknüpfung im traditionell-konventionellem Rahmen bewegt. Die alttestamentlichen Hintergrund-elemente für die Darstellung „des Herrn" werden dann aber von der fulminanten Auferstehungsszenerie, die wohl als innovativ bezeichnet werden kann – alttestamentliche Bezüge begegnen jedenfalls nicht –, in den Schatten gestellt.

Aus dieser Perspektive heraus wird klar, warum für das EvPetr die Kreuzigung des Herrn einem Verbrechen von historischer oder kosmischer Dimension gleichkommt (vgl. die ausführlich thematisierte „Finsternis am Mittag") – sie steht in der Schwere der damit verbundenen Schuld mindestens auf der Ebene der Verfehlungen, die zum Exil geführt haben. Die alt-testamentlichen Bezüge in diesem Kontext lassen zugleich die Kreuzigung als Auftakt des Gerichts erscheinen, als Reaktion auf gravierendes menschliches Fehlverhalten seitens der jüdischen Autoritäten. Die fatale Wirkungsgeschichte

---

[63] Diese Tendenz wird vielfach festgestellt, vgl. z.B. Vaganay, L'Évangile de Pierre, 104; Brown, Gospel of Peter, 340; idem, Death, 1339; Koester, Ancient Christian Gospels, 217. Denker, Stellung, 81, sagt zwar, die apologetische Tendenz des EvPetr sei nicht antijüdisch, fährt aber dann fort, dass der Verfasser des EvPetr den Juden „die Größe der Schuld, in die sie durch die Verwerfung Jesu geraten sind, deutlich machen will." Insgesamt wolle daher das EvPetr die Juden zur Buße und zum Glauben an den Herrn rufen und richte sich gegen antichristliche jüdische Polemik. Zur Rolle der „Juden" im Petrusevangelium vgl. zudem T. Nicklas, Die „Juden" im Petrusevangelium (P.Cair. 10759). Ein Testfall, NTS 47, 2001, 206-221, sowie den Beitrag von J. Verheyden im vorliegenden Band.

derartiger Darstellungen für das Verhältnis von Christen und Juden muss hier nicht mehr eigens thematisiert werden.

Meist kann nicht mit Sicherheit gesagt werden, ob die vorgestellten Schriftbezüge und die damit verbundenen Deutungen dem oder den Autor(en) des EvPetr bewusst waren. Auch ist hier kein Urteil darüber gefällt, ob diese Bezüge und Implikationen „berechtigt" sind. Das wären keine dem Befund angemessene Fragerichtungen. Deutlich wird jedoch auf der Leserebene, dass die Aktivierung des alttestamentlichen intertextuellen Resonanzraumes zu bemerkenswerten, teils erschreckenden Sinnzuwächsen führt – so gewinnt die Lektüre des nicht-kanonischen Textes Petrusevangelium im Bezug zum Kanon der christlichen Bibel erheblich an Dynamik.

The *Gospel of Peter* and the Canonical Gospels

by

JOHN DOMINIC CROSSAN

This article examines three main answers on the relationship of the *Gospel of Peter* to the gospels in the New Testament in recent United States scholarship and argues once again for my own solution to that question. Those three views are chosen because they are the more-or-less obvious responses to that problem. The first solution is *independence*, the second one is *dependence*, and the third one is a combination of both *independence and dependence*.

Introduction

First, the *Gospel of Peter* is an actual not a hypothetical document and, whether any solution be deemed adequate or inadequate, the document will still be there demanding explanation.

 Second, it exists today as P.Cair. 10759 in the Library of Alexandria with five folios of a *parchment codex* already in fragmentary form when copied into our extant text. It was discovered in 1886-87 at modern Akhmîm or ancient Panopolis and published in 1892-93.[1] It is dated between the sixth and seventh centuries.[2] It also exists as POxy 2949 in Oxford's Ashmolean Museum with two tiny and badly mutilated *papyrus scroll* fragments. It was discovered after 1897 at modern El Bahnasa or ancient Oxyrhynchus and published in 1972.[3] It is dated to the end of the second or start of the third century.[4]

---

[1] U. Bouriant, Fragments du texte grec du livre d'Énoch et de quelques écrits attribués a Saint Pierre, in: Mémoires publiés par les membres de la Mission archéologique française au Caire 9.1, Paris 1892, 91-147; A. Lods, Evangelii secundum Petrum et Petri Apocalypseos quae supersunt, in: Mémoires publiés par les membres de la Mission archéologique française au Caire 9.3, Paris 1893, 217-235, with Plates I-XXXIV [Pp. 232-235 are mispagnated as 333-335]. For a critical Greek text, see M.G. Mara, Évangile de Pierre. Introduction, Texte Critique, Traduction, Commentaire et Index, SC 201, Paris 1973, and now T.J. Kraus/T. Nicklas, Das Petrusevangelium und die Petrusapokalypse. Die griechischen Fragmente mit deutscher und englischer Übersetzung, GCS.NF 11, Neutestamentliche Apokryphen 1, Berlin-New York 2004.

[2] See now Kraus/Nicklas, Petrusevangelium.

[3] G.M. Browne/R.A. Coles/J.R. Rea/J.C. Shelton/E.G. Turner, The Oxyrhynchus Papyri XLI, Cambridge 1972. Coles edited P.Oxy. xli 2949 = *Gos. Pet.* 2, on pp.15-16; see also Plate II; he noted on p. 15 that: "The verso is blank; the book therefore was apparently not a codex." See

Third, there are textual discrepancies between *Gos. Pet.* 2:3-5a in those earlier Oxyrhynchus and later Akhmîm versions[5] similar to those between the *Gospel of Thomas* in its earlier Oxyrhynchus (POxy 1, 654, & 655) and its later Nag Hammadi versions.[6] Such divergences are to be expected in both extracanonical and intracanonical texts.[7] That evident textual instability may make any specific word somewhat questionable but it cannot justify ignoring the *Gospel of Peter* any more than the *Gospel of Thomas*.

First Proposal: Independence

I take Helmut Koester as representative of the *independence* solution and this is his general thesis: "[T]here are indications that the basis of the *Gospel of Peter* was a very early form of the passion and resurrection narratives."[8] I emphasize every word in that assertion and summarize his arguments under four points.

First, Koester, drawing on Denker,[9] argues that the passion narrative in the *Gospel of Peter* is older and more original than those in the canonical gospels. Koester's presupposition is that the origins of that story derive not from a record of history but from a meditation on prophecy, the "according to the Scriptures" of 1 Cor 15:3-4.[10] It is, in my terms, not history remembered but prophecy historicized.

Second, Koester also presumes a common passion story behind Mark and John which ended with the women at the empty tomb but which lacked any direct resurrection-apparition as such. But there is an account of the actual resurrection itself in the *Gospel of Peter* 8:28-11:49 and that raises the question whether it has preserved older resurrection traditions possibly now fragmented into such units as the centurion in Mark 15:39; the guards in Matt

---

also D. Lührmann, POx 2949: EvPt 3-5 in einer Handschrift des 2./3. Jahrhunderts, ZNW 72, 1981, 216-226; idem, POx 4009: Ein neues Fragment des Petrusevangeliums?, NT 35, 1993, 390-410; idem, Ein neues Fragment des Petrusevangeliums, in: The Synoptic Gospels: Source Criticism and the New Literary Criticism, ed. by C. Focant, BEThL 110, Leuven 1993, 579-581.

4   J. van Haelst, Catalogue des Papyrus Littéraires Juifs et Chrétiens, Paris 1976, 209 Nr. 592. It should be added to his index on p. 410.

5   J.C. Treat, The Two Manuscript Witnesses to the Gospel of Peter, SBLSP 29, 1990, 391-399.

6   M. Marcovich, Textual Criticism on the Gospel of Thomas, JThS 20, 1969, 53-74; O. Hofius, Das koptische Thomasevangelium und die Oxyrhynchus-Papyri Nr. 1, 654 und 655, EvTh 20, 1960, 21-42. 182-192; J.A. Fitzmyer, The Oxyrhynchus Logoi of Jesus and the Coptic Gospel according to Thomas, in: idem, Essays on the Semitic Background of the New Testament, SBLSBS 5, Missoula 1974 (= London 1971), 355-433 [Updated revision of article in TS 20, 1959, 505-560].

7   F. Bovon, The Synoptic Gospels and the Noncanonical Acts of the Apostles, HThR 81, 1988, 19-36; H. Koester, The Text of the Synoptic Gospels in the Second Century, in: Gospel Traditions in the Second Century. Origins, Recensions, Text, and Transmission, ed. by W.L. Petersen, Christianity and Judaism in Antiquity 3, Notre Dame 1989, 19-37.

8   H. Koester, Apocryphal and Canonical Gospels, HThR 73, 1980, 105-130, esp. 126.

9   J. Denker, Die theologiegeschichtliche Stellung des Petrusevangeliums. Ein Beitrag zur Frühgeschichte des Doketismus, EHS XXIII.36, Bern-Frankfurt/Main 1975.

10   Denker, Die theologiegeschichtliche Stellung, 127-128.

27:62-64 & 28:2-4; and maybe, as a "very faint echo," the Transfiguration in Mark 9:2-8.[11]

Third, Koester returned to those two points a few years later. He argued for an early written "Passion Narrative" independently behind *Peter*, Mark, and John.[12] But was it a passion only or a passion and resurrection narrative? Is the basic common source used by *Peter*, Mark, and John a passion or a passion-resurrection story? Or does *Peter* know, but quite separately, a very early passion *and* a very early resurrection story?

Fourth, in a later study Koester decided clearly for that second option but the resurrection story was not a direct epiphany of the risen Jesus but only an indirect epiphany about the risen Jesus. That single *passion* story used by *Peter*, Mark, and John ended with the *youth-epiphany* to the women at the empty tomb. All other *epiphany* stories are separate and gospel-specific. But the *Jesus-epiphany* story from the *Gospel of Peter* was known to Mark and Matthew. Notice, by the way, how that last item somewhat complicates the situation.[13]

To make those claims convincing, however, Koester would have to continue his analysis into at least these two points. First, what is the basic content of his proposed passion-epiphany source common to the *Gospel of Peter*, Mark, and John? It would, presumably, contain at least those items common to all three redactions. Second, he would have to explain in each case how and why those three redactions adapted their common source as each did.

Second Proposal: Dependence

For Helmut Koester the *Gospel of Peter* is independent of the canonical gospels but for Raymond Brown it is dependent upon them. Once again, I summarize the argument over four points for convenience and emphasis.

First, the basic relationship between the canonical gospels and the *Gospel of Peter* [GP] is not one of written dependence or scribal copying but of "oral dependence of GP on some or all of the canonical Gospels." He proposed the analogy "of an intelligent Christian today whose knowledge of the Gospel story does not come from reading a Bible but from hearing Sunday pericopes read in church."[14] Those "memories preserved through their having been heard

---

11   Denker, Die theologiegeschichtliche Stellung, 129-130.
12   H. Koester, Introduction to the New Testament 2, Hermeneia Foundations and Facets, Philadelphia 1982, 49. 68. 163.
13   H. Koester, Ancient Christian Gospels. Their History and Development, London-Philadelphia 1990. Under the general heading of "The Passion Narrative and the Gospel of Peter" (pp. 216-240) he discusses separately "The Passion Narrative" in the singular (220-230) and then "Epiphany Stories" in the plural (231-240).
14   R.E. Brown, The *Gospel of Peter* and Canonical Gospel Priority, NTS 33, 1987, 321-343, esp. 335-336.

and recounted orally" involved Matthew, Mark, Luke, and John.[15] In summary, then, the *Gospel of Peter* "was not produced at a desk by someone with written sources propped up before him but by someone with a memory of what he had read and heard (canonical and noncanonical) to which he contributed imagination and a sense of drama."[16]

Second, Brown concludes that, while the *Gospel of Peter* "may well have known" the guards-at-the-tomb story from Matt 27:62-66, it also knew the story of the guarded tomb and the story of the visible resurrection in a version which was both "consecutive" and "independent" of that canonical version.[17] This other account involved all of these items: "The supplying of the centurion's name, the seven seals, the stone rolling off by itself, the account of the resurrection with the gigantic figures, the talking cross, the confession of Jesus as God's Son by the Jewish authorities, and their fear of their own people."[18] I return to this point in the Conclusion at the end of this article.

Third, Brown agrees with Koester that Mark and John had independent passion narratives. But there is also, apart from them, another and also independent stream of passion tradition. He describes this passion tradition repeatedly in various places as "popular, imaginative, oral, romanticized, and vivid."[19] Brown proposes that those popular traditions now appear only in Matthew and *Peter*, but at an earlier stage in Matthew and at a more developed stage in *Peter*.[20] Those popular traditions included these items: "A consecutive story about the guard at the sepulcher ... the suicide of Judas and the blood money (27:3-10); the dream of Pilate's wife (27:19); Pilate's washing his hands of Jesus' blood while the people accepted responsibility for it (27:24-25); the extraordinary phenomena on earth and in heaven when Jesus died (27:51b-53)."[21]

Fourth, Brown also adduces independent oral traditions to explain the minor agreements of Matthew and Luke against Mark in the passion narratives.[22] Examples cited are Matt 26:68 and Luke 22:64 against Mark 14:65 for, "Who is it that struck you?" and Matt 26:75 and Luke 22:62 against Mark 14:72 for, "And he went out and wept bitterly."[23]

---

[15] R.E. Brown, The Death of the Messiah: From Gethsemane to the Grave. A Commentary on the Passion Narratives in the Four Gospels, ABRL, New York 1994, 1001. 1057. 1306. 1334-1335.
[16] Brown, The Death of the Messiah, 1336.
[17] Brown, The Death of the Messiah, 1287. 1301 n. 35. 1305-1306.
[18] Brown, The Death of the Messiah, 1307.
[19] Brown, The Death of the Messiah, 42. 287 n. 10. 784. 860. 1118. 1287. 1288. 1304. 1345.
[20] Brown, The Death of the Messiah, 1335. 1345.
[21] Brown, The Death of the Messiah, 1287.
[22] Brown, The Death of the Messiah, 44-45. 784. 857.
[23] Brown, The Death of the Messiah, 579. 609. 611 n. 43.

Third Proposal: Independence and Dependence

This is my own solution and I propose it both negatively and positively. The negative section gives my most basic disagreements with Koester and Brown. The positive section outlines my own position on the *Gospel of Peter* as a second-century conflation of extracanonical and canonical passion-resurrection narratives.

Negative Section

First, my most important disagreement with *both* Koester and Brown concerns their claim for the independence of John from the Synoptic tradition in its passion-resurrection complex. They argue for independence – in general – but I think that John's passion-resurrection narrative – in particular – is dependent on the Synoptic versions. And one's decision on that issue is fundamental for many others concerning the *Gospel of Peter*'s own relationship with those canonical gospels, I leave aside for now any wider consideration of John/Synoptic relations[24] but, for background, I also imagine here a combination of independence and dependence: I do not think that John's sayings-tradition and miracles-tradition are synoptically dependent and even less that his combination of miracles and sayings into signs-discourses is synoptically dependent. But I focus here only on John's passion-resurrection tradition (with resurrection here meaning the indirect witness of the empty tomb and youth-epiphany).[25]

What convinces me that John knew specifically the Markan passion story is that the intercalation of Peter's denial and Jesus' confession in Mark 14:53-72 is found also in John 18:13-27. I presume, of course, that the presence of something uniquely or even characteristically redactional (not just traditional)

---

24   F. Neirynck, John and the Synoptics, 1965-1975, in: L'Évangile de Jean. Sources, rédaction, théologie, ed. by M. De Jonge, BEThL 44, Leuven 1977, 73-106 (also in: Evangelica [I: 1966-1981]. Gospel Studies. Études d'Évangile. Collected Essays by Frans Neirynck, ed. by F. Van Segbroeck, BEThL 60, Leuven 1982, 365-398, with Additional Note on pp. 398-400). See also in: Evangelica [II: 1982-1991]. Collected Essays by Frans Neirynck, ed. by F. Van Segbroeck, BEThL 99, Leuven 1991, 798-799; and: John and the Synoptics: 1975-1990, in: John and the Synoptics, ed. by A. Denaux, BEThL 101, Leuven 1992, 3-62.

25   For the dependence of John's passion-narrative in 18:1-19:42 on the written Synoptic tradition, see M. Sabbe, The Arrest of Jesus in Jn 18,1-11 and Its Relation to the Synoptic Gospels. A Critical Evaluation of A. Dauer's Hypothesis, in: idem, Studia Neotestamentica. Collected Essays, BEThL 98, Leuven 1991, 355-386 with Additional Note on 387-388 (also in: L'Évangile de Jean. Sources, rédaction, théologie, ed. by M. de Jonge, BEThL 44, Leuven 1977, 203-234); idem, The Denial of Peter in the Gospel of John, Louvain Studies 20, 1995, 219-240; idem, The Trial of Jesus before Pilate in John and Its Relation to the Synoptic Gospels, in: Studia Neotestamentica. Collected Essays, BEThL 98, Leuven 1991, 467-513 (also in: John and the Synoptics, ed. by A. Denaux, BEThL 101, Leuven 1992, 341-385) and idem, The Johannine Account of the Death of Jesus and Its Synoptic Parallels (Jn 19, 16b-42), EThL 70, 1994, 34-64.

from Mark into John is the strongest possible argument for dependence. Three points:

(1) By *intercalation* I do not mean the simple *juxtaposition* of two units. A simple juxtaposition of Peter's denials and Jesus' confession could easily happen in separate texts independently of one another since both are linked to the same event: the night judgment before Jewish religious authority. But Markan intercalation is not, emphatically not, a general juxtaposition.

(2) One of the most peculiar and distinctive Markan compositional devices has been called an *intercalation* or *sandwich*. The device has two elements. First, literary presentation: Event A begins (A¹), then Event B begins and finishes (B), and finally, Event A finishes (A²). Second, theological meaning: the purpose of the intercalation is not mere literary show; it presumes that those two events, call them the framing event and the insert event, are mutually interactive, that they interpret one another to emphasize Mark's theological intention. It is this combination of literary structure *and* theological import that makes those intercalations particularly if not uniquely Markan.

Frans Neirynck cites seven instances,[26] John Donahue also suggests seven cases,[27] and Edwards offers nine examples.[28] They agree on these six examples which include the one under discussion here:

---

[26] F. Neirynck, Duality in Mark. Contributions to the Study of the Markan Redaction, BEThL 31, Leuven 1972, 133 n. 28.

[27] J.R. Donahue, Are You the Christ? The Trial Narrative in the Gospel of Mark, SBLDS 10, Cambridge/Ma 1973, 42 n. 2. 58-59. Brown, The Death of the Messiah, 427, mentions Markan intercalations, but he insists, against Donahue, that one is *not* present in the specific case of Mark 14:53-72. He says that, "Donahue is right: If this clear Marcan pattern is found in 14:53-72, there is every reason to think that Mark put the whole scheme together and, since John has some of the same sequence, perhaps to think that John drew on Mark." But he rejects Donahue here because, "Mark is not filling in between the beginning of Peter's denial scene and its conclusion; he is describing two simultaneous actions, and that is not a feature of intercalation." – First, simultaneity or non-simultaneity between the two events is irrelevant to intercalations. It is the theological dialectic created by their relationship that is the significant point. Indeed, Brown himself mentions that "Mark surrounds Jesus' cleansing of the Temple with the cursing and withering of the fig tree (11:12-14 and 20-21 around 11:15-19) as a symbolic interpretation of how he will treat the Temple" (p. 447). He does not call that an intercalation, does not include it in his index under "Mark/style/intercalation" (p. 1570), but Neirynck, Donahue, and Edwards include it in the six instances on which they all agree. It is, in fact, a classic Markan intercalation involving two simultaneous events but – once again – simultaneity or its lack is not the point. Markan intercalation is about what Brown sees clearly in this one case – it is about "symbolic interpretation" of framed unit by framing unit (and vice versa). – Second, elsewhere, Brown repeatedly misinterprets Markan intercalation as a simple literary device to fill in time between the start and finish of some action: "to fill in the time" (p. 119 n. 4), "allows time .... to take up the time" (p. 427), and "filling in the time" (p. 1356). But to repeat, Markan intercalation is a literary device employed for theological dialectic.

[28] J.R. Edwards, Markan Sandwiches: The Significance of Interpolations in Markan Narratives, NT 31, 1989, 193-216, esp. 197-198.

A¹	B	A²
3:20-21	3:22-30	3:31-35
5:21-24	5:25-34	5:35-43
6:7-13	6:14-29	6:30
11:12-14	11:15-19	11:20-21
14:1-2	14:3-9	14:10-11
14:53-54	14:55-65	14:66-72

Edwards also notes that "of Mark's nine sandwiches, Matthew retains Mark's A¹-B-A² pattern five times and Luke retains it four times."[29] In the present instance the A¹-B-A² inclusion of Mark 14:53-72 is retained in Matt 26:57-75 but eliminated in Luke 22:56-71 where Peter's denials in 22:54-62 simply precede Jesus' confession in 22:63-71. John, on the other hand, not only presents the same A¹-B-A² pattern but, if anything, he intensifies it by having one denial precede (18:13-18) and two others follow (18:25-27) Jesus' confession (18:19-24). His purpose was probably not just to contrast Jesus and Peter, as Mark did, but also to contrast Peter and "the other [Beloved?] disciple" (18:15-16). Nothing is said about *that* disciple denying Jesus!

(3) The transposition of that peculiarly or even uniquely Markan literary-theological structure from Mark 14:53-72 into John 18:13-27 persuades me to accept, at least as a working hypothesis, the dependence of John's passion account on Mark's. This is confirmed by the presence of two other *subsidiary* elements not uniquely or even peculiarly but at least characteristically Markan within that same A¹-B-A² structure.

The first subsidiary element is an example of Mark's penchant for duplication. This usually concerns smaller rather than larger Markan inserts and it involves the repetition of the same word or phrase both before and after the insert. It is much harder to distinguish from a simple repetition and is thus much less clearly Markan than those larger intercalations. What I emphasize here is its presence in conjunction with the larger intercalation under discussion. Neirynck gives 36 examples of such "inclusions."[30] Donahue cites 45 or 46 examples but emphasizes 22 cases where "(a) close verbal agreement, (b) a superfluous or tautological quality to one of the phrases, and (c) synoptic alteration" are present.[31] The example of present interest is this one:

---

[29]   Edwards, Markan Sandwiches, 199.
[30]   Neirynck, Duality in Mark, 131-133 n. 27.
[31]   Donahue, Are You the Christ, 241-243, see also 78-81.

A¹: PETER – start denial in Mark 14:53-54:
"*Peter* had followed him at a distance, right into the *courtyard* of the high priest; and he was sitting with the guards, *warming himself* at the fire."

B: JESUS – start & finish confession in Mark 14:55-65.

A²: PETER – restart & finish denial in Mark 14:66-67:
"While *Peter* was below in the *courtyard*, one of the servant-girls of the high priest came by. When she saw Peter *warming himself*, she stared at him and said, 'You also were with Jesus, the man from Nazareth.'"

That specific example is given by Neirynck[32] but not by Donahue although its seems to fit his three just-cited criteria for framing inclusions. Those repetitions are usually within a few verses of each other but that separation between Mark 14:53-54 and 14:66-67 is no farther apart than the one he suggests between Mark 5:10 (καὶ παρεκάλει αὐτὸν πολλά) and 5:23 (καὶ παρεκάλει αὐτὸν πολλά).

The second subsidiary element is an example of Mark's penchant for triplication. As there are, for example, three prophecies of the passion-resurrection 8:31-33; 9:31; 10:33-34 or three visits to the sleeping disciples in 14:37-39, 40, 41-42, so there are three denials by Peter in 14:66-68, 69-70a, 70b-72.

In summary, therefore, that denial/confession/denial *intercalation* along with, on a subsidiary and less significant level, that *duplication* of outer frames (Peter, courtyard, warming himself) and that *triplication* of inner content (three denials) are as redactionally Markan as I can imagine and their presence in John renders dependence the safest working hypothesis. One might object, I suppose, that it only proves (literary) dependence of John on Mark for that *intercalation* alone, but I see it as the strongest argument for the Sabbe and Neirynck proposals concerning the general dependence of John on the Synoptic tradition for his entire passion-resurrection narrative.

Second, my most significant disagreement with Brown concerns his discussion of "anti-Judaism" in the *Gospel of Peter*. Brown claims that the *Gospel of Peter* is more anti-Jewish than any of the intracanonical gospels, a feature which indicates, he says, that it is later than they are and also popular rather than official, heterodox rather than orthodox. In other words, its author could have read them and deliberately made them more anti-Jewish. This is a vital point because it proposes a redactional reason for the creation of that extracanonical text from the intracanonical sources. This claim of "anti-Judaism" is repeated again and again throughout his analysis:[33]

---

32 Neirynck, Duality in Mark, 132.
33 Brown, Death of the Messiah, 63. 834. 868. 912. 929. 1037. 1065. 1235. 1347 n. 62. Brown does not say that the *Gospel of Peter* was redacted exclusively, primarily, especially, or even deliberately in order to increase the anti-Judaism of the intracanonical passion-resurrection narratives. But that claim is made clearly and brutally in two other studies: (1) S.E. Schaeffer, The Gospel of

[I]n the later *GPet*, where one finds a popularization freer from the controls of the standardized preaching and teaching discernible in much of Matt, the anti-Jewish feeling is even more unnuanced .... sharply more anti-Jewish than the canonical Gospels .... this work is quite hostile to the Jews .... overtly anti-Jewish spirit .... anti-Jewish thrust .... anti-Jewish implication of hypocrisy .... the anti-Jewish sentiment that is much more prominent in *GPet* than in the canonical Gospels .... strong anti-Jewish prejudice of *GPet* .... I would hope that today Christians would recognize another heterodox tendency in *GPet*: its intensified anti-Jewish depictions.

(By the way, I read such terms as "anti-Jewish" to mean anti-some-or-even-all-other-forms-of-Judaism-except-our-own-most-righteous-one! I am much more willing to talk, looking backwards from later history, about "roots of anti-Judaism" or "roots of anti-Semitism" than about "anti-Judaism" or "anti-Semitism" when at this early stage one Jewish group calls any or all other Jewish groups by nasty names or bitter epithets). My main point, however, is that Brown's comments are flatly wrong, not just interpretively wrong from my viewpoint but factually wrong from anyone's viewpoint. Here is what *actually* happens in the *Gospel of Peter*.

It is "the Jews" and not the Romans who condemn Jesus and it is "the people" who abuse and execute him. Only here is Pilate fully innocent and capable of true hand-washing, a gesture somewhat hypocritical in Matthew's account since he alone can and does condemn Jesus to death and supplies the soldiers for his execution. In the *Gospel of Peter* his soldiers are not at all involved in the execution. So far Brown is absolutely correct. This is more anti-Jewish than anything in the canonical gospels. And if the story stopped with that, the *Gospel of Peter* would be certainly the most anti-Jewish of the five passion accounts. But then something very strange happens and that must be read within the unfolding narrative development. Those marvellous signs at the death of Jesus result in this reaction:

Peter, the Canonical Gospels, and Oral Tradition, Ann Arbor 1991 (Ph.D. dissertation, Union Theological Seminary, NY, under Raymond E. Brown). She says that "The Jews are revealed as cruel, murderous, hypocritical, and stupid. The *GosPet*'s portrait of the Jews is scathing, they are depicted as being sadistic, foolish, and hypocritical. The *GosPet* also implies that the Jewish leaders themselves might have believed in the resurrection but that they are afraid of being stoned by the Jews (11:49), that is by those who have not become apostates ... In their last official act in the gospel (as far as we know it), the Jewish leaders seem weak and almost pitiable. In the background, behind their actions, stands a murderous, faceless force of apostate-hating Jews. If actual persecution is in the background, the *GosPet* could have come from the post-Bar Cochba period, ca. 135-140 C.E." (226. 244. 254-255). – (2) A. Kirk, Examining Priorities: Another Look at the *Gospel of Peter*'s Relationship to the New Testament Gospels, NTS 40, 1994, 572-595. He claims that "the reshaping of the Lukan (and Matthean, Markan, and Johannine) material .... [was] driven by an anti-Jewish *Tendenz* ... the intention was to focus on the evil actions of the Jews ... to focus the narrative upon the 'villainous Jews' ... [on the] sadistic, hard-hearted Jews who inhabit the narrative ... putting the Jews in as bad a light as possible ... the Jews are depicted as the cruel torturers and murderers of Jesus and as dour legalists." (577. 578 and 582 n. 23).

Then the Jews and the elders and the priests, perceiving what great evil they had
done to themselves, began to lament and to say, "Woe on our sins, the judgment
and the end of Jerusalem is drawn nigh." (7:25)

At this point the Jewish *authorities* know they have done wrong, know that they
will be punished but, far from being repentant, seek guards from Pilate for
Jesus' tomb lest the *people* harm them:

> But the scribes and Pharisees and elders, being assembled together and hearing that
> all the people were murmuring and beating their breasts, saying, "If at his death
> these exceeding great signs have come to pass, behold how righteous he was!" The
> elders were afraid and came to Pilate, entreating him and saying, "Give us soldiers
> that we may watch his sepulchre for three days, lest his disciples come and steal
> him away and the people suppose that he is risen from the dead, and do us harm."
> (8:28-30)

A crucial distinction is now established between Jewish *authorities* and Jewish
people and this distinction reaches a climax in what follows. In the *Gospel of
Peter*, both Roman and Jewish authorities are actually at the tomb and witness
the resurrection of Jesus. The Roman authorities confess Jesus but the Jewish
authorities conspire with Pilate to deceive their own *people*:

> Then all came to him, beseeching him [Pilate] and urgently calling upon him to
> command the centurion and the soldiers to tell no one what they had seen. "For it is
> better for us," they said, "to make ourselves guilty of the greatest sin before God
> than to fall into the hands of the people of the Jews and be stoned." Pilate therefore
> commanded the centurion and the soldiers to say nothing. (11:47-49)

That is a strange phrase, "the people of the Jews." For this author there are two
Jewish groups: first, the authorities, including several groups, also called
simply "the Jews"; and "the people" or "the people of the Jews."

My reading of the *Gospel of Peter* is that it is more anti-Jewish with regard to
the *authorities* than any of the canonical gospels but also more pro-Jewish with
regard to the *people* than any of them.[34] I return to this point below.

There is, furthermore, a disconcerting element in Brown's reiteration of the
"anti-Jewish" context of Peter. He knows those texts I have just cited from the
Gospel of Peter just as well as I do and he spells out their implications clearly
and accurately but only in one single place:[35]

> *GPet* 7:25-8:29 offers an interesting insight into the author's attitude towards the
> Jews, whom (having left the Romans completely out of the execution) he has
> described as responsible for the crucifixion and death of Jesus. One gets the
> impression that overall *GPet* envisions two Jewish groups, one unrepentant and one
> repentant ... As for repentant Jews, one gets the impression that *GPet* differentiates
> between 'the Jews and the elders and the priests' who beat themselves in 7:25 and
> 'all the people' who beat their breasts in 8:28b. The former do so because by their
> sins they have made inevitable God's wrathful judgment and the end of Jerusalem,
> and thus they have done wrong to themselves. The latter do so, after they have

---

34 For a quite similar view see now also T. Nicklas, Die „Juden" im Petrusevangelium (P.Cair.
    10759). Ein Testfall, NTS 47, 2001, 206-221, but compare J. Verheyden's article in this volume.
35 Brown, Death of the Messiah, 1190.

murmured against the authorities, because the great signs have shown them how just Jesus was. In having this differentiation *GPet* is close to the twofold Lukan picture of reactions to Jesus before the crucifixion and after his death.

But that statement invalidates all those other comments throughout *The Death of the Messiah* about the anti-Jewish nature of the *Gospel of Peter*, comments made both before and after it in the list of places I gave earlier. Even his very last mention of that motif is still inadequate although better than most others: "There is a strong anti-Jewish animus [in *GPet*], especially amongst the religious authorities ... Although there are instances of Jewish repentance."[36]

Furthermore, Brown has argued that increasing "anti-Judaism" may be used as a norm for chronological progression and dating within the trajectory of the passion narratives. In other words, and in general, the hostility tends to deepen and widen from earlier to later gospel texts. He proposes the following sequence:[37]

(a) Mark: "the crowd' ... at the end of Mark ... is not friendly to Jesus. To describe a collectivity hostile to Jesus Mark does not use in the PN [Passion Narrative] 'the people,' 'the nation' or 'the Jews.'"

(b) Matthew: "Matt describes as hostile 'all the people' (27:25), 'the Jews' (28:15), and 'the sons of Israel' (27:9)."

(c) Luke: "in the Lucan Gospel taken by itself, one finds little emphasis on a collective group hostile to Jesus."

(d) Acts: "The reader of the whole work Luke-Acts ... would come away with a strong sense that there was a Jewish collectivity very hostile to Jesus."

(e) John: "John 18:35 uses 'nation' for those who with the chief priests gave Jesus over to Pilate. The phrase 'the Jews' is used at least nine times in the PN to describe those hostile to Jesus and who want his death. The latter usage makes the Johannine picture of collective agency very strong."

Presuming that trajectory of increasing "anti-Judaism," and presuming also that the *Gospel of Peter* is as "anti-Jewish" as Brown claims, it would be correct to consider it the latest of the five passion-narratives. But, of course, if one grants, as I have argued, its strong and emphatic distinction between Jewish *authority* and Jewish *people*, it would be the earliest and not the latest of those five narratives of deepening and widening "anti-Judaism":

Cross Gospel:	Jewish authorities bad & Jewish people (become) good
Mark:	Jewish authorities bad & Jewish "crowd" bad
Luke/Acts:	Jewish authorities bad & Jewish people bad
Matthew:	Jewish authorities bad & Jewish people bad
John:	Jews (no distinction) bad.

---

36 Brown, Death of the Messiah, 1339.
37 Brown, Death of the Messiah, 1421-1423.

I am sure of that reading for the initial *Cross Gospel* but much less secure about it for the final *Gospel of Peter*. When, for example, the final author/redactor speaks of "the Jews" in sections dependent on the canonical passion accounts such as 6:23 or 12:50,52, should it be taken narrowly (= the Jewish authorities, as in the *Cross Gospel*) or broadly (= all those other Jews except ourselves, as in John)? Be that as it may, the *Cross Gospel*'s vision bespeaks a situation where a Jewish-Christian author can still imagine *the Jewish people* as ready, willing, and able to accept Christianity if only *the Jewish authorities* had not lied, deceived, and misled them.

Finally, the invalidity of Brown's "anti-Judaism" position can be seen most clearly by comparing the following two verses, one from the *Gospel of Peter* and the other from Matthew, both with almost the exact same Greek expression:

> All the people (ὁ λαὸς ἅπας) were murmuring and beating their breasts, saying, 'If at his death these exceeding great signs have come to pass, behold how righteous he was!' (*Gospel of Peter* 8:28)

> The people as a whole (πᾶς ὁ λαός) answered, 'His blood be on us and on our children!' (Matthew 27:25)

If, as Brown claims, the *Gospel of Peter* knew Matthew and Luke, he must at least have preferred Luke 23:47-48 to Matt 27:25 in rendering his 8:28 less and not more "anti-Jewish."

Positive Section

For convenience, emphasis, and clarity, I also summarize my own solution over four points.

First, what is most important for me is whether the *details* of the passion-resurrection narrative came originally from, in my terms, history remembered or prophecy historicized. I have four major reasons for preferring Koester's choice of *prophecy* rather than Brown's choice of *memory* as the matrix for those details. Those reasons also make it unlikely for me that memory retained a far wider passion narrative but only those elements were kept that could be linked to prophecy.

(1) Outside the canonical gospels, for about a hundred years after the event itself, nobody shows independent knowledge of any linked and detailed passion-resurrection narrative. I do not think, for example, that we can presume such a consecutive narrative from, say, Paul in 1 Cor 11:23 or even from 1 Cor 15:3-7.

(2) Inside the canonical gospels, it is extremely difficult to find independent versions of this consecutive passion-resurrection story as remembered history. Matthew and Luke do not know an alternative to Mark and, at least in this area, John is, in my judgment, dependent on the synoptic versions. In effect, John is Mark rewritten with Jesus in total control of events.

(3) All four gospels are in remarkable general agreement until Mark ends at the empty tomb in 16:8, but when Mark stops they all go their very separate ways. What happened to history remembered when Mark stopped and left the others on their own? Why is everyone so dependent on Mark's sequential story?

(4) The individual units, the general sequences, and the overall frames of the passion-resurrection stories are so linked to prophetic fulfillment that its removal leaves nothing but the barest facts, almost as in Josephus, Tacitus, or the Apostles' Creed. By *individual units* I mean such items as: the garments and lots from Psalm 22:18; the darkness at noon from Amos 8:9; or the gall and vinegar drink from Psalm 69:21. *By general sequences* I mean such items as: the Mount of Olives situation from 2 Samuel 15-17; the trial collaboration from Psalm 2; or the abuse description from the Day of Atonement ritual in Leviticus 16. By *overall frames* I mean the narrative genre of innocence vindicated, righteousness redeemed, and virtue rewarded.[38]

Second, the purpose or function of the *Gospel of Peter* was to conflate together two quite divergent versions of the passion-resurrection narrative and that places it securely within such second-century attempts at apologetic harmonization.[39]

(1) By *apologetic harmonization* I mean that the author/redactor is aware of problems with having two very divergent accounts of the passion-resurrection narrative. Those problems could be internal, for example, the canonical gospels and Petrine leadership pressing from inside Christianity, and/or external problems, for example, polemical opponents criticizing discrepancies from outside Christianity. The solution chosen was not to abandon either account but to make a harmonized narrative out of those two contradictory versions. Apologetic interests are quite evident in other facets of the final text as well but this integration of discordant base-narratives is the text's primary purpose. Those discordant versions are still evident in the *Gospel of Peter* as follows and they focus on whether enemies or friends are involved in terms of the burial and resurrection:

Version I: (a) *Execution*: Jesus is tried and crucified by his *enemies*
              (*Gos. Pet.* 1:1-2 & 2:5b-6:22)
          (b) *Tomb*: Jesus is buried and his tomb *guarded* by his *enemies*
              (*Gos. Pet.* 7:25 & 8:28-9:34)
          (c) *Resurrection*: Jesus rises and appears to his *enemies*
              (*Gos. Pet.* 9:35-10:42 & 11:45-49).

---

38 J.D. Crossan, Who Killed Jesus? Exploring the Roots of Anti-Semitism in the Gospel Story of the Death of Jesus, San Francisco 1995. See, respectively, 76. 82. 120. 141. 143 and 191-195.

39 J.D. Crossan, Four Other Gospels. Shadows on the Contours of Canon, Minneapolis 1985, 123-187 (Repr. Sonoma 1992, 85-127); idem, The Cross that Spoke. The Origins of the Passion Narrative, San Francisco 1988; idem, The Birth of Christianity. Discovering What Happened in the Years Immediately after the Execution of Jesus, San Francisco 1998, 481-525.

Version II: (a) *Execution*: Jesus is tried and crucified by his *enemies*

(b) *Tomb*: Jesus is buried and his tomb *visited* by his *friends*
(*Gos. Pet.* 6:23-24 & 12:50-13:57)

(c) *Resurrection*: Jesus rises and appears to his *friends*
(*Gos. Pet.* 14:60)

In order clearly and emphatically to distinguish that Version I from the canonical accounts in Version II, I gave it a specific name, the *Cross Gospel*, but that was done only for specificity – any distinguishing name is acceptable. It is, I repeat, part of but not the whole of the *Gospel of Peter*. Also, of course, if titles such as I and II imply priority, just reverse them mentally in what follows.

(2) In that harmonization, Version I is privileged over Version II because there is neither an equal conflation of both versions nor is Version I inserted into Version II. It is Version II that is fitted into Version I. That happens in two ways:

(a) One is that Version Ia is chosen rather than Version IIa for the passion account. I see no secure indication there of material from the passion accounts of the canonical gospels. The reason is that both versions agree that, of course, the execution was conducted by Jesus' enemies in both versions.

(b) Another is that, in Version 1 Jesus' enemies are: (i) the Jewish authorities; (ii) initially but not ultimately the Jewish crowd/people/all; (iii) neither the Roman soldiers nor the Roman authorities. But in Version II, Jesus' enemies are: (i) the Jewish authorities; (ii) initially and ultimately the Jewish crowd/people/all; (iii) the Roman soldiers *but not* the Roman authorities.

(3) Harmonization rather than simple juxtaposition is effected by placing within the three units of Version I certain preparatory verses which serve to smooth the conflation of Version II:

(a) Request for Burial in *Gos. Pet.* 2:3-5a as preparation for burial by *friends* rather than enemies in 6:23-24.

(b) Action of Disciples in *Gos. Pet.* 7:26-27 & 14:58-59 as preparation for apparition to *friends* rather than enemies in 14:60.

(c) Arrival of Youth in *Gos. Pet.* 11:43-44 as preparation for a tomb visited by *friends* and not just guarded by enemies in 12:50-13:57.

(4) Finally, that harmonization was sealed by an overall consistency of vocabulary, syntax, and style characterized by a pedantic use of words untypical of early Christian literature and by a modish nostalgia for Atticizing forms of speech typical of the second century.[40]

Third, I concentrate now on that extracanonical source, the *Cross Gospel* or Version I above, used by the author/redactor of the *Gospel of Peter*. I have five basic arguments for its existence.

---

[40]   This agrees with Schaeffer, Gospel of Peter, 92-93. 112.

(1) Text. The separation of Versions I and II has little to do with separate or distinguishable vocabulary, syntax, or style. Not every ancient redactor makes life that easy for the contemporary critic. My textual basic for proposing it is, however, those redactional preparations suggested in the preceding point (3abc).

(2) Narrative. My argument is not that this extracanonical story is a "better" story than the intracanonical ones but simply that, as a *separate* complex involving three stages (Execution, Tomb, Resurrection), its narrative logic holds together quite well:

(a) *Execution*: Jewish authorities and Jewish people but not Roman authorities or Roman soldiers crucify Jesus; at his death and deposition miracles take place so that Jewish authorities and Jewish people know they have done wrong; hence

(b) *Tomb*: the Jewish authorities demand Roman guards for Jesus' tomb "for three days," that is, until Jesus is securely dead and cannot be resuscitated and removed by his followers so that the now-repentant people might believe him resurrected;[41] hence

(c) *Resurrection*: Jewish authorities and Roman soldiers are present at the tomb to see the resurrection; the former persuade the latter to stay silent lest their own people stone them for leading them astray.

(3) Genre. Nickelsburg's seminal studies on the narrative genre of vindicated innocence indicated two successive moments in its development: (a) an earlier tradition in which the just, innocent, or righteous one is saved *before* death and vindicated *on earth* before his enemies under the control of a just king; (b) a later tradition in which the just, innocent, or righteous one is saved *after* death and vindicated *in heaven* before his enemies under the control of the Just King.[42] The *Cross Gospel* fits better into that former tradition while Mark's passion fits better into that latter one. Hence it is absolutely necessary for the *Cross Gospel* that the Jewish authorities as Jesus' enemies, are present at the tomb to witness the resurrection and that the just ruler Pilate, whose soldiers took no part in the execution, confesses to them after it that, "I am clean from the blood of the Son of God, upon such a thing have you decided" (11:47).

(4) Theology. The theology of the *Cross Gospel* is that of communal passion linked to communal resurrection. Passion prophecy was not just about the sufferings of Jesus as Messiah but about the sufferings of all the righteous, just, and innocent ones of Israel's past history. Jesus died as the climax of their passion and rose as the head of their resurrection. This is all serenely mythological: the Son of God breaks open the prison-house of death and leads

---

[41] See Crossan, The Cross that Spoke, 27; Brown, The Death of the Messiah, 1309 n. 55. Note that there is no mention of Jesus' prophecy about his resurrection or that the disciples will have to claim resurrection — the people are ready to believe it just from an empty tomb alone!

[42] G.W.E. Nickelsburg, Resurrection, Immortality, and Eternal Life in Intertestamental Judaism, HThS 26, Cambridge/Ma 1972. See pp. 48-111 and its application in his article, The Genre and Function of the Markan Passion Narrative, HThR 73, 1980, 153-184.

forth the imprisoned ones. But it is also profoundly Jewish: it shows a concern for Jesus and his Jewish past and not just for Jesus and his Christian future. I find that theology profoundly beautiful and mourn the fact that it was fast disappearing even as the New Testament writings were being composed.

Fourth, what is the most plausible chronological and geographical location for a story in which: (a) the Romans are absolutely innocent – Pilate's hand-washing is more valid in the *Gospel of Peter* than in Matthew where his soldiers execute Jesus; (b) the Jewish authorities are supremely guilty – much more so than in any canonical account – because they have actually witnessed the resurrection itself; but (c) the "people of the Jews" are so repentant that their own leaders dare not tell them the truth of the resurrection which they themselves have just seen? It is, of course, especially that final point that is decisive for my dating but the conjunction of all three is very important as well.

Gerd Theißen has recently proposed that the passion narrative "underwent its critical shaping ... in light of the persecutions that occurred during Agrippa I's reign" in 41-44 C.E.[43] I agree, but his arguments hold better for the *Cross Gospel* or Version I than for any version imagined behind Mark and/or John.

Two potentially catastrophic events precipitated the creation and dictated the content of that *Cross Gospel* or Version I in the early 40s C.E. The first was the threatened desecration of the Temple by Caligula's statue, the danger of invasion and war, the almost saintly intervention of the Syrian governor, Petronius, who risked his own life and almost lost it by deliberate procrastination.[44] That made the local Romans look very good indeed and they would have looked even better as the 40s progressed. The second event was Agrippa I's assumption of royal rule over the entire Jewish homeland between 41 and 44 C.E.[45] He was now, like Herod the Great before him, King of the Jews by imperial Roman designation. Josephus praised his piety profusely: "He enjoyed residing in Jerusalem and did so constantly; and he scrupulously observed the traditions of his people. He neglected no rite of purification, and no day passed for him without the prescribed sacrifice."[46]

But what would Herod Agrippa I have thought about dissident Jewish Christians and their attitudes towards the laws of his fathers, especially in Jerusalem? We know from Acts 12:1-3.11 that he executed James, son of Zebedee, and imprisoned Peter. Those twin crises, with Petronius as Saint and Herod (Agrippa) as Villain, served to generate the popular narrativity of the passion story in which Jesus' enemies are updated to fit Christian experience in the early 40s. Rome (Pilate = Petronius) is innocent and even pro-Christian

---

[43] G. Theißen, The Gospels in Context. Social and Political History in the Synoptic Tradition, Minneapolis 1991, esp. 198 and all of 166-199.

[44] Josephus, *bell. Iud.* 2:201 and *ant.* 18:278. 282. 285. 306-309.

[45] D.R. Schwartz, Agrippa I. The Last King of Judaea, TSAJ 23, Tübingen 1990.

[46] Josephus, *ant.* 19:331.

because that is how those Jewish Christians had most recently experienced it at the start of the 40s and "Herod" (Antipas = Agrippa I) is responsible and anti-Christian because that is how they have experienced it as the 40s continued.

For Jewish Christians who thought like that, the restoration of direct Roman rule over the Jewish homeland when Herod Agrippa I died after a very short reign in 44 C.E. must have been very good news indeed. That situation was significant enough to generate the by-no-mean-necessary leap from scholarly passion prophecy to popular passion narrative. It also dictated the innocence of the Romans who had withdrawn entirely from the execution process, the responsibility of "Herod" rather than Pilate, the guilt (not just responsibility) of the Jewish authorities who knew and hid the truth of the resurrection, and first the responsibility, then the repentance, but finally the inculpable ignorance of "the people of the Jews." If only, as it were, the Jewish *people* had been told the truth by the Jewish *authorities*, they would all have become Christian! That, of course, is simply a dream but it is one from earlier rather than later in the night of Jewish and Christian relations.

Conclusion

This conclusion does not simply summarize those preceding three positions on the relationship of the *Gospel of Peter* to the intracanonical passion-resurrection narratives but will draw particular attention to one convergence between my own independence-and-dependence position and the apparently irreconcilable dependence-one of Raymond Brown.

As noted above, Brown argues that the *Gospel of Peter*, apart from knowing Matthew's story of the guards at the tomb, also knew a "consecutive" and "independent" version which contained not only that story but all of *Gos. Pet.* 8:28-11:49. Here are some key texts:[47]

> The author of *GPet* drew not only on Matt but on an independent form of the guard-at-the-sepulcher story .... The author of *GPet* may well have known Matt's account of the guard (a judgment based on his use of Matthean vocabulary), but a plausible scenario is that he also knew a consecutive form of the story and gave preference to that .... Matt broke up a consecutive guard-at-the-sepulcher story to interweave it with the women-at-the-tomb story [from Mark], while *GPet* preserved the original consecutive form of the guard story .... *GPet* ... had a source besides Matt, namely, a more developed account of the guard at the tomb. (That point is also supported by the consecutiveness of the story in *GPet*.) The supplying of the centurion's name, the seven seals, the stone rolling off by itself, the account of the resurrection with the gigantic figures, the talking cross, the confession of Jesus as God's Son by the Jewish authorities, and their fear of their own people – all those elements could plausibly have been in the more developed form of the story known to the author of *GPet* and absent from the form known to Matt.

---

[47]   Brown, Death of the Messiah, 1287. 1301 n. 35. 1305-1306. 1307.

In summary, Brown is not postulating random nuggets of tradition but an independent and sequential story involving about a third of the extant *Gospel of Peter*. And that, of course, covers the last two of the three units I (*Execution, Tomb, Resurrection*) proposed for the *Cross Gospel* or Version I above.

On the one hand, those two units could never have existed without some preceding one which, first, detailed the condemnation and execution or at least the death of Jesus and, second, explained why his *Tomb* needed to be guarded. But, on the other, such an explanation is adequately presented in the preceding *Execution* unit which records popular reaction to the cosmic miracles at Jesus' death. Surely, then, if Brown accepts a consecutive and independent story for *Tomb* and *Resurrection* units, he might as well concede the independence of that *Execution* unit as well. In other words, he may have to concede a three-unit consecutive and independent narrative such as I proposed for the *Cross Gospel* or Version I.

Frans Neirynck disagrees completely with my position on the *Gospel of Peter*,[48] but he noted that Brown "comes close to Crossan's *Cross Gospel* in his approach to the guard-at-the-sepulcher story (GP 28-49); the author knew an independent form of this long story, and a less developed pre-Matthean form of the same story is preserved in the Gospel of Matthew."[49] But, of course, that "long story" in *Gos. Pet.* 28-49 includes both the guarded *Tomb* and the visible *Resurrection* units, much more, that is, than simply the "guard-at-the-sepulcher" unit. In any case, Neirynck also recognizes that, "regarding Brown's hypothesis [about that independent source in *Gos. Pet.* 28-49] Crossan's reply makes sense: 'there could never have been such an independent story without some preceding account of condemnation and crucifixion.'"[50] And one, I repeat, that would have explained why a guarded tomb was necessary.

Finally, since I maintain my own independence-and-dependence solution despite its almost universal scholarly rejection, I must ask myself what would change my mind, what would convince me that I am wrong. If anyone can show me how a person who knows the canonical versions either as scribal documents or oral traditions got from them to the present *Gospel of Peter*, I would withdraw my proposed solution. It is not enough to speak of memory and/or orality in general theory without explaining how memory and/or orality worked in this particular instance.[51] What theory of memory and/or what exercise of oral tradition or scribal transmission gets one from any or all of our intracanonical gospels to the very coherent narrative in the *Cross Gospel* or Version I?

---

48   F. Neirynck, The Apocryphal Gospels and the Gospel of Mark, in: The New Testament in Early Christianity. La réception des écrits néotestamentaires dans le christianisme primitif, ed. by J.-M. Sevrin, BEThL 86, Leuven 1989, 123-175, esp.140-157.

49   F. Neirynck, The Historical Jesus: Reflections on an Inventory, EThL 70, 1994, 221-234, esp. 229.

50   F. Neirynck, Review of John Dominic Crossan, "Who Killed Jesus? Exposing the Roots of Anti-Semitism in the Gospel Story of the Death of Jesus [etc.]," EThL 71, 1995, 455-457, esp. 456 (citing "Who Killed Jesus?", p. 7).

51   For my own understanding of memory and orality, see my "The Birth of Christianity", 47-89.

Tradition and Memory in the *Gospel of Peter*

by

Alan Kirk

Cultural memory approaches and orality theory offer powerful new ways to conceptualize problems of tradition, writing, and canonization.[1] These are precisely the issues at stake in determining the location of the *Gospel of Peter* (*GosPet*) in the history of the gospel literature, a problem usually construed in terms of determining its relationship to the synoptic gospels. We will use cultural memory and orality theory to critique Crossan, Brown, and in particular Koester not just as regards their proposed solutions to this problem, but at the more fundamental level of method. Having thus prepared the terrain, we will bring these approaches to bear upon the *GosPet*, arguing that its distinctive profile arises from the fact that it enacts a *nachsynoptische* Passion-narrative tradition within the memory frameworks of the second century.

I

Analysis has generally operated within the literary paradigm, which is to say that the question of dependence or independence is construed in terms of relationships among literary sources. We can observe the influence of the literary paradigm in Crossan, Brown, and Koester respectively.

Crossan argues that *GosPet* is the product of a second-century redaction, drawing upon the intracanonical Passion narratives, of the *Cross Gospel*, a mid-first century document that was a source for the synoptic and Johannine Passion narratives, the point of this subsequent redaction being to bring the *Cross Gospel* into alignment with emerging orthodoxy.[2] Crossan's utilization hypothesis is markedly situated within the literary, redaction-of-sources paradigm, with "sources," "redaction," "stages," and "stemma" his operative terms throughout.[3] The literary paradigm also provides the perspective from

---

[1]   I am indebted to Werner Kelber, whose influence has directed my research toward the problem of orality, and to Barry Schwartz, who has been a generous mentor in memory studies.
[2]   J.D. Crossan, The Cross that Spoke. The Origins of the Passion Narrative, San Francisco 1988, 16-30. See also Crossan's article in the present volume.
[3]   Crossan's literary assumptions have been pointed out by H. Koester, Ancient Christian Gospels, Philadelphia-London 1990, 219.

which he rejects arguments for *GosPet*'s dependence upon the Gospels, pointing to the implausibility of accounting for the former as being a "composite digest" of the latter.[4] The *GosPet*'s Thief on the Cross episode is assigned priority over Luke's because, reversing the redactional scenario, Crossan "can see no reason" for the *GosPet*'s "textual dismemberment" of Luke's story.[5] Most previous analysis of the *GosPet*'s relationship to the Gospels has operated within this text-and-redaction framework, and Crossan's hypothesis remains securely within it.[6] While considering the possibility that oral tradition might be a complicating factor, Crossan ultimately adverts to the view that oral and literary processes are incommensurable.[7]

Helmut Koester in his comprehensive approach to gospels and their history makes far more allowance for the variable of oral tradition. Like Crossan, however, Koester remains within the literary framework. This is particularly apparent in his tendency to sharply distinguish oral and written lines of transmission. In his study of synoptic tradition in the Apostolic Fathers he programmatically posits as alternatives *either* literary dependence on analogy with Matthew and Luke's utilization of Mark, *or* independent recourse to common oral tradition:

> An welchem Ort stehen die AVV [die apostolischen Väter] in ihrem Verhältnis zu den synoptischen Evangelien in dieser Geschichte [der synoptischen Tradition]? Müssen letztere für die Zitate und Anführungen der AVV bereits vorausgesetzt werden? *Oder* [emphasis added] erklären sich solche Zitate aus einer Traditionsgeschichte, die aus der vorsynoptischen Überlieferung her parallel zur Überlieferung schriftlicher Evangelien verläuft?[8]

Koester utilizes much the same literary criteria as Crossan, namely, indications of copying and redaction of (a) written source(s). Synoptic influence upon *1 Clem* 46:6-8 is ruled out, for example,

> wegen der trotz dieser Übereinstimmungen verbleibenden bedeutenden Abweichungen. Die Rückführung auf eines der synoptischen Evangelien *kommt schon gar nicht in Frage. Es bleibt nur die Annahme*, daß 1 Clem. 46,8 mit einer Vorstufe der Synoptiker … verwandt ist [emphasis added].[9]

---

4   Crossan, Cross that Spoke, 14-15.
5   Crossan, Cross that Spoke, 173.
6   In a subsequent essay Crossan claims that "I never presumed that synoptic-style copying was the best or only model," but acknowledges that "I [am] not at all clear yet on how exactly these processes happened." Idem, The *Gospel of Peter* and the Canonical Gospels: Independence, Dependence, or Both?, Forum n.s. 1, 1998, 7-51, esp. 24.
7   Crossan seems to conceive of oral processes in terms of deep structure generative dynamics constantly giving rise to variants. This, he suggests, cannot be reconciled with scribal processes, in his view characterized by production of strict sequences bound to "established original[s]." In other words, how can oral processes possibly be implicated in a scribal *Gospel of Peter*? "How … can an author with a written tradition … sustain an override from an oral tradition …?" (The *Gospel of Peter*, 33-34).
8   H. Koester, Synoptische Überlieferung bei den Apostolischen Vätern, TU 65, Berlin 1957, 2.
9   Koester, Synoptische Überlieferung, 18.

In other words, if variations from the synoptic parallel are significant enough to make direct copying of a *Vorlage* unlikely, Koester adverts to his default position – independent appropriation "aus der freien Überlieferung."[10] Koester's analysis of Ignatius, *Pol.* 2:1-2 is a case in point, for here the proximity of Matthean (2:2) and Lukan (2:1) – sounding materials rules out influence of these synoptics upon Ignatius (and rules in synoptic-independent oral tradition), for such proximity is not comprehensible on the model of utilization of literary *Vorlagen*.[11] Similarly indebted to this model is Koester's practice of assigning synoptic-type materials occurring in the Apostolic Fathers *sans* the literary context and accompanying redactional features of the synoptic parallel likewise to the "freie Überlieferung." Conversely, "Whenever one observes words or phrases that derive from the author or redactor of a gospel writing, the existence of a written source must be assumed."[12] Absent these indicators, Koester routinely shifts to the other pole: independent recourse to independent oral tradition. The indebtedness of his approach to the literary paradigm leads him, like Crossan, to construe dependence in terms of redaction of literary *Vorlagen* and, accordingly, whenever difficulties arise in understanding materials in those terms, assigning as their source the distinct sphere of the "freie Überlieferung." In short, Koester has virtually no concept, let alone a working model for the *interface* of oral and written traditions.

This latter point accounts for another marked feature of Koester's approach: his tendency to identify with the "ältere Form," vis à vis the corresponding materials in the Gospels, traditions he determines have been drawn out of the "freie Überlieferung." With respect to synoptic-related traditions in Ignatius, for example, Koester argues,

> Die meisten dieser Stücke zeigen keinerlei für die Redaktionsarbeit der Evangelisten charakteristische Züge, könnten vielmehr in der von Ign. dargebotenen Form bereits aus älterer freier Überlieferung stammen (Eph. 5,2; 14,2; 17,1; Pol 2,2; wohl auch Pol. 2,1), bzw. von einer solchen älteren Form aus weiterentwickelt worden sein (Trall. 11,1; Phld. 3,1; 6,1).[13]

Given a conceptual model inherently incapable of positing reciprocal feedback between written and oral tradition, it is inevitable that a tradition in a non-canonical source, determined according to this model to have been drawn from the "freie Überlieferung," will additionally be viewed either as more primitive than its counterpart in the written gospels or as occupying an identical position vis à vis the textual appropriation of common oral tradition.[14]

---

10   Koester, Synoptische Überlieferung, 43, here in reference to Ignatius, *Pol.* 2:2.
11   Koester, Synoptische Überlieferung, 43: "Es ist wahrscheinlicher, daß beide Logien aus der freien Überlieferung stammen, als daß eines aus Mt., das andere (Pol. 2,1) aus Luk. entnommen ist."
12   H. Koester, Written Gospels or Oral Tradition?, JBL 113, 1994, 293-297, esp. 297.
13   Koester, Synoptische Überlieferung, 60.
14   Koester's analysis of of the relationship between Ignatius, *Sm.* 3:2-3 and the resurrection story in Luke 24:36-43 is a case in point: "In den Worten ψηλαφήσατέ με καὶ ἴδετε stimmen sie beide wörtlich überein. In dem jeweils folgenden Satze wird der Verdacht, es erscheine nur ein Geist,

Koester supports these judgments by recourse to classical form-critical approaches to working out tradition-histories. These are predicated on the view that oral tradition develops according to particular tendencies that make it possible to assess whether a given tradition is primitive or secondary.[15] The viability of this approach, however, has been dealt a blow by research in the phenomenology of oral tradition demonstrating that the morphology of tradition depends not upon developmental or de-pristinating tendencies but upon social variables impinging upon the different performance arenas in which a given tradition is enacted (see below).

Koester's model guides his analysis of the *GosPet*. Invoking oral tradition makes it possible for him to assert without recourse to laborious source and redaction scenarios that a number of the *GosPet*'s constituent traditions are independent of and more primitive than their synoptic parallels. The *GosPet*'s divergence from the synoptics in narrative logic and the low number of direct verbal agreements manifestly raise serious difficulties for any literary utilization hypothesis. Koester's view that dependence is largely to be understood as redaction-of-*Vorlagen* permits him therefore to uncouple *GosPet* from the Gospels at that level (and judiciously to reject the possibility of re-instituting the connection in a reverse stemma). Accordingly he then accounts for parallel episodes by arguing that they came to the *GosPet* independently through the oral tradition. Koester closes the circle by applying form-critical criteria to assert that these traditions embedded in *GosPet* preserve a more primitive stage of the oral tradition than their synoptic counterparts. In the case of the Guard at the Tomb and Resurrection episode (*GosPet* 8:28-11:49; Matt 27:62-68; 28:2-4, 11-15), for example, Koester argues that because the *GosPet* tradition when purged of its elaborative accretions stands closer to the form of the epiphany genre than can be recovered from Matthew's version, it is the most primitive, a line of reasoning predicated on the form-critical postulate of

---

abgewehrt; doch geschieht das nicht mit denselben Worten ... Zum Schluß wird jedesmal berichtet, daß der Auferstandene mit den Jüngern gegessen habe. Nicht gering sind aber auch die Verschiedenheiten beider Berichte ... *Kann die Vorlage des Ign. der Luk.-Bericht gewesen sein?* [emphasis added] Dafür scheint die genaue Übereinstimmung beider in den Worten ψηλαφήσατέ με καὶ ἴδετε ὅτι zu sprechen. Doch handelt es sich dabei um die Wiedergabe von Worten des Auferstandenen, die sicher, wie die Herrenworte überhaupt, getreuer aufbewahrt worden sind als etwa der Rahmen einer solchen Erzählung. Deshalb wird man aus dieser Übereinstimmung allein noch keine literarische Abhängigkeit von Luk erweisen können. Doch macht diese Übereinstimmung es wenigstens sicher, daß Sm. 3,2 und Luk. 24,36ff. Varianten ein und desselben Berichtes sind" (Synoptische Überlieferung, 46-47). Koester's line of analysis and the assumptions informing it are patent. It is decided that the agreements are not significant enough to indicate dependency, *understood as redaction of a literary Vorlage*. The only possible alternative, on Koester's model, is that *Sm.* 3,2 and Luke 24:36-43 are independent enactments of an oral tradition.

15   See Koester, Synoptische Überlieferung, 2.

the original form.[16] In the case of the mocking scene (*GosPet* 3:6-9) Koester brings to bear the simple-to-complex form-critical canon:

> The narrative version of this [exegetical] tradition as it is preserved in the *GosPet* has not yet split the mocking account into several scenes [as in the Gospels].[17]

We stated above that Koester's approach is beset with problems in light of research on orality and writing in the ancient world. John Miles Foley designates writing and orality as distinct communication "channels" or "media" that when present within a particular cultural sphere cannot be insulated from each other. In traditional cultures with even highly restricted literacy, reciprocal feedback occurs across the interface of the oral and written registers.[18] Foley notes that

> scholarship over the past twenty years, especially field research on living oral traditions, has taught us to distrust the false dichotomy of 'oral versus written' and to expect complex inventories and interactions of oral and literate in the same culture and even in the very same individual.[19]

These advances likewise render the form-critical canon of developmental tendencies in the oral tradition all but a dead letter. Theo Heckel has pointed out that literary appropriation – "Redaktionsarbeit" – unleashes a different set of utilization forces that cut across the grain of putative tradition-history tendencies.[20] We can state this even more strongly. Separate forces are not at work in the enactment of oral tradition in various performance arenas (Foley's apt term) on the one hand and in the literary appropriation of tradition within particular social contexts on the other. Variants in oral tradition (multiforms) arise from the diverse social contexts in which it is performed in the same way as literary composition and redaction are wired into living social contexts. Oral tradition by definition exists in its actualization in performance. Contemporary theorists emphasize that an audience's horizon of expectations and the impinging social variables are *constitutive* of tradition as it is iteratively embodied in particular performances, a process W.F. Hanks refers to as "internalizing reception into the production process itself."[21] Performance is nothing if not a *recreation* of tradition within multiplex performance arenas, a recreation essential to the very life of the tradition inasmuch as it enables it

---

16 See Koester's discussion in his Ancient Christian Gospels, 232-38. N. Walter, Eine vormatthäische Schilderung der Auferstehung Jesu, NTS 19, 1972-73, 415-429, makes a similar argument, identifying the primitive tradition as a *Befreiungswunder*, and likewise works within a literary *Vorlage* model of dependency.

17 Koester, Ancient Christian Gospels, 227.

18 J.M. Foley, Homer's Traditional Art, University Park/Penn. 1999, 3-4. See also R. Finnegan, Oral Traditions and the Verbal Arts. A Guide to Research, London-New York 1992, 178-179, and eadem, Literacy and Orality: Studies in the Technology of Communication, Oxford 1988, 62.

19 Foley, Homer's Traditional Art, 3; see also J. Vansina, Oral Tradition as History, Madison 1985, 156.

20 T.K. Heckel, Vom Evangelium des Markus zum viergestaltigen Evangelium, Tübingen 1999, 274.

21 W.F. Hanks, Texts and Textuality, Annual Review of Anthropology 18, 1989, 95-127, esp. 112.

unceasingly and ever afresh to speak in the crises, contingencies, and
exigencies of the group that reveres it.[22] Accordingly, no fixed original form is
recoverable in relation to which variants can be viewed as defective
derivatives. Each multiform is uniquely affected by social factors whose
configuration defines a particular performance arena.[23]

This compressed survey of research developments gives us a vantage point
to assess Raymond E. Brown's and Susan Schaeffer's solution, which makes
use of orality theory. The "remarkably little exact verbal identity" lead them to
rule out any scenario in which the *GosPet*'s dependence on the Gospels is
understood as direct literary appropriation, noting that neither redaction on
the synoptic model nor harmonization on Tatian's model can account for the
GosPet's profile.[24] Instead, that profile indicates dependence upon the Gospels
via memory mediated by second orality.[25] The paucity of copies in the second
century entailed that the exposure of most Christians to the Gospels was *aural*,
from the liturgy. By this means narratives and sayings from the written
Gospels re-entered the stream of popular oral tradition where they would have
been subject to significant alterations. This in Brown and Schaeffer's view
accounts for the characteristic features of *GosPet* vis à vis the Gospels. The
author's access to the latter was not as *Vorlagen*, but was mediated aurally and
from secondary oralization.[26] Hence it was an easy matter for transpositions of
motifs and combination and confusion of details to occur. These features mark
the *GosPet* relative to the Gospels and accordingly suggest "oral dependence of
GP on some or all of the canonical Gospels."[27]

This explanation is more sensitive to the realities of literacy and orality in
the ancient world. Moreover, papyrus remains confirm, in Christoph
Markschies' words, that "a large number of Christians knew the Bible only

---

[22] A.B. Lord, The Singer of Tales, Cambridge/Mass.-London ²2000, 101; J. Goody, The Interface
      Between the Written and the Oral, Cambridge 1987, 295-297.
[23] Tradition-histories are nevertheless possible as histories of reception. See J. Assmann, Das
      kulturelle Gedächtnis. Schrift, Erinnerung und politische Identität in frühen Hochkulturen,
      München 1992, 120 (characterizing "Rezeptionsakt" as "selegierende[r] Zugriff auf Tradition");
      J. Schröter, Erinnerung an Jesu Worte: Studien zur Rezeption der Logienüberlieferung in
      Markus, Q und Thomas, WMANT 76, Neukirchen-Vluyn 1997; J.K. Olick, Genre Memories and
      Memory Genres. A Dialogical Analysis of May 8, 1945 Commemorations in the Federal
      Republic of Germany, American Sociological Review 64, 1999, 381-402, and idem, Collective
      Memory. The Two Cultures, Sociological Theory 17, 1999, 333-348.
[24] R.E. Brown, The Gospel of Peter and Canonical Gospel Priority, NTS 33, 1987, 321-343, esp. 333;
      S.E. Schaeffer, The 'Gospel of Peter', the Canonical Gospels, and Oral Tradition, Diss. Union
      Theological Seminary 1991, 119-120.
[25] R.E. Brown, The Death of the Messiah 2, New York-London 1994, 1336; see also K. Beyschlag,
      Die verborgene Überlieferung von Christus, München-Hamburg 1969, 51-52.
[26] Brown, Gospel of Peter, 335; idem, Death of the Messiah, 1334-1335 (Brown vacillates on
      whether the author had reading knowledge of Matthew); Schaeffer, Gospel of Peter, 155-161.
[27] Brown, Gospel of Peter, 335.

from short passages in the liturgy."[28] In a number of respects, however, Brown and Schaeffer's solution is not satisfying. A case in point is their attempt to argue that its use of direct discourse and parataxis are indicators of the "spoken background of the *GPet*."[29] This tells us little, however, for in the ancient world most writing was calibrated for oral performance. Furthermore, as we stated they aggregate the author of the *GosPet* with unlettered audiences with only aural exposure to the Gospels, and accordingly suggest that the gospel is a textualization of this popular oral tradition.[30] However, Schaeffer herself recognizes that the *GosPet* is a literary artifact with some claim to stylistic refinement and in her own fine analysis demonstrates the complexity of its narrative design.[31] Moreover, the dense texture of allusions to the Jewish scriptures,[32] long recognized as definitive of the *GosPet*, points to learned scribal activity. These features rule out viewing the *GosPet* as a collocation of popular tradition, and they weaken the claim that *GosPet*'s Passion narrative is told the way it is because its author's channel to the Gospels was a non-elite oral tradition which in the course of things had deformed the written narratives.[33] This scenario cannot explain its characteristic transformations. Another set of forces must have been in play, which Brown and Schaeffer's popular-tradition hypothesis cannot account for. Schaeffer moves in these alternative directions with her detailed canvassing of social and ideological frameworks germane to second-century churches that, she argues, affected the *GosPet*'s shaping of the synoptic Passion narratives. She never reconciles these factors, however, with the popular oral tradition component of her hypothesis, that is, it is not clear whether it is ideological or transmissional factors that are crucial in bringing about the *GosPet*'s difference with respect to the Gospels.

In the final analysis Brown and Schaeffer leave us without a coherent account of the *GosPet*'s relationship to the written Gospels. In significant measure this is because despite their promising experimentation with orality theory, like Crossan and Koester they reason largely within the framework of a literary paradigm that envisions *either* written reception, on the model of Tatian's redaction of Gospel *Vorlagen*, *or* oral reception, the latter understood as a stream of pure orality functioning as the middle term between the *GosPet* and the Gospels, which because of its supposed innate instability acts as an expedient to account for the *GosPet*'s deformations of the Gospel episodes.[34]

---

28 C. Markschies, The Canon of the New Testament in Antiquity. Some New Horizons for Future Research, in: Homer, the Bible, and Beyond. Literary and Religious Canons in the Ancient World, ed. by M. Finkelberg/G. Stroumsa, JSRC 2, Leiden-Boston 2002, 175-194, esp. 186.

29 Brown, Death of the Messiah, 1335; also Schaeffer, Gospel of Peter, 196-197.

30 Brown, Death of the Messiah, 1336.

31 Schaeffer, Gospel of Peter, 26-27. 89. On the sophisticated design of the *GosPet*'s narrative see also T. Nicklas, Die 'Juden' im Petrusevangelium (PCair 10759): Ein Testfall, NTS 46, 2000, 206-221.

32 See, e.g., Thomas Hieke's article in this volume.

33 Schaeffer, Gospel of Peter, 159, in fact concludes in light of these features that the author's "reliability as a direct witness to the oral tradition … is questionable."

34 Brown, Death of the Messiah, 1333-1334; Schaeffer, Gospel of Peter, 207.

While their introduction of the category of second orality is an important complication of the literary paradigm, their approach has difficulties taking the measure of the complexity of interaction along the oral and written axes. Finally, their depiction of the written Gospels aurally received in the liturgy begs the question of the status of the Gospels at this point. On the one hand their solution posits a status for the written Gospels so privileged as to be received aurally by the *GosPet*'s author in the liturgy, but on the other the *GosPet* if anything shows that the Gospels were hardly regulative for its composition, a fact underscored by its claim to Petrine authority.

We turn now to cultural memory approaches and to orality theory to lay out a more adequate methodological framework. This will then be applied in a provisional analysis of gospel traditions in the sub-apostolic writings, using data analyzed by Koester in his seminal study. With the ground thus prepared we will use this framework to specify the location of the *GosPet* within the history of the gospel literature.

II

Cultural memory theorists focus upon how certain elements of a community's past are transformed into group-constitutive *Erinnerungsfiguren*. A community marks and commemorates certain elements of its past as being of fundamental significance to its identity, typically events and persons foundational to its origins and epitomizing its values.[35] These key events and persons are configured in the *Erinnerungsfigur* of a foundational narrative, the rehearsal of which enables the community to relate itself to its core identity and values in ever-changing circumstances and in the face of contemporary crises. In Jan Assmann's words, "Es handelt sich um die Transformation von Vergangenheit in fundierende Geschichte," the latter referred to by Yael Zerubavel as a community's "master commemorative narrative."[36] These "Große Erzählungen [sind] … immer im Überlieferungsschatz eines Volkes lebendig oder reaktivierbar."[37] The *Iliad*, Margalit Finkelberg points out, "became the foundation myth of the new Greek civilization at the beginning of the first millennium B.C.E.," while the Exodus is the primary *Erinnerungsfigur* in Jewish cultural memory.[38] Clearly the Passion narrative came to fill this position in early Christian cultural memory.

---

[35] Assmann, Das kulturelle Gedächtnis, 30-38. 132-133; also B. Schwartz, The Social Context of Commemoration. A Study in Collective Memory, Social Forces 61, 1982, 374-402, esp. 377.

[36] Assmann, Das kulturelle Gedächtnis, 77; Y. Zerubavel, Recovered Roots. Collective Memory and the Making of Israeli National Tradition, Chicago 1997, 4-7.

[37] J. Assmann, Religion und kulturelles Gedächtnis. Zehn Studien, München 2000, 18.

[38] M. Finkelberg, Homer as Foundation Text, in: Homer, the Bible, and Beyond. Literary and Religious Canons in the Ancient World, ed. by M. Finkelberg/G. Stroumsa, JSRC 2, Leiden-Boston 2002, 74-96, esp. 90; Assmann, Das kulturelle Gedächtnis, 52.

A master commemorative narrative shapes and sustains the core identity of a group; its recitation in ritual and festival settings secures "die Reproduktion der kulturellen Identität."[39] Accordingly the salient *past*, immanent in the semantically dense narrative patterns in which it has become engrained in the collective memory, provides the cognitive frameworks and hermeneutical resources by which a community orients itself to and masters its *present*.[40] A master commemorative narrative provides, in Barry Schwartz's words, "an expressive symbol – a language as it were, for articulating present predicaments."[41] By the same token, the present social realities of a community acutely affect its representation of its past. The father of social memory studies, Maurice Halbwachs, argued that to remember is not to *retrouver*, but to *reconstruire*, to align the image of the past with present social realities.[42] Assmann expresses this point as follows:

> Das Gedächtnis verfährt also rekonstruktiv. Die Vergangenheit vermag sich in ihm nicht als solche zu bewahren. Sie wird fortwährend von den sich wandelnden Bezugsrahmen der fortschreitenden Gegenwart her reorganisiert.[43]

Schwartz accordingly points out that "to remember is to place a part of the past in the service of the needs and conceptions of the present."[44] Current crises and preoccupations determine what elements of a community's past are awarded prominence, that is, commemorated, or conversely, are so to speak forgotten.[45] Hence *Erinnerungsfiguren* are not static, immobile objects but are themselves subject to renovation as external and internal factors in the community's existence change. Finkelberg provides an illuminating example of this dynamic in her discussion of geographical anomalies in the *Iliad*:

> Tiryns and Amyclae, whose functions as the administrative and cult centers of pre-Dorian Greece were well known to the Greeks of the Archaic period, were replaced by the more up-to-date Argos and Sparta and, accordingly, marginalized. That is to

---

[39] Assmann, Religion und kulturelles Gedächtnis, 55; also 22-23. 43; idem, Das kulturelle Gedächtnis, 89. 139.

[40] Assmann, Das kulturelle Gedächtnis, 16. 52; also Zerubavel, Recovered Roots, 229; J. Fentress/C. Wickham, Social Memory, Oxford 1992, 51; P. Connerton, How Societies Remember, Cambridge 1989, 2.

[41] B. Schwartz, Memory as a Cultural System. Abraham Lincoln in World War II, American Sociological Review 61, 1996, 908-927, esp. 910. Assmann articulates this point as follows: "Sie [the connective structure formed by the cultural memory] bindet aber auch das Gestern ans Heute, indem sie die prägenden Erfahrungen und Erinnerungen formt und gegenwärtig hält, indem sie in einen fortschreitenden Gegenwartshorizont Bilder und Geschichten einer anderen Zeit einschließt und dadurch Hoffnung und Erinnerung stiftet" (Das kulturelle Gedächtnis, 16).

[42] M. Halbwachs, On Collective Memory, trans. by L.A. Coser, Chicago 1992, 40, from Halbwachs's Les cadres sociaux de la mémoire, 1952 edition (1st ed. 1925). Halbwachs states, "Les cadres collectifs de la mémoire ... sont ... les instruments dont la mémoire collective se sert pour recomposer une image du passé qui s'accorde à chaque époque avec les pensées dominantes de la société" (cited by G. Namer, Mémoire et société, Paris 1987, 34).

[43] Assmann, Das kulturelle Gedächtnis, 41-42.

[44] Schwartz, Social Context of Commemoration, 374.

[45] Assmann, Das kulturelle Gedächtnis, 224.

say, although it was a matter of common knowledge that the Dorians were post-Mycenaean newcomers into the Peloponnese, their descendants could nevertheless easily locate themselves on the map of Heroic Greece that Homer supplied [i.e. the Argos of Diomedes reflecting the Dorian Argos and the Sparta of Menelaus corresponding to the Dorian Sparta]. This suggests that in drawing his picture of Heroic Greece Homer systematically updated the past in such a way that it might fit the present.[46]

In John Thompson's words, traditions can "become increasingly remote from their contexts of origin and increasingly interwoven with symbolic contents derived from the new circumstances in which they are re-enacted."[47]

This is the dynamic at work in the *GosPet*. It can hardly be a matter of indifference that the *GosPet* presents a version of the Passion narrative, one of early Christianity's leading *Erinnerungsfiguren*. As is the case with the synoptic and Johannine Passion narratives, in the *GosPet* we see a community's salient past, embodied in its master commemorative narrative, being told in such a way as to illuminate present predicaments. Likewise the community's conflicted present shapes the master narrative, not just cosmetically, but to its core. Having pointed to the relevance of cultural memory approaches to the *GosPet*, however, we will defer further analysis of the narrative while we clarify how the *phenomenology of tradition* can likewise be comprehended within the cultural memory framework. This will make it possible to coordinate synchronic analysis of the narrative with the diachronic question of its location within the history of the gospel tradition.

III

The key factors identified by Assmann in this regard are the breakdown of *communicative memory* and the critical transition to *cultural memory*. Broadly conceived, communicative memory encompasses all dimensions of face-to-face communication in primarily oral societies:

> Dieses Gedächtnis gehört in den Zwischenbereich zwischen Individuen, es bildet sich im Verkehr der Menschen untereinander heraus.[48]

The concept draws upon Halbwachs's insight that memory is constituted by social frameworks, which is to say that the social realities and communicative practices of communities give substance, shape, and duration to the memory of the people belonging to those communities. A particularly important dimension of communicative memory is that through the medium of ceremonial orality it acts as the framework for the transmission of a commu-

---

[46]   Finkelberg, Homer as Foundation Text, 81.
[47]   J.B. Thompson, Tradition and Self in a Mediated World, in: De-traditionalization. Critical Reflections on Authority and Identity in a Time of Uncertainty, ed. by P. Heelas/S. Lash/P. Morris, Oxford 1996, 89-103, esp. 103.
[48]   Assmann, Religion und kulturelles Gedächtnis, 13.

nity's formative narratives and normative wisdom. Despite his desire to reserve the term "cultural memory" for the artifact-based "Mnemotechnik" that arises in the wake of breakdowns of communicative memory, Assmann states:

> [E]ine mündliche Überlieferung gliedert sich genau so nach kommunikativer und kultureller, alltäglicher und feierlicher Erinnerung wie die Erinnerung einer Schriftkultur.[49]

Brian Stock notes that in communities in which orality predominates,

> the continuity of culture depends on individuals who verbally transmit the heritage from one generation to the next. The form and content of knowledge … are passed on in a series of face to face encounters. Such meetings are rich in gesture, ritual, and ceremony … The human sensorium is oriented around the ear.[50]

Communicative memory, understood as transmission of cultural traditions primarily through oral means, in long-standing societies can operate efficiently for centuries. But it is also through the operations of communicative memory that oral traditions coalesce within *emergent groups*, particularly when a salient past is being distilled out of the flux of contemporaneous events.[51] In both cases, the morphology of oral tradition is responsive to the present realities, that is social frameworks, of the diverse performance arenas in which it is enacted. This phenomenon viewed in its totality – oral traditions intersecting vitally with the shifting social frameworks of diverse performance arenas – can be identified with Assmann's "communicative memory," through whose operations a community's salient past and the exigencies of its ever-changing present are constantly brought into reciprocally influential alignment.[52]

Oral tradition, the bearer of a community's formative narratives and normative ethos, possesses no innate tendency towards writing, even when writing technologies are available.[53] Concern for its transposition to written media arises in the wake of a *Traditionsbruch*, brought about by a crisis in the functioning of communicative memory. In such cases a community, confronted with loss of connection to memory and hence with the threat of its own dissolution, must turn toward more enduring media capable of carrying memory in a vital manner across generations, that is, toward the artifactual forms of "cultural memory," a process that entails reworking connections to

---

49 Assmann, Das kulturelle Gedächtnis, 59.
50 B. Stock, The Implications of Literacy. Written Language and Models of Interpretation in the Eleventh and Twelfth Centuries, Princeton/N.J. 1983, 14-15.
51 Halbwachs discussed the constitution of foundational memories through communicative practices in groups, though he avoided the term "tradition" for these memories. Assmann devotes less attention to these dynamics.
52 See for example R. Thomas's analysis of family traditions of aristocratic Athenian families, brought into alignment with 5th and 4th century democratic values (Oral Tradition and Written Record in Classical Athens, Cambridge 1989, 108).
53 J. Assmann, Fünf Stufen auf dem Wege zum Kanon. Tradition und Schriftkultur im frühen Judentum und seiner Umwelt, Münster 1999, 13-14.

the past in the midst of drastically altered circumstances.[54] In the case of Egypt the millennia-long succession of dynasties that provided the framework for cultivation and transmission of cultural traditions was destroyed by the Persians. This touched off a counter-movement to codify tradition in monumental media, that is, a "großangelegte[s] Bauprogramm" of Egyptian temples, "beschriftet" inside and out with representations of formative myths and *Lehren*.[55] In politically unstable Mesopotamia

> sehen wir ... jede größere politische Umbruchsphase begleitet von einer Bemühung um die Kodifizierung und Sicherung der Tradition.[56]

Greece is characterized by two fractures that produced new ways of establishing connections with the foundational past across the *Umbruchszeit*. The first was the collapse of archaic society and with it the social frameworks it supplied for oral epic performance. This led on the one hand to writing down the disappearing epic tradition in the *Iliad* and *Odyssey* and on the other to the rise of the practice of rhapsodic performance of these epics in the social frameworks supplied by the *polis* festivals. The second was the collapse of the society centered on the classical *polis*, which accounts for the intense efforts of the Alexandrian scholars of the Hellenistic age to standardize the texts of these monumental epics from the many performance variants that had arisen.[57] In deportation and exile Israel experienced a potentially calamitous *Traditionsbruch*.

> Deportation bedeutete in der damaligen Welt das Ende einer kollektiven Identität. Mit dem Verlust der Heimat brachen alle notwendigen Rahmen kollektiver Erinnerung zusammen, die konnektive Struktur der Kultur riß ab, und die deportierte Gruppe ging spurlos in ihrer neuen Umwelt auf.[58]

This crisis led to production of Torah as a written artifact, in which the catastrophes of the present acted as social frameworks for reconstruction of the salient past.[59] That the writing down and systematization of oral interpretation of Torah and Mishnah in the Talmud was another such undertaking is clear from David Stern's description:

> The Gemara's project ... is ... to harmonize and unify the many fragmentary and seemingly inconsistent pieces of tradition ... What is most important, however, is the attempt – that is, the desire to construct a unified tradition which can assemble and encompass the manifold heritage of the past.[60]

---

[54] Assmann, Das kulturelle Gedächtnis, 165. 218-221. 275; also idem, Religion und kulturelles Gedächtnis, 53-54. 87-88; idem, Fünf Stufen, 20.

[55] Assmann, Das kulturelle Gedächtnis, 159. 193.

[56] Assmann, Das kulturelle Gedächtnis, 165, expressed in books and monumental libraries.

[57] Assmann, Das kulturelle Gedächtnis, 274-278.

[58] Assmann, Das kulturelle Gedächtnis, 294.

[59] Assmann, Das kulturelle Gedächtnis, 253-254.

[60] D. Stern, On Canonization in Rabbinic Judaism, in: Homer, the Bible, and Beyond. Literary and Religious Canons in the Ancient World, ed. by M. Finkelberg/G. Stroumsa, JSRC 2, Leiden-Boston 2002, 227-252, esp. 249.

Such cultural memory projects encompass the narrative and moral traditions foundational to the community's collective identity.

For emergent communities, that is, groups still in close proximity to their charismatic period of origins, *Traditionsbrüche* likewise arise from crises in communicative memory:

> Dieses Gedächtnis wächst der Gruppe historisch zu; es entsteht in der Zeit und vergeht mit ihr, genauer, mit seinen Trägern. ... Dieser allen durch persönlich verbürgte und kommunizierte Erfahrung gebildete Erinnerungsraum entspricht biblisch den 3-4 Generationen.[61]

In other words, for such communities the outer limit for the operations of communicative memory is the cohort of those still able to claim direct contact with those who knew the first generation, hence three or at the most four generations, that is, eighty to one hundred years.[62] Assmann argues that the limitations of communicative memory force themselves upon an emergent community as a crisis of memory at approximately the forty-year threshold, the point at which it is becoming apparent that the cohort of its living carriers – those who experienced the charismatic period of origins – is disappearing. It is at this point that the community, if it is not eventually to dissolve along with its memory, must accelerate the transformation of communicative memory into the enduring artifacts of cultural memory, a process Assmann characterizes as "die Objektivationen gemeinsam erinnerten Wissens in Gestalt kultureller Formen."[63]

> Wenn wir den typischen Dreigenerationen-Zeitrahmen des kommunikativen Gedächtnisses als einen synchronen Erinnerungsraum auffassen, dann bildet das kulturelle Gedächtnis anhand weit in die Vergangenheit zurückreichender Überlieferung eine diachrone Achse.[64]

The fact that Deuteronomy utilizes the forty-year threshold of communicative memory, that is, the passing of the generation that had experienced the liberation from Egypt, as its dramatic setting to address what is in truth the civilizational memory crisis brought in the wake of the *Traditionsbruch* of the Exile shows that these two types of memory crisis are in fact cognate. In both cases the exigency is the securing of long-term cultural viability in the face of breakdown in the social practices for communicating normative and formative tradition.[65]

---

61 Assmann, Das kulturelle Gedächtnis, 50.
62 Assmann, Das kulturelle Gedächtnis, 37. R. Thomas's study of Athenian family traditions is a striking confirmation of the three-to-four generation life-span of communicative memory (Oral and Written Tradition, 125-129).
63 Assmann, Religion und kulturelles Gedächtnis, 117; also pp. 29. 37-38. 53-54. 87-88, and idem, Das kulturelle Gedächtnis, 11. 32-38. 50-56. 218-221. See also S. Farmer, Martyred Village. Commemorating the 1944 Massacre at Oradour-sur-Glane, Berkeley-Los Angeles 1999, 197-213.
64 Assmann, Religion und kulturelles Gedächtnis, 19, drawing here expressly upon A. Assmann's Zeit und Tradition: kulturelle Strategien der Dauer, Köln 1999.
65 See Assmann, Religion und kulturelles Gedächtnis, 29-30.

Accordingly, the large-scale shifting of tradition from oral to written media, that is, from communicative to cultural memory, is hardly a matter of whimsy or mere convenience. Rather, it arises out of the crisis of memory. "Traditionsbrüche bedeuten Verschriftungsschübe" is Assmann's aphoristic way of expressing it.[66] As cultural memory artifacts, texts emerging out of a *Traditionsbruch* crisis innately possess an "erhöhte Normativität."[67] This is because as "exkarnations" of a community's normative and formative traditions, they embody what Assmann refers to as "eine Überlebensstrategie kultureller Identität," and accordingly, they have the capacity to develop further along that strategic course into a canon.[68] It is important to view the absolute normativity and textual inviolability typically associated with "canon" as the *terminus ad quem* of a historically protracted project of cultural identity.[69]

Precisely because it is "eine Überlebensstrategie kultureller Identität," canonization for emergent communities correlates, as an ascending line, with the three-to-four generation life-span of communicative memory. Written artifacts of cultural memory do not appear belatedly, at the last wheeze of communicative memory when the circle of tradents made up those who can claim direct or directly mediated contact with participants in the charismatic period of origins is on the verge of completely dying out. Rather, as we saw above, they spring up relatively early in the multi-generational lifespan of communicative memory – around the *Traditionsbruch* opened up by the passing of the first generation of tradents. So at this point communicative memory still has much of its cycle to run through, and accordingly both the dynamics and the authority of the unbroken oral tradition remain unabated. We can illustrate this through its natural analogy with the civilizational memory crisis that spurred textualization of the Greek epic tradition. With the appearance of the *Iliad* Foley points out that

> we most assuredly do not posit the immediate demise of the large tradition and the smaller local traditions out of which the poems were fashioned.[70]

---

[66] Assmann, Fünf Stufen, 20. 22; idem, Religion und kulturelles Gedächtnis, 88. Highly formalized orality, usually entailing memorization, also can function as a cultural memory technique. See S. Shaked, Scripture and Exegesis in Zoroastrianism, in: Homer, the Bible, and Beyond. Literary and Religious Canons in the Ancient World, ed. by M. Finkelberg/G. Stroumsa, JSRC 2, Leiden-Boston 2002, 63-74, esp. 65.

[67] Assmann, Fünf Stufen, 20; see idem, Das kulturelle Gedächtnis, 169.

[68] Assmann, Das kulturelle Gedächtnis, 127. 294; also M. Finkelberg/G.G. Stroumsa, Introduction: Before the Western Canon, in their: Homer, the Bible, and Beyond. Literary and Religious Canons in the Ancient World, JSRC 2, Leiden-Boston 2002, 1-8, esp. 5.

[69] Assmann, Das kulturelle Gedächtnis, 127. 159. Finkelberg and Strousma emphasize that "canonization of the text is an ongoing process, and fixation is only one of the stages in canon formation" (Finkelberg/Stroumsa, Before the Western Canon, 7).

[70] J.M. Foley, Traditional Oral Epic: the Odyssey, Beowulf, and the Serbo-Croatian Return Song, Berkeley-Los Angeles 1990, 23. In this case the pure oral epic tradition of archaic society modulated into the rhapsodic performance tradition of the *polis* festivals. Rhapsodic performance, while oral and free, orbited around the written epics.

Oral and written transmission do not run along separate channels; rather the boundaries between them are both indistinct and active. Cultural memory texts, their "erhöhte Normativität" notwithstanding, exist subject to the dynamics of this oral environment. Particularly important for our purposes is the fact that in the ancient world oral practices, performance in particular, were regulative for traffic with written texts. The *Iliad*, for example, after its transposition into the written medium, was typically enacted in rhapsodic performance. In accordance with the dynamics of performance, local rhapsodes "would continue to modify the received text and to shape it to their conception of what Homer must have said or meant," giving rise to local variants that provided the grist for the Alexandrian scholars' work of standardizing the text, undertaken after the collapse of the classical *polis* society.[71] In the same vein, the embedding of texts within oral performance practices entailed, in Jocelyn Penny Small's words, that "public performance before an audience physically in attendance remained a dominant form of transmission" of written texts.[72] The implications of this are important, for it renders the notion of isolated lines of literary transmission nonsensical, particularly for any period in which communicative memory and cultural memory practices coexist. With regard to the transmission of the authoritative Peisistratian version of the *Iliad* Foley writes,

> The practice of Homeric poetry must have been alive in some form all over the Greek world … by insisting on a simple, literary model for the transmission of the Homerid, Athenian text directly to Alexandria and beyond we miss that essential point.[73]

Ruth Finnegan notes that

> the written word was read *aloud*, literary works were commonly composed for *oral* performance and thus circulated among the population by word of mouth.[74]

We see again how blurred are the boundaries, and while communicative memory is in its unabated strength even how arbitrary the categories of oral and written transmission, as materials from cultural memory texts easily pass into the oral existence of communicative memory, in which they continue to be subject to all the transformative performance arena dynamics associated with the phenomenology of oral tradition. It is clear that in the period in which communicative memory is still operating effectively, cultural memory artifacts, without prejudice to their "erhöhte Normativität," will possess a relatively weak prescriptive capacity with respect to oral tradition. Likewise, these written texts will not be treated as off-limits to appropriation and interpretive transformation not just in oral performance but in fresh acts of writing, since writing itself is an act of performance that shapes tradition for the exigencies of

---

[71] Foley, Traditional Oral Epic, 28-29.
[72] J.P. Small, Wax Tablets of the Mind: Cognitive Studies of Memory and Literacy in Classical Antiquity, London-New York 1997, 35.
[73] Foley, Traditional Oral Epic, 28
[74] Finnegan, Literacy and Orality, 28.

new social contexts. In short, while communicative memory remains highly functional, oral dynamics set the terms for the writing and utilization even of cultural memory artifacts.

It would be an error, however, to re-subsume writing, particularly writing associated with cultural memory undertakings, totally under the rubric of oral processes. Written artifacts of the cultural memory possess material ingrediency that enables diffusion and iteration, rendering them resistant to complete re-assimilation to oral tradition dynamics.[75] Moreover,

> [D]er unerbittliche Wille, etwas Beständiges in die flüchtige Substanz des Lebens zu gravieren, der Drang, Spuren zu hinterlassen und die eigene Identität oder die eigene Wahrheit unauslöschlich zu machen – das sind hier wie dort Manifestationen eines Schriftpathos.[76]

Inscription enables tradition "die Interaktionssituation [zu] überdauern und späteren Wiederaufnahmen zugänglich werden zu können."[77] Nor is it possible to view the appearance of written cultural memory artifacts in the wake of a *Traditionsbruch* as anything other than epochal for an emergent community or, on a larger scale, a civilization. Foley characterizes the written Homeric epics as "monumental poems that bear the burden of a long tradition," and as "the flower" of their epic tradition.[78] We saw that as commemorative artifacts constituted from a community's normative and formative traditions, such texts possess "erhöhte Normativität" and embody "eine Überlebensstrategie kultureller Identität."[79] They emerge in response to a community's recognition of the transience of its communicative memory, and accordingly of the fragility of its own identity. They are orally deployed within ceremonial performance arenas,[80] whence they exert a heightened influence upon oral tradition.[81]

As we have emphasized oral tradition retains unbroken its innate authority and free scope for operation when cultural memory artifacts first appear, for the communicative memory frameworks that enable it are still securely in place. According to our model, however, oral tradition's authority wanes and that of the written texts waxes as the three-to-four generation lifespan of

---

[75] E.S. Casey, Remembering. A Phenomenological Study, Bloomington 1987, 227; E. Shils, Tradition, Chicago 1981, 91.

[76] A. and J. Assmann, Schrift, Tradition und Kultur, in: Zwischen Festtag und Alltag. Zehn Beiträge zum Thema 'Mündlichkeit und Schriftlichkeit,' ed. by P. Goetsch/W. Raible/H.-R. Roemer, Tübingen 1988, 25-49, esp. 48; see also Connerton, How Societies Remember, 102.

[77] Assmann, Das kulturelle Gedächtnis, 284.

[78] Foley, Traditional Oral Epic, 23.

[79] Assmann, Das kulturelle Gedächtnis, 22. See also J. Goody, The Power of the Written Tradition, Washington-London 2000, 56.

[80] See Assmann, on the performance settings of the Homeric epics: "Die Homerischen Epen zirkulieren in der typischen Form der 'zeremoniellen Kommunikation' und fundieren in unauflöslichem Zusammenhang mit den panhellenischen Festen das Projekt einer Ethnogenes" (Das kulturelle Gedächtnis, 276).

[81] Goody, Power of the Written Tradition, 56. Foley uses the word "inertia" to characterize the effect of a "manuscript text" upon the oral performance tradition of Homer (Traditional Oral Epic, 27).

communicative memory gradually plays itself out. Canonization is the cultural memory response to the *Traditionsbruch* brought about by the demise of communicative memory. In canonization,

> die Texte werden ... in ihrer Verbindlichkeit gesteigert. Diese gesteigerte Verbindlichkeit bezieht sich auf ihre Gestalt (ihren Wortlaut), sowie auf ihre Autorität, was eng miteinander zusammenhängt.[82]

Because the intensification of the drive to canonization corresponds to the decline and expiration of communicative memory, it is the indispensable culminating element in the "Konstruktion kultureller Kontinuität ... [der] Verfestigung kulturellen Sinns."[83]

Utilization practices alter correspondingly. We saw above that during the period of the effective operation of communicative memory, cultural memory texts are appropriated in modes of oral performance and re-performance. This entails free interpretive play with the texts themselves, in oral performance, in re-writing (calibrated for oral performance), or in redactional transformation, to render the normative and formative contents of tradition hermeneutically responsive to shifting social frameworks. Canonization, however, to ensure cultural continuity in response to the loss of the communicative connection to the salient past further hardens the written tradition into a durable artifact. The ground rules for appropriation of the written tradition shift to *citation* and *commentary*. Interpretive commentary takes over the task of ensuring cultural continuity:

> Wenn das ganze Gewicht der kulturellen Kontinuität auf die fundierenden Texte gelegt wird, kommt alles darauf an, sie lebendig zu erhalten und die unabwendbar wachsende Distanz zwischen ihnen und der sich wandelnden Lebenswirklichkeit zu überbrücken. Zunächst geschieht das textintern, durch Umschreiben und Fortschreiben, durch redaktionelle Anpassung an veränderte Verstehens-verhältnisse. Dann, wenn der Text kanonisiert, d.h. in seinem Wortlaut und Umfang unveränderbar festgelegt wird, kann diese Brücke nur noch durch einen Metatext geschlagen werden: den Kommentar.[84]

IV

The importance of cultural memory approaches to describing the history of the gospel traditions and the gospel literature is patent. In emergent Christianity the *Traditionsbruch* at the forty-year threshold is marked by the appearance of the Gospel of Mark, followed over the next two decades by the Gospels of Matthew and Luke and perhaps other writing events that have left only indistinct traces. As our interest here is the *GosPet*, we will pass over this early

---

[82] Assmann, Fünf Stufen, 14.
[83] Assmann, Das kulturelle Gedächtnis, 278.
[84] Assmann, Das kulturelle Gedächtnis, 295, also 176. 278-279; idem, Religion und kulturelles Gedächtnis, 59; idem, Fünf Stufen, 14. See Stock, Implications of Literacy, 56.

stage of Christian cultural memory to assess data from the sub-apostolic period gathered in Koester's seminal work on synoptic traditions in the Apostolic Fathers. It is in Justin that citation formulae such as γέγραπται and εἴρηκεν, signaling reference to writings approaching scriptural status, first begin to appear with measurable frequency applied to gospel materials.[85]

> Hier [*Dial*. 100.1] tauchen also zum ersten Male in der altchristlichen Literatur die *termini* γέγραπται und εὐαγγέλιον nebeneinander auf.[86]

This pattern corresponds to the winding-down of the three-to-four generation lifespan of the effective operation of communicative memory. Prior to this *Traditionsbruch* we can expect to find utilization practices that accord with the sub-scriptural status possessed by written artifacts during the period in which communicative memory sustains the operations and authority of oral tradition. Accordingly, we can expect for this period that what evidence there is of synoptic traditions will appear under the signs of oral processing and performance rather than citation or close copying. In Ignatius, for example,

> finden sich ... keine ausdrücklichen Zitate von synoptischen Stücken. Doch sind stillschweigende Anführungen von Sätzen, die in den synoptischen Evangelien als Jesusworte überliefert sind, nicht selten. Hinzu kommen Erwähnungen von bei den Synoptikern berichteten Ereignissen und mehrere terminologische Anklänge an die Synoptiker.[87]

Similarly with *2 Clement*:

> So ist also der Gebrauch von λέγει in den Anführungen zu synoptischen Zitaten ... eine Bestätigung für Vermutung, daß die synoptischen Zitate des 2 Clem. aus einer schriftlichen Quelle stammen, die aber nicht die Autorität der Schrift hatte.[88]

Such references in the case of *Didache* and *2 Clem* and other pre-Justin writings tend to be placed under the direct authority of "der in ihnen redende Kyrios." "An keiner dieser Stellen ist von der 'Schrift' die Rede."[89] At this point things were unlikely to be otherwise.

The sub-scriptural status of the literary gospel tradition for the balance of the lifespan of communicative memory entails that its textualized form is not prescriptive for its utilization. Hence in performance and re-performance it will be subjected to forces characteristically at work in orality, resulting in the production of oral "multiforms" of the literary tradition. Certain features of gospel traditions in the writings of the Apostolic Fathers can be plausibly attributed to this phenomenon. Koester and others have noted, for example,

---

[85] Koester, Synoptische Überlieferung, 200-201.
[86] Koester, Synoptische Überlieferung, 12. Koester's claim that in Justin "the formula does not mean 'it is written in Holy Scripture,' but 'it is recorded in a written document that Jesus said' (*Dial*. 100.1)" (Ancient Christian Gospels, 41) should be understood in light of his novel views on the origins of the canonical status of the Gospels (see below).
[87] Koester, Synoptische Überlieferung, 24.
[88] Koester, Synoptische Überlieferung, 66.
[89] Koester, Synoptische Überlieferung, 11-12. 64-65; see also Heckel, Evangelium des Markus, 277-278.

the frequent conflation of Lukan and Matthean materials. The *Didache*'s version of the "Love Enemies" instruction (1:3-5) is characterized by

> eine[r] Mischung der Mt.- und Luk.-Parallelen. Diese synoptischen Logien haben ferner Erweiterungen und Änderungen erfahren,

moreover,

> aus Mt. und Luk. stammende Logien sind – teils stark verändert – mit einem anderen offenbar jüdischen Traditionsstück (1,5) und einem apokryphen Schriftwort (1,6) zu einem Ganzen verbunden.[90]

This points to the flexibility characteristic of oral appropriation, or if the actual sources lie close to hand (as Koester thinks), their re-arrangement and re-writing.[91] The close contextual integration of non-synoptic *Traditionsgut* likewise points to the prominence of oral modes of trafficking with tradition in a scenario in which the written artifacts with their "erhöhte Normativität" are a significant factor in the traditioning process while not yet being totally definitive of the shape of the tradition or its extent, nor, because of the enduring efficacy of communicative memory, being the sole reference points for the tradition's authority. The *Didache*'s instruction on fasts (8:1), which re-orients the Matthean version (6:16-18) from the proper demeanor for fasting to the proper days for fasting while anomalously retaining Matthew's "hypocrite" epithet, shows how oral modes, in which the social exigencies of new performance arenas generate fresh configurations of the tradition, can strip synoptic materials of their literary contexts.[92] With regard to 2 *Clem* 5:2, where the "Sheep among Wolves" saying is combined with sayings from Q 12:4-5, Jens Schröter observes "[dass] Logien aus der synoptischen Tradition in neuer Weise verknüpft werden, der Kontext aus den Synoptikern dabei jedoch nicht überliefert wird."[93] *Did* 1:3-5, the "Love Enemies" instruction touched on above, is a diagnostic case of synoptic materials appropriated in oral performance modes, with the present social realities of the performance arena acting as the force reconfiguring the normative tradition. The *Didache* passage, for example, features προσεύχεσθε ὑπὲρ τῶν ἐχθρῶν instead of the synoptic ἀγαπᾶτε τοὺς ἐχθρούς, "was die Einstellung der Christenheit den Feinden gegenüber auszeichnete."[94] This is to say that later community practice was marked liturgically by prayer for enemies.

> So erklärt sich, weshalb das 'Liebet eure Feinde' bald zu einem 'Betet für eure Feinde' werden konnte. ... Die kirchliche Sitte hat alterierend auf den synoptischen Wortlaut dieses Gebots eingewirkt. Die gleiche Einwirkung der kirchlichen Sitte zeigt sich auch in dem Satz νηστεύετε δὲ ὑπὲρ τῶν διωκόντων ὑμᾶς. Ohne Zweifel ist

---

[90] Koester, Synoptische Überlieferung, 238.
[91] Koester, Synoptische Überlieferung, 230.
[92] Koester, Synoptische Überlieferung, 202-203. This of course is hardly the inference Koester draws.
[93] Schröter, Erinnerung an Jesu Worte, 173.
[94] Koester, Synoptische Überlieferung, 224.

auch diese Ermäßigung zur praktisch-sittlichen Mahnung ein Zeichen späterer Zeit.[95]

Koester characterizes the time framework for the literary productions of the Apostolic Fathers, "etwa zwischen 90 und 150 p. Chr.," as the period during which "unsere kanonischen Evangelien sich … gegenüber der mündlichen Überlieferung durchgesetzt haben."[96] This corresponds with the on-going vitality yet ultimate decline of communicative memory and the corresponding trend of the written artifacts towards scriptural status. These shifts correlate with a decline in oral performance modes of appropriating the literary tradition in favor of commentary on increasingly off-limits texts. Because his analysis is so determined by the literary paradigm, however, Koester draws mistaken inferences from his data. As we discussed earlier, his model is unable to conceptualize let alone assess the interface of written and oral media. By the same token, it posits transmission involving written sources in terms of redaction of *Vorlagen*. This leads Koester to construe written transmission and oral tradition as distinct and accordingly, when little evidence of direct redaction of the synoptics in the literature of the Apostolic Fathers can be found, to default to the "freie [and 'ältere'] Überlieferung" as their primary source. He marvels at

> wie sehr die Geschichte der Tradition bei den AVV *eine neben den synoptischen Evangelien liegende Geschichte ist,* die weit zurückreicht bis in die Quellen der Entstehung der synoptischen Evangelien hinein [emphasis added].[97]

His further inference, that the written gospels though present lacked significant normativity, follows inevitably:

> Auch diese Erwägungen zeigen, wie wenig die synoptischen Evangelien, auch wenn sie schon bekannt waren, irgendeine besondere Stellung innehatten.[98]

Research in orality, showing interaction of oral and written registers to be the norm, really negates this line of reasoning. It also calls in question Koester's methodology at another primary point. For Koester the *Sitz im Leben* of a tradition is a constant in oral transmission: "When pieces of tradition are quoted and used in early Christian authors, their function in the life of the community is usually maintained," e.g. catechetical applications.[99] *Verschriftlichung*, on the other hand, entails the transposition of oral materials from community settings into a context in the life of Jesus. In Koester's view this brings about "fundamental changes in [form and] function and meaning."[100]

---

[95] Koester, Synoptische Überlieferung, 224. Koester's literary approach to the issue of dependency makes it difficult for him to account for this phenomenon.

[96] Koester, Synoptische Überlieferung, 3.

[97] Koester, Synoptische Überlieferung, 267, see also 258.

[98] Koester, Synoptische Überlieferung, 267. In context Koester is referring to the weak presence of gospel narratives in the AVV, in contrast to kerygmatic statements, but the statement is representative.

[99] Koester, Written Gospels or Oral Tradition, 296-297.

[100] Koester, Written Gospels or Oral Tradition, 296 n. 12.

This literary context, in other words, supposedly leaves an indelible mark on the tradition. Absence of the ambient synoptic literary context thus for Koester functions as an indicator that a given piece of tradition is both distinct from and more primitive than its gospel counterpart.[101] This account is notable for the absence of any reference to performance, the core dynamic in the phenomenology of tradition. Performance settings guide the contextualization and re-contextualization of tradition. Previous contextualizations, that is, previous receptions of tradition, are certainly a factor, but not the sole or necessarily determinative one. Literary contexts are not necessarily transmitted when written tradition is taken up again in oral tradition (one need only think of free-floating quotations from Shakespeare). The literary paradigm that frames Koester's analysis is innately incapable of assessing the capacity of orality to digest and re-contextualize written tradition.[102] Accordingly, Koester's conclusions, namely, that the oral tradition runs "neben" the written tradition, and correspondingly that the latter is a negligible factor with respect to the former, are virtually inevitable. Oral performance also generates multiformity, an attribute emblematic of the *authority* of tradition, but for Koester such variability equates to lack of authority. From the fact that the written gospels in the sub-apostolic period "could be freely altered and changed according to the existing needs" he draws the inference that "there was no special authority attached to their existence in written form."[103]

Øvind Andersen notes that "in a still essentially oral culture, tradition does not strive towards transcription."[104] Given his view on the negligible authority of the gospels in the sub-apostolic period, Koester does not adequately problematize the very *existence* of written gospels. Consistently with this view of their status, Koester represents their initial appearance as being likewise a matter of little consequence. The gospels were simply

> alternative forms of the continuing oral tradition ... optional and convenient aids designed to strengthen the role the tradition about Jesus played in the churches.[105]

Similarly, this marginality of the gospels makes it necessary for Koester to account for their second-century apotheosis. Their canonization is conceptualized by Koester within his characteristic framework:

> Erst um diese Zeit [mid-second century] begannen Mt. und Luk. ... *sich gegen die freie vorsynoptische Überlieferung durchzusetzen* [emphasis added].[106]

---

[101]   Koester, Written Gospels or Oral Tradition, 296.
[102]   Koester is not entirely without a concept of second orality, e.g. "freie Zitation" (Synoptische Überlieferung, 91-92), but it is not a factor in his deliberations.
[103]   Koester, Written Gospels or Oral Tradition, 295; also idem, Synoptische Überlieferung, 241.
[104]   Ø. Andersen, Oral Tradition, in: Jesus and the Oral Gospel Tradition, ed. by H. Wansbrough, JSNT.S 64, Sheffield 1991, 17-58, esp. 46.
[105]   Koester, Written Gospels or Oral Tradition, 294. Koester here contradicts his characterization, in the same essay, of the composition of synoptics as a weighty *Verschriftlichung* of tradition standing in distinction to "the casual written fixation of oral materials" (296 n. 12).
[106]   Koester, Synoptische Überlieferung, 122-123.

(We mark here the written tradition's shift in course from tacking "neben" to "gegen" the "freie Überlieferung.") Lacking a diagnostic framework capable of accommodating the cross-cultural phenomenon of canonization, Koester brings forward *ad hoc* explanations. It was Justin who is responsible for elevating the Gospels from nullity to repute, as an *ad hoc* strategic reaction to Marcion's canon. Justin, however, stopped short of ascribing to the gospels scriptural status. That fateful step was taken by the Alexandrian theologians Clement and Origin, who took over from the Gnostics the notion that books containing the words of Jesus were inspired.[107]

V

The extended criticism to which we have subjected Koester's views indicates at a general level the need for a re-description of the history of the gospel traditions within the framework of cultural memory analysis. More to our purposes, however, it shows that much work on the *GosPet* has taken place in the context of unsound analytical models. Accordingly we can now connect with our discussion initiated earlier on *Erinnerungsfiguren* to show how cultural memory approaches can point the way towards resolution of the problems raised by the *GosPet*. The power of this approach lies in its capacity to integrate advanced understandings of the phenomenology of tradition with an account of the mechanism, namely, social memory, that drives transformations of tradition. We recall that tradition is the deposit of the salient past of a community. It is constituted by *Erinnerungsfiguren* that manifest a given community's memory in its formative (master narratives) and normative (instructional) dimensions. A group constantly establishes connections with its salient past, deposited in its tradition, within the memory frameworks of its present social realities. Stated from the perspective of the dynamics of tradition, this is to say that immediate social contexts guide enactments of tradition in performance.

The *GosPet* is a site in which the *Erinnerungsfigur* of the Passion narrative intersects with the social memory frameworks of the second century. The distinctiveness of the *GosPet* arises from the fact that in it the Passion narrative tradition is being brought into dramatic alignment with the social realities impinging upon this community. It has been frequently pointed out how alien to the *GosPet's* narrative are the cultural realities, ritual practices, and topography of first-century Jewish Palestine and conversely, how saturated it is in ecclesiastical conditions and practices of the second century. A few examples will suffice to illustrate this well-documented feature. Peter Head has shown that martyrological motifs characteristic of second-century Christian

---

[107] H. Koester, Writings and the Spirit. Authority and Politics in Ancient Christianity, HThR 84, 1991, 353-372, esp. 365-372.

sources pervade the *GosPet*'s narration of Jesus' sufferings.[108] Dieter Lührmann argues that the relatively small role granted to Mary Magdalene in the *GosPet* Resurrection account is intelligible in light of second-century rivalries among competing strands of Christianity.[109] It is widely recognized that an anti-Jewish *Tendenz*, mirroring the acrimonious rivalry between church and synagogue and corollary Christian attitudes towards Jews attested for the second century, has exerted a formative effect upon the entire narrative.[110] In this regard the absence of Romans from the Crucifixion, their role as executioners filled by the Jews, is a classic example of the "forgetting" of an element of a master narrative that does not conform to a community's present realities. Assmann states that such

> Vergessen bedingt [wird] durch Rahmenwechsel, durch die völlige Veränderung der Lebensbedingungen und sozialen Verhältnisse.[111]

We can further account for these transformations by correlating them with the communicative memory/cultural memory axis. This will make it possible to coordinate synchronic analysis of the narrative with the diachronic question of its location within the history of the gospel tradition. The *GosPet* appears *after* the production of the synoptics as cultural memory artifacts in the wake of the forty-year *Traditionsbruch*, but *prior* to the cessation of the unbroken operations of communicative memory, which will persist well into the middle of the second century. This means, given the oral-written interface now activated, that the synoptic Passion narratives with their "erhöhte Normativität" will have a significant though not prescriptive effect upon the stream of early Christian tradition that the *GosPet* moves within. On the other hand it entails that the ground rules for the *GosPet*'s reception of the *nachsynoptische* tradition are the performance dynamics of communicative memory. Since elevation of the synoptics to canonical, textually prescriptive status occurs in the wake of the *Traditionsbruch* brought about by the final breakdown of communicative memory, we can expect a utilization mode in which no gap has opened up between the formative tradition and its interpretation. In other words, the Passion narrative itself will be transformed to make it responsive to contemporary social exigencies.

It is important to emphasize, however, that the *GosPet* registers an innate, independent claim to authority, which its fictive authorship simply under-scores. This is because during the lifecycle of communicative memory,

---

[108] P.M. Head, On the Christology of the Gospel of Peter, VigChr 46, 1992, 209-224; also Beyschlag, Die verborgene Überlieferung, 62-63.

[109] D. Lührmann, Die apokryph gewordenen Evangelien. Studien zu neuen Texten und zu neuen Fragen, NT.S 112, Boston-Leiden 2004, 40.

[110] See Brown, The Gospel of Peter, 331. 339; Schaeffer, Gospel of Peter, 227. 242-253; Beyschlag, Die verborgene Überlieferung, 45-52; also A. Kirk, The Johannine Jews in the *Gospel of Peter*. A Social Memory Approach, in: Jesus in Johannine Tradition, ed. by R.T. Fortna/T. Thatcher, Louisville 2001, 313-322.

[111] Assmann, Das kulturelle Gedächtnis, 224; see also Schaeffer, Gospel of Peter, 214-215, and Thomas, Oral Tradition and Written Record, 141-178.

performance in a "diskursimmanent" mode, in which "Tradition und Interpretation untrennbar miteinander verknüpft [sind],"[112] is precisely the means by which the enormous authority of tradition is directly enacted in new contexts. On the same basis, nothing prevents fresh articulations of the *nachsynoptische* tradition from being calibrated to complement, update, compete with, displace, or transcend the written gospels, or for that matter to coalesce from that stream of tradition apart from significant contact with the written artifacts at all. Cultural memory analysis, therefore, while enabling us to comprehend the course followed by the gospels from their writing in the last third of first century to their canonization by the last third of the second allows us to take full account of the historical contingencies and contestations that attended this process along the way.

---

[112] Assmann, Das kulturelle Gedächtnis, 175.

Das Petrusevangelium als Evangelium

von

JUDITH HARTENSTEIN

1. Einleitung: Evangelienliteratur

Der folgende Beitrag versucht, das EvPetr in die Vielfalt frühchristlicher Evangelienliteratur einzuordnen, um so sein spezifisches Profil genauer zu erfassen. Dabei geht es mir einerseits um grundsätzliche Überlegungen zu Evangelien und ihren Gemeinsamkeiten und Unterschieden, andererseits um einen spezielleren Vergleich des EvPetr mit einzelnen anderen Schriften, zu denen es Berührungen aufweist. Hier ist vor allem das „Unbekannte Berliner Evangelium" (UBE)[1] interessant und bisher noch wenig ausgewertet.

Das für heutige LeserInnen grundlegendste Merkmal bei der Differenzierung von Evangelien ist die Frage der Zugehörigkeit zum Kanon: das EvPetr ist ein apokryphes, kein kanonisches Evangelium. Es gehörte über Jahrhunderte nicht zu den kirchlich als heilige Schrift anerkannten Evangelien. Dies impliziert nicht nur ein theologisches Werturteil – das ja gegebenenfalls kritisch hinterfragt werden könnte –, sondern wirkt sich auch ganz praktisch auf den Überlieferungszustand und die Vertrautheit mit dem Text aus. Zudem sind für heutige LeserInnen die kanonischen Evangelien ein natürlicher und sachlich sinnvoller Bezugspunkt, von dem aus das EvPetr gedeutet wird (nicht umgekehrt).[2] Diese Unterscheidung kanonisch – nichtkanonisch gilt jedoch weder für die Abfassung noch für die frühe Rezeption der Evangelien, wie z.B. die ältesten Papyrusfunde zeigen.[3] Die Entstehung des Kanons war ein historischer Prozess, in dem einige schon vorhandene Evangelien kanonisch

---

[1] Im englischsprachigen Raum ist der von der Erstedition gewählte Titel „Gospel of the Savior" üblich. Näheres zu dieser Schrift siehe unten, Textausgabe und Übersetzungen Anm. 36f.

[2] Vgl. T. Nicklas, Ein „neutestamentliches Apokryphon"? Zum umstrittenen Kanonbezug des sog. „Petrusevangeliums", VigChr 56, 2002, 260-272, hier 268-271.

[3] Vgl. H. Koester, Apocryphal and Canonical Gospels, HThR 73, 1980, 105-130, hier 107-111. Er belegt durch die Funde von Handschriften und Zitate bei Kirchenvätern die weite Verbreitung verschiedener Evangelien und das Fehlen einer Grenze zwischen kanonischen und nichtkanonischen. Dieser Befund widerlegt meines Erachtens die Annahme von H.-J. Klauck, dass die 4-Evangelien-Sammlung schon ab der Mitte des 2. Jahrhunderts eine feste Bezuggröße ist; vgl. H.-J. Klauck, Apokyphe Evangelien. Eine Einführung, Stuttgart 2002, 282.

wurden, andere apokryph. Er beginnt im 2. Jahrhundert, ist aber dann noch keineswegs abgeschlossen.[4] Noch lange Zeit später zeigen sich regionale und individuelle Differenzen und eine hohe Flexibilität in der Wertschätzung von Evangelien.[5]

Aufgrund dieses Befundes halte ich es für sinnvoll, die Evangelienliteratur im 2. Jahrhundert als einen gemeinsamen Bestand an Schriften anzusehen, ohne sofort zwischen kanonisch und nichtkanonisch zu differenzieren und ohne die kanonisch gewordenen Evangelien zum Maßstab oder zur Norm dieser Literatur zu machen.[6] Daraus ergibt sich allerdings als Folgeproblem die Frage, was eigentlich ein Evangelium ist, denn unter dieser Bezeichnung sind sehr unterschiedliche Schriften erhalten.[7] Meines Erachtens lassen sie sich nicht einer gemeinsamen Gattung zuordnen, trotzdem lässt sich beschreiben, was ein Evangelium ausmacht und von anderer Literatur unterscheidet. Meine Definition schließt dann auch Schriften ein, von denen kein Titel bekannt ist oder die eine andere Bezeichnung tragen: Als Evangelien bezeichne ich diejenige frühchristliche Literatur, die vom irdischen Wirken Jesu berichtet und damit den Lesenden heilsrelevante Information geben will.

Diese Definition ist in vielem Helmut Koesters Ansatz verpflichtet, der ebenfalls die Vielfalt der Evangelienliteratur beschreibt, in der die kanonisch gewordenen Evangelien nur einen relativ spezifischen Teil bilden. Er definiert Evangelienliteratur so:

---

4   Vgl. D. Lührmann, Die apokryph gewordenen Evangelien. Studien zu neuen Texten und neuen Fragen, NT.S 112, Leiden-Boston 2004, 54. Seine Bezeichnung der Evangelien als kanonisch bzw. apokryph *geworden* macht diesen Punkt auch sprachlich deutlich.

5   Siehe z.B. die Handschrift P.Cair. 10759, die – abgefasst im 6./7. Jahrhundert – u.a. einen Ausschnitt des EvPetr enthielt und vermutlich eine Grabbeigabe war.

6   So begründet Schneemelcher die Zusammenstellung der Schriften im Band 1 (Evangelien) der neutestamentlichen Apokryphen damit, „daß alle Texte sich in irgendeiner Weise auf Person, Leben und Werk Jesu beziehen, und zwar nicht im Stil einer theologischen Reflexion, sondern in Anlehnung an die Gattung Evangelium" (W. Schneemelcher, Einleitung, in: NtApo 1, Tübingen [6]1990, 65-75, hier 66). Ähnlich definiert auch Klauck, Evangelien, 282: „Es handelt sich bei ihnen um theologische Gebrauchstexte der frühen Christen (nicht: der einen Kirche), die formale, inhaltliche und terminologische Affinitäten zu jenen Schriften aufweisen, die als Evangelien kanonisch geworden sind." Ein solcher Ansatz passt aus einer rezeptions-orientierten Perspektive, die ja dem Unterfangen, apokryphe Evangelien zu sammeln, schon an sich zugrunde liegt. Aber der Begriff „Anlehnung" bei Schneemelcher impliziert meiner Meinung nach, dass die apokryph gewordenen Evangelien schon im Bezug auf die kanonisch gewordenen entstanden sind. Klauck vermeidet eine solche Festlegung, führt aber durch die Bezeichnung als „Gebrauchstexte" eine inhaltliche Wertung ein. Mir fehlt bei beiden Ansätzen die Möglichkeit, dass apokryph gewordene Evangelien eigenständig und gleichwertig neben kanonisch gewordenen stehen.

7   Völlig ausgeklammert soll hier bleiben, dass „Evangelium" ursprünglich allgemein die Heilsbotschaft von Jesus Christus bezeichnet. Erst im 2. Jahrhundert wurde der Begriff für Schriften üblich, ohne dass die erste Bedeutung damit verschwand. Vgl. hierzu z.B. J.A. Kelhoffer, „How soon a book" revisited: ΕΥΑΓΓΕΛΙΟΝ as a Reference to „Gospel" Materials in the First Half of the Second Century, ZNW 95, 2004, 1-34.

This corpus should include all those writings which are constituted by the transmission, use, and interpretation of materials and traditions from and about Jesus of Nazareth.[8]

Auf den ersten Blick klingt dies sehr ähnlich wie meine Beschreibung. Allerdings ist für Koester die Einbindung der Evangelienschriften in die traditionsgeschichtliche Überlieferung ein entscheidendes Kriterium: Nach Koester sind Evangelien nur diejenigen Schriften, die formgeschichtlich der frühen Jesusüberlieferung entsprechen bzw. als ihre Weiterentwicklung anzusehen sind.[9] Dazu gehören z.B. Spruchüberlieferung und ihre dialogische Ausgestaltung und Erzählungen wie Wundergeschichten und die Passionsgeschichte; Evangelien können sowohl auf einen Bereich beschränkt sein als auch eine Mischung bieten – letzteres liegt in den kanonischen Evangelien vor, ist aber nach Koester eine spätere Entwicklung.

Anders als bei Koester ist in meiner Definition die Darstellung in der Schrift selbst entscheidend, es genügt mir, wenn sie nach eigenem Anspruch Jesustradition überliefert.[10] Der Unterschied wird z.B. in der Einschätzung der Sophia Jesu Christi (NHC III,4; BG,3) deutlich: Ich halte diese Schrift für ein Evangelium, weil in ihr nach eigenem Anspruch heilsrelevante Worte Jesu übermittelt werden – Koester schließt sie (und einige andere vergleichbare Schriften) aus, weil sie nachweislich ein vermutlich nichtchristliches philosophisches Traktat verarbeitet, den Eugnostosbrief (NHC III,3; V,1), also einen der Jesustradition ganz fremden Stoff.[11]

Ebenfalls an der literarischen Endgestalt, nicht der formgeschichtlichen Einordnung der Schriften ist Lührmann orientiert. Entscheidend ist für ihn die Verwendung der Bezeichnung „Evangelium" in den alten Texten selbst (bzw. in ihrer frühen Rezeption). Denn bei einem solchen Titel „handelt es sich nicht einfach um eine formale Kategorie, mit ihm verbindet sich vielmehr ein Anspruch an Verbindlichkeit."[12] Diese Annahme ist meines Erachtens berechtigt und kommt dem nahe, was ich mit Heilsrelevanz umschrieben habe. Schwierig ist aber, dass die Titel nicht immer fester Bestandteil einer Schrift sind – sie können sekundär zugefügt sein, sind auch noch später variabel und bei manchen fragmentarischen Schriften nicht mehr erhalten.[13] Deshalb sehe

---

8   H. Koester, Ancient Christian Gospels. Their History and Development, London-Philadelphia 1990, 46.

9   Vgl. Koester, Gospels, 46-47. Maßgeblich ist für Koester die formgeschichtliche Einordnung, es geht nicht um die historische Verlässlichkeit des Stoffes!

10   Allerdings kommt auch meine Definition nicht ohne ein „weiches", das heißt ein nicht immer unmittelbar im Text greifbares, Kriterium aus, das Evangelien von Jesusbüchern aller Art abgrenzt: den Anspruch, Heil zu vermitteln. Diese Frage nach der Absicht gehört aber zur Kommunikationssituation einer Schrift, eignet sich also durchaus als Merkmal – und in den allermeisten Fällen ist ein solcher Anspruch auch einigermaßen deutlich ersichtlich.

11   Vgl. Koester, Gospels, 47.

12   Lührmann, Evangelien, 33.

13   Ein Beispiel für die Veränderung eines Titels bietet das Apokryphon des Johannes. In der vermutlich älteren kürzeren Fassung (NHC III,1; BG,2) heißt diese Schrift ⲡⲁⲡⲟⲕⲣⲟⲫⲟⲛ ⲓ̄ⲱ̄ⲁⲛⲛⲏⲥ also „das Apokryphon des Johannes". Der Titel der Langfassung (NHC II,1; IV,1)

ich den überlieferten Titel als einen wichtigen, aber nicht den entscheidenden Hinweis für die Einordnung einer Schrift, mein Gebrauch von „Evangelium" ist eine moderne Klassifizierung.

Evangelien im Sinn dieser Definition lassen sich von anderen früh-christlichen Schriften wie der Acta-Literatur, Apokalypsen oder auch theologischen Traktaten oder Homilien unterscheiden. Denn sie berichten primär von Jesus, sie reflektieren nicht über ihn (auch wenn dies indirekt natürlich auch dazu gehört) und beziehen sich so auf einen bestimmten, zeitlichen und räumlich abgrenzbaren Bereich.[14] Sie können den Zeitraum von Geburt, auch mit einer Vorgeschichte von Ankündigung und Schwangerschaft, bis zur Auferstehung einschließlich Erscheinungen umfassen, aber auch nur einen Teil davon. Berichtet werden kann von Ereignissen und Handlungen, aber auch von dem, was Jesus sagt. Alle Evangelien haben den Anspruch, dass das in ihnen vermittelte Wissen zum Heil (im weiten Sinne) führt – das unterscheidet sie z.B. von modernen wissenschaftlichen oder populären Jesusbüchern. Aber meines Erachtens wurde keines geschrieben, um Bestandteil eines Kanons zu werden.

Diese Definition passt auf die neutestamentlichen Evangelien, auf außerkanonische Evangelien, wie sie z.B. in den „neutestamentlichen Apokryphen" von Hennecke/Schneemelcher gesammelt sind, und auf erschlossene Schriften wie Q. Sie gehören aber unterschiedlichen literarischen Gattungen an, zu denen jeweils unterschiedliche Paralleltexte in jüdischer oder paganer antiker Literatur genannt werden können. So gibt es narrative Evangelien mit einem Schwerpunkt auf der Passionsgeschichte wie Mk, Mt, Lk, Joh, soweit ersichtlich auch EvPetr und UBE und eventuell weitere fragmentarisch erhaltene Schriften. Andere narrative Evangelien konzentrieren sich auf die Kindheit und Vorgeschichte Jesu.[15] Wieder andere Evangelien bestehen im Wesentlichen aus Worten Jesu (Thomasevangelim, Q), die auch dialogisch ausgeformt sein können (Dialog des Erlösers (NHC III,5); Ägypterevangelium bei Clemens Alexandrinus). Schließlich gibt es noch die

---

ⲕⲁⲧⲁ ⲓⲱⲑⲁⲛⲛⲏⲛ ⲁⲡⲟⲕⲣⲟⲫⲟⲛ lässt sich am ehesten als „das apokryphe (Evangelium) nach Johannes" wiedergeben. Denn ⲁⲡⲟⲕⲣⲟⲫⲟⲛ ist hier attributiv angeschlossen, kann also nicht das Bezugswort für ⲕⲁⲧⲁ ⲓⲱⲑⲁⲛⲛⲏⲛ sein, sondern braucht selber ein Bezugswort. Da „nach Johannes" eine gängige Kurzform für den Evangelientitel ist, bietet sich die Ergänzung von „Evangelium" an. Das bedeutet, diese Schrift hat ihre Bezeichnung im Laufe der Überlieferung gewechselt. Vgl. J. Hartenstein, Die zweite Lehre. Erscheinungen des Auferstandenen als Rahmenerzählungen frühchristlicher Dialoge, TU 146, Berlin 2000, 64.

14   Dies gilt auch z.B. für das Thomasevangelium, in dem die Worte Jesu zwar überzeitliche Gültigkeit beanspruchen und der „lebendige Jesus" auch mehr umfasst als sein irdisches Wirken, aber in dem durch zumindest minimale Rahmung der Worte und weitere vorkommende Personen doch eine Verortung gegeben ist.

15   Falls es auch einmal Sammlungen von Wundergeschichten (z.B. die vermutete Semeiaquelle) gab, ließen sie sich als narrative Evangelien mit einem Schwerpunkt auf Taten des erwachsenen Jesus, aber ohne Passion beschreiben. Einen Grenzfall bildet das Protevangelium des Jakobus, das das Leben Marias bis zur Geburt Jesu behandelt – fraglich ist aber auch, ob diese Schrift tatsächlich den Anspruch erhebt, den Weg zum Heil zu weisen.

Evangelien, in denen eine Erscheinung des Auferstandenen den Erzählrahmen für einen Dialog bildet (Sophia Jesu Christi, Apokryphon des Johannes, Epistula Apostolorum, Evangelium nach Maria, Brief des Petrus an Philippus, erste Apokalypse des Jakobus, apokrypher Jakobusbrief, Pistis Sophia).[16] Es gibt aber auch Schriften, die in der Antike Evangelien genannt wurden, die nach meiner Definition nicht zur Evangelienliteratur gehören, sondern eher theologische Abhandlungen sind.[17]

Neben diesen mehr oder weniger vollständig erhaltenen Evangelien gab es vermutlich noch viele weitere, die einfach nicht erhalten sind bzw. bisher noch nicht entdeckt wurden.[18] Auch schriftliche Quellen zu den bekannten Evangelien lassen sich vermuten, aber mit Ausnahme von Q nur sehr hypothetisch rekonstruieren; auch sie würden aber zur Evangelienliteratur gehören.[19] Neben diesen Schriften ist aber auch mit einer breiten mündlichen Tradition zu rechnen, die sich nicht immer grundsätzlich von den Verschriftlichungen abgrenzen lässt. Ich spreche von Evangelientradition, wenn ich die mündliche Tradition ausdrücklich mit einbeziehen will.

In dieses grob skizzierte Feld von Evangelienliteratur ordnet sich das EvPetr ein. Auch wenn es nur fragmentarisch erhalten ist, wird der narrative Charakter deutlich: Es umfasste jedenfalls auch eine Passionsgeschichte. Dies verbindet das EvPetr mit den kanonisch gewordenen Evangelien, aber auch mit UBE. Eine Besonderheit des EvPetr liegt in der Autorenfiktion, zu der andere Evangelien ebenfalls Parallelen bieten. Im Folgenden soll auf solche Verbindungen genauer eingegangen werden. Ausklammern will ich dabei die Frage der literarischen Abhängigkeit des EvPetr von den synoptischen Evangelien und Joh. Dieser Punkt ist vielfach untersucht worden, ohne zu einem Konsens zu führen. Ich will stattdessen versuchen, das EvPetr in seiner Eigenart als Evangelium im Zusammenhang der ganzen Vielfalt frühchristlicher Evangelienliteratur zu verstehen.

---

16 Meines Erachtens gehören auch diese Schriften zur Evangelienliteratur, und zwar unabhängig vom Inhalt des Dialogs. Auch sie handeln vom irdischen Wirken Jesu und seinen JüngerInnen, und zwar im Zeitraum zwischen Auferstehung und Himmelfahrt. Zudem bilden sie dem eigenen Anspruch nach eine Art Fortsetzung zu den Evangelien, die das Wirken Jesu bis zu Tod und Auferstehung beschreiben; vgl. dazu Hartenstein, Lehre, 295-296. 316.

17 Z.B. das Evangelium Veritatis (NHC I,3) und das Ägypterevangelium (NHC III,2 und IV,2). „Evangelium" scheint bei diesen Schriften den Inhalt als gute Botschaft zu charakterisieren. Schwierig ist die Einordnung des Evangeliums nach Philippus (NHC II,3), das gewisse Ähnlichkeit mit dem Thomasevangelium aufweist, aber im Ganzen eher eine Sammlung von einzelnen theologischen Aussagen (u.a. über Jesus, die Sakramente) darstellt als eine Sammlung von Jesusworten oder Episoden aus seinem Leben.

18 Dass stetig neue Entdeckungen möglich sind, zeigt nicht nur das UBE, sondern auch ein der Forschung erst seit Kurzem zugänglicher koptischer Kodex, der neben Abschriften des Briefs des Petrus an Philippus und der ersten Apokalypse des Jakobus vermutlich auch das von Irenäus, *haer.* I 31,1 erwähnte Judasevangelium enthält.

19 Vgl. Koester, Gospels, 45-46; Klauck, Evangelien, 281.

2. Das EvPetr als Erzählung des Petrus

a) Erzählstimme und Autorenfiktion

Im EvPetr – soweit es erhalten ist – erzählt Petrus die Geschehnisse (EvPetr 14,60). Das Evangelium hat also in narratologischer Terminologie keine externe Erzählstimme, sondern eine interne: Ein Charakter aus der erzählten Welt fungiert zugleich als Erzähler.[20] Eine solche Erzählform kommt auch in anderen Evangelien vor, so ist Johannes der Erzähler im Apokryphon des Johannes, Jakobus im apokryphen Jakobusbrief und der ersten Apokalypse des Jakobus, die ganze Gruppe der Zwölf bzw. der Apostel in der Epistula Apostolorum und im UBE. Wechsel zwischen Erzählen in erster und dritter Person in einer Schrift sind durchaus möglich.[21] Im EvPetr wird die Identität der Erzählstimme besonders betont, indem das Ich oder Wir ausdrücklich identifiziert wird (EvPetr 14,59.60).

In allen vollständig erhaltenen Evangelien, die in der ersten Person erzählen, wird diese Erzählsituation näher ausgeführt. Es gibt entweder eine ausdrückliche Anweisung zum Aufschreiben, so im Apokryphon des Johannes (BG p. 75,15-19 par.) und in komplizierterer Form in der ersten Apokalypse des Jakobus[22]. Oder das Evangelium ist gerahmt durch einen Brief bzw. ein persönliches Vorwort, das die Erzählsituation erklärt, so in der Epistula Apostolorum 1-2 und im apokryphen Jakobusbrief (NHC I p. 1,1-18). In jedem Fall wird erklärt, wie die erzählende Person zu dieser Rolle kommt, der Erzähler ist zugleich auch Autor bzw. Schreiber der Schrift.[23] Es ist demnach wahrscheinlich, dass auch das EvPetr entweder eine ausdrückliche Aufforderung an Petrus zum Aufschreiben seiner Erlebnisse enthielt oder Petrus dies selbst als Erzähler begründet – beides vermutlich entweder am Anfang oder am Ende des Evangeliums, also in leider nicht erhaltenen Teilen. Wenn das so ist, dann hatte für die ursprüngliche Schrift die Funktion des Petrus als Erzähler und Autor noch größeres Gewicht, als aus den erhaltenen Fragmenten ersichtlich ist.

---

[20] Vgl. T. Nicklas, Erzähler und Charakter zugleich: Zur literarischen Funktion des „Petrus" in dem nach ihm benannten Evangelienfragment, VigChr 55, 2001, 318-326.

[21] Durchgehend in der Wir-Form bleiben die Epistula Apostolorum und das UBE. Das Apokryphon des Johannes beispielsweise beginnt und endet in der dritten und wechselt zwischendurch zur ersten Person – und zwar in den unterschiedlichen Versionen der Schrift an verschiedenen Stellen. Die Wir-Berichte der Apg zeigen, dass Wechsel in die erste Person auch in einem überwiegend in der dritten Person erzählten Text möglich sind.

[22] Hier wird Jakobus zum Übermitteln der Lehre an Addai aufgefordert, der sie dann später, zu einem bestimmten Zeitpunkt, aufschreiben soll (erste Apokalypse des Jakobus NHC V p. 36,12-23).

[23] Bei Apokalypsen scheint das nicht durchgehend der Fall zu sein.

Dies gilt auch im Vergleich mit Evangelien, die zwar eine externe Erzählstimme haben, in denen aber der Autor bzw. Schreiber trotzdem mit einer der beteiligten Personen identifiziert wird. So werden der geliebte Jünger bei Joh und Thomas im Thomasevangelium als diejenigen genannt, die das vorliegende Evangelium geschrieben haben (Joh 21,24; Thomasevangelium Kapitel 1). Sie kommen aber in der Erzählung selbst vor wie andere Charaktere. Auch hier liegt also eine Legitimation der Schrift durch die Berufung auf eine bestimmte, wichtige Person vor – aber sie hat keine so prägende Bedeutung für die ganze Schrift, da sie nur an einer Stelle greifbar ist. Interessant ist die besondere Rolle gerade von Petrus, der weit verbreitet der bedeutendste Jünger Jesu ist, während Thomas oder der „geliebte Jünger" wohl nur in begrenzten Kreisen wichtig waren. Das EvPetr knüpft hier an eine besondere Autorität an,[24] könnte aber zugleich auch Bestandteil einer Petrustradition sein.

b) Erzählstimme und Perspektive (Fokussierung)

Obwohl die Erzählstimme im EvPetr an den Charakter Petrus gebunden ist, ist sie trotzdem allwissend. Das heißt es wird auch von Ereignissen berichtet, bei denen Petrus eindeutig nicht anwesend ist – er und die übrigen JüngerInnen halten sich versteckt (EvPetr 7,26) – und auch von Gefühlen und Gedanken verschiedener Personen.[25] Wo aber von Petrus und den anderen erzählt wird, da wird deutlich, dass sie zu dem Zeitpunkt noch über sehr begrenztes Wissen verfügen. Insbesondere haben sie noch keine Ahnung von der Auferstehung Jesu, als sie sich nach Hause aufmachen (EvPetr 14,59), obwohl von dieser zuvor ausführlich berichtet wurde.

Diese Spannung in der Erzählstimme zwischen Allwissenheit und Bindung an Petrus lässt sich noch zu einem anderen Phänomen in Beziehung setzen: die Frage der Perspektive oder Fokussierung in der Erzählung. In der Narratologie wird unterschieden zwischen denjenigen, die das Erzählte sehen, und denjenigen, die es erzählen. Beides muss nicht übereinstimmen, die Perspektive einer Erzählung ist nicht unbedingt die der Erzählstimme bzw. lässt sich noch differenzierter beschreiben. M. Bal, die das Phänomen genauer analysiert hat, spricht von Fokussierung (*focalization*): Die Fokussierung beschreibt die Beziehung zwischen dem Sehen und dem, was gesehen wird.[26] Grundsätzlich gibt es ein Subjekt, das fokussiert, und ein Objekt, auf das fokussiert wird. Das Subjekt kann sich innerhalb der Erzählung befinden, aber

---

24 Vgl. Nicklas, Erzähler, 325-326; T.V. Smith, Petrine Controversies in Early Christianity. Attitudes towards Peter in Christian Writings of the First Two Centuries, WUNT 2.15, Tübingen 1985, 41-42.

25 Vgl. Nicklas, Erzähler, 322.

26 Vgl. M. Bal, Narratology. Introduction to the Theory of Narrative, Toronto et. al. ²1997, 142-143 – in Einzelheiten 142-161.

auch außerhalb; Wechsel sind leicht möglich, ebenso verschiedene Ebenen der Fokussierung. Ein weiteres Unterscheidungsmerkmal ist, ob das, was gesehen wird, allgemein erkennbar ist oder nicht.

Im EvPetr ist nun ausgesprochen auffällig, dass über weite Strecken des erhaltenen Fragments P.Cair. 10759 die GegnerInnen Jesu, die ihn verspotten, kreuzigen und das Grab bewachen, die Subjekte der Fokussierung sind. Die Ereignisse werden aus ihrer Sicht geschildert, sie sehen Jesus, aber auch die Vorgänge bei der Auferstehung. Von ihnen werden auch Gefühle und Motive genannt.[27] Jesus dagegen ist nur Objekt, er steht aber nicht einmal im Mittelpunkt der Fokussierung. Seine GegnerInnen sind bei den Ereignissen um die Kreuzigung viel eher auf sich selbst und ihre Absichten fokussiert, die sich dann indirekt auf Jesus beziehen.[28] Ein gewisser Bruch in der Darstellung entsteht jedoch durch die Verwendung von christologischen Titeln für Jesus (EvPetr 3,6.9). Wenn sie Jesus wirklich als Sohn Gottes ansehen, ist nicht plausibel, wieso sie sich gegen ihn wenden.[29] Aber die Titel kommen in den eigenen Äußerungen vor, sie entsprechen innerhalb der Erzählung der Einschätzung dieser Charaktere.

Diese Fokussierung macht die Erzählung dramatischer und das Geschehen an sich drastischer. Die Schilderung der Motive und Absichten verstärkt auch die negative Sicht der GegnerInnen. Für ihr Verhalten lässt sich wirklich keine Rechtfertigung finden.[30] Dass die Erzählung mit den Augen der GegnerInnen sieht, lenkt aber auch die LeserInnen. Die Darstellung legt eigentlich eine Identifikation mit den Subjekten der Fokussierung nahe, obwohl sie so negativ gezeichnet sind. Dies ist im Zusammenhang mit der Auferstehung wirklich sinnvoll, denn so führt die ungläubige Perspektive zu einer um so stärkeren Überzeugung. Auch Petrus und die JüngerInnen stehen zunächst jedem Gedanken an die Auferstehung fern. Ein Umschwung ist anzunehmen, kommt aber im erhaltenen Fragment nicht mehr vor. Hier ergänzt sich also die wechselnde Fokussierung der GegnerInnen und der JüngerInnen und gibt den LeserInnen eine ähnliche Rolle.

Aber auch bei der Kreuzigung bringt die Schilderung der Ereignisse aus der Perspektive der GegnerInnen einschließlich ihrer Motive und Gefühle diese den LeserInnen nahe. Dazu passt, dass die verwendeten Titel vermutlich dem entsprechen, was die LeserInnen über Jesus denken. Andererseits macht

---

[27] Darin unterscheidet sich das EvPetr von den Passionsgeschichten anderer Evangelien, in denen eine externe Fokussierung überwiegt, aber mitunter auch Jesus fokussiert.

[28] Die Nichtbeteiligung Jesu zeigt sich z.B. im Gespräch mit dem einen Mitgekreuzigten. Dieser beschimpft in EvPetr 4,13 die Kreuzigenden, ohne mit Jesus selbst zu reden, während er in Lk 23,40-43 mit dem dritten Gekreuzigten und mit Jesus spricht, der dann das entscheidende Schlusswort hat.

[29] Nicklas sieht dies als eine Verspottung des eigenen Gottes, vgl. T. Nicklas, Die „Juden" im Petrusevangelium (P.Cair 10759). Ein Testfall, NTS 47, 2001, 206-221, hier 216. Siehe auch den Beitrag von T. Hieke im vorliegenden Band.

[30] Dies wird durch den Erzählkommentar in EvPetr 5,17 ausdrücklich festgehalten. Anders dagegen z.B. die Darstellung in Joh 19,23-24, wo auch die kreuzigenden Soldaten als schrifterfüllend dargestellt sind.

die negative Wertung des Verhaltens eine auch nur annähernde Identifizierung eigentlich unmöglich.

Diese Spannung und Widersprüchlichkeit der Darstellung lässt sich eindeutig erheben. Sie ist schon im Inhalt der Erzählung durch die auffällige Verwendung von christologischen Titeln im Mund der GegnerInnen greifbar und wird durch die Erzähltechnik der Fokussierung noch verstärkt. Schwieriger ist eine Deutung des Befundes – möglich sind auch unterschiedliche Wirkungen auf die Lesenden.[31] Nahe liegend ist zunächst, dass durch die Darstellung ein Erschrecken und größere Abscheu produziert wird, also die Nähe, die die Erzählung herstellt, letztlich zu einer größeren Distanz führt. Aber ich halte es auch für denkbar, dass auch christliche LeserInnen zumindest ansatzweise mit den GegnerInnen Jesu fühlen, also die vom Text gebotenen Möglichkeiten der Identifizierung nutzen.[32] Vielleicht wird so eine Bekehrung nacherlebt oder eine eigene Schuld der LeserInnen aufgegriffen. Dazu passt, dass das Volk nach der Kreuzigung bereut (EvPetr 7,25; 8,28) und für die Grabbewachung dann nur noch eine Führungsschicht – die sich ausdrücklich im Gegensatz zum Volk sieht (EvPetr 11,48) – verantwortlich ist.[33] Leider ist im erhaltenen Text nicht deutlich, ob und wie diese Wende im Volk in einen größeren Zusammenhang eingebunden ist – und wie weit es Parallelen zur Darstellung von Petrus und den JüngerInnen (z.B. die Verleugnung des Petrus, falls sie erzählt wurde) gibt.

3. EvPetr und UBE

Das EvPetr weist nicht nur zu den kanonisch gewordenen Evangelien enge Beziehungen auf, sondern auch zum UBE. Nur in diesen Evangelien aus einer relativ frühen Zeit spielt die Passionsgeschichte eine wesentliche Rolle. Speziell UBE und EvPetr ist der Erzählstil in der ersten Person gemeinsam und außerdem einige Einzelheiten der Darstellung wie die Kreuzigung Jesu durch das Volk Israel und die besondere Rolle des Kreuzes, das personifiziert auftritt.[34] Ein Vergleich zwischen den Schriften ist aber nicht nur wegen dieser

---

[31]   Die Frage, welche Absicht beim Abfassen der Erzählung bestand, lässt sich meines Erachtens noch viel schlechter greifen. Es ist fraglich, wie weit die Autorenintention überhaupt eine Rolle für die Bedeutung eines Textes spielt oder ob dessen Sinn nicht in erster Linie in der Rezeption durch die LeserInnen entsteht.

[32]   Eine gewisse Analogie bieten manche Passionslieder, in denen das Besingen des Leidens Jesus „für mich" in ein „durch mich" übergehen kann. Das ist zumindest ansatzweise eine Identifikation mit denjenigen, die Jesus kreuzigen, auch wenn sie nicht als Passionserzählung ausgeführt wird.

[33]   Vgl. Nicklas, Juden, 219-220.

[34]   Schenke hat aufgrund dieser Beziehungen sogar vermutet, das Berliner Fragment sei ein Teil des EvPetr, vgl. H.-M. Schenke, Das sogenannte „Unbekannte Berliner Evangelium" (UBE), ZAC 2, 1998, 199-213, hier 205-207. Allerdings sprechen dagegen Unterschiede in der Wortwahl und in Einzelheiten: So wird Jesus im EvPetr stets als κύριος bezeichnet, im UBE als ; die Gruppe seiner AnhängerInnen heißt im EvPetr μαθηταί, im UBE ⲛⲁⲡⲟⲥⲧⲟⲗⲟⲥ; und auch die

Übereinstimmungen interessant, sondern auch weil das UBE aller Wahrscheinlichkeit nach zur Wirkungsgeschichte des EvPetr gehört: Es zeigt, wie das EvPetr selbst oder die in ihm ausgedrückten Gedanken und Traditionen weiter verarbeitet wurden. Diese Perspektive kann nicht die Entstehung des EvPetr erhellen, aber sie kann den Ort des EvPetr im Rahmen frühchristlicher Evangelienliteratur beschreiben helfen.

a) Das UBE

Das UBE besteht aus 7 teilweise erhaltenen Blättern und einigen kleineren Fragmenten eines koptischen Pergamentkodex, die 1967 vom Berliner Ägyptischen Museum gekauft und katalogisiert wurden, dann aber in Vergessenheit gerieten. 1991 wurden sie wiederentdeckt und der wissenschaftlichen Öffentlichkeit in einer kritischen Edition mit englischer Übersetzung sowie Fotos zugänglich gemacht.[35] Auch über die Wissenschaft hinaus erregte der Fund einiges Aufsehen. Inzwischen hat S. Emmel aufgrund von kodikologischen Überlegungen die Anordnung der Blätter gegenüber der Erstedition korrigiert und sie in eine weitaus überzeugendere Abfolge gebracht, die zudem auch inhaltlich einen besser zusammenhängenden Text ergibt.[36] Ebenfalls von Emmel stammt die Identifizierung des „Straßburger Koptischen Papyrus"[37] als Abschrift derselben Schrift.[38]

Ankündigung des Lanzenstichs im UBE hat in der Passionsdarstellung des EvPetr keine genaue Entsprechung. Diese Einwände nennt schon Schenke.

[35] C.W. Hedrick/P.A. Mirecki, Gospel of the Savior. A New Ancient Gospel, Santa Rosa 1999; eine erste deutsche Übersetzung in Schenke, Evangelium, 208-213.

[36] Vgl. S. Emmel, The Recently Published *Gospel of the Savior* („Unbekanntes Berliner Evangelium"): Righting the Order of Pages and Events, HThR 95, 2002, 45-72. Der Aufsatz enthält auch eine neue englische Übersetzung (52-60). Eine deutsche Übersetzung des UBE in der neuen, korrekten Abfolge bei U.-K. Plisch, Verborgene Worte Jesu – verworfene Evangelien. Apokryphe Schriften des frühen Christentums, Brennpunkt: Die Bibel 5, Erfurt 2000, 27-34. Hedrick hat die Rekonstruktion der Erstedition verteidigt (C.W. Hedrick, Caveats to a „Righted Order" of the *Gospel of the Savior*, HThR 96, 2003, 229-238), kann damit aber die in jeder Hinsicht plausible Darlegung von Emmel nicht erschüttern. Vgl. auch U.-K. Plisch, Zu einigen Einleitungsfragen des Unbekannten Berliner Evangeliums (UBE), Vortrag auf der SNTS 2004, erscheint in ZAC. Ich verwende im Folgenden die Seitenzählung nach der Rekonstruktion von Emmel für Verweise auf das UBE. Sie ist durch seine Begründung der Reihenfolge und durch auf zwei der Blätter erhaltene Paginierung gut gesichert. Textzitate folgen, wenn nicht anders angegeben, der Übersetzung von Plisch.

[37] Vgl. W. Schneemelcher, Der Straßburger koptische Papyrus, in: NTApo 1, Tübingen 61990, 87-89.

[38] Vgl. S. Emmel, Unbekanntes Berliner Evangelium = the Strasbourg Coptic Gospel: Prolegomena to a New Edition of the Strasbourg Fragments, in: For the Children, Perfect Instruction, FS Hans-Martin Schenke, NHMS 54, Leiden-Boston 2002, 353-374, hier 353. 364-370. P. Nagel hat diese Identifizierung in Frage gestellt, vgl. idem, „Gespräch Jesu mit seinen Jüngern vor der Auferstehung": Zur Herkunft und Datierung des „Unbekannten Berliner Evangeliums", ZNW 94, 2003, 215-257, hier 217-223. Die Zuordnung ermöglicht die Ergänzung einiger Textlücken im UBE und bietet etwas zusätzlichen Text. Eine Übersetzung sowie den koptischen Text unter Einbeziehung der Straßburger Fragmente bei S. Emmel, Preliminary

Die erhaltenen Seiten des UBE berichten von Gesprächen zwischen Jesus und den JüngerInnen[39] vor der Passion, vermutlich handelt es sich um Abschiedsreden in einem narrativen Evangelium. Im Gespräch kündigt Jesus Passions- und Auferstehungsereignisse an und gibt viele Ermutigungen und Mahnungen. Besonders auffällig ist ein Visionsbericht, der Elemente der Gethsemane-Erzählung enthält – nämlich ein dreifaches Gebet Jesu zum Vater mit der Bitte, der Kelch möge an ihm vorübergehen, was sich aber nicht auf die Passion als Ganze bezieht, sondern auf die Tötung Jesu durch Israel. Dieser Visionsbericht knüpft aber auch an die Verklärung an und beteiligt die JüngerInnen.[40] Weitere Besonderheiten sind ein längeres Responsorium, bei dem die JüngerInnen jeweils mit Amen auf Worte Jesu antworten,[41] sowie eine Rede Jesu an das Kreuz.[42] Das UBE setzt die Existenz mindestens von Joh und Mt in schriftlicher Form voraus,[43] verwendet aber auch nichtkanonisches Spruchgut.[44] Vermutlich ist es ursprünglich auf Griechisch verfasst und in das Ende des 2. Jahrhunderts oder etwas später zu datieren.[45]

Typisch für das UBE ist eine neue Verknüpfung von bekannten Worten, z.B. das von Mk, Mt und im Fayûm-Fragment[46] auf Jesu Passion bezogene Zitat

---

Reedition and Translation of the *Gospel of the Savior*: New Light on the *Strasbourg Coptic Gospel* and the *Stauros-Text* from Nubia, Apocrypha 14, 2003, 9-53. Emmel zieht hier außerdem altnubische Stauros-Texte heran.

[39] Namentlich genannt sind nur Andreas, Johannes und vermutlich Judas. Die Nähe zu Joh spricht aber dafür, dass zur Gruppe auch Jüngerinnen gehörten.

[40] Ausführlicher zu dieser Szene als Entschärfung der Gethsemane-Perikope J. Frey, Leidenskampf und Himmelsreise: das Berliner Evangelienfragment (Papyrus Berolinensis 22220) und die Gethsemane-Tradition, BZ 46, 2002, 71-96.

[41] UBE p. 108,42-53: *Weint von nun an nicht mehr, sondern freut euch doch! – Amen – Ich habe die Welt besiegt. Ihr aber, lasst nicht zu, dass euch die Welt besiegt! – Amen – Ich habe mich von der Welt befreit, und auch ihr, befreit euch von [ihr]! – Amen.*

[42] UBE p. 110,9-26: *Weine [nicht], o [Kreuz], sondern freue dich doch, und erkenne [deinen] Herrn, der [zu] dir kommt ...* (einige Zeilen schlecht erhalten) *... sondern [ich bin] reich, und ich werde [dich] mit meinem Reichtum [erfüllen]. Noch kurze Zeit, o Kreuz, und das Mangelhafte wird sich vervollkommnen, und das Geringe wird sich füllen* (Übersetzung nach der Textergänzung von Emmel, Reedition, 51).

[43] Vgl. Frey, Leidenskampf, 75-76; Emmel, Gospel, 51. Eindeutig ist der Rückgriff auf Joh 19,34-35 in UBE p. 108,59-64: *Man wird mich mit einer Lanze in die Seite stechen. Der es gesehen hat, soll Zeugnis geben. Und sein Zeugnis ist wahr.*

[44] Z.B. den Spruch vom Feuer, Thomasevangelium 82 und etliche andere Belege, vgl. Nagel, Gespräch, 232-234.

[45] Hedrick/Mirecki, Gospel, 23, vermuten eine Abfassung in der zweiten Hälfte des 2. Jahrhunderts. Etwas später datieren Plisch, Worte, 28, und Frey, Leidenskampf, 95: nicht vor Ende des 2. Jahrhunderts. Nagel plädiert dagegen für eine Datierung erst im 5. Jahrhundert und hält das UBE zudem für auf Koptisch verfasst, vgl. idem, Gespräch, 234-248. Eine kritische Auseinandersetzung mit den Argumenten von Nagel bei Plisch, Einleitungsfragen.

[46] Dies könnte ein Fragment des EvPetr sein, so vorsichtig D. Lührmann, Fragmente apokryph gewordener Evangelien in griechischer und lateinischer Sprache, MThSt 59, Marburg 2000, 73-74; anders T.J. Kraus/T. Nicklas, Das Petrusevangelium und die Petrusapokalypse. Die griechischen Fragmente mit deutscher und englischer Übersetzung, GCS.NF 11; Neutestamentliche Apokryphen 1, Berlin-New York 2004, 68.

(Sach 13,7) vom Schlagen des Hirten mit der johanneischen Formulierung vom guten Hirten, der sein Leben für die Schafe lässt (UBE p. 98,47-99,14):

> Steht auf, lasst uns diesen Ort verlassen! Denn genaht hat sich der, der mich verraten wird. Und ihr werdet alle fliehen und euch an mir ärgern. Ihr werdet alle fliehen und mich allein [lassen], aber ich bleibe nicht allein, denn mein Vater ist bei mir. Ich und mein Vater, wir sind ein einziger. Denn es steht geschrieben: ‚Ich werde den Hirten schlagen und (p. 99) die Schafe der Herde werden sich zerstreuen.' Ich aber bin der gute Hirte und werde mein Leben für euch geben. Auch ihr sollt euer Leben geben für eure Freunde, damit ihr meinem Vater wohlgefällig seid, denn es gibt kein größeres Gebot als dieses, dass ich mein Leben ...

Insgesamt wird eine „johanneisierende" Tendenz im UBE deutlich. Außerdem werden an vielen Stellen Ereignisse angesagt, die in anderen Evangelien berichtet werden. So gibt es die Ankündigung einer Erscheinung, für die ein Berühren Jesu vor seinem Aufstieg zum Vater (vgl. Joh 20,17) verboten wird – verbunden mit der Selbstbezeichnung Jesu als Feuer, die dieses Verbot begründet.[47]

b) Beziehungen zum EvPetr

Parallel zum EvPetr ist zunächst die Erzählform: im UBE ist das die erste Person Plural, dieses Wir ist auf p. 101,2-3 einmal als „wir, die Apostel" aufgelöst (vgl. EvPetr 14,59). Andreas und Johannes, eventuell auch Judas, sind namentlich genannt, aber im nicht erhaltenen Text waren das wohl noch weitere Personen – und es ist sowohl ein durchgängiger Wir-Stil denkbar als auch der Wechsel mit einem Ich-Stil ähnlich wie im EvPetr.

Außerdem gibt es einige Übereinstimmungen mit dem EvPetr, an denen beide gemeinsam von anderen Passionsdarstellungen abweichen. So wird im UBE vorausgesetzt, dass Jesus durch das Volk Israel getötet wird (UBE p. 102,4-6; EvPetr 2,5-6; 6,23; 7,25). Außerdem wird ein Abstieg ins Totenreich angekündigt (UBE p. 97,59-63), nach dem in EvPetr 10,41 gefragt wird. Und schließlich ist das Kreuz Jesu in beiden Schriften personifiziert, es tritt als fast lebendige Größe und Gesprächspartner auf.[48] Vor allem angesichts des schlechten Erhaltungszustands beider Schriften – ihr Text überschneidet sich nicht! – sind das bemerkenswert viele Übereinstimmungen. Allerdings handelt es sich jeweils um eine Parallelität von Motiven, nicht um Zitate oder Anlehnungen, die eine Kenntnis des Textes zwingend voraussetzen. Sie sind

---

[47] Es gibt keine ausdrücklich kausale Verbindung zwischen beiden Aussagen, aber die Zusammenstellung ist vermutlich so zu verstehen. UBE p. 107,30-48: *Aber berührt mich ja nicht, bis ich zu meinem Vater aufgestiegen bin, der auch euer Vater ist, und zu [meinem Gott], der auch euer Gott ist, und zu meinem Herrn, der auch euer Herr ist. Wenn aber einer mir zu nahe kommt, wird er verbrennen. Ich bin das lodernde Feuer. Wer [mir nah ist], ist dem Feuer nah. Wer mir fern ist, ist dem Leben fern.*

[48] Im UBE wird es zwar nur angeredet, aber ihm werden auch Gefühle zugesprochen.

alle auch in anderer Überlieferung bekannt, das EvPetr ist also nicht die einzige mögliche Quelle.[49]

Aber ergänzt sich die Aufnahme und Einbettung dieser Motive in den jeweiligen Kontexten, das heißt werden sie tatsächlich in einem ähnlichen Sinn verwendet? Beide Evangelien gehen von einer jüdischen Verantwortung für Jesu Tod aus, aber die Deutung ist durchaus unterschiedlich: Im UBE drückt Jesus schon im Voraus Trauer über diesen Umstand aus, er weint um seine Geliebten (Abraham, Isaak und Jakob) und versucht, diese Tötung durch Israel abzuwenden (p. 102,4-13). Das ist eine völlig andere Stimmung als die Feindseligkeit des jüdischen Volkes in der Kreuzigungsszene im EvPetr, in der Jesus passiv und unbeteiligt ist. Es ist schwer vorstellbar, dass auf die Vorausschau im UBE im selben Evangelium eine Umsetzung ähnlich wie im EvPetr folgte.[50] Verständlich ist die Darstellung im UBE aber als eine Verarbeitung (und Entschärfung) der anstößigen Passagen im EvPetr. Das UBE könnte eine Passionsdarstellung wie im EvPetr voraussetzen,[51] die dann im Gebet Jesu theologisch gedeutet wird, was die Fakten nicht ändert, aber sie in einen größeren Zusammenhang einbindet. Gemeinsam ist in beiden Schriften dabei die hohe emotionale Bedeutung des Ereignisses: Die Art der Darstellung der Kreuzigenden im EvPetr fühlt jedenfalls mit ihnen mit, ob nun identifizierend oder Abscheu auslösend. Es ist nur eine kleine Verschiebung, dieses Mitfühlen auf Jesus zu übertragen.[52]

Auch bei der Rolle des Kreuzes bestehen trotz der grundlegenden Gemeinsamkeit der Personifizierung Unterschiede. Im EvPetr scheint das Kreuz vor allem ein Triumphzeichen bei der Auferstehung zu sein, das die vollständige Überwindung des Todes deutlich macht.[53] Es besteht aber auch eine gewisse Identifizierung mit Jesus, weil es für ihn spricht. Diese Funktion hat das Kreuz aber nur bei der Auferstehung, in der Kreuzigungsszene ist nichts Derartiges angedeutet. Der fehlende bestimmte Artikel in EvPetr 10,39 spricht ebenfalls dafür, dass es vorher keine Ankündigung gab. Im UBE

---

[49] Eine Hadesfahrt ist auch 1Petr 3,19 und Epistula Apostolorum 27 angedeutet, ein personifiziertes und angesprochenes Kreuz findet sich in den Andreas-Akten und eine jüdische Schuld am Tod Jesu in den Petrus-Akten.

[50] Dies ist noch ein Argument gegen eine Zugehörigkeit der Fragmente zu einer Schrift. Es ist aber auch an anderen Stellen im UBE schwierig, sich vorzustellen, wie eine spätere Erzählung die im erhaltenen Text angekündigten Ereignisse konkret ausgestaltete. Denn eigentlich ist das Wichtigste schon vorweggenommen, was bleibt noch zu erzählen?

[51] So auch Frey, Leidenskampf, 84.

[52] Auch an anderen Stellen im UBE lässt sich eine Konzentration auf Jesus beobachten: So verbürgt z.B. in UBE p. 108,61-64 anders als in Joh 19,35 Jesus selbst die Wahrheit des Zeugnisses von dem, der den Lanzenstich gesehen hat. Vgl. dazu Lührmann, Evangelien, 43. Auch die Aussage Jesu über sich als kleines Kind (UBE p. 107,58-60) könnte durch eine solche Konzentration vielleicht auf der Basis von Mt 18,2-5 oder Thomasevangelium 21-22 erklärt werden. Anders aber die Deutung von Nagel, Gespräch, 243-244.

[53] J.D. Crossan, The Cross that Spoke. The Origins of the Passion Narrative, San Francisco et al. 1988, 385-386, hält das Kreuz für die Jesus in Kreuzform folgenden auferweckten Heiligen. Näher liegend ist aber meines Erachtens eine Deutung von der Funktion bei der Parusie in Epistula Apostolorum 16 oder ApkPetr 1 her.

dagegen wird das Kreuz schon vor der Kreuzigung angesprochen. Die Worte Jesu zeigen eine dichte Beziehung und Identifikation und zugleich eine Deutung des Leidens. Die Verbindung mit dem Kreuz erscheint als sehr positiv und erstrebenswert, inhaltlich erinnern die Gedanken an die johanneische Vorstellung von Erhöhung und Verherrlichung Jesu bei der Kreuzigung. Allerdings ist nicht eindeutig, ob alle futurischen Aussagen nur auf die Kreuzigung oder nicht auch auf die Auferstehung vorausweisen. Eine Teilhabe des Kreuzes an der Auferstehung Jesu wäre jedenfalls eine logische Fortsetzung der Ausführungen.

Erneut passt also die Darstellung im EvPetr und UBE nicht ganz genau zusammen, aber wieder könnte das UBE gut eine weiterführende Interpretation sein. Wenn das UBE eine Rolle des Kreuzes bei der Auferweckung voraussetzt, dann ist die erhaltene Rede Jesu an das Kreuz eine vorwegnehmende Thematisierung, so wie auch andere Passionsereignisse im UBE zuvor angekündigt werden. Außerdem liegt wieder eine Konzentration auf Jesus (sein Handeln am Kreuz) vor, auch dies ist typisch. Ein weiteres inhaltliches Anliegen könnte sein, die Kreuzigung im Voraus zu deuten und die Souveränität Jesu bei ihr zu betonen. Ähnlich wie in der Gethsemane-Szene (siehe unten) wird so die Anstößigkeit des Todes Jesu entschärft.

Weitere Parallelen zum EvPetr ergeben sich bei einigen Lückenergänzungen von S. Emmel. So findet sich direkt vor der Ankündigung des Lanzenstiches in UBE p. 108,54-58 eine Ankündigung, dass Jesus zu trinken bekommt – sie ist eindeutig lesbar, das Getränk muss aber teilweise in Textlücken ergänzt werden. Emmel rekonstruiert:

> [I will be] given [vinegar and gall] to drink. But [you], acquire life [and rest for yourselves]! – Amen![54]

Von Galle (χολη) sind noch Buchstabenreste erkennbar, statt Essig ließe sich aber meines Erachtens auch Wein ergänzen – Emmel beruft sich für seine Lückenfüllung auf die koptische (mittelägyptische) Überlieferung von Mt, wo in 27,34 (und in einer Handschrift auch in 27,48) ebenfalls diese Kombination begegnet.[55] Mir scheint aber an dieser Stelle EvPetr 5,16 trotz anderer Wortreihenfolge die nahe stehendste Parallele zu sein, weil die Ankündigung im UBE meiner Meinung nach impliziert, dass Jesus auch trinkt, was Mt 27,34 nicht so ist. Außerdem passt der im EvPetr unmittelbar folgende Tod – möglicherweise sogar ausgelöst durch den Trank – genau zur Fortsetzung in UBE, in der die JüngerInnen Leben empfangen sollen. Auch sonst werden Analogien zwischen dem Schicksal Jesu und dem der JüngerInnen hergestellt, hier wäre die Analogie genau gegenläufig.

Noch an einer anderer Stelle bietet Emmel eine Lückenergänzung, die eine Nähe zum EvPetr herstellt: In UBE p. 100,33-51 sehen die Apostel eine Vision, bei der sich die Himmel öffnen und der Erlöser alle Himmel durchquert. Von

---

[54]   Vgl. Emmel, Gospel, 59; idem, Reedition, 42.
[55]   Vgl. Emmel, Gospel, 59. Auch z.B. im Barnabasbrief 7,3 sind Essig und Galle genannt.

den folgenden Zeilen sind jeweils nur wenige Buchstaben erhalten, Emmel ergänzt:

> [his] feet [placed firmly on] the [mountain with us, his head penetrating the seventh] heaven.[56]

Wenn dies auch nur ungefähr zutreffend sein sollte, dann besteht hier eine Parallele zu EvPetr 10,40, wo Jesus aus dem Grab geführt wird und sein Haupt die Himmel überragt.[57] Die Visionsschilderung des UBE würde dann nicht nur Elemente der Gethsemane-Szene und der Verklärung aufnehmen, sondern auch der Auferstehungsschilderung des EvPetr.[58] Zum Stil des UBE, der häufige zeitliche Verschiebungen von Ereignissen umfasst, würde das gut passen.

Auch wenn die Rekonstruktion der Lücken mit großen Unsicherheiten belastet ist, spricht das Ergebnis doch dafür, mit manchen weiteren motivischen oder sprachlichen Parallelen zwischen dem UBE und dem EvPetr zu rechnen, die sich vielleicht erhärten lassen, wenn weiterer Text in beiden Schriften gesichert werden kann.[59] Beim derzeitigen Stand lässt sich eine klare Bezugnahme auf das EvPetr als Schrift nicht nachweisen, sie ist aber meines Erachtens angesichts der Vielzahl der Berührungen trotz des geringes Textbestandes wahrscheinlich. Die vorliegenden Verbindungen zeigen dann, dass das EvPetr im Ganzen vom UBE in ähnlicher Weise verarbeitet wird wie die kanonischen Evangelien: Motive und möglicherweise auch Formulierungen werden aufgenommen, in neue Zusammenhänge gestellt und so interpretierend verarbeitet. Zudem besteht eine inhaltliche Nähe, so dass die Theologie des EvPetr möglicherweise beinahe so prägend für das UBE war wie die des Joh.

c) Vergleich der Verwendung von Evangelientradition in UBE und EvPetr

Neben diesen direkten Beziehungen ist der Vergleich zwischen UBE und EvPetr noch in einem anderen Punkt interessant. Beide Schriften enthalten viele Einzelheiten, die auch aus anderen Evangelien bekannt sind, aber dort in einem anderen zeitlichen oder sachlichen Zusammenhang stehen. An diesen Stellen wird also sowohl die Verbindung zur Tradition – in welcher Weise auch immer – deutlich als auch die je eigenständige Ausprägung des Stoffes. Meiner Meinung nach ist nun ein vielleicht mehr gradueller als grundsätzlicher

---

56 Vgl. Emmel, Gospel, 54; Reedition, 39. Diese Ergänzung ist durch eine ähnliche Formulierung im Bartholomäusevangelium inspiriert – einer deutlich späteren und vermutlich original koptischen Schrift. Vgl. M. Westerhoff, Auferstehung und Jenseits im koptischen „Buch der Auferstehung Jesu Christi, unseres Herrn", Wiesbaden 1999, 227.

57 Es handelt sich aber nur um eine sachliche, nicht eine wörtliche Parallele.

58 Dazu passt auch das Öffnen der Himmel (UBE p. 100,41-42; EvPetr 9,36; 11,44), das aber auch einfach zu einer Vision gehört.

59 Es wäre z.B. denkbar, dass der Spruch vom Feuer (UBE p. 107,42-48) aus dem EvPetr stammt.

aber doch vorhandener Unterschied zwischen UBE und EvPetr im Verhältnis zur Tradition erkennbar, den ich gerne näher ausführen und dann zur Charakterisierung des EvPetr nutzen will.

Der oben zitierte Abschnitt des UBE über das Schlagen des Hirten erscheint als eine Kompilation von Einzelsätzen, die sich verschiedenen Evangelien zuordnen lassen – insbesondere Mk 14,27 par. und Joh 16,32; 10,14-15.30; 15,13-14.[60] Sie bilden einen zusammenhängenden Text, der die Passion Jesu und das Verhalten der JüngerInnen deutet. Trotzdem ist auffällig, dass die Formulierung sich sprachlich an andere Texte anlehnt, nicht eigene Worte nutzt, und dabei außerdem Abschnitte mit durchaus unterschiedlicher Aussage verbindet. Dieses Verfahren scheint mir nicht nur schriftliche Evangelien vorauszusetzen, sondern auch ihre Anerkennung als maßgeblich. Die Neukombination bestätigt dann ihre Bedeutung, schafft aber zugleich einen neuen Sinn. Ich sehe den Text des UBE als eine Exegese anderer Evangelien, aber ohne dabei die Gattung zu wechseln (und einen Kommentar zu einem Evangelium zu verfassen).

Auch das Gethsemane-Gebet Jesu im Visionsbericht des UBE legt andere Evangeliendarstellungen aus. J. Frey hat gezeigt, dass die theologische Anstößigkeit vor allem der markinischen Fassung der Szene zu verschiedenen Entschärfungen geführt hat und das UBE hier einzuordnen ist.[61] Auffällig ist dabei aber die wörtliche Aufnahme der entscheidenden Stelle, nämlich der Bitte um das Vorübergehen des Kelches.[62] Dieser Satz bleibt bestehen, wird aber ganz anders bezogen als in Mk und außerdem in einen erzählerischen Kontext gestellt, wo das Problem der Niedrigkeit des Gottessohnes vermieden wird. Auch dies lässt sich meines Erachtens deuten als eine Neuinterpretation eines bekannten und maßgeblichen Textes durch eine literarische Verarbeitung.[63]

Zum Vergleich nun einige Beispiele für die besondere Platzierung und Verwendung von Einzelheiten im EvPetr – schon vorab lässt sich feststellen, dass anders als im UBE kaum sprachliche Anlehnungen an andere bekannte Evangelien vorliegen.[64] Das Fragment P.Cair. 10759 beginnt mit der Feststellung, dass sich weder Herodes noch seine Richter die Hände waschen (1,1) – vermutlich war zuvor vom Händewaschen des Pilatus die Rede (vgl.

---

[60] Vgl. T. Nagel, Das „Unbekannte Berliner Evangelium" und das Johannesevangelium, ZNW 93, 2002, 251-267, hier 265.

[61] Vgl. Frey, Leidenskampf, 84-94.

[62] Der koptische Text des UBE entspricht weitgehend – nicht ganz wortgetreu – der sahidischen Übersetzung von Mk 14,36 bzw. Mt 26,39. Die Unterschiede lassen sich meines Erachtens plausibler durch eine unabhängige Übersetzung erklären als durch das Aufgreifen einer einzelnen sahidischen Handschrift und ihrer Fassung von Mt 26,39, wie Nagel vermutet, vgl. idem, Gespräch, 235-236. So auch Plisch, Einleitungsfragen.

[63] Vgl. dagegen Joh 12,27-28, wo vermutlich ebenfalls eine Auseinandersetzung mit der Gethsemane-Tradition vorliegt, aber einfach eine ganz andere Geschichte erzählt wird.

[64] Dies zeigt ein Vergleich der Texte, bei dem auch viele kleine Veränderungen in der Reihenfolge auffallen. Eine Auflistung der längsten Übereinstimmungen bietet P.M. Head, On the Christology of the Gospel of Peter, VigChr 46, 1992, 209-224, hier 220 n. 8.

Mt 27,24). Josef bittet schon vor der Kreuzigung Pilatus um den Leichnam Jesu, wofür dieser sich an Herodes wendet (EvPetr 2,3-4). Es ist das Volk, nicht Soldaten (Mk 15,16-20 par.) oder Herodes (Lk 23,11), das Jesus verspottet. Bei der Kreuzigung ist vom Schweigen Jesu die Rede (EvPetr 4,10) – ein Verhör vor dem Hohen Rat (Mk 14,61 par. Mt 26,63) gehört nicht zum erhaltenen Text.[65] Die Beine nicht zu brechen hat eine Straffunktion (EvPetr 4,14) und das Tränken mit Galle und Essig soll vermutlich als Vergiftung wirken (EvPetr 5,16). Ein Erdbeben entsteht nach der Kreuzabnahme (EvPetr 6,21). Die Soldaten bekennen Jesus nach den Auferstehungsereignissen als Gottes Sohn (EvPetr 11,45), während dies Mk 15,39 par. nach dem Tod Jesu erfolgt. Maria Magdalena und ihre Gefährtinnen fürchten sich vor „den Juden" (EvPetr 12,50) – Joh 20,19 ist es die ganze Gruppe, und zwar zeitlich vor der Erscheinung Jesu.

Die meisten dieser Besonderheiten haben eine erzählerische Funktion. Im EvPetr werden viele beteiligte Personen anders charakterisiert als in den kanonisch gewordenen Evangelien. Die Verantwortung für die Kreuzigung Jesu liegt im EvPetr bei jüdischen Stellen bzw. Herodes und wird zugleich besonders negativ gewertet. Dieser Tendenz lassen sich viele Einzelheiten zuordnen. Auch die Person Jesus ist spezifisch akzentuiert: Die Bedeutung des Leidens für ihn selbst steht nicht im Zentrum des Interesses – er ist weder ein verzweifelter noch ein vorbildlicher oder ein souveräner Leidender. Der Ton scheint eher auf der wunderbaren göttlichen Parteinahme für Jesus zu liegen, die sich vor allem in den Auferstehungsereignissen zeigt.[66] Es ist daher hoch plausibel, z.B. das Bekenntnis dort einzubinden. Wo auch immer das EvPetr die Einzelheiten seiner Darstellung her hat, es erzählt eine eigene Geschichte. Manche Motive werden vielleicht wissentlich anders gedeutet, bei anderen ergibt sich ein neuer Bezug vielleicht einfach aus der Erzähllogik.

Diese Art des Neuerzählens setzt einerseits die Vertrautheit mit zahlreichen Einzelheiten voraus, andererseits eine Unabhängigkeit und Freiheit, die eine eigene Gestaltung des Stoffes ermöglicht. Deshalb lässt sich zwar an vielen Einzelmotiven begründen, ob sie jeweils eine ältere oder jüngere Stufe der Traditionsentwicklung repräsentieren.[67] Auf die ganze Passionserzählung des EvPetr bezogen lässt sich aber nicht eindeutig sagen, dass sie eine interpretierende Fortschreibung anderer Evangelien ist. Gerade im Vergleich mit der Technik des UBE wird deutlich, dass das EvPetr weder eine schon maßgebliche Tradition neu interpretiert noch überwiegend auf literarischer Ebene arbeitet. Es ist gut möglich – und ich halte es auch für wahrscheinlich –, dass das EvPetr viele Einzelheiten seiner Erzählung aus den synoptischen Evangelien und Joh kennt. Aber der Bezug auf diese voraus-

---

65 Vgl. auch das Nichtantworten Jesu gegenüber Herodes (Lk 23,9) und Pilatus (Joh 19,9).
66 Vgl. Head, Christology, 218.
67 Beispielsweise ist die Tendenz zur Entlastung des Pilatus eine spätere Entwicklung, während die Darstellung in Anlehnung an alttestamentliche Formulierungen aber ohne direkten Schriftverweis möglicherweise eher früh ist. Vgl. Koester, Gospels, 217-218.

gehende Tradition ist nicht wie beim UBE ein Bezug auf schon maßgebliche Schriften und ihre Neuinterpretation, sondern die eigenständige Gestaltung eines Entwurfes, der einfach neben anderen stehen kann. Dies ist eher dem Umgang des Joh mit synoptischer Tradition vergleichbar.

4. Beziehungen zwischen Evangelien

Um den Unterschied in der Bezugnahme auf andere Evangelien bzw. Evangelientradition, die ich in UBE und EvPetr erkenne, auf eine etwas breitere Basis zu stellen, will ich weitere Evangelien heranziehen. Dabei interessieren mich zunächst die Aussagen in den Evangelien selbst: In erstaunlich vielen Evangelien wird ausdrücklich über die Beziehung zu anderen reflektiert.

a) Beispiele für ausdrückliche Reflexion von Evangelien über andere

In Lk 1,1 wird erwähnt, dass sich schon viele zuvor an der Abfassung von Berichten, wie auch Lk ihn beabsichtigt, versucht haben. Lk kennt also andere Evangelienliteratur, scheint aber nicht sehr viel von ihr zu halten.[68] Zumindest ist das eigene Evangelium eine sowohl gelungene als auch allein völlig ausreichende Darstellung der Ereignisse (Lk 1,3-4). Diese Selbsteinschätzung deckt sich mit der Art des Erzählens: Lk lässt sich ohne Weiteres lesen und verstehen, ohne ein anderes Evangelium zu kennen. Ein Bezug auf andere Darstellungen ist nicht nötig und eigentlich auch nicht sinnvoll. Faktisch hat die Existenz von Lk zumindest Anteil daran, dass mindestens eines der früheren Evangelien – nämlich Q – nicht mehr weiter überliefert wurde und auch Mk gefährdet war.

Auch Joh 20,30; 21,25 sagt ausdrücklich, dass es noch mehr über Jesus zu berichten gibt. Es wird zwar nicht direkt von vorhandenen Büchern gesprochen, aber der Verweis auf das eigene und die vielen potentiell möglichen Bücher legt eine solche Deutung nahe. Betont wird der Wert der eigenen Darstellung (Joh 20,31; 21,24), aber ohne eine direkte Herabsetzung anderer. Dieses Verhältnis zu anderen Zeugnissen bestätigt sich an vielen Stellen im Text: Es werden oft bestimmte Kenntnisse vorausgesetzt, zu denen sich die eigene Darstellung interpretierend in Beziehung setzt, ohne sie aber aufzuheben.[69]

---

[68] Vgl. die beiden anderen Belege für ἐπιχειρέω in Apg 9,29; 19,13, die jeweils ein vergebliches Bemühen beschreiben.

[69] Vgl. U. Wilckens, Das Evangelium nach Johannes, NTD 4, Göttingen [17]1998, 4-5. Klar im Text greifbar ist beispielsweise die Einführung von Maria von Betanien in Joh 11,1-2. Die Person wird ebenso als bekannt vorausgesetzt wie die Salbungsgeschichte, aber beide werden aufeinander bezogen.

Im Thomasevangelium sind laut Aussage des *Incipit* die geheimen (apokryphen) Worte Jesu niedergeschrieben. Diese Qualifizierung des Inhalts könnte implizieren, dass das Thomasevangelium auch nichtgeheime Worte Jesu kennt, sei es schriftlich, sei es mündlich.[70] Der eigenen Schrift gilt hohe Wertschätzung, die Worte in ihr führen zum Leben – wenn sie richtig gedeutet werden (Thomasevangelium 1). In einigen wenigen Sprüchen findet eine ausdrückliche Auseinandersetzung mit anderen Positionen statt,[71] die meisten sind sich selbst genug. Dieser Befund lässt sich meines Erachtens am besten so verstehen, dass das Thomasevangelium von anderer, inhaltlich divergenter Jesusüberlieferung weiß, aber in erster Linie die eigene Position darstellt, weniger Interesse an Abgrenzung hat. Die vorhandenen Hinweise sprechen jeweils von mündlicher Lehre, es gibt keine Verweise auf andere Bücher – dies ist ein Indiz für einen Bezug auf mündliche Traditionen.[72]

Im Brief des Petrus an Philippus (NHC VIII,2) sagt der gerade erschienene Jesus auf Fragen der Apostel hin zunächst:

> Ihr selbst seid es, die bezeugen können, dass ich euch all das (bereits) gesagt habe. Aber wegen eures Unglaubens werde ich es noch einmal sagen! (p. 135,4-8)

Auch wenn dies ein Redebeitrag innerhalb der Erzählung, kein Kommentar der Erzählstimme über die Bedeutung des eigenen Werkes ist, so ist es doch ein Hinweis auf frühere Zeugnisse der Apostel. Hier könnten also andere Evangelien im Blick sein.[73] Der Brief des Petrus an Philippus sieht sich selbst dann als eine einfache Wiederholung, das heißt vorausgehende Evangelien werden anerkannt und zur Legitimation der eigenen Lehre genutzt. Die folgenden Ausführungen Jesu entsprechen dann aber keineswegs dem, was aus anderen Schriften über ihn bekannt ist – dargelegt werden gnostisch-mythologische Vorstellungen. Diese inhaltliche Spannung macht die erste

---

[70] Im apokryphen Jakobusbrief werden in der Rahmenerzählung ausdrücklich sowohl die verborgenen als auch die öffentlichen Worte Jesu als Grundlage der Bücher der Jünger erwähnt (NHC I p. 2,10-14). Vgl. auch E. Rau, Jenseits von Raum, Zeit und Gemeinschaft. „Christ-Sein" nach dem Thomasevangelium, NT 45, 2003, 138-159, hier 140-141, mit weiteren Indizien, dass das Thomasevangelium andere Jesusüberlieferung voraussetzt.

[71] Im Thomasevangelium Kapitel 3 werden Positionen zum Ort des Reiches Gottes widerlegt, die ausdrücklich als Aussagen derjenigen „die euch vorangehen" (eventuell Führungs- oder Amtspersonen?) gekennzeichnet sind. Auch im Thomasevangelium Kapitel 13 spiegelt sich in den verschiedenen Antworten von Jüngern (erst Petrus und Matthäus, dann Thomas) zur Beschreibung Jesu möglicherweise ein Meinungsstreit. Vgl. dazu Lührmann, Evangelien, 45-46, der dies als Auseinandersetzung mit Mt versteht. Auch Rau, Jenseits von Raum, 147, sieht hier eine Auseinandersetzung mit anderer Jesusüberlieferung (aber keinen Bezug auf ein konkretes Evangelium). Im Thomasevangelium Kapitel 92 wird eine aktuelle umfassende Lehre Jesu einer früheren unvollständigen gegenübergestellt – auch dies lässt sich auf verschiedene Traditionen beziehen (aber auch anders deuten).

[72] Vor allem im Vergleich mit Lk und Joh, wo Hinweise auf andere Schriften vorliegen. Es ist aber nicht ausgeschlossen, dass das Thomasevangelium sich auf Lehre bezieht, die in schriftlicher Form bekannt war.

[73] Zumal eine Kenntnis anderer Evangelien wahrscheinlich ist. Die Bemerkung könnte sich aber auch auf mündliche Tradition/Predigt der Apostel beziehen.

Behauptung um so interessanter, denn sie drückt eine Beziehung und Wertschätzung aus, die vom Inhalt her gar nicht nahe liegt.[74]

Im apokryphen Jakobusbrief (NHC I,2) wird in der Rahmenerzählung von den Zwölf berichtet, die die ihnen jeweils bekannten Worte Jesu zu Büchern ordnen (NHC I p. 2,10-15). In diese Situation hinein erscheint Jesus und gibt weitere Belehrungen nur an Jakobus und Petrus, die Jakobus später als entscheidende Offenbarung aufschreibt, wie er im Prolog erläutert. Hier werden also eindeutig Evangelien vorausgesetzt, aber anders als im Brief des Petrus an Philippus werden sie als unvollkommen abgewertet, da sie die entscheidende Belehrung noch nicht enthalten.[75]

Auch im Evangelium der Maria gibt es einen, allerdings indirekten, Hinweis auf andere Evangelientradition: Nachdem Maria ausführlich von ihr bekannten Worten Jesu berichtet hat, wendet Andreas ein, er glaube nicht, dass der Erlöser dies gesagt habe, denn diese Lehren seien „andere Gedanken" (Evangelium der Maria (BG p. 17,13-15)). Dem folgt ein weiterer Einwand von Petrus und die Verteidigung der Worte durch Maria und Levi. Das Argument des Andreas setzt voraus, dass bekannt ist, was Jesus gesagt hat. „Neue" Worte müssen sich an dieser Basis messen lassen – und das scheint für das Evangelium der Maria und seine Lehre nicht ganz einfach gewesen zu sein, wie der apologetische Aufwand zugunsten von Maria zeigt.[76] Zu dieser Anerkennung von dem, was Jesus gesagt hat, passt auch ein Stück im Evangelium der Maria, in dem ähnlich wie im UBE Sätze aus anderen Evangelien miteinander zu einem neuen Sinn verbunden werden.[77]

b) Auswertung: Unterschiedliche Bezugnahmen auf andere Evangelien

Dieser knappe Überblick zeigt zunächst, wie viele Evangelien ausdrücklich oder implizit auf andere Evangelien verweisen.[78] Dies gilt schon für eine

---

[74] Wie dies doch möglich ist, zeigt etwa die (gnostische) Deutung der Passion Jesu in einer Rede des Petrus (Brief des Petrus an Philippus (NHC VIII p. 139,15-28)), vgl. Hartenstein, Lehre, 178.

[75] Im Prolog ist ausdrücklich betont, dass die Lehre des apokryphen Jakobusbriefes eben nicht allen zwölf anvertraut wurde. Vgl. auch Hartenstein, Lehre, 242-243.

[76] Allerdings wird auf den Einwand des Andreas gar nicht näher eingegangen, die Argumentation konzentriert sich auf den leichter zu entkräftenden Angriff des Petrus auf Maria. Vgl. Hartenstein, Lehre, 134. 149-151.

[77] Evangelium der Maria (BG p. 8,14-9,4): *Friede sei mit euch. Bringt euch meinen Frieden hervor. Passt auf, dass niemand euch irreführt, indem er sagt: „Siehe hier" oder „siehe da". Denn in eurem Innern ist der Menschensohn. Folgt ihm nach! Die nach ihm suchen, werden ihn finden. Geht also und predigt das Evangelium vom Reich! Erlasst keine Regel neben dem, was ich euch angeordnet habe, und gebt auch kein Gesetz wie der Gesetzgeber, damit ihr nicht in ihm ergriffen werdet.*

[78] Aber auch in Evangelien ohne ausdrückliche Reflexion über den Bezug zu anderen lässt sich mitunter eine Kenntnis anderer Schriften auf anderem Wege belegen (Mt). Eine genaue Analyse kann auch dann eine Auseinandersetzung mit anderer Evangelienliteratur (oder mündlicher Tradition) aufzeigen, wenn sie nur implizit erfolgt. Dies ist für Mt im Vergleich mit Mk und Q einfach. Aber auch in Mk lässt z.B. das Jüngerunverständnis gegenüber dem Leiden

frühere Zeit (Lk, Joh, Thomasevangelium) und sowohl für kanonische wie für nichtkanonische Schriften. Es besteht ein breites Bewusstsein dafür, dass es auch andere Versuche und andere Möglichkeiten gibt, über den irdischen Jesus zu berichten. Dieser Traditionskontext kann explizit schriftlich, aber eventuell auch nur mündlich sein. Die geäußerte Beziehung eines Evangeliums zu den anderen kann dabei eine sehr unterschiedliche Ausrichtung haben. Ich sehe als Tendenzen: Überbietung – gleichberechtigtes abgrenzendes, ergänzendes oder dialogisches Nebeneinander – Aufbau auf vorhandene Grundlage. Zum ausdrücklich geäußerten Bezug gehört auch jeweils ein entsprechender Umgang mit bzw. Verarbeitung von vorausgehender Tradition.

Die erste Tendenz, nämlich die zur Überbietung, sehe ich in Lk. Nach eigener Aussage wird das Wichtigste aus den Vorgängern aufgenommen – das heißt andere Schriften werden so aufgehoben im doppelten Sinn des Wortes, sie sind im Stoff vorhanden, aber werden als eigene Schriften überflüssig.[79] Dazu passt die über weite Strecken wörtliche Aufnahme von anderen Schriften. Diese Form des Bezugs auf andere Evangelien setzt voraus, dass die Vorgänger noch nicht weit verbreitet und anerkannt sind, funktioniert also vor allem in der Frühzeit der Evangelienliteratur oder bei eher regional verbreiteten Evangelien.

Die zweite Tendenz bedeutet das gleichberechtigte Nebeneinander verschiedener Evangelien, die weder völlig aufgenommen werden können noch einen Maßstab für die Darstellung bilden, auch wenn Informationen aus anderen Evangelien stammen. Es gibt also je eigene Darstellungen der wichtigen Dinge – zu anderen Evangelien ist sowohl eine Abgrenzung möglich als auch eine positive dialogische Bezogenheit. Abgrenzend wirkt z.B. das Thomasevangelium, das anderen Schriften keine eigene Relevanz zuzusprechen scheint. Joh dagegen scheint andere Tradition (oder vorhandene Evangelien) eher durch zusätzlichen Stoff oder eine neue Sicht bereichern zu wollen, das heißt es lässt sich gut neben und im Dialog mit diesen lesen, bietet aber trotzdem eine ganz eigene Perspektive. Bei diesen Arten von Nebeneinander ist keine wörtliche Übernahme zu erwarten, sondern eher eigene Traditionen, Variationen von Erzählungen und Eigenständigkeit in der Darstellung. Typisch ist aber auch die Notwendigkeit, das eigene Evangelium in der Konkurrenz zu behaupten und zu legitimieren, etwa durch die Berufung auf ZeugInnen.

Schließlich ist als dritter Weg der Aufbau auf andere, schon anerkannte Schriften möglich wie im Brief des Petrus an Philippus und im Evangelium der Maria. Andere Evangelienliteratur wird als existent und wichtig vorausgesetzt, zu ihr muss sich das eigene Evangelium in Beziehung setzen. Eine Weiterentwicklung und Neuinterpretation ist dabei durch eine literarische Verarbeitung des vorhandenen Stoffs möglich, aber auch durch zusätzliches

---

Jesu vermuten, dass hier eine andere Sicht und Deutung des Geschicks Jesu vorausgesetzt, aber nicht übernommen wird.

[79] Vgl. Lührmann, Evangelien, 30.

Material[80] oder eine neue Perspektive. Auch eine deutliche Abwertung wie im apokryphen Jakobusbrief ist möglich.

Diese Tendenzen der Beziehung eines Evangeliums auf andere lassen sich ansatzweise auch zeitlich ordnen: Ein gleichberechtigtes Nebeneinander setzt voraus, dass es schon anerkannte Evangelien gibt. Ein Aufnehmen und Verdrängen ist dann nicht mehr möglich. Wenn die Bedeutung der vorhandenen Evangelien noch größer geworden ist, dann ist für eine neue Schrift eine ausdrückliche Auseinandersetzung mit ihnen nötig. Aber die Übergänge sind sicher fließend und auch durch das jeweilige Anliegen eines Evangeliums, sein Interesse an Abgrenzung und Anknüpfung bestimmt. Einen noch weiteren Schritt bedeutet es, vorhandene Evangelium als kanonisch, als heilige Schrift anzusehen – und dies schließt die Abfassung von neuen Evangelien als heilsvermittelnden Schriften eigentlich aus. Möglich ist dann die Auslegung der schon vorhandenen.

Wenn diese Tendenzen des Umgangs von Evangelien miteinander ungefähr zutreffen, dann ist leicht verständlich, wieso bei vielen Evangelien der Nachweis von literarischer Abhängigkeit so schwer zu führen ist. Wörtliche Übereinstimmungen sind nämlich nur im ersten und im dritten Fall zu erwarten. Bei einem abgrenzenden oder dialogischen Nebeneinander mit anderen Evangelien ist die sprachliche Anlehnung sachlich nicht sinnvoll. Hier lässt sich zwar oft sagen, dass ein Bezug auf andere Evangelientradition vorliegt, aber eben nicht, um welche Evangelien es sich genau handeln könnte.

Nur fragmentarisch erhaltene Schriften hier einzuordnen ist schwierig, weil insgesamt weniger Text zur Verfügung steht und außerdem möglicherweise eine besonders relevante Selbstreflexion nicht erhalten ist. Trotzdem lässt sich vermuten, dass das UBE der dritten Gruppe zuzuordnen ist. Dafür spricht, dass im Evangelium der Maria eine ganz ähnliche Technik der Verbindung von bekannten Sätzen aus Evangelien erfolgt.

Das EvPetr lässt sich als ein Evangelium, gleichberechtigt unter anderen, beschreiben. Es ist auf andere erhaltene Evangelien weder so bezogen, dass es sie weitgehend aufnimmt,[81] noch setzt es sie als maßgebliche Grundlage voraus. Vielmehr bietet es einen eigenen Entwurf, der neben anderen steht – und die Berufung auf Petrus hilft dabei auch zur Legitimation. Mit allem Vorbehalt wegen der schmalen Textbasis sehe ich eher eine Nähe zum Thomasevangelium und seiner abgrenzenden Tendenz – das EvPetr könnte sich gut als „die wahre Geschichte vom Wirken, Leiden und Auferstehen des Herrn, wie Petrus sie erlebt hat," angesehen haben. Jedenfalls scheint nicht unbedingt nötig zu sein, neben ihm noch weitere Evangelien zu lesen. Joh strahlt demgegenüber eine etwas positivere Bezugnahme aus. Für alle drei Evangelien gilt jedoch, dass sie die Bedeutung und Legitimität ihrer Darstellung ausdrücklich rechtfertigen. Sie alle stehen in Konkurrenz zu

---

[80] Möglicherweise sind die Kindheitsevangelien hier einzuordnen, die den vorausgesetzten Stoff anderer Evangelien ergänzen.

[81] Denkbar ist ein solches Verhältnis aber gegenüber einem nicht bekannten Evangelium!

anderen Evangelientraditionen und müssen sich in ihr zumindest ansatzweise behaupten, z.B. durch die Berufung auf einen wichtigen Zeugen. Für Lk und Mt gilt das nicht in gleicher Weise.

Diese Sicht des EvPetr deutet die Gemeinsamkeiten und Unterschiede mit anderen Evangelien nicht primär als Hinweis auf die Kenntnis von Schriften oder anderer Tradition in dieser oder jener Form. Entscheidend ist vielmehr die eigene Absicht des EvPetr, das sicher Beziehungen zu anderer Evangelienliteratur hat, aber vor allem ein autonomer Entwurf ist. Das EvPetr erzählt eine eigene Geschichte – dass es von anderen weiß, machen die vielen auch sonst bekannten Einzelheiten wahrscheinlich, und die Berufung auf Petrus ist ein Indiz für eine Behauptung in Konkurrenz. Aber warum dann dieser neue Entwurf? Mir scheint hinter dem EvPetr vor allem eine Konflikt- oder Bedrängnissituation deutlich zu werden. Sie spiegelt sich in der emotionalen Charakterisierung von verschiedenen Personen und Gruppen – Trauer und Furcht der JüngerInnen, Feindseligkeit von jüdischem Volk und Führung, Umkehr des Volkes – ohne dass sich eine ganz konkrete Zuordnung anbietet. Sie zeigt sich aber auch in der Absicherung der wichtigen Punkte: die Zeichen und Sichtbarkeit der Auferstehung und ihre Verbürgung durch GegnerInnen. Die Berufung auf Petrus ist auch nach innen eine Absicherung und Verbürgung des Erzählten.

Das Petrusevangelium und die spätere großkirchliche Literatur

von

MARTIN MEISER

In der Einschätzung der Wirkungsgeschichte *des Textes* P.Cair. 10759 (im Folgenden der Kürze halber ohne Rücksicht auf die Zuordnung anderer Fragmente „Petrusevangelium" genannt), messbar an Parallelen und literarischen Berührungen, ist die anfängliche Entdeckerfreude[1] bereits in dem Beitrag von A. Stülcken in der ersten Auflage der von E. Hennecke herausgegebenen „Neutestamentlichen Apokryphen",[2] vor allem dann aber in den Arbeiten von L. Vaganay, O. Perler, M.G. Mara und J. Denker[3] einer tief greifenden Zurückhaltung gewichen.[4] Auch dieser Aufsatz wird trotz einer möglichen Analogie zu EvPetr XI 45 bei Kyrill von Alexandrien[5] keinen Anlass zu einer veränderten Einschätzung geben. Eher bleibt zu fragen, wie dieser nicht nur für das Petrusevangelium gültige Befund zu interpretieren ist und ob

---

[1] Vgl. etwa A. Harnack, Bruchstücke des Evangeliums und der Apokalypse des Petrus, TU 9.2, Leipzig 1893, 59-60; A. Hilgenfeld, Das Petrusevangelium über Leiden und Auferstehung, ZWissTh 36, 1893, I 439-454; II 220-267, hier 232. 256; H.B. Swete, Εὐαγγέλιον κατὰ Πέτρον. The Akhmîm Fragment of the Apocryphal Gospel of St Peter. Edited with an Introduction, Notes and Indices, London 1893, 31.

[2] „Die angeblichen Benutzungen bei Tatian, Justin, ja im Barnabasbrief, bei Papias, Ignatius und gar in der Didache sind ausnahmslos preiszugeben" (in: E. Hennecke, Neutestamentliche Apokryphen in Verbindung mit Fachgelehrten in deutscher Übersetzung und mit Einleitungen herausgegeben, 1. Aufl. Tübingen 1909, 29).

[3] L. Vaganay, L'Évangile de Pierre, ÉtB, Paris 1930, 163-176; O. Perler, L'Évangile de Pierre et Méliton de Sardes, RB 71, 1964, 584-590; M.G. Mara, Évangile de Pierre, SC 201, Paris 1973, 20-24; J. Denker, Die theologiegeschichtliche Stellung des Petrusevangeliums. Ein Beitrag zur Frühgeschichte des Doketismus, EHS XXIII/36, Bern-Frankfurt/Main 1975, 9-31, sowie M.G. Mara, Il Vangelo di Pietro, Bologna 2003, 18-19.

[4] So schon Vaganay, L'Évangile de Pierre, 164.

[5] Kyrill von Alexandrien beschreibt zu Sach 12,10 Jesu Geschick nach Tod und Hadesfahrt: ἀνεβίω τε αὖ, σεισμοῦ γενομένου, παρὰ τὸ μνημεῖον οἱ προσεδεύοντες ἐθαύμαζον, λέγοντες· Ἀληθῶς υἱὸς θεοῦ ἦν οὗτος· πολλὴ δὲ παρὰ πολλοῖς ἡ μετάγνωσις ἦν (Kyrill von Alexandrien, *Zach.* 5, PG 72, 224 B). Der Wortlaut des Bekenntnisses stammt aus Mt 27,54 B D; die Akoluthie der Aussagen kommt EvPetr XI 45 nahe. Es fiele freilich leichter, diese Stelle bei Kyrill als unmittelbaren Niederschlag von EvPetr XI 45 oder einer analogen Erzähltradition zu werten, wenn nicht auch sonst gelegentlich bei Kyrill Verwechslungsfehler zu beobachten wären: Die Verspottung Jesu durch die römischen Soldaten lässt Kyrill begleitet sein durch die Aufforderung „Weissage uns, Christus: Wer ist es, der dich schlug?" (Kyrill von Alexandrien, *Is.* 5/1, PG 70, 1173 A).

das bekannte Negativurteil Serapions als der einzige Grund dafür angesehen werden muss.

Zwar sollte die Mahnung im Bewusstsein bleiben, das Studium der Wirkungsgeschichte apokryph gewordener Werke nicht unter der Voraussetzung der Höherwertigkeit der kanonischen christlichen Schriften zu betreiben.[6] Vielleicht noch ernster zu nehmen ist das methodische Bedenken, dass ein literarkritisch allzu strenges Maß ungewollt unser notwendig zurückhaltendes Urteil zu einer vermeintlichen Gewissheit über den minimalen Einfluss eines in Frage stehenden Werkes verfälschen kann. Die richtige Erkenntnis, dass ein Einfluss etwa des Petrusevangeliums auf andere Literatur in vielen Fällen nicht zweifelsfrei nachweisbar ist, darf nicht als stringenter Beweis dafür gewertet werden, dass es diesen in Frage stehenden Einfluss nicht gegeben *hat*. Antike Autoren, auch christliche antike Autoren, pflegen die Quellen ihrer Behauptungen nur nach Belieben zu nennen. Dass ein Erzählzug unterschiedlich begründet werden,[7] in einem anderen Kontext begegnen[8] oder unterschiedlichen Zwecken dienen kann, schließt nicht von vornherein die literarische Bekanntschaft aus. Auch kann man, wie der Vergleich zwischen P.Cair. 10759 und P.Oxy. 2949 zeigt, nicht davon ausgehen, in P.Cair. 10759 den „Urtext" dessen vor sich zu haben, was bei Kirchenschriftstellern des dritten und vierten Jahrhunderts als „Petrusevangelium" bekannt ist.[9] Ferner ist davon auszugehen, dass die Masse der uns heute vorliegenden Quellen immer noch ein wohl einseitiges Bild dessen bietet, was früher tatsächlich von Bedeutung war. Vermutlich war die sich in P.Cair. 10759 sowie in dem von D. Lührmann in die Diskussion eingebrachten Ostrakon *van Haelst* 741[10] aussprechende Wertschätzung des Petrus als Evangelisten in Kreisen zu Hause, die in dem uns zur Verfügung stehenden Quellenmaterial unterrepräsentiert sind, und noch die folgende Aufstellung lässt erkennen, dass eine mögliche Nachwirkung des Petrusevangeliums in volkstümlicher Literatur auch noch für einen späteren Zeitraum diskutabel ist, während sich andere Textsorten und Texte für andere Schichten von dem Gattungsmodell schon verabschiedet haben. Trotz dieser methodischen Vorbehalte ist es jedoch zweifellos richtig, von „spärlichen Spuren"[11] des Petrusevangeliums in der altkirchlichen Literatur zu sprechen, denn die eben genannten generellen Bedenken gegen eine zu große Sicherheit im Negativurteil ersetzen nicht den geforderten positiven Nachweis im Einzelfall.

---

[6]   So Mara, Évangile de Pierre, 25-26, zu Vaganay.

[7]   Denker, Stellung, 16.

[8]   Vaganay, L'Évangile de Pierre, 167.

[9]   Vgl. auch den Beitrag von P. van Minnen im vorliegenden Band.

[10]   Vgl. D. Lührmann, Die apokryph gewordenen Evangelien. Studien zu neuen Texten und zu neuen Fragen, NT.S 112, Leiden 2004, 90-98. Kritisch hierzu allerdings T.J. Kraus, Petrus und das Ostrakon *van Haelst* 741, ZAC 7, 2003, 203-211. Vgl. auch Lührmanns Beitrag im vorliegenden Band.

[11]   T. Nicklas, Ein „neutestamentliches Apokryphon"? Zum umstrittenen Kanonbezug des sog. „Petrusevangeliums", VigChr 56, 2002, 260-272, hier 268.

Zunächst gilt es, sich Bekanntes zu vergegenwärtigen; Vollständigkeit wird dabei nicht erstrebt. Festzuhalten sind für das zweite Jahrhundert Berührungen mit dem Barnabasbrief[12] sowie mit Justin (?) und Meliton von Sardes,[13] für das dritte Jahrhundert mögliche Berührungen mit Origenes,[14] Tertullian,[15] Cyprian,[16] Pseudo-Cyprian[17] und der Himmelfahrt des Jesaja,[18] für das vierte Jahrhundert Berührungen mit der syrischen Didaskalia[19] und dem syrischen

---

[12] Auffällig ist die gleichlautende Wendung χολὴν μετὰ ὄξους in Barn 7,5 und EvPetr V 16 als Kontraktion aus Ps 69 (68),22, doch rechne ich eher mit Analogien der Formulierung als mit literarkritischer Abhängigkeit. Barn 7,5 wie EvPetr V 16 setzen voraus, dass Jesus gegen den Willen die Galle getrunken habe. Barn 5,14 und Barn 6,7 belegen, dass Jes 50,6 sowie Jes 3,9-10 schon bald auf Christi Passion bezogen wurden, und zeigen, dass EvPetr III 8-9 und EvPetr VII 25 erzählerisch umsetzen, was andernorts mit der Technik des Schriftbeweises bewältigt wird. Auch in EvPetr II 9 kann wie in Barn 7,8 auf Jes 50,6 als Voraussage der Bespeiung Jesu zurückgegriffen sein. Andere diskutierte Analogien sind nicht gegeben: Das „zu Fall kommen" wird in EvPetr V 18 wörtlich, in Barn 12,5 übertragen verstanden, die Übeltäter von Barn 5,13 (vgl. dazu Ps 22 [21],17) sind nicht die Übeltäter von EvPetr IV 13.

[13] Zu den Berührungen des Petrusevangeliums mit Justin und Meliton vgl. auch die Beiträge von K. Greschat und T.J. Karmann im vorliegenden Band.

[14] Zu erwähnen sind vor allem Parallelen zu EvPetr I 1 bei Origenes, comm. in Mt. Ser. 124, GCS 38, 259 (Juden waschen sich nicht die Hände) und zu EvPetr IV 10b in dem Satz Et in his omnibus unigenita virtus nocita non est, sicut nec passa est aliquid (Origenes, comm. in Mt. Ser. 125, GCS 38, 262, der den Satz aber auf die Verspottungsszene bezieht). Zu weiteren Fällen möglicher Berührungen bei Origenes und bei Dionysios von Alexandrien vgl. Denker, Stellung, 15-16. Allerdings schließt die ungenaue Angabe bei Origenes, comm. in Mt. 10,17, GCS 40, 21 („sich auf die Überlieferung des Petrusevangeliums oder des Jakobusbuches stützend") die unmittelbare Kenntnis des Petrusevangeliums durch den Alexandriner wohl eher aus, Denker, Stellung, 14, verweist auf die Strittigkeit der exklusiven oder inklusiven Deutung der Partikel ἤ.

[15] Vgl. Tertullian, resurr. 20,5, CC.SL 2, 945: Herodes Antipas gilt als der Hauptverantwortliche für die Kreuzigung Jesu, und Jesu Tränkung soll ihm Qualen bereiten.

[16] Auch nach Cyprian, patient. 7, CC.SL 3 A, 122, soll die Tränkung Jesu diesem Qualen bereiten.

[17] Zu EvPetr I 1; VII 26; VI 21.23 (in dieser Reihenfolge!) ist Ps.-Cyprian, adv. Iud. 4, CSEL 3/3, 137 zu vergleichen: plebs autem nec alienum nec exterum imitata est (das Beispiel des Pilatus, die Hände zu waschen) ... lugebant apostoli, et populus gloriabat: tremebat terra, et plebs laetabatur.

[18] In AscJes 3,16-17 wird erzählt, dass „der Engel des Hl. Geistes und Michael, der Oberste der Engel, am dritten Tage sein Grab öffnen werden und daß der Geliebte, auf ihren Schultern sitzend, hervortreten und seine zwölf Jünger aussenden wird". Denker, Stellung, 22, rechnet nicht mit einer unmittelbaren literarischen Abhängigkeit, sondern mit dem voneinander unabhängigen Rückgriff auf eine Wächtererzählung, wie sie auch in Mt 28 herangezogen wird. – In rhetorischer Übersteigerung wird den Juden bei (Ps.?-)Leo, serm. 9,4, PL 54, 498 C beschieden: In vanum dumtaxat vigilatis ad sepulcrum nocturnum. Natürlich ist daraus ebenso wenig eine Kenntnis des Petrusevangeliums abzuleiten wie aus der Vorstellung bei Ps.-Augustin, serm. 155,9-11, PL 39, 2051-2052, am Jüngsten Tag werde Christus mit dem Kreuz erscheinen ut ostendat quoniam ipse est qui crucifixus est (serm. 155,11, PL 39, 2052).

[19] Mit EvPetr I 2 teilt Didasc. 21 die Vorstellung, Herodes Antipas habe den Befehl zur Kreuzigung gegeben (vgl. dazu noch den Dialog des Adamantius 5,1; aus dem 6. Jahrhundert (vielleicht) Act Andr et Matth 26, p. 105,3). Mit EvPetr X 41 teilt Didasc. 26 die Vorstellung vom descensus ad inferos, wie EvPetr V 15 wird in Didasc. 26 Dtn 21,22-23 betont. Wie EvPetr 18 werden die drei Stunden der Finsternis als Nacht gerechnet (Didasc. 21). Wie EvPetr 35 wird die Auferstehung in der Nacht zum Sonntag vorausgesetzt (Didasc. 21) und wie in EvPetr 17 wird vom Vollenden der Übeltat gesprochen. Didasc. 21 und EvPetr 16 nennen eine Erscheinung (auch) vor Levi (vgl. dazu auch das Evangelium der Maria, BG 8502); in EvPetr 60 ist er aber Teil einer Gruppe von Jüngern, denen der Herr, vermutlich am See, erscheint, nicht allein und im Haus.

Evangelientext,[20] mit dem „Unbekannten Berliner Evangelium" (PBerol. 22220)[21] sowie mit den Johannesakten[22] und den Pilatusakten,[23] ferner Berührungen mit der manichäischen Literatur,[24] so dass J. Denkers Verortung des Petrusevangeliums „in einem breiten Strom westsyrischer Evangelienüberlieferung"[25] das Richtige treffen wird. Mit dem Begriff „Berührungen" soll dabei lediglich auf ähnliche Formulierungen hingewiesen, aber kein literarkritisches Urteil insinuiert werden. Die vor allem in älterer Literatur behaupteten Parallelen zu Ignatius von Antiochien[26] und Polykarp[27] halte ich für nicht gegeben, die Analogien mit Kyrill von Jerusalem[28] oder Aphrahat[29]

---

20 Belege bei Denker, Stellung, 26-29.

21 H.-J. Klauck, Apokryphe Evangelien. Eine Einführung, Stuttgart 2000, 48. Vgl. hierzu auch den Beitrag von J. Hartenstein im vorliegenden Band.

22 Zu EvPetr III 9 (Stechen mit dem Rohr) vgl. ActJoh 97. Zu Berührungspunkten zwischen EvPetr und apokryphen Apostelakten vgl. auch den Beitrag von I. Czachesz in diesem Band.

23 Nach EvPetr III 8 sowie ActPil A 10,1 wird die Dornenkrone Jesus erst an der Stätte der Kreuzigung aufgesetzt (W. Bauer, Das Leben Jesu im Zeitalter der neutestamentlichen Apokryphen, Tübingen 1909, 203-204). Denker, Stellung, 24-25, vermutet nur bei der jüngeren Rezension der Pilatusakten eine Abhängigkeit vom Petrusevangelium.

24 Vgl. W. Sundermann, Christliche Evangelientexte in der Überlieferung der iranisch-manichäischen Literatur, MIO 14, 1968, 386-405, hier 344-399; Denker, Stellung, 29-30; H.-Ch. Puech/W. Schneemelcher, in: NtApo 1, Evangelien, Tübingen ⁵1987, 320-329; H.-J. Klimkeit, Hymnen und Gebete der Religion des Lichts. Iranische und türkische liturgische Texte der Manichäer Zentralasiens, eingeleitet und aus dem Mittelpersischen, Parthischen, Sogdischen und Uigurischen (Alttürkischen) übersetzt, Abhandlungen der Rheinisch-Westfälischen Akademie der Wissenschaften 79, Opladen 1989, 109. 115 (Parallelen zu EvPetr XI 4-48 bzw. zu EvPetr III 7-9). Zu verweisen ist auch auf die Anordnung des Lanzenstichmotivs innerhalb der Verspottungsszene in dem bei C.R.C. Allberry, A Manichaean Psalm-Book. Part II, Stuttgart 1938, 193,13-197,8 gebotenen Hymnus aus der Sammlung der „Psalmen des Herakleides", hier 196,7, sowie auf das Motiv der Tränkung mit Galle und des Lanzenstichs (am Kreuz, aber noch vor dem Tod) in dem manichäischen „Teil der Erzählung von der Kreuzigung" bei H.J. Polotsky (Hg.), Manichäische Homilien 1, Stuttgart 1934, 42-85, hier 68, Z. 27-29. Zur Rolle der Passionsgeschichte bei den Manichäern vgl. auch M. Tardieu, Le procès de Jésus vu par les Manichéens, Apocrypha 8, 1997, 9-24.

25 Denker, Stellung, 30.

26 Harnack, Bruchstücke, hatte zwischen Ignatius, *Smyrn*. 3,2 und EvPetr 60 eine Parallele vermutet. Mara, Évangile de Pierre, 21 n. 1, bemerkt dazu: „La ressemblance vue par Harnack ... est très douteuse."

27 Zwischen *EpPolyk* 7,1 und EvPetr 41-42 wäre eine Verbindung nur über den Begriff μαρτύριον im Zusammenhang mit dem Kreuz möglich; der Begriff wird aber in beiden Fällen grundlegend anders verstanden.

28 Kyrill von Jerusalem, *catech*. 13,14, und EvPetr I 2 kommen meines Erachtens nur in dem volkstümlichen, aber biblisch belegten (vgl. Mk 6,14; Mt 14,9) Titel „König" für Antipas überein; *catech*. 13,26 und EvPetr IV 12 kommen im Gebrauch der selteneren Vokabeln λαχμός und λαγχάνω überein; *catech*. 13,24 berichtet wie EvPetr VI 22 vom Wiedererstrahlen des Lichtes; das wird sich unabhängig Rückgriff auf Sach 14,6-7 verdanken. *catech*. 13,28 und EvPetr 21 erwähnen die Nägel, vgl. aber Joh 20,25 sowie Meliton und Leo den Großen); dass sich die Apostel vor Schmerz verbergen (*catech*. 13,25 = EvPetr 54. 26), kann aus Mk 14,50 par. Mt 26,56b herausgesponnen sein oder ist möglicherweise ein unabhängig voneinander erfolgender Versuch der Abmilderung gegenüber der Tradition der Jüngerflucht (Bauer, Leben Jesu, 180). Vaganay, L'Évangile, 172, und Denker, Stellung, 21, haben wohl recht: Wenn Kyrill gegen Doketen kämpft, wird er kaum ein im Verdacht des Doketismus stehendes Werk benutzt haben.

sind meines Erachtens zu allgemein gehalten, als dass sie eine breitere Nachwirkung des Petrusevangeliums stichhaltig belegen könnten.

Die Belege für eine Nachwirkung des Petrusevangeliums in der altkirchlichen Literatur vermehren sich auch dann nicht, wenn man auf Grund der bei M. Dibelius und J. Denker[30] gegebenen Hinweise auf einen fortlaufenden und eigenständigen Rückbezug des Petrusevangeliums auf das Alte Testament die spätere Kommentierung der einschlägigen Stellen auf Nähe oder Distanz zu Traditionen des Petrusevangelium untersucht. Gelegentliche Ähnlichkeiten in Formulierung und Motivik können sich gemeinchristlicher Sprache ebenso verdanken wie unabhängigem Rückgriff auf das Alte Testament, dessen Erfüllung im Leidensgeschehen nachzuweisen das Petrusevangelium bestrebt ist. Deshalb bleiben in diesem Aufsatz Berührungen zwischen EvPetr V 16 und der späteren großkirchlichen Kommentierung von Ps 69,22 ebenso unberücksichtigt[31] wie die Kommentierung von Jes 3,9-10, das als Vorlage für EvPetr VII 25 gedient haben wird. Von der Kommentierung von Ps 2,2 bzw. Apg 4,26-27 – daraus wird auch in großkirchlicher Literatur im allgemeinen Sinn die Mitwirkung des Herodes Antipas bei der Kreuzigung Jesu erschlossen – muss nur die dem Petrusevangelium noch am nächsten kommende Bemerkung von Beda Venerabilis notiert werden, dem gemäß Herodes Antipas dem römischen Präfekten „Konsens" zur Kreuzigung Jesu gewährt habe.[32] In anderen Fällen werden die alttestamentlichen Weissagungen auf die aus den kanonischen Passionsdarstellungen bekannten Erzählmotive bezogen, ohne dass eine Nähe zu Traditionen oder auch Textlesarten des Petrusevangeliums sichtbar würde. Das gilt für die Auslegung von Jes 53,7[33] wie für die Exegese von Ps 22,17.

---

29 Die vermuteten Berührungen zwischen *hom.* 12,6 und EvPetr 35-45 sowie zwischen *hom.* 14,45; 17,10 und EvPetr 1-25 sind mir zu undeutlich; der Verweis auf *hom.* 20,11 mit der Sendungsaussage (vgl. EvPetr 56) verliert angesichts von Mt 28,6 und Joh 16,5 an Evidenz.

30 M. Dibelius, Die alttestamentlichen Motive in der Leidensgeschichte des Petrus- und des Johannesevangeliums, in: idem, Botschaft und Geschichte. Gesammelte Aufsätze, Bd. 1, Zur Evangelienforschung, hg. v. G. Bornkamm, Tübingen 1953, 221-247; Denker, Stellung, 58-77. Siehe jetzt auch den Beitrag von T. Hieke im vorliegenden Band.

31 Hinweise auf die Verbindung von ποτίζω, ὄξος und χολή nebeneinander in Schriften des 4. Jahrhunderts gibt F. Prostmeier, Der Barnabasbrief, KAV 8, Göttingen 1999, 289.

32 Beda Venerabilis, *retract. in Act.*, CC.SL 121, 125: *qui* (scil. Herodes Antipas) *in nece domini Pilato consensum praebuit.* Von einer aktiven Beteiligung des Antipas geht Beda auch in seinem Lukaskommentar aus und wendet das antijüdisch: *Verum diuina prouidentia neque Iudaeis excusatio remaneret quasi non ipsi sed Romani Christum crucifixerint Herodes quoque qui natu et religione erat Iudaeus ... quid de illo senserit est ostentare permissus* (Beda Venerabilis, *in Lc.*, CC.SL 120, 395. – Das Motiv fehlt bei Johannes Chrysostomus, *hom. in Act.* 11,1, PG 60, 93.

33 So wird Jes 53,7 auf das in Mk 14,61; 15,5 par. Mt 26,63; 27,14 genannte Schweigen Jesu bezogen, vgl. Eusebius, *Is.* II 42, GCS, 336; Ps.-Chrysostomus, *in sancta et magna Parasceve et in sanctam Passionem Domini hom.* 1, PG 62, 721; Theodoret von Kyros, *in Jes.* 17, SC 315, 154; Kyrill von Alexandrien, *Is.* 5/1, PG 70, 1177 A-C; Hieronymus, *in Is.* 14, CC.SL 73 A, 591.

Andererseits sind manche der in der Forschung vermuteten Bezugnahmen des Petrusevangelium auf das Alte Testament von späteren frühchristlichen Autoren nicht oder zumindest nicht durchgehend verfolgt worden. So lassen sich beispielsweise weder zu Jes 58,2[34] noch zu Jes 59,9-10[35] Anklänge an die in EvPetr III 7 bzw. EvPetr V 18 verarbeitete Tradition nachweisen, dasselbe gilt für die Kommentierung von Ps 118 (117),13, der vermuteten Vorlage für EvPetr III 6. Was sich in der späteren großkirchlichen Exegese dieser Stellen bemerkbar macht, ist die Ausdifferenzierung der geistlichen Schriftauslegung, die nunmehr die Aussagen der Psalmen auch als vorbildhafte Weisungen für die christlichen Gläubigen versteht, und diese Ausdifferenzierung hängt mit dem Umstand zusammen, dass christliche Literatur neben apologetischen Zwecken auch anderen Belangen dienen muss, vor allem der Sicherung bzw. Hebung christlicher Disziplin.

Der Grund für die „spärlichen Spuren" ist natürlich zumindest teilweise in Serapions Häresieverdacht zu suchen.[36] Eine eingehende Widerlegung der angeblich doketischen[37] Lehren des P.Cair. 10759 findet sich in großkirchlicher Literatur nirgends – dieses Schicksal teilt das Petrusevangelium mit den meisten anderen „apokryph gewordenen"[38] Literaturwerken. Im vierten Jahrhundert wurde zwischen den verschiedenen sich befehdenden Lagern auf dem Boden der kanonisch gewordenen Schriften gestritten, eine Argumentation mit apokryph gewordenen Texten hätte nicht mehr dem neuen Diskussionsstand entsprochen.

---

[34] Jes 58,2 wird bei Justin, *1 apol.* 35 und EvPetr III 7 auf Jesu Verspottung bezogen, aber nicht mehr auf Jesu Passion bezogen bei Eusebius von Cäsarea, *Is.* II 47, GCS 56, 357; Hieronymus, *in Is.*, CC.SL 73 A, 659-663.

[35] Jes 59,9-10 wird nicht auf die Sonnenfinsternis bei Jesu Passion bezogen bei Theodoret von Kyros, *in Jes.* 18, SC 315, 224-236; Hieronymus, *in Is.* 16, CC.SL 73 A, 683; Kyrill, *Is.* 5/4, PG 70, 1309 D-1313 C.

[36] Man wird freilich zu fragen haben, wie schnell sich Serapions Urteil verbreiten und durchsetzen konnte. Hier stellt sich natürlich auch die Frage: Steht Serapion vielleicht beispielhaft für vergleichbare Urteile, die wir nicht kennen, oder für einen Einzelfall, der erst durch Eusebius bekannt gemacht wird?

[37] Zur Problematik des Begriffs „Doketismus" als eines terminus der Wissenschaftssprache vgl. N. Brox, „Doketismus" – eine Problemanzeige, ZKG 95, 1984, 301-314. – Neben EvPetr V 19 wird immer wieder auch EvPetr IV 10b als möglicher Hinweis auf einen doketischen Charakter des Petrusevangeliums diskutiert. Indessen mag sich die Aussage einem anderen Anliegen verdanken: Jes 53,4b LXX (ἡμεῖς ἐλογισάμεθα αὐτὸν εἶναι ἐν πόνῳ; die Wendung „von Gott", אלהים, ist nicht übersetzt worden) ist isoliert betrachtet im Lichte von Jes 53,5 ein Fehlurteil, das der Verfasser des Petrusevangeliums erzählerisch umsetzen wollte und mit der Aussage über das Schweigen Jesu aus Jes 53,7 verband (so auch Denker, Stellung, 69). Die Verkennung dieses exegetischen Verfahrens kann freilich eine Rezeption der Stelle im Sinne eines nur scheinbaren Leidens Jesu (gegen den Willen des Verfassers) begünstigen und so zu Serapions Urteil führen. Anders P.M. Head, On the Christology of the Gospel of Peter, VigChr 46, 1992, 209-224: Er deutet EvPetr IV 10b mit Hilfe der Märtyrerterminologie. Zur Christologie des EvPetr vgl. aber auch den Beitrag von M. Myllykoski im vorliegenden Band.

[38] Vgl. den Titel bei D. Lührmann, Fragmente apokryph gewordener Evangelien in griechischer und lateinischer Sprache, MThSt 59, Marburg 2000.

Bekanntlich sind die Grenzen zwischen dem, was später als Häresie bzw. Orthodoxie gilt, im zweiten Jahrhundert noch fließend, doch kann man durchaus fragen, ob die Autorfiktion allein schon ein Konkurrenzverhältnis zum Johannesevangelium, die Jüngerliste in EvPetr XIV 60 ein Konkurrenzverhältnis zu anderen Dialogevangelien insinuieren[39] und die Einordnung des Petrusevangeliums in die unterschiedlichen Versuche begründen kann, „eine verbindliche Fassung der grundlegenden Geschichte Jesu zu finden ... eine bestimmte zu der einzigen zu machen".[40] Gerade hier ist an den fragmentarischen Charakter von P.Cair. 10759 zu erinnern. Vermutlich hat der Text in seiner Fortsetzung ähnlich wie Joh 21 von einer Erscheinung Jesu vor den Jüngern am „Meer" berichtet, doch bleibt der Inhalt dieser Erzählepisode unbekannt, der uns in der Suche nach einer Textpragmatik des Petrusevangeliums insgesamt weiterhelfen könnte. Denkbar wären Belehrungen mit verschiedener Thematik, z.B. der Schrifterfüllung (vgl. Lk 24,44); denkbar wäre aber auch, dass „lediglich" der Wahrheitsgehalt der ausführlichen Auferstehungserzählung EvPetr IX 35-X 44 durch ein Wort des Auferstandenen bekräftigt werden soll. Wird in EvPetr XI 45-48 die Auferstehung Jesu als Widerlegung der Position des nicht an Jesus glaubenden Israel[41], vor allem seiner Eliten[42] interpretiert, so könnte das Petrusevangelium unter anderem (!) zum Ziel gehabt haben, seine christlichen Leserinnen und Leser gegen den jüdischen Vorwurf des Leichendiebstahls zu immunisieren, wie das auf seine Weise auch Mt 28,9-10 tut.[43] Zu diesem Zweck aber eignet sich der Augenzeuge[44] Petrus durchaus, so dass die Doppelung des Petrus als Erzähler und zugleich als literarische Figur in seiner Erzählung dem christlichen Leser das Vertrauen auf den Wahrheitsgehalt seiner Darstellung zu vermitteln vermag.[45]

---

[39] So Lührmann, Die apokryph gewordenen Evangelien, 38-41.

[40] So Lührmann, Die apokryph gewordenen Evangelien, 102.

[41] Geleitet von dem Anliegen, das Petrusevangelium als theologische Literatur zu würdigen (T. Nicklas, Die „Juden" im Petrusevangelium [PCair 10759]: Ein Testfall, NTS 47, 2001, 206-221, hier 209), kann man EvPetr XI 48 als grausame Steigerung gegenüber der Aussage 2 Sam 24,14 und als Gegengeschichte zu Jer 26 lesen: Die „Oberen" von EvPetr XI 48 verlassen sich nicht einmal auf die Barmherzigkeit Gottes (2 Sam 24,14), sondern riskieren selbst eine Versündigung (man muss ergänzen: „mit erhobener Hand"), um ja nicht dem Volk der Juden (nicht: der Menschen, so 2 Sam 24,14) in die Hände zu fallen, und sie sind zu einer Selbstkorrektur, wie sie in Jer 26,16-19 berichtet wird, nicht fähig oder nicht willens.

[42] Die von Nicklas, Die Juden, 219, herausgestellte Tendenz des Petrusevangeliums, zwischen den Eliten und den Nichteliten zu differenzieren, findet sich teilweise auch in synoptischer Tradition. Vgl. M. Meiser, Die Reaktion des Volkes auf Jesus. Eine redaktionskritische Studie zu den synoptischen Evangelien, BZNW 96, Berlin-New York 1998, 214-215. 240-242.

[43] Dieser Text signalisiert ja erst dem christlichen Leser, den der Autor von einem Schauplatz zum anderen mitnimmt, die Haltlosigkeit, ja Lächerlichkeit der in Mt 28,11-15 berichteten Aktivitäten der Gegner.

[44] Er ist nach urchristlicher Anschauung der erste, dem der Auferstandene erschienen war (vgl. 1 Kor 15,5; Lk 24,34).

[45] „Die Identifikation des Erzählers mit dem Charakter ‚Petrus' stiftet ... Autorität, indem sie diesen Charakter zum Letztgültiges aussprechenden Interpreten und Zeugen der Ereignisse um die Passion Jesu hochstilisiert" (T. Nicklas, Erzähler und Charakter zugleich. Zur

Unter dieser Voraussetzung wäre das Petrusevangelium zu interpretieren als Zeuge einer christlichen relativen „haggadischen" Freiheit, die im Zug der Auseinandersetzung um Häresie und Orthodoxie im Raum des Christentums später reduziert wurde auf die Auffüllung der von den kanonischen Darstellungen übrig gelassenen größeren (!) Lücken im Ablauf eines Geschehens oder im Lebenslauf einer Person. So ist es nicht verwunderlich, dass traditionsgeschichtlich oder gar literarkritisch verwertbare Bezüge auf das Petrusevangelium auch da nicht zweifelsfrei nachweisbar sind, wo immerhin eine ähnliche Motivik vorliegt.

Wenigstens die Fundstellen für eine solche ähnliche Motivik sollen genannt sein, angeordnet nach den in Frage stehenden Parallelen im Petrusevangelium.

(1) Dass (auch) die Juden als Subjekte der Verspottung Jesu nach der Verurteilung durch Pilatus zu benennen sind[46], ergibt sich für spätere großkirchliche Exegese wohl aufgrund des Rückschlusses von der Vorstellung, die Juden hätten Christus gekreuzigt;[47] diese wiederum war durch Aussagen wie 1 Thess 2,15; Apg 3,15 und durch die zweideutige Darstellung Lk 23,15 unter damaligen (!) hermeneutischen Bedingungen plausibel.

(2) Der Ruf „Meine Kraft, Kraft, du hast mich verlassen" in EvPetr V 19 kann sich, sofern man den Fortfall der Fragepartikel hier vernachlässigen darf,[48] einer Kenntnis der von Aquila zu ψ 21,2a gebotenen Lesart verdanken und muss daher keineswegs als intentional doketisch gebrandmarkt werden.[49] In den mir bekannt gewordenen Psalmenkommentaren wird diese Lesart allerdings erst[50] bei Paschasius Radbertus diskutiert; völlig unpolemisch

---

   literarischen Funktion des „Petrus" in dem nach ihm benannten Evangelium, VigChr 55, 2001, 318-326, hier 325-326).

[46]   Vgl. z.B. Chromatius von Aquileia, *serm*. 19,1 (*Haec quidem Iudaei et gentiles irrisionis fecerunt*), CC.SL 9 A, 89. Die Beispiele ließen sich vermehren.

[47]   Für Belege für die Mitwirkung der Juden bei der Hinrichtung Jesu vgl. Bauer, Leben Jesu, 201 (für die Frühzeit); ferner u.a. Hieronymus, *Zach*. III, CC.SL 76 A, 868; Ps.-Athanasius, *de passione et cruce Domini* 11, PG 28, 204 A; Basilius von Seleukia, *or*. 38,3, PG 85, 412 A; Prokop von Gaza, *Is.*, PG 87/2, 1845 A. Die Vorstellung ist im Diatessaron belegt, aber auch im Manichäismus bekannt (vgl. dazu Kephalaia 13,3-4 sowie die bei A. Adam [Hg.], Texte zum Manichäismus, kT 175, Berlin ²1969, 9, mitgeteilte Kapitelüberschrift aus dem Mysterienbuch). Darüber hinausgehend heißt es bei Ps.-Athanasius (Basilius von Seleukia?), *sermo in passionem Domini* 3, PG 28, 1057 B, die Juden hätten unter Außerachtlassung anderer Todesarten just die Kreuzigung als Todesstrafe gewählt, τιμωρίας ὁμοῦ καὶ ἀτιμίας ἐπινοήσαντες ὄργανον.

[48]   Ps 22,2a wird, soweit ich sehen kann, in später großkirchlicher Schriftauslegung ausnahmslos mit der Fragepartikel gelesen und kommentiert.

[49]   Zur Christologie des Petrusevangeliums vgl. auch den Beitrag von M. Myllykoski im vorliegenden Band.

[50]   Auffällig ist, dass nicht einmal Hieronymus, *in psalm.*, CC.SL 72, 202, auf diese Variante zu sprechen kommt. Überprüft wurden Origenes, *comm. in Mt. Ser.* 135, GCS 38, 278-281; Eusebius, *Ps*. 21, PG 23, 201 C-216 C; Ps.-Hieronymus, *Brev.*, PL 26, 931 C; Didymus, PG 39, 1276 C-1277 A; Theodoret, *in psalm.*, PG 80, 1009 A-1012 B; Augustinus, *en. Ps.*, CC.SL 38, 123; Cassiodor, *expos. in psalm.*, CC.SL 97, 190.

vermerkt der Kommentator, diese Lesart ergebe die etymologische Grundlage der Gottesbezeichnung El.[51]

(3) Die in EvPetr VI 21 vorliegende spezielle Erwähnung der Nägel begegnet auch bei Meliton von Sardes und bei Leo dem Großen, der von Naturphänomenen angesichts der Annagelung Jesu (nicht angesichts der Abnahme der Nägel!) zu phantasieren weiß.[52]

(4) Die EvPetr VI 22 vergleichbare Angabe vom Wiedererstrahlen des Lichtes zur neunten Stunde wird teilweise explizit aus Sach 14,7 erschlossen.[53] Geht man den von D. Lührmann gegebenen Hinweisen auf eine Nachwirkung von EvPetr VIII 28 in der handschriftlichen Überlieferung zu Lk 23,48 nach,[54] so ergibt eine Sichtung der Kommentarliteratur als Fund den gelegentlichen Gedanken, dass auch einige Juden denen, die Jesus kreuzigten, Vorwürfe machten,[55] ohne dass tatsächlich auf eine Bekanntschaft mit dem Petrusevangelium geschlossen werden könnte: die Erweiterungen erweisen sich als erzähltechnisch einfacher, doch nicht ungeschickter Zug, die gespaltene Haltung Israels gegenüber Jesus in nachösterlicher Zeit (vgl. Apg 2 mit Apg 13 etc.) zu motivieren.

Das bisher Gesagte mag als Selbstverständlichkeit empfunden werden. Freilich sind nun auch einige Fälle zu beobachten, in denen ein andersartiger Zugriff späterer großkirchlicher Literatur auf alt- und neutestamentliche Motive, die auch im Petrusevangelium verarbeitet sind, eine weitere Antwort nahe legen könnten.

Gehört nämlich das Petrusevangelium der apologetischen Literatur an,[56] so legt sich die Frage nahe, ob neben Serapions Häresieverdacht nicht auch sachliche Gründe für den geringen Grad an Rezeption verantwortlich zu

---

[51] Paschasius Radbertus, *expositio in Matthaeum* 12, zu Mt 27,46, PL 120, 957 A: *Eli interpretatur Deus meus, quia El unum est nomen ex decem nominibus Dei. Quod Aquila etymologiam eius volens exprimere,* ἰσχυρόν *interpretatus est, quod est fortis.* – Im Bereich der Septuaginta-Überlieferung begegnet die Variante חיל statt אל (wohl als Verschreibung zu deuten) auch andernorts, vgl. 2 Kön 22,31.33 (die καί-γε-Rezension liest החיל, der antiochenische Text האל).

[52] Vgl. Leo den Großen, *serm.* 57, CC.SL 138 A, 336: *Exaltatum autem Jesum ad se traxisse omnia, non solum nostrae substantiae passione, sed etiam totius mundi commotione monstratum est. Pendente enim in patibulo creatore, universa creatura congemuit, et Crucis clauos omnia simul elementa senserunt. Nihil ab illo supplicio liberum fuit.*

[53] Verwiesen wird gelegentlich auf Kyrill von Jerusalem, *catech.* 13,24, im Vergleich mit EvPetr 22. Auf den Todestag Jesu wird Sach 14,7 auch in *Const. App.* 5,14,16 sowie bei Theodoret von Kyros, *in Zach.*, PG 81, 1953 BC gedeutet (zur Geschichte der weiteren Deutung von Sach 14,7 siehe unten).

[54] Lührmann, Die apokryph gewordenen Evangelien, 103, verweist auf Spuren der Nachwirkung des Petrusevangeliums in der Vetus Syra zu Lk 23,48 und auf Erweiterungen in den lateinischen Handschriften g1 (8./9. Jahrhundert) zu Lk 23,48 (vgl. EvPetr VII 25) und k (4./5. Jahrhundert) zu Mk 16,3 (vgl. EvPetr IX 36). Zu Parallelen zwischen EvPetr und textlichen Tendenzen in der Vetus Syra vgl. auch T. Nicklas, Die altsyrische Sinaiticus-Handschrift (Sy^s) als Zeuge antijüdischer Tendenzen, Aramaic Studies 1, 2003, 29-54, bes. 50. 52.

[55] Vgl. Kyrill von Alexandrien, *in Lc.*, PG 72, 940 B, idem, *in Mt* (sic!), PG 72, 468 C, in beiden Fällen als Erfüllung des Wortes Joh 12,32 gedeutet; vgl. ferner Theophylakt, *in Lc.*, PG 123, 1108 C.

[56] Bauer, Leben Jesu, 482; Denker, Stellung, 24.

machen sind. D. Lührmann hat als einen Gesichtspunkt die Materialfülle des
seit Irenäus favorisierten viergestaltigen Evangeliums zu bedenken gegeben;
daneben konnten sich, so Lührmann, „auf Dauer nur solche Werke halten, die
für die Vorgeschichte Jesu und seine Passion mehr boten".[57] Ein weiterer
möglicher Gesichtspunkt ist meines Erachtens der, dass zumindest für die
Ebene der Schuldiskussionen und der Streitgespräche zwischen Christen und
Juden die Kombination des kanonischen neutestamentlichen Textes mit der
explizit benannten alttestamentlichen Aussage in den Augen der Christen eine
wirkungsvollere Argumentation versprach[58] als die freie Nacherzählung
mündlicher Tradition mit nur indirekten Anspielungen in Form der
erzählerischen Umsetzung des im Alten Testament Geweissagten.[59] Justins
„Dialog mit dem Juden Trypho" würde nach dieser Vermutung dann
gegenüber dem Petrusevangelium den für die Folgezeit wirkungsmächtigeren
Typus von Apologetik und antijüdischer Polemik verkörpern.

Großkirchliche Exegese hat in der Auslegung einiger Motive der
Leidensgeschichte eine andere Richtung genommen, als sie im Petrusevangelium eingeschlagen wird: Motive aus den kanonischen Evangelien, die
gewisse Leerstellen ihrerseits begründen können, oder andere, zusätzliche
Bibelzitate oder eine genauere Beachtung des AT-Textes, auch im Hinblick auf
die Christentumskritik eines Porphyrius und eines Julian Apostata notwendig
geworden, oder innerchristliche theologische Weiterentwicklungen machen
den Gebrauch der älteren außerkanonischen Traditionen überflüssig.

Die erstgenannte Möglichkeit erklärt z.B., warum das Motiv der
Freundschaft des Joseph von Arimathia zu Pilatus nicht mehr weitertradiert
wird: Nach Meinung großkirchlicher Auslegung ist es Josephs Reichtum, der
ihm den Weg zu dem römischen Präfekten ebnet.[60]

Die an zweiter Stelle genannte Möglichkeit ist zu EvPetr I 1 und zu EvPetr
II 3 zu bedenken. Zu Mt 27,25 wird der Hinweis darauf, dass die Juden sich die
Hände nicht wuschen, dann überflüssig, wenn im Sinne von Jes 1,15[61] auch das

---

[57] Lührmann, Die apokryph gewordenen Evangelien, 102.
[58] Christen behaupten über die Disputation mit den Juden, der Schriftbeweis u.a. aus Jes 53 und
      Ps 69,22 etc. hätte die Wirkung bei den jüdischen Gesprächspartnern nicht verfehlt, sie seien im
      Gespräch eine Zeitlang unfähig gewesen, sich zu verteidigen (Ps.-Gregentius von Taphar, disp.,
      PG 86, 664 C). Selbst die textinterne bloße Behauptung ist textextern Indiz für die
      entsprechende Erwartungshaltung seitens der Christen.
[59] Nach P. Vielhauer, Geschichte der urchristlichen Literatur. Einleitung in das Neue Testament,
      die Apokryphen und die Apostolischen Väter, GLB, durchges. Nachdr. Berlin-New York 1985,
      646, ist die im Petrusevangelium vorliegende Art des Schriftbezuges „traditionsgeschichtlich
      älter als der explizite Schriftbeweis". Zu dem traditionsgeschichtlichen Argument wäre der
      Verweis auf eine mögliche andere Intention des Petrusevangeliums zu ergänzen.
[60] Bruno von Segni, in Mt., PL 165, 308 A: *Quia enim iste Joseph dives et novilis erat, ideo Christi
      corpus tam facile a Pilato potuit impetrare.* Johannes Chrysostomus spricht von der εὔνοια des
      Joseph von Arimathia Jesus gegenüber (Johannes Chrysostomus, hom. in Mt. 882, PG 58, 778),
      und Photius von Konstantinopel bezeichnet ihn als κρύφιος φίλος des Herrn (Photius, in Lc., PG
      101, 1226 D), sonst gilt Joseph aufgrund von Joh 19,38 meist als (heimlicher) *discipulus* Jesu.
[61] Einen erstmaligen Bezug von Jes 1,15 auf die Verschuldung der Juden bei Jesu Passion
      vermutet Bauer, Leben Jesu, 200, für Irenäus, *haer.* 4,18,4.

äußere Händewaschen nicht als wirkliche Lossagung von der Sündhaftigkeit anerkannt wird.[62] Die schon in den kanonischen Evangelien beginnende Belastung der Juden mit dem Vorwurf, für das Urteil gegen Jesus verantwortlich zu sein, hatte im Petrusevangelium zur völligen Entlastung des Pilatus geführt;[63] ungeachtet des großkirchlichen Antijudaismus ist das Pilatusbild der Großkirche keineswegs immer dieser Tendenz der *völligen* Entlastung gefolgt. Zwar kann die Auslegung bei Ps.-Diodor von Tarsus und bei Theodoret im Sinne dieser Entlastung verstanden werden,[64] doch ist das nicht das einzige, was hierzu zu vermelden ist: Erfrischend anders, nämlich unter Betonung der Wendung *inter innocentes*, kommentiert Cassiodor wie folgt: *Et bene addidit* (scil. David als Subjekt) *inter innocentes quia possunt lavare manus etiam qui nocentes sunt, sicut fecit Pontius Pilatus qui dum animam suam nefanda Domini traditione pollueret, manus suas saeculi istius liquore mundabat.*[65] Cassiodor schwenkt dann auf die übliche Deutung der Stelle auf das geforderte oder verwirklichte Verhalten der Gläubigen ein.[66] Cassiodors Auslegung von Ps 25,6 ist zugleich ein Musterbeispiel dafür, dass eine genauere Wahrnehmung eines alttestamentlichen Textes und ein wachsendes hermeneutisches Problembewusstsein unter altkirchlichen Voraussetzungen (!) die Weiterführung bestimmter im Petrusevangelium vorliegender Verknüpfungen zwischen dem Alten Testament und dem Passionsgeschehen nicht mehr nahe legt. Ein weiteres Beispiel ist die Kommentierung von Ps 34 (33),21 (*custodit Dominus omnia ossa eorum*), einer Stelle, die nur im ungefähren Sinn, aber nicht im Wortlaut christologisch (als Voraussage von Joh 19,36[67]) und anagogisch verwertbar war. Einige Autoren verzichten auf die christologische Auslegung,[68] was sich aber auch anderweitigen Tendenzen verdanken kann.

---

[62] Vgl. Eusebius von Cäsarea, *Is.* 16, GCS 56, 8; Hieronymus, *in Ionam* 1,14, FC 60, 134; ähnlich idem, *in Mt.*, CC.SL 77, 267; ferner Theodoret von Kyros, *in Jes.* 1, SC 276, 170; Rhabanus Maurus, *in Mt.*, PL 107, 1132 D; Paschasius Radbertus, *in Mt.*, PL 120, 940 A. – Auch zu Jes 1,16 wird auf eine entsprechende Selbstverweigerung der Juden nicht Bezug genommen, der Vers kann aufgrund des Imperativs z.B. als Aufforderung zur Taufe gedeutet werden, auch an die Adresse der Juden gerichtet (die Situation der Kirche im 5. Jahrhundert fließt natürlich ein), so bei Kyrill von Alexandrien, *Is.* 1,1, PG 70, 40 D-41 A.

[63] „Hier die Juden und Herodes – dort Jesus, Pilatus und ihre Freunde, das ist die Parteigruppierung, wie sie unserem Verfasser vorschwebt" (Bauer, Leben Jesu, 192-193). Vgl. aber den Beitrag von H. Omerzu im vorliegenden Band.

[64] Ps 25,6 wird auf die Distanzierung des Pilatus von den Juden bezogen bei (Ps.?-)Diodor von Tarsus, *Ps.*, CC.SG 6, 150f.; Theodoret, *in psalm.*, PG 80, 1048 A.

[65] Cassiodor, *in psalm.*, CC.SL 97, 232.

[66] Vgl. Eusebius, *Ps.*, PG 23, 236 BC; Didymus, *in ps.* (Mühlenberg I, Frgm. 233, S. 250); (Ps.?-)Athanasius von Alexandrien, *exp. Ps.*, PG 27, 148 B; Arnobius der Jüngere, *in psalm.*, CC.SL 25, 33 – die Unschuldigen von Ps 25,6 sind dort die *catholici* im Gegensatz zu den *haeretici* –; Augustinus, *en. Ps.* 25,1,6, CC.SL 38, 141; *en. Ps.* 25,2,10, CC.SL 38, 147; Hieronymus, *in psalm.*, CC.SL 72, 200; Julian von Eclanum, *epit. in psalm.*, CC.SL 88 A, 123.

[67] Das Motiv kann aber auch mit Ex 12,46 begründet werden, so u.a. Isidor von Sevilla, *fid. cath.* 1,46,1, PL 83, 489 C.

[68] Ps 33,21 wird von Arnobius dem Jüngeren, *in psalm.*, CC.SL 25, 45, auf die Bewahrung der Gebeine der verstorbenen Gläubigen hin zur Auferstehung der Toten, von Kyrill von

Explizit greifbar wird die Problematik in der Kommentierung der Stelle durch
Augustinus: Wenn der Text hieße *custodit Dominus omnia ossa Filii sui*, wäre er
in Christus erfüllt (vgl. Joh 19,33), doch ist die Verheißung in Ps 33,21 aufgrund
der Wendung *ossa eorum* auch den Christen gegeben, deshalb ist die Stelle
geistlich auszulegen.[69] Auch Cassiodor warnt vor einem naiven wörtlichen
Verständnis des Satzes: Die wörtlich zu verstehenden Gebeine können auch bei
den Gläubigen sehr wohl gebrochen werden, wie das Beispiel des reuigen
Schächers am Kreuz (Lk 23,42 in Verbindung mit Joh 19,32) und das der vielen
Märtyrer beweist; deswegen ist die Bewahrung der *ossa* auf die Bewahrung der
Tugenden der Gläubigen zu beziehen.[70] Eine solche Problematik war jedoch
mit der Technik der erzählerischen Umsetzung des in der Heiligen Schrift
Geweissagten im Rahmen eines Textes, der auf das Element des Lehrdialoges
verzichtet, nicht mehr zu bewältigen.

Jes 53,4 wird in späterer Exegese nicht mehr isoliert von Jes 53,5 betrachtet,
vielmehr wird um der Aussage διὰ τῆς ἁμαρτίας ἡμῶν in Jes 53,4 der Gedanke
eingetragen, dass der Gottesknecht nicht aufgrund eigener Verschuldung ἐν
πόνῳ sei;[71] für eine mögliche Vereinnahmung von Jes 53,4 zugunsten einer
Aussage wie ὡς μηδένα πόνον ἔχων (EvPetr IV 10b) ist somit keine Grundlage
mehr gegeben.

Sach 6,11, von J. Denker als Vorlage für das Motiv der Dornenkrone
genommen,[72] wird entweder auf die Krönung Serubbabels[73] oder geistlich auf
die Verherrlichung des Herrn durch unsere Tugenden[74] oder auf unsere
Rechtgläubigkeit bzw. unsere guten Werke bezogen.[75] Dass die Stelle in
späterer altkirchlicher Schriftauslegung nicht mit der Dornenkrönung Jesu in
Verbindung gebracht wird, liegt vermutlich daran, dass Sach 6,11 einen positiv
bewerteten Vorgang, die Dornenkrönung hingegen eine Verspottung

---

Alexandrien, *Ps.*, PG 69, 893 A, auf die δυνάμεις der Seele und deren Bewahrung im Glauben
gedeutet.

[69]   Augustinus, *en. Ps.* 33, s. II, CC.SL 38, 297.

[70]   Cassiodor, *exp. in Ps.* 33, CC.SL 97, 302; ähnliche Bedenken bei Ps.-Hieronymus, *Brev.*, PL 26,
978 B.

[71]   Vgl. Kyrill von Alexandrien, *Is.* 5/1, PG 70, 1173C; Theodoret , *in Jes.* 17, SC 315, 441 BC; Prokop
von Gaza, *Is.*, PG 87/2, 2521 A; Hieronymus, *in Is.* 14,53,7, CC.SL 73 A, 590. Ohnehin ist das ἐν
πόνῳ εἶναι für die großkirchlichen Autoren aufgrund von Mt 26,38 und Joh 12,27 (darauf
verweist Hieronymus) kein Gegenstand der Diskussion. Hieronymus leitet aus Jes 53,3-4 gegen
„alte und neue Häresien" ab, dass Christus *uere ... non putative, id est* τὸ δοκεῖν, gelitten habe (*Is.*
14, CC.SL 73 A, 589).

[72]   Denker, *Stellung*, 65. – Anastasius Sinaita, *disputatio adversus Judaeos*, PG 89, 1244 B, verweist
auf Jeremia: Ταῖς ἀκάνθαις τῶν ἀνιμιῶν αὐτῶν ἔστεψαν με; Isidor von Sevilla, *fid. cath.* 1,31,2, PL
83, 482 C, verweist ebenfalls auf einen angeblichen Satz Jeremias: *Spinis peccatorum suorum
circumdedit me populus hic*. Leider ist der Satz bei Jeremia nicht zu finden. Isidor, *fid. cath.* 31,1.2,
PL 83, 482 C, verweist jedoch zusätzlich auf Hld 3,11 und Jes 5,2.

[73]   Theodoret, *in Zach.*, PG 81, 1905 CD.

[74]   Hieronymus, *in Zach.* I, CC.SL 76 A, 798.

[75]   Kyrill von Alexandrien, *in Zach.* 2, PG 72, 96 D-97 A. Die Rechtgläubigkeit ist das in Sach 6,11
erwähnte Gold, die guten Werke sind das dort genannte Silber.

beschreibt.[76] Sach 14,7 wird aufgrund des Kontextes Sach 14,6 in der Regel auf den Jüngsten Tag hin ausgelegt, nicht mehr auf den Todestag Jesu, und entfällt damit als Grundlage einer Aussage, wie sie in EvPetr VI 22 geboten wird.[77]

Für den Verweis auf theologische Weiterentwicklungen ist vor allem die spätere großkirchliche Exegese zu Ps 22,2a namhaft zu machen. Die Auslegung der Frage „Warum hast du mich verlassen" kann sich auf das Faktum beziehen, dass Christus aus der Hl. Schrift zitiert, und wird dann als Apologetik dergestalt verstanden, dass Jesus sich nicht im Widerspruch mit der Schrift befinde und Gott den Vater ehren wolle.[78] Antidoketisch verhindert Ps 22,2a *ne secundum quosdam phatasma totum pietatis eius opus et mysterium crederetur.*[79] Die christologische Problematik der Aussage ist hier nicht im Einzelnen zu erörtern. Wichtig ist, dass gerade Ps 22,2a viele Autoren zu prägnanten und eingängigen Formulierungen veranlasst, die unter den Voraussetzungen altkirchlicher Christologie das Heilsgeschehen beschreiben. Ps 22,2a ist Ausweis der völligen Selbsterniedrigung des sündlosen[80] Gottessohnes, der unser Verlassensein von Gott auf sich lenkt, um dem Fluch ein Ende zu setzen,[81] der das, was wir sind, in sich selbst abbildet,[82] der so spricht, wie wir als Sünder sprechen müssen.[83] Das Verlassensein Christi ist eine ἐγκατάλειψις οἰκονομική;[84] betont wird das *propter nos*,[85] das *pro nobis*.[86] Zugleich ist die Aussage im Munde Christi auch eine Mahnung zur Geduld.[87]

---

[76] Allerdings ist das Motiv nicht immer zwingend. Von Chromatius von Aquileia, *serm.* 19,3, CC.SL 9 A, 90-91, wird die Dornenkrone geistlich auf die Kirche bezogen und mit Ps 21 (20),4 biblisch unterlegt: *Posuisti super caput eius coronam de lapide pretioso.*

[77] Kyrill von Alexandrien, *in Zach.*, PG 72, 248 D; Hieronymus, *in Zach.*, CC.SL 76 A, 882. Dass Theodoret von Kyros, *in Zach.*, PG 81, 1953 BC, noch der alten Deutung von Sach 14,7 folgt, ist angesichts seiner sonstigen exegetischen Qualitäten eher erstaunlich.

[78] Ps.-Petrus von Laodicea, *in Mt.* (C.F.G. Heinrici, Des Petrus von Laodicea Erklärung des Matthäusevangeliums, Leipzig 1908, 332).

[79] Julian von Eclanum, *epit. in psalm.*, CC.SL 88 A, 108.

[80] Vgl. Didymus den Blinden, bei E. Mühlenberg, Psalmenkommentare aus der Katenenüberlieferung 1, PTS 15, Berlin-New York 1975, Frgm. 176, S. 224.

[81] (Ps.?-)Athanasius von Alexandrien, *exp. Ps.*, PG 27, 132 B: τὰ ἡμῶν εἰς ἑαυτὸν μετατιθεὶς ἵνα παύσῃ τὴν ἀράν.

[82] Grundlegend formuliert Gregor von Nazianz, *or.* 30,5, FC 22, 232: Ἐν ἑαυτῷ ... τυποῖ τὸ ἡμέτερον. Wir waren vorher die Verlassenen und Verachteten, sind aber jetzt, durch die Leiden des Leidensunfähigen, die Aufgenommenen und Geretteten.

[83] Vgl. Kyrill von Alexandrien, bei Reuss, Matthäuskommentare, Frgm. 312: Die Worte „Warum hast du mich verlassen" auszusprechen ist nur für die Reinen und Sündlosen unnötig; vgl. ferner Beda Venerabilis, *in Mt.*, PL 92, 125 A; Rhabanus Maurus, *in Mt.*, PL 107, 1142 CD: *Ostenditque quantum flere debeant qui peccant, quando sic flevit qui nunquam peccavit.*

[84] Ammonius von Alexandrien, *fr. in Mt.*, PG 85, 1389 C.

[85] Maximus von Turin, *hom.* 45, PL 57, 330 A: *Haec autem dicit, ut manifestaret propter nos se esse derelictum, quorum peccata portabat, ac videntes disceremus et nos pro ipso sancto et iusto mori, cum pro peccatoribus et ille moreretur.*

[86] Ebenso Leo, *serm.* 67,7, CC.SL 138 A, 412-413: *Vox ista ... doctrina est, non querela. Nam cum in Christo Dei et hominis una persona sit, nec ab eo potuerit relinqui a quo non poterat separari, pro nobis trepidis et infirmis interrogat cur caro pati metuens exaudita non fuerit.*

[87] Vgl. ferner wiederum Beda Venerabilis, *in Mt.*, PL 92, 125 A; Rhabanus Maurus, *in Mt.*, PL 107, 1142 CD, die nach den vorhin genannten Zitaten fortfahren: *Et ostendit quam patientes et*

Die Möglichkeit, Ps 22,2a auf die *intercessio* Jesu zu beziehen, ergibt sich nach altkirchlicher Hermeneutik durch den notwendigen Ausgleich zwischen der dank 2 Kor 5,21 feststehenden Sündlosigkeit Jesu mit den Worten *uerba delictorum meorum* aus Ps 22,2b, die nicht ohne Zwischengedanken christologisch gedeutet werden können.[88]

Der Verweis auf die geänderten theologischen Voraussetzungen betrifft aber auch die Auferweckungsaussagen des Petrusevangeliums. Die Erzähl-folge in Mt 28 (erstmals *nach* der bereits stattgefundenen Auferstehung kommt ein Engel) lässt gerade um der zu bezeugenden Macht Christi keinen Raum für die zusätzliche Erwähnung der zwei Männer, die den Gottessohn bei der Auferstehung begleiten und ihn stützen.[89]

Wie ist das Überleben dieses P.Cair. 10759 genannten Fragmentes des Petrusevangeliums bis ins sechste, eventuell siebte Jahrhundert zu erklären? In Akhmîm mag es als erbauliche Evangelienharmonie gelesen (!) worden sein. D. Lührmann verweist auf den Nutzeffekt für die christologische Diskussion für die ägyptische Theologie jener Zeit hinsichtlich des Auferstehungsleibes.[90]

All diese vorgenannten Ausführungen haben nicht den Zweck, das Urteil Serapions im Nachhinein zu rechtfertigen. Im zweiten Jahrhundert standen viele der später drängenden Probleme noch nicht vor Augen, und die kirchen-wie theologiegeschichtlichen Umstände haben vermutlich die Entstehung von Texten in der Art des Petrusevangeliums begünstigt. Die Einsicht, dass ein zu seiner Zeit adäquater Text die Fragen kommender Generationen zumeist nicht beantworten kann, gilt ja auch für die eigene wissenschaftliche Arbeit.

---

sperantes debeant esse inter flagella, qui peccatores sunt, quomo ipse ad immortalitatem non nisi per mortem transivit.

[88]   Noch (Ps.?-)Diodor von Tarsus, *Ps.*, CC.SG 6, 127, hatte um dieser Worte willen abgelehnt, den ganzen Psalm auf Christus zu deuten.

[89]   Petrus Chrysologus, s. 75, PL 52, 413 A: *Revolvit lapidem, non ut egredienti Domino praeberet aditum, sed ut Dominum mundo jam resurrexisse monstraret.* Vgl. auch Paschasius Radbertus, *expositio in Matthaeum* 12, PL 120, 979 C: *Angelus enim Domini descendit de caelo, imo angeli. Non ut resuscitent Dominum sed ut annuntient eum resurrexisse a mortuis.* Vgl. ferner Christian Duthmarus, *in Mt.*, PL 106, 1498 B: *Revolvit (scil. Angelus) lapidem. Non ut Domino viam panderet, sed et mulieribus monstraret iam abiisse Dominum.*

[90]   Lührmann, Die apokryph gewordenen Evangelien, 104.

Justins „Denkwürdigkeiten der Apostel"
und das Petrusevangelium

von

KATHARINA GRESCHAT

„Hat Justin, der ja offensichtlich bereits Evangelientexte kannte, in seinen Schriften auf das apokryphe Petrusevangelium Bezug genommen?"

Diese Frage beschäftigt nicht nur diejenigen, die sich für die Geschichte des neutestamentlichen Kanons interessieren.[1] Denn selbst wenn sich keine Anhaltspunkte dafür finden lassen, dass Justin unmittelbar aus einem ihm bekannten Petrusevangelium zitiert hat, bleibt immer noch das Problem, wie man sich die zweifellos bestehenden Gemeinsamkeiten zwischen beiden sonst erklären soll.

Im Rahmen dieses Beitrags möchte ich versuchen, eine mögliche Lösung für dieses Problem vorzustellen. Zuvor muss jedoch kurz auf die Bezeugungen für das Petrusevangelium eingegangen werden, um anschließend etwas ausführlicher auf die von Justin verwendeten Evangelientexte, die er die „Denkwürdigkeiten der Apostel" nennt, zu sprechen zu kommen. Erst danach lässt sich diskutieren, ob Justin das Petrusevangelium gekannt hat, und worauf sich die Gemeinsamkeiten zwischen den „Denkwürdigkeiten der Apostel" und dem Petrusevangelium gründen.

I. Die Bezeugungen für das Petrusevangelium

Bischof Serapion von Antiochien verfasste um das Jahr 200 ein kurzes Werk, vielleicht auch nur einen Brief, in dem er sich mit häretischen Lesern eines so genannten Petrusevangeliums auseinander setzte. Von der Existenz dieses Evangeliums hatte er erst anlässlich eines Besuches im nahe gelegenen Rhossus erfahren.[2]

---

[1] Vgl. dazu beispielsweise die Beiträge von C.H. Cosgrove, Justin Martyr and the Emerging Christian Canon. Observations on the Purpose and Destination of the Dialogue with Trypho, VigChr 36, 1982, 209-232; C.E. Hill, Justin and the New Testament Writings, Studia Patristica 30, 1997, 42-48; B. Aland/W.L. Petersen, Hg., Gospel Traditions in the Second Century. Origins, Recensions, Text and Transmission, Christianity and Judaism in Antiquity 3, Notre Dame 1989; G.N. Stanton, Jesus and Gospel, Cambridge 2004, 92-105, der Cosgrove energisch widerspricht.

[2] Euseb, *h.e.* VI,12,2-6 (GCS 9,2 544,9-546,7).

In seiner Kirchengeschichte bezieht sich nun Euseb von Caesarea auf diese kleine Schrift des Serapion, weil sie ihm vorzüglich dazu geeignet erscheint, seine eigene Ansicht zu stützen, dass man nämlich seit alters her nur einen einzigen Petrusbrief kirchlicherseits anerkannt und verwendet habe. Die übrige Petrusliteratur – Euseb nennt hier Petrusakten, ein Petrusevangelium, eine Petruspredigt und eine Petrusapokalypse – habe man seiner Meinung nach bereits in der Frühzeit verworfen.[3] Papias und Polykarp, Eusebs kirchliche Gewährsleute für das frühe zweite Jahrhundert, kannten und benutzten ebenso wie die späteren nur den ersten Petrusbrief.[4] Um nun besonders hervorzuheben, dass das Petrusevangelium schon früh für häretisch gehalten wurde,[5] lässt Euseb den Bischof Serapion selbst zu Wort kommen[6].

Dieser bezeichnete das Petrusevangelium als eine Pseudepigraphie[7] und meinte damit, dass es eine Schrift sei, die zwar den Namen eines Apostels trägt, jedoch nicht zuverlässig überliefert ist.[8] Ohne dieses Evangelium selbst gelesen zu haben, hielt er es, als er in Rhossus weilte, zunächst für unbedenklich. Nach seiner Rückkehr erfuhr er jedoch, dass die Leser des Petrusevangeliums von anderen Gemeindegliedern der Häresie verdächtigt wurden. Erst jetzt zog Serapion genauere Erkundigungen ein und konnte in Erfahrung bringen, dass dieses Evangelium von Leuten, οὓς Δοκητὰς καλοῦμεν, benutzt wurde.[9] Daraufhin ließ er es genauer überprüfen und fand heraus, dass „das meiste der wahren Lehre unseres Erlösers entsprach, manches aber auch hinzugefügt wurde."[10] Die folgende Auflistung dieser Unterschiede im Einzelnen, die für uns äußerst aufschlussreich gewesen wäre, hat uns Euseb jedoch leider nicht überliefert.[11] Für seine Argumentation war sie nicht notwendig.

---

3   Euseb, *h.e.* III,3,1-3 (GCS 9,188,17-190,11).
4   Euseb, *h.e.* III,39,17 (GCS 9,292,7-8) und IV,14,9 (GCS 9,334,16-18). Irenaeus, V,8,7 (GCS 9,4461-4462) und Origenes, VI,25,8 (GCS 9,2 578,1-3).
5   Euseb, *h.e.* III,25,6 (GCS 9,252,15), rechnet das Petrusevangelium zur häretischen Literatur.
6   Euseb, *h.e.* VI,12,3-5 (GCS 9,2 544,15-546,7). Vgl. auch A.D. Baum, Pseudepigraphie und literarische Fälschung im frühen Christentum, WUNT 2.138, Tübingen 2001, 100-103.
7   Zur antiken Pseudepigraphie vgl. vor allem N. Brox, Falsche Verfasserangaben. Zur Erklärung der frühchristlichen Pseudepigraphie, SBS 79, Stuttgart 1975; idem, Pseudepigraphie in der heidnischen und jüdisch-christlichen Antike, WdF 484, Darmstadt 1977.
8   Euseb, *h.e.* VI,12,3 (GCS 9,2 544,15-18).
9   Nicht alles, was im modernen Sinne für Doketismus gehalten wird, musste auch in der Spätantike als Doketismus bezeichnet werden; vgl. N. Brox, „Doketismus" – eine Problemanzeige, ZKG 95, 1984, 301-314. Zu den sehr verschiedenen doketischen Vorstellungen des zweiten Jahrhunderts vgl. auch M.D. Goulder, Ignatius' „Docetists", VigChr 53, 1999, 16-30.
10   Euseb, *h.e.* VI,12,6 (GCS 9,2 546,6-7): τὰ μὲν πλείονα τοῦ ὀρθοῦ λόγου τοῦ σωτῆρος, τινὰ δὲ προσδιεσταλμένα. Vgl. auch E. Junod, Eusèbe de Césarée, Sérapion d'Antioche et l'Évangile de Pierre. D'un évangile à un pseudépigraphe, RSLR 24, 1988, 3-16; idem, Comment l'Évangile de Pierre s'est trouvé écarté des lectures de l'Église dans les années 200, in: Le mystère apocryphe. Introduction à une littérature méconnue, hg. von J.-D. Kaestli/D. Marguerat, EssBib 26, Genf 1995, 43-46.
11   Euseb, *h.e.* VI,12, 6 (GCS 9,2 546,7).

Dass das Petrusevangelium nicht zweifelsfrei von Petrus selbst stammte, war für Bischof Serapion noch kein hinreichender Grund, es abzulehnen.[12] Solange die Rechtgläubigkeit und Einheit der Gemeinde gewahrt blieb, gab es für ihn offenbar noch nicht einmal die Notwendigkeit, sich mit dem Inhalt dieses Evangeliums näher zu befassen. Erst nachdem seine Leser der Häresie bezichtigt wurden, sah sich der Bischof zur Lektüre genötigt. Was man in diesem Evangelium einmal lesen konnte, deutet Origenes an, der von einem Petrusevangelium zumindest vom Hörensagen wusste:

> Die Brüder Jesu seien, sagen einige, durch die Überlieferung des nach Petrus benannten Evangeliums oder des Jakobusbuchs verleitet, Söhne Josefs von einer früheren Frau, die mit ihm vor Maria verheiratet gewesen war.[13]

Mit dem Jakobusbuch ist wohl das mit „Geburt der Maria – Offenbarung des Jakobus" betitelte so genannte Protevangelium des Jakobus gemeint.[14] Dort sind die Brüder Jesu tatsächlich nicht seine leiblichen Brüder. Ob das Petrusevangelium tatsächlich eine solche Erzählung enthielt, ist für uns jedoch nicht mehr nachprüfbar.[15] Bislang wurde im oberägyptischen Akhmîm lediglich ein handschriftlich auf das Ende des 6. Jahrhunderts zu datierender Pergamentcodex mit einem Evangelienfragment (*P.Cair.* 10759) entdeckt, das die Passion und Auferstehung aus der Sicht des Petrus schildert. Deshalb hat man angenommen, dass es sich hierbei um einen Teil des Petrusevangeliums handelt.[16] Zwei kurze Fragmente des 2./3. Jahrhunderts (*P.Oxy.* XLI 2949), die Textvarianten zu dem Fragment aus Akhmîm bezeugen, lassen darauf schließen, dass dieses Evangelium sehr viel älter als der genannte Textzeuge aus dem 6. Jahrhundert sein muss.[17] Im Jahre 1994 wurde mit *P.Oxy.* LX 4009 das Fragment einer bisher unbekannten Aussendungsrede entdeckt, die ebenfalls aus der Sicht des Petrus erzählt wird. Man könnte diese Rede, falls sie denn wirklich zum Petrusevangelium gehören sollte, vor oder auch nach der Passions- und Ostergeschichte platzieren.[18] Ob darüber hinaus auch andere,

---

[12] Junod, Eusèbe de Césarée, 14: „ ... ce n'est pas d'abord l'Evangile de Pierre que Sérapion met sur la sellette, mais bien ses lecteurs."

[13] Origenes, *comm. in Mt.* X 17 (GCS 40,21).

[14] Vgl. H. Koester, Überlieferung und Geschichte der frühchristlichen Evangelienliteratur, ANRW II. 25.2, 1984, 1463-1542, hier 1483.

[15] J. Denker, Die theologiegeschichtliche Stellung des Petrusevangeliums. Ein Beitrag zur Frühgeschichte des Doketismus, EHS XXII.36, Frankfurt 1975, 14, erwägt, dass Origenes die Partikel ἤ an dieser Stelle inklusiv gemeint haben könnte.

[16] Vgl. P. Vielhauer, Geschichte der urchristlichen Literatur. Einleitung in das Neue Testament, die Apokryphen und die Apostolischen Väter, Berlin-New York 1995, 642: „Es gilt als ausgemacht, daß es sich bei diesem [sc. dem von Serapion gemeinten Evangelium] und bei dem Fragment von Akhmim um dasselbe PetrEv handelt. Das ist zwar nicht zu beweisen, aber auch nicht zu widerlegen."

[17] Vgl. D. Lührmann, POx 2949: EvPt 3-5 in einer Handschrift des 2./3. Jahrhunderts, ZNW 72, 1981, 216-226; T. Nicklas, Ein „neutestamentliches Apokryphon"? Zum umstrittenen Kanonbezug des sog. „Petrusevangeliums", VigChr 56, 2002, 260-272, hier 263.

[18] Vgl. D. Lührmann, POx 4009: Ein neues Fragment des Petrusevangeliums?, NT 35, 1993, 390-410. Vorsichtig äußert sich hingegen T. Nicklas, Die „Juden" im Petrusevangelium (PCair 10759): Ein Testfall, NTS 47, 2001, 206-221, hier 211.

bislang nicht zu identifizierende Evangelienfragmente dem Petrusevangelium zuzurechnen sind, muss nach dem bisherigen Stand der Forschung fraglich bleiben.[19]

II. Justin und die „Denkwürdigkeiten der Apostel"

Der erste kirchliche Schriftsteller, der nachweislich bereits vorliegende Evangelienbücher benutzte und ausgiebig aus ihnen zitierte, war Justin der Märtyrer, dessen erhaltene Schriften vermutlich kurz nach dem Jahre 150 in Rom entstanden.[20] Die Frage, welche Evangelien Justin kannte, hat die Forschung schon lange beschäftigt.[21] Nach der Entdeckung des Fragments aus dem Petrusevangelium meinte man, endlich nachweisen zu können, dass sich Justin auch auf dieses Evangelium beruft.[22] Justin nennt jedoch keine Namen, er bezeichnet die ihm vorliegenden Evangelientexte vielmehr grundsätzlich als die ἀπομνημονεύματα der Apostel,[23] wie folgende Stelle zeigt:

> Die Apostel haben nämlich in den von ihnen stammenden Denkwürdigkeiten, die Evangelien genannt werden, folgendermaßen überliefert ...[24]

Diese ἀπομνημονεύματα der Apostel, so berichtet Justin weiter, wurden im sonntäglichen Gottesdienst neben den Schriften der Propheten verlesen.[25] Man darf also vermuten, dass die römische Gemeinde die prophetischen Schriften als Verheißung auf Christus hin verstand und dementsprechend in den

---

[19] Vgl. D. Lührmann, Fragmente apokryph gewordener Evangelien in griechischer und lateinischer Sprache, MThSt 59, Marburg 2000, 72-74. Vgl. auch idem, Die apokryph gewordenen Evangelien. Studien zu neuen Texten und zu neuen Fragen, NT.S 112, Leiden 2004, 55-104. Zur Diskussion vgl. die Textausgabe von T.J. Kraus/T. Nicklas, Das Petrusevangelium und die Petrusapokalypse. Die griechischen Fragmente mit deutscher und englischer Übersetzung, GCS.NF 11; Neutestamentliche Apokryphen 1, Berlin-New York 2004, 5-6.

[20] Vgl. Koester, Überlieferung,1467.

[21] Vgl. E.F. Osborn, Justin Martyr, Tübingen 1973, 120, der darauf hinweist, dass B.L. Gildersleeve bereits im Jahre 1877 schrieb, dass die Frage, ob man die Denkwürdigkeiten der Apostel mit den synoptischen Evangelien identifizieren könne, bereits seit einem Jahrhundert diskutiert werde. Vgl. auch W. Bousset, Die Evangeliencitate Justins des Märtyrers in ihrem Wert für die Evangelienkritik, Göttingen 1891.

[22] Vgl. vor allem A. Harnack, Bruchstücke des Evangeliums und der Apokalypse des Petrus, TU 9,1/2, Leipzig 1893.

[23] Zu diesem Begriff vgl. auch Bousset, Evangeliencitate, 14-18, und R. Heard, The ΑΠΟΜΝΗΜΟΝΕΥΜΑΤΑ in Papias, Justin, and Irenaeus, NTS 1, 1954/55, 122-129.

[24] Justin, 1 apol. 66,3 (Paradosis 39,120): οἱ γὰρ ἀπόστολοι ἐν τοῖς γενομένοις ὑπ' αὐτῶν ἀπομνημονεύμασιν, ἃ καλεῖται εὐαγγέλια ...

[25] Justin, 1 apol. 67,3-4 (Paradosis 39,122). Vgl. dazu auch H. von Campenhausen, Die Entstehung der christlichen Bibel, BHTh 39, Tübingen 1968, 196-197. Zu Form und Gestalt der frühchristlichen Gottesdienste vgl. jetzt auch P.F. Bradshaw, The Search for the Origins of Christian Worship, London 1992; J.C. Salzmann, Lehren und Ermahnen. Zur Geschichte des christlichen Wortgottesdienstes in den ersten drei Jahrhunderten, WUNT 59, Tübingen 1994; L.W. Hurtado, At the Origins of Christian Worship, Grand Rapids 2000; P. Wick, Die urchristlichen Gottesdienste, BWANT 150, Stuttgart 2002.

ἀπομνημονεύματα der Apostel die Erfüllung dieser Verheißung fand. Genauso geht Justin auch in seiner ausführlichen Auslegung des 22. Psalms (Psalm 21 nach der Zählung der Septuaginta) im *Dialog mit Tryphon* vor.[26] In der Psalmdeutung führt er immer wieder Belege aus den Denkwürdigkeiten der Apostel an,[27] um seinen jüdischen Gesprächspartner Tryphon[28] davon zu überzeugen, dass all das, was in diesem Psalm beschrieben steht, bereits mit der Person Christi erfüllt sei.[29] Justin verweist Tryphon zunächst grundsätzlich auf „das Evangelium",[30] bevor er dann genauer von den ἀπομνημονεύματα der Apostel spricht, die über Christi Präexistenz und seine menschliche Geburt, sein Leben und Sterben, sowie über seine Auferstehung von den Toten Auskunft geben. Alle wichtigen Glaubensaussagen über Christus werden in der Schrift angekündigt und sodann von den ἀπομνημονεύματα der Apostel bestätigt.[31] Für Justin sind diese Texte vollkommen zuverlässig, weil sie von den Aposteln selbst und von deren Nachfolgern verfasst worden sind.[32] Er möchte sie offenbar bewusst zur Gattung der ἀπομνημονεύματα gerechnet haben, vielleicht in Anlehnung an die von den Platonschülern Erastos und Asklepiades verfassten Denkwürdigkeiten des Platon oder an Xenophons Denkwürdigkeiten des Sokrates.[33] Dem Tryphon konnte er auf diese Weise glaubhaft machen, dass die schriftlichen Hinterlassenschaften von Aposteln und deren Nachfolgern für die Zuverlässigkeit ihrer Aussagen über die wichtigen christologischen Glaubensinhalte bürgen.

Fragt man nun etwas genauer danach, was in diesen ἀπομνημονεύματα der Apostel zu lesen stand, so bezeugen sie für Justin zunächst einmal, dass der

---

26 Nach O. Skarsaune, The Proof from Prophecy. A Study in Justin Martyr's Proof-Text Tradition. Text-Type, Provenance, Theological Profile, Leiden 1987, stützt sich Justin hier auf ältere Sammlungen von Weissagungen, die christologisch gedeutet werden konnten. Skarsaune unterscheidet zwischen einer ursprünglich judenchristlichen „kerygma source" und einer eher paulinisch geprägten „recapitulation source".

27 L. Abramowski, Die Erinnerungen der Apostel bei Justin, in: Das Evangelium und die Evangelien, hg. von P. Stuhlmacher, WUNT 28, Tübingen 1983, 341-353, vermutet, dass Justin an dieser Stelle einen von ihm selbst verfassten antignostischen Traktat aufnimmt und in der Auseinandersetzung mit Tryphon weiter ausarbeitet.

28 Man wird kaum mit N. Hyldahl, Philosophie und Christentum. Eine Interpretation der Einleitung zum Dialog Justins, Acta theologica danica 9, Kopenhagen 1966, 81, davon ausgehen können, dass Justin an dieser Stelle „die Erinnerung an tatsächlich geführte Gespräche" mit einem gesetzeskundigen Juden wiedergibt.

29 Vgl. auch C.D. Allert, Revelation, Truth, Canon, and Interpretation. Studies in Justin Martyr's Dialogue with Trypho, VigChr.S 64, Leiden 2002, 188-190.

30 Justin, *dial.* 100,1 (PTS 47,241). Von dem Evangelium im Singular spricht sonst nur Tryphon in *dial.* 10,2 (PTS 47,87).

31 Vgl. auch Justin, *1 apol.* 33,5 (Paradosis 39,78).

32 Justin, *dial.* 103,7 (PTS 47,248-249). Vgl. auch Allert, Revelation, 193.

33 Vgl. C.-J. Thornton, Justin und das Markusevangelium, ZNW 84, 1993, 93-110, hier 109-110, n. 64, und T. Zahn, Geschichte des neutestamentlichen Kanons I.2, Erlangen 1888, 471. Die Analogie stimmt aber nicht ganz, Justin müsste konsequenterweise von den Denkwürdigkeiten Christi sprechen, vgl. dazu auch A. Hilgenfeld, Kritische Untersuchungen über die Evangelien Justin's, der clementinischen Homilien und Marcions, Halle 1850, 23.

Gottessohn der Sohn einer Jungfrau war[34] und in Betlehem geboren wurde.[35] Sie berichten offenbar von der Verkündigung des Engels Gabriel an Maria,[36] die ähnlich wie im Protevangelium des Jakobus[37] selbst aus dem Geschlechte Davids stammte.[38] In den Denkwürdigkeiten konnte man außerdem nachlesen, dass die Magier bei der Geburt des Gottessohnes einen Stern als himmlisches Zeichen sahen, und eigens aus Arabien herbei kamen, um den Gottessohn anzubeten.[39]

Gemäß der Prophezeiung des Psalms war der Gottessohn von Anfang an von jüdischen Widersachern bedroht, wie der Bericht über die Flucht nach Ägypten aus Furcht vor dem jüdischen König Herodes verdeutlicht.[40] Direkt nach seiner Taufe im Jordan und der göttlichen Stimme, die ihn als den Sohn Gottes anerkannte, trat der Teufel zu ihm und versuchte ihn, indem er göttliche Verehrung von ihm verlangte.[41] Jesus antwortete jedoch ähnlich wie in Mt und Lk mit Dtn 6,13: „Du sollst den Herrn, deinen Gott, anbeten und ihm allein dienen."

Der aus den ἀπομνημονεύματα der Apostel stammende Satz: „Wenn eure Gerechtigkeit nicht die der Schriftgelehrten und Pharisäer übertrifft, werdet ihr nicht in das Himmelreich eingehen,"[42] dokumentiert für Justin die kontinuierliche Auseinandersetzung Jesu und seiner Nachfolger mit den Juden, das heißt mit dem Geschlecht, das nach einem Zeichen verlangt, obwohl ihm doch das Zeichen des Jona gegeben ist.[43] Auch die Einzelheiten des Leidens und Sterbens des Erlösers sieht Justin mit den Worten von Ps 22 vorhergesagt und durch das Zeugnis der Denkwürdigkeiten der Apostel bestätigt. In den Hunden, die den Beter umzingeln, und in den Bösewichtern, die ihn umlagern, kann er mit Bezug auf die ἀπομνημονεύματα wiederum nur die Widersacher Jesu entdecken, die gierig Jagd auf ihn machen und ihn schon seit jeher verurteilen wollten.[44] Die Aussage des Psalms: „Wie Wasser ist hingegossen und zerdehnt ist all mein Gebein" ist für Justin mit Jesu Gefangennahme erfüllt, denn nach den Denkwürdigkeiten rann sein Schweiß wie Tropfen zur Erde, während er darum bat, der Kelch möge, wenn es möglich sei, an ihm vorübergehen.[45] Wie vom Psalm vorhergesagt, schwieg Jesus während seines Prozesses und verhielt sich damit vollkommen anders als zuvor, als er Pharisäer, Schriftgelehrte und

---

[34] Justin, *dial.* 100,3-4 (PTS 47,244); *dial.* 105,1 (PTS 47,250).
[35] Justin, *dial.* 102,2 (PTS 47,246-247).
[36] Justin, *dial.* 100,5 (PTS 47,242-243). Vgl. *Protevangelium des Jakobus* 11 und insbesondere 12,2.
[37] *Protevangelium des Jakobus* 10.
[38] Justin, *dial.* 100,3 (PTS 47,243). Vgl. auch *dial.* 23,3 (PTS 47,108); *dial.* 43,1 (PTS 47,140).
[39] Justin, *dial.* 102,2 (PTS 47,244); *dial.* 103,3 (PTS 47,247); *dial.* 106,4 (PTS 47,253).
[40] Justin, *dial.* 102,2 (PTS 47,244). Justin meint hier ganz offensichtlich Herodes den Großen, dem dann Herodes Antipas folgte; vgl. auch *dial.* 103,3 (PTS 47,247).
[41] Justin, *dial.* 103,5 (PTS 47,248).
[42] Justin, *dial.* 105,6 (PTS 47,251): Ἐὰν μὴ περισσεύσῃ ὑμῶν ἡ δικαιοσύνη πλεῖον τῶν γραμματέων καὶ Φαρισαίων, οὐ μὴ εἰσέλθητε εἰς τὴν βασιλείαν τῶν οὐρανῶν.
[43] Justin, *dial.* 107,1 (PTS 47,253).
[44] Justin, *dial.* 104 (PTS 47,249-250).
[45] Justin, *dial.* 103,8 (PTS 47,249). Vgl. Mt 26,39 und Lk 22,42.

die verschiedenen Lehrer der Juden wortreich widerlegte.[46] Dass eben diese jüdischen Widersacher nun auch den Gekreuzigten verspotteten, kann den Leser des Psalms nicht verwundern und wird durch die Denkwürdigkeiten der Apostel bestätigt, wo gesagt wird: „Zum Sohn Gottes hat er sich gemacht, er steige herab und wandle! Gott möge ihn erlösen!"[47] Eine vergleichbare Szene ist uns aus den synoptischen Evangelien bekannt, doch heißt es dort, er möge sich selbst erlösen und herabsteigen, wenn er der Sohn Gottes sei, dann werden ihm auch die Spötter glauben.[48]

Im Psalm wird ferner vorhergesagt und von den ἀπομνημονεύματα bestätigt, dass um sein Gewand das Los geworfen wurde.[49] Auch für Jesu letzte Worte zitiert Justin die Denkwürdigkeiten der Apostel[50] ebenso wie für die Auferstehung von den Toten am dritten Tage.[51]

Abschließend berichtet Justin davon, dass die Denkwürdigkeiten bezeugen, Jesus sei inmitten der Apostel erschienen und habe ihnen erläutert, dass seine Passion von den Propheten und von ihm selbst im Voraus verkündigt worden war und der Auferstandene in der Gemeinschaft mit seinen Aposteln Gott lobte.[52] Damit bezieht sich Justin offenkundig wiederum auf das Geschehen im christlichen Gottesdienst, in dem aus den Propheten und den Denkwürdigkeiten der Apostel gelesen und anschließend Gott gelobt wurde. Was hier wie eine einheitliche Szene erscheint, kennen wir nur als einzelne Elemente aus verschiedenen Evangelien. Vom unerwarteten Erscheinen des Auferstandenen inmitten des Apostelkreises berichten sowohl Mt als auch Lk,[53] während der Verweis auf die bereits in den Schriften enthaltene Verkündigung des Auferstandenen typisch lukanisch ist und sich sowohl in der Emmauserzählung als auch im Lukasschluss findet.[54] Vom Lobpreis Gottes ist nur bei Mk und Mt die Rede, dort bildet er jedoch den Abschluss des Abendmahls vor dem Gang auf den Ölberg.[55]

Im Rahmen seiner christologischen Deutung von Psalm 22 zitiert Justin zwar immer wieder aus den Denkwürdigkeiten der Apostel und damit aus Evangelienschriften, die ihm aber vermutlich kaum in der heutigen Form vorgelegen haben dürften.[56] Nicht nur die hier angesprochenen Bezugnahmen

---

46 Justin, *dial.* 102,5 (PTS 47,248); *dial.* 103,9 (PTS 47,249).
47 Justin, *dial.* 101,3 (PTS 47,244).
48 Vgl. Mt 27,40-43; Mk 15,29-30; Lk 23,35. Thornton, Justin, 95, stellt zu Recht fest: „Justin […] gibt diese Passage aber keineswegs wörtlich wieder."
49 Justin, *dial.* 104 (PTS 47,249-250). Vgl. Mt 27,35; Mk 15,24; Lk 23,34.
50 Justin, *dial.* 105,5 (PTS 47,251).
51 Justin, *dial.* 107,1 (PTS 47,253).
52 Justin, *dial.* 106,1 (PTS 47,252). Vgl. auch Thornton, Justin, 96.
53 Mt 28,10; Lk 24,36.
54 Vgl. Lk 24,25-26 und 44-46.
55 Vgl. Mt 26,30; Mk 14,26.
56 Vgl. auch die Tabelle zum Textbestand von Ps 22,8-9 bei Justin und bei Mt und Lk von H. Koester, The Text of the Synoptic Gospels in the Second Century, in: Gospel Traditions in the Second Century. Origins, Recensions, Text and Transmission, hg. von B. Aland/W.L. Petersen, Christianity and Judaism in Antiquity 3, Notre Dame 1989, 19-37, hier 31. Für Koester ist damit

und Zitate zeigen eine unübersehbare Tendenz zur Verknüpfung und Vereinheitlichung insbesondere des Stoffes aus Mt und Lk, der darüber hinaus durch anderes, uns zum Teil unbekanntes Material ergänzt wird.[57] Will man nicht meinen, dass Justin die synoptischen Evangelien noch nicht gekannt und deshalb vorsynoptische Traditionen verarbeitet habe,[58] oder aber, dass er unter einem schwachen Gedächtnis gelitten und deswegen nur sehr ungenau zitiert habe,[59] liegt es nahe anzunehmen, dass er, wie bereits Harnacks kirchengeschichtlicher Lehrer Moritz von Engelhardt vermutet hatte, aus so etwas wie einer nachsynoptischen Evangelienharmonie zitiert.[60] Kaum zufällig hören wir ab der Mitte des zweiten Jahrhunderts häufiger von der Existenz solcher Evangelienharmonien. Tatians Diatessaron war vielleicht die prominenteste, aber wohl keineswegs die erste Evangelienharmonie.[61] Und: Tatian war ein römischer Schüler des Justin.[62] Für Justins Verwendung einer Evangelienharmonie spricht auch, dass die von ihm wörtlich wiedergegebenen Aussprüche Jesu mehrfach in der gleichen harmonisierten Weise wiederkehren.[63] Ähnliches gilt aber auch für das narrative Material.[64] Als Beispiel mag an dieser Stelle ein kurzer Abschnitt aus der Geburtsgeschichte genügen, dessen einzelne Bestandteile im Dialog mit Tryphon noch häufiger begegnen:

> Damals aber, als der Knabe in Bethlehem geboren wurde, nahm Josef, da er in jenem Dorfe nirgends Unterkunft finden konnte, in einer Höhle in der Nähe des Dorfes Quartier. Als sie damals an jenem Ort weilten, hatte Maria Christus geboren und ihn in eine Krippe gelegt. Hier haben ihn die Magier aus Arabien gefunden.[65]

---

sehr deutlich, dass Justin den Text aus Mt und Lk verbessert, um die Erfüllung der Verheißung noch stärker herausstreichen zu können.

57 Vgl. auch Stanton, Jesus, 103, der jedoch Justins Tendenzen zur Vereinheitlichung herunterspielt. Stanton kann sich lediglich vorstellen, dass Justin zu katechetischen Zwecken neben den synoptischen Evangelien zusätzlich noch eine Zusammenstellung von verschiedenen Aussprüchen Jesu verwendet hat.

58 So Bousset, Evangeliencitate, 114-116.

59 So K. Semisch, Die apostolischen Denkwürdigkeiten des Märtyrers Justinus, Hamburg 1848, 389-392; ähnlich auch Zahn, Geschichte, 463-465.

60 So bereits M. von Engelhardt, Das Christenthum Justins des Märtyrers. Eine Untersuchung über die Anfänge der katholischen Glaubenslehre, Erlangen 1878, 335-348.

61 Vgl. auch M.-É. Boismard, Le Diatessaron. De Tatien à Justin, ÉtB N.S. 15, Paris 1992, sowie die kritische Auseinandersetzung von W.L. Petersen, Tatian's Diatessaron. Its Creation, Significance, and History in Scholarship, VigChr.S 25, Leiden 1994.

62 Vgl. dazu auch die höchst interessanten Ausführungen von W.L. Petersen, Textual Evidence of Tatian's Dependence upon Justin's ΑΠΟΜΝΗΜΟΝΕΥΜΑΤΑ, NTS 36, 1990, 512-534.

63 A.J. Bellinzoni, The Sayings of Jesus in the Writings of Justin Martyr, NT.S 17, Leiden 1967; vgl. auch L.K. Kline, Harmonized Sayings of Jesus in the Pseudo-Clementine Homilies and Justin Martyr, ZNW 66, 1975, 223-241.

64 Vgl. auch Allert, Revelation, 197-199.

65 Justin, *dial.* 78,5 (PTS 47,205): Γεννηθέντος δὲ τότε τοῦ παιδίου ἐν Βηθλεέμ, ἐπειδὴ Ἰωσὴφ οὐκ εἶχεν ἐν τῇ κώμῃ ἐκείνῃ ποῦ καταλῦσαι, ἐν σπηλαίῳ τινὶ σύνεγγυς τῆς κώμης κατέλυσε. καὶ τότε αὐτῶν ὄντων ἐκεῖ, ἐτετόκει ἡ Μαρία τὸν Χριστὸν καὶ ἐν φάτνῃ αὐτὸν ἐτεθείκει, ὅτου ἐλθόντες οἱ ἀπὸ Ἀραβίας μάγοι εὗρον αὐτόν.

Die Verknüpfung zwischen Lk 2,7 (Krippe) und Mt 2,1-25 ist überdeutlich. Darüber hinaus finden sich jedoch auch andere Elemente wie die Höhle, die vermutlich aus dem Protevangelium Jakobi stammt, sowie die Herkunft der Magier aus Arabien, die bei Justin offenbar niemals fehlen durfte.[66] Justins Evangelienharmonie enthielt offenbar neben dem synoptischen noch zusätzliches Material, das wahrscheinlich aus anderen Evangelien stammte.[67] Einen Hinweis auf dessen Herkunft gibt Justin vielleicht sogar selbst.

III. Bezieht sich Justin auf das Petrusevangelium?

Im Zuge seiner Auslegung der Schlussdoxologie des besagten Psalms muss Justin erläutern, dass mit dem Namen des Herrn kein anderer als Christus und mit den Nachkommen Jakobs und Israels nur die Christen gemeint sein können. Auch hier hilft ihm ein Rückgriff auf die Denkwürdigkeiten der Apostel:

> Wenn es heißt, er habe den Namen eines der Apostel in Petrus geändert, und wenn in dessen Denkwürdigkeiten geschrieben steht, dass er außerdem auch noch zwei Brüdern, den Söhnen des Zebedäus, den Namen Boanerges, das meint Donnersöhne, beigelegt habe, so war damit angedeutet, dass er derjenige ist, durch welchen auch die Namen Jakob und Israel verliehen worden sind.[68]

Da zuvor ausdrücklich von Petrus die Rede war, kann sich die Formulierung ἀπομνημονεύματα αὐτοῦ hier nur auf Petrus zurückbeziehen. Justin spräche demnach hier eindeutig von den Denkwürdigkeiten des Petrus und meinte damit offenbar das Petrusevangelium.[69] Vollkommen zu Recht wurde jedoch darauf hingewiesen, dass diese Formulierung bei Justin absolut singulär sei.[70] Einfacher wäre es also, die Aussage zu ἀπομνημονεύματα τῶν ἀποστόλων αὐτοῦ zu ergänzen.[71] Diejenigen, die den Wortlaut des Textes bewahren wollen, vermuten nun aber, Justin meine an dieser Stelle gar nicht das Petrus-, sondern das Evangelium seines Nachfolgers Markus, weil nur dieses von einer wirklichen Umbenennung des Simon in Petrus ausgeht und vom Beinamen der Zebedaïden berichtet.[72] Sie berufen sich dafür zusätzlich auf Papias von Hierapolis[73] und auf Irenaeus[74], die den in ihren Augen so wenig prominenten

66 Justin, *dial.* 77,4 (PTS 47,203-204); *dial.* 78,1.2.7 (PTS 47,204-205); *dial.* 88,1 (PTS 47,222).
67 Vgl. auch Allert, Revelation, 199.
68 Justin, *dial.* 106,3 (PTS 47,252).
69 Harnack, Bruchstücke, 40; vgl. auch P. Pilhofer, Justin und das Petrusevangelium, ZNW 81, 1990, 60-78.
70 Denker, Theologiegeschichtliche Stellung, 12; Thornton, Justin, 96-97.
71 So die Konjektur von M. Marcovich, Iustini Martyris Dialogus cum Tryphone, PTS 47, Berlin-New York 1997, 252.
72 Dafür hat sich zuletzt Thornton, Justin, ausgesprochen. Ohne Thorntons Forschungen zu erwähnen, schließt sich auch Stanton, Jesus, 101, dieser Ansicht an.
73 Euseb, *h.e.* III,39,15 (GCS 9,290,21-292,2).
74 Irenaeus, *haer.* III,1,1

Evangelisten Markus mit der großen Gestalt des Apostels Petrus in Verbindung brachten und ihn deshalb den Nachfolger des Petrus nannten. Ob jedoch auch Justin von dieser Interpretation wusste[75] und sie darüber hinaus ohne jede Erklärung als allgemein bekannt voraussetzen konnte,[76] muss jedoch sehr zweifelhaft bleiben. Es ist jedenfalls keineswegs zwingend anzunehmen, dass Justin das synoptische Markusevangelium gemeint habe,[77] wenn er hier von den ἀπομνημονεύματα αὐτοῦ spricht.

Doch leider lässt sich auch umgekehrt nicht mehr nachweisen, dass die Umbenennung des Petrus und die Beinamen der Zebedaïden einmal im Petrusevangelium gestanden haben, weil das Akhmîmfragment lediglich die Erzählungen von Passion, Tod und Auferstehung Jesu umfasst.[78] Schon Harnack klagte darüber, dass uns „ein neidisches Geschick" sowohl den Anfang als auch das Ende des Petrusevangeliums vorenthalten habe.[79] Was auch immer man dort über Jesu Geburt und seine irdische Wirksamkeit einmal gelesen haben mag, lässt sich nach dem gegenwärtigen Stand der Forschung beim besten Willen nicht mehr rekonstruieren. Doch uns fehlt nicht nur einiges an Text aus diesem Evangelium, sondern – und das ist nicht minder bedauerlich – auch seine frühe Textgestalt, da das einzig überlieferte längere Fragment aus dem sechsten Jahrhundert stammt.[80] Damit wird jede Argumentation, die sprachliche Ähnlichkeiten feststellen und auf dieser Basis literarische Abhängigkeiten konstatieren will, ausgesprochen schwierig, wenn nicht gar unmöglich.[81] Doch selbst wenn sich Justins ἀπομνημονεύματα der Apostel nicht direkt auf das Petrusevangelium bezogen haben, gibt es nichtsdestoweniger eine ganze Reihe von auffälligen Berührungen zwischen beiden Texten.[82]

Sie lassen sich vielleicht am ehesten mit einer durch die historische Situation geprägten Gleichartigkeit erklären, in der sich Christen genötigt

---

[75] Heard, The ΑΠΟΜΝΗΜΟΝΕΥΜΑΤΑ, behauptet ohne jeden Beweis, dass Justin das Werk des Papias gelesen habe.

[76] Vgl. auch Pilhofer, Justin, 68: „Man müßte in diesem Fall annehmen, daß um die Mitte des zweiten Jahrhunderts jedem potentiellen Leser des Dialogs die Gleichsetzung 'Memoiren des Petrus = Markusevangelium' eine Selbstverständlichkeit gewesen sei."

[77] Anders als Thornton annimmt, könnte die Bezeichnung der Donnersöhne auch von Mk her in die Synoptikertexte eingewandert sein, ein später Zeuge dafür ist Codex Bezae zu Lk 6,14. Dass von einer Umbenennung des Petrus die Rede ist, dürfte eher vom Auslegungsziel als vom Text selbst bestimmt sein, vgl. etwa auch Tertullian, adv. Marc. IV,13,5 (SC 456,170).

[78] Vgl. zur Christologie des Fragments vor allem P.M. Head, On the Christology of the Gospel of Peter, VigChr 46, 1992, 209-224; J.W. McCant, The Gospel of Peter. Docetism Reconsidered, NTS 30, 1984, 258-273, sowie den Beitrag von M. Myllykoski im vorliegenden Band.

[79] A. Harnack, Über die jüngsten Entdeckungen auf dem Gebiete der ältesten Kirchengeschichte, PJ 92, 1898, 191-219, hier 200.

[80] Darauf macht Nicklas, Ein „Neutestamentliches Apokryphon", 261-265, aufmerksam.

[81] Vgl. auch Nicklas, Juden, 211-212 n. 19.

[82] Das geben auch diejenigen zu, die meinen, Justin habe sich bei seiner Auslegung des 22. Psalms nicht auf das Petrusevangelium berufen; vgl. Denker, Theologiegeschichtliche Stellung, 10-12; Thornton, Justin, 105 n. 51.

sahen, in der Auseinandersetzung mit Juden[83] nachzuweisen, dass ihre Erzählungen von Jesus Christus im Einklang mit den alttestamentarischen Schriften stehen.[84] Bei aller Abgrenzung den Juden gegenüber wird diesen aber zugleich auch die Möglichkeit zu Umkehr und Buße eröffnet, wenn sie denn Christus als den in den alttestamtlichen Schriften verheißenen Sohn Gottes anerkennen.

IV. Die Gemeinsamkeiten zwischen Justin und dem Petrusevangelium

Bereits auf den ersten Blick fällt auf, dass sowohl Justin als auch das Petrusevangelium darum bemüht sind, allein den Juden die Schuld an Jesu Tod zu geben. Für Justin waren sie es, die Christus gekreuzigt haben,[85] und für das Petrusevangelium sie sind es noch heute, die die Christen bekämpfen und als κακοῦργοι beschimpfen.[86] Dass die Juden allein für den Tod Jesu verantwortlich waren, wird bereits zu Beginn des Fragments aus dem Petrusevangelium mit einer kleinen Szene veranschaulicht, der offenbar das Verhör Jesu vorangegangen ist: von den Juden, so heißt es dort, reinigte sich keiner die Hände, weder Herodes noch einer seiner Richter. Statt dessen ließ Herodes Jesus abführen, während Pilatus demgegenüber ganz und gar unbeteiligt bleibt.[87] Dahinter steckt keineswegs – wie man vielleicht zunächst annehmen könnte – eine prorömische Tendenz, die Pilatus von der Schuld am Tod Jesu freisprechen möchte,[88] „es geht dem Verfasser des Petrusevangeliums vielmehr darum, die Juden und ihr Verhalten in den Vordergrund zu rücken."[89] Er will nicht die Römer entlasten, sondern die Juden belasten, weil es ihm vor allem um die Juden zu tun ist.[90] Demgegenüber mag man nun aber einwenden, dass der Vorwurf, die Juden träfe die Hauptschuld am Tode Jesu, nicht sehr charakteristisch ist und sich auch bei anderen frühchristlichen Schriftstellern häufiger findet.[91] Das ist zweifellos richtig. Und doch kann anhand von einigen aufschlussreichen Beispielen die besondere und sehr

---

[83]   Vgl. dazu auch J. Carleton Paget, Anti-Judaism and Early Christian Identity, ZAC 1, 1997, 195-225.
[84]   Sowohl dem Verfasser des Petrusevangeliums als auch Justin wird in jüngster Zeit immer wieder vorgeworfen, von massiver antijüdischer Polemik geprägt zu sein; vgl. Nicklas, Juden, 209-211. In aller Deutlichkeit äußert sich jetzt auch D. Rokéah, Justin Martyr and the Jews, Jewish and Christian Perspectives Series 5, Leiden 2002, in diese Richtung.
[85]   Das betont auch Pilhofer, Justin, 69-71.
[86]   EvPetr 26 (GCS.NF 11,38).
[87]   EvPetr 1-2 (GCS.NF 11,32).
[88]   Vgl. auch Denker, Theologiegeschichtliche Stellung, 79.
[89]   Döpp, Deutung, 53.
[90]   Vgl. dazu auch ausführlich Denker, Theologiegeschichtliche Stellung, 78-87, der das Petrusevangelium für ein judenchristliches Evangelium hält.
[91]   Vgl. Denker, Theologiegeschichtliche Stellung, 11; Pilhofer, Justin, 71, sowie Döpp, Deutung, 29-30, der in diesem Zusammenhang beispielsweise auf Melito von Sardes hinweist.

charakteristische Nähe zwischen Justin und dem Petrusevangelium deutlich
werden, die über diese noch eher allgemeine Gemeinsamkeit hinausgeht.

1. Die Verspottung Jesu

Beide Texte schildern die Verspottung Jesu entgegen der synoptischen
Tradition und erzählen davon, dass die Juden bzw. das jüdische Volk und
nicht die römischen Soldaten Jesus verspotteten, indem sie ihn auf einen
Richterstuhl setzten und dazu aufforderten, über sie zu richten.[92] Dieser
Darstellung liegt ein offenbar schon älterer Weissagungsbeweis nach Jes 58,2
zugrunde, wonach festgestellt wird, dass das Volk nur scheinbar gerecht ist
und darüber ein Urteil von seinem Herrn fordert.[93] Um die Sache noch
deutlicher zu machen, verknüpft Justin diese Aussage zusätzlich mit Jes 65,2,
wo erneut der Widerspruch des halsstarrigen Volkes gegen seinen Messias
zum Ausdruck gebracht wird.[94] Trotz einiger Unterschiede der Texte im
Einzelnen[95] zeigen die beiden Erzählungen insofern strukturelle Gemeinsamkeiten,[96] als sie Jesu Leiden und Passion ganz im Licht der alttestamentarischen Weissagungen erscheinen lassen. Sie konzentrieren sich darauf
zu zeigen, dass die Schrift mit Jesus Christus erfüllt ist[97] und wenden sich
damit in großer Eindringlichkeit an die Juden, die das noch immer nicht
begreifen wollen, obwohl sie doch durch die Weissagungen der Schrift
eigentlich schon längst überführt sind.[98]

2. Die Verlosung der Kleider Jesu unter dem Kreuz

Ähnliches gilt nun auch von der Verlosung der Kleider Jesu unter dem Kreuz,
die auch in allen kanonischen Evangelien als die Erfüllung der Weissagung

---

[92]   Justin, 1 apol. 35,6 (Paradosis 39,80) und EvPetr 7 (GCS.NF 11,7); vgl. zu beiden Texten auch
       Pilhofer, Justin, 72-73, der ausdrücklich betont: „Hier wie bei Justin sind die Juden die
       Handelnden." Justin, 1 apol. 35, steht insofern in enger Verbindung zu dial. 98-107, als auch hier
       intensiv auf den 22. Psalm Bezug genommen wird, vgl. auch P. Prigent, Justin et l'Ancien
       Testament. L'argument scripturaire du traité de Justin contre toutes les hérésies comme source
       principale du dialogue avec Tryphon et de la première Apologie, ÉtB, Paris 1964, 279-281.
[93]   Vgl. zu diesem Weissagungsbeweis auch M. Dibelius, Die alttestamentlichen Motive in der
       Leidensgeschichte des Petrus- und des Johannesevangeliums, Botschaft und Geschichte I
       (1953), 221-247, hier 224-225. Vgl. auch den Beitrag von T. Hieke im vorliegenden Band.
[94]   Vgl. dazu Denker, Theologiegeschichtliche Stellung, 9-10; Prigent, Justin, 281-282, und
       Skarsaune, Proof, 147.
[95]   Diese Unterschiede betont insbesondere Denker, Theologiegeschichtliche Stellung, 9-10.
[96]   Vgl. auch Pilhofer, Justin, 73.
[97]   Vgl. Denker, Theologiegeschichtliche Stellung, 65-67, für das Petrusevangelium. Für Justin gilt
       das jedoch ganz genauso.
[98]   Vgl. auch Nicklas, Juden, 216.

von Ps 22,19 gedeutet wird.[99] Doch nur bei Justin[100] und im Petrusevangelium,[101] nicht aber für die Verfasser der kanonischen Evangelien, sind es wiederum allein die Juden, die dort um die Kleider ihres Herrn losen.[102] Somit zeigt sich auch die Gestaltung dieser Szene ganz auf die Erfüllung der Verheißung und damit auf die Auseinandersetzung mit den Juden zugeschnitten.

3. Das Herausziehen der Nägel nach dem Tode Jesu

Das Petrusevangelium und Justin erzählen davon, dass die Juden Jesus bei der Kreuzabnahme die Nägel aus seinen Händen und Füßen zogen, während man das aus den kanonischen Evangelien nur indirekt erschließen kann.[103] Diese an sich unwichtig erscheinende Einzelheit ist offenbar deshalb für Justin und das Petrusevangelium von Bedeutung, weil sie von beiden Autoren als Erfüllung der Aussage von Ps 22,17 „sie haben meine Hände und Füße durchgraben" durch das seinem Messias gegenüber noch immer halsstarrige Volk der Juden gewertet wird.[104]

4. Die mangelnde Buße der Juden und die Zerstörung von Tempel und Stadt

Sowohl Justin als auch das Petrusevangelium verstehen die Zerstörung des Tempels und der Stadt Jerusalem als die gerechte Strafe für die Ablehnung Jesu.[105] Für den Verfasser des Petrusevangeliums erkennen die Juden, Ältesten und Priester nach dem von verschiedenen Zeichen begleiteten Tod Jesu[106]

---

[99] Mk 15,24; Mt 27,35; Lk 23,34 sowie Joh 19,24; vgl. auch Pilhofer, Justin, 73-74, und Denker, Theologiegeschichtliche Stellung, 68.

[100] Justin, *1 apol.* 35,8 (Paradosis 39,80), im unmittelbaren Zusammenhang mit der eben interpretierten Verspottungsszene sowie in *dial.* 97,3 (PTS 47,237) und 104 (PTS 47,249-250).

[101] EvPetr 12 (GCS.NF 11,34).

[102] Pilhofer, Justin, 74, urteilt: „Dies ist eine Übereinstimmung, der als solcher schon entscheidendes Gewicht zukommt."

[103] EvPetr 21 (GCS.NF 11,36) und Justin, *1 apol.* 35 (Paradosis 39,80), im unmittelbaren Kontext zum Losen um das Gewand. Die Auferstehungserzählungen bei Lk 24,39-40 und Joh 20,25 setzen voraus, dass man Jesus ans Kreuz genagelt hatte, vgl. auch Denker, Theologiegeschichtliche Stellung, 76. Gleichzeitig macht er (11) aber auch deutlich, dass dieses Motiv nicht nur bei Justin und im Petrusevangelium begegnet.

[104] Vgl. auch Denker, Theologiegeschichtliche Stellung, 77, zum Petrusevangelium. In *1 apol.* 35 nimmt Justin mit der Schilderung des Herausziehens der Nägel und dem Losen um das Gewand Bezug auf zwei Verse aus Ps 22, auf die sich eben auch das Petrusevangelium stützt, vgl. auch Skarsaune, Proof, 147.

[105] EvPetr 25 (GCS.NF 11,36-37) und Justin, *dial.* 107-108 (PTS 47,253-255). Das Thema begegnet bei Justin jedoch noch häufiger, vgl. Döpp, Deutung, 27-28.

[106] Nach EvPetr 15-17 (GCS.NF 11,34-35) herrschte Finsternis, nachdem Jesus ans Kreuz geschlagen wurde; EvPetr 21 (GCS.NF 11,36) berichtet davon, dass die Erde bebte, als Jesu Leichnam vom Kreuz genommen wurde. Für das Volk geben die Zeichen bei seinem Tod

plötzlich ihre eigenen Verfehlungen und beginnen zu wehklagen: „Wehe unseren Sünden! Nahe gekommen ist das Gericht und das Ende Jerusalems!"[107] Der folgende Vers macht klar, dass nunmehr auch mit der Zerstörung des Tempels zu rechnen ist.[108] In der Tötung Jesu kulminieren demnach die Sünden des Volkes Israel,[109] ihr Maß ist mit der Kreuzigung des Gottessohnes endgültig voll.[110] Und doch will der Hinweis auf den Untergang Jerusalems die Juden zur Buße und zum Glauben an den Herrn bringen.[111] Während die Anführer des Volkes verstockt bleiben und gleichsam wider besseres Wissen handeln, zeigt das Volk nunmehr deutliche Anzeichen von Reue, schlägt sich an die Brust und murrt über seine Anführer: „Wenn bei seinem Tod diese überaus großen Zeichen geschehen sind, seht, wie gerecht er war!"[112] Damit gibt der Verfasser des Petrusevangeliums seiner Hoffnung Ausdruck, dass zumindest einige Juden die geschehenen Zeichen zum Anlass nehmen, Buße zu tun und umzukehren.[113]

In eben diesen Zusammenhang stellt auch Justin seine ausführliche Erörterung über die den Juden gegebenen Zeichen.[114] In den Denkwürdigkeiten der Apostel wird erzählt, dass die Juden ein Zeichen forderten und daraufhin lediglich das Zeichen des Jona erhielten, welches sie damals jedoch nicht verstanden.[115] Doch spätestens nach der Auferstehung hätten sie das Zeichen deuten und dementsprechend umkehren und wie die Niniviten Buße tun müssen, „damit nicht euer Volk und eure Stadt vernichtet werden, wie es geschehen ist."[116] Einsicht und Umkehr der Juden hätten also offenbar die Zerstörung Jerusalems und die Exilierung des Volkes verhindern können.

---

hingegen den Anlass, umzudenken und Jesus für einen Gerechten zu halten (EvPetr 28 GCS.NF 11,38).

107 EvPetr 25 (GCS.NF 11,36-37): οὐαὶ, ταῖς ἁμαρτίας ὑμῶν. ἤγγισεν ἡ κρίσις καὶ τὸ τέλος Ἰερουσαλήμ. Vgl. auch Denker, Theologiegeschichtliche Stellung, 81-82, und Döpp, Deutung, 54-55.

108 EvPetr 26 (GCS.NF 11,38), vgl. auch Döpp, Deutung, 55.

109 Vgl. zum Topos des Prophetenmordes auch die Untersuchung von O.-H. Steck, Israel und das gewaltsame Geschick der Propheten. Untersuchungen zur Überlieferung des deuteronomistischen Geschichtsbildes im Alten Testament, Spätjudentum und Urchristentum, WMANT 23, Neukirchen 1967.

110 Vgl. auch EvPetr 17 (GCS.NF 11,36) und Denker, Theologiegeschichtliche Stellung, 82.

111 Vgl. auch Denker, Theologiegeschichtliche Stellung, 82; Döpp, Deutung, 55-56: „Doch verbindet das Petrusevangelium damit kein Verwerfungsurteil. Vielmehr paßt sich die Erwähnung der Zerstörung Jerusalems in die allgemeine apologetische Tendenz ein. Mit dem Topos der Tötung der Propheten – einschließlich Jesu – durch Israel in Verbindung mit der Zerstörung Jerusalems als direkte Folge zielt das Petrusevangelium auf Umkehr zumindest eines Teiles der Juden."

112 EvPetr 28 (GCS.NF 11,38): εἰ τῷ θανάτῳ αὐτοῦ ταῦτα τὰ μέγιστα σημεῖα γέγονεν. ἴδετε ὅτι πόσον δίκαιός ἐστιν. Vgl. auch Nicklas, Juden, 219-220.

113 Vgl. auch Denker, Theologiegeschichtliche Stellung, 82: „Mit der Umkehr der Führer der Juden rechnet der Verfasser des PE nicht mehr."

114 Justin, dial. 107-108 (PTS 47,253-255.).

115 Justin, dial. 107,1 (PTS 47,253), vgl. auch Prigent, Justin, 218-219.

116 Justin, dial. 108,1 (PTS 47,255): καὶ τὸ ἔθνος καὶ ἡ πόλις ὑμῶν μὴ ἁλῷ καταστραφεῖσα ὡς κατεστράφη, vgl. auch Döpp, Deutung, 28.

Aber selbst dieses Zeichen, so Justin, missachten die Juden bis auf den heutigen Tag:

> Ja, nicht einmal nach der Eroberung eurer Stadt und der Verwüstung eures Landes tut ihr Buße, sondern erkühnt euch, Jesus und alle seine Gläubigen zu verfluchen.[117]

Justin versteht also den Untergang der Stadt Jerusalem als ein weiteres Zeichen auf der Linie des Jonazeichens, das den Juden gegeben ist, um sie auch weiterhin zur Umkehr zu mahnen.[118] Denn noch ist die Chance nicht vertan, noch haben sie die Möglichkeit, ihren Herrn zu erkennen, Buße zu tun und zu ihm umzukehren.[119]

5. Die Grabeswache und die Angst vor dem Jüngerbetrug

In je eigener Weise setzen sich beide Texte mit dem jüdischen Einwand auseinander, die Jünger hätten den Leichnam Jesu weggeschafft und daraufhin behauptet, er sei auferstanden, den wir auch aus dem Sondergut des Mt kennen.[120] Für Justin zeigt sich die Halsstarrigkeit und mangelnde Bußfertigkeit der Juden darin, dass sie die Auferstehung zum Anlass nehmen, wie bei Mt befürchtet, den Auferstandenen als einen Verführer (πλάνος)[121] zu verleugnen und zu behaupten, dass sie ihn gekreuzigt haben, während seine Jünger ihn gestohlen haben und nun den Leuten weismachen, er sei auferstanden und in den Himmel aufgefahren.[122] Dagegen verbindet das Petrusevangelium den Einwand der Juden wie in Mt mit dem Wunsch nach einer Grabeswache. So bitten die Anführer der Juden Pilatus aus Angst vor ihrem eigenen Volk, das ja schon deutliche Anzeichen von Reue erkennen lässt, um die Gewährung einer Grabeswache, damit die Jünger Jesu Leichnam nicht stehlen können und das Volk dann die Möglichkeit hätte zu behaupten, er sei von den Toten auferstanden.[123] Im Einzelnen zeigt die Erzählung jedoch nur wenig Gemeinsamkeiten mit Mt;[124] insbesondere fällt auf, dass der Verfasser des Petrusevangeliums der Grabeswache aus römischen Soldaten auch die

---

117 Justin, *dial.* 108,3 (PTS 47,255): Πρὸς τούτοις δὲ καὶ ἁλούσης ὑμῶν τῆς πόλεως καὶ τῆς γῆς ἐρημωθείσης οὐ μετανοεῖτε, ἀλλὰ καὶ καταρᾶσθαι αὐτοῦ καὶ τῶν πιστευόντων εἰς αὐτὸν πάντων τολμᾶτε, vgl. auch Döpp, Deutung, 29.

118 Vgl. auch Skarsaune, Proof, 290: „In Justin, as in the tradition before him, the accusation is addressed directly to Israel – the Jewish guilt is emphasized in an effort to bring Israel to repentence."

119 Justin, *dial.* 108,3 (PTS 47,255): εὐχόμεθα κἂν νῦν μετανοήσαντας πάντας ἐλέους τυχεῖν παρὰ τοῦ εὐσπλάγχνου καὶ πολυελέου πατρὸς τῶν ὅλων θεοῦ.

120 EvPetr 30 (GCS.NF 11,38-39) und Justin, *dial.* 108,2 (PTS 47,255) sowie Mt 27,64 und Mt 28,13, vgl. dazu auch Denker, Theologiegeschichtliche Stellung, 11.

121 Justin, *dial.* 108,2 (PTS 47,255) vgl. Mt 27,63. Vgl. zu dieser bekannten jüdischen Polemik auch Denker, Theologiegeschichtliche Stellung, 85.

122 Justin, *dial.* 108,2 (PTS 47,255), vgl. dazu auch Allert, Revelation, 51: „Justin complains about the Jews spreading misconceptions about Christianity. "

123 EvPetr 30 (GCS.NF 11,38-39).

124 Zum Vergleich mit Mt 27,62-64 auch Denker, Theologiegeschichtliche Stellung, 45-47.

Anführer der Juden zugesellt, damit diese anschließend auf unfreiwillige
Weise zu Auferstehungszeugen werden.[125] Deutlicher kann dann auch das
vollständige Versagen der jüdischen Anführer, die wider besseres Wissen alles
daran setzen, dem Volk das Zeugnis der Auferstehung vorzuenthalten,[126]
kaum zum Ausdruck gebracht werden.

V. Fazit

Die hier vorgestellten Beispiele haben eine gewisse Nähe zwischen Justins
Denkwürdigkeiten der Apostel und dem Petrusevangelium erkennen lassen,
die nicht mit direkter literarischer Abhängigkeit erklärt werden muss. Bei
beiden Texten handelt es sich um je verschiedene Erzählungen des
Christusereignisses, denen jedoch gemeinsam ist, dass alles auf die Erfüllung
der Schrift durch Christus im Unterschied zu den Juden ankommt. Damit
gehören sie in die Situation der Auseinandersetzung zwischen einem
zunehmend von ehemaligen Heiden geprägten Christentum,[127] das nicht so
recht verstehen konnte, wieso die Juden trotz der Ereignisse der Jahre 70 und
132-135 weiterhin als Juden existieren und in der Mehrzahl ohne den für sie
bestimmten Messias auskommen wollten.[128] Darüber hinaus sah man sich
offenbar auch mit jüdischer Polemik gegenüber dem Christentum
konfrontiert.[129] Justin behauptete sogar, die Juden in Jerusalem hätten einige
Männer aus ihren Reihen ausgewählt und mit verleumderischen An-
schuldigungen gegen die „gottlose Sekte der Christen" in alle Welt
hinausgeschickt.[130] Dennoch wird man von jüdischer Seite kaum mit
systematischer Gegenpropaganda gegen die Christen rechnen dürfen.[131]
Vielmehr wird man davon ausgehen müssen, dass sich Juden und Christen in

---

[125] EvPetr 31 (GCS.NF 11,40) und EvPetr 38 (GCS.NF 11,42), vgl. dazu auch Denker, Theologiegeschichtliche Stellung, 80, und Döpp, Deutung, 53.

[126] Vgl. auch EvPetr 48 (GCS.NF 11,44): συμφέρει γάρ, φασίν [die Anführer der Juden], ἡμῖν ὀφλῆσαι
μεγίστην ἁμαρτίαν ἔμπροσθεν τοῦ θεοῦ καὶ μὴ ἐμπεσεῖν εἰς χεῖρας τοῦ λαοῦ τῶν Ἰουδαίων καὶ
λιθασθῆναι. Schon allein, dass die Anführer der Juden hier geradezu formelhaft vom „Volk der
Juden" sprechen, ist auffällig, vgl. zu dieser Stelle auch Nicklas, Juden, 219.

[127] Denker, Theologiegeschichtliche Stellung, 78-80, hält das Petrusevangelium jedoch für ein
judenchristliches Evangelium.

[128] Vgl. dazu auch Nicklas, Juden, 220.

[129] Der bereits erwähnte Bischof Serapion von Antiochien hat nach dem Bericht des Euseb auch
eine Schrift an einen uns ansonsten unbekannten Domnus geschrieben, der angesichts der
Verfolgungssituation vom Christentum zum Judentum übergetreten war, vgl. Euseb, h.e.
VI,12,1 (GCS 9,2 544,4-8). Offensichtlich sah sich der Bischof von Antiochien, wo es einen
starken jüdischen Anteil an der Bevölkerung gab, in besonderer Weise genötigt, zu diesem
Problem Stellung zu nehmen. Vgl. auch W.A. Meeks/R.L. Wilken, Jews and Christians in
Antioch. In the First Four Centuries of the Common Era, Michigan 1978, 19-22.

[130] Justin, dial. 108,2 (PTS 47,255).

[131] Dazu, dass das Judentum begreiflicherweise viel weniger Notwendigkeit sah, sich mit dem
Christentum auseinanderzusetzen, vgl. auch J. Maier, Jüdische Auseinandersetzung mit dem
Christentum, EdF 177, Darmstadt 1982.

ihren Missionsbestrebungen häufiger als heftige Konkurrenten um die Gruppe der so genannten „Gottesfürchtigen" erfuhren.[132] Denn trotz vehementer Abgrenzung bleibt dennoch in beiden Texten ein intensives Bemühen um die Juden und ein eindringliches Werben um zumindest einige von ihnen spürbar. Die Hoffnung auf ihre Buße und Bekehrung ist weder in den Denkwürdigkeiten der Apostel noch im Petrusevangelium aufgegeben.[133] Beide Texte beziehen sich dabei immer wieder auf das Zeugnis der Schrift, die in ihren Augen für jeden nachvollziehbar mit dem Christusereignis erfüllt ist.[134] Wie wichtig gerade dieser Zugang für die Verbreitung des Christentums auch noch in der Mitte des zweiten Jahrhunderts war, zeigt Justins Rückgriff auf die Denkwürdigkeiten der Apostel in dem von ihm selbst auf die Zeit des 2. Jüdischen Krieges datierten Dialog mit dem Juden Tryphon.[135] Mit diesem Dialog wandte sich Justin nicht nur an Juden „aus der Beschneidung" wie Tryphon,[136] sondern auch und vor allem an dessen Gefährten, und damit wohl in erster Linie an Heiden, die sich mit dem Gedanken trugen, zum Judentum überzutreten.[137] Gegenüber diesen schilderte Justin seinen eigenen Weg zum Christentum als einen Weg, der ihn durch die verschiedenen Philosophenschulen führte. Doch keine dieser Schulrichtungen brachte ihn der Wahrheit näher. Schließlich begegnete dem mit den philosophischen Lehren unzufriedenen Justin ein alter Mann, der in ihm die Liebe zu der in der Schrift bezeugten prophetischen Verkündigung und zu jenen Männern weckte,[138] welche als die „Freunde Christi" bezeichnet werden.[139] Offenbar wies ihn der alte Mann auf die Übereinstimmung zwischen der prophetischen Verkün-

---

[132] Vgl. auch Skarsaune, Proof, 429: „This is probably to be explained by the phenomenon of missionary competition: The Church addressed the Gentile God-fearers who had already been the adressees of Jewish proselytizing efforts. "

[133] Das betont auch Denker, Theologiegeschichtliche Stellung, 78.

[134] Vgl. zu diesem Kanonbezug des Petrusevangeliums neben Denker, Theologiegeschichtliche Stellung, auch Nicklas, Juden, 221. Gleiches gilt aber auch für Justin und seine Denkwürdigkeiten.

[135] Nach Justin, *dial.* 1,3 (PTS 47,69-70) ist Tryphon vor dem Krieg nach Kleinasien geflohen; vgl. auch *dial.* 9,2 (PTS 47,85-86), wo es heißt, dass die Gefährten des Tryphon über den Jüdischen Krieg beratschlagten.

[136] Justin, *dial.* 1,3 (PTS 47,70) stellt sich Tryphon folgendermaßen vor: εἰμι δὲ ῾Εβραῖος ἐκ περιτομῆς.

[137] Die Gefährten des Tryphon spielen nicht nur in den ersten neun Kapiteln des Dialogs eine wichtige Rolle, vgl. etwa Justin, *dial.* 23,3 (PTS 47,108). Vgl. zu den anvisierten Adressaten des Dialogs mit Tryphon auch J. Nilson, To Whom is Justin's Dialogue with Trypho Addressed?, TS 38, 1977, 538-546. Allert, Revelation, 37-39, bleibt jedoch sehr unbestimmt und hält es für möglich, dass sich der Dialog in erster Linie an Juden richtet, aber auch von einem christlichen Publikum gelesen worden ist.

[138] Hyldahl, Philosophie, 81, sieht in der Figur des alten Mannes die Verkörperung der verlorenen Urphilosophie, vgl. auch A. Hofer, The Old Man as Christ in Justin's Dialogue with Trypho, VigChr 57, 2003, 1-21.

[139] Justin, *dial.* 8,2 (PTS 47,84). Vgl. zu den ersten Kapiteln des Dialogs auch Hyldahl, Philosophie, und J.C.M. van Winden, An Early Christian Philosopher. Justin Martyr's Dialogue with Trypho Chapters One to Nine, Philosophia Patrum 1, Leiden 1971.

digung und den Aussagen der Apostel hin.[140] Im Unterschied zu den
Philosophen erschienen Justin die Propheten zudem frei von aller Ruhmsucht
zu sein. In seinen Augen haben sie nur das niedergelegt, was sie selbst, vom
Heiligen Geist erfüllt, über Gott gehört und gesehen haben.[141] Ihre Schriften
sind damit nicht nur ungleich älter, sondern sie geben auch sehr viel
glaubwürdiger und verlässlicher als alle philosophischen Lehren über Gott den
Weltschöpfer und Vater Auskunft und verkündigen darüber hinaus das
Kommen seines Sohnes.[142] Justin fand hier die „allein zuverlässige und
nützliche Philosophie,"[143] die er nun, vom Zeugnis der Apostel immer wieder
und in allen Einzelheiten bestätigt, im Rahmen einer ausführlichen Erläuterung
und Diskussion um das richtige Schriftverständnis an andere, vorzugsweise an
die Gruppe der Gottesfürchtigen im Umkreis der Synagoge, weitergeben
wollte.[144]

---

[140] Vgl. auch Allert, Revelation, 216.

[141] Justin, *dial.* 7,1 (PTS 47,82-83), vgl. auch Allert, Revelation, 216.

[142] Justin, *dial.* 7,2 (PTS 47,83), vgl. auch Allert, Revelation, 216.

[143] Justin, *dial.* 8,1 (PTS 47,84): εὕρισκον φιλοσοφίαν ἀσφαλῆ τε καὶ σύμφορον. Vgl. dazu, dass die
Christen seit der Mitte des zweiten Jahrhunderts häufiger von ihrem Glauben als „unserer
Philosophie" sprachen und das Christentum ihrer Umwelt als eine philosophische Schullehre
darstellten, die es mit den paganen Lehren durchaus aufnehmen konnte, auch G. Bardy,
„Philosophie" et „philosophe" dans le vocabulaire chrétien des premiers siècles, RAM 25, 1949,
97-108.

[144] Vgl. auch Skarsaune, Proof, 425: „Justin indicates that he was converted to Christianity by
encountering a proclamation of the Christian kerygma in which the argument from prophecy
played a dominant role. This way of presenting the Christian Gospel deeply influenced Justin –
he adopts it himself. "

Die Paschahomilie des Melito von Sardes und das Petrusevangelium

von

Thomas R. Karmann

Einleitung

Einer der ältesten direkten Hinweise auf ein Petrusevangelium (ὀνόματι Πέτρου εὐαγγέλιον) und dessen Kenntnis im frühen Christentum findet sich in der Kirchengeschichte des Euseb von Caesarea und zwar im Kapitel über Serapion, den Bischof von Antiochien.[1] Euseb berichtet dort, dass Serapion wohl um 200 n.Chr. eine Schrift, vielleicht auch nur einen Brief an die Gemeinde von Rhossus über ein dem Petrus zugeschriebenes Evangelium verfasst habe, und zitiert auch daraus.[2] Aufgrund dieser eher dürftigen Aussagen in der Kirchengeschichte Eusebs wurde es in der Forschung immer wieder unternommen, einen *terminus ante quem* für einen 1886/87 im oberägyptischen Akhmîm gefunden Text (P.Cair. 10759), der allgemein als Fragment des Petrusevangeliums betrachtet wird, zu gewinnen.[3] Da sich bei Serapion bzw. im Werk des Bischofs von Caesarea aber kaum Angaben über den Inhalt des damals bekannten Petrusevangeliums finden und so letztlich auch keine Übereinstimmungen mit dem heute vorliegenden Fragment dieses Apokryphons aufgezeigt werden können, ist ein solches Vorgehen mit einer gewissen Vorsicht zu beurteilen.[4]

---

* Herrn Prof. em. Dr. Norbert Brox in Verehrung und Dankbarkeit zum 70. Geburtstag gewidmet.

1 Vgl. Euseb, *h.e.* VI, 12, 1-6 (GCS 9, 544-546).
2 Vgl. u.a. É. Junod, Eusèbe de Césarée, Sérapion d'Antioche et l'Évangile de Pierre. D'un évangile d'un pseudépigraphe, RSLR 24, 1988, 3-16; T.J. Kraus/T. Nicklas, Das Petrusevangelium und die Petrusapokalypse. Die griechischen Fragmente mit deutscher und englischer Übersetzung, GCS.NF 11; Neutestamentliche Apokryphen 1, Berlin-New York 2004, 12-16. Zu Serapion vgl. R. Hanig, Art. Serapion von Antiochien, in: LACL³ (2002), 631.
3 Vgl. z.B. J. Denker, Die theologiegeschichtliche Stellung des Petrusevangeliums. Ein Beitrag zur Frühgeschichte des Doketismus, EHS XXIII.36, Frankfurt/Main 1975, 57; C. Maurer/W. Schneemelcher, Petrusevangelium, in: NTApo⁶ 1, 184.
4 Eine Identität des von Serapion erwähnten Petrusevangeliums mit dem Text des Akhmîm-Codex kann letztlich nicht bewiesen werden, von daher kann aus dem Hinweis in der Kirchengeschichte des Euseb auch kein sicherer *terminus ad quem* für diese Schrift gewonnen

Nicht zuletzt, um einen früheren, vielleicht auch zuverlässigeren *terminus ad quem* zu ermitteln, versuchte man, in anderen Werken der antiken christlichen Literatur Hinweise auf das Petrusevangelium zu finden, vor allem aber auch Parallelen zu den Resten des Textes aus Akhmîm anzuführen, um neben Anhaltspunkten für die Datierung Hinweise auf die Kenntnis und den Einfluss dieser apokryphen Schrift in der frühen Kirche zu gewinnen. Eine breitere Debatte entstand dabei etwa um die Frage, ob Justin das Petrusevangelium gekannt und benutzt habe.[5] Mögliche Übereinstimmungen zwischen dem Text des Akhmîm-Codex und anderen frühchristlichen Werken wurden bisher meines Wissens am ausführlichsten von Léon Vaganay und Jürgen Denker aufgearbeitet.[6] In die Diskussion über Anspielungen und Parallelen zum Petrusevangelium in der patristischen Literatur wurde bereits vor über vierzig Jahren von Othmar Perler die Paschahomilie des Melito von Sardes eingebracht.[7] Ziel des vorliegenden Beitrags ist es, die These des Schweizer Patristikers vorzustellen, seine Argumente auf ihre Stichhaltigkeit zu überprüfen und die Frage nach dem Verhältnis der beiden Schriften etwas weiterzuführen. Dem seien aber noch einige Hinweise auf Melito und seine Osterpredigt vorangestellt.

Melito von Sardes und seine Paschahomilie

Die wichtigsten Informationen zur Biographie Melitos[8] finden sich in der Kirchengeschichte Eusebs, u.a. in einem dort überlieferten Brief Polycrates' von Ephesus an Victor von Rom. Diesem Schreiben ist zu entnehmen, dass der Sardianer zur Zeit der Abfassung des Briefes an Victor, also um 190 n.Chr., bereits tot war. Daneben wird Melito darin einer der Wortführer der quartodezimanischen Osterpraxis genannt.[9] Ob er Bischof der lydischen Stadt Sardes war, ist fraglich.[10] Aus dem umfangreichen Verzeichnis der Schriften

---

werden. Darüber hinaus ist ja auch fraglich, ob der ursprüngliche Text des Akhmîm-Fragments den Titel „Petrusevangelium" trug. Vgl. Kraus/Nicklas, Petrusevangelium, 15-16.

5   Vgl. den Beitrag von K. Greschat in diesem Band.
6   Vgl. L. Vaganay, L'Évangile de Pierre, ÉtB, Paris ²1930, 147-196; Denker, Stellung, 9-30, sowie den Beitrag von M. Meiser in diesem Band. Zu weiteren direkten Hinweisen auf ein Petrusevangelium in der frühen Kirche vgl. Kraus/Nicklas, Petrusevangelium, 11-23.
7   Vgl. O. Perler, L'Évangile de Pierre et Méliton de Sardes, RB 71, 1964, 584-590. Wieder-abgedruckt in: idem, Sapientia et Caritas. Gesammelte Aufsätze zum 90. Geburtstag (Par. 29), hg. von D. Van Damme/O. Wermelinger/M. v. F. Nuvolone, Freiburg/Schweiz 1990, 331-337.
8   Allgemein zu Melito vgl. z.B. I. Angerstorfer, Melito und das Judentum, Regensburg 1985, 1-5; S.G. Hall, Art. Melito von Sardes, in: TRE 22 (1992), 424-428; G. Röwekamp, Art. Melito von Sardes, in: LACL³ (2002), 499-500.
9   Vgl. Euseb, *h.e.* V, 24, 5 (GCS 9, 492); Hall, Melito, 424.
10   In Euseb, *h.e.* IV, 26, 1 (GCS 9, 380) wird Melito als Bischof von Sardes bezeichnet, während Polycrates ihn nicht als solchen nennt, obwohl andere Autoritäten der Quartodezimaner im Brief an Victor mit ihren Amtsbezeichnungen aufgeführt werden. Vgl. Euseb, *h.e.* V, 24, 2-7 (GCS 9, 490-491).

Melitos bei Euseb ist jedoch zu erschließen, dass er zu den bedeutendsten christlichen Theologen der zweiten Hälfte des 2. Jahrhunderts zu zählen ist. Von seinen zahlreichen Werken, deren Titel Euseb überliefert hat, sind jedoch größtenteils nur Fragmente erhalten.[11]

Aus dem Werkverzeichnis in der Kirchengeschichte des Bischofs von Caesarea geht auch hervor, dass Melito zwei Bücher bzw. Schriften über das Pascha (τὰ Περὶ τοῦ πάσχα δύο) verfasst haben soll.[12] In den 30er Jahren des vergangenen Jahrhunderts wurde in einem Papyruscodex aus dem 4. Jahrhundert (P.Beatty VIII + P.Mich. inv. 5553) eine Homilie entdeckt, die *editio princeps* erstellte Campbell Bonner 1940 und identifizierte die Paschapredigt als Schrift des Melito.[13] Ein zweiter griechischer Zeuge befindet sich in der Bibliotheca Bodmeriana in Genf (P.Bodm. XIII). Dieser Textzeuge, Teil eines umfangreicheren Codex,[14] überliefert auch eine Überschrift, die die Zuschreibung an einen Melito sicherstellt. Diesen Text veröffentlichte Michel Testuz 1960.[15] Auf der Grundlage dieser beiden griechischen Textzeugen und unter Einbezug alter Übersetzungen[16] erarbeiteten Othmar Perler und Stuart George Hall die beiden bis heute maßgeblichen kritischen Editionen, jeweils mit Einleitung, Text, Übersetzung und kurzem Kommentar.[17] Dass es sich bei dieser Predigt um die beiden bei Euseb erwähnten Schriften bzw. Bücher über das Pascha handelt, ist zwar eher unwahrscheinlich, doch die Verfasserschaft Melitos von Sardes wird größtenteils akzeptiert. Aufgrund der Zuweisung der Osterhomilie zum Œuvre des Sardianers wird üblicherweise eine Entstehungszeit der Predigt zwischen 160 und 170 angenommen.[18]

Die Paschahomilie Melitos erfreute sich seit ihrer Entdeckung in der Forschung regen Interesses, vor allem die Untersuchung von Stil, Aufbau und Gattungsfragen, des Verhältnisses zur quartodezimanischen Osterpraxis, der Christologie und des Verhältnisses zum Judentum standen dabei im

---

[11] Vgl. Euseb, *h.e.* IV, 26, 1-14 (GCS 9, 380-388). Hall, Melito, 424-425.

[12] Vgl. Euseb, *h.e.* IV, 26, 2-3 (GCS 9, 380-382).

[13] Vgl. The Homily on the Passion by Melito Bishop of Sardis and Some Fragments of Apocryphal Ezekiel, StD 12, hg. von C. Bonner, London 1940 [= Text A].

[14] Zu diesem Codex weiterführend T. Nicklas/T. Wasserman, Theologische Linien im *Codex Bodmer Miscellani?*, in: T.J. Kraus/T. Nicklas (Hg.), New Testament Manuscripts, their Text and their World, TENT 2, Leiden-Boston 2006, 161-188.

[15] Vgl. Papyrus Bodmer XIII. Méliton de Sardes. Homélie sur la Pâque, hg. von M. Testuz, Genf 1960 [= Text B].

[16] Es gibt koptische, georgische und lateinische Übersetzungen sowie syrische Fragmente der Paschahomilie. Vgl. hierzu u.a. CPG I bzw. CPG.S 1092.

[17] Vgl. Méliton de Sardes, Sur la pâque et fragments. Introduction, texte critique, traduction et notes, SC 123, hg. von O. Perler, Paris 1966. Melito of Sardis, On Pascha and Fragments. Texts and Translations, OECT, hg. von S.G. Hall, Oxford 1979. Von Gregor Wurst wird derzeit eine Neuedition der Paschahomilie unter konsequenter Einbeziehung der orientalischen Textzeugen erarbeitet. Eine deutsche Übersetzung des kritischen Textes liegt bis heute noch nicht vor, Josef Blank stützte sich bei seiner Übertragung vor allem auf die Edition von Testuz. Vgl. Meliton von Sardes, Vom Passa. Die älteste christliche Osterpredigt, Sophia 3, übers. von J. Blank, Freiburg i.Br. 1963.

[18] Vgl. u.a. Perler, Méliton, 16-24; Hall, Melito, XVII-XXII; Angerstorfer, Melito, 2-5.

Vordergrund.[19] Die Osterpredigt lässt sich anhand der vier Doxologien[20] folgendermaßen gliedern: 1. Prolog (*pass*. 1-10). 2. Das alttestamentliche Pascha (*pass*. 11-45). 3. Die Vorbereitung des christlichen Pascha im Alten Testament (*pass*. 46-65). 4. Das neutestamentliche Pascha (*pass*. 66-105).[21] Für die Frage nach Gemeinsamkeiten zwischen der Homilie und dem Petrusevangelium kann man sich fast ausschließlich auf den letzten Abschnitt der Predigt beschränken, dort werden das Leiden und der Tod Christi sowie sein Triumph thematisiert. Dies ist mit einer langen Anklagerede gegen Israel verbunden.[22]

Die These einer literarischen Abhängigkeit Melitos vom Petrusevangelium

Ausgehend von dem eher negativen Urteil, das Léon Vaganay über die Benutzung des Petrusevangeliums in der frühchristlichen Literatur vor Origenes gefällt hatte, unternahm es Perler, anhand der Paschahomilie Melitos den Gegenbeweis anzutreten.[23] Als Hauptindiz für eine literarische Abhängigkeit dieser Predigt vom Petrusevangelium wertete Perler, dass in beiden Texten die Schuld für den Tod Jesu allein bei den Juden liege, während Pilatus hier wie dort entlastet werde.[24] Als Hauptargumente für seine These führte er die Händewaschung des Pilatus bzw. die Nichtdurchführung dieser durch die Juden und die Anordnung des Herodes zur Tötung Jesu sowohl bei Melito von Sardes als auch im Akhmîm-Codex an.[25] Daneben sah Perler die These literarischer Abhängigkeit zwischen beiden Schriften dadurch gestützt, dass

---

[19] Die ältere Literatur bis 1980 ist in zwei Bibliographien zusammengestellt. Vgl. R.M. Mainka, Melito von Sardes. Eine bibliographische Übersicht, Clar. 5, 1965, 225-255; H.R. Drobner, 15 Jahre Forschung zu Melito von Sardes (1965-1980). Eine kritische Bibliographie, VigChr 36, 1982, 313-333. Neuere Veröffentlichungen finden sich z.B. in den Bibliographien folgender Monographien: A. Stewart-Sykes, The Lamb's High Feast. Melito, *Peri Pascha* and the QuartoDeciman Paschal Liturgy at Sardis, VigChr.S 42, Leiden-Boston-Köln 1998, 207-218; L.H. Cohick, The *Peri Pascha* Attributed to Melito of Sardis. Setting, Purpose, and Sources, BJSt 327, Atlanta 2000, 159-177. Ein knapper, aber hilfreicher Überblick vor allem über die englischsprachige Forschung findet sich bei H.M. Knapp, Melito's Use of Scripture in *Peri Pascha*. Second-Century Typology, VigChr 54, 2000, 343-348.

[20] Vgl. Melito, *pass*. 10. 45. 65. 105 (SC 123, 64, 84, 94, 126).

[21] Zum Aufbau der Paschapredigt vgl. u.a. Perler, Méliton, 42-44; Hall, Melito XXII-XXIII; H.R. Drobner, Der Aufbau der Paschapredigt Melitos von Sardes, ThGl 80, 1990, 205-207.

[22] Othmar Perler beschränkte sich bei seinem literarkritischen Vergleich der beiden Schriften ebenfalls auf diesen Abschnitt. Vgl. Perler, Évangile, 584.

[23] Vgl. Perler, Évangile, 584; Vaganay, Évangile, 161-167. Vaganay konnte einen Einfluss des Petrusevangeliums auf die Predigt Melitos von Sardes natürlich noch nicht untersuchen, da die Homilie zu dieser Zeit ja gar nicht bekannt war.

[24] Vgl. Perler, Évangile, 584.

[25] Vgl. Perler, Évangile, 585-586. „Les coïncidences que nous venons de relever concernent le contenu, rarement les expressions. Elles sont certes d'une valeur inégale. Elles veulent être appréciées dans leur senssemble [!]. Celles du lavement des mains et des ordres par Hérode nous semblent décisives." Perler, Évangile, 590.

die Hinrichtung Jesu hier wie dort allein durch die Juden vollzogen werde, dass in beiden Texten entgegen kanonischen Passionstraditionen das Motiv der Entehrung des Herrn durch die Juden begegne und als Kreuzestitel „König Israels" benutzt werde. Daneben wurden die explizite Thematisierung von Nägeln bei der Kreuzigung, die Nennung von Galle und Essig, der Hinweis auf die Wohltaten Jesu an Israel und dessen Undankbarkeit sowie die Andeutung der Bestrafung Israels durch den Untergang Jerusalems als Übereinstimmungen zwischen der Paschahomilie und dem Petrusevangelium angeführt.[26] Obwohl Othmar Perler auch Divergenzen zwischen beiden Schriften wahrnahm, diese aber durch die Unterschiede im Genus wie auch in der Zielsetzung von Melitos Predigt und dem Petrusevangelium erklärte, kam er zu folgenden Ergebnis: „Nonobstant cela, une dépendance littéraire paraît certaine."[27] Daraus zog er zum einen die Konsequenz, dass der *terminus ante quem* für das Petrusevangelium, für dessen Bestimmung man ansonsten allgemein das Zeugnis Serapions bei Euseb heranzog, auf die Zeit um 170 n.Chr. herabgesetzt werden könne und dass andererseits die gängige Lokalisierung dieses Apokryphons im syrischen Raum durch dessen frühe Benutzung in Kleinasien als gar nicht mehr so sicher zu gelten habe.[28] Die These Perlers wurde in der Forschung weitgehend zustimmend aufgenommen, so z.B. von Maria Grazia Mara.[29] Daneben führte etwa auch Hall im Index seiner Edition der Paschapredigt Übereinstimmungen mit dem Petrusevangelium auf.[30]

---

[26] Vgl. Perler, Évangile, 587-590.

[27] Perler, Évangile, 590.

[28] Vgl. Perler, Évangile, 590. Darüber hinaus wurde in der Forschung auch die Benutzung bzw. Kenntnis anderer frühchristlicher Apokryphen, etwa der Johannesakten, durch Melito diskutiert. Vgl. z.B. S.G. Hall, Melito's Paschal Homily and the Acts of John, JThS NS 17, 1966, 95-98.

[29] Vgl. Évangile de Pierre. Introduction, texte critique, traduction, commentaire et index, SC 201, hg. von M.G. Mara, Paris 1973, 21-24 und Index s.v. Méliton. Il Vangelo di Pietro. Introduzione, versione, commento, SOCr 30, hg. v. M.G. Mara, Bologna 2003, 12. 19-22 und Index s.v. Melitone di Sardi.

[30] Vgl. Hall, Melito, 99. Hall verzeichnete im Index Parallelen, auf die schon Perler hingewiesen hatte: die Rolle des Herodes, den Kreuzestitel, Galle und Essig sowie die Erwähnung von Nägeln. Darüber hinaus wies er aber auch noch auf andere Übereinstimmungen hin: die Verwendung des Verbs σύρω in EvPetr III, 6 (GCS.NF 11, 32) und Melito, *pass.* 71 (SC 123, 98, 515), den Zeitpunkt der Finsternis während der Kreuzigung in EvPetr V, 15 (GCS.NF 11, 34) und Melito, *pass.* 94 (SC 123, 116,725 = OECT 52,705), das Schreien Jesu in EvPetr V, 19 (GCS.NF 11, 36) und Melito, *pass.* 98 (SC 123, 118,752) sowie die Geschehnisse bei seinem Tod, die Finsternis in EvPetr V, 15 (GCS.NF 11, 34) und Melito, *pass.* 97 (SC 123, 116,741), das Zerreißen des Vorhangs in EvPetr V, 20 (GCS.NF 11, 36) und Melito, *pass.* 98 (SC 123, 118,748f), das Beben der Erde und das Aufkommen von Furcht in EvPetr V, 21 (GCS.NF 11, 36) und Melito, *pass.* 98 (SC 123, 118,744-747).

Überprüfung möglicher Übereinstimmungen

Da die These Perlers in der bisherigen Forschung zumeist ohne nachmalige
Prüfung übernommen wurde, sollen im Folgenden seine Argumente kritisch
diskutiert werden.[31] Auf weitere Parallelen, auf welche z.B. Hall hinwies, soll
hier nicht eingegangen werden, da diese teils recht vage sind und es sich teils
um Motive handelt, die sowohl im Akhmim-Codex als auch in den kanonischen Passionsberichten begegnen. Eine Übernahme dieser durch Melito aus
dem Petrusevangelium muss deshalb nicht angenommen werden.[32]

Es soll jedoch an dieser Stelle noch auf ein methodisches Problem
hingewiesen werden, das die literarkritische Untersuchung des Verhältnisses
der Paschahomilie zum Petrusevangelium grundsätzlich erschwert. Von der
Predigt Melitos besitzen wir durch zwei griechische Textzeugen und diverse
alte Übersetzungen einen einigermaßen gesicherten Text, beim Petrusevangelium ist dies anders: Es liegt nämlich nur ein ausführlicher Textzeuge
vor, der Akhmîm-Codex (P.Cair. 10759). Dieser stammt aus dem späten 6. oder
frühen 7. Jahrhundert und beinhaltet wohl nur einen Teil des ehemaligen
Petrusevangeliums.[33] Nicht zuletzt P.Oxy. XLI 2949, der möglicherweise eine
Parallele zum Akhmîm-Fragment bietet, zeigt, mit welchen textlichen Varian-

---

[31] Die meines Wissens bisher einzige kritische Überprüfung stellt die knappe Diskussion der
Abhängigkeit Melitos vom Petrusevangeliums bei Denker dar. Vgl. Denker, Stellung 17-18.

[32] Dass sowohl in EvPetr III, 6 (GCS.NF 11, 32) und Melito, *pass.* 71 (SC 123, 98,515) vom
Wegschleifen bzw. -schleppen Jesu die Rede ist, kann Zufall sein, da die Kontexte in beiden
Texten nicht völlig identisch sind. Das Lexem σύρω kommt auch in Apg 8,3; 14,19 und 17,6 vor,
wo von Verfolgungen von Christen berichtet wird. Dies könnte die Verwendung in der
Paschahomilie eventuell erklären. EvPetr V, 15 (GCS.NF 11, 34) spricht ähnlich, wie Mt 27,45,
davon, dass bei der Kreuzigung gegen Mittag eine Finsternis anbrach, Melito, *pass.* 94 (SC 123,
116,725 = OECT 52,705) hingegen davon, dass Jesus „mitten am Tag" ermordet wurde.
Letzteres ist textkritisch aber unsicher, denn in Melito, *pass.* 71 und 78 (SC 123, 100,516 und
104,571) ist die Rede davon, dass Christus am Abend getötet wurde. Die Übereinstimmung
zwischen EvPetr V, 19 (GCS.NF 11, 36) und Melito, *pass.* 98 (SC 123, 118,752) ist ebenfalls recht
undeutlich, wenn doch vorhanden, z.B. auch aus einer Abhängigkeit Melitos von Mt
27,46.50 zu erklären. Die Finsternis in EvPetr V, 15 (GCS.NF 11, 34) und Melito, *pass.* 97 (SC
123, 116,741) kommt z.B. auch in Mt 27,45 vor. Die Parallele zwischen EvPetr V, 20 (GCS.NF 11,
36) und Melito, *pass.* 98 (SC 123, 118,748-749) ist eigentlich nicht vorhanden, da der Sardianer
wohl davon spricht, dass sich beim Tod Christi zwar nicht Israel, aber die Engel aus Trauer
ihre Kleider zerrissen haben. Wenn er hier doch vom Zerreißen des Tempelvorhangs sprechen
sollte, hätte er dieses Motiv z.B. auch aus Mt 27,51 kennen können. Das Beben der Erde in
EvPetr V, 21 (GCS.NF 11, 36) und Melito, *pass.* 98 (SC 123, 118,744-745) begegnet auch in Mt
27,51-52. In EvPetr V, 21 (GCS.NF 11, 36) wird davon gesprochen, dass beim Tod Jesu Furcht
entstand, als Subjekt dazu sind wohl die Juden anzunehmen, während in Melito, *pass.* 98 (SC
123, 118,746-747) davon die Rede ist, dass sich Israel nicht fürchtete, im Gegensatz dazu aber
die Himmel.

[33] Vgl. Kraus/Nicklas, Petrusevangelium, 25-31. Zur Datierung von P.Cair. 10759 vgl. vor allem
G. Cavallo/H. Maehler, Greek Bookhands of the Early Byzantine Period A.D. 300-800, BICS.S
47, London 1987, Nr. 41. Vgl. auch den Beitrag von P. Van Minnen im vorliegenden Band.
Andere Texte, wie die Fragmente P.Oxy. LX 4009 und P.Vindob.G. 2325 wie auch das Ostrakon
van Haelst 741 sollten wegen ihres unsicheren Bezugs zum Petrusevangelium nicht als dessen
direkte Textzeugnisse herangezogen werden. Vgl. ebd., 59-68. 20-23.

ten beim Petrusevangelium zu rechnen ist.[34] Sollte Melito dieses Apokryphon wirklich gekannt haben, wäre es sehr fraglich, was für einen Text des Petrusevangelium er vor sich hatte. Dies erschwert einen literarkritischen Vergleich von Übereinstimmungen und Unterschieden zwischen den beiden frühchristlichen Schriften natürlich erheblich.[35]

Das Nicht-Händewaschen der Juden

Das Petrusevangelium im Akhmîm-Codex beginnt bekanntlich völlig unvermittelt folgendermaßen: τ[ῶν] δὲ Ἰουδαίων οὐδεὶς ἐνίψατο τὰς χεῖρας οὐδὲ Ἡρώδης οὐδέ τις τῶν κριτῶν αὐτοῦ, καὶ μὴ βουληθέντων νίψασθαι ἀνέστη Πειλᾶτος.[36] Perler schloss daraus, dass in einem ursprünglichen, vollständigen Text zuvor von einem entsühnenden Händewaschen des Pilatus berichtet worden sein muss.[37] Die Durchführung dieser Handlung durch den römischen Beamten bzw. die Nichtdurchführung dieser durch die Juden, Herodes und die Richter brachte er mit folgenden Stellen bei Melito in Verbindung: ἐφ' ᾧ [Jesus] καὶ ἐνίψατο Πιλᾶτος τὰς χεῖρας und οὐδὲ ἀφωσίωσαι [Israel] τῷ δεσπότῃ.[38] Als besonderes Indiz für literarische Abhängigkeit wurde dabei gewertet, dass sowohl im Petrusevangelium, als auch in der Paschahomilie das Verbum νίπτω und nicht, wie in Mt 27,24, dessen Kompositum ἀπονίπτω verwendet wird. Darüber hinaus brachte Perler einige weitere Stellen aus anderen frühchristlichen Schriften ein[39] und zog daraus den Schluss, dass Pilatus in dem verloren gegangenen Teil des Petrusevangeliums als ἀλλόφυλος bezeichnet wurde. Dieser Ausdruck kommt auch in der Predigt des Sardianers vor,[40] wodurch Perler seine These ebenfalls gestützt sah.[41]

Diese im ersten Moment recht bestechende Argumentation, eine der Hauptstützen der These, verliert bei näherer Betrachtung durch die zahlreichen Unwägbarkeiten jedoch stark an Überzeugungskraft. Ein erstes

---

[34] Vgl. Kraus/Nicklas, Petrusevangelium, 55-58. P.Oxy. XLI 2949 fr. 1 bietet wohl eine Parallele zu EvPetr II, 3-5 (GCS.NF 11, 32).

[35] Vgl. T. Nicklas, Ein „neutestamentliches Apokryphon"? Zum umstrittenen Kanonbezug des sog. „Petrusevangeliums", VigChr 56, 2002, 261-265. Nicklas weist hier auf die methodischen Schwierigkeiten bei einem literarkritischen Vergleich zwischen dem Petrusevangelium und den kanonischen Evangelien hin. Die genannten Probleme begegnen aber auch bei der Anwendung dieser Methode auf den Akhmîm-Codex und andere Texte der antiken christlichen Literatur.

[36] EvPetr I, 1 (GCS.NF 11, 32).

[37] Dies könnte man eventuell auch aus EvPetr XI, 46 (GCS.NF 11, 44) schließen.

[38] Melito, *pass.* 92 und 77 (SC 123, 114,693 und 102,560).

[39] Perler wies an dieser Stelle, zum Teil ohne genaue Angaben, auf Origenes, *comm. ser.* 124 *in Mt* (GCS 38, 259), Ps.-Cyprian, *adv. Iud.* IV, 4-5 (CCL 4, 269), *Didasc.* XXI (CSCO 407, 214f) und *Const. apost.* V, 19, 4 (SC 329, 272) hin.

[40] Vgl. Melito, *pass.* 92 und 76 (SC 123, 114,692 und 102,554).

[41] Vgl. Perler, Évangile 585-586.

Problem im Beweisgang Perlers besteht darin, dass er einen nicht erhaltenen
Teil des Petrusevangeliums, die Händewaschung des Pilatus, rekonstruiert
und dies dann als Übereinstimmung zu Melito ausgibt. Auch wenn eine
derartige Rekonstruktion als Parallele des Petrus- zum Matthäusevangelium
(Mt 27,24) denkbar, ja vielleicht sogar wahrscheinlich ist,[42] ist ein Vorgehen,
das Übereinstimmungen zu einem nicht erhaltenen Text postuliert, methodisch
nicht unproblematisch. Richtig ist, dass von einer Nicht-Entsühnung der Juden
im Neuen Testament nirgends die Rede ist, ob allerdings inhaltliche Parallelen
bei fehlenden wörtlichen Übereinstimmungen notwendigerweise literarkritisch
gelöst werden müssen, ist mehr als fraglich. Melito hätte die Formulierung οὐδὲ
ἀφωσίωσαι τῷ δεσπότῃ, die darüber hinaus textkritisch gewisse Unsicherheiten
aufweist,[43] auch ohne Kenntnis des Petrusevangeliums entwickeln können, z.B.
in Aufnahme des so genannten „Blutrufs" des Matthäusevangeliums (Mt
27,25).[44] Aus dem Kontext der Osterhomilie ist zu erschließen, dass Melito hier
in erster Linie nochmals auf die Schuld Israels am Tod Christi verweisen will.
Ob an dieser Stelle explizit das Motiv des Nicht-Händewaschens der Juden im
Hintergrund steht, ist jedoch ungewiss.[45] Daneben ist auch festzustellen, dass
bei Melito hier nur allgemein von Israel gesprochen wird, jedoch nicht wie im
Petrusevangelium auch von Herodes und den Richtern. Auch die Übereinstimmung bei der Benutzung des Simplex in der Osterpredigt und im
Akhmîm-Codex anstelle des Kompositums, wie bei Mt, überzeugt nicht recht,
da zum einen die jeweils zum Verb νίπτω gehörenden Subjekte verschieden
sind und zum anderen bei Melito als Variante auch das Kompositum ἀπονίπτω
belegt ist.[46] Außerdem ist eine solch eher marginale Parallele nicht besonders
aussagekräftig. Äußerst fragwürdig ist Perlers Vorgehen hinsichtlich der
Bezeichnung des Pilatus als ἀλλόφυλος. Einerseits ist dies im Text des Akhmîm-
Codex nicht belegt, sondern muss aus möglichen Vergleichsstellen postuliert
werden, andererseits bringt eine solche Rekonstruktion keine Übereinstimmung zur Osterpredigt Melitos, da dieses Lexem dort zwar vorkommt,

---

[42] Vgl. Denker, Stellung, 58; Nicklas, Apokryphon, 270; Mara, Vangelo, 35-37.
[43] Anstelle der Emendation ἀφωσίωσαι steht in B αποσειωσαι, als Variante in A hingegen αφερεισω, was man als ἀπερείσω lesen kann. Vgl. Perler, Méliton, 103 App. und 179-180.
[44] Denker, Stellung, 59, schreibt im Bezug auf das Petrusevangelium Folgendes: „Ob diese Worte [Mt 27,25] im PE gestanden haben, läßt sich nicht mehr mit Sicherheit feststellen. Immerhin will die Aussage, daß die Juden sich nicht die Hände gewaschen haben, dasselbe sagen." Auf diesem Hintergrund wäre es nicht verwunderlich, wenn Melito und das Petrusevangelium ausgehend von demselben Motiv, aber literarisch unabhängig voneinander zu ähnlichen Formulierungen gelangten.
[45] Selbst wenn es aber so wäre, könnte man in Betracht ziehen, ob nicht sowohl das Petrus-evangelium wie auch die Paschahomilie das Nicht-Händewaschen der Juden unabhängig voneinander aus dem Alten Testament, z.B. aus Dtn 21,6-7 und Ps 26 (25),4-6, entwickelt haben, um die Schuld der Juden an der Verurteilung Jesu klar zum Ausdruck zu bringen. Zum Petrusevangelium vgl. u.a. Denker, Stellung, 58. Zur Rolle alttestamentlicher Bezüge im EvPetr vgl. den Beitrag von T. Hieke im vorliegenden Band.
[46] Vgl. Perler, Méliton, 114 App. Die Benutzung des Simplex anstelle des Kompositum ist im zweiten Jahrhundert nicht unüblich. Vgl. Denker, Stellung, 66.

aber in den beiden Fällen jeweils im Plural und ohne unmittelbaren Bezug zu Pilatus.[47]

Die Rolle des Herodes und der Juden beim Prozess Jesu

Die führende Rolle des Herodes und jüdischer Richter beim Prozess gegen Jesus im Petrusevangelium brachte Perler mit einigen Passagen der Paschahomilie in Verbindung, wo ebenfalls die Verurteilung Christi durch Israel thematisiert wird.[48] Einen der wichtigsten Belege für literarische Abhängigkeit zwischen beiden Schriften sah Perler darin, dass im Petrusevangelium der Befehl zur Hinrichtung des Herrn von Herodes und nicht von Pilatus ausgesprochen wird: καὶ τότε κελεύει Ἡρῴδης ὁ βασιλεὺς παρ[αλη]μφθῆναι τὸν κ(ύριο)ν εἰπὼν αὐτοῖς ὅτι ὅσα ἐκέλευσα ὑμῖν ποιῆσαι αὐτῷ ποιήσατε[49] und dass ersterer auch bei Melito von Sardes eine ähnliche Funktion einnimmt: Πικρός σοι [Israel] Ἡρῴδης ᾧ ἐξηκολούθησας.[50] Diese Übereinstimmung entgegen der kanonischen Evangelientradition, für welche Perler auch noch Belegstellen aus anderen altkirchlichen Werken einbrachte,[51] wertete er als weiteres Hauptargument seiner These.[52]

Richtig ist, dass in beiden Texten die Juden bezüglich der Verurteilung Jesu belastet werden, wohingegen Pilatus entlastet wird.[53] Diese Schuldzuweisung widerspricht historisch wahrscheinlichen Gegebenheiten, ist aber auch im Neuen Testament anzutreffen.[54] Daraus weitergehende Schlüsse zu ziehen,

47 Vgl. Melito, *pass*. 76 und 92 (SC 123, 102,554 und 114,692).
48 Vgl. EvPetr I, 1 (GCS.NF 11, 32); Melito, pass. 75-76 (SC 123, 102, vor allem 548 und 555). In der Paschahomilie heißt es z.B.: Ἔδει αὐτὸν κριθῆναί, ἀλλ᾽ οὐχ ὑπὸ σοῦ [Israel].
49 EvPetr I, 2 (GSC.NF 11, 32). Zu Herodes im Petrusevangelium und der apokryphen Literatur vgl. Mara, Évangile, 74-77; Nicklas, Apokryphon, 269.
50 Melito, *pass*. 93 (SC 123, 114,704).
51 Perler führte hierzu, teilweise ohne genaue Fundstelle, *Didasc*. XXI (CSCO 407, 215), *Const. apost.* V, 19, 5 (SC 329, 272), *EvGam* II, 54-55 (SpicFri 4, 28) und *AscJes* XI, 19-21 (CCA 7, 123) an.
52 Vgl. Perler, Évangile, 586-587.
53 Eine Ausnahme bezüglich Melitos von Sardes könnte Fragment 15 darstellen, dort wird die Verurteilung Jesu durch Pilatus und nicht durch die Juden angesprochen. Vgl. Melito, *fr.* 15 (SC 123, 242,34). Dieser Text sollte meines Erachtens aber nicht als Gegenargument zur These Perlers herangezogen werden, da es doch eher fraglich ist, ob dieses Fragment auf Melito zurückgeht. Vgl. Hall, Melito XXXVII-XXXVIII. Und selbst wenn, ist es nicht ausgeschlossen, dass derselbe Autor in unterschiedlichen Kontexten verschiedene Aussagen macht. Auch in Fragment 14 erscheint Pilatus und zwar entgegen der Predigt in wohl richterlicher Funktion. Hierzu gilt wohl dasselbe. Vgl. Melito, *fr.* 14 (SC 123, 240,13); Hall, Melito XXXVII. Die Erwähnung des Herodes in Fragment 15 kann nicht als Argument herangezogen werden, da es sich hier um eine unsichere Ergänzung des ursprünglichen Textes handelt. Sollte man dieser folgen, würde Herodes hier eher seiner Rolle im Lukas- als der im Petrusevangelium entsprechen. Vgl. Melito, *fr.* 15 (SC 123, 242,34). – Zur Rolle des Pilatus im Petrusevangelium vgl. zudem den Beitrag von H. Omerzu im vorliegenden Band.
54 Vgl. z.B. W. Bösen, Der letzte Tag des Jesus von Nazaret. Was wirklich geschah, Freiburg i.Br. ³1995, 66-67. Zu Pilatus in der apokryphen Literatur vgl. J.K. Elliott, The Apocryphal Jesus. Legends of the Early Church, Oxford-New York 1996, 88-96.

geht meines Erachtens zu weit, da sich Melitos Formulierungen bezüglich einer Verurteilung des Herrn durch Israel auch auf den Prozess Jesu vor dem Synhedrium, wie ihn die kanonischen Evangelien berichten (z.B. Mt 26,66; 27,1), beziehen können. Eine grundsätzlich durchaus positive Sicht der Heiden findet sich darüber hinaus auch sonst in der Homilie, ebenso wie in den Fragmenten der Apologie Melitos an Kaiser Marc Aurel im Blick auf das *Imperium Romanum*.[55] Diese und sein Antijudaismus müssen aber nicht vom Petrusevangelium her erklärt werden, sondern zeigen doch eher vergleichbare Grundhaltungen im frühen Christentum. Bezüglich der Funktion des Herodes im Petrusevangelium und seiner Erwähnung in der Paschahomilie muss man Perler zugestehen, dass darin das wohl stärkste Indiz für eine literarische Abhängigkeit zwischen beiden Schriften liegt. Allerdings ist festzuhalten, dass die oben zitierte Stelle die einzige bei Melito von Sardes ist, in der Herodes überhaupt eine Rolle spielt. Im Gegensatz zum Petrusevangelium wird in der Osterpredigt jedoch nicht direkt davon gesprochen, dass Herodes den Befehl zur Hinrichtung Jesu gab, sondern dies wird, wenn überhaupt, nur angedeutet.[56] Diese nicht ganz deutliche Nennung des Herodes bei Melito könnte darüber hinaus auch auf dessen Erwähnungen in den lukanischen Schriften zurückgehen (Lk 23,6-12; Apg 4,27). Außerdem könnten das Petrusevangelium und die Paschahomilie unabhängig voneinander, wie schon die Apostelgeschichte, auf Ps 2,1-2 zurückgegriffen haben.[57]

Die Rolle der Juden bei der Hinrichtung Jesu

Dass Jesus laut Petrusevangelium von den Juden verspottet, misshandelt und schließlich gekreuzigt wird und dass dabei die römische Besatzungsmacht keine Rolle spielt, brachte Perler mit Aussagen der Paschahomilie in Verbindung, die ebenfalls alleine Israel die Tötung Christi zuschreiben.[58] Eine besondere Übereinstimmung sah Perler zwischen der sarkastischen Aufforderung der Juden: ταύτῃ τῇ τιμῇ τιμήσωμεν τὸν υἱὸν τοῦ θεοῦ,[59] durch die im Petrusevangelium die Verhöhnung und Misshandlung des Herrn abgeschlossen wird, und Formulierungen in der Predigt Melitos, z.B. Ἠτίμησας

---

55 Vgl. Melito, *pass.* 92 (SC 123, 114,690-692); *fr.* 1, 2 und 3 (SC 123, 218-220). Zur Apologie Melitos vgl. u.a. W. Schneemelcher, Heilsgeschichte und Imperium. Melito von Sardes und der Staat, Kl. 5, 1973, 257-275.
56 Es könnte bei Melito mit der Formulierung: Πικρός σοι Ἡρώδης ᾧ ἐξηκολούθησας ja auch nur ausgesagt sein, dass sich Israel gegenüber Jesus so verhalten habe, wie dies von Herodes in Lk 23,11 erzählt wird. Der Text der Predigt ist hier recht offen, die Ausführung des Befehls zur Hinrichtung Jesu muss an dieser Stelle nicht unbedingt angesprochen sein.
57 Melito verwendet diesen Psalmtext als Zitat auch an anderer Stelle in der Paschapredigt. Vgl. Melito, *pass.* 62 (SC 123, 94). Zu Ps 2,1-2 als Hintergrund für das Petrusevangelium vgl. z.B. Denker, Stellung, 59-60. Interessanterweise wird Herodes im Text des Akhmîm-Codex als König bezeichnet, in der Osterpredigt jedoch nicht.
58 Vgl. EvPetr III, 6-9; IV, 10-23; VII, 25 (GCS.NF 11, 32-38); Melito, *pass.* 75-76 (SC 123, 102).
59 EvPetr III, 9 (GCS.NF 11, 34).

τὸν τιμήσαντά σε,[60] die ebenfalls von einer Entehrung Christi durch Israel sprechen und dieser das ehrende Verhalten des Herrn an seinem Volk gegenüberstellen.[61]

Zu Ersterem gilt Gleiches wie oben. Die Belastung der Juden und Entlastung der Römer bezüglich der Hinrichtung Christi findet sich zwar in beiden Texten. Da sich diese Tendenz allerdings in Ansätzen schon im Neuen Testament verifizieren lässt (z.B. Apg 4,10; 7,52) und leider auch in der sonstigen altkirchlichen Literatur begegnet, muss dies nicht literarkritisch erklärt werden.[62] Auch die Übereinstimmung bezüglich der Formulierung der Entehrung des Herrn mit dem Verb ἀτιμάζω bzw. τιμάω muss meines Erachtens nicht aufgrund von literarischer Abhängigkeit erklärt werden. Zum einen begegnet in der Osterhomilie die Antithese ἀτιμάζω – τιμάω und Ableitungen von dieser Wurzel nicht nur in Bezug auf das Passionsgeschehen, sondern auch in anderen Zusammenhängen,[63] zum anderen greift die Formulierung Ἡτίμησας τὸν τιμήσαντά σε als Ausdruck für das Verhalten Israels an Christus bei Melito wohl auf Jes 53,3 zurück,[64] zum dritten scheint die Wendung im Petrusevangelium direkt auf die Verspottung bzw. Misshandlung Jesu bezogen zu sein, während in der Paschapredigt das Lexem ἀτιμάζω wohl breitere Bedeutung hat und ganz allgemein das Verhalten Israels gegenüber Christus von dessen Ablehnung bis zu seiner Kreuzigung ausdrücken kann. Auch findet sich im Petrusevangelium nicht die bei Melito gängige Antithese ἀτιμάζω – τιμάω, so dass das Petrusevangelium als Quelle für die Formulierung des Sardianers wohl eher nicht anzunehmen ist.

Der Kreuzestitel

Einen Hinweis auf die Benutzung des Petrusevangeliums durch Melito sah Perler auch darin, dass in beiden Texten im Gegensatz zu den kanonischen Passionsberichten als *titulus crucis* βασιλεὺς τοῦ Ἰσραήλ angegeben wird.[65] Im Petrusevangelium ist es anders als im Neuen Testament nicht Pilatus, der diesen anbringen lässt, sondern es sind die Juden.[66]

---

[60] Melito, *pass.* 73 (SC 123, 100,535). Vgl. auch Melito, *pass.* 87-90 (SC 123, 110-112).

[61] Vgl. Perler, Évangile 587-588.

[62] Außerdem könnte sich die Paschahomilie auch auf die Verspottung und Misshandlung Jesu durch das Synhedrium, wie z.B. Mt 26,67-68 berichtet, beziehen.

[63] Zur Verwendung dieser Wurzel in der Paschahomilie ohne Bezug auf die Passion vgl. z.B. Melito, *pass.* 37; 43-45; 49 (SC 123, 78,256-257; 82-84; 86,352) und mit Bezug auf das Leiden Christi vgl. z.B. Melito, *pass.* 69; 75; 81 (SC 123, 98,505; 102,547; 106,601).

[64] Vgl. Perler, Méliton, 179. Das vierte Gottesknechtslied wurde von Melito auch an anderer Stelle immer wieder aufgenommen, z.B. Jes 53,4 in Melito, *pass.* 66 (SC 123, 96,469-472) oder Jes 53,7 u.a. in Melito, *pass.* 1; 64; 71 (SC 123, 60,5-6; 94,460-463; 98,515). Denker, Stellung, 64, hält es auch für möglich, dass Jes 53,3 den Hintergrund der Formulierung im Petrusevangelium bildet.

[65] EvPetr IV, 11 (GCS.NF 11, 34). Melito, *pass.* 96 (SC 123, 118,736).

[66] Vgl. Perler, Évangile, 588.

Auch diese Argumentation kann letztlich nicht recht überzeugen: Die Paschahomilie erwähnt zwar den Kreuzestitel, wofür sie jedoch anders als das Petrusevangelium den aus dem Johannesevangelium bekannten Begriff τίτλος (Joh 19,19-20) benutzt, Melito aber will im Folgenden nicht, wie das Petrusevangelium, die Aufschrift zitieren, sondern in Antithesen aufzeigen, wer hier getötet wird und von wem: Ὁ βασιλεὺς τοῦ Ἰσραὴλ ἀνήρεται ὑπὸ δεξιᾶς Ἰσραηλίτιδος.[67] Dabei wird der Ermordete nicht nur als König Israels bezeichnet, sondern auch als Herr und Gott, wie auch in seiner Funktion als Schöpfer beschrieben.[68] Zum anderen wäre, selbst wenn man davon ausgehen will, dass Melito mit βασιλεὺς τοῦ Ἰσραήλ den genauen Wortlaut der Kreuzesaufschrift angeben möchte, dies nicht unbedingt ein Hinweis auf die Kenntnis bzw. Benutzung des Petrusevangeliums, da in der ganzen Osterpredigt niemals der Begriff Ἰουδαῖοι, sondern immer Ἰσραήλ verwendet wird.[69] Melito von Sardes möchte hier ausdrücken, wer der Ermordete ist, und dazu passt der messianische Hoheitstitel, der auch neutestamentlich im Kontext der Passion begegnet (z.B. Mt 27,42), besser als der aus den kanonischen Evangelien bekannte Text der Kreuzesaufschrift βασιλεὺς τῶν Ἰουδαίων (z.B. Mt 27,37). Dies hat literarkritisch mit dem Petrusevangelium aber wohl nichts zu tun. In der Paschahomilie wird außerdem nicht direkt gesagt, wer den Kreuzestitel anbringt. Es ist zwar möglich, dass auch hier, wie im Petrusevangelium, an die Juden gedacht ist, durch die passivische Formulierung wird dies jedoch nicht ausdrücklich angesprochen.

Die Nägel bei der Kreuzigung

Othmar Perler führte als kleinere Stütze seiner Argumentation an, dass in beiden Vergleichstexten anders als in den neutestamentlichen Passionsberichten ausdrücklich die Verwendung von Nägeln (ἧλοι) bei der Kreuzigung Jesu angesprochen wird.[70] Allerdings maß er dieser Übereinstimmung zu Recht keine allzu große Bedeutung bei.[71]

---

67 Melito, *pass.* 96 (SC 123, 118,736-737).
68 Vgl. Melito, *pass.* 95-96 (SC 123, 116-118). Manche der Formulierungen Melitos scheinen auf monarchianische Züge seiner Christologie hinzudeuten. Hierzu vgl. z.B. R.M. Hübner, Melito von Sardes und Noët von Smyrna, in: D. Papandreou/W.A. Bienert/K. Schäferdiek (Hg.), Oecumenica et Patristica (FS W. Schneemelcher), Stuttgart et al. 1989, 219-240; A. Grillmeier, Jesus der Christus im Glauben der Kirche 1: Von der Apostolischen Zeit bis zum Konzil von Chalcedon (451), Freiburg i.Br. ³2004, 207-212.
69 Vgl. Perler, Méliton, 263. Im Akhmîm-Codex wird von Israel hingegen nur in der Verbindung βασιλεὺς τοῦ Ἰσραήλ in EvPetr III, 7 und IV, 11 (GCS.NF 11, 32-34) gesprochen, ansonsten aber von den Ἰουδαῖοι.
70 Vgl. EvPetr VI, 21 (GCS.NF 11, 36). Melito, *pass.* 78 und 93 (SC 123, 104,572 und 114,698)
71 Vgl. Perler, Évangile, 588: „La coïncidence ne prouve donc pas par elle-même." Perler verweist in diesem Zusammenhang auch auf Melito, *pass.* 76 und 80 (SC 123, 102,556 und 106,591) sowie auf *fr.* 15 (SC 123, 242,35). Dies bringt aber für seine Argumentation meines Erachtens keinen

Dass bei einer Kreuzigung Nägel verwendet werden können, war einem antiken Menschen sicher bewusst.[72] Auf diesem Hintergrund ist es auch verständlich, dass diese Selbstverständlichkeit in den kanonischen Texten nicht ausdrücklich gesagt werden muss, aber z.B. in Joh 20,25 anklingen kann. Wie andere frühchristliche Autoren haben Petrusevangelium und Paschahomilie die Verwendung von Nägeln erwähnt[73] und darin die Erfüllung von Ps 22 (21),17 gesehen. Dies hat aber wohl nichts mit literarischer Abhängigkeit zu tun, worauf auch die eher unterschiedlichen Kontexte der Erwähnung von Nägeln in beiden Texten schließen lassen.[74]

Das Reichen von Galle und Essig

Auch in der Tatsache, dass in beiden Texten Jesus bei der Passion Galle (χολή) und Essig (ὄξος) gegeben, und dadurch die Schrift erfüllt wird,[75] sah der Autor zu Recht nur ein Argument von eher geringer Bedeutung.[76]

Richtig ist, dass in beiden Texten Galle und Essig in direkter Verbindung miteinander vorkommen. In den kanonischen Passionsberichten finden sich Galle und Essig zwar nur im Matthäusevangelium (Mt 27,34.48), aber auch dort nicht unmittelbar nebeneinander. Essig wird hingegen auch in Mk 15,36; Lk 23,36 und Joh 19,28-30 genannt.[77] Die Übereinstimmung zwischen den beiden frühchristlichen Schriften muss aber nicht literarkritisch erklärt werden. Alle genannten Texte greifen nämlich auf Ps 69 (68),22 zurück. Dass dies das Petrusevangelium und die Osterpredigt unabhängig voneinander tun, ist dabei wohl sogar wahrscheinlicher als literarische Abhängigkeit, da im Petrusevangelium davon die Rede ist, dass dem Herrn ein Mischtrank χολὴ μετὰ ὄξους zum Trinken gereicht wird, während der Sardianer in enger Anlehnung an den Psalm vom Trinken des Essig und vom Essen der Galle spricht.[78]

---

weiteren Gewinn, da das Verbum προσηλόω z.B. auch in Kol 2,14 begegnet, im Akhmîm-Codex hingegen nicht.

72   Vgl. u.a. Bösen, Tag, 277-281. Auch archäologisch ist die Annagelung als übliche Praxis durch den Gekreuzigten von Giv'at ha Mivtar, der 1968 im Nordosten Jerusalem gefunden wurde, belegt.

73   Perler wies hier auf Ignatius, *Smyrn.* 1, 2 (SUC 1, 204), *Barn.* 5, 13 (SUC 2, 150), Justin, *dial.* 97, 3 (PTS 47, 237) und *1 apol.* 35, 7 (PTS 38, 83) hin.

74   Im Akhmîm-Fragment ist davon die Rede, dass Jesus nach seinem Tod zur Kreuzesabnahme die Nägel aus den Händen gezogen werden, während bei Melito von Sardes vom Annageln Christi und vom Zuspitzen der Nägel gegen Jesus gesprochen wird.

75   Vgl. EvPetr V, 16-17 (GCS.NF 11, 34-36); Melito, *pass.* 79; 80; 93 (SC 123, 104,573-574 [578]; 104,583; 114,706-707).

76   Vgl. Perler, Évangile, 588-589.

77   Vgl. hierzu auch die entsprechenden Passagen im Beitrag von T. Hieke im vorliegenden Band.

78   Vgl. Melito, *pass.* 80 (SC 123, 104,582-583). Die Osterpredigt stellt das Trinken von Essig und Essen von Galle durch Jesus dem Trinken von Wein und Essen von Brot durch Israel während des Paschamahles gegenüber.

Die Wohltaten Jesu an Israel und dessen Undankbarkeit

Auch darin, dass im Petrusevangelium von den guten Taten Jesu gesprochen
wird und dass diese in Antithese zur Undankbarkeit Israels an mehreren
Stellen auch in der Paschahomilie begegnen,[79] sah Othmar Perler ein Indiz für
die Benutzung des Petrusevangeliums durch Melito von Sardes.[80]

Die Argumentation Perlers ist hier äußerst problematisch. Zum einen ist zu
bedenken, dass im Petrusevangelium die guten Taten des Herrn nur in einem
Nebensatz angesprochen werden und zwar als Begründung für die Bestattung
Jesu durch Josef, während die Wohltaten Christi an Israel – hier werden von
Melito nicht nur die des irdischen Jesu in den Blick genommen, sondern auch
diejenigen, die das Alte Testament Gott selbst zuschreibt – ein beherrschendes
Thema des letzten Teils der Osterpredigt darstellen. Zum anderen werden in
der Paschahomilie die Wohltaten Christi an Israel zum Grund für seine Tötung
und die Undankbarkeit Israels wird ihnen gegenübergestellt. Beides findet sich
im erhaltenen Text des Petrusevangeliums aber nicht. Wenn hier überhaupt
von einer Übereinstimmung gesprochen werden kann, hat diese jedoch sicher
nichts mit literarischer Abhängigkeit zu tun.

Der Fall Jerusalems als Strafe

Im Petrusevangelium sagen die Juden nach dem Tod Jesu und den damit
verbundenen erschreckenden Geschehnissen Folgendes: οὐαί, ταῖς ἁμαρτίαις
ἡμῶν· ἤγγισεν ἡ κρίσις καὶ τὸ τέλος Ἰερουσαλήμ.[81] Dadurch wird der Untergang
der jüdischen Hauptstadt als Bestrafung der Juden für die Tötung Jesu
gedeutet. Eine Übereinstimmung sah Perler hier mit folgender Stelle aus der
Paschapredigt: Ἠδάφισας τὸν κύριον, ἠδαφίσθεις χαμαί. Καὶ σὺ [Israel] μὲν κεῖσαι
νεκρός ...[82] Auch die häufige Benutzung des Adjektivs πικρός bei Melito brachte
der Autor mit der gerade angeführten Stelle aus dem Petrusevangelium in
Verbindung.[83] Er bemerkte zwar auch den bedeutenden Unterschied zwischen
beiden Texten in diesem Zusammenhang, nämlich dass im Petrusevangelium
von der Bestürzung bzw. Reue der Juden gesprochen wird,[84] während dieses
Motiv bei Melito von Sardes völlig fehlt,[85] er versuchte die Differenz aber

---

79   Vgl. EvPetr VI, 23 (GCS.NF 11, 36); Melito, *pass.* 72-73; 78-79; 81-90 (SC 123, 100-102; 102-104;
      106-112).
80   Vgl. Perler, Évangile, 589.
81   EvPetr VII, 25 (GCS.NF 11, 38).
82   Melito, *pass.* 99 (SC 123, 120,762-764).
83   Vgl. Melito, *pass.* 93 (SC 123, 114,695-709). An dieser Stelle wird das Adjektiv πικρός dreizehn-,
      nicht zwölfmal, wie Perler behauptet, gebraucht. Vgl. Perler, Évangile, 589.
84   Perler weist in seinem Aufsatz nicht direkt auf EvPetr VIII, 28 (GCS.NF 11, 38) hin – vielleicht
      auch deswegen, weil die dortige Reaktion des Volkes in einem noch stärkeren Widerspruch
      zur Paschahomilie steht als der Ausruf von EvPetr VII, 25 (GCS.NF 11, 38).
85   Vgl. Melito, *pass.* 98-99 (SC 123, 118,744-120,759).

dadurch zu erklären, dass dies nicht zum Thema und der Rhetorik der Sardianers gepasst hätte.[86]

Auch dieses Argument Perlers kann nicht recht überzeugen. Die Ähnlichkeiten zwischen der Osterpredigt und dem Petrusevangelium sind nämlich nicht besonders groß. Bei Melito wird der Untergang Jerusalems nicht ausdrücklich thematisiert und es ist recht fraglich, ob das Lexem πικρός direkt auf das Schicksal des jüdischen Volkes in den ersten zwei Jahrhunderten christlicher Zeit zu beziehen ist.[87] Dass sich in beiden Texten Anspielungen auf den Ausgang des 1. und 2. Jüdischen Krieges finden und dies als Bestrafung für das Verhalten gegenüber Jesus interpretiert wird, ist zuzugeben, muss aber nicht literarkritisch gelöst werden. Dieser geschichtstheologische Triumphalismus des frühen Christentums gegenüber Israel findet sich leider auch in anderen altkirchlichen Texten.[88] Ob man den Unterschied zwischen den beiden Schriften bezüglich des Motivs der Reue der Juden einfach so wegdiskutieren kann, wie Perler dies tat, ist meines Erachtens fraglich. Die gegenüber dem Petrusevangelium bei Melito noch verschärfte Darstellung der Juden bezüglich der Schuld am Tod Jesu ohne jegliche Reue sollte inhaltlich wahrgenommen und nicht nur rhetorisch erklärt werden.

Unterschiede zwischen Melito und dem Petrusevangelium

Mit dem zuletzt genannten Motiv der Reue der Juden im Petrusevangelium, das in der Paschahomilie nicht begegnet, ist bereits eine erste deutliche Differenz zwischen diesen beiden Texten angesprochen. Othmar Perler nannte in seinem Beitrag von 1964 auch noch andere Unterschiede, z.B. dass die Gestalt des Josef und des guten Schächers aus dem Petrusevangelium bei Melito von Sardes keine Rolle spielen, dass in der Paschahomilie das Motiv der Finsternis nicht so breit ausgemalt ist wie im Petrusevangelium, während etwa der Engel, welcher in der Osterpredigt im Zusammenhang mit den Geschehnissen beim Tod Jesu erwähnt wird, im Apokryphon gar nicht auftritt.[89] Diese Aufzählung ließe sich leicht fortführen – die Schilderung der

---

[86] Vgl. Perler, Évangile, 589-590.
[87] Melito von Sardes greift hier die Aufforderung aus Ex 12,8, ungesäuertes Brot mit Bitterkräutern zu essen, auf und stellt somit indirekt das Verhalten Israels gegen Jesus der Befreiungstat Gottes im Exodusgeschehen gegenüber. Vgl. Melito, *pass.* 93 (SC 123, 114,695-710).
[88] Vgl. z.B. Lk 23,48 var. lect.; H.-M. Dopp, Die Deutung der Zerstörung Jerusalems und des zweiten Tempels im Jahre 70 in den ersten drei Jahrhunderten n.Chr., TANZ 34, Tübingen et al. 1998, vor allem 29-30. 52-70. 267-268.
[89] Vgl. Perler, Évangile, 590. Perler weist hier auf die Rolle Josefs in EvPetr II, 3-5 und VI, 23-24 (GCS.NF 11, 32 und 36) und des guten Schächers in EvPetr IV, 13-14 (GCS.NF 11, 34) hin. Perler spricht in diesem Zusammenhang von Josef von Arimathäa, das Petrusevangelium jedoch nur von Josef ohne Herkunftsbezeichnung. Unbewusst hat Perler hier bei der Lektüre des Akhmîm-Fragments wohl Informationen eingetragen, die sich in den kanonischen Evangelien finden; vgl. Nicklas, Apokryphon 269. Bezüglich des Motivs „Finsternis" vergleicht

Auferstehung in der Predigt Melitos zeigt sich beispielsweise völlig unberührt von der im Petrusevangelium[90] –, jedoch ist der Aussagewert dieser Differenzen nicht allzu hoch einzuschätzen, da es sich hierbei ja ausschließlich um *argumenta e silentio* handelt. Man könnte nämlich behaupten, dass Melito das Petrusevangelium kannte, aber manche Züge der Passions- und Ostererzählungen dieses Textes in seiner Homilie beiseite ließ, da sie zu seiner Aussageabsicht thematisch oder stilistisch nicht passten bzw. sich für seine Darstellung als überflüssig erwiesen. Hier ist Perler aus methodischen Gründen zuzustimmen, eine literarische Abhängigkeit Melitos vom Petrus-evangelium ist durch die eben genannten Unterschiede nicht ausgeschlossen – man könnte diese ja auch nur als Beleg für das jeweilige Eigenprofil eines Textes werten –, wenn eine größere Anzahl solcher Differenzen ein Abhängig-keitsverhältnis auch nicht gerade wahrscheinlicher macht.

Perler wies als für ihn wohl bedeutendsten Unterschied zwischen den beiden Texten auch auf die differierende Terminierung des Todestages Jesu hin.[91] Das Petrusevangelium datiert, ähnlich wie Joh 19,14.31 und historisch wohl korrekt, die Ereignisse folgendermaßen: πρὸ μιᾶς τῶν ἀζύμων, τῆς ἑορτῆς αὐτῶν.[92] Die Osterhomilie des Sardianers spricht hingegen mehrmals davon, dass Christus ἐν τῇ μεγάλῃ ἑορτῇ hingerichtet wurde.[93] Dies entspricht der Chronologie der Synoptiker (vgl. z.B. Mt 26,17-19). Trotz dieser Differenz hielt Perler aber an einem literarischen Abhängigkeitsverhältnis zwischen beiden Schriften fest. Auch hier ist ihm zuzugestehen, dass dies trotz eines solchen Unterschieds nicht auszuschließen ist. Zum einen geht es nämlich Melito in seiner Predigt wohl nicht zuvorderst darum, eine genaue Datierung des Todestages Christi vorzulegen, sondern er möchte das Pascha Israels dem der Christen gegenüberstellen und das Skandalöse der Ermordung Jesu durch die Terminierung auf den Festtag noch steigern. Zum anderen ist durch seine Formulierung der Rüsttag des Festes ja auch nicht direkt ausgeschlossen.[94]

Perler die Passagen von EvPetr V, 15-VI, 23 (GCS.NF 11, 34-36) und Melito, *pass.* 97-98 (SC 123, 118). Bezüglich der Gestalt des Engels verweist er auf Melito, *pass.* 98 (SC 123, 118, 748-749). Fraglich ist jedoch, ob Perler die Funktion des Engels in der Paschahomilie nicht etwas überinterpretiert.

90 Vgl. EvPetr VIII, 28-XI, 37 (GCS.NF 11, 38-48); Melito, *pass.* 100-102 (SC 123, 120-122).
91 Vgl. Perler, Évangile, 590.
92 EvPetr II, 5 (GCS.NF 11, 32). Vgl. Mara, Vangelo, 41-45.
93 Melito, *pass.* 79 und 92 (SC 123, 104,579 und 114,694). Vgl. auch *pass.* 93 (SC 123, 114,995). In Melito, *pass.* 80 (SC 123, 104,580-106,595) wird die Festfreude Israels dem Leiden Christi gegenübergestellt. Vgl. Perler, Méliton, 181-183.
94 Auf der Maur geht unter Bezugnahme auf Melito, *pass.* 80 (SC 123, 104,580-106,595), was er als Hinweis darauf wertet, dass Jesus am Tag des jüdischen Paschamahles starb, davon aus, dass die Osterpredigt der Chronologie des Johannesevangeliums folgt. Somit wäre zwischen den beiden Texten kein Unterschied, sondern eine Übereinstimmung festzuhalten. Er schränkt seine Aussage jedoch, wie auch die entgegengesetzte These, folgendermaßen ein: „Hier wird wohl eine Fragestellung [bezüglich der Chronologie] des 20. Jahrhunderts an einen alten Text herangetragen. Die Antwort muss so oder anders falsch sein, sofern man nicht zugibt, daß der Text auf diese Frage gar keine Antwort geben kann oder will." H. Auf der Maur, Die Osterfeier

Außerdem wäre es auch denkbar, dass er das Petrusevangelium zwar kannte, aber z.B. aus Rücksicht auf die Terminierung des Osterfestes in seiner Gemeinde oder wegen der Kenntnis anderer Datierungen dessen Chronologie nicht übernahm.[95] Jürgen Denker wollte daneben auch noch eine Differenz in der Lokalisierung der Kreuzigung zwischen dem apokryphen Evangelium und der Paschapredigt sehen.[96] Melito spricht zwar mehrmals davon, dass Jesus ἐν μέσῳ Ἰερουσαλέμ getötet wurde,[97] im erhaltenen Text des Petrusevangeliums wird die Hinrichtungsstätte hingegen nicht näher lokalisiert.[98] Ein wirklicher Gegensatz liegt hier meines Erachtens nicht vor.[99]

Fazit

Perlers These von der literarischen Abhängigkeit der Paschahomilie Melitos von Sardes vom Petrusevangelium, die sowohl in der Forschung zu diesem apokryphen Text als auch zur Predigt des Sardianers Eingang gefunden hat und breit rezipiert wurde,[100] scheint bei näherer Überprüfung der Übereinstimmungen zwischen diesen beiden frühchristlichen Texten ins Wanken zu

---

in der Alten Kirche, Liturgica Oenipontana 2, hg. von R. Meßner/W.G. Schöpf, Münster 2003, 69-70. Vgl. Mara, Vangelo, 44.

[95]   In Euseb, *h.e.* V, 24, 5 (GCS 9, 492) wird Melito als einer der führenden Quartodezimaner genannt. Inwieweit dies der Chronologie der Paschahomilie entspricht, ist fraglich. Vgl. u.a. Angerstorfer, Melito, 8-36; Stewart-Sykes, Lamb, 141-206; Auf der Maur, Osterfeier, 63-70. Teilweise wird auch das Petrusevangelium mit quartodezimanischer Praxis in Verbindung gebracht. Vgl. Denker, Stellung, 87-92. Hieraus literarkritisch relevantes Vergleichsmaterial zu erheben, ist aber wohl kaum möglich, da bei beiden Texten hinsichtlich dieser Thematik zu wenige eindeutige Aussagen zugrunde gelegt werden können.

[96]   Vgl. Denker, Stellung, 18.

[97]   Vgl. Melito, *pass.* 73; 93; 94 (SC 123, 100,523-524; 114,710; 116,712). In Melito, *pass.* 94 (SC 123, 116) wird Jerusalem zugleich als religiöses Zentrum Israels und als Hinrichtungsort Jesu dargestellt, dabei begegnet auch die Formulierung ἐν μέσῳ πόλεως. Melito will damit wohl ausdrücken, dass die Kreuzigung Jesu nicht im Geheimen, sondern in aller Öffentlichkeit und zwar in der Stadt der Verheißung geschah. Vgl. Perler, Méliton, 193-194.

[98]   Dies mag auch an den geringen Ortskenntnissen, die sich im EvPetr zeigen, liegen.

[99]   Hier eine Differenz anzunehmen, die literarkritisch bedeutsam ist, liegt wohl nicht nahe, da davon auszugehen ist, dass Melito sicher die kanonischen Passionserzählungen kannte, wo die Kreuzigung nicht inmitten der Stadt, sondern vor den Mauern Jerusalems lokalisiert wird (vgl. z.B. Joh 19,17). Die Lokalisierung des Sardianers hängt wohl damit zusammen, dass er selbst eine Reise in die biblischen Länder unternahm und sich zu seiner Zeit die Kreuzigungsstätte tatsächlich innerhalb der Mauern von Jerusalem bzw. Aelia Capitolina befand. Vgl. Melito, *fr.* 3 (SC 123, 222,16-17); A.E. Harvey, Melito and Jerusalem, JThS NS 17, 1966, 401-403.

[100] Dies soll hier beispielhaft nochmals an der Rolle des Herodes in EvPetr I, 2 (GSC.NF 11, 32) und Melito, *pass.* 93 (SC 123, 114,704) verdeutlicht werden. In den Kommentaren zum Petrusevangelium wird hier auf die Paschapredigt verwiesen und umgekehrt. Vgl. Mara, Évangile, 76-77; eadem, Vangelo, 39; Perler, Méliton, 192-193; Hall, Melito, 53 n. 54. Selbst Denker, Stellung, 17, der ja der literarischen Abhängigkeit zwischen den beiden Texten skeptisch gegenübersteht, spricht von „eine[r] wichtige[n] Rolle" des Herodes bei Melito und schließt eine Benutzung des Petrusevangeliums hier nicht direkt aus. Da Herodes in der Osterhomilie nur an dieser Stelle vorkommt, ist meines Erachtens der Beurteilung Denkers aber nicht unbedingt zu folgen.

geraten. Die vielen Unwägbarkeiten und Unsicherheiten in der Argumentation Perlers lassen es wohl als eher problematisch erscheinen, Gemeinsamkeiten zwischen der Osterpredigt und dem Petrusevangelium literarkritisch lösen zu wollen. Die Differenzen zwischen den beiden Schriften können ein Abhängigkeitsverhältnis zwischen diesen zwar nicht widerlegen, machen ein solches aber doch eher unwahrscheinlich. Das oben zitierte Urteil Othmar Perlers: „... une dépendance littéraire parait certaine"[101] kann meines Erachtens in seiner Eindeutigkeit nicht aufrecht erhalten werden, wenngleich auch methodisch korrekt zugegeben werden muss, dass eine Benutzung des apokryphen Evangeliums durch Melito nicht völlig auszuschließen ist.[102]

Vor diesem Hintergrund sind natürlich auch die Konsequenzen, die Perler bezüglich Datierung und Lokalisierung des Petrusevangeliums aus seiner These zog, fraglich:[103] Da ein literarisches Abhängigkeitsverhältnis zwischen den beiden Schriften nicht bewiesen werden kann, kann die Paschahomilie, deren Abfassungszeitpunkt letztlich ja auch nicht ganz sicher ist,[104] nicht mehr als *terminus ante quem* für das Petrusevangelium herangezogen werden. Da auch das Zeugnis Serapions von Antiochien bei Euseb keine wirklich verlässliche Datierungshilfe bietet, sollte künftig nur mehr auf das Papyrusfragment P.Oxy. XLI 2949, welches wohl auf das ausgehende 2. oder frühe 3. Jahrhundert zu datieren ist, zurückgegriffen werden, um eine Entstehung dieses apokryphen Evangeliums bzw. entsprechender Traditionen vor 200 belegen zu können.[105] Gleiches gilt für den Entstehungsort. Da sich eine Abhängigkeit der Osterpredigt vom Petrusevangelium nicht nachweisen lässt, fehlt einer Diskussion über eine mögliche Lokalisierung dieser Schrift in Kleinasien der Bezugspunkt. Da auch für Syrien als Entstehungsort keine letztlich überzeugenden Argumente vorgebracht werden können, sollte diese Frage im Moment als kaum lösbar betrachtet werden. Durch das Fragment aus Oxyrhynchus ist das Petrusevangelium zu Beginn des 3. Jahrhunderts nur in Ägypten sicher bezeugt.[106]

---

[101] Perler, Évangile, 590.

[102] Zu einem ähnlichen Ergebnis kam auch Denker, Stellung, 18: „Es ist wohl möglich, daß Melito das PE benutzt hat, wahrscheinlicher aber scheint mir zu sein, daß er sich wie das PE auf bestimmte Traditionen, das AT auszulegen, stützt."

[103] Die Folgerungen aus der These Perlers hinsichtlich Zeit und Ort der Entstehung des Petrusevangeliums wurden z.B. auch von Mara in ihrem aktuellen Kommentar rezipiert. Vgl. Mara, Vangelo, 19. 21.

[104] Eine Datierung der Predigt auf 160-170, genauso wie ihre Lokalisierung in Kleinasien, hängt ja von der Identität des Autors der Osterhomilie mit Melito von Sardes ab. Diese wurde in letzter Zeit z.B. von Lynn H. Cohick infrage gestellt. Vgl. L.H. Cohick, Melito of Sardis's *PERI PASCHA* and Its „Israel", HThR 91, 1998, 354-357; eadem, Pascha, 11-51.

[105] „Inhaltlich eher unergiebig, hat besonders das erste Fragment POxy 2949 doch seine Bedeutung, weil es eine Datierung des EvPetr vor 200 n.Chr. absichert ..." H.-J. Klauck, Apokryphe Evangelien. Eine Einführung, Stuttgart 2002, 112. Vgl. Kraus/Nicklas, Petrusevangelium, 55-58. Hierzu inzwischen aber ebenfalls kritisch P. Foster, Are There Any Early Fragments of the So-Called Gospel of Peter?, NTS 52, 2006, 1-26.

[106] Zur Datierung und Lokalisierung des Petrusevangeliums vgl. u.a. die Überblicke bei Maurer/Schneemelcher, Petrusevangelium, 184-185, und Mara, Vangelo, 19-22. Auf die

Auch wenn das Verhältnis zwischen den beiden frühchristlichen Texten mit Hilfe der literarkritischen Methode kaum gelöst werden kann, sind Berührungspunkte zwischen dem Petrusevangelium und der Paschahomilie zu konstatieren. Diese könnten dadurch erklärt werden, dass beide Schriften die Passion Christi im Licht des Alten Testaments deuten und so aufgrund ähnlicher Bezugstexte, z.B. Ps 2,1-2; Jes 53,3, zu vergleichbaren Formulierungen gelangen.[107] Darüber hinaus wäre es auch denkbar, dass das Petrusevangelium wie auch Melito auf die kanonischen Evangelien rekurrieren und deren Traditionen weiterentwickeln. Diese Möglichkeit soll jedoch hier nicht weiterverfolgt werden, da das Verhältnis zwischen dem apokryphen Text und den Passionsberichten des Neuen Testaments zu den umstrittensten Fragen der Forschung zum Petrusevangelium zählt.[108] Natürlich kann man die Ähnlichkeiten auch durch den Rückgriff beider Schriften auf vergleichbare mündliche Traditionen zu erklären suchen. Dies ist zwar gut denkbar, Belege und tragfähige Argumente sind aber wohl nur schwer beizubringen.[109] Auf der Ebene eines produktionsorientierten Paradigmas ist die Beziehung zwischen diesen beiden Texten der antiken christlichen Literatur kaum zufriedenstellend lösbar.

Ausblick

Als wichtigster Berührungspunkt zwischen dem Petrusevangelium und der Paschapredigt Melitos von Sardes ist die antijüdische Tendenz beider Schriften

---

umfangreiche Forschungsdiskussion dazu soll hier nicht näher eingegangen werden, in diesem Beitrag wird als Arbeitshypothese davon ausgegangen, dass das Petrusevangelium in der ersten Hälfte des 2. Jahrhunderts entstanden ist.

[107] Vgl. Denker, Stellung, 17-18. Zum Verhältnis des Petrusevangeliums zum Alten Testament vgl. den Beitrag von T. Hieke im vorliegenden Band. Zum Verhältnis der Paschapredigt zum Alten Testament vgl. u.a. Angerstorfer, Melito, 100-115; Knapp, Use, 353-374; Cohick, Pascha, 139-142. Welche Bedeutung das Alte Testament für Melito hatte, belegt u.a. Melito, *fr.* 3 (SC 123, 222-224). Dort berichtet der Sardianer von einer Reise ins Heilige Land. Das Ziel dieser war, den alttestamentlichen Kanon genau zu überprüfen. Der bei Melito aufgeführte Umfang des Kanons entspricht übrigens dem der hebräischen Bibel, ausgenommen das Buch Esther. In diesem Fragment berichtet er darüber hinaus auch davon, ἐξ βιβλία διελών aus dem Alten Testament verfasst zu haben.

[108] Einen knapper Forschungsüberblick findet sich z.B. bei Maurer/Schneemelcher, Petrusevangelium, 182-183; Mara, Vangelo, 18-19. Vgl. auch den Beitrag von J. Verheyden im vorliegenden Band.

[109] Brown hat für die Verhältnisbestimmung zwischen dem Petrusevangelium und den kanonischen Evangelien das Modell einer *second orality* entwickelt – zu dieser Fragestellung weiterführend auch der Beitrag von A. Kirk im vorliegenden Band. Man könnte z.B. versuchen, dies in modifizierter Form auch auf die hier diskutierte Fragestellung anzuwenden. Vgl. R.E. Brown, The Gospel of Peter and Canonical Gospel Priority, NTS 33, 1987, 321-343. Daneben wäre z.B. auch denkbar, dass Melito neutestamentliche Passionstraditionen aufnahm und weiterentwickelte, während das Petrusevangelium diese zwar nicht kannte, aber doch vergleichbare mündliche Traditionen.

zu nennen.[110] Da diese Übereinstimmung literarkritisch wohl nicht aufgelöst werden kann, wäre es auch denkbar, zu versuchen, die Hintergründe des Antijudaismus in beiden Schriften zu erheben, und dann danach zu fragen, ob diese vergleichbar sind. Bei der Paschahomilie gab es hierzu eine breite Diskussion in der Forschung, vor allem wurden dabei die divergierenden Lebensbedingungen von Juden und Christen in Sardes als möglicher Einflussfaktor auf Melitos Haltung gegenüber Israel geltend gemacht.[111] Da über die Hintergründe des Apokryphons und dessen Antijudaismus jedoch kaum etwas Gesichertes ausgesagt werden kann, ja selbst bei der Osterpredigt derartige Schlüsse in gewisser Weise hypothetisch bleiben müssen,[112] ist auch dieser Weg, das Verhältnis zwischen den beiden frühchristlichen Texten näher zu bestimmen, letztlich zum Scheitern verurteilt.

Übereinstimmungen und Unterschiede zwischen dem Petrusevangelium und der Paschahomilie Melitos von Sardes können auf einer diachronen Ebene derzeit also wohl kaum befriedigend erklärt werden, trotzdem kann es interessant sein, aus synchroner Perspektive Berührungen zwischen den beiden Texten festzustellen, aber auch ihr jeweiliges Eigenprofil herauszuarbeiten. Abschließend soll dies am Beispiel des Antijudaismus skizzenhaft angedeutet werden: In beiden frühchristlichen Schriften sind es die

---

[110] Ein direkter Antijudaismus wurde aber auch für beide frühchristliche Texte infrage gestellt bzw. zumindest stark relativiert. Zum Petrusevangelium vgl. Denker, Stellung, 78-87. Zur Paschahomilie vgl. Cohick, Melito, 371-372, eadem, Pascha, 52-87.

[111] Ingeborg Angerstorfer fasst die gängige Forschungsmeinung folgendermaßen zusammen: „Vergleicht man nun die Situation der jüdischen und der christlichen Gemeinde in Sardes, so ergibt sich auf der einen Seite das Bild einer sozial-wirtschaftlich relativ starken und gesellschaftspolitisch anerkannten jüdischen Bürgerschaft, auf der anderen Seite das Bild einer sozial-wirtschaftlich geschädigten und gesellschaftspolitisch nicht nur nicht anerkannten, sondern im Gegenteil unterdrückten christlichen Einwohnerschaft. Eine solche Konstellation zweier gesellschaftlicher Gruppen läßt an sich schon erwarten, daß die schlechter gestellte Gruppe Aggressionen gegen die besser situierte hegt. Falls wirklich auch Juden – direkt oder indirekt – an der Verfolgung der Christen beteiligt waren, steigerte dies gewiß erst recht den Zorn der Christen auf die Juden." Angerstorfer, Melito, 220. Diese Sicht geht vor allem auf die Auswertung der archäologischen und literarischen Zeugnisse für Sardes zurück. Vgl. z.B. A.T. Kraabel, Melito the Bishop and the Synagogue at Sardis: Text and Context, in: Studies Presented to G.M.A. Hanfmann, hg. von D. Mitten/J.G. Pedley/J.A. Scott, Mainz 1971, 77-85; K.W. Noakes, Melito of Sardis and the Jews, StPatr 13 = TU 112, 1975, 244-249; A.R. Seager/A.T. Kraabel, The Synagogue and the Jewish Community, in: Sardis from Prehistoric to Roman Times. Results of the Archaeological Explorations, 1958-1975, hg. von G.M.A. Hanfmann, Cambridge/MA 1983, 168-190. Daneben wurde Melitos Antijudaismus aber auch durch seine besonders starke Nähe zum Judentum und durch den deswegen umso stärkeren Hang zur Abgrenzung erklärt. Vgl. z.B. S.G. Wilson, Passover, Easter and Anti-Judaism. Melito of Sardis and Others, in: To See Ourselves as Others See Us. Christians, Jews, „Others" in Late Antiquity, hg. von J. Neusner, Chico 1985, 337-356; A. Stewart-Sykes, Melito's Anti-Judaism, JECS 5, 1997, 271-283.

[112] Da die Identität des Autors der Paschapredigt mit Melito von Sardes als nicht völlig gesichert angenommen werden kann, aber auch weil fraglich ist, ob die für Sardes erhobenen archäologischen und literarischen Quellen für das 2. Jahrhundert aussagekräftig sind, ist in gewisser Weise doch unsicher, ob man den Hintergrund der Osterhomilie so zutreffend beschreiben kann. Vgl. z.B. H. Botermann, Die Synagoge von Sardis: eine Synagoge aus dem 4. Jahrhundert?, ZNW 81, 1990, 103-121.

Juden bzw. Israel, die Jesus verurteilen, verspotten, misshandeln und schließlich kreuzigen. Ihnen wird in beiden Texten die Schuld am Tode Christi gegeben, Pilatus und die römische Besatzungsmacht werden hingegen entlastet.[113] Die beiden Texte lassen sich also bezüglich der Schuldfrage an der Hinrichtung Jesu komplementär verstehen, sie ergänzen sich gegenseitig. Darüber hinaus ist auch festzustellen, dass für einen Leser der Paschahomilie, der auch das Petrusevangelium kennt, manche Aussagen Melitos deutlicher werden. Beispielsweise wird die Lektüre folgender Stelle aus der Osterpredigt: οὐδὲ ἀφωσίωσαι [Israel] τῷ δεσπότῃ bei einem solchen Leser sofort den ersten Satz des Petrusevangeliums ins Gedächtnis rufen: τ[ῶν] δὲ Ἰουδαίων οὐδεὶς ἐνίψατο τὰς χεῖρας οὐδὲ Ἡρῴδης οὐδέ τις τῶν κριτῶν αὐτοῦ. καὶ μὴ βουληθέντων νίψασθαι ἀνέστη Πειλᾶτος.[114] Die beiden Texte können also in Dialog miteinander gebracht werden, auch wenn sie wohl literarisch unabhängig voneinander sind. Ein Leser, der beide Schriften kennt, wird aber auch Differenzen wahrnehmen, z.B. dass in dem apokryphen Evangelium Reue oder zumindest Bestürzung der Juden nach dem Tod Jesu anklingt, während Melito das Bild des verstockten Israels zeichnet.[115] Im Petrusevangelium lässt sich hinsichtlich der Schuld am Tod Jesu vielleicht auch eine gewisse Differenzierung zwischen Herodes und der jüdischen Führungsschicht auf der einen Seite und dem Volk auf der anderen erkennen, die Paschahomilie hingegen beschuldigt Israel als Ganzes der Ermordung Christi, ja Gottes.[116] Auf einer solchen, synchronen Ebene könnte man wohl noch viele weitere frühchristliche Schriften mit dem Petrusevangelium und der ersten uns bekannten Osterpredigt ins Gespräch bringen, ohne dass damit etwas über Abhängigkeitsverhältnisse ausgesagt wäre.[117] Leider würde sich dabei herausstellen, dass diese beiden Texte mit ihrer antijüdischen Tendenz keine Ausnahmen in der christlichen Literatur des 2. Jahrhunderts darstellen.[118]

---

[113] Vgl. zum Petrusevangelium z.B. T. Nicklas, Die „Juden" im Petrusevangelium (PCair 10759): Ein Testfall, NTS 46, 2000, 212-219 und zur Paschahomilie z.B. Angerstorfer, Melito, 221-227.

[114] Melito, *pass.* 77 (SC 123, 102,560). EvPetr I, 1 (GCS.NF 11, 32). Als ein weiteres Beispiel könnte man auch die Stelle: Πικρός σοι [Israel] Ἡρώδης ᾧ ἐξηκολούθησας in Melito, *pass.* 93 (SC 123, 114,704) nennen, die sofort an: καὶ τότε κελεύει Ἡρώ(ι)δης ὁ βασιλεὺς παρ[αλη]μφθῆναι τὸν κ(ύριο)ν εἰπὼν αὐτοῖς ὅτι ὅσα ἐκέλευσα ὑμῖν ποιῆσαι αὐτῷ ποιήσατε in EvPetr I, 2 (GSC.NF 11, 32) denken lässt. Texte können also unabhängig von ihrer Entstehungsgeschichte im Dialog miteinander stehen.

[115] Vgl. EvPetr VII, 25 und VIII, 28 (GCS.NF 11, 38); Nicklas, Juden, 219-221; Melito, *pass.* 98-99 (SC 123, 118-120).

[116] Vgl. EvPetr I, 1-2 und VIII, 28 (GCS.NF 11, 32 und 38); Melito, *pass.* 73-75 und 96 (SC 123, 100-102 und 116-118). Es ist in gewisser Weise jedoch fraglich, ob sich eine solche Differenzierung im Petrusevangelium wirklich nachweisen lässt. Vgl. Nicklas, Juden, 212-214 und 219 sowie den Beitrag von J. Verheyden in diesem Band.

[117] Vgl. auch den Beitrag von T. Nicklas im vorliegenden Band.

[118] Vgl. u.a. S.G. Wilson (Hg.), Anti-Judaism in Early Christianity. Bd. 2: Separation and Polemic, SCJud 2, Waterloo/Ont. 1986; C.A. Evans/D.A. Hagner (Hg.), Anti-Semitism and Early Christianity. Issues of Polemic and Faith, Minneapolis 1993, vor allem 215-289; J.M. Lieu, Image and Reality. The Jews in the World of the Christians in the Second Century, Edinburgh 1996; H. Schreckenberg, Die christlichen Adversus-Judaeos-Texte und ihr literarisches und historisches Umfeld (1.-11. Jh.), EHS XXIII.172, Frankfurt/Main et al. [4]1999, 171-225.

The Gospel of Peter in Pseudo-Clementine Recognitions 1,27-71

by

F. STANLEY JONES

Pseudo-Clementine *Recognitions* 1,27-71 preserves a Jewish Christian repartee to Luke's Acts of the Apostles. It describes how James the brother of the Lord convinced the High Priest and the entire nation to be baptized. Paul, however, disrupted this event through a violent ruckus at the Temple. Here, he personally killed James. Dating from about 200 C.E., this source is a relatively unexplored gold mine for early Jewish Christianity.[1] It finally presents, for example, primary evidence for Jewish Christian chiliastic views: Jewish Christians will occupy the land and the holy city without a temple and will be filled with food and drink in an earthly kingdom of heaven prior to the resurrection of the dead.[2] Alongside its critical use of Acts, this source also employed the Gospel of Matthew, the Gospel of Luke, and probably the *Gospel of the Ebionites*. Recently, questions have been raised about whether this source used the *Gospel of Peter*, too.[3] Though a review of the literature reveals that

---

[1] The Greek has not been preserved. Access to the ancient Syriac and Latin versions in English translation, along with a historical investigation, is provided in my book F.S. Jones, An Ancient Jewish Christian Source on the History of Christianity. Pseudo-Clementine Recognitions 1.27-71, SBL.TT 37. SBL.CA 2, Atlanta 1995 = 1998 = 2001. Exploration of this passage as a counter-Acts of the Apostles, with the texts in parallel columns, is found in my study F.S. Jones, An Ancient Jewish Christian Rejoinder to Luke's Acts of the Apostles: Pseudo-Clementine Recognitions 1.27-71, Sem. 80, 1997, 223-245. Current critical editions of the Pseudo-Clementines are B. Rehm, ed., Die Pseudoklementinen I. Homilien, ed. by G. Strecker, GCS, Berlin ³1992; B. Rehm, ed., Die Pseudoklementinen II. Rekognitionen in Rufins Übersetzung, ed. by G. Strecker, GCS, Berlin ²1994; W. Frankenberg, Die syrischen Clementinen mit griechischem Paralleltext. Eine Vorarbeit zu dem literargeschichtlichen Problem der Sammlung, TU 48.3, Leipzig 1937. Particularly in the case of the Syriac, my work is based on a direct reading of the manuscripts.

[2] See my study F.S. Jones, Jewish-Christian Chiliastic Restoration in Pseudo-Clementine Recognitions 1.27-71, in: Restoration. Old Testament, Jewish, and Christian Perspectives, ed. by J.M. Scott, JSJ.S 72, Leiden-Boston-Cologne 2001, 529-547.

[3] A recent discussion is J.D. Crossan, The Birth of Christianity. Discovering What Happened in the Years Immediately after the Execution of Jesus, San Francisco 1998, 512-519. For the source's use of the other writings listed above, see Jones, An Ancient Jewish Christian Source, 140-149.

these questions are not actually new,[4] the debate can possibly help clarify the standing of the *Gospel of Peter* at the end of the second century and will be addressed in the following.

To start with a seemingly innocuous parallel between the two writings, it may be observed that both the *Gospel of Peter* and *Recognitions* 1 mention that the sun "shone" or "showed itself."

Gospel of Peter 22
τότε ἥλιος ἔλαμψε

PsCl R 1,42,3 (Syriac/Latin)
.ﺟ‌ﺪ‌ﺮ‌ ﺮ‌ﺟ‌ﺪ‌ﺮ‌   *sole reddito*

"The sun appeared."

This is, of course, a natural thing for the sun to do. The context of the remark, however, is significant. Both texts are referring to the end of the darkness at Jesus' crucifixion. The synoptic accounts of the death of Jesus state only that darkness came over the land from the sixth to the ninth hour or, in the Western and Byzantine text of Luke, that the sun was darkened during this period. The synoptics fail to state explicitly that the sun shone again, and this silence dominates in patristic literature. Cyril of Jerusalem, around 350 C.E., is apparently the first patristic writer to make the explicit statement that the sun shone again at the ninth hour.[5]

The remark in the *Gospel of Peter* that the sun shone thus starts to seem distinctive. Furthermore, this gospel's continuation that when the sun shone, it was found to be the ninth hour seems clearly motivated by the *Gospel of Peter's* preceding description of the fear of the Jews that the sun should have set on one being put to death (15), which it justifies by twice citing the scriptural proof text of the prohibition (5, 15). So it is not only distinctive of the *Gospel of Peter* but also characteristic of this gospel to have the explicit remark that the sun shone.

J. Rendel Harris, in any event, found it remarkable that Ephrem also had this statement about the sun in his *Commentary on the Diatessaron*.[6]

---

[4] H. Waitz, Das Evangelium der zwölf Apostel, ZNW 14, 1913, 38-64, already noted the parallels to R 1,41-42 (p. 54). J. Denker, Die theologiegeschichtliche Stellung des Petrusevangeliums. Ein Beitrag zur Frühgeschichte des Doketismus, EHS.T XXIII.36, Frankfurt/Main 1975, 22, also discussed R 1,42,3-4.

[5] Catech. 13,24. A. Harnack, Bruchstücke des Evangeliums und der Apokalypse des Petrus, TU 9,2, Leipzig ²1893, 59, reports that it was J.H. Bernard who pointed out that Cyril mentions that "there was light again from the ninth hour." This passage, along with the others listed on pp. 59-60 in Harnack, raise the possibility that Cyril knew and used the Gospel of Peter, but the case that can be made for this perspective is not entirely convincing.

[6] J.R. Harris, A Popular Account of the Newly-Recovered Gospel of Peter, London 1893, 81-82. For Ephrem's Commentary on the Diatessaron, see L. Leloir, ed. and trans., Saint Éphrem

Ephrem *Commentary on the Diatessaron* 21,5 to Lk 23:45 (210,8-9 Leloir)

ܫܡܫܐ ... ܚܫܟ ܘܗܝܕܝܢ ܢܗܪ.

"The sun ... darkened and then shone."

To explain this coincidence, Harris suggested that the *Gospel of Peter* might have used Tatian's *Diatessaron*. A careful reading of Ephrem's *Commentary*, however, reveals another, more persuasive explanation. As is evident from the following parallel texts, Ephrem's *Commentary* apparently knew and used the Syriac translation of the Pseudo-Clementine *Recognitions*.

Mt 27:51-52
Καὶ ἰδοὺ τὸ καταπέτασμα τοῦ ναοῦ ἐσχίσθη ... καὶ ἡ γῆ ἐσείσθη καὶ αἱ πέτραι ἐσχίσθησαν, καὶ τὰ μνημεῖα ἀνεῴχθησαν.

PsCl R 1,41,3 (Syriac)

ܘܛܘܪܐ ܐܫܬܪܝܘ. ܘܩܒܪܐ ܐܬܦܬܚܘ. ܘܐܦܝ ܬܪܥܐ ܕܗܝܟܠܐ
ܐܨܛܪܝ. ܕܐܝܟ ܕܒܐܒܠܐ ܕܥܠ ܚܘܪܒܗ ܕܕܘܟܬܐ ܕܥܬܝܕ ܗܘܐ
ܐܠܐ ܗܘܐ

"And the mountains were shattered, and the graves were opened, and the veil of the temple was torn so that it was lamenting as if in mourning over the destruction of the place that was imminent."

PsCl R 1,41,3 (Latin)
montesque disrupti et sepulchra patefacta sunt, velum templi scissum est, velut lamentans excidium inminens loco.

Ephrem *Commentary on the Diatessaron* 21,5 to Mt 27:51-52 (210,10-12 Leloir)

ܘܛܘܪܐ ܙܥܘ. ܘܩܒܪܐ ܐܬܦܬܚܘ. ܘܐܦܝ ܬܪܥܐ ܐܨܛܪܝ. ܘܐܝܟ
ܕܒܐܒܠܐ ܥܠ ܚܘܪܒܗ ܕܕܘܟܬܐ ܕܥܬܝܕ ܐܠܐ ܗܘܐ.

"And the mountains shook, and the graves were opened, and the veil was torn and was lamenting as if in mourning over the destruction of the place that was imminent."

The underlined material displays distinctive wording, content, and order shared by Ephrem and *Recognitions* 1. It is true that I. Ortiz de Urbina accepted

Commentaire de l'évangile concordant: Text syriaque (Manuscrit Chester Beatty 709), CBM 8, Dublin 1963.

this passage from Ephrem into his reconstruction of the *Diatessaron*.[7] But Ortiz de Urbina overlooked the verbatim parallel in the *Pseudo-Clementines* and neglected other readings in Ephrem's other works that would indicate that the *Diatessaron* had a different text. Furthermore, there is yet another instance of parallel material in Ephrem's *Commentary* and *Recognitions* 1:

> Ephrem *Commentary on the Diatessaron* 16,22 to Mt 22:23 (180,6-9 Leloir)
>
> ܡܬܩܪܝܢ ܕܝܢ ܙܕܘܩܝܐ. ܗܘ ܕܝܢ ܙܕܝܩܐ. ܕܠܐ ܠܡ ܚܠܦ ܐܓܪܐ
> ܦܠܚܝܢܢ ܠܐܠܗܐ. ܠܐ ܓܝܪ ܡܣܟܝܢ ܠܢܘܚܡܬܐ. ܡܛܠ ܗܢܐ
> ܙܕܝܩܐ ܩܪܝܢ ܠܢܦܫܗܘܢ. ܕܠܐ ܐܓܪܐ ܠܡ ܙܕܩ ܠܢ ܕܢܪܚܡܝܘܗܝ
> ܠܐܠܗܐ.
>
> "Now they are called Sadducees, which is 'righteous,' for 'We do not serve God for a reward.' For they do not expect the resurrection. For this reason they call themselves righteous, 'because it is proper for us to love God without a reward.'"
>
> PsCl R 1,54,2 (Syriac)
>
> ... ܕܡܬܩܪܝܢ ܙܕܘܩܝܐ ... ܙܕܝܩܐ ... ܘܒܢܘܚܡܬܐ ܕܡܝܬܐ
> ܟܦܘܪܘ܆ ... ܕܐܡܪܘ ܕܠܐ ܠܡ ܘܠܐ ܕܒܐܓܪܐ ܕܛܝܒܘܬܐ
> ܢܦܠܚ ܘܢܕܚܠ ܠܐܠܗܐ܂
>
> "... who are called Sadducees ... righteous ... and they deny the resurrection of the dead ... since they said, 'It is not proper for us to serve and fear God for a reward of goodness.'"
>
> PsCl R 1,54,2 (Latin)
>
> *Qui dicebantur Sadducaei. ... hique ... iustiores ... mortuorum resurrectionem negare ... dicentes non esse dignum ut quasi sub mercede proposita colatur deus.*

No one, to my knowledge, has postulated that this material came from the *Diatessaron*. In sum, then, there are good indications that Ephrem's *Commentary* knew and used the Syriac translation of the Pseudo-Clementine *Recognitions*.

The true parallel to the *Gospel of Peter*'s statement that the sun shone is found not in Ephrem's *Commentary* but rather in the Pseudo-Clementine *Recognitions* – and not merely in the Syriac translation of the *Recognitions* but even in the original, though lost, Greek *Recognitions*, as the preserved Latin

---

7 I. Ortiz de Urbina, ed., Vetus Evangelium Syrorum et Exinde Excerptum Diatessaron Tatiani, BPM 6, Madrid 1967, 294, cf. p. 192 no. 2448.

translation demonstrates.[8] Since the *Gospel of Peter* has an obvious motivation for this statement, whereas the *Recognitions* does not, it seems quite possible that the source of *Recognitions* 1 knew the *Gospel of Peter*.

A review of the literature opens up one other possibility, however. Hans Waitz thought many passages in the *Pseudo-Clementines* derived from the *Gospel of the Ebionites*, and he included this current passage, about the sun reappearing, in his list of excerpts from the *Gospel of the Ebionites*.[9] Waitz's contributions stand as a permanent reminder of the uncertainties when it comes to both the compass of the *Gospel of the Ebionites* and the origin of the evangelical materials in the *Pseudo-Clementines*, particularly in the source of *Recognitions* 1, which indeed apparently did employ the *Gospel of the Ebionites* elsewhere. Waitz's position, that the statement that the sun reappeared in *Recognitions* 1 came from the *Gospel of the Ebionites*, must be left on the table and indeed raises a more disturbing question about the relationship between the *Gospel of Peter* and the *Gospel of the Ebionites*.[10]

Without dismissing Waitz, then, and setting his position to one side now only because it leads into deeper and darker realms, this paper will proceed to ask about other possible correspondences between *Recognitions* 1 and the *Gospel of Peter*. There seem to be only two or three further cases:[11]

---

8   Attention was drawn to this parallel also by E. Norelli, L'Ascensione di Isaia. Studi su un apocrifo al crocevia dei cristianesimi (Origini n.s. 1), Bologna 1994, 148-149 n. 302.

9   Waitz, Das Evangelium der zwölf Apostel, 54.

10   W.L. Petersen, Tatian's Diatessaron. Its Creation, Dissemination, Significance, and History in Scholarship, VigChr.S 25, Leiden-New York-Cologne 1994, 414-420, examines another case (the variant of the Old Syriac, etc., after Lk 23:48 [the crowds cry, "Woe to us, etc."]) and concludes that "both Tatian and Peter took the variant from the same Judaic-Christian gospel" (p. 420), though he does not specify which Judaic-Christian gospel he has in mind. H.J.W. Drijvers/G.J. Reinink, Taufe und Licht. Tatian, Ebionäerevangelium und Thomasakten, in: Text and Testimony. Essays on New Testament and Apocryphal Literature in Honour of A.F.J. Klijn, ed. by T. Baarda et al., Kampen 1988, 91-110, argued that the Gospel of the Ebionites was dependent on Tatian's Diatessaron, and A.F.J. Klijn, Jewish-Christian Gospel Tradition, VigChr.S 17, Leiden-New York-Copenhagen-Cologne 1992, 73, accepted this conclusion, though the argument is not truly convincing.

11   Crossan's use, The Birth of Christianity, 514-517, of R.E. Van Voorst's translations, The Ascents of James. History and Theology of a Jewish-Christian Community, SBL.DS 112, Atlanta 1989, has led him to identify some specious correspondences. For example, the contrast between "all the people" with "some" in R 1,41,4 that Crossan (pp. 515-518) finds also in the Gospel of Peter 28 is based on an improbable reconstruction of the text by Frankenberg, Die syrischen Clementinen, 48, that Van Voorst adopted. The older Syriac manuscript and the Latin read "world" instead of "people" and are thus overwhelming evidence that the original reading of the later Syriac manuscript ("people"), which was soon revised by the corrector, is wrong. On pages 516-517, Crossan similarly relies on Van Voorst's mistranslation of R 1,43,1 (Syriac).

Gospel of Peter 15
ἐθοροβοῦντο καὶ ἠγωνίων

PsCl R 1,41,4 (Syriac/Latin)
ܟܠܗ ܥܡܐ ܐܬܪܓܫ ܗܘܐ. *omnis mundus commotus sit*

"The entire nation was disturbed."

Gospel of Peter 29
ἐφοβήθησαν οἱ πρεσβύτεροι

PsCl R 1,53,1-2 (Syriac)
ܗܢܘܢ ܕܠܐ ܗܝܡܢܘ ܡܢ ܝܗܘܕܝܐ ܝܬܝܪܐܝܬ ܫܢ̈ܝܗܘܢ ܥܠܝܢ
ܡܚܪܩܝܢ ܗܘܘ. ܟܕ ܡܬܦܠܓܝܢ ܗܘܘ. ܕܕܠܡܐ ܟܝ ܗܘ ܐܝܬܘܗܝ
ܗܘ ܕܒܗ ܩܕܡ ܚܛܘ ܘܐܣܟܠܘ ܘܬܘܒ ܫܪܝܪܐܝܬ ܗܝ ܕܚܠܬܐ
ܒܗܘܢ ܪܒܐ ܗܘܬ ܘܣܓܝܐ ܗܘܬ.

"Those from the Jews who did not believe were excessively gnashing their teeth over us, as they were undecided, lest the one against whom they had previously sinned and offended truly be [sc. the Christ]. And again, fear was growing in them and becoming great …."

PsCl R 1,53,1-2 (Latin)
Infideles quique ex Iudaeis inmensa adversum nos insania commoventur, verentes ne forte ipse sit, in quem peccaverunt; et eo magis metus increscit ...

PsCl R 1,43,1 (Syriac/Latin)
ܟܗ̈ܢܝܗܘܢ ܕܚܝܠܝܢ *pertimescerent sacerdotes*

"Their priests were afraid."

The statement in the *Gospel of Peter* that the Jews "were disturbed and in agony" lest the sun had set (15) corresponds with the statement in *Recognitions* 1,41,4 that after the portents at Jesus' death the entire nation or world was disturbed (cf. also *Gospel of Peter* 25, 28). Such a statement is not found in the canonical gospels.[12] The dependency of the *Recognitions* on the *Gospel of Peter* thus seems quite possible.

In the *Gospel of Peter* 29, the statement that the elders were afraid after hearing the people's reactions to the portents provides a ready explanation for

---

12 Cf. L. Vaganay, L'Évangile de Pierre, ÉtB, Paris ²1930, 250: « un motif inconnu de la tradition évangélique ».

the statement in *Recognitions* 1,53,1-2 that fear was becoming great among the unbelievers of the Jews (because of the portents, because the body was not found, and because many were coming to the faith) as well as for the statement in *Recognitions* 1,43,1 that "their priests were afraid," even though the object of the fear in this last instance is only that the entire nation should come to the (Christian) faith. Again, the notion that Jewish leaders were in fear after the crucifixion is not found in the canonical gospels.[13] Finally, the reference to the sin of the unbelievers against Christ in *Recognitions* 1,53,1 finds a parallel in the *Gospel of Peter* 25 (οὐαὶ ταῖς ἁμαρτίαις ἡμῶν) though this concept is also found in a text-critical variant to Lk 23:48 that has a complex history (*Diatessaron* from an uncertain source).[14]

The conclusion to these observations is that the *Gospel of Peter* provides a possible explanation for the presence of these several motifs in *Recognitions* 1. The shared elements are indeed evidence that the source of *Recognitions* 1 might well have known and used the *Gospel of Peter*, and in the absence of an explanation other than sheer narrative coincidence or the postulation of yet another uncertain source,[15] this seems to be the most likely conclusion. The *Gospel of the Ebionites* remains a factor that could possibly affect this conclusion, but there is nothing in the assured fragments of the *Gospel of the Ebionites* that shows affinities with these motifs. Several myths about the *Diatessaron*, however, could be dismissed in the course of this paper, though of course that is just a drop in the bucket of difficult questions about the text of the *Diatessaron*.

The author of *Recognitions* 1,27-71 seems to have been parodying Acts in a rather detailed way; this author also apparently used Jubilees. While the *Gospel of the Ebionites* was yet another writing known to the author and remains something of a wildcard in the evaluation of the other gospel material, it seems likely that the author also employed at least the gospels of Matthew and Luke. In view of this context and the evidence presented above, it seems likely that the Jewish Christian author of *Recognitions* 1,27-71 also knew and used the *Gospel of Peter*. Given the nature of the *Gospel of Peter*, this Jewish Christian author knew and used it as a writing accepted not so much by fellow Jewish Christians but rather by the rising Gentile Christian church of the day that was also promoting the horrid book of Acts. In this manner, Pseudo-Clementine *Recognitions* 1 somewhat liberates Rhossos north of Antioch from its isolation

---

13   The concept is known for other moments in the canonical evangelical story; see Vaganay, L'Évangile de Pierre, 281.

14   Alongside Petersen's discussion of this variant mentioned above in note 10 (and the literature he cites), see Vaganay, L'Évangile de Pierre, 268-271. The voice of the Pseudo-Clementines should be included in the discussion.

15   Crossan, The Birth of Christianity, 519, has indeed proposed another explanation: Pseudo-Clementine Recognitions 1 is dependent on a source of the Gospel of Peter that he entitles the Cross Gospel. Along with others, I am not persuaded by the arguments that have been advanced for this supposed source. Furthermore, substituting "the Cross Gospel" for "the Gospel of Peter" would not materially alter the results of this study.

for its use of the *Gospel of Peter* at the end of the second century (though I would tend to include both the *Didascalia* and the *Toledoth Jeshu* in this West Syrian group).[16] The Jewish Christian author of *Recognitions* 1 apparently thought the *Gospel of Peter* was current among Gentile Christians in and around Aelia Capitolina. His witness is parallel to that of Bishop Serapion for the region north of Antioch.

---

[16]   Cf. Denker, Die theologiegeschichtliche Stellung des Petrusevangeliums, 30 with n. 143 on p. 141. For the *Didascalia*, see especially Vaganay, L'Évangile de Pierre, 167-169. A similar scriptural proof text that the body should not remain on the cross at night is found in the Toledoth Jeshu (e.g., S. Krauss, Das Leben Jesu nach jüdischen Quellen, Berlin 1902, 45. 58. 120. 126; H.J. Schonfield, According to the Hebrews, London 1937, 51; W. Horbury, A Critical Examination of the Toledoth Jeshu, Ph.D. diss., Cambridge 1970, 86. 107. 193. 244. 293. 303). See the comments on this parallel to the Gospel of Peter by Schonfield, According to the Hebrews, 102-103.

The Gospel of Peter and the Apocryphal Acts of the Apostles

Using Cognitive Science to Reconstruct Gospel Traditions

by

ISTVÁN CZACHESZ

This contribution compares the *Gospel of Peter* with gospel traditions in the Apocryphal Acts of the Apostles. I will restrict my investigation to the second and early third century, when the earliest, so-called 'major' Apocryphal Acts were written. In those writings, both references to Jesus' passion as well as reports of the apostles' martyrdom will receive attention. In the final part of the article, proposals will be made about the formation of the common tradition, relying on models of memory and orality from cognitive science.

1. The Gospel of Peter and the Apocryphal Acts

a. The Gospel of the Acts of John

That the *Acts of John* 88-104 contains a short gospel has been acknowledged by various scholars, yet this apocryphal gospel did not receive much attention in the discussion of the gospel tradition.[1] The *Gospel of the Acts of John* begins with a prologue and the call of the disciples, reports various details from Jesus' ministry, particularly, the transfiguration (in two versions), a visit in the house of a Pharisee, and the multiplication of bread. A number of episodes are unique to this *Gospel*: John watches Jesus on several occasions, Jesus never blinks his eyes, leaves no footprints on the ground, and once he pulls John's beard. The

---

[1] There is no discussion, to my knowledge, of this passage as a gospel. Cf. K. Beyschlag, Die verborgene Überlieferung von Christus, München 1969, 97-116; E. Junod/J.-D. Kaestli, Acta Iohannis 2, Turnhout 1983, 595-600, writing about 'the use of gospel traditions'; P. Lalleman, The Acts of John. A Two-Stage Initiation Into Johannine Gnosticism, Leuven 1998, 42-46; I. Czachesz, Apostolic Commission Narratives in the Canonical and Apocryphal Acts of the Apostles, Diss. Groningen 2002, 96-110.

last supper is replaced by a ritual dance of Jesus and the disciples, and the Gospel concludes with a passion narrative. For the time being, we will focus on details of the text that can be directly related to the *Gospel of Peter*.[2]

In the passion of *Acts of John* 97-102, while the crowd thinks they are crucifying the Saviour, the *real* Jesus teaches John in a cave on the Mount of Olives. We first have to consider his words, 'John, to the multitude down below in Jerusalem I am being crucified, and pierced with lances and reeds, and gall and vinegar is given me to drink'.[3] Both piercing with reeds (νύσσω, καλάμος) and the mention of gall and vinegar together (χολή, ὄξος) are found in the *Acts of John* 101 and the *Gospel of Peter* (9 and 16, respectively) but none of the other gospels.[4] Interestingly, the same combination occurs in one of the Nag Hammadi texts, *The Second Treatise of the Great Seth*: 'Another, their father, was the one who drank the gall with the vinegar (ⲙ̄ⲡⲥⲓϭⲉ ⲙ︱ⲛ ⲡⲓ︤ⲏ︦ⲙ︦ⲏ︦ⲅ︥︡) it was not I. They were hitting me with the reed (ⲙ̄ⲡⲓⲕⲁⲥ̄); another was the one who lifted up the cross on his shoulder, who was Simon.'[5]

In the following section, *Acts of John* 98-101, a cross of light appears to John, and the voice of the Lord talks to him from the cross.[6] The motif evidently parallels the resurrection scene of the *Gospel of Peter* 41-42, where the question whether Christ had preached to the dead is answered by a voice from the cross. There is, however, no literal agreement (beyond σταυρός) between the two texts in this case.[7]

Later, the voice from the cross explains to John, 'Therefore I have suffered none of the things which they will say of me.' This is parallel to the remark of the *Gospel of Peter* 11: 'But he held his peace as (if) he felt no pain.' Again, there is no verbatim agreement between the two texts.[8]

---

2   For the text of the Gospel of Peter, see T.J. Kraus/T. Nicklas, Das Petrusevangelium und die Petrusapokalypse. Die griechischen Fragmente mit deutscher und englischer Übersetzung, GCS.NF 11; Neutestamentliche Apokryphen 1, Berlin-New York 2004.

3   Text in E. Junod/J.-D. Kaestli, Acta Iohannis. Praefatio – Textus, Turnhout, 1983. The translation of the major Apocryphal Acts, the Gospel of Peter, and some other Christian apocrypha has been adapted from J.K. Elliott, The Apocryphal New Testament. A Collection of Apocryphal Christian Literature in an English Translation based on M.R. James, Oxford 1993.

4   Gospel of Peter 9 and 16; cf. Lalleman, Acts of John, 129-130. Piercing with reeds occurs in Sibylline Oracles 1.374 and 8.296; cf. L. Vaganay, L'Évangile de Pierre, Paris 1930, 228; M.G. Mara, Évangile de Pierre. Introduction, texte critique, traduction, commentaire et index, Paris 1973, 103-104. 'Gall' and 'vinegar' occur in Psalm 68:22, Barnabas 7:3-5, and a number of later Christian texts; cf. Vaganay, Évangile, 246; Mara, Évangile, 129-132.

5   The Second Treatise of the Great Seth (NHC VII,2) 56.6-10, text and translation G. Riley, in: B.A. Pearson (ed.), Nag Hammadi Codex VII, Leiden 1996, 165; cf. Junod/Kaestli, Acta Iohannis 1, 595 n. 7.

6   Cf. J.-M. Prieur, La croix vivante dans la littérature chrétienne du IIe siècle, RHPhR 79, 1999, 435-444, esp. 435-437.

7   Another passage of the Acts of John contains an important parallel. The occurrence of ὑπακούω in the meaning of 'answer' in Acts of John 94 is an early evidence of the liturgical use of the word, supporting the reading ὑπακοή in Gospel of Peter 42; cf. Vaganay, Évangile, 302-303; Mara, Évangile, 190; Kraus/Nicklas, Petrusevangelium, 43.

8   Lalleman, Acts of John, 131-132, writes about 'conceptual intertextuality', claiming that both texts were influenced by docetic Christology. His explanation will be criticised below.

According to the *Acts of John* 102, 'When [Jesus] had spoken to me these things and others which I know not how to say as he would have me, he was taken up (...).' The same verbal form, 'taken up' (ἀνελήφθη) is used here as in the *Gospel of Peter* 19: 'And having said this, he was taken up.' In the Synoptics we find at this place 'breathed his last, expired' (ἀφῆκεν τὸ πνεῦμα, ἐξέπνευσεν), in John 'gave up his spirit' (παρέδωκεν τὸ πνεῦμα).[9]

A motif of the resurrection scene in the *Gospel of Peter* 40, Christ's head reaching beyond the heavens (κεφαλὴν ... ὑπερβαίνουσαν τοὺς οὐρανούς), is found also in *Acts of John* 90. In the *Acts of John,* there is no resurrection (Christ is not actually crucified and ascends directly to heaven, as we have seen above). However, when John describes the appearance of Jesus in different shapes, he mentions that on one occasion, 'his feet were whiter than snow, so that the ground there was lit up by his feet, and his head reached to heaven (τὴν κεφαλὴν εἰς τὸν οὐρανὸν ἐρειδομένην)'.

The list of agreements between the two gospels against other gospel texts is impressive and needs explanation. The *Gospel of Peter* has traditionally been stamped as docetic; this view has been challenged by recent scholarship.[10] Even if we admitted that both the *Gospel of Peter* and the *Acts of John* were influenced by docetism, this would hardly explain the range of agreements. Christ's head reaching to (or beyond) heaven as well as the verbatim agreements of 'pierce', 'reed', 'gall' and 'vinegar' are difficult to connect with docetic christology; also, whereas 'taken up' in the *Acts of John* reflects a docetic concept (Christ did not suffer), the *Gospel of Peter* follows the sequence of death, burial, and resurrection.

A further interesting agreement is found between the *Gospel of Peter* 59 and the *Acts of John* by Pseudo-Prochorus.[11] In both texts, the author writes in the first person plural about 'we the twelve'. Both the use of first person and the number of twelve deserve our attention. After Judas' betrayal and death, the synoptics refer to the apostles as 'the eleven'.[12] The expression 'we the twelve' also occurs in *Apocalypse of Peter* 5, and is implied by the *Acts of Peter and the Twelve* (cf. also the Ethiopic text of *Epistula Apostolorum* 19).[13]

---

9   Matt 27:50; Mark 15:37; Luke 23:46; John 19:30. The passive voice of ἀναλαμβάνω normally refers to the ascension (e.g., Mark 16:19; Acts 1:2).
10 For an overview, see R.E. Brown, The Death of the Messiah. From Gethsemane to the Grave 2, New York 1994, 1137-1138. See also M. Myllykoski's article in the present volume.
11 T. Zahn, Acta Joannis, Erlangen 1880, 32. Cf. Vaganay, Évangile, 337.
12 Matt 28:16; Mark 16:14; Luke 24:9,33; cf. Acts 1:26.
13 *Acts of Peter and the Twelve* (NHC VI,1) 1:9-13 and passim, cf. the title (12:20-22): 'The acts of Peter with the twelve apostles'. In 1 Cor 15:5 Paul mentions Christ's appearance 'to Kefas and then to the twelve'. In Acts 1:26, Codex Bezae has 'twelve' rather than 'eleven'.

b. The Acts of Peter

In the *Acts of Peter* there are only few direct references to Jesus' passion. As in the *Gospel of Peter* 1-2, in *Acts of Peter* 8 Herod is made responsible for Jesus' death: 'You (the devil) hardened the heart of Herod' (*Tu Herodis cor indurasti*). The motif also appears in the *Acts of Thomas* 32 (see below).[14]

The *Acts of Peter*, however, show significant parallels to the passion narrative in another way. That Peter's martyrdom imitates the passion of Christ is explicitly stated in the famous *quo vadis* episode: 'When he (Peter) went out of the gate he saw the Lord come into Rome. And when he saw him he said, "Lord, where are you going?" And the Lord said to him, "I go to Rome to be crucified" ' (ch. 35).

Peter is arrested by four soldiers and taken before prefect Agrippa. Given the emphasis on Herod's responsibility for Jesus' crucifixion in the *Acts of Peter* (see above), it would not be surprising if this were an allusion to another 'Herod', namely king Agrippa I (10 BC-44 CE).[15] In Acts 12, Agrippa I is called Herod and presented as a persecutor of Christianity. After executing James, the brother of John, he

> proceeded to arrest Peter also. This was during the festival of Unleavened Bread. When he had seized him, he put him in prison and handed him over to four squads of soldiers to guard him, intending to bring him out to the people after the Passover.

The use of the name Herod as well as the mention of Unleavened Bread in the Lukan account allude to Jesus' passion. The mentions of four soldiers in *Acts of Peter* 36 and four times four in Acts 12 suggest that the two accounts of Peter's arrest derive from a common tradition.[16] This makes it even more plausible that the name Agrippa in the *Acts of Peter* is meant as an allusion to the Herods involved in the executions and imprisonments of Jesus and his disciples.

Only in the *Gospel of Peter* is Jesus actually *ordered* to be crucified, and this order comes from Herod (v. 2: τότε κελεύει Ἡρώδης).[17] Agrippa's command to crucify Peter (ἐκέλευσεν αὐτὸν σταυρωθῆναι) parallels that passion narrative. Again, the explicit mention of Herod's responsibility in Jesus death earlier in the *Acts of Peter* makes the link even more plausible.

The *Gospel of Peter* gives special attention to Joseph of Arimathea in contrast to the other gospels. Joseph is introduced as a 'friend of Pilate as well as of the Lord' (v. 2). Peter is buried by a prominent character of the *Acts of Peter*, senator Marcellus, who is rebuked by Nero for his charitable deeds with the Christians (ch. 8). Marcellus washes the body with costly cosmetics and buries

---

[14]   Cf. *Acts of Andrew and Matthias* 26, 'We will kill you as Herod killed your teacher called Jesus'; Vaganay, Évangile, 205; Mara, Évangile, 74-77.

[15]   Cf. I. Karasszon, Agrippa, King and Prefect, in: The Apocryphal Acts of Peter: Magic, Miracles and Gnosticism, ed. by J.N. Bremmer, Leuven 1998, 21-28.

[16]   Four soldiers execute Thomas (*Acts of Thomas* 164-168), but they are not mentioned at his arrest.

[17]   According to the other gospels Pilate handed him over (παρέδωκεν) to be crucified.

him in his own tomb. Two verbatim agreements draw our attention in this scene. The washing of the body is not mentioned in any other gospel, except for *Gospel of Peter* 24; the same verbal form, ἔλουσε(ν), occurs in the *Acts of Peter* 60. Only the *Gospel of Peter* uses the adjective ἴδιος to emphasise the tomb was Joseph's *own* one; again, the same word is used in the *Acts of Peter* in connection with Marcellus' tomb.

There are also details in the *Acts of Peter* which clearly parallel other gospel traditions than that of the *Gospel of Peter*. For example, Peter 'gave up his spirit (to the Lord)' (τὸ πνεῦμα τῷ κυρίῳ παρέδωκεν / ἀπέπνευσεν / *deposuit spiritum*), as Jesus did in the canonical gospels, and was not 'taken up' as Jesus in the *Gospel of Peter* and the *Gospel of the Acts of John* (see above).[18]

c. The Acts of Paul

Although Paul is beheaded with a sword rather than crucified, his martyrdom in the *Acts of Paul* parallels Jesus' passion narrative at several points.[19] Paul was sentenced to death by the emperor Nero, who 'commanded (ἐκέλευσεν) all the prisoners [i.e. Paul's fellow-Christians] to be burned with fire, but Paul to be beheaded according to the law of the Romans' (Martyrdom 3). Similarly as in the *Gospel of Peter*, a direct command of execution is given.

When Paul was beheaded, the *Acts of Paul* reports, 'milk splashed on the tunic of the soldier' (Martyrdom 5). After seeing this,

> the soldier and all who stood near by were astonished at this sight and glorified God who had thus honoured Paul. And they went away and reported everything to Caesar. When he heard of it he was amazed and did not know what to say.

In the synoptic tradition, the signs accompanying Jesus' death make the centurion confess that Jesus was 'son of God' or 'a righteous man'.[20] There is no mention in the gospels, however, of the soldiers reporting this to Pilate or Herod. In the *Gospel of Peter*, in contrast, the confession of the centurion occurs after the resurrection (45-46):

> When those who were of the centurion's company saw this they hurried by night to Pilate, leaving the sepulchre which they were guarding, and reported everything that they had seen, being greatly agitated (ἀγωνιῶντες) and saying, 'In truth he was (the) Son of God.' Pilate answered and said, 'I am clean from the blood of the Son of God; it was you who desired it.'

---

[18] The usage is consistently retained in later versions of Peter's Martyrdom: *Martyrium Petri et Pauli* / *Passio sanctorum apostolorum Petri et Pauli* 62 (παρέδωκεν τὸ πνεῦμα τῷ κυρίῳ / *emissit spiritum*); *Acta Petri et Pauli* 83 (παρέδωκεν τὸ πνεῦμα), both in R.A. Lipsius, Acta apostolorum apocrypha 1, Leipzig 1891, 172-173. 216, respectively.

[19] *Martyrium Pauli* (Greek) and *Passionis Pauli fragmentum* (Latin) in Lipsius, Acta apostolorum apocrypha 1, 104-117; C. Schmidt, ΠΡΑΞΕΙΣ ΠΑΥΛΟΥ. Acta Pauli, Glückstadt-Hamburg 1936, 60-73 (Hamburg Papyrus); idem, Acta Pauli. Aus der Heidelberger Koptischen Papyrushandschrift Nr. 1, Leipzig 1905, 48*-50* (Coptic Heidelberg Papyrus).

[20] Matt 27:54; Mark 15:39; Luke 23:47.

The soldiers' report of Paul's death to Nero, although in a different vocabulary, parallels the soldiers' rushing to Pilate in the *Gospel of Peter*. When hearing the report of the miracle at Paul's execution, Nero is amazed and confused (θαυμάζοντος καὶ διαπορῦντος), but his amazement will soon turn into fear (ταραχθείς).[21] Unlike John and Peter in their respective *Acts*, Paul is resurrected in the *Acts of Paul*. He predicts to Nero that he (Paul) would be raised from the dead and would appear to him (Nero) (ch. 4), and announces his resurrection again to two of Nero's soldiers (ch. 5). Before his death, he instructs two new converts, Longus and Cestus, to come to his tomb early in the morning following his death (ch. 5). Soon after Nero receives the report of the soldiers, Paul himself, resurrected, appears to him:

> While many philosophers and the centurion were assembled with the emperor, Paul came about the ninth hour, and in the presence of all he said, 'Caesar, behold, here is Paul, the soldier of God; I am not dead but live in my God. But upon you, unhappy one, many evils and great punishments will come because you have unjustly shed the blood of the righteous not many days ago.' ... When Nero heard this he was very frightened and commanded that the prisoners be released.

The statement of Nero's guiltiness in 'unjustly shedding the blood of the righteous' parallels the self-defence of Pilate, 'I am clean from the blood of the Son of God', and his command to release the prisoners the command of Pilate to keep Jesus' resurrection in secret.

Paul also appears to the two converts whom he ordered to visit his tomb. When Longus and Cestus approach the tomb, they take sight of 'two men in prayer and Paul between them'. They explain to Paul's companions, Titus and Luke, that they came to the tomb on Paul's command, 'whom we have seen in prayer between you before a little while' (implying that Paul disappeared meanwhile). This passage shows agreements with *Gospel of Peter* 39, where two men 'support' (ὑπορθόω) Christ as he ascends to heaven.

Again, motifs that typically resemble other traditions than that of the *Gospel of Peter* are also found in the text. For example, before his execution, Paul 'prayed at length' and 'conversed in Hebrew with the fathers'. In the Hamburg Papyrus, Paul also prays 'Father ... I commit my spirit, receive it!' Although the last sentence is not totally clear in the manuscript,[22] the motif of praying in Hebrew is best associated with Jesus' cry 'Eloi, Eloi, lema sabachthani?',[23] and his last words in Luke 23:46, 'Father, into your hands I commend my spirit.'[24]

---

[21] According to the later *Passio Sancti Pauli Apostoli* 18, when Pilate heard the news about Paul's execution, he was 'amazed and horrified' (miratus est horrifice). Lipsius, Acta apostolorum apocrypha 1, 42.

[22] Schmidt's conjecture: 'Father of my Lord Jesus Christ (?), in his (?) hands I commit my soul, and Lord Jesus, receive it!'

[23] Mark 15:34 and Matt 27:46. *Gospel of Peter* 19 has 'My power, O power, you have forsaken me', without indicating that the words were spoken in Hebrew or Aramaic.

[24] Cf. Stephen's last words in Acts 7:59: 'Lord Jesus, receive my spirit!'

d. The Acts of Andrew

Andrew in his Acts is crucified in Patras by Aegeates, proconsul of Achaea.[25] His conviction by the proconsul and his death on the cross can be readily compared to the passion of Jesus. According to *Acts of Andrew* 51, Aegeates

> commanded that Andrew be scourged with seven whips. Then he sent him off to be crucified and commanded the executioners to leave his knees uncut, supposing that by so doing he would punish Andrew even more cruelly.

As in the *Acts of Peter* and the *Acts of Paul*, the proconsul actually commanded that the apostle was executed. Even more interesting is, however, Aegeates' order that the executioners do not cut Andrew's knees. The author finds this point especially important, because he later reports,

> they tied up only his feet and armpits, without nailing up his hands or feet *nor severing his knees because of what the proconsul had commanded them, for Aegeates intended to torment him* by being hung and being eaten by dogs if he were still alive at night.

This passage is a perfect parallel to *Gospel of Peter* 14, 'And they were angry with him and commanded that his legs should not be broken so that he might die in torment.' An intertextual link is even the more likely since the motif is not frequent in ancient literature.[26]

The proconsul's brother, Stratocles, converted to Christianity. When he heard of Andrew's arrest, 'he arrived running and saw the executioners violently dragging off (βίᾳ συρόμενον) the blessed one like a criminal' (ch. 52). That the soldiers were 'dragging' Jesus at his arrest is not mentioned in the canonical gospels, but receives much attention in *Gospel of Peter* 6. It also occurs in *Acts of Thomas* 106, where parallels with the *Gospel of Peter* are even more explicit (see below).

The personification of the cross in *Acts of Andrew* 54 is a motif that we have already seen in the *Acts of John* and the *Gospel of Peter* (see above). Andrew calls the cross 'pure, radiant, full of life and light',[27] which is very similar to the image of the cross of light in *Acts of John* 98-100. The personified cross does not speak in the *Acts of Andrew*, which makes the analogy with the *Gospel of Peter* less direct in this writing than in the *Acts of John*.[28]

---

25 Text in J.-M. Prieur, Acta Andreae. Textus, Turnhout 1989, 507-549. Cf. J.-M. Prieur, Acta Andreae. Prefatio – Commentarius, Turnhout 1989, 45-56.

26 J.N. Bremmer, Man, Magic, and Martyrdom in the Acts of Andrew, in: idem (ed.), The Apocryphal Acts of Andrew, Leuven 2000, 15-34, esp. 33-34. Cf. John 19:31-33.

27 For the various versions of Andrew's address to the cross, see Prieur, Acta Andreae. Textus, 737-745.

28 An even less direct parallel is found in *Acts of Peter* 37, where Peter personifies the 'name of the cross', cf. *Armenian Martyrdom of Andrew* 72-73 (Prieur, Acta Andreae. Textus, 741). In the Gospel of the Savior (UBE; Pap. Berolinensis 22220) Jesus addresses the cross (C.W. Hedrick/P.A. Mirecki, Gospel of the Savior. A New Ancient Gospel, Santa Rosa/Cal. 1999, 38-39, 52-63; and S. Emmel, The Recently Published Gospel of the Savior ["Unbekanntes Berliner Evangelium"]. Righting the Order of Pages and Events, HThR 95, 2002, 45-72). In the Ethiopic

Andrew's death is reported similarly as that of Paul (and Peter). In his last prayer he entreats Christ, 'But you yourself, O Christ, you whom I desired ... receive me, so that by my departure to you there may be a reunion of my many kindred, those who rest in your majesty.' When he said this, 'he handed over his spirit' (παρέδωκεν τὸ πνεῦμα, ch. 63).

e. The Acts of Thomas

Among the few references to the gospel narrative, the serpent in the *Acts of Thomas* 32 underlines the role of the Jewish leaders, Herod and Caiaphas, in Jesus' death: 'I (the serpent) am he who kindled Herod (ὁ τὸν Ἡρώδην πυρώσας) and inflamed Caiaphas to the lying accusation before Pilate.' The passage is similar to *Acts of Peter* 8 (see above); given the assumed dependence of the *Acts of Thomas* on the *Acts of Peter*,[29] it might be drawn from the latter, rather than from the *Gospel of Peter*.

The martyrdom of Thomas in *Acts of Thomas* 105-170 is the longest among the major Acts.[30] Thomas is arrested at the house of Charisius, a near relative of king Misdaeus, whose wife Mygdonia became a follower of apostle. Misdaeus sent 'many soldiers' to Charisius' house (ch. 105), where Charisius

> took a mantle from one of his servants, put it on the neck of the apostle and said, 'Drag him off (σύρατε) and take him away; I shall see whether God can save him from my hands.' And they dragged him off (σύραντες) and took him to King Misdaeus (ch. 106).

The first detail that catches our attention at Thomas' arrest is Charisius' command to 'drag him off'. We have seen that the motif does not occur in the canonical gospels, but both in *Acts of Andrew* 52 (see above) and in *Gospel of Peter* 6:

> So they took the Lord and pushed him as they ran and said, 'Let us drag (σύρωμεν) the Son of God along now that we have got power over him.' And they put upon him a purple robe and set him on the judgement seat ....[31]

Not only do soldiers 'drag' the victims in both the *Gospel of Peter* and the *Acts of Thomas*, their torturers also claim they have them in their power, saying, 'I shall

---

Apocalypse of Peter 1, the cross is said to 'come before Jesus' face' at the Parousia. For other writings, cf. Vaganay, Évangile, 298-299; Mara, Évangile, 188-189; Prieur, La croix vivante.

[29] D.R. MacDonald, Which Came First: Intertextual Relationships Between the Apocryphal Acts of the Apostles, Sem. 80, 1997, 11-41; A.F.J. Klijn, Acts of Thomas. Introduction – Text – Commentary, Leiden ²2003, 26.

[30] Greek: Acta apostolorum apocrypha 2/2, Leipzig 1903, 217-287; Syriac: P. Bedjan, Acta martyrum et sanctorum syriacae 3, Leipzig 1892, 107-175.

[31] Justin, *1 apol.* 35:6 seems to report the same tradition: "And as the prophet spoke, they tormented (διασύροντες) him, and set him on the judgement-seat, and said, 'Judge us.'" Cf. 4 Macc 6:1; Acts 8:3 and 17:6; *Acts of Andrew and Matthias* 25-26; *Acts of Philip*, Martyrdom 14; Vaganay, Évangile, 223-224; Mara, Évangile, 89 n. 3. On the question whether Justin used the Gospel of Peter, see Kraus/Nicklas, Petrusevangelium, 11-12, and the article of K. Greschat in the present volume.

see whether God can save him from my hands' and 'we have got power over him', respectively. Charisius' casting a mantle[32] on Thomas' neck might parallel the purple robe put on Jesus; the latter episode, however, is not restricted to the *Gospel of Peter* among the gospels.

The rest of Thomas' martyrdom contains various agreements with other gospels and apostolic Acts, but no particular references to the *Gospel of Peter*. The four soldiers, already known to us from Acts 12 and *Acts of Peter* 36 (see above), are given theological importance at Thomas' execution (ch. 165). Thomas' appearance to his followers at his tomb includes parallels with different gospels; the apostle instructs Siphor and Vazan, 'Why do you sit here and keep watch over me? I am not here but I have gone up and received all that I was promised. But rise up and go down hence; for after a little time you also shall be gathered to me;' he also comforts Mygdonia and Tertia, 'Do not be deceived: Jesus the holy, the living one, shall quickly send help to you.'

2. The common tradition of the Gospel of Peter and the major Apocryphal Acts

In the first part of the chapter we have searched each of the major Apocryphal Acts for elements which are found in the *Gospel of Peter* but not in the canonical gospels. Before proceeding with the explanation of the textual evidence, it will be helpful to summarise our findings in a table, this time from the perspective of the *Gospel of Peter*. The words in italics in the table indicate verbatim agreement.[33] In the last column other important early Christian parallels are listed, including references to some later Apocryphal Acts.

GosPet	AJ	APet	APaul	AAndr	AThom	Other
Herod and judges do not wash hands		devil hardened Herod			serpent kindled Herod and Caiaphas	Andrew and Matthias
Herod's *command*		Agrippa's *command*	Nero's *command*	Aegeates' *command*	Charisius' *command*	
dragging Jesus, having power over him				*dragging* Andrew	*dragging* Thomas, see if he is rescued	Justin; Acts; Andrew and Matthias

---

[32] In Origen, *Selecta in Ezechielem* 13:812.28, ἡμιφύριον explains περιβόλαιον, worn by the personified Jerusalem. In the Septuagint, περιβόλαιον is any clothing that covers the body; in 1 Cor 11:15 it means women's headcovers. Passages referred by Lampe, s.v., show that ἡμιφύριον was later worn by monks. In the Syriac, *ma'phrâ* is worn by women and priests, cf. Payne Smith, Thesaurus, s.v.; Klijn, Acts of Thomas, 119, translates 'turban', cf. his commentary on p. 273.

[33] Verbatim agreement does not always extend to the grammatical form.

throwing robe on Jesus				throwing mantle on Thomas	
pierce with reeds	*pierce with reeds*				Sib. Or.; Sec. Treat. of Great Seth
no pain	no suffering				docetism?
gall with *vinegar*	*gall* and *vinegar*				Barn.; Sec. Treat. of Great Seth
bones not broken to prolong suffering				knees uncut to prolong suffering	
taken up	*taken up*				ascension
high-status Joseph *washes* the body; buries it in his *own* grave	high-status Marcellus *washes* the body; buries it in his *own* grave				
ascension between two men			appearance between two men		AscIsa 15-17
head reaching beyond *heaven*	*head* reaching to *heaven*				
voice from the cross	voice from the cross	(personified cross)		personified cross	UBE; Rev. of Peter
soldiers agitated, confess, report			soldiers astonished, confess, report		
Pilate's confession; clean from *blood; orders* guard			Nero's confusion; shedding righteous *blood; orders* release of Christians		
we the Twelve					Ps.-Prochorus; Peter and the Twelve

    A general look at the table reveals that the passages extend to the entire plot of the *Gospel of Peter* as well as involve all of the major Acts. The parallels include verbatim agreements as well as similar content expressed in different words. Most verbatim parallels are found in the *Acts of John*, but all of the major Acts contain at least one verbatim or otherwise very strong agreement. The extent and strength of the agreements makes it unlikely that we have to do with an ensemble of coincidences. Consequently, some kind of intertextual relation has to be established between the *Gospel of Peter* and the Apocryphal Acts.

Technically speaking, we have four major options to establish an intertextual link between the *Gospel of Peter* and any of the Apocryphal Acts. (1) The author used a copy of the *Gospel of Peter*. Were the parallels sentence-long verbatim agreements, this option would be very plausible. This is, however, not the case. If the author had a written copy of the *Gospel of Peter*, he opted to use it freely. (2) The author did not have a copy of the *Gospel of Peter* at hand, but read or heard it earlier and relied on his memory. (3) The author had access to a document related to the *Gospel of Peter*, such as a source or a different version. (4) The author relied on oral tradition connected with the *Gospel of Peter*. This might have been an oral source, parallel tradition, or a result of 'secondary orality'.

These four solutions actually can be reduced to two major options. The third solution, that the author used a written document related to the *Gospel of Peter*, immediately raises the question of how the *Gospel of Peter* used that hypothetical document (or vice versa). Consequently, both the first and third solution mount to the problem of reconstructing the scribal manoeuvres that transform the readings of the extant *Gospel of Peter* into their parallels in the Apocryphal Acts (or vice versa). Also the second and fourth solutions are close relatives. Citing a text from memory is basically the first stage of secondary orality. That is, the second major option is to consider oral transmission and its possible effects on texts to explain the connection between the extant *Gospel of Peter* and its parallels in the Apocryphal Acts.

Before going into more detail, a comparison with the use of other early Christian literature in the Apocryphal Acts may provide us with a good starting point. Studies on the use of the New Testament and other early Christian texts in the Apocryphal Acts show that parallels with such literature are of a similar nature as parallels with the *Gospel of Peter*.[34] Most agreements extend to one to a few words, regard phrases and expressions, include ideas reformulated in different words, or are due to conceptual similarities. This includes references to the epistles of Paul, which undoubtedly were the earliest written documents of Christianity in broad circulation.[35] In general, it is extremely difficult to locate extended verbatim quotations (such as complete sentences) of literary texts in the Apocryphal Acts. This overall picture yields

---

[34] P. Herczeg, New Testament Parallels to the Apocryphal Acta Pauli documents, in: The Apocryphal Acts of Paul, ed. by J.N. Bremmer, Kampen 1996, 142-149; Lalleman, Acts of John, 71-75. 110-135.

[35] H. Gamble, Books and Readers in the Early Church. A History of Early Christian Texts, New Haven-London 1995, 95-101.

the preliminary conclusion that the Apocryphal Acts of the Apostles came to existence in an oral context, including probably both primary and secondary orality. In the rest of my article I will outline a model which is capable of explaining the type of intertexuality found in the *Gospel of Peter* and the Apocryphal Acts, and which is potentially extensible to other texts of earliest Christianity.

3. Martyrdom texts in a cognitive perspective

The use of cognitive science in orality studies provides biblical scholars with hitherto unexploited resources for understanding early Christian tradition.[36] The model that I will briefly outline relies on two findings of cognitive science: (1) the use of narrative scripts in remembering events; and (2) the mechanism of serial recall in retrieving texts. There are a number of additional aspects of (oral) transmission that cannot be discussed here, such as the role of innate mental structures and rituals in the transmission of cultural information.[37]

Let us first consider narrative scripts. Human perception and memory make use of various levels of filtering and schematisation. Inherited and culturally learned structures of the mind determine what kind of information we perceive and in which ways we deal with that information.[38] Events that we experience are stored in memory as narrative scripts.[39] Any particular experience is perceived using the relevant script in our memory as well as it modifies the exact form of that script. When we receive a sufficient amount of information that is related to a given script, the script is evoked (instantiated).[40] The interpretative power of scripts lies in that once a script is evoked it supplies information that is not immediately available in the actual situation.[41] At the same time, reality is distorted by (or better: experienced in terms of) the expectations and limits imposed on it by our available scripts. We extend the original use of scripts inasmuch as we apply them not only to remembering real-life (autobiographical) events but other information as well.[42]

---

[36] Cf. I. Czachesz, Cognitive Science and the Gospels, in: Learned Antiquity. Scholarship and Society in the Near-East, the Greco-Roman World, and the Early Medieval West, ed. by A.A. MacDonald et al., Leuven 2003, 25-36; idem, Toward a Cognitive Psychology of Early Christian Tradition, Studies in Religion 2006 [forthcoming]; R. Uro, Explaining Radical Family Ethos. A Critique of Theories Concerning the Synoptic Antifamilial Traditions, NTT 2006 [forthcoming].

[37] For those aspects, cf. Czachesz, Toward a Cognitive Psychology, and the literature discussed there.

[38] A representative study is S. Pinker, How the Mind Works, London 1997.

[39] Our starting point is R.C. Schank/R.P. Abelson, Scripts, Plans, Goals and Understanding. An Inquiry into Human Knowledge Structures, Hillsdale/N.J. 1977.

[40] Schank/Abelson, Scripts, 46-50, describe very precise rules for the application of scripts.

[41] Schank/Abelson, Scripts, 41.

[42] See E. Minchin, Homer and the Resources of Memory. Some Applications of Cognitive Theory to the Iliad and the Odyssey, Oxford 2001, for an attempt to use script theory in Homeric studies.

In early Christian literature it is easy to identify a number of frequently used scripts, such as the 'martyrdom script', the 'gospel script', the 'healing script', or 'divine call'.[43] A script is evoked when typical motifs occur in the information to be processed, such as illness, resurrection, or epiphany. The blueprint of the story is immediately made up in the listener's mind using the known details, whereas unknown details are filled up with default values of the relevant script. The importance of thinking in scripts is that the occurrence of a typical motif makes other details predictable: once 'martyrdom script' is evoked, the listener will predict a particular story pattern, excluding, for example, the possibilities that the hero was assassinated, or was acquitted during the trial.

Stories of martyrdom were well-known in Hellenistic (Jewish) literatures. That tradition probably began with classical Athenian civilisation, which nurtured a degree of interest in individuality unparalleled in other ancient cultures. An important consequence of this interest was the appearance of biography as a literary convention, of which the first example is Plato's *Apology of Socrates*.[44] The courage of the individual was powerfully represented by Socrates' martyrdom. Socrates' example gave later a decisive impetus to Christian images of martyrdom.[45] In Jewish literature, biographies mainly followed idealised patterns rather than portraying individual personalities.[46] And the ideal, it seems, was peaceful death rather than martyrdom. Even the martyrdom of a suffering prophet like Jeremiah is missing in the earliest tradition. In the Hellenistic period the situation changed. Paradoxically, it was likely under the influence of the Greek ideal that the story of the Maccabees, the emblematic figures of Jewish national pride, was coloured by the martyrdom narratives of Eleazar and the mother with seven sons.[47] The martyrdom narratives preserved in the books of the Maccabees contributed an important element to the martyrdom script: it was coloured by an Oriental interest in gruesome details.[48]

---

[43] Cf. Czachesz, Cognitive Science, 29-32; idem, Apostolic Commission Narratives, 213-248.

[44] A. Dihle, Studien zur griechischen Biographie, Göttingen ²1970, 18. 19. 35. 36 and passim; P. Cox, Biography in Late Antiquity. A Quest for the Holy Man, Berkeley 1983, 7.

[45] As various scholars suggested, Acts 17 probably alludes to Socrates (e.g., J.C. O'Neill, The Theology of Acts in Its Historical Setting, London ²1970, 160-171). Lucian, *Passing of Peregrinus* 12, reports that Christians called Peregrinus, when he was in prison, 'the new Socrates'. For the second and third century Fathers, see K.W. Döring, Exemplum Socratis, Wiesbaden 1979, 143-161. For Eusebius' *Life of Origen* 6:3.7, see Cox, Biography, 87.

[46] K. Baltzer, Die Biographie der Propheten, Neukirchen-Vluyn 1975.

[47] 2 Macc. 6-7; 4 Macc. 5-12. Explicit references to those passages are found in *Martyrdom of Marian and James* 13:1 and *Martyrdom of Montanus and Lucius* 16:4. Cf. A. Hilhorst, Fourth Maccabees in Christian Martyrdom Texts, in: Ultima Aetas. Time, Tense and Transience in the Ancient World, ed. by C. Kroon/D. Den Hengst, Amsterdam 2000, 107-122.

[48] For the sources of torture in early Christian imagination, see I. Czachesz, Torture in Hell and Reality, in: The Apocalypse of Paul, ed. by J.N. Bremmer/I. Czachesz, Leuven 2006, [forthcoming].

At the time when Christianity was emerging, the ideal of martyrdom became increasingly valued in the Roman world. Beginning with the early principate, Stoic contempt of death was famous, and accounts of Stoic martyrs circulated.[49] A particularly remarkable group of martyrdom texts is preserved in the so-called *Acta Alexandrinorum*, containing records of the processes of Alexandrian noblemen, written probably between the middle of the first and the end of the second century CE.[50] Christian martyrdom is characterised by a twofold emphasis: on the one hand, Socratic wisdom during the trial, including a testimony or farewell speech; on the other hand, a detailed description of ordeals and death.[51]

The earliest Christian martyr texts include various reports of Jesus' passion, the martyrdom of the apostles, particularly in the major Apocryphal Acts, and the acts of the martyrs. Most examples of this literature follow the standard *martyrdom script*: 1. arrest; 2. imprisonment and tortures; 3. reaction of the martyr's companions; 4. significant words of the martyr; 5. conviction; 6. way to the place of execution; 7. last words of the martyr; 8. death; 9. miraculous signs; 10. reaction of friends and enemies; 11. resurrection; 12. appearances.

Narrative scripts not only predict an expected sequence of episodes, they also determine a set of narrative functions. In case of the Christian martyrdom script, it comprises the hero, the judge (monarch, proconsul, or other high-standing official), soldiers, the hero's companions, crowds etc. Their expected behaviour, their relation with each other, and the possible changes in their relation and character (conversion, betrayal, confession) are also predicted by the script.[52] Already from a limited number of cues it is not difficult to construct a whole martyrdom narrative, filling up most details according to the default values of the scripts: proconsuls are hostile but impressed by the signs, some enemies convert, soldiers are struck with awe, the hero will resurrect and appear to his enemies and followers. That most Christian passion narratives, Apocryphal Acts, and martyrdom stories are rather similar to each other is not a matter of literary influence, but due to the constraints that the martyrdom script imposes on cognition.

At the same time, the narratives under examination are very different from each other. Verbatim agreement beyond the length of a few words is the exception, even among the synoptic gospels. A traditional way of explaining

---

[49] H.A. Musurillo, Acts of the Pagan Martyrs. Acta Alexandrinorum, Oxford 1954, 239-242.

[50] Musurillo, Acts, 83-232.

[51] Whereas the Socratic, stoic, and cynic martyr ideal probably inspired formative Christianity, a direct influence of the Acta Alexandrinorum on the earliest Christian martyrdom narratives is unlikely; cf. Musurillo, Acts, v. 244. 262; K. Berger, Hellenistische Gattungen im Neuen Testament, ANRW 2.25.2, 1984, 1031-1432, esp. 1250-1251.

[52] A full analysis of the martyrdom script would require a description of the narrative plot as well as of the narrative functions. Plot and functions are two interconnected aspects of the script: on the one hand, the plot emerges from the interaction of the characters; on the other hand, the function of the characters can be understood by analysing the plot. For an analysis of the 'commission script', see Czachesz, Apostolic Commission, 242-248.

this phenomenon is to attribute sophisticated editorial work to the authors, who rephrased each sentence in their sources according to their own theological views. It is not our task at this time to evaluate the documentary approaches to the gospel tradition. As for the comparison of the *Gospel of Peter* and the Apocryphal Acts, we have already provided arguments that compel us to solve the problems within the framework of orality.

When people recall and perform (or write down) texts, they also use another technique to fill up the blueprint provided by scripts. This technique is effective, *mutatis mutandis*, with narratives as well as poetic, legal, or other texts. In a process called *serial recall*, speakers depart from genre-specific constraints and some initial phrase, which gives cues to produce the next word or phrase, proceeding in this way from word to word, phrase to phrase, to build up sentences, episodes, up to very extensive and complex texts.[53] It seems that professional performers and casual ones alike follow basically the same strategy.[54] Different cues, including sound patterns, rhythm, rhymes, as well as syntactic and semantic features, help the speaker choose the next word in the text. Although professionals may make use of mnemonic techniques, this is not essential for the mechanism to work.

The set of words and phrases that can be used in telling a Christian martyrdom narrative is delimited by tradition. For example, expressions meaning 'gave up his spirit' (ἐξέπνευσεν, ἀπέπνευσεν, ἀφῆκεν … / παρέδωκεν / ἀπέδωκεν τὸ πνεῦμα) are preferred to report the death of the martyr in the gospels, the Apocryphal Acts, and often the acts of the martyrs,[55] above other alternatives. When the speaker or writer arrives at this detail, he knows that a phrase with 'spirit' is appropriate, but the actual formulation (using one of the above-mentioned phrases) is a matter of individual choice and momentary inspiration. Sometimes other alternatives are chosen, such as 'taken up' in *Gospel of Peter* 19, or other expressions, for example, in many acts of the martyrs. In this paradigm, the actual form of the text is a result of a delicate interplay of convention and improvisation.

Some details in the script are optional, but when they occur, they are frequently expressed with the same word. An example is the 'dragging' of the martyr in *Gospel of Peter* 6 and some Apocryphal Acts. Optional details may themselves form a 'sub-script' (a shorter chain of stereotyped events), such as the burial of the martyr. The burial script is implemented in a similar way in *Gospel of Peter* 24 and *Acts of Peter* 60, including verbal agreements (washing, 'own' grave). Such multiple verbal agreements may refer to a particular

---

53 D. Rubin, Memory in Oral Traditions. The Cognitive Psychology of Epic, Ballads, and Counting-out Rhymes, New York 1995, 175-176.

54 For example, American students were found to use this technique when recalling the Preamble of the Constitution; Rubin, Memory, 182.

55 E.g., *Martyrdom of St. Carpus* 47; *Martyrdom of Pionius* 21:9; *Martyrdom of St. Conon* 6:5. For comparing the Apocryphal Acts with the Acts of the Martyrs, see A. Hilhorst, The Apocryphal Acts as Martyrdom Texts. The Case of the Acts of Andrew, in: The Apocryphal Acts of John, ed. by J.N. Bremmer, Kampen 1995, 1-14.

'dialect' in oral tradition, in which the formulation of an episode consistently made use of different words than in other dialects. Dialects of the tradition may be explained by social, linguistic (Greek, Latin, Syriac), or geographic relations between the respective implementations of the martyrdom script. For example, if particular dialects sympathised with high-status, influential Christians (possibly because such persons played a positive role in the respective communities), the burial script may have also paid special attention to persons like Joseph and Marcellus.

At other times, similarities are conceptual rather than textual, such as in the case of the personified cross. Within that larger concept, however, various textual traditions can be identified: the *Gospel of the Savior*, the *Acts of Peter* and the *Acts of Andrew* seem to follow a closely related textual pattern of the address to the cross. The models of narrative scripts and serial recall, used in this article, are not particularly strong at explaining the evolution of concepts.[56]

For the time being, I do not attempt a whole-scale explanation of the textual agreements between the *Gospel of Peter* and the Apocryphal Acts. Through a few examples I illustrated how a cognitive model of oral transmission can account for various types of textual relations between those writings. In the final part of the article, I want to ask about the historical framework in which such interactions between the respective texts may have occurred.

4. Did the Gospel of Peter influence the Apocryphal Acts?

If the similarities between the Apocryphal Acts and the gospels are due to the rules of remembering and orality, from the historical point of view we have the following possibilities: either the gospels (or some of them) influenced the Apocryphal Acts through *secondary orality*,[57] or the gospels (at least some of them) were in an oral-formative period at the very time during which the Apocryphal Acts (or their relevant parts) were composed. A definite answer to this question bears various implications for the dating of the gospels and the Apocryphal Acts. In this article I obviously cannot undertake such a large-scale investigation.

According to the opinion of recent scholarship, the major Apocryphal Acts were composed between the middle of the second and the first quarter of the third century.[58] The *Acts of John* have recently been dated even earlier, to the second quarter of the second century.[59] Our first, very careful conclusion is that beginning from the first half of the second century the Apocryphal Acts used either oral tradition that later became incorporated in the *Gospel of Peter*, or the

---

[56]   Cf. Czachesz, Toward a Cognitive Psychology.
[57]   Concerning the problem of secondary orality see also A. Kirk's article in the present volume.
[58]   For the respective dates, see J.N. Bremmer, The Apocryphal Acts. Date, Time, and Readership, in: idem, The Apocryphal Acts of Thomas, Leuven 2001, 149-170.
[59]   Lalleman, Acts of John, 268-270.

Gospel of Peter itself from secondary orality. The literary fixation of the gospels (including the *Gospel of Peter*), as well as of the Apocryphal Acts, did not put an end to the oral transmission of the material included in them. Therefore, the dividing line between 'primary' and 'secondary' orality is far from being clear-cut: a cross-fertilisation of written and oral texts likely characterised the composition of the Apocryphal Acts.

Traditions of the apostles' death pre-dated the final composition of the Apocryphal Acts.[60] A more progressive conclusion, therefore, may date the use of the respective gospel traditions by the martyrdom narratives of the apostles to the end of the first and the beginning of the second century.

The third, provocative, conclusion sounds like this. Given that tradition set the martyrdom of Jesus under Pontius Pilate and the death of Paul (and Peter) under Nero, but the first written gospels are not dated earlier than 70 CE, we cannot *a priori* exclude that the respective martyrdom narratives circulated simultaneously before their fixation in writing. In that case, traditions of the martyrdom of Jesus and the apostles could have influenced each other within the framework of oral transmission, as outlined in the previous section. In principle, even some Apocryphal Acts could have been written before some of the (canonical) gospels.[61] In that case, the intertextual relations between the gospels and the apocryphal (and canonical) Acts must be approached in a radically different way than it has been done in earlier scholarship.

---

[60] The martyrdom of Peter and Paul is reported first in 1 Clement 5; cf. recently H. Löhr, Zur Paulus-Notiz in 1 Clem 5.5-7, in: Das Ende des Paulus. Historische, theologische, und literaturgeschichtliche Aspekte, ed. by F.W. Horn, Berlin 2001, 197-213, esp. 212-213; U. Schnelle, Paulus. Leben und Denken, Berlin 2003, 425-431. Early martyrdom traditions include the Stephen story (Acts 6:8-8:1) and the death of James (brother of John, Acts 12:1-3).

[61] Cf. A. Hilhorst, Tertullian on the Acts of Paul, in: The Apocryphal Acts of Paul, ed. by J.N. Bremmer, Kampen 1996, 150-163, esp. 162, for a possible early dating of the Acts of Paul.

Apokryphe Passionstraditionen im Vergleich:
Petrusevangelium und Sibyllinische Orakel (Buch VIII)

von

TOBIAS NICKLAS

1. Einleitung: Einige grundsätzliche Vorbemerkungen zu den Sibyllinischen Orakeln

Die heute erhaltene Sammlung der *Oracula Sibyllina* (*OrSib*), eigentlich zusammengesetzt aus zwei Sammlungen, besteht aus insgesamt 12 Büchern unterschiedlicher Länge.[1] Diese Texte, insgesamt etwa 4230 Verse in Hexametern,[2] dürften in einem Zeitraum von mehr als einem halben Jahrtausend entstanden sein. Der älteste erhaltene Text ist wohl das jüdische 3. Orakel,[3] die jüngsten stammen aus christlicher Hand bzw. sind von christlicher Hand überarbeitet.[4] Die gesamte Sammlung ist uns nur über ihre Tradierung in christlichen Kreisen überliefert.[5]

---

[1] Die eigenartige Zählung 1-8 // 11-14 erklärt sich aufgrund der geteilten Manuskript-Tradition. Weiterführend J.J. Collins, The Sibylline Oracles, in: Jewish Writings of the Second Temple Period. Apocrypha, Pseudepigrapha, Qumran Sectarian Writings, Philo, Josephus, ed. by M.E. Stone, CRINT II.2, Assen-Philadelphia 1984, 357-381, bes. 357.

[2] Zählung entsprechend V. Nikoprowetzky, Oracles Sibyllins, in: La Bible. Écrits intertestamentaires, hg. von A. Dupont-Sommer/M. Philonenko, Paris 1987, 1037-1140, bes. 1037.

[3] So etwa J.J. Collins, The Development of the Sibylline Tradition, ANRW II.20.1, 1987, 421-459, bes. 430.

[4] Ausführlich hierzu Collins, Development, 422 (nimmt eine Spanne von 700 Jahren an). Vgl. aber auch J. Bartlett, Jews in the Hellenistic World: Josephus, Aristeas, the Sibylline Oracles, Eupolemos, Cambridge Commentaries on Writings of the Jewish and Christian World 200 BC to AD 200, Cambridge et al. 1985, 35 (2. Jh. v.Chr. - 4. Jh. n.Chr.), oder U. Treu, Christliche Sibyllinen, in: NtApo 2: Apostolisches, Apokalypsen und Verwandtes, Tübingen ⁶1997, 591-619, bes. 592: „Die einzelnen Bücher sind etwa in der Zeit von 180 vor Chr. bis zum dritten nachchristlichen Jahrhundert entstanden." Die Endfassung der Sammlung allerdings ist erst um das 6. Jh. unserer Zeitrechnung anzusetzen. Hierzu vgl. J.H. Charlesworth, Jewish and Christian Self-Definition in Light of the Christian Additions to the Apocryphal Writings, in: Jewish and Christian Self-Definition II: Aspects of Judaism in the Graeco-Roman Period, ed. by E.P. Sanders et al., Philadelphia 1981, 27-55, bes. 48; J.-D. Gauger, Sibyllinische Weissagungen. Griechisch-deutsch. Auf der Grundlage der Ausgabe von Alfons Kurfeß neu übersetzt und herausgegeben, Tusculum, Düsseldorf-Zürich ²2002, 333.

[5] Ausführlich zur Überlieferungslage vgl. A.-M. Denis, Introduction à la littérature religieuse judéo-hellénistique II (Pseudepigraphes de l'Ancien Testament), Turnhout 2000, 953-962. Der

Auch wenn die in der Sammlung zusammengestellten Texte außer der Stimme, die sie spricht, nicht viel gemeinsam haben, werden in der Forschung doch einige gemeinsame Linien gezogen:

(1) Regelmäßig wird die These vertreten, dass die jüdisch-christlichen Sibyllinen anders als viele apokalyptische Texte[6], die nach innen wirken sollen, sich nach außen richteten – den ältesten Texten ging es um Heidenmission in der jüdischen Diaspora Ägyptens.[7]

(2) Darüber hinaus lasse sich in vielen der jüdisch-christlichen Sibyllinen neben einer Verurteilung heidnischer Religion ein eklatanter Hass auf Rom und seine Herrschaft beobachten.[8]

Für den hier vorliegenden Zusammenhang ist vor allem bedeutsam, dass die Teile der sibyllinischen Orakel, die von christlichen Händen überarbeitet wurden bzw. erst von christlicher Hand entstanden, auch apokryphe Passagen über die Passion Jesu von Nazaret enthalten, die sich in einen Bezug zu anderen Passionserzählungen bringen lassen. So wurde bei der Suche nach Texten, die möglicherweise von der Darstellung von Passion und Auf-erstehung, wie sie sich im *EvPetr* finden, beeinflusst sind, auch immer wieder das achte Buch der *OrSib* genannt. Bereits L. Vaganay hat in seinem großen Kommentar zum *EvPetr* (1930) Parallelen zwischen *OrSib* VIII 288-311 und *EvPetr* 8-10.16.18.41 herausgearbeitet. Diese Parallelen aber ließen nicht auf literarische Abhängigkeit schließen, sondern könnten viel leichter über den gemeinsamen Hintergrund alt- und neutestamentlicher Texte erklärt werden.[9] Auch in J. Denkers Übersicht über Texte, die vom *EvPetr* beeinflusst sein

---

früheste christliche Text, in dem eine Sibylle (die Sibylle von Cumae) begegnet, ist der *Hirt des Hermas* II 4,1. Hierzu weiterführend N. Brox, Der Hirt des Hermas, KAV 7, Göttingen 1991, 104-105.

6   Auch wenn die *OrSib* traditionell in die Nähe der Apokalyptik eingeordnet werden (so z.B. ihre Einordnung NtApo 2; Denis, Introduction II, 947), lassen sie sich streng genommen nicht als „Apokalypsen" gemäß der heute weitgehend akzeptierten Definition von J.J. Collins, Towards the Morphology of a Genre, in: Sem. 14, 1979, 1-20, bes. 9, einordnen. Zur religions-geschichtlichen Herleitung der jüdisch-christlichen Sibyllinen vgl. Collins, Development, 424-426.

7   Vgl. etwa J.J. Collins, The Sibyl and the Potter. Political Propaganda in Ptolemaic Egypt, in: idem, Seers, Sibyls and Sages in Hellenistic-Roman Judaism, JSJ.S 54, Leiden-New York-Köln 1997, 199-210, bes. 199; Gauger, Sibyllinische Weissagungen, 334.

8   So auch R. Van den Broek, Juden und Christen in Alexandrien im 2. und 3. Jahrhundert, in: Juden und Christen in der Antike, hg. von J. Van Amersfoort/J. Van Oort, Kampen 1990, 101-115, bes. 106; Gauger, Sibyllinische Weissagungen, 334.

9   Vgl. L. Vaganay, L'Évangile de Pierre, ÉtB, Paris 1930, 164-165. Vaganays Beobachtungen werden auch bei M.G. Mara, Évangile de Pierre, SC 201, Paris 1973, 23; eadem, Il Vangelo di Pietro, Scritti delle origini cristiane 30, Bologna 2003, 19; M. Erbetta, Gli apocrifi del Nuovo Testamento: Vangeli I,1: Scritti affini ai vangeli canonici – composizione gnostiche – materiale illustrativo, Turin 1975, 141, knapp wieder aufgenommen. – Nicht erwähnt werden die Passionstraditionen der *OrSib* überraschenderweise bei R.E. Van Voorst, Extracanonical Passion Narratives, in: The Death of Jesus in Early Christianity, ed. by J.T. Carroll/J.B. Green, Peabody 1995, 148-161.

könnten, begegnet *OrSib* VIII.[10] Anders als Vaganay aber sucht Denker nicht nur nach wörtlichen Übereinstimmungen, die er dann auflistet, sondern betrachtet zumindest bei einzelnen Motiven, wie dem Schweigen Christi, deren Funktion im Kontext. Der Hintergrund der Gemeinsamkeiten, die zwischen beiden Texten zu erkennen sind, finde seinen Ursprung in den alttestamentlichen „Vorlagen" der gemeinsamen Züge begründet – „die Übereinstimmungen zwischen der christlichen Interpolation im achten Buch der Sib und dem PE" könnten sich „aus einer gemeinsamen Auslegungstradition"[11] erklären.

Mit den Mitteln der klassischen Literarkritik, die vergleichbare Wörter und Strukturen zweier Texte zunächst auf synchroner Ebene miteinander in Verbindung bringt und anschließend nach möglichen Beziehungen zwischen beiden Texten (auf Autorebene) fragt, das heißt literarische Abhängigkeiten festzustellen sucht, dürfte in der genannten Frage nicht mehr zu erbringen sein, als bisher bereits der Fall ist. Dass diese Methodik gerade im Falle christlicher Apokryphen darüber hinaus durchaus problematisch sein kann, habe ich an anderer Stelle gezeigt.[12] Vielleicht aber ist es möglich, an beide Texte gemeinsame Fragen heranzutragen, deren Antwort jeweils gegenüber gestellt die Möglichkeit zur gegenseitigen genaueren Profilierung der Texte erbringen kann. Ein derartiger Vergleich könnte dann – punktuell – mithelfen, sowohl das *EvPetr* als auch die Passionstraditionen der *OrSib* in ein „Universum antiker Literatur" einzubetten und ihren (keineswegs statisch zu denkenden) Ort in diesem „Universum" näher zu beschreiben.[13]

Die folgende Untersuchung geht der Frage nach Gemeinsamkeiten und Unterschieden in der Darstellung der Passion und Auferstehung Jesu von Nazaret in *OrSib* VIII 217-336 und *EvPetr* nach.[14] Die bereits von Denker eingeschlagene Linie soll dabei im Detail aufgezeichnet werden: Wo finden sich gemeinsame Motive in der Darstellung der Passion – auch solche, die vergleichbar in kanonischen Texten begegnen? Welche Funktion besitzen diese Motive im jeweiligen Kontext? Vielleicht gelingt damit nicht nur eine noch präzisere Antwort auf die Frage nach dem intertextuellen Zueinander von *EvPetr* und dem christlichen Abschnitt von *OrSib* VIII, möglicherweise gelingt

---

10 Vgl. J. Denker, Die theologiegeschichtliche Stellung des Petrusevangeliums. Ein Beitrag zur Geschichte des Doketismus, EHS XXIII.36, Bern-Frankfurt/Main 1975, 19-20.

11 Denker, Stellung, 20.

12 Vgl. z.B. T. Nicklas, Ein „neutestamentliches Apokryphon"? Zum umstrittenen Kanonbezug des sog. „Petrusevangeliums", VigChr 56, 2002, 260-272; idem, Fragmente christlicher Apokryphen und die Textgeschichte des Neuen Testaments, ZNW 96, 2005, 129-142.

13 Zur Rede von einem „Universum antiker (christlicher) Literatur" vgl. die entsprechenden Gedanken in meiner Habilitationsschrift „Christliche Apokryphen lesen".

14 Die Untersuchung setzt so mit dem Beginn des Akrostichons ein. Nach VIII 336 ist wiederum ein inhaltlicher Einschnitt zu beobachten (Untergang der Welt und allen Lebens). Insgesamt wird *OrSib* VIII in zwei recht unterschiedliche Teile gegliedert: Z. 1-216, die mit J.J. Collins, Art. Sibylline Oracles, in: AncB.Dictionary 6 (1992), 2-6, bes. 5, wohl zum Teil jüdischen Ursprungs sind, und der klar christliche Teil Z. 217-500. Den gesamten christlichen Abschnitt zu untersuchen, würde den Rahmen der vorliegenden Arbeit sprengen.

gerade im Gegenüber der beiden Texte auch eine schärfere Profilierung der „Position"[15] dieser beiden Passionsdarstellungen in einem möglichen „Universum christlicher Literatur".

2. Zum Text: *OrSib* VIII 217-336 und *EvPetr*

2.1 Das Weltengericht (*OrSib* VIII 217-250)

Zwar erwähnt der erhaltene Teil des *EvPetr* streng genommen keine Szene, in der die Ereignisse des Endgerichts geschildert werden,[16] trotzdem sollte die für das Verständnis der Szene in *OrSib* VIII so wichtige Beschreibung des Endgerichts (im *Akrostichon*) nicht zu schnell außer Acht gelassen werden.

2.1.1 Das von der Sibylle geschilderte *Endgericht* ist auf die ganze Menschheit und den gesamten Kosmos bezogen (VIII 219.222); nicht ganz klar wird, wen sich die Sibylle als Richter vorstellt:[17] VIII 218 spricht vom „Ewigkeitsherrscher, dem künftigen König"[18], VIII 220 von der unmittelbaren Gottesschau der Gläubigen wie auch der Ungläubigen (vgl. auch VIII 221). Stellt sich die Sibylle Gott als eigentlichen Weltenrichter vor? In diese Richtung ließe sich vielleicht auch VIII 230 interpretieren, wo wiederum der θεός als der Handelnde dargestellt wird, oder VIII 242, wo vom „Richtstuhl Gottes" (βῆμα θεοῦ) die Rede ist. Das Erscheinen des Zeichens des Kreuzes (VIII 244-245) jedoch kündigt zumindest an, dass auch das Christusereignis für das Gericht eine entscheidende Rolle spielt. Allerdings bieten erst Z. 249-250 eine Antwort auf die Frage: Der unsterbliche König, σωτήρ, der gelitten hat – damit eindeutig Christus – wird als „unser Gott" bezeichnet. Offensichtlich liegt hier also ein Beispiel eines modalistischen Monarchianismus[19] vor, Gottvater und Sohn werden zumindest in einigen Aussagen völlig miteinander identifiziert.

Die erhaltenen Teile des *EvPetr* zeigen keine derartige christologische Tendenz. Immerhin begegnet eine – äußerst ironisch geschilderte – Gerichts-

---

[15] Der Begriff „Position" darf dabei durchaus als dynamisch angesehen werden.

[16] Diese Aussage hängt von der Entscheidung ab, dass das zweite apokryphe Fragment des Akhmîm-Codex mit der Mehrheit der Forscher der *Offenbarung des Petrus* und nicht dem *EvPetr* zuzuschreiben ist. Vgl. hierzu jetzt T. Nicklas, Zwei petrinische Apokryphen im Akhmîm-Codex oder eines? Kritische Anmerkungen und Gedanken, Apocrypha 16, 2005, 75-96.

[17] Wie vielfältig jüdische und christliche Gerichtsvorstellungen in der Antike – selbst im literarischen Corpus eines einzigen Autors, Paulus – ausfallen können, zeigt exemplarisch M. Konradt, Gericht und Gemeinde. Eine Studie zur Bedeutung und Funktion von Gerichtsaussagen im Rahmen der paulinischen Ekklesiologie und Ethik in 1Thess und 1Kor, BZNW 117, Berlin-New York 2003.

[18] Übersetzung: Gauger, Sibyllinische Weissagungen, 185.

[19] Zur Definition vgl. D.W. Winter, Art. Monarchianismus, in: Lexikon der christlichen Antike, hg. von J.B. Bauer/J. Hutter, Darmstadt 1999, 260-261.

szene, *EvPetr* 7-9. Auch wenn der erhaltene Text nicht davon spricht, dass Jesus – oder besser: der κύριος[20] – formal zum Kreuzestod verurteilt worden sei, ist sein Schicksal bereits in V. 3 deutlich vorgezeichnet: Josef – eine Parallelgestalt zum kanonischen Josef von Arimathaia[21] – weiß schon von der geplanten Kreuzigung und bittet um den Leib Jesu; man könnte dabei aber durchaus auch die Bedeutung „Leichnam" für σῶμα mitlesen.[22] Auch V. 5 wirft Licht auf das Zukünftige: Wenn Herodes davon spricht, dass die Sonne nicht über einem „Ermordeten" untergehen dürfe (vgl. Dtn 21,22-23)[23], ist damit klar, was mit Jesus geschehen und wie diese Tat vom Text beurteilt werden wird. Jesus wird dem „Volk", also den „Juden" (V. 5) ausgeliefert. Daraus entspinnt sich eine Szene, in deren Verlauf der todgeweihte Jesus als Richter und König Israels verspottet wird. Der „Sohn Gottes" (V. 6.9) und „König Israels" (V. 7) – auch das Bekleiden mit einem purpurnen Gewand (V. 7) und Aufsetzen des Dornenkrone (V. 8) erfüllt die Funktion, Jesu Königtum zu verspotten – wird auf einen Richtstuhl (καθέδρα κρίσεως) gesetzt und soll als gerechter Richter über Israel urteilen (vgl. Jes 58,2).[24] Was aus der Perspektive der „Juden" als Charaktere der erzählten Welt Verspottung eines Verurteilten ist, wird aus der Perspektive des *EvPetr* – in beißend-antijüdischer Ironie[25] geschildert – zur Vorwegnahme des Gerichts über Israel. Zumindest vage Ähnlichkeiten, vor allem aber klare Unterschiede zum genannten Abschnitt der *OrSib* lassen sich von daher erkennen:

(1) Während es der Sibylle um das Gegenüber von Gläubigen und Ungläubigen geht (VIII 220), die im Gericht voneinander geschieden werden – der Schwerpunkt liegt auf den Gläubigen, die als die „Erwählten" eine endzeitliche „Taufe"[26] empfangen –, liegt das alleinige Interesse der Szene im *EvPetr* auf der Selbstverurteilung des jüdischen Volks vor dem Richtstuhl des „Sohnes Gottes."

---

20 Das *EvPetr* erwähnt in seinem erhaltenen Fragment weder den Namen Jesus von Nazaret, noch dessen Bezeichnung als „Christus".
21 Diese aus den kanonischen Evangelien bekannte Herkunftsbezeichnung begegnet im *EvPetr* nicht.
22 Belege bei LSJ, 1749. Vgl. auch K. Beyschlag, Die verborgene Überlieferung von Christus, München-Hamburg 1969, 34.
23 Weiterführend der Beitrag von T. Hieke im vorliegenden Band.
24 Die Szene könnte sich diachron möglicherweise von Joh 19,13 ableiten. So z.B. M. Dibelius, Die alttestamentlichen Motive in der Leidensgeschichte des Petrus- und des Johannes-Evangeliums, in: Botschaft und Geschichte 1: Zur Evangelienforschung, Tübingen 1953, 221-247, bes. 226-227; F.F. Bruce, Außerbiblische Zeugnisse über Jesus und das frühe Christentum, hg. von E. Güting, Gießen-Basel 1991, 80 n. 18. Zur Problematik vgl. allerdings Mara, Vangelo, 49-50.
25 Zum Bild, das das *EvPetr* von den „Juden" entwickelt, vgl. T. Nicklas, Die „Juden" im Petrusevangelium (PCair 10759). Ein Testfall, NTS 47, 2001, 206-221, sowie die Beiträge von J.D. Crossan und J. Verheyden im vorliegenden Band.
26 Liegt hier eine Parallele zu der „Taufe im Acherusischen See" vor, die die *Offenbarung des Petrus* (P.Vindob. G 39756) kennt? Vgl. hierzu T.J. Kraus, Acherousia und Elysion: Anmerkungen im Hinblick auf deren Verwendung auch im christlichen Kontext, Mn. 66, 2003, 145-163.

(2) Eine Parallele ist in der Bezeichnung des Richters – in *OrSib* VIII 222 und 242 auf einer βῆμα sitzend vorgestellt, in *EvPetr* 7 auf der καθέδρα κρίσεως – als „König" (*OrSib* VIII 218.250) zu sehen. Der Unterschied zwischen dem „König Israels" (*EvPetr* 7), der als „Sohn Gottes" bezeichnet wird (*EvPetr* 6.9), und dem die Welt beherrschenden endzeitlichen König der Sibyllinen, in denen Christus mit Gott identifiziert ist, wird jedoch deutlich.

2.1.2 Interessant ist die in *OrSib* VIII 244-245 deutlich werdende *Rolle des Kreuzes* bei den Ereignissen des „Jüngsten Gerichts." Dieses erscheint als Zeichen (σῆμα) wohl am Himmel. Diese Aussage ist zu offen, um einen sicheren Bezug zu der in manchen altkirchlichen Texten begegnenden Vorstellung vom „lebendigen Kreuz" herzustellen, das bei der Parusie vor dem auferstandenen Christus einhergeht (z.B. *Offenbarung des Petrus* 1 [in Exegese von Mt 24], *Epistula Apostolorum* 16[27]). Immerhin lässt der parallele Kontext es möglich erscheinen, dass hier eine ähnliche Vorstellung wie etwa in der *Elija-Apokalypse* 31,19-32,4 angedeutet ist, wo das Kreuz als Unterscheidungszeichen zwischen dem wahren Messias und dem „Sohn der Gesetzlosigkeit" dient. Dafür könnte auch die Bezeichnung des Kreuzes als „deutliches Siegel" (σφραγὶς ἐπίσημος; VIII 244) sprechen. Ist von hier aus auch ein Bezug zur Vorstellung des *EvPetr* denkbar, dass am Morgen der Auferstehung das Kreuz dem Auferstandenen folgt und offensichtlich mit ihm zum Himmel hinaufsteigt (V. 39-42)? Diese eigenartige Darstellung wurde unterschiedlich interpretiert.[28] Mir scheint aber am wahrscheinlichsten, dass das *EvPetr* davon ausgeht, das Kreuz müsse, wenn es bei der Parusie als Siegeszeichen des Auferstandenen wieder eine wichtige Rolle spielen und somit am Himmel erscheinen soll, dem Auferstandenen auch in den Himmel folgen. Sollte dies zutreffen, dann lägen in *OrSib* VIII 244-245 und *EvPetr* 38-42 zwei Vorstellungen vor, die zumindest entfernt miteinander in Bezug stünden.

2.2 Das „Wort" vor seinem irdischen Leben (VIII 251-268)

Der folgende Abschnitt *OrSib* VIII 251-269 bietet kaum Ansätze, um Bezüge zum *EvPetr* herzustellen. Der Verfasser von *OrSib* VIII 251ff. zeigt sich hier als Schriftexeget bzw. setzt bei seinen Lesern bereits Traditionen christlicher Exegese der Schrift, das heißt aus unserer Sicht des Alten Testaments, voraus: So wird z.B. in VIII 251-252 die Mose-Amalek-Szene (Ex 17,9-16) offensichtlich

---

[27]   Hier ist vor allem der koptische Text interessant, der vom „Zeichen des Kreuzes" spricht.

[28]   Mit Recht kritisiert J.D. Crossan, The Cross That Spoke. The Origins of the Passion Narrative, San Francisco 1988, 385-386, die Interpretation, das Kreuz stehe hier als Zeichen der Macht bzw. des Triumphes Jesu. Vielmehr sei ernst zu nehmen, dass es unabhängig von dem Auferstandenen agiere und ihm folge, nicht vorausgehe. Er selbst schlägt deshalb vor, die V. 39-41 als Beschreibung einer Szene, in der Jesus die Heiligen aus der Scheol befreit, zu interpretieren. Das Kreuz sei von daher als kreuzförmige Prozession der Heiligen Israels, die im Namen Jesu antworten, zu interpretieren. Vgl. auch den Beitrag von S.E. Porter im vorliegenden Band.

in einer Weise interpretiert, wie sie auch in *Barn* 12,2 zu finden ist:[29] Das Ausstrecken der Arme durch Mose (Ex 17,11), der damit zum Bild des Kreuzes wird, ist in VIII 251 als Zeichen auf den σωτήρ hin gedeutet (vgl. auch Firmicus Maternus, *err.* 21,6; Mitte 4. Jh.).[30]

Die angekündigte Inkarnation wird als Vollendung der Schöpfung dargestellt (VIII 258-268), womit bereits jetzt eine Einbettung der Passion in den Spannungsbogen von Schöpfung und Gericht deutlich wird, ein Hintergrund, der für das erhaltene Fragment des *EvPetr* nicht erkennbar ist.[31]

2.3 Das irdische Leben bis zur Passion (VIII 269-284)

Die Aussagen über die Inkarnation des „Wortes" (VIII 267) lassen sich weitgehend aus den kanonischen Evangelien ableiten.[32] Immerhin finden sich Aspekte, die apokryphen Traditionen zu entstammen scheinen bzw. nicht in den kanonischen Texten zu finden sind wie z.B. die Rede davon, dass der Inkarnierte mit fünf Broten und *einem* Fisch die 5000 gespeist habe (VIII 275) oder die Deutung der 12 Körbe, in die die übrigen Brocken eingefüllt werden εἰς ἐλπίδα λαῶν („zur Hoffnung der Völker"). Ein Nachweis darüber, ob irgendetwas davon mit dem *EvPetr* zusammenhängen könnte, ist natürlich aufgrund der Quellensituation nicht möglich.

Interessant zumindest scheint, dass für die Sibyllinen auch hier die das Fragment des *EvPetr* so deutlich bestimmende Perspektive der jüdisch-christlichen Auseinandersetzung völlig fehlt: Der Logos wird auf die Erde gesandt, bringt das „nachahmende Ebenbild" (ἀντίτυπον μίμημα)[33] zur „heiligen Jungfrau" (VIII 270). Das Ziel seines Auftrages wird bereits in VIII 267-269 in das Schöpfungswerk Gottes an der ganzen Welt eingebettet; er richtet sich von daher an alle Menschen; die Inkarnation des Logos als „jüdischer Mensch"[34] in den zeitgeschichtlichen Kontext Israels wird hier nicht einmal auf polemische Weise gespiegelt.

---

[29] Zur Interpretation der Szene in *Barn* 12 vgl. F.R. Prostmeier, Der Barnabasbrief, KAV 8, Göttingen 1999, 436-437.

[30] Vgl. Gauger, Sibyllinische Weissagungen, 523-524.

[31] Ein Bezug zwischen Passion, Auferstehung, Endgericht und Jenseits wird allerdings durch die im Akhmîm-Codex zusammengestellten Texte *EvPetr*, *ApkPetr* (?) und *Hen* geschaffen.

[32] Hierzu vgl. vor allem É. Massaux, Influence de l'Évangile de Saint Matthieu sur la littérature chrétienne avant Saint Irénée, Neuauflage hg. von F. Neirynck, BEThL 75, Leuven 1986, 227-246 (nicht nur zu Mt, sondern zum gesamten NT).

[33] Obwohl Gen 1,27 LXX die Erschaffung des Menschen mit der Wendung κατ' εἰκόνα θεοῦ umschreibt, liegt hier auch aufgrund des Schöpfungskontextes, in dem vom Abbilden sterblicher Menschen nach unserem Bilde (ἄμφω εἰκόνος ἡμετέρην VIII 265-266) die Rede ist, ein Bezug hierauf vor.

[34] Diese Redeweise lehnt sich bewusst an F. Mußner, Der „Jude" Jesus, in: Jesus von Nazareth im Umfeld Israels und der Urkirche, hg. von M. Theobald, WUNT 111, Tübingen 1999, 89-97, bes. 97, bereits auf das Jahr 1971 zurückgehende Rede von Jesus Christus als „vere homo judaeus" an.

2.4 Die Passion des „Wortes" (VIII 285-309)

Die deutlichsten Verbindungslinien zwischen *EvPetr* und *OrSib* VIII sind im
nun folgenden Abschnitt zu erwarten, in dem die Passion des „Logos" (VIII
285) beschrieben wird. Auch dieser Abschnitt von *OrSib* VIII 285-309 ist bereits
in seinen ersten Worten mit der Schöpfung verbunden; der Inkarnierte wird als
λόγος ὁ κτίζων μορφάς bezeichnet (VIII 285). Dieser wird nun in die Hände der
„Ungesetzlichen" und „Ungläubigen" ausgeliefert (VIII 287), die dann auch für
seinen Tod verantwortlich werden. Soll mit den Begriffen ἄνομος und ἄπιστος
ausgedrückt werden, dass es sich – anders als im *EvPetr* – um Römer, also nicht
um Juden handelt, die ja den νόμος haben? Wahrscheinlicher erscheint mir, dass
diese Fragestellung für *OrSib* hier gar keine Rolle spielt: Eingebettet in das
Orakel vom Endgericht ist nur noch das Gegenüber von „Gerechten" und
„Ungerechten" bzw. „Gläubigen" und „Ungläubigen" von Interesse.

2.4.1 Die in VIII 288-290 begegnende Schilderung der *Folterung* des
inkarnierten Logos wurde – wie oben bemerkt – bereits von L. Vaganay mit der
Erzählung im *EvPetr* in Verbindung gebracht.[35] Tatsächlich begegnen drei der
in *EvPetr* 9 geschilderten Arten von Tätlichkeiten gegenüber dem Gefolterten –
das Stoßen des „Herrn" mit einem κάλαμος hingegen findet sich in den *OrSib*
erst deutlich später, in VIII 296 (vgl. auch *OrSib* I 374).

(1) In den *OrSib* allerdings ist weder ganz klar, in welchem Kontext der
Passion sich diese Tätlichkeiten ereignen: Das „Spucken" wird ja in den
neutestamentlichen Parallelen an zwei verschiedenen Stellen erwähnt: Mk
14,65 par. Mt 27,67 (Verhör vor dem Synhedrium) sowie – vom Kontext her
noch näher an der Szene des *EvPetr* – Mk 15,19 par. Mt 27,30 (Verspottung
durch die römischen Soldaten).

(2) In den *OrSib* ist nicht vom Spucken *ins Gesicht*[36] (*EvPetr* 9) die Rede;
vielmehr liegt der Schwerpunkt auf dem „befleckten Mund" der Spuckenden,
aus dem „giftiger Speichel" kommt. Gerade die Erwähnung des „giftigen
Speichels" macht es meines Erachtens äußerst unwahrscheinlich, dass *OrSib*
hier auf das *EvPetr* zurückgreift. Viel wahrscheinlicher erscheint mir, dass das
Motiv des Spuckens an dieser Stelle aus dem dritten Lied vom Gottesknecht
(Jes 50,6) mit dem Motiv des Gifts aus Ps 69 (68),22 in Bezug gesetzt wird.
OrSib verbindet also das Leiden des inkarnierten Logos mit dem des
jesajanischen Gottesknechts wie auch des leidenden Gerechten des Psalters.[37]

(3) Das Schlagen (ῥαπίζω) auf die Wangen (*EvPetr* 9) erinnert an eine
bekannte Forderung der Bergpredigt (Mt 5,39). Vor diesem Hintergrund lässt
sich die Szene des *EvPetr* so lesen, dass der verspottete Kyrios die eigene, in
der Bergpredigt gestellte Forderung erfüllt, auch die andere Wange

---

[35] Vgl. Vaganay, Évangile de Pierre, 164.

[36] Wörtlich: „in die Augen".

[37] Ob diese alttestamentlichen Bezüge bewusst gesetzt oder nur indirekt über nicht mehr auf
      ihren Hintergrund reflektierte christliche Auslegungstraditionen hereinspielen, lässt sich
      allerdings nicht mehr mit Sicherheit entscheiden. Ich halte eher Letzteres für wahrscheinlich.

hinzuhalten, wenn man geschlagen wird.[38] In der Parallele der Sibyllinen ist wiederum die Beflecktheit derer, die schlagen, im Zentrum. Die ῥαβδύσματα (VIII 288) werden hier zwar mit den Händen ausgeführt, streng genommen muss es sich aber dabei nicht unbedingt um „Ohrfeigen" wie in *EvPetr* 9 halten. Dass diese trotzdem gemeint sein könnten, macht der mögliche Hintergrund Jes 50,6 – in *EvPetr* 9 wie auch in *OrSib* VIII 288 – denkbar.[39]

(4) Noch problematischer wird die Parallele dadurch, dass *OrSib* VIII 288 davon spricht, dass die Schläge der „unheiligen Hände" Gott (θεῷ) gelten! Während für *EvPetr* 9 das umstehende Volk (λαός; V. 5) seinen König, den „Sohn Gottes," höhnisch zum Richter macht und ihn quält, liegt der Fokus des Orakels darin, dass Gott selbst, der Schöpfer und Richter der Welt, von seinem Geschöpf (handgreiflich) geschlagen wird. Dass dieser Tat das Gericht folgen muss, ist unumgänglich.

(5) Eine Geißelung Jesu wird auch in den kanonischen Evangelien erzählt. Das Verbum μαστίζω allerdings wird im Kontext der Passion nur vom *EvPetr* verwendet, in den *OrSib* VIII 290 entsprechen ihm die „Geißeln". Der letztere Text interessiert sich offenbar weniger für die Folterer als den Gegeißelten selbst. Dieser Perspektivenwechsel ist notwendig, um das Motiv des Schweigens einzuführen.

Die Detailanalyse dieser ersten möglichen literarischen Beziehung zwischen beiden Texten zeigt meines Erachtens recht deutlich, dass die Unterschiede in der Darstellung der beiden Szenen, ja zum Teil auch in der Funktion der Einzelszenen die Gemeinsamkeiten deutlich überwiegen.

2.4.2 Dies wird noch deutlicher beim zweiten möglichen Motiv der Übereinstimmung:[40] In beiden Vergleichstexten begegnet kurz nach der Erwähnung der „Verspottung" das Motiv des *Schweigens* des „Herrn" bzw. des „Logos" (*EvPetr* 10; *OrSib* VIII 291). Doch bereits die Verbindung zum Vorhergegangenen unterscheidet sich deutlich voneinander. Im *EvPetr* hat bereits die Szene gewechselt. Der „Herr" ist bereits zwischen zwei Übeltätern gekreuzigt, die eigentliche Verspottungs- bzw. Folterungsszene bereits verlassen, während *OrSib* VIII 291 das Schweigen ganz eng mit den Misshandlungen der Folter (Partizip: κολαφιζόμενος) verbindet. Zwar mag in beiden Fällen Jes 53,7, die Rede von der Widerstandslosigkeit des Gottesknechts, eine Rolle spielen bzw. traditionsgeschichtlich der Auslöser für das Eindringen des Schweigemotivs in die Passionstradition sein.[41] Beide Texte haben sich aber meines Erachtens schon recht weit von diesem Hintergrund entfernt – und das in durchaus unterschiedliche Richtungen.

(1) Das Schweigen des „Herrn" in *EvPetr* 10 ist mit großer Wahrscheinlichkeit dahingehend zu deuten, dass dieser zwar den Schmerz spürt, aber dies

---

[38]   Dies bedeutet natürlich nicht, dass das ursprüngliche *EvPetr* eine Form der Bergpredigt enthalten haben muss.

[39]   Zur Funktion dieses Bezugs im *EvPetr* vgl. den Beitrag von T. Hieke im vorliegenden Band.

[40]   Vgl. Vaganay, Évangile de Pierre, 164.

[41]   Weiterführend der Beitrag von T. Hieke im vorliegenden Band.

gegenüber seinen Peinigern nicht zu erkennen gibt. Eine derartige
Verarbeitung des Schweigemotivs rückt die Passion des Herrn in die Nähe zu
Märtyrertexten (z.B. *Martyrium des Polykarp* 2,2), in denen die Standhaftigkeit
des bzw. der Leidenden durch ähnliche Aussagen ausgedrückt wird.[42]

(2) Die Funktion des Schweigemotivs in der Parallele der *OrSib* VIII 291
unterscheidet sich davon erheblich: Der Logos wird hier nicht als Märtyrer
gezeichnet; vielmehr hat sein „Schweigen" die Funktion, die heilsgeschichtliche Bedeutung seines Leidens zu verhüllen. Der Logos darf nicht als
der erkannt werden, der er ist. Er, der noch VIII 285 als Schöpfer eingeführt
wurde, wird hier als der bezeichnet, der die Toten rufen wird. Endzeitliches
„Rufen" (λαλέω) und „Schweigen" des „Logos" in der Passion ergeben somit
ein hoch interessantes strukturelles Gegenüber: Am Anfang der Schöpfung
steht das „Wort", der „Logos", an seinem Ende das „Rufen" zum Gericht;
dazwischen das rettende „Schweigen" des Wortes, das nicht als Wort erkannt
werden darf. Passion ist so in ungeheuerer, meines Erachtens auch in den
kanonischen Texten nirgends ganz vergleichbarer Konsequenz auch strukturell
in das Gegenüber von Schöpfung und Eschatologie eingespannt.

2.4.3 Auch das Motiv des *Dornenkranzes* (στέφανον ἀκάνθινον) begegnet in
beiden Texten (*OrSib* VIII 294; *EvPetr* 8).[43] Ähnlich wie in den kanonischen
Parallelen (Mk 15,16-20a; Mt 27,27-31a sowie Joh 19,1-3) hat das Motiv im
EvPetr die Funktion, Jesus zum Spottkönig – *EvPetr* 7 als „König Israels" – zu
machen. Auch hier verarbeitet *OrSib* VIII 294 das Motiv in anderer Weise.
Zwar ist im Kontext auch vom „Königtum" die Rede (strukturell wichtig: VIII
218). Dieses Königtum Gottes, der mit dem Logos identifiziert wird, ist aber an
keiner Stelle auf Israel bezogen, vielmehr wird es auf den gesamten Kosmos
ausgedehnt. Dies scheint aber im engeren Kontext gar nicht angezielt; vielmehr
wird der Dornenkranz offensichtlich nicht als Königskrone interpretiert,
sondern in Beziehung gebracht mit dem Kranz, der die Erwählten schmücken
wird (VIII 294-295).[44] Erneut zieht der Text an dieser Stelle also eine
Verbindung zwischen Passion und eschatologischem Heil, bringt beide in
bildhaften Zusammenhang.

2.4.4 Die Parallele zwischen *OrSib* VIII 296 und *EvPetr* 9 wurde oben (2.4.1)
bereits kurz erwähnt. Das *Stoßen* bzw. *„Stechen" mit dem Rohr* (κάλαμος)
begegnet tatsächlich in beiden Texten und erinnert natürlich auch an Mk 15,19

---

[42] Die Diskussion, ob das Motiv auf einen möglichen Doketismus des Textes schließen lasse,
muss hier nicht erneut geführt werden. Vgl. zum Problem z.B. G.W. McCant, The Gospel of
Peter: Docetism Reconsidered, NTS 30, 1984, 258-273; P.M. Head, On the Christology of the
Gospel of Peter, VigChr 46, 1992, 209-224, sowie der Beitrag von M. Myllykoski im vorliegenden Band. – Allgemein die Frage nach dem Verhältnis zwischen *EvPetr* und Märtyrertexten vor allem des 2. Jh.s stellt M. Cambe, Les récits de la Passion en relation avec différents
textes au IIᵉ siècle, FV 81.4, 1982, 12-24, bes. 18-21.

[43] Vgl. Vaganay, Évangile de Pierre, 164. – Die kanonischen Parallelen haben: ἀκάνθινον στέφανον
(Mk 15,17); στέφανον ἐξ ἀκανθῶν (Mt 27,29; Joh 19,2). Damit stimmen *OrSib* und *EvPetr* an dieser
Stelle gegen die kanonischen Texte überein. Diese Übereinstimmung ist aber so wenig
signifikant, dass aus ihr keine literarkritischen Schlüsse gezogen werden sollten.

[44] ἄγαλμα hier möglicherweise „Schmuckstück".

bzw. Mt 27,30. In beiden kanonischen Texten wird die Tätigkeit aber mit dem Verbum τύπτω, nicht νύσσω beschrieben. Damit stimmen die beiden apokryphen Texte in diesem Punkt gegen die kanonischen Parallelen miteinander überein.[45] Trotzdem erscheint es gerade in diesem Fall äußerst unwahrscheinlich, dass *OrSib* VIII 296 hier von *EvPetr* 9 abhängig ist. Die Szene in *EvPetr* 9 scheint tatsächlich eine Parallele der genannten synoptischen Texte zu bieten; νύσσω dürfte als sprachliche Variation zu τύπτω aufzufassen sein und sich am ehesten als „Stoßen" übersetzen lassen. Der Kontext in *OrSib* VIII 296 aber deutet an, dass die Verspottungsszene bereits verlassen ist: Objekt von νύσσω ist in *OrSib* πλευρά, das heißt die „Seite". Dies aber erinnert stark an Joh 19,34,[46] wo der Gekreuzigte nach seinem Tode – allerdings von einer Lanze – in die Seite gestoßen bzw. gestochen wird. Ist möglicherweise der „Logos" auch in *OrSib* VIII 296 schon als gekreuzigt vorgestellt? Dann dürfte νύσσω hier am besten als „stechen" zu verstehen sein. Dieses „Stechen" geschieht „wegen ihres Gesetzes": Für den Kontext der Szene in *OrSib* VIII schimmert an dieser Stelle erstmals – und dies auch nur angedeutet – die jüdische Perspektive auf.[47] Welche Schriftstelle dabei gemeint ist, bleibt offen – möglicherweise könnte an Sach 12,10 gedacht sein;[48] andererseits ist auch möglich, dass gar keine *konkrete* Anspielung angezielt ist.

2.4.5 Auch das *Bild des Gekreuzigten* selbst wird von der Sibylle in kosmischen Dimensionen interpretiert: Das Ausbreiten der Hände (ἐκπετάννυμι; vgl. *OrSib* VIII 302) wird zum Messen des gesamten Weltalls.[49] Bei der eigentlichen Kreuzigungsszene des *EvPetr* begegnet dieses Motiv nicht. Immerhin ist zumindest denkbar, dass das dem Auferstandenen aus dem Grab folgende Kreuz, dessen Ausmaße zwar nicht beschrieben werden, das aber doch mit den beiden riesigen Gestalten, die den noch größer geschilderten Auferstandenen stützen, in Verbindung steht, im weitesten Sinne als eine Art „kosmisches Kreuz" verstanden werden will.[50]

2.4.6 Kontrast zu diesem Blick auf die kosmische Bedeutung der Kreuzigungsszene ist die Schilderung vom „Tisch der Gastfeindschaft" (*OrSib* VIII 304), der dem Logos bereitet werde, was sich an *Galle und Essig* zeige (*OrSib* VIII 303). Alttestamentlicher Hintergrund dieser Darstellung ist in beiden Fällen Ps 68,22 LXX, der hier sogar noch konsequenter verarbeitet ist als

---

45 Vgl. Vaganay, Évangile de Pierre, 164.
46 Diesen Bezug sehen viele Autoren. Vgl. z.B. Treu, Christliche Sibyllinen, 612.
47 Es ist unklar, was mit „jedem Gesetz" in *OrSib* VIII 300 gemeint ist: Ist hier der Blick auf das Judentum bereits wieder ausgeweitet? Dagegen spricht die Rede vom „ungehorsamen Volk" in *OrSib* VIII 301.
48 Diese Prophetenstelle wurde in der altkirchlichen Literatur breit rezipiert, z.B. *Barn* 7,8-9; *Protevangelium des Jakobus* 24,3; Justin, *dial.* 32,2; 1 *apol.* 52,11; Irenäus, *haer.* IV 33,11 u.a. bereits im 2. Jh.
49 Verwandte Ideen, wie die Vorstellung vom kosmischen Leib Christi finden sich bereits im Kolosserbrief; ein kosmisches (Licht-)Kreuz begegnet z.B. in den *Acta Iohannis* 97-102; dieses ist sogar mit Christus bzw. dem Logos selbst zu identifizieren (Kap. 98). Die Verbindung zwischen Kreuzigung und Schöpfung stellt auch Melito, *pass.* 96 her.
50 Vgl. auch Mara, Évangile de Pierre, 188-189.

in den kanonischen Parallelen.[51] In der engen Verbindung von „Galle" und
„Essig" aber stimmt *OrSib* VIII 303 mit *EvPetr* 16 gegen die kanonischen Texte
der kritischen Ausgaben überein. Bereits die Tatsache, dass diese Verbindung
einerseits in der neutestamentlichen Textgeschichte, andererseits aber auch
häufig in altkirchlichen Texten begegnet,[52] sollte davor warnen, aus dieser
Beobachtung Schlüsse auf mögliche literarische Abhängigkeiten zu ziehen.
Zudem ist auch in diesem Fall das Motiv in beiden Texten auf unterschiedliche
Weise verarbeitet: Für *OrSib* VIII 303-304 werden Galle und Essig zum Zeichen
für die Ungastlichkeit der Menschen (bzw. der Schöpfung) gegenüber dem
Schöpfer; in *EvPetr* 16 aber vermischt man beides zu einem Getränk, das – aus
dem Kontext erschließbar – in der am Mittag herangebrochenen Finsternis,
wegen der das Volk fürchtet, gegen das Gesetz verstoßen zu haben (*EvPetr* 15)
den Tod Jesu schneller herbeiführen soll. Mit der Überreichung dieses
(offensichtlichen) Gifttrankes macht das Volk das Maß seiner Sünden voll – der
Tod des Herrn wird unmittelbar damit in Verbindung gebracht (*EvPetr* 19).

2.4.7 Der Tod Jesu wird in *OrSib* VIII nicht direkt geschildert. Der Text
verlangt hier die Einspielung anderer Passionserzählungen, so z.B. der
kanonischen Texte, um dem Leser zu erlauben, das Zerreißen des Vorhangs im
Tempel mit dem Tod des Inkarnierten in Verbindung zu bringen. Diese
Darstellung passt natürlich zur bisherigen Tendenz des Textes, Christus und
Gott zu identifizieren – und die menschliche Natur des Inkarnierten in den
Hintergrund zu rücken. Vom Zerreißen des Vorhangs im Tempel ist bei allen
Synoptikern die Rede, auch von einer *Finsternis*, die drei Stunden lang währt.
Die Synoptiker verwenden dabei das Wort σκότος (Mt 27,45; Mk 15,33; Lk
23,44), das auch im *EvPetr* vorkommt (V. 15). Wie in den *OrSib* begegnet im
EvPetr im Kontext der Kreuzigung allerdings auch die Vokabel νύξ „Nacht"
(*OrSib* VIII 306; *EvPetr* 18).[53] Beide apokryphen Texte sprechen auch nicht von
der „sechsten Stunde", sondern vom Mittag, wenn auch nicht in identischen
Vokabeln (*EvPetr* 15: μεσημβρία; *OrSib* VIII 305: ἤματι μέσσῳ). Auch diese
Übereinstimmungen gegen die kanonischen Texte sollten nicht literarkritisch
überbewertet werden, denn die einzige wörtliche Übereinstimmung, das Wort
„Nacht", ist wieder in beiden Texten ganz unterschiedlich gebraucht. Während
OrSib von der „finsteren, furchtbaren Nacht" spricht, erzählt das *EvPetr*, dass

---

[51] Vgl. hierzu auch H. Koester, Ancient Christian Gospels. Their History and Development,
     Harrisburg 1990, 228. Explizit gemacht wird die Verbindung dieses Motivs mit Ps 68,22 bereits
     bei Origenes, *comm. in Mt* ser. 137 zu Mt 27,47-49.

[52] Nur einige Beispiele seien genannt: Die Verbindung „Galle" plus „Essig" scheint bereits auf
     das *Diatessaron* Tatians zurückzugehen. Von daher dürfte sie Eingang in östliche (z.B. Ephräm,
     comm. in Diat. 20.27; *Cruc.* 5,10-11.16; Romanos der Melode, *Hymnus* 36,33-34 zur Passion) und
     westliche Zeugen (z.B. die altlateinischen Ms. c f h und q) für den Einfluss des *Diatessaron*
     genommen haben. Vgl. aber auch Mt 27,34 A W und 𝔐, *Barn* 7,3.5; die syrische *Didaskalie* 19
     u.v.a.

[53] Vgl. schon Vaganay, Évangile de Pierre, 165. Von der „Nacht" ist in diesem Zusammenhang
     aber auch in anderen frühchristlichen Texten die Rede. Vgl. z.B. Amphilochius von Iconium,
     or. in diem Sabbati Sancti 1, wogegen Cyrill von Jerusalem, *catech.* 13,24, explizit betont, dass am
     Tag der Kreuzigung weder „Tag" noch „Nacht" war (vgl. Sach 14,6-7).

viele der Anwesenden *irrtümlich* davon ausgehen, dass Nacht sei. Der Unterschied ist noch deutlicher: Für die Szene der *OrSib* im Kontext der Spanne Schöpfung – Gericht, in deren Mitte der gekreuzigt Inkarnierte mit seinen ausgebreiteten Händen den Kosmos fasst, kann die Nacht nur als tatsächlicher finsterer Wendepunkt, der die gesamte Schöpfung betrifft, interpretiert werden; dem *EvPetr* geht diese kosmische Dimension dagegen völlig ab: die Finsternis bezieht sich auf „ganz Judäa" (*EvPetr* 15).

2.4.8 Auch die Rede vom *Zerreißen des Vorhangs im Tempel* begegnet zwar in beiden Texten, will aber wohl je unterschiedlich interpretiert werden: Für *OrSib* VIII 305 verliert mit dem Zerreißen des Vorhangs das Gesetz – offensichtlich die jüdische Tora[54] – seine Gültigkeit, ebenso der Tempel als Ort, an dem Gott gedient werden kann. Bedeutet die Rede von den φαντασίαι κόσμου („Erscheinungen des Kosmos"[55]), denen nun nicht mehr gedient werden muss, dass jede bisherige Anbetung Gottes, also auch die jüdische Gottesverehrung, als Götzendienst verstanden wird? Der Kontext „Tempel" und „Gesetz" legt dies hier immerhin nahe; in späteren Abschnitten wie VIII 328, wenn offensichtlich von der Lösung der „gottlosen Gesetze" Israels – bezeichnet als „Tochter Zion" (VIII 324) – die Rede ist, wird diese Vorstellung ganz deutlich ausgedrückt.

Das *EvPetr* interpretiert das Zerreißen des Vorhangs zunächst nicht: Die Wendung „zur gleichen Stunde"[56] stellt jedoch eine ganz enge temporale Verbindung zwischen dem Ereignis und dem Tode Jesu her. Eine Interpretation des Ereignisses findet sich erst viel später (*EvPetr* 28), wo davon die Rede ist, dass das Volk wegen der „großartigen Zeichen", die beim Tode Jesu geschehen sind, sich (wohl aus Reue) an die Brust schlägt.[57] Zu diesen Zeichen gehören sicherlich das Beben der Erde, als diese mit dem Leichnam des Herrn in Berührung kommt (*EvPetr* 21), wie auch das Zerreißen des Vorhangs. Eine theologisch tiefere Deutung des Motivs ist von daher im *EvPetr* nicht angebracht: Der Text scheint zeigen zu wollen, welch gewaltige wunderbare Ereignisse mit dem Tode des „Herrn" einhergingen – vielleicht auch noch darum, dass diese fast eine Umkehr des Volkes bewirkt hätten.

---

54 Was die Rede vom „geheimen Gesetz" aussagen will, ist mir nicht ganz klar. Ist hier die in apokalyptischer Tradition immer wieder angespielte geheime Zusatzoffenbarung zur Tora gemeint? Der Kontext jedoch scheint dies nicht zu tragen.

55 Das Wort φαντασία kann grundsätzlich neutral gebraucht werden, dürfte an dieser Stelle aber einen negativen Beigeschmack haben.

56 Zum griechischen Text vgl. T.J. Kraus/T. Nicklas, Das Petrusevangelium und die Petrusapokalypse. Die griechischen Fragmente mit deutscher und englischer Übersetzung, GCS.NF 11; Neutestamentliche Apokryphen 1, Berlin-New York 2004, 37.

57 Zur Bedeutung dieser Aktion für die Israel-Theologie des Petrusevangeliums vgl. Nicklas, „Juden" im Petrusevangelium.

2.5 Tod und Auferstehung (*OrSib* VIII 310-312)

Die Aussagen, die nun noch zu Tod und Auferstehung selbst gemacht werden, berühren sich nur noch in ganz geringem Maße mit denen des *EvPetr*.

Selbst das gemeinsame *descensus ad inferos*-Motiv,[58] das zumindest in den kanonischen Evangelien nicht begegnet, ist in beiden Texten sehr unterschiedlich verarbeitet. Der „ewige Herrscher" steigt laut *OrSib* in den „Hades" hinab, er wendet sich an alle Heiligen (VIII 310-311), während im *EvPetr* von einer Predigt an die „Entschlafenen" (V. 41) und nicht *nur* die Heiligen die Rede ist.[59] Der Inhalt dieser Predigt ist im *EvPetr* nicht ausgeführt. Laut *OrSib* VIII geht es um die Hoffnung, die mit dem Ende der Zeiten und dem „jüngsten Tag" (ἔσχατον ἦμαρ) zusammenhängt: Erneut erweist sich der Text als von der Perspektive Schöpfung – Endgericht her bestimmt.

3. Fazit

Vor allem die eigentlichen Passionsszenen in *OrSib* VIII und dem *EvPetr* weisen, wie bereits von mehreren Autoren erkannt, immer wieder wörtliche Übereinstimmungen gegen die entsprechenden Parallelen der kanonischen Evangelien auf. Zumindest von dieser Beobachtung „auf der Textoberfläche" könnte von daher der Schluss gezogen werden, beide Texte seien möglicherweise literarisch voneinander abhängig.

Ein Detailvergleich der relevanten Abschnitte im Kontext lässt daran aber eher zweifeln:[60] Das deutlich voneinander unterschiedene Eigenprofil beider Texte wird mit jedem Abschnitt klarer. Die wörtlichen Berührungspunkte sind derart gering, dass sie vor allem bei den so unterschiedlichen theologischen Eigenprofilen der beiden Texte kaum ins Gewicht fallen. Wo sich der Text der *OrSib* gerade in Einzelbegriffen und Formulierungen von dem der kanonischen Evangelien unterscheidet, sollte dies zudem nicht zu schnell damit erklärt werden, dass *OrSib* dann auf eine von den kanonischen Texten unterschiedender Tradition zurückgreift. Vielmehr zwingt bereits die poetische Form der Texte wie auch die mit der Form des Orakels verbundene Vorliebe für (nicht nur im Vergleich mit dem neutestamentlichen Sprachgebrauch) seltene Begriffe den Autor/die Autoren der *OrSib* zu einer Darstellung des Christusereignisses, die immer wieder von der der

---

[58] Zum *descensus ad inferos*-Motiv und seiner Entwicklung in der antiken christlichen Literatur vgl. ausführlich R. Gounelle, La descente du Christ aux enfers. Institutionalisation d'une croyance, Collection des Études Augustiniennes. Serie Antiquité 162, Paris 2000.

[59] Erinnert sei in diesem Zusammenhang allerdings an die bereits erwähnte Deutung der *EvPetr*-Szene durch Crossan, The Cross That Spoke, 385-386, der das „Kreuz" als eine Art kreuzförmiger Prozession der Heiligen Israels interpretiert.

[60] Selbst wenn man die wörtlichen Anklänge als Indizien literarischer Abhängigkeit auffassen wollte, so wäre damit bestenfalls ein hypothetisches Indiz zur Einordnung des Textes *EvPetr* gewonnen, für die Interpretation eines der beiden Texte wäre aber nichts gewonnen.

kanonischen Texte abweicht.[61] Daneben spielt das von Vaganay und Denker vorgebrachte Argument gemeinsamer Auslegungstraditionen biblischer Motive sicherlich eine Rolle – beide parallelen Texte entfernen sich aber immer wieder (z.B. beim Schweigemotiv) recht weit von den alttestamentlichen Wurzeln des jeweiligen Motivs, so dass hier nur sehr oberflächliche Übereinstimmungen entstehen. In nahezu allen Punkten, in denen die Ebene der „Wörter" Verbindungen nahe legt, zeigen sich in der Funktion der Motive, die bearbeitet sind, solch deutliche Unterschiede, dass gerade von diesen Berührungspunkten aus das Eigenprofil beider Texte gut zum Tragen kommt. Das im Hinblick auf literarische Abhängigkeit der Texte negative Ergebnis geht somit mit dem positiven Ergebnis einher, dass der Vergleich beider Texte die Bandbreite der Möglichkeiten der Verarbeitung von Motiven der Passionsgeschichten anzudeuten hilft. Mit dem Vergleich auf synchroner Ebene kommen ganz unterschiedliche Perspektiven der Rezeption von der Passion Jesu von Nazaret zum Tragen. Gerade an den Punkten, an denen auf „Oberflächenebene" Übereinstimmung wahrscheinlich erscheint, hilft der Vergleich, das Eigenprofil der Texte zu erarbeiten.

Zumindest einige Aspekte seien noch einmal zusammengefasst. Von ihnen aus lassen sich zudem einige Rückfragen an die einleitenden Bemerkungen zu den *OrSib* stellen:

(1) Eindeutig bestätigt sich für *OrSib* VIII die eingangs formulierte Aussage, dass Geschichte in den *OrSib* von der Perspektive des Gerichts aus beschrieben wird. Im untersuchten Text kommt dabei noch eine zweite Dimension hinzu: Heilsgeschichte wird – auch strukturell – als eingespannt zwischen Schöpfung und Vollendung im Endgericht gezeichnet, eine Dimension, der zumindest im erhaltenen Fragment des *EvPetr* die eher partikularistische Sicht mit dem Gegenüber „Juden" entspricht.

(2) Beide Texte weisen eine sehr hohe, weit entwickelte Christologie auf. Keiner der beiden erwähnt im eigentlichen (erhaltenen) Text den Namen Jesus von Nazaret oder den Titel Christus. Während das *EvPetr* vor allem vom „Herrn", aber auch dem „Sohn Gottes" spricht, verwendet *OrSib* VIII zumindest in seinem Text v.a. die schöpfungstheologisch wichtige Bezeichnung „Logos", die sich hervorragend in das Gesamtkonzept des Textes einfügt.[62] Bei einer Beurteilung der Christologie des Orakeltextes darf aber

---

61 W.-D. Köhler, Die Rezeption des Matthäusevangeliums in der Zeit vor Irenäus, WUNT II 24, Tübingen 1987, 313, schreibt: „Als unwahrscheinlich erscheint mir aus mehreren Gründen, daß die Sib auf Evangelientraditionen rekurrieren, die zeitlich vor die Abfassung unserer Evangelien anzusetzen sind. Zum einen ist ein Bezug auf solche Traditionen angesichts der zu vermutenden Abfassungszeit(en) der entsprechenden Passagen *a priori* unwahrscheinlich. Zum anderen erklären sich die Abweichungen von den synoptischen Evangelien in der Sache oder in der Formulierung hinreichend durch den Weissagungs- und Orakelcharakter der sibyllinischen Sprüche."

62 Collins, Development, 448; idem, Sibylline Oracles, 380, bezeichnet die Proklamation Christi als das Hauptthema des christlichen Abschnitts von *OrSib* VIII. Damit hat er sicherlich Recht – dieses Thema aber lässt sich konkreter als Proklamation des an der Schöpfung teilhabenden „Logos", der zum Gericht erscheinen wird, fassen.

nicht das Akrostichon der Z. 217-250 vergessen werden, das mit den Worten
ΙΗΣΟΥΣ ΧΡΕΙΣΤΟΣ ΘΕΟΥ ΥΙΟΣ ΣΩΤΕΡ ΣΤΑΥΡΟΣ („Jesus Christus Gottes
Sohn Heiland Kreuz") ein ganz klassisches Bekenntnis in biblischer
Begrifflichkeit abgibt.[63]

(3) Zwar tritt die Darstellung der „Juden" im untersuchten Text der *OrSib*
gegenüber der zentralen Rolle, die diese in der Passion des *EvPetr* spielen,
deutlich zurück, was mit der oben angesprochenen umfassenden kosmischen
Perspektive des *OrSib*-Textes zusammenhängt. Dieser Unterschied zeigt sich
deutlich daran, dass *OrSib* anders als *EvPetr* nicht die „Juden" für den Kreuzestod Jesu verantwortlich macht.[64] Wenn sie auch nur in einigen wenigen
Bemerkungen begegnen, sind die antijüdischen Spitzen im untersuchten Text
der *OrSib* theologisch jedoch äußerst problematisch. Die Vorstellung von der
Auflösung des Gesetzes, vor allem aber die Idee, dass jeder Gottesdienst vor
dem Christusereignis als Anbetung von Götzen zu verstehen sei, entzieht dem
Judentum jegliche Glaubensbasis, ja erinnert an Marcions ablehnende Haltung
gegenüber der jüdischen Schrift.

(4) Gerade der untersuchte christliche Abschnitt zeigt meines Erachtens
aber keinerlei Anzeichen der Romfeindschaft anderer Texte der *OrSib*.[65] Zwar
sind Darstellungstendenzen wie in *EvPetr*, wo Josef von Arimathaia zum
Freund des Pilatus (*EvPetr* 3) wird und letzterer von jeglicher Schuld am Tode
Jesu freigesprochen wird, nicht zu erkennen. Dies liegt sicherlich daran, dass
der große heilsgeschichtliche Bogen der *OrSib* sich für derartige Details nicht
interessiert – immerhin aber begegnen keinerlei Aussagen, die in irgendeiner
Weise Rom kritisieren.

(5) Obwohl in beiden Passionstraditionen Motive begegnen, die auf
alttestamentliche Texte zurückgehen, würde ich zögern, einen der beiden
Autoren als „schriftgelehrt" argumentierend zu bezeichnen. Vielmehr scheinen
beide bereits auf christliche Auslegungstraditionen von Schrifttexten
zurückgreifen zu können, die sie in ihren Texten (auf zum Teil völlig
unterschiedliche Weise) verarbeiten. Nicht immer wird dabei ganz klar, ob der
alttestamentliche Hintergrund des jeweils verarbeiteten Motivs für das
Verstehen des Textes, der dabei entsteht, *immer* wirklich bedeutsam ist.
Zumindest *in einigen Abschnitten* der *OrSib* scheint dies jedoch trotzdem
unabdingbar – vielleicht am deutlichsten in VIII 251-252 mit dem Rückgriff auf
Mose-Amalek, wo nicht nur der Text Ex 17,9-11, sondern auch eine spezielle
Auslegungstradition, die diesen mit dem Kreuz in Verbindung bringt,
vorausgesetzt werden muss, um den Text zu verstehen. Kann von daher
wirklich davon ausgegangen werden, dass ein christlicher Text wie *OrSib* VIII

---

[63]   Aus diesem Akrostichon (zitiert bei Konstantin, *or. s.c.* 18; Augustinus, *civ.* 18,23 [ohne *stauros*])
ergibt sich dann weiter das bekannte ΙΧΘΥΣ, das seit dem Ende des 1. Jh.s nachgewiesene
„Fisch-Symbol".

[64]   So auch Charlesworth, Christian and Jewish Self-Definition, 52.

[65]   Der erste, möglicherweise zum Teil auf jüdische Ursprünge zurückgehende Teil von *OrSib* VIII
(1-216) weist allerdings mehrfach antirömische Prophezeiungen auf, so z.B. VIII 37-49. 73-130.

217-219 wirklich *nach außen* – und wenn, dann wohin? – gerichtet ist? Heidnische Leser dürften keine Chance gehabt haben, in einem derartigen Text mehr als geheimnisvolle, etwas abstruse Weissagungen zu verstehen.[66] Jüdische Leser dürften spätestens durch die Aussagen vom Gesetz abgeschreckt worden sein. Die Tatsache, dass in manchen Abschnitten (z.B. bei der Rede vom Zerreißen des Vorhangs im Tempel) offensichtlich die Kenntnis anderer (z.B. kanonischer) Passionstraditionen vorausgesetzt ist, scheint mir eher darauf zu verweisen, dass hier von christlicher Seite ein Orakeltext zur Selbstvergewisserung der eigenen Situation vor dem Gericht Gottes verfasst wurde.[67]

---

[66] Deswegen zögere ich damit, der Einschätzung von Charlesworth, Christian and Jewish Self-Definition, 53, zu folgen, nach der die Gruppe, auf die der christliche Part von *OrSib* VIII zurückgehen soll, vor allem im Dialog mit Griechen und Römern ihre Identität entwickelte.

[67] Von hier aus wäre es interessant, nach Spuren der tatsächlichen Rezeption der Sibyllinischen Orakel zu fragen. Meines Wissens sind solche aber nur aus dem christlichen Bereich erhalten. Weiterführend vor allem Denis, Introduction, 958-960.

Some Reflections on Determining the Purpose of the "Gospel of Peter"

by

Joseph Verheyden

The Gospel of Peter (GP) again enjoys a lot of attention. It has been edited twice in the past five years.[1] Much of the discussion and research of the last two or three decades has centred on literary-critical questions regarding the sources and composition history of GP and its relationship to the New Testament gospels, and on various other issues, of which the characterisation GP gives of the Jewish leaders and people is commonly regarded as maybe the most crucial one. For several of these questions established views were challenged and tested again, and not all of them stood the test. Most recently perhaps the more surprising, not to say unpleasant, results were reached with regard to such introductory matters as the date of the so-called Akhmîm Fragment (AF), the circumstances of its discovery, and its current location, all of them questions that were thought to have been settled long ago. Here widely accepted positions are open for questioning again, or had to be put aside.

Thus the dating of AF in the eighth or ninth century, which was first tentatively proposed by H. Omont on the basis of a comparison with another papyrus in the same find[2] and was followed by many afterwards, is most probably

---

[1] See D. Lührmann, Fragmente apokryph gewordener Evangelien in griechischer und lateinischer Sprache, MThSt 59, Marburg 2000, 72-95; T.J. Kraus/T. Nicklas, Das Petrusevangelium und die Petrusapokalypse. Die griechischen Fragmente mit deutscher und englischer Übersetzung, GCS.NF 11; Neutestamentliche Apokryphen 1, Berlin-New York 2004, 1-77.

[2] As quoted by A. Lods, L'Évangile et l'Apocalypse de Pierre, Paris 1893, 15: "M. Baillet attribue au VIIe ou VIIIe siècle l'écriture du papyrus mathématique, rien ne s'y oppose au point de vue paléographique. J'avoue cependant que je serais porté à rajeunir quelque peu la minuscule de l'évangile de saint Pierre et à la reporter plutôt au VIIIe ou IXe siècle." U. Bouriant, who was responsible for the first edition, was far less confident: "Nulle date, nulle indication qui puisse nous aider à établir l'époque même approximative où ils [i.e., the various texts contained in the codex] ont été transcrits. Seules, les particularités qu'on relève dans l'écriture ou dans la langue elle-même, peuvent nous mettre sur la voie, et montrent que le manuscrit n'est pas antérieur au VIIIe siècle ni postérieur au XIIe" (93): J. Baillet, Le papyrus mathématique d'Akhmîm – U. Bouriant, Fragments du texte grec du livre d'Énoch et de quelques écrits attribués à Saint Pierre, in: Mémoires publiés par les Membres de la Mission archéologique française au Caire 9.1, Paris 1892, 93-94 (Introduction) and 137-142 (Text). Somewhat surprisingly, Lods, who in a previous publication had cited Bouriant correctly (Evangelii secundum Petrum et Petri Apocalypseos quae supersunt, Paris 1892, 2), continues after the quotation from Omont by

to be brought further back towards the end of the sixth century.[3] Attention has also been drawn to the fact that we do not have any hard evidence that the Fragment had been discovered in a monk's tomb as can be read in Bouriant's introduction and has been commonly accepted since then.[4] Of a somewhat different kind, but certainly no less disturbing, is the conclusion that we do no longer seem to know the whereabouts of our most important direct and indirect witnesses to GP. Intensive research and correspondence by the latest editors has made it clear that both the AF and the ostracon figuring Peter as an evangelist are not to be found – at least for now – at the locations where they were thought to have been stored long ago.[5] It can only be hoped that these witnesses, after they had been buried for so many years in the sands of Egypt finally to be recovered, are not now "preserved" in the archives of our modern Institutes to be lost forever!

These examples may illustrate that certain "obvious" things about GP can again become a puzzle upon closer examination. They may also remind us that some other issues too with regard to this gospel have perhaps been misunderstood or have not yet been sufficiently explored and explained. One such issue

---

saying that the date given by Bouriant would refer to the period that the cemetery in which the papyri were found had been in use. Lods here confuses Bouriant's dating of the papyrus (8th-9th century) with that of the use of the cemetery (5th-15th century).

3   Cf. G. Cavallo/H. Maehler, Greek Bookhands of the Early Byzantine Period A.D. 300-800, BICS.S 47, London 1987, 90 (no. 41). See now also Lührmann, Fragmente, 72; P. Van Minnen, The Greek Apocalypse of Peter, in: The Apocalypse of Peter, ed. by J.N. Bremmer/I. Czachesz, Studies on Early Christian Apocrypha 7, Leuven 2003, 15-39, esp. 16-17 (with a brief survey of alternative suggestions) and 21-24 (a balanced and expert account of the evidence, settling for the late sixth or early seventh century as the most probable dating) and Van Minnen's article in the present volume. The conclusions reached by Van Minnen are also accepted by Kraus/Nicklas, Petrusevangelium, 29.

4   Bouriant is more interested in explaining why the text has been preserved only fragmentarily. "Les fragments reproduits dans le volume pourraient cependant être d'une époque plus ancienne que celle où vivait le moine dans le tombeau duquel ils ont été déposés. ... On peut donc supposer qu'ils proviennent de manuscrits en mauvais état" (Fragments, 94). His alternative suggestion, that the copyist thrice (Gospel of Peter , Apocalypse of Peter, Enoch) would have begun copying a text but had left his work unfinished, seems to be rather implausible. On the location, see again Van Minnen, Apocalypse of Peter, 17-19: "This was no doubt merely an inference from the content of the codex, not based on actual indications in the tomb itself. The inference may be correct, but it should not be used as an independent fact in discussing the codex" (17-18). Basically repeated by Kraus/Nicklas, Petrusevangelium, 26-27. Lührmann did not yet know the article by Van Minnen in his latest monograph and still keeps to the common position: Die apokryph gewordenen Evangelien. Studien zu neuen Texten und zu neuen Fragen, NT.S 112, Leiden 2004, 59-60 and 90-98 (there 59: "im Grab eines Mönches"). – When I concluded a recent study on the Empty Tomb story in GP and (as I read it) its somewhat depreciating presentation of the women by observing that "It may not be accidental that GP was discovered in a monk's tomb", I had of course no intention to use this as an argument for my interpretation; see J. Verheyden, Silent Witnesses. Mary Magdalene and the Women at the Tomb in the Gospel of Peter, in: Resurrection in the New Testament. Festschrift Jan Lambrecht, ed. by R. Bieringer et al., BEThL 165, Leuven 2002, 457-482, here 481-482.

5   See D. Lührmann, Petrus als Evangelist – ein bemerkenswertes Ostrakon, NT 43, 2001, 348-367, here 348-350; Kraus/Nicklas, Petrusevangelium, 8-9 (location of AF "schleierhaft"; the ostracon, "das nunmehr als verschollen gilt").

is that of the purpose of GP, of where to look for it and of how to interpret the evidence that can be gathered from the text. It is a most difficult question to answer for a writing that is only partially preserved and that, in the part that is preserved, does not formally describe its purpose, as indeed is unfortunately so often the case in ancient literature, Christian and other. In the following I will briefly comment upon three ways that may help to shed some light on this question.

1. The Gospel "of Peter" or "according to Peter"

It is a plausible suggestion that maybe something can be said about the purpose of a "Gospel of Peter" by looking at the character of Peter who is here presented as the narrator.[6] At first, turning Peter into the narrator of the story may seem to be a revolutionary move. Christians were given yet another access, in addition to the Gospel of John, to the story of Jesus as it was told by one who had lived with Jesus and could speak from his own experience, one who, moreover, had been the first among the Twelve to have met with the risen Lord (1 Cor 15:5), the first also to have preached the gospel to Jews and Gentiles alike (Acts 2:14-36; 15:7) and thereby to have used the very word εὐαγγελίζομαι in addressing Cornelius (Acts 10:36). Unfortunately for GP the move failed to impress or to convince a broader audience. The earliest generations of Christians apparently did not know of a "Gospel of" or "according to Peter", and they did not seem to have cared or to have felt a need for it. And when towards the end of the second century bishop Serapion stumbled upon such a gospel, his initial enthusiasm, to his own embarrassment, soon had to give way to a more critical attitude that was only to be reinforced by others later on, most of whom, unlike Serapion, probably had not even read the text they were condemning.[7]

But perhaps the move was not so revolutionary after all. By the time GP was most likely being composed Peter had already been made an author himself (1 Peter). In another letter transmitted under his name, Peter is said to be among those who were present at the transfiguration (2 Peter 1:16-18), "und zwar unter ausdrücklicher Betonung seiner Augenzeugenschaft,"[8] though this last implication is open to discussion and certainly is not the only way to inter-

---

[6]   Cf. on this aspect of GP, T. Nicklas, Erzähler und Charakter zugleich. Zur literarischen Funktion des "Petrus" in dem nach ihm benannten Evangelienfragment, VigChr 55, 2001, 318-326.

[7]   On this testimony of Serapion (and Patristic evidence in general), see, a.o., L. Vaganay, L'Évangile de Pierre, ÉtB, Paris 1930, 1-12 (Serapion: 1-8); É. Junod, Eusèbe de Césarée, Sérapion d'Antioche et l'Évangile de Pierre. D'un Évangile à un Pseudépigraphe, RSLR 24, 1981, 3-16. Kraus/Nicklas, Petrusevangelium, 11-19 (Serapion: 12-16). Much in Serapion's account, as related by Eusebius, remains puzzling (see below).

[8]   Lührmann, Fragmente, 73.

pret this passage.[9] Moreover, according to Papias, Peter by longstanding tradition had also closely been linked to the Gospel of Mark, which if not authored,
he at least had authorised.[10] We do not know, and I am afraid we have no clue
to find out, whether the author of GP was in some way acquainted with that
tradition, but the evidence of AF does not allow us to conclude without further
ado that he had indeed positively identified the narrator with the author.[11] If
not, GP would have looked somewhat like an adaptation of the tradition that is
reported by Papias for Mark (an author noting down the words of a narrator,
but while preserving the narrator's use of the first person).[12]

As far as can be judged from AF and from the other fragments that may
have belonged to GP, Peter's role does not differ from the one he has in our
canonical gospels, nor is he in any way a more prominent character still than
he already was in these gospels. He is mentioned only twice in AF (vv. 26 and
60), both times as a member of a group of disciples. And if he is put in first
position, this has probably more to do with complying to the way Peter usually
figures in a list of disciples (see Mark 1:16 par. Matt 4:18; John 21:1) than with a
conscious attempt at promoting his character, for on both occasions the scene is

---

[9] The author is here using the first person plural. While this may be a case of "pluralis maiesta-
tis", it should be noted that there is a certain contrast with the immediately preceding verses
(1,12-15) where the author/Peter speaks in the first singular. The latter fits well with the
genre of the "farewell discourse", as Vögtle has noted (158), but the "we" in v. 16 could also be a way
to express, "dass die einheitliche apostolische Parusieverkündigung auf Augenzeugenschaft
beruht, somit glaubwürdig ist" (166); cf. A. Vögtle, Der Judasbrief / Der 2. Petrusbrief, EKK 22,
Solothurn-Düsseldorf-Neukirchen-Vluyn 1994.

[10] It is worth recalling that later on Jerome, while rejecting Peter's authorship of various writings
that circulated under his name, including a gospel, as a matter of fact makes him the author of
the Gospel of Mark: *Sed et evangelium iuxta Marcum, qui auditor eius et interpres fuit, huius dicitur*
(*vir. ill.* 1,3). Jerome does not actually call Peter "an evangelist", but that is of course what he
then should be called. Since Jerome's Catalogue was known in the East (there is a Greek
translation dated to the seventh century), should one also take this into account for
understanding the ostracon?

[11] As is well known, AF does not contain a title, and the presentation by Lührmann, who adds
Εὐαγγέλιον κατὰ Πέτρον at the end of the Greek text (Fragmente, 93), is in this respect
misleading. See Kraus/Nicklas, Petrusevangelium, 15 n. 43 and 46 (also 5 n. 15) and T. Nicklas,
Ein "neutestamentliches Apokryphon"? Zum umstrittenen Kanonbezug des sog.
"Petrusevangelium", VigChr 56, 2002, 260-272, esp. 265-267.

[12] Probably some time after GP Peter was also made the narrator (– author) in various other
writings: see the Ethiopic *Apocalypse of Peter* (note, however, the Greek in which the first person
narrator is not formally identified with Peter), the *Acts of Peter and the Twelve Apostles* (1,30-31;
NH VI,1), and the Coptic-Gnostic *Apocalypse of Peter* (NH VII,3). On the latter, see now F.
Lapham, Peter: The Myth, the Man and the Writings. A Study of Early Petrine Texts and
Tradition, JSNT.S 239, Sheffield 2003, 217-236 (as a "visionary" Peter is a much more crucial
figure than in GP). – But it cannot be completely excluded either that GP used the first person
merely as a stylistic device. Thus J. Gnilka, Petrus und Rom. Das Petrusbild in den ersten zwei
Jahrhunderten, Freiburg-Basel-Wien 2002, 270: "Auch vermittelt die Ich-Form ... für den Leser
den Eindruck, unmittelbar beteiligt zu sein."

all but heroic and after being mentioned as an individual Peter quickly is absorbed into the group again.[13]

GP does not offer any additional information on the character of Peter to what is already known from the canonical gospels. He is among those who grieved and returned to their homes and their previous jobs as fishermen in vv. 59-60, as he is in John 21:1-2, and he is among those who are hiding from the Jewish authorities in v. 26, as he is naturally supposed to be in John 20:19 ("the disciples", and see v. 24 "the twelve"). GP makes a moderate use of the figure of Peter that does not go beyond what is found in the canonical gospels.[14] It does not introduce him in scenes where he was not mentioned in these gospels to make him a privileged witness of the crucifixion or of the burial of Jesus, let alone of his resurrection. It even completely leaves him out from the Empty Tomb story where he had been mentioned by Mark (16:7), by Luke (24:12), and by John (20:3-10). It is of course always hazardous to argue from an argument from silence. It is just possible that the version of Luke GP had read or known did not contain v. 12 that is also missing in D and part of the Old Latin tradition with which it concurs elsewhere as well.[15] GP's version agrees best with what Mark has to say about Peter: he did not know about the empty tomb, and it is of secondary importance only whether or not this was because the women failed to inform him. If GP gave preference to Mark's version over that of John because the latter in some sense makes Peter look the lesser of the two disciples, this would signal an interest of GP in preserving Peter's role as an independent witness, but only at the expense of sacrificing his presence at the empty tomb and thus by opting for a solution that actually is attested in one of

---

[13] See v. 26 ἐγὼ δὲ μετὰ τῶν ἑταίρων μου ἐλυπούμην, but then it changes to the first person plural (ἐκρυβόμεθα, ἐζητούμεθα, etc.) and v. 60 ἐγὼ δὲ Σίμων Πέτρος καὶ Ἀνδρέας ὁ ἀδελφὸς μου ... καὶ ἦν σὺν ἡμῖν Λευεὶς ...

[14] This would be true also for P.Vindob. G 2325, if this is a fragment of GP as Lührmann "versuchsweise" has suggested (Fragmente, 73-74); but see T.J. Kraus, P. Vindob. G 2325. Das sogenannte Fayûm-Evangelium – Neuedition und kritische Rückschlüsse, ZAC 5, 2001, 197-212 and Kraus/Nicklas, Petrusevangelium, 68. – More disputed still is P. Oxy. 4009 (see Kraus/Nicklas, Petrusevangelium, 62-63). Here Peter is made the addressee of the first half of the saying (see the singular ending ἀκέ]ραιος on l. 5), but immediately after Peter's intervention, who seems to speak for others too when using the first plural [σπαραχθῶ]μεν in l. 10 (as, e.g., also in Luke 9:33 or in 8:45 v.l.), Jesus apparently goes on addressing all the disciples (l. 15 ὑ]μῖν). Peter is not presented in any way as a privileged witness. – P. Oxy. 4009, if an authentic part of GP, is of singular importance as it would be our sole positive attestation that GP was "anything more than a Passion Gospel" (Lapham, Peter, 25), unless one is prepared to read Origen's comment at Matt 13,55 as proof that, besides the "Book of James" (most probably the *Protevangelium Jacobi* is meant), GP also contained a similar section on the brothers of the Lord, but that is far from certain (see Kraus/Nicklas, Petrusevangelium, 16).

[15] Though I think that the combination of παρακύπτω (cf. also John 20:5.10) and the notion of unbelief in GP 56 is best explained if GP knew Luke 24:11-12 (Silent Witnesses, 476). – On the agreements of GP with the Western text, see Vaganay, Pierre, 70-72; A.F.J. Klijn, Het Evangelie van Petrus in de Westerse tekst, NTT 15, 1961, 264-269; J. Denker, Die theologiegeschichtliche Stellung des Petrusevangeliums. Ein Beitrag zur Frühgeschichte des Doketismus, EHS XXIII.36, Bern-Frankfurt/Main 1975, 26-29; T. Nicklas, Fragmente christlicher Apokryphen und die Textgeschichte des Neuen Testaments, ZNW 96, 2005, 129-142, here 139-141.

its sources and not by a more drastical intervention in the traditional accounts and making Peter the sole or primary witness at the tomb.

GP does not show any explicit interest either in promoting Peter as a disciple or as a witness of the risen Lord (he is with some of the other disciples when that is supposedly going to happen in what follows after vv. 59-60), nor in disclaiming any accusations or in defending his authority against that of other disciples. It does not seem to know of such discussions as can be found in other gospels, but it is of course not possible to be absolutely positive and certain about this as such episodes naturally only follow after the disciples have experienced the presence of the Lord.[16]

All in all then, GP is content to stick to what could be found about Peter in other gospels with which it was acquainted, as probably were its readers. GP apparently had no specific purpose in making Peter the narrator of the story.[17] On the contrary it seems to display a rather "unreflected" interest in the character and person of Peter. At best, this is the gospel "as told by Peter", not a "Petrine" gospel.

2. GP and the Canonical Gospels

A second place possibly to look for clues about what may have been the purpose of GP is the way it has made use of the accounts in the canonical gospels. The once fairly generally accepted hypothesis that GP basically relies upon these accounts has now been challenged again, most prominently, and in different ways, by J.D. Crossan and H. Koester.[18] However, so far their efforts

---

[16] On Peter as a subject of discussion, with Mary Magdalene as the major opponent, see, a.o., T.V. Smith, Petrine Controversies in Early Christianity. Attitudes towards Peter in Christian Writings of the First Two Centuries, WUNT II.15, Tübingen 1985, 102-142. Cf. also my comments in Silent Witnesses, 469-470 and 480-481. To the works mentioned there, now add A. Graham Brock, Mary Magdalene, the First Apostle. The Struggle for Authority, HThS 51, Cambridge, MA-London 2003, 65-69.

[17] And it could in any case have made much more of its attempt to have Peter play the double role of character and narrator. Nicklas points out that the two "wenigstens ansatzweise konvergieren" and even speaks of a "zumindest grundlegende Kontinuität zwischen ihrer [i.e., Peter and the disciples, not Peter alone!] evaluativen Perspektive und der des nahezu allwissend auftretenden Erzählers" (Erzähler und Charakter, 324. 325), but that may be a somewhat too optimistic conclusion in light of the evidence in GP: One can assume that Peter as a character would agree with the narrator's comment in v. 17 and likewise would have a high esteem of the figure of Jesus, but the narrator makes no effort to emphasise this in any way and, most significantly, to explain to the reader how he, let alone the reclusive Peter, would have had knowledge of the details of the trial and execution: "Woher dieser [the narrator] sein Wissen, welches ja weit über das des Charakters 'Petrus' hinausgeht, bezieht, wird zumindest im erhaltenen Fragment nicht thematisiert" (325).

[18] Cf. J.D. Crossan, Four Other Gospels. Shadows on the Contours of Canon, Minneapolis 1985, 125-181; idem, The Cross That Spoke. The Earliest Narrative of the Passion and Resurrection, Forum 3, 1987, 3-22; idem, The Cross That Spoke. The Origins of the Passion Narrative, San Francisco 1988; idem, Who Killed Jesus? Exposing the Roots of Anti-Semitism in the Gospel Story of the Death of Jesus, San Francisco 1995, 137-141. 195-202; idem, The Gospel of Peter &

have met with less success than they may have hoped for and they have not (yet) won the hearts and the minds of the greater majority of their colleagues. This is perhaps not so much because both Crossan and Koester do reckon with some influence of the canonical accounts at one stage in the development from a pre-GP towards the "final" text as it is known to us in (the version of) AF, but rather because their position involves a literary-critical operation on a fragmentarily preserved document that cannot sufficiently be counterchecked. On the positive side one should mention that this kind of criticism of the received position has led others, with I think some good results, systematically to re-examine the evidence for GP's dependence on the other gospels. W.-D. Köhler is admittedly less impressed by the verbal parallels with Matt than was É. Massaux before him, but the structural agreements between GP and Matt finally bring him to the conclusion that GP must have used Matthew's gospel.[19] F. Neirynck, in dialogue with Crossan and Koester, has once more stated the case for GP's dependence on Mark in vv. 50-57.[20] Evidence for GP's acquaintance with Luke is by no means limited to the episode of the Two Thieves (vv. 10-14), though this is probably the clearest example.[21] That GP also knew the Fourth Gospel has most recently been argued again by C.E. Hill.[22] And if some have expressed doubts whether this should have been a matter of literary dependence only, speculating about the circumstances in which GP may have become acquainted with the gospels,[23] this is as much a warning against overplaying one's hand in trying to be too precise about how we should envisage this relationship as it is against too mechanical or too rigid an understanding of the concept of literary dependence itself.

---

the Canonical Gospels. Independence, Dependence, or Both?, Forum 1 NS, 1998, 7-51; H. Koester, Apocryphal and Canonical Gospels, HThR 73, 1980, 105-130, esp. 126-130; idem, Ancient Christian Gospels. Their History and Development, London 1990, 216-240.

19   See É. Massaux, Influence de l'Évangile de saint Matthieu sur la littérature chrétienne avant saint Irénée, Leuven-Gembloux 1950; repr. BEThL 75, Leuven 1986, 358-388; ET: The Influence of the Gospel of Saint Matthew on Christian Literature before Saint Irenaeus, 3 vols., New Gospel Studies 5/1-3, Macon-Leuven 1990-1993; W.-D. Köhler, Die Rezeption des Matthäusevangelium in der Zeit vor Irenäus (WUNT II.24), Tübingen 1987, 437-448: "sicher ist der Verfasser Zeuge für die große Bedeutung des Matt dadurch, daß er die Struktur seines Evangeliums in Anlehnung an das Matt entwickelt" (447-448). Köhler also puts less emphasis on the fact that GP would contain *Sondergut* material from all four of the canonical gospels (445: "ein zusätzliches, aber nicht ganz so starkes Argument für Abhängigkeit"), which has traditionally been considered a crucial argument for dependence: see now again T.K. Heckel, Vom Evangelium des Markus zum viergestaltigen Evangelium, WUNT 120, Tübingen 1999, 291-298.

20   F. Neirynck, The Apocryphal Gospels and the Gospel of Mark (1989), in: Evangelica II, BEThL 99, Leuven 1991, 715-772, here 735-740.

21   Cf. Vaganay, Pierre, 554-59; Massaux, Influence, 377-381. But traces of influence from Luke-Acts can also be found in the Empty Tomb story (cf. Verheyden, Silent Witnesses, 466-476).

22   C.E. Hill, The Johannine Corpus in the Early Church, Oxford 2004, 306-309. 330-332.

23   See R.E. Brown, The Gospel of Peter and Canonical Gospel Priority, NTS 33, 1987, 321-343; idem, The Death of the Messiah. From Gethsemane to the Grave, ABRL, New York 1994, 1317-1349; S.E. Schaeffer, The "Gospel of Peter", the Canonical Gospels, and Oral Tradition, diss. Union Theological Seminary, New York 1991; M.K. Stillman, The Gospel of Peter. A Case for Oral-Only Dependency?, EThL 73, 1997, 114-120.

I will not retrace here the history of this discussion that has taken up so much energy.[24] What may still have been left more or less untouched, however, is the question of how to evaluate GP's use of these other gospels in terms of defining its purpose.

There is to my opinion no evidence to argue that GP is primarily interested in correcting or superseding its predecessors, let alone one of these in particular.[25] The categories just mentioned are difficult to handle when applied to a writing that just too often seemingly indiscriminately makes use of several of these sources at a time. What criteria are there to ascertain that a choice for one version was by the same token a conscious choice against an other? GP also contains just too little "substantial" information that is not covered by one of the other gospels, or could have been inspired by them, to make this its prime purpose. Moreover, such material there is does not seem to be coherent enough to argue that it was added or inserted with one specific purpose. As a "correction" some of this material is really irrelevant. What was won by adding Levi's name in v. 60 (unless he was to become a major character in what followed, but that we cannot certify)? The detailed description of the resurrection certainly fills what could be felt to be a lacuna in the narrative, but in what sense would it have been a correction?[26] As a demonstration of the superiority of GP's account on this point over that of the other gospels – but again in what sense, as a historically more reliable source? –, it seems to have missed its goal for then it would have helped if GP had made Peter the sole witness of this event, or would have indicated how Peter had come to know about it. Such additions do not necessarily have to be taken as corrections.

---

[24] See, e.g., Crossan, The Gospel of Peter, 7-51; Verheyden, Silent Witnesses, 461-465.

[25] And it would be utterly wrong to conceive of such a "struggle" in terms of "canonical" versus "non-canonical", as is rightly noted by Gnilka, Petrus und Rom, 270. – It remains a mere assumption that GP at one time rivalled Matt in Syria, as was suggested (rather than argued) by B.A. Johnson, Empty Tomb Tradition in the Gospel of Peter, diss. Harvard University 1965, 124-125; "alles andere als wahrscheinlich" (Köhler, Rezeption, 448). – According to Heckel (Evangelium, 299-300), the title κατὰ Πέτρον and GP's alleged intention to supersede the Gospel of Mark would indicate that it already presupposes the existence of a collection of the four canonical gospels, though as yet without "canonical" status. However, the title, while obviously patterned after the canonical gospels, is not attested before Origen, and so it may be risky to build too much on it. As for the second argument, the Peter-Mark tradition as transmitted by Papias may be evidence that no "Gospel of Peter" was known at that time, but I do not see how this would support Heckel's thesis that GP was acquainted with a four-gospel collection, nor on what basis it can be called a "nachträglicher Versuch" (299) to do away with "Mark's version of Peter's account", for after all that is what Papias really says about Mark and Peter and the early Church apparently could live with such a variety of versions.

[26] See already the comment of Vaganay, Pierre, 298, who is sceptical of any attempt to find in the description of Jesus leaving the tomb a sense of heresy. While comparing this scene with the similar one in the Ascension of Isaiah (3:17-18), he prefers to call it "une image pittoresque" and "la marque de l'imagination populaire interprétant à sa façon le ἀνεφέρετο εἰς τὸν οὐρανόν (ferebatur in celum) de Lc., xxiv, 51". On GP and AscIs, see Verheyden, L'Ascension d'Isaïe et l'Évangile de Matthieu. Examen de AI 3,13-18, in: The New Testament in Early Christianity, ed. by J.-M. Sevrin, BEThL 86, Leuven 1989, 247-274.

There are also other, more subtle, changes. Thus GP differs from all four canonical gospels in that it does not have the women inform the disciples about the empty tomb (so Matt, Luke, John), nor has the angel order them to do so with the women disobeying him (Mark 16:7-8). Instead, GP completely leaves out the disciples and creates a radical break between what happened to the women at the tomb and to the disciples at the sea (on the assumption that the women were not mentioned here after the text breaks off). This is one way to see things. But in fact, GP's "correction" stays close to Mark, as I already indicated above, or alternatively seems to be very much inspired by the "contradictions" it found in the gospels for the result looks like a conflation of Mark 16:8 (the women do not tell anyone) and of Luke 24:7-8 (they are not formally ordered to inform the disciples). It is possible that GP's version of the empty tomb reflects a certain depreciation of the role of the women, but we have no way to check whether that was also the case in other passages, and thus a major interest of the author, or just one more expression of the kind of unreflected "anti-feminist" feelings that were widely spread in society in general.[27] GP with its adaptation was then just continuing a development that had already begun in the canonical gospels by changing the focus away from the empty tomb (and the women) to the appearance stories (involving the male disciples) as the more important stage in convincing the disciples that the Lord had indeed risen from the death.

A better category to describe GP's handling of its sources might be that of gospel harmony, but then only if taken in a rather broad sense.[28] GP is not so much occupied with consistently preserving as many elements or as much information as possible from the various accounts, or with finding ways to reconcile all the differences there are between these, nor is there any indication that it wanted to replace the other accounts with this one and only, which clearly are all primary concerns of prototypical gospel harmonies in the Diatessaron tradition. Too often indeed GP is content with paraphrasing or freely rendering parts of the story, or with picking out certain episodes, and after all that may be the better way to describe what is going on here. It involves a good deal of freedom and far less of strategy or "patterning". If so, we should then

---

[27]   See Verheyden, Silent Witnesses, 480-481. Graham Brock, Mary Magdalene, 69, rightly regards "the diminished role of Mary Magdalene", together with the negative view of Herod, the anti-Jewish sentiments, and the elaboration of the resurrection scene, as one of four characteristic features of GP, but the question I am interested in is whether there was much of theological reflection involved.

[28]   That GP was itself dependent upon a gospel harmony has been suggested by H.B. Swete, Εὐαγγέλιον κατὰ Πέτρον. The Akhmîm Fragment of the Apocryphal Gospel of St. Peter, London 1893, xx-xxv, and by a few others (see the discussion in Vaganay, Pierre, 75-77). Vaganay is equally critical of attempts to label GP as a gospel harmony (with reference to von Schubert and several others) or as a compilation (contra Zahn). In light of such criticism it is perhaps not wise to characterise GP's proceeding as "to amalgamate and to harmonise the Gospel accounts" (so Hill, Johannine Corpus, 309). Of these two "amalgamate" would be the better qualification, on condition not to bring together GP under the same heading as P. Egerton or the Longer Ending of Mark, or the way Tatian rewrote the gospels.

perhaps again settle for the qualification "unreflected" as the one that best characterises what GP has been doing to its sources.[29]

3. GP's "Anti-Jewish" Stand

Admittedly maybe the more promising place to find out about the purpose of GP is to look for characteristic features of its content. Two such features are often mentioned: its alleged docetism and its anti-Jewish sentiments.

More than one scholar has doubted that GP is an utterly docetic document, and with good reason.[30] The allegations rest on little more than the opinion of Serapion, as voiced by Eusebius, of whom we do not know for certain what he actually meant by docetism,[31] nor whether he made up the charge and just read too much in certain passages because he had found the gospel to be in use among people he considered to be docetists and therefore wanted to discredit it,[32] or whether the work really was more outspokenly docetic in some other sections that have not been preserved. The latter is a priori rather improbable as this would mean that GP would only be moderately docetic in precisely those sections (the passion and death of Jesus) where such a doctrine could have been expressed most clearly. The few verses that are cited as evidence from AF (vv. 10 and 19) certainly do not warrant the conclusion that GP wanted to promote in some way a docetic theology or doctrine.[33] At best one

---

[29] Cf. Vaganay's comment: "Il y a dans le fragment d'Akhmîm une note personnelle, une liberté dans la composition ... Il pourrait bien s'être inspiré surtout de l'histoire de Jésus, telle qu'on la racontait dans son milieu d'après nos quatre évangiles. Lorsqu'on parle de ses emprunts, on ne doit pas l'entendre de l'emploi formel et direct de telle parole scripturaire. Il vaut mieux penser à un emprunt au sens large, à une connaissance moins immédiate du passage en question" (Pierre, 81).

[30] Denker's forceful defense for the opposite has remained an isolated position in current research (Doketismus, 111-117, and 126-130 on Ignatius). See J.M. McCant, The Gospel of Peter. Docetism Reconsidered, NTS 30, 1984, 258-273; P.M. Head, On the Christology of the Gospel of Peter, VigChr 46, 1992, 209-224; Heckel, Evangelium, 290-291; Lapham, Peter, 25-29; Hill, Johannine Corpus, 307-309.

[31] See on this issue in general, N. Brox, "Doketimus" – eine Problemanzeige, ZKG 95, 1984, 301-314. M.D. Goulder, Ignatius' "Docetists", VigChr 53, 1999, 16-30 (Docetism would be a modern misunderstanding for a form of Ebionism).

[32] So Junod, Eusèbe de Césarée, 15. Serapion's initial appreciation of GP would argue against the view that he rejected the book because it was a pseudepigraphon, and not because of its contents, as has recently been defended by A.D. Baum, Pseudepigraphie und literarische Fälschung im frühen Christentum, WUNT II.138, Tübingen 2001, 100-103.

[33] Thus Lührmann, Die apokryph gewordenen Evangelien, 56-57: "Die klassische Lehre der Doketen, dass Jesus nicht selbst gelitten habe und nicht selbst gekreuzigt worden sei, ergibt sich jedenfalls nicht aus dem uns zugänglichen Text des Evangeliums". For Hill, "the entire emphasis on the resurrection of 'the Lord' in this document is a major stumbling block to a patently docetic motive" (Johannine Corpus, 308). Lapham is less affirmative: "it is difficult to read the text without suspecting that it originates from a milieu which, while not rejecting the humanity of Christ, was more concerned by far to emphasize his exaltation than his suffering" (Peter, 29).

can say that it contains a couple of rather faint docetic-like elements – to speak of an tendency would already go too far –, which again would point towards some kind of "unreflectedness" on the part of its author.

GP is very negative about the role of the Jewish leaders in the trial of Jesus. For Denker GP was moved by pedagogical motives and meant to win over some individuals from the Jewish population by exposing the scandalous behaviour of its leaders in concealing for the masses what really had happened to Jesus after his death.[34] Crossan, in his critique of Brown, sees in GP's polemics an echo of the situation in the early years of Christianity when tensions with official representatives of Judaism were rising, but had not yet exploded into fullblown and indiscriminate anti-Jewish feelings as was happening somewhat later and is witnessed in the canonical gospels (Matt 27:24-25). "My reading of the Gospel of Peter is that it is more 'anti-Jewish' with regard to the authorities than any of the canonical gospels but also more 'pro-Jewish' with regard to the *people* than any of them."[35] A. Kirk has criticised Crossan for underestimating the anti-Jewish bias of GP and making this into an argument – indeed his core argument – for the early dating of his alleged Cross Gospel that would not yet have been taunted by this more hostile characterisation of the Jews as a whole.[36] Kirk argues that GP combines several purposes – he lists three – by presenting the Jews the way it does, and addresses a twofold audience – Jews and Jewish-Christian converts alike. "It rationalizes the limited Jewish response to the Christian proclamation ('their leaders keep them in ignorance of the truth of the resurrection') while at the same time makes a case to Jews as to why they should leave the synagogue and join the church ('your leaders are untrustworthy and are deceiving you'). The same propaganda served to hinder defections to the synagogue"[37]. T. Nicklas in turn has presented a close reading of the relevant passages and concluded that GP is looking for an answer to the question why the Jews have denied and put to death their Messiah. "Der Autor scheint von der Frage bewegt zu sein, wie es dazu kommen konnte, dass Gottes Volk den 'Herrn' abgelehnt, ja seiner Meinung nach gekreuzigt hat."[38] Nicklas focuses on the way GP makes use of Scripture to drive home its point. The Jews play their part in God's plan and help fulfil what was prophesied about the fate of the Messiah. However, GP also explains, and here it goes beyond what was announced in the Scriptures, how the people had been prevented from repenting for what they allowed to happen to Jesus by their own leaders who had done everything in their power to keep the masses from hearing about the resurrection. Nicklas finds here in GP's story a twofold positive as-

---

[34] Doketismus, 78-92.

[35] Crossan, The Gospel of Peter, 28. Cf. The Birth of Christianity. Discovering What Happened in the Years Immediately after the Execution of Jesus, San Francisco 1998, 496-498.

[36] A. Kirk, The Johannine Jesus in the Gospel of Peter. A Social Memory Approach, in: Jesus in Johannine Tradition, ed. by R.T. Fortna/T. Thatcher, Louisville 2001, 313-321, here 319-321.

[37] Ibid., 321.

[38] T. Nicklas, Die "Juden" im Petrusevangelium (PCair. 10759). Ein Testfall, NTS 47, 2001, 206-221, here 220.

pect of hope that the Jewish people would at last confess the Lord and, on a more general basis, that repentance always remains possible for all.[39]

I am rather more reserved about how much of conscious reflection there really is behind GP's presentation of the role of the Jews. Reading GP may have prevented some from relapsing in their old faith, as Kirk suggests as a third purpose, but we have little to go on that this was still a major concern early on in or towards the middle of the second century and in GP's community. No more evidence is there for Kirk's second purpose that GP was actually also addressing the Jews of the neighbouring synagogue. Here Nicklas is closer to Kirk than his criticism of Denker in this regard seems to suggest,[40] for if GP indeed still believes that the Jews might repent and convert upon hearing the truth about Jesus and its own leaders it must somehow have worked to make this message known to those for whom it was meant.

Moreover, I am not convinced either that it was GP's goal to adapt the story of Jesus' trial and passion so as to explain to its readers the reasons for the limited response of the Jewish populations to the Christian mission. On this point Nicklas agrees with Kirk. The latter calls it a "rationalisation". For Nicklas this reflection even takes the form of a developing "theology" that includes making sense of why the Jews at first had denied Jesus by integrating certain passages from Scripture into the story. But that the leaders of the Jews had prevented the people from hearing about the empty tomb could already be found in Matt (27:62-66; 28:11-15). Moreover, if it was GP's purpose to develop this theme to some extent, it could have made much more of it just by keeping to the text of Matt. There one reads not only that the chief priests and the Pharisees make common cause with Pilate (27:62-66), but also that they cover up for the "failure" without even consulting Pilate when bribing the guard (28:11-15, and esp. v. 14a). All this would have made excellent stuff for someone who wished to put the blame for the limited success of the Jewish mission squarely on the shoulders of the Jewish authorities.

Instead, GP makes Pilate co-responsible, or even just the chief responsible,[41] for the cover-up (49 ἐκέλευσεν οὖν ὁ Πειλᾶτος, the only time in GP that Pilate is said to give a command) and turns the meeting between the governor and the Jewish leaders into a repetition of the confrontation in Matt 27:24-25, with Pilate confessing his innocence (v. 46) and the others accepting the fate they had

---

[39] "Aus der Darstellung der 'Juden' im PE lassen sich somit immerhin zwei durchaus positiv zu beurteilende Gedanken herausschälen, die zumindest implizit im Text erhalten sind: dies ist einerseits der Gedanke möglicher Umkehr bei noch so großer Sünde, andererseits mag auch die zumindest aus christlicher Perspektive verstehbare Hoffnung mitschwingen, daß das 'Volk der Juden' sich doch noch zu seinem 'Herrn' bekehrt" (ibid., 220-221).

[40] Ibid., 220 n. 57.

[41] Cf. M.G. Mara, Évangile de Pierre, SC 201, Paris 1973, 196: "Pilate reste toujours l'autorité suprême, même si elle est seulement une autorité instrumentale." See also H. Omerzu's article in the present volume.

sworn to take upon them (v. 48), while it omits to mention the bribing[42] and does not know how to exploit the irony of 28:13 when the Jews can do no better than to propose as a solution the very thing they previously had tried to avoid at all cost (i.e., that the disciples would steal away the body of Jesus).

One thing, however, is obvious to the author of GP: it is the Jews who, as of one, have put Jesus to death. This is not something that has to be "demon-strated". The author is not so much intent on "arguing a thesis", as on just tell-ing the story in this way, because that is how Christians like himself commonly saw it: Jesus was killed by the Jews, not by an individual, or by one faction, but simply by "the Jews". It is the "normal" way of telling the passion story, rooted in a kind of "unreflected" and "self-evident" anti-Jewish sentiments. It was something that by and large was taken for granted. And it is a way of telling the story that for a good deal was inspired by and could rely on the accounts that were found in other gospels without all too much complicating or altering them.[43] Nicklas tends to disregard this factor and solely concentrates on GP's indebtedness to Scripture, but that may precisely be crucial in appreciating the way it presents the story.

Let me illustrate this somewhat further. For GP there can be no discussion that it is Herod, rather than Pilate, who ordered Jesus to be killed (v. 2). This is of course not found as such in any of the gospels. Yet GP in no way seems to think it is necessary to account for it. In its view, that is just how it went. But on the other hand, GP's version is not completely out of way with what could be found in the canonical gospels. There, too, Pilate had been excused – or rather, had himself excused – for the condemnation of Jesus. He had washed his hands. What GP has to tell about this does not significantly differ, except that it explicitly adds that the Jews who were with him did not wash their hands, which prepares for the next verse. It is difficult to say more, because we do not know what preceded v. 1 of AF. Was there a last confrontation with the people, as in Matt 27:24-25, which GP would then have duplicated somewhat clumsily in vv. 46-49? Or was it simply not further interested in the character of the gov-ernor who immediately leaves the scene (ἀνέστη)?[44] It is Herod who steps in and takes full responsibility for condemning Jesus. The way he formulates his command in v. 2 seems to suppose that he already had made his decision clear at the trial itself.[45] But on this point as well, GP may after all be more in line

---

42 Compare again Mara: "il n'y a pas d'allusion qu'on ait cherché à corrompre les soldats pour qu'ils se taisent, comme dans Matth. 28,11-15" (Pierre, 195).
43 Cf. J.M. Lieu, Image and Reality. The Jews in the World of the Christians in the Second Century, Edinburgh 1996, 261: "A narrative may generate its own momentum towards intensification of characterisation, such as typifies the reworking in the Gospel of Peter of the canonical(-type) passion traditions, themselves already on a trajectory of increasing hostility to the Jews."
44 Mara, Pierre, 69, translates the verb paraphrastically as "Pilate se leva (pour s'en aller)."
45 "À première vue, cela ne paraît qu'un ordre qui ratifie quelque chose de déjà dit précédem-ment mais dont nous ne savons rien, et qui rend évidente la responsabilité du roi Hérode dans la condamnation du Christ" (ibid., 75).

with at least one of the canonical accounts than one might suspect. That Herod was in a decisive way involved in the trial of Jesus may have been inspired by the account of Luke in 23:6-12 and 23:15. Commentators and translations as a rule interpret or render ἀλλ' οὐδὲ ʿΗρῴδης in the latter verse as "neither did Herod" (so NRSV) or the like. Herod and Pilate would stand united in their opposition against the people and its leaders. But it is possible to read, or mis-read, ἀλλ' οὐδέ in another way. In 23:14 a contrast was created between the Jews who are charging Jesus of perverting the people and Pilate who does not find any guilt in him (καὶ ἰδού). The contrast is continued in v. 15 with Herod now contradicting Pilate (ἀλλ' οὐδέ) and the latter repeating his position (again, καὶ ἰδού). The mocking scene in 23:11 and the fact that Jesus is sent back to Pilate (23:11.15) is not proof that Herod thinks Jesus to be an innocent fool. It can be read, rather to the contrary, as a sign that Herod indeed has initiated the process of one who is condemned. The mocking will also be the first step after Pilate has given up Jesus in Mark 15:15-20 (par. Matt and John) and Luke's ἐξου-θενέω in 23:11 is probably stronger than just "treating with contempt", as it may be an echo of Jesus' prediction in Mark 9:12 (there with παθεῖν). That Herod has Jesus sent back indicates that he wants the procedure to be continued, as it is the case also with Paul in Acts 23:29. Luke does not say in the gospel that Herod was also present with Pilate at the trial of Jesus, but he had emphasised that the two had befriended (23:12) and when in Acts 4:27 Luke recalls the trial scene his interpretation of Ps 2:1-2 leads him to write that Herod and Pilate had indeed "come together" (συνήχθησαν γὰρ ἐπ' ἀληθείας ἐν τῇ πόλει ταύτῃ ... ʿΗρῴδης τε καὶ Πόντιος Πιλᾶτος). This may perhaps not be the most orthodox interpretation of Luke 23:15, but it would be an understandable one from an author who wanted to make Herod a key figure in the condemnation of Jesus, and a similar interpretation of ἀλλ' οὐδέ can be found elsewhere in Luke.[46]

Nicklas points out the influence of Ps 2:1-2 for the role of Herod in the trial of Jesus,[47] but he does not take into account the possibility that this influence may have been mediated by Luke and that the latter's influence was not limited to this one element. The influence of passages such as Dtn 21:6-7, Ps 25:4-6 (LXX) and 72:13 (LXX), and of Dan 13:46 (Susanna) that others have drawn attention to[48] may likewise have been mediated by Matthew's account in 27:24-25. It is not necessary, however, to assume that each and every detail of GP's version must go back to one of these texts. When Pilate raises from his seat at the end of v. 1, this clearly marks that for him the trial has come to an end and at the same time could express his dissatisfaction with the course the events

---

46 Compare the strong adversative use of ἀλλ' οὐδ' in Acts 19:2. R. Pesch translates here as "im Gegenteil", as part of "die polemische Überspitzung der Unwissenheit" of those who are addressed: cf. idem, Die Apostelgeschichte (Apg 13-28), EKK 5/2, Zürich et al. 1986, 163. 165.

47 Nicklas, Die "Juden", 214 n. 33, with reference to Denker, Doketismus, 59. The qualification "king" for Herod may also come from the same passage, if it is not a conflation by GP with Herod the Great (214 n. 33).

48 See Denker, Doketismus, 58 (Ps 25); Crossan, The Cross That Spoke, 96-99.

had taken, but ἀνέστη may as well have been inspired by Matt 27:19 (καθημένου) or by John 19:13 (Pilate pronounces judgement while seated; in GP he openly declines to exercise his function), as it could be an echo of Ps 25:5b (μετὰ ἀσέβων οὐ μὴ καθίσω).

Herod is the one who hands over Jesus, not to the soldiers, however, but directly to the people (v. 5 παρέδωκεν τῷ λαῷ). The latter are most probably already mentioned in v. 2, – at least if αὐτοῖς does not refer back to the judges who accompany Herod, but this is quite implausible and would create a contrast with v. 5, where the people are explicitly made Herod's partners in crime.[49] However, in what follows in GP 6-24 it is then no longer explicitly and consistently said who is doing what, except for the one general οἱ Ἰουδαῖοι at the very end of this section (v. 23). Grammatically οἱ λαβόντες τὸν κύριον (v. 6), τις αὐτῶν (v. 8), ἕτεροι ... ἄλλοι ... ἕτεροι ... τινες (v. 9), τις αὐτῶν (v. 16), and the many verbs in third plural would all refer to the people of v. 5. If this is not merely the result of some inaccuracy on the part of GP, forgetting to point out that the ones in vv. 6-8 are soldiers, one would at least have expected GP to have been more explicit about the identity of those who mock and crucify Jesus, if it really was its intention and purpose actually to "argue" that the Jews – and they alone – were actively involved in killing Jesus. Is it not rather because this seems so self-evident to GP that it does not feel the need to be more precise (and so to "correct" in a sense the canonical accounts on this point), and that it can suffice with the kind of indirect and general references that are now found in vv. 6-24? "They" killed Jesus.

GP's version for this part of the passion narrative certainly differs from the story as it is told by Mark and by Matthew who at first do not say to whom Jesus is handed over (15:15 par. 27:26)[50], but in the next verse they make it plain clear for the reader that it is the – obviously Roman – soldiers (Matt τοῦ ἡγεμόνος) who mock Jesus and then take him to the cross. However, Luke and John are rather less explicit on this point. In John it are the soldiers who mock Jesus (19:2). It is possible that the same are still mentioned, together with the chief priests, in 19:6. But from the next verse on it is "the Jews", supported in v. 16 by the chief priests, who confront Pilate. It is "to them" (αὐτοῖς) that Pilate hands over Jesus in v. 16a, and it is "they" who take and crucify him in vv. 17-18 and who intervene with Pilate in v. 21. Only in v. 23 the reader hears about the soldiers, who apparently also are the subject of vv. 17-18, but that John had not said immediately. The situation is not much different in Luke. Jesus is "delivered up to 'their' will" (23:25), but those present are "the chief priests and

---

49 Cf. Vaganay, Pierre, 206: "Ce qu'il y a de plus choquant d'ailleurs, c'est moins le libellé de la sentence que cette demi-obscurité qui entoure les agents d'exécution (αὐτοῖς, ὑμῖν). Non pas qu'il y ait doute sur leur caractère juif ou païen. Les subordonnés auxquels Hérode s'adresse ne peuvent être que des Juifs."

50 There is a variant reading in Matt with αὐτοῖς which may have resulted from ἀπέλυσεν αὐτοῖς in the first half of the verse, or from confusion with John 19:16, and would refer to the people (27:25 ὁ λαός). See on the variant, Nicklas, Textgeschichte, 140, who notes that such similarities may not be enough to establish a direct link between the Western text and GP.

the rulers and the people", not, however, the soldiers (23:13). Only in v. 36, when Jesus is already put on the cross, the soldiers are mentioned, and presumably they had been present right from the outset, but again that was not said so clearly. In addition, it should also be reminded that in both Mark and Matt (some of) the people (15:29 par. 27:39 οἱ δὲ παραπορευόμενοι ἐβλασφήμουν αὐτόν), together with the chief priests and the scribes (in Matt also the elders), play an active role in deriding Jesus at the cross, using precisely the same two titles as "they" do in GP.[51]

It is only from v. 15 on that the reader is made more aware of the fact that it are "the Jews" who have killed Jesus. All of vv. 15-24 is dominated by GP's interest in depicting the concern of the Jews to comply with the Law by not leaving somebody hang from the cross after dark and by providing for a burial. GP's fascination with this issue results in a rather more free rendering of what happened at the death of Jesus in which certain details of the story as told in the gospels are re-used in quite a different way, thus contributing to almost caricaturise the behaviour of the Jews. The episode of the two thieves that is reported in great detail (10-14) ends with a very brutal scene in v. 14, that is lacking in Luke, in which "they", contrary to John 19:31-33, do not break the legs of one of those who are crucified to make him suffer longer. It is not said who the victim is – Jesus or the "good thief" –, but if there is any link with the next scene, it must be Jesus.[52] The sudden darkness that falls upon the land shortly after causes great panic (15 ἐθορυβοῦντο), lest they would have left somebody on the cross after sunset. They decide to poison Jesus to hasten his death, for that obviously is how GP – in line with Mark, Matt, and John – interprets their offering Jesus vinegar to drink in Mark 15:36 and parr. that immediately precedes his death.[53] They then hurriedly proceed to take Jesus down from the cross – there is no time to ask permission from Pilate, as in John 19:31 –, only to find out that none of this was needed, for the sun starts shining again as it was not later yet than the ninth hour. Jesus had not been left on the cross at night. This causes the Jews great joy (v. 23), but they apparently do not seem

---

51 Βασιλεὺς τοῦ Ἰσραήλ: GP 7 and, without the article, Matt 27:42 par. Mark 15:32; and υἱὸς τοῦ θεοῦ: GP 9 (with ὁ) and Matt 27:40 (cf. also the ἄρχοντες in Luke 23:25 and the soldiers in v. 37).

52 So also Mara, Pierre, 120, diff. Vaganay, Pierre, 242. It would be one more illustration of the somewhat inaccurate style of the author who also "failed" to mention the soldiers before.

53 The poisonous effect is also pointed out by Nicklas, Die "Juden", 218. Mara is sceptical (Pierre, 131: "un moyen pour hâter sa mort. Il me paraît abusif de tirer cette interprétation des textes cités") and would like to see in it only a concern to imitate Ps 68:22 (LXX) ("le désir de refléter le plus fidèlement possible le Ps. 68"). However, that there is an immediate link between Jesus drinking the cup and his death is at least also suggested by John (19:29.30) and, if Jesus is thought to have already drunk before the others intervene, also by Matt and by Mark (27:48.50 par. 15:36a.37). That GP has "mixed gall with vinegar" (χολὴν μετὰ ὄξους. καὶ κεράσαντες) is not in itself an indication that its author would here directly allude to Ps 68. For one, the LXX does not speak of "mixing" the two; moreover, the gall and vinegar are not presented to someone who is dying. The latter is the case, however, in the canonical accounts. And it is there that one finds both elements offered to Jesus, be it on separate occasions and with gall mixed up in wine (Matt 27:34 μεμιγμένον).

to realise how great a fool they have made of themselves. The doubly ironic scene of v. 18, having them running around as when they were trying to arrest Jesus (John 18:3-7) at a time that in Matt the dead are wandering around in the city (Matt 27:51-53), and the observation in v. 17, possibly echoing John 19:28 (see ἐτελείωσαν and ἵνα τελειωθῇ ἡ γραφή[54]), only add to this mixture of ridicule and tragedy that characterises this whole episode and that to me reflects rather more the kind of popular anti-Jewish feelings on which GP is built and from which it lives, than that such a story would be the result of a well-thought and theologically well-motivated re-telling of the passion story that should bring the Jewish neighbours to the faith.

Finally, the way GP presents the reaction of the Jews in v. 25 and mixes up the various categories of Jewish leaders in what follows is so careless and clumsy that it obscures its major intention of distinctively separating the leaders from the masses to blame the former for the ignorance of the latter, and again rather seems to be symptomatic of an "unreflected" dependence on the canonical accounts. Most significant is v. 25. GP may have been acquainted with a different form of Luke 23:48 than the one that is found in our modern editions.[55] But why change Luke's πάντες οἱ συμπαραγενόμενοι ὄχλοι and have "the elders and the priests" join "the Jews" (the masses?) in their lament? After the short remark on the situation of the disciples in vv. 26-27, GP continues with describing the reaction of the leaders, and at least the elders (but not the priests?) now have joined forces with the scribes and the Pharisees in their critique of the people, without a word of comment on the part of GP about this "defection."[56] It is this same group ("the elders") that seeks to convince Pilate to seal and guard the tomb (v. 29), and they even remain with the soldiers (v. 38, note the emphatical parenthesis). But in the meantime the reader has also been informed that the elders had been accompanied by the scribes (v. 31), and maybe by others still (v. 32), but apparently these did not stay on for the night. When the guard after the resurrection rushes to Pilate, the elders are not specifically mentioned again, but others, who remain unidentified, were present there too (v. 47 "all") and are much concerned about the enmity of the people

---

54 Mara again would rather like to see here a direct allusion to the Psalm, be it "en suivant une interprétation particulière" (Pierre, 131). It is true, of course, that GP has the Jews fulfill their own fate (pl. ἐπλήρωσαν πάντα), while in John 19:28 it is Jesus who takes the initiative. But should such a difference surprise in a writing that has reduced Jesus' role to merely uttering the words of dereliction (v. 19), foregoing the scene with his mother and the disciple (John 19:26-27) and even omitting Jesus' promise to the good thief, to focus so consistently on what "they" were doing?

55 See Klijn, Westerse tekst, 267; Denker, Doketismus, 28.

56 Mara notes the difference but does not explain it beyond the general observation that "toutes ces catégories sont présentes dans les Évangiles canoniques, même si on ne les rencontre pas réunies de la sorte dans les mêmes circonstances" (Pierre, 165). In their edition Kraus/Nicklas regard the plural λέγοντες in v. 28 (λαὸς γογγύζει καὶ κόπτεται ... λέγοντες) as a "constructio ad sensum" and translate in the sg. ("und sagte"), but see the English translation (51: "and they said"). Or is this one more illustration of the inaccurateness of an author who in v. 25 had written, more appropriately, ἤρξαντο κόπτεσθαι καὶ λέγειν?

towards them. Mary Magdalene and the women, however, do not seem to be aware of all this and continue to be afraid of "the Jews" (vv. 50 and 52), as were the other disciples before (v. 26).[57] Is there anything more behind this than the kind of "unreflected" use of these various categories that can also be found in Matt 27:62-66 (the chief priests and the Pharisees) and 28:11-15 (only the chief priests), and in several other instances in the gospels?[58]

Conclusion

The story that GP wants to tell had already been told many times before and had even been put to writing by several others on whom it relied with no clear intention whatsoever to fundamentally challenge or counter these accounts. It is a story in which both Peter and the Jews and their leaders obviously were major characters. By making Peter the narrator (and author?) of its own account GP adds a dimension to this character that was not found in the other gospels but that did not significantly alter the story as such or the role of Peter in it. By having the Jews take part in the trial and death of Jesus in the way as this happens in GP, its author gives witness to what cannot be otherwise described than as a general and "unreflected" utterance of anti-Jewish sentiments that were probably widely spread throughout all levels of society but that when formulated in a purely narrative way, without any more systematical reflection, as this is the case in GP, rather echoes the voice of somebody living in and addressing a more popular, though perhaps not completely uncultivated, milieu[59]. The few really "novel" things, such as the detailed description

---

[57] The disciples are thus virtually excluded from participation in the events. But they are as much the victim of the vengeance of the Jews as was Jesus himself. Being accused of planning to destroy the temple is not only a most ironic and historically implausible accusation, but it is also a crude example of anti-Jewish polemics as is rightly observed by Nicklas (Erzähler und Charakter, 325: "Diese erklärt sich m.E. am besten als Seitenhieb gegen die 'Juden'").

[58] See "the chief priests" in Mark 15:3.11, to which Matt adds "the elders" (27:12.20), but in 15:31 the chief priests are joined by the scribes at the cross, to which Matt again adds the elders (27:41), while Luke keeps to "the rulers" (23:35). Cf. also the chief priests in Luke 23:4, who are then joined by "the scribes" before Herod in 23:10, and by "the rulers" in 23:13.

[59] It has often been observed that GP seems to be rather well-informed about certain Jewish practices, which would indicate that its author lived in an ethnically mixed society with a relatively strong Jewish component, but in which the various groups already have distanced themselves from each other and it is precisely this situation that may have fuelled an anti-Jewish atmosphere on a broader scale. Cf. Lieu, Image and Reality, 261: "Although there is no inclusive terminology for the faithful nor any reference to the gentiles, the former undoubtedly saw themselves as fully separate from 'the Jews'". S.G. Wilson, Related Strangers. Jews and Christians 70-170 C.E., Minneapolis 1995, rightly points out that the intense hostility towards Judaism in general that springs from the pages of GP and many other writings should not yield the impression "that Jews and Christians were constantly at each other's throats" (290). – It is difficult to be more specific beyond this. Lapham refers to the many communities of Jewish-Christian origin that flourished in the regions east of Antioch, but from there to say that "it is not unreasonable to speculate that Gos. Pet. was produced in and for a community (Nazaraean or Elchasaite, perhaps) for whom the observance of the law was still important" (Peter, 32) may

of the resurrection, would only demonstrate that GP indeed is the kind of popularising account that would have appealed to these circles.[60] GP does not want to be innovating. It does not want to sanction other accounts, and I would not call it the work of an "impostor" either (cf. Vaganay's "faussaire"). Its author has no great design or theologically profound message to offer. His agenda is far more modest. He tells a story that was known to all, and he does this in a way that appeals to an audience that was probably as little concerned with doctrine as it was eager for being confirmed in its opinions and prejudices about those who it was convinced had murdered Jesus. In short, the author does not so much give "his" but rather "the" account of the story of Jesus as it was readily understood and accepted by his readers.

---

be one step too far taking into account not only our limited knowledge of the history and composition of these communities but also the fact that GP's interest in the disciples observing the law basically repeats what is already found in the canonical accounts.

[60] The most important aspect here is perhaps not that the resurrection is presented in terms of an ascension, nor whether or not this represents ancient tradition (see Harnack versus Vaganay), but the interest GP takes in combining the miraculous and the spectacular in describing the resurrection as an event that was witnessed by the guard. See J.-M. Prieur, La croix vivante dans la littérature chrétienne du IIe siècle, RHPR 79, 1999, 435-444, esp. 439-440. Cf. K.E. Corley, Women and the Crucifixion and Burial of Jesus, Forum 1 NS, 1998, 181-225, esp. 211: "the Gospel of Peter should be considered a late novelistic account of the crucifixion and the empty tomb."

Die Kraft des Herrn
Erwägungen zur Christologie des Petrusevangeliums

von

MATTI MYLLYKOSKI

Laut Eusebius von Caesarea (*h. e.* 6,12) war Serapion, in den Jahren 193-211 Bischof von Antiochien, bei seinem Besuch in der Gemeinde von Rhossus dem Petrusevangelium begegnet. Obwohl Serapion das dort diskutierte Evangelium zunächst akzeptierte, verbot er es später als eine Schrift der „Doketen". Zwar akzeptierte er den größten Teil des Evangeliums als „wahre Lehre des Erlösers", identifizierte aber auch Stellen, die angeblich von dieser Lehre abwichen. Leider zitiert Eusebius Serapions Liste dieser Stellen nicht. Als 1892 mit dem Akhmîm-Fragment ein Stück der Passions- und Auferstehungs- geschichte des Petrusevangeliums entdeckt wurde, hat man daher die den kanonischen Evangelien unbekannten Stellen dieses apokryphen Textes immer wieder als Zeichen doketistischer Christologie interpretiert. Heutzutage dagegen weist man diese Interpretation oft zurück. Sowohl der Passus des Eusebius über Serapion als auch die angeblich doketischen Belegstellen im Fragment des EvPetr enthalten zahlreiche Probleme, die in der Geschichte der Forschung unterschiedlich gedeutet wurden. Einige Ausleger haben sogar daran gezweifelt, dass das Akhmîm-Fragment und das von Serapion als doketisch abgestempelte Petrusevangelium identisch sind.[1] Im Folgenden werden zunächst das Zeugnis des Eusebius und der Brief des Serapion[2] und

---

[1] M.G. Mara, L'Évangile de Pierre, SC 201, Paris 1973, 19, mit Hinweis auf A. Vitti, Rez. L. Vaganay, L'Évangile de Pierre, Bib. 12, 1931, 247-248. Vorsichtig äußern sich auch T.J. Kraus/T. Nicklas, Das Petrusevangelium und die Petrusapokalypse. Die griechischen Fragmente mit deutscher und englischer Übersetzung, GCS.NF 11; Neutestamentliche Apokryphen 1, Berlin- New York 2004, die immer wieder vom „so genannten Petrusevangelium" sprechen. Zur Problematik der Identifikation von Fragmenten vgl. jetzt auch ausführlich T. Nicklas, Zwei petrinische Apokryphen im Akhmîm-Codex oder eines? Kritische Anmerkungen und Gedanken, Apocrypha 16, 2005, 75-96.

[2] Literatur: J.A. Robinson, The Gospel according to Peter, and the Revelation of Peter. Two Lectures on the Newly Recovered Fragments together with the Greek Text, London 1892; A. Harnack, Bruchstücke des Evangeliums und der Apokalypse des Petrus, Leipzig ²1893, 4-5; A. Hilgenfeld, Das Petrus-Evangelium über Leiden und Auferstehung Jesu, ZWTh 36.1, 1893, 439- 454, bes. 452-454 und 36.2, 1893, 220-267, bes. 226-232; H.B. Swete, ΕΥΑΓΓΕΛΙΟΝ ΚΑΤΑ ΠΕΤΡΟΝ. The Akhmîm Fragment of the Apocryphal Gospel of St. Peter, London 1893, x-xii; T. Zahn, Das Evangelium des Petrus. Das kürzlich gefundene Fragment seines Textes aufs neue herausgegeben, übersetzt und untersucht, Erlangen-Leipzig 1893; L. Vaganay, L'Évangile de Pierre, ÉtB, Paris 1930, 1-8; J.D. Crossan, The Cross That Spoke. The Origins of the Passion

dann die umstrittene Frage nach Doketismus im Akhmîm-Fragment[3] kritisch untersucht.

Bischof Serapion, der Doketismus und das Petrusevangelium

In *h. e.* 6,12 beschreibt Eusebius zunächst kurz Karriere und Schriften Serapions, um dann die Rhossus-Episode zu berichten und den Brief des Bischofs an die Gemeinde zu zitieren:[4]

1 Τοῦ μὲν οὖν Σεραπίωνος τῆς περὶ λόγους ἀσκήσεως καὶ ἄλλα μὲν εἰκὸς σῴζεσθαι παρ' ἑτέροις ὑπομνήματα, εἰς ἡμᾶς δὲ μόνα κατῆλθεν τὰ Πρὸς Δόμνον, ἐκπεπτωκότα τινὰ παρὰ τὸν τοῦ διωγμοῦ καιρὸν ἀπὸ τῆς εἰς Χριστὸν πίστεως ἐπὶ τὴν Ἰουδαϊκὴν ἐθελοθρησκείαν, καὶ τὰ Πρὸς Πόντιον καὶ Καρικόν, ἐκκλησιαστικοὺς ἄνδρας, καὶ ἄλλαι πρὸς ἑτέρους ἐπιστολαί, 2 ἕτερός τε συντεταγμένος αὐτῷ λόγος Περὶ τοῦ λεγομένου κατὰ Πέτρον εὐαγγέλιου, ὃν πεποίηται ἀπελέγχων τὰ ψευδῶς ἐν αὐτῷ εἰρημένα διά τινας ἐν τῇ κατὰ Ῥωσσὸν παροικίᾳ προφάσει τῆς εἰρημένης γραφῆς εἰς ἑτεροδόξους διδασκαλίας ἀποκείλαντας ἀφ' οὗ εὔλογον βραχείας παραθέσθαι λέξεις, δι' ὧν ἣν εἶχεν περὶ τοῦ βιβλίου γνώμην προτίθησιν, οὕτω γράφων·

3 ἡμεῖς γάρ, ἀδελφοί, καὶ Πέτρον καὶ τοὺς ἄλλους ἀποστόλους ἀποδεχόμεθα ὡς Χριστόν, τὰ δὲ ὀνόματι αὐτῶν ψευδεπίγραφα ὡς ἔμπειροι παραιτούμεθα, γινώσκοντες ὅτι τὰ τοιαῦτα οὐ παρελάβομεν. 4 ἐγὼ γὰρ γενόμενος παρ' ὑμῖν, ὑπενόουν τοὺς πάντας ὀρθῇ πίστει προσφέρεσθαι, καὶ μὴ διελθὼν τὸ ὑπ' αὐτῶν προφερόμενον ὀνόματι Πέτρου εὐαγγέλιον, εἶπον ὅτι εἰ τοῦτό ἐστιν μόνον τὸ δοκοῦν ὑμῖν παρέχειν μικροψυχίαν, ἀναγινωσκέσθω· νῦν δὲ μαθὼν ὅτι αἱρέσει τινὶ ὁ νοῦς αὐτῶν ἐφώλευεν, ἐκ τῶν λεχθέντων

Narrative, San Francisco 1988, 10-12; E. Junod, Eusèbe de Césarée, Sérapion d'Antioche et l'Évangile de Pierre: D'un Évangile à une Pseudepigraphe, RSLR 24, 1988, 3-16; A.D. Baum, Literarische Echtheit als Kanonkriterium in der alten Kirche, ZNW 88, 1997, 97-110, bes. 104-105; M. Bockmuehl, Syrian Memories of Peter: Ignatius, Justin and Serapion, in: The Image of the Judeo-Christians in Ancient Jewish and Christian Literature, ed. by P.J. Tomson/D. Lambers-Petry, WUNT 158, Tübingen 2003, 124-146, bes. 128-132; B.D. Ehrman, Lost Christianities. The Battles for Scripture and the Faiths We Never Knew, Oxford 2003, 13-28, bes. 14-16; T.J. Kraus/T. Nicklas, Petrusevangelium, 12-16.

3   Literatur: J. Kunze, Das Petrusevangelium, NJDTh 2, 1893, 583-604; NJDTh 3, 1894, 58-104; A. Lods, L'Évangile et l'Apocalypse de Pierre, Paris 1893; H. von Schubert, Die Composition des pseudopetrinischen Evangelienfragments, Berlin 1893, 46-47. 170-172; Swete, ΕΥΑΓΓΕΛΙΟΝ, xxxvii-xliii; T. Zahn, Das Evangelium des Petrus, NKZ 4, 1893, 143-218, bes. 171-180. 213-218; Vaganay, Évangile, 106-122. 236-237. 255-257; Mara, Évangile, 105-111. 132-140; J. Denker, Die theologiegeschichtliche Stellung des Petrusevangeliums. Ein Beitrag zur Geschichte des Doketismus, Frankfurt/Main 1975, 118-125; Crossan, Cross, 174-187. 220-224; J.W. McCant, The Gospel of Peter: Docetism Reconsidered, NTS 30, 1984, 258-273; P.M. Head, On the Christology of the Gospel of Peter, VigChr 46, 1992, 209-224; R.E. Brown, The Death of the Messiah. From Gethsemane to the Grave. A Commentary on the Passion Narrative in the Four Gospels, vol. 1-2, New York 1994, 2:1056-1058, 1337-1338; M.G. Mara, Il Vangelo di Pietro. Introduzione, versione, commento, Bologna 2002, 22-23. 54-59. 70-75.

4   Text: G. Bardy, Eusèbe de Césarée. Histoire ecclésiastique, Bd. 2, SC 41, Paris 1955, 102-104. Übersetzung: Eusebius, Kirchengeschichte. Übers. von P. Haeuser (Bibliothek der Kirchenväter, 2. Reihe, Band 1) München 1932, sprachlich überarbeitet durch H.-A. Gärtner, Kempten 1967. Diese Übersetzung habe ich an einigen Stellen modifiziert.

μοι, σπουδάσω πάλιν γενέσθαι πρὸς ὑμᾶς, ὥστε, ἀδελφοί, προσδοκᾶτέ με ἐν τάχει. 5 ἡμεῖς δέ, ἀδελφοί, καταλαβόμενοι ὁποίας ἦν αἱρέσεως ὁ Μαρκιανός, <ὃς> καὶ ἑαυτῷ ἐναντιοῦτο, μὴ νοῶν ἃ ἐλάλει, ἃ μαθήσεσθε ἐξ ὧν ὑμῖν ἐγράφη, 6 ἐδυνήθημεν γὰρ παρ' ἄλλων τῶν ἀσκησάντων αὐτὸ τοῦτο τὸ εὐαγγέλιον, τοῦτ' ἐστὶν παρὰ τῶν διαδόχων τῶν καταρξαμένων αὐτοῦ, οὓς Δοκητὰς καλοῦμεν, τὰ γὰρ πλείονα φρονήματα ἐκείνων ἐστὶ τῆς διδασκαλίας, χρησάμενοι παρ' αὐτῶν διελθεῖν καὶ εὑρεῖν τὰ μὲν πλείονα τοῦ ὀρθοῦ λόγου τοῦ σωτῆρος, τινὰ δὲ προσδιεσταλμένα, ἃ καὶ ὑπετάξαμεν ὑμῖν.

Von der schriftstellerischen Tätigkeit Serapions sind wohl noch andere Denkmäler bei andern vorhanden. Zu unserer Kenntnis gekommen sind jedoch nur die Schrift „An Domnus", welcher zur Zeit der Verfolgung vom christlichen Glauben zum jüdischen Eigenkult abgefallen war, die Schrift „An die kirchlich gesinnten Männer Pontius und Karikus", ferner noch Schreiben an verschiedene Anschriften und schließlich eine Arbeit „Über das so genannte Petrusevangelium". Diese verfasste er, um die in diesem Evangelium enthaltenen falschen Sätze zu widerlegen; denn einige Glieder der Kirche zu Rhossus hatten sich durch die erwähnte Schrift zu falschen Lehren verleiten lassen. Es dürfte zweckmäßig sein, aus jener Arbeit einige wenige Worte anzuführen, welche seine Ansicht über die Schrift wiedergeben. Serapion schreibt:

„Meine Brüder, wir empfangen Petrus und die übrigen Apostel wie Christus.[5] Wenn aber Schriften fälschlich unter ihrem Namen gehen, so sind wir erfahren genug, sie zurückzuweisen; denn wir wissen, dass uns solche Schriften nicht überliefert worden sind. Als ich bei euch war, meinte ich, dass alle den rechten Glauben hätten. Und ohne das von ihnen vorgelegte, den Namen Petri führende Evangelium durchgelesen zu haben, hatte ich erklärt: Wenn dies allein euer Verdruss[6] ist, dann möge man es lesen! Da ich aber nun vom Hörensagen[7] weiß, dass ihr Sinn sich in einer Häresie einnistete,[8] werde ich mich beeilen, wieder zu euch zu kommen. Daher, Brüder, erwartet mich in Bälde! Wir kennen, Brüder, die Häresie des Marcian. Er widersprach sich selbst und wusste nicht, was er sagte. Ihr könnt dies aus dem, was euch geschrieben ist, ersehen.[9] Durch andere, die eben dies Evangelium benützten, das heißt durch die Nachfolger seiner Urheber,[10] die wir Doketen nennen, da ja seine Ideen größtenteils dieser Richtung angehören, kamen wir in die Lage, dasselbe von ihnen zu erhalten und durchzulesen und zu finden, dass zwar das meiste mit der wahren Lehre unseres Erlösers übereinstimmt, manches aber auch davon abweicht, was wir unten für euch anfügten."

---

5   Haeuser und Gärtner: „... wir halten an Petrus und den übrigen Aposteln ebenso fest wie an Christus."
6   Rufinus: *simultas*; Vaganay, Évangile, 2; Junod, Eusèbe, 9 Anm. 17: contrariété.
7   Junod, Eusèbe 10: „d'après ce que l'on m'a dit"; Mara, Vangelo, 8: „Ma da quanto mi si è detto poi".
8   Handschrift A liest ἐνεφώλευεν. Zur Übersetzung vgl. auch Junod, Eusèbe, 10: „leur esprit se nichait dans quelque hérésie", und Mara, Vangelo, 8: „loro mente si annidava l'eresia". Einige Autoren interpretieren den Ausdruck ὁ νοῦς αὐτῶν ἐφώλευεν hier als „eine heimliche Zuneigung"; s. Haeuser und Gärtner: „dass ihr Sinn heimlich einer Häresie zuneigt"; so auch Vaganay, Évangile, 2: „leur esprit se dissimulait dans quelque hérésie".
9   Mit Junod, Eusèbe, 10: „par ce qui vous a été écrit". Haeuser und Gärtner übersetzen: „was ich euch geschrieben habe".
10   Das Verb κατάρχομαι hat Schwierigkeiten bereitet. Swete, ΕΥΑΓΓΕΛΙΟΝ, xxxvii, erklärt, das EvPetr sei laut Serapion „emanated from the Docetic party"; Junod, Eusèbe, 10 n. 22: „à savoir grace aux successeurs de ceux qui furent à ses débuts". Anders Vaganay, Évangile, 3 n. 1: „c'est-à-dire par les successeurs de ceux qui l'ont intronisé".

Die ersten Ausleger des Akhmîm-Fragments nahmen das Zeugnis des Eusebius mehr oder weniger als Beweis des „Doketismus" in der Gemeinde von Rhossus. Der kurze Forschungsbericht von Vaganay[11] aus dem Jahr 1930 verrät trotz einer Menge von Differenzen im Detail eine der damaligen Forschung gemeinsame Fragestellung und Argumentation. Laut Harnack wurde das EvPetr von der Gemeinde in Rhossus gelesen und war „bei der Secte der Doketen um 200 im Gebrauch, gleichzeitig mindestens in *einer* Gemeinde des antiochenischen Sprengels, wurde aber aus dieser von Serapion entfernt" [Hervorhebung im Original].[12] Vaganay dagegen greift die Idee des langfristigen Gebrauchs des EvPetr in Rhossus auf und fragt: Wenn das EvPetr wirklich in Rhossus ein hochgeschätztes liturgisches Buch war, wie konnte Serapion, der vollmächtige Bischof von Antiochien, es überhaupt nicht kennen und dann trotzdem ohne Lesung akzeptieren?[13] Daneben will Vaganay auch die Interpretation von Hilgenfeld – eine abgeschwächte Variante der Harnackschen Theorie – widerlegen. Nach Hilgenfeld habe das EvPetr erst relativ kurz vor dem Besuch des Bischofs in der Gemeinde von Rhossus einen kanonischen Status erhalten und sei daher diskutiert worden. Der von Serapion erwähnte Markianos sei der Führer der dortigen Befürworter des EvPetr gewesen.[14] Vaganay findet diese Erklärung immer noch unbefriedigend, da die Beschreibung Serapions keineswegs voraussetzen kann, dass die Doketen in Rhossus die Mehrheit der Gemeindemitglieder repräsentiert hätten. Im Gegenteil, sie könnten nur eine *faible minorité* gewesen sein.[15] Zuletzt weist Vaganay den Vorschlag von Kunze zurück, dem zufolge Marcian das EvPetr erst kurz vor dem Besuch Serapions in Rhossus eingeführt habe.[16] Der Bischof könne selbst unter solchen Umständen keine öffentliche, sondern nur eine private Lesung der unbekannten Schrift erlaubt haben. Serapion habe also einen kleinen Fehler gemacht, der aber trotzdem unter den guten Christen der Stadt zum Anlass heftiger Polemik geworden war.[17] Wie Zahn und viele andere argumentieren, wollte ein kleiner Kreis von Christen der Gemeinde von Rhossus, die das EvPetr privat lasen, diese Praxis vom Bischof selbst anerkannt haben.[18] Der Erfolg des EvPetr in Rhossus war also dünn und kurzfristig.[19]

---

11   Vaganay, Évangile, 3-8. 9-11. Laut Junod, Eusèbe, 3, ist dieser Bericht „[l]e commentaire le plus approfondi de ce témoignage de Sérapion et de la notice d'Eusèbe qui l'introduit."
12   Harnack, Bruchstücke, 4-5 n. 1.
13   Vaganay, Évangile, 4.
14   Hilgenfeld, Petrus-Evangelium, 226-232.
15   Vaganay, Évangile, 4-5. Er kontrastiert die häretische Minderheit (τὸ ὑπ' αὐτῶν προφερόμενον ὀνόματι Πέτρου εὐαγγέλιον) mit der Mehrheit der Gemeinde, die Serapion anspricht (εἰς τοῦτό ἐστιν μόνον τὸ δοκοῦν ὑμῖν παρέχειν μικροψυχίαν, ἀναγινωσκέσθω).
16   Kunze, Petrusevangelium (1893), 603-604 und (1894), 58-59.
17   Vaganay, Évangile, 5-6. Mit Verweis auf drei Texte (Joh 19,20; Justin, *1. apol.* 44,12; Cyrill von Jerusalem, *catech.* 4,36), plädiert er dafür, dass das Verb ἀναγινώσκω im Brief des Serapion auf private Lesung des Evangeliums hinweist.
18   Zahn, Evangelium, 2-5. 76-77.
19   Vaganay, Évangile, 8.

Vaganays Forschungsbericht verrät, dass viele Wissenschaftler bei ihren Erwägungen zum Zeugnis Serapions vier entscheidende Grundannahmen teilten. Erstens: Da der Bischof von Antiochien das EvPetr nicht kannte, sei dieses Evangelium auch im Allgemeinen relativ unbekannt gewesen. Im Vergleich zu den kanonischen Evangelien, die im Laufe des 2. Jahrhunderts allgemein akzeptiert wurden, habe es bestimmt keine bemerkenswerte Stellung eingenommen. Zweitens wurde oft angenommen, dass das EvPetr in Rhossus nahezu allein von einer kleinen Gruppe von Doketen gelesen wurde. Daraus zog man – drittens – den Schluss, dass das EvPetr mit den allgemein anerkannten vier Evangelien konkurrierte und in breiten kirchlichen Kreisen als ein heterodoxes Evangelium abgelehnt wurde. Viertens vermuteten viele Forscher aufgrund der drei genannten Punkte, dass die Doketen von Rhossus den Serapion nicht gefragt hätten, ob das EvPetr *im Gottesdienst* verlesen werden könne, sondern ob sie selbst dieses Evangelium *privat* lesen dürften.

Zu (1): Schon Harnack war mit der erstgenannten These nicht ganz zufrieden. Er hielt es für „höchst merkwürdig, ja rätselhaft", dass das EvPetr am Ende des 2. Jahrhunderts in Syrien gelesen, vermutlich schon im Anfang des 3. Jahrhunderts in Ägypten bekannt und noch einige Jahrhunderte später wenigstens von einigen ägyptischen Mönchen gebraucht wurde.[20] Er nennt aufgrund seiner Untersuchung auch weitere Trägergruppen, Autoren und Schriften, die mit unterschiedlicher Wahrscheinlichkeit das EvPetr rezipierten. Die Geschichte der Verwendung des EvPetr bei folgenden Texten und Autoren sollte beweisen, dass dieses Evangelium

> „nicht für eine Secte geschrieben worden ist": Nazaräer (?), Didache, Ignatios (?), Papias (?), Justin, ein Abschreiber des Johannesevangeliums im 2. Jahrhundert, Tatian (??), Clemens von Alexandrien (?), Doketen in Syrien, die Gemeinde von Rhossos, Serapion, Versio Syr. Cureton, Origenes, Didaskalia, Eusebios (?), Pseudo-Ignatios, Codices Sangerm. und Bobbiensis, und das Fragment von Akhmîm[21] bezeugten die Rezeption des Textes.

Anders urteilte Vaganay, der den Einfluss des EvPetr lediglich auf dem syrischen Boden für nachweisbar hielt: Origenes habe dieses Evangelium in der Spätphase seines Lebens in Cäsarea kennen gelernt, während die syrische Didaskalie und vielleicht Aphrahat es als Quelle verwendeten.[22] Den Akhmîm-Fund erklärte er damit, dass die in Syrien verfolgten monophysitischen Mönche das EvPetr im 6. Jahrhundert nach Ägypten gebracht hätten.[23] Jürgen Denker, dessen Dissertation aus dem Jahr 1972 im Jahr 1975 gedruckt wurde, wiederholt Vaganays Urteil über die Rezeption des EvPetr in gemäßigter Form:

---

20 Harnack, Bruchstücke, 5.
21 Harnack, Bruchstücke, 37-61. Die Liste findet sich ibid., 80; die Fragezeichen stammen von Harnack.
22 Vaganay, Évangile, 163-176, bes. 176.
23 Vaganay, Évangile, 178.

Nur die Verbreitung über Westsyrien lässt sich erweisen, zumindest in späterer Zeit ist es in Ägypten gelesen worden, möglicherweise bereits von Origenes und Clemens.

Das EvPetr sei mit dem aus Syrien stammenden „westlichen Text" der kanonischen Evangelien und mit Tatians Diatessaron verwandt; daher gehört es deutlich zur westsyrischen Evangelienüberlieferung. Die Parallelen zu den Schriften Justins seien mit gemeinsamen Traditionen zu erklären.[24]

Das in Ägypten gefundene und auf das Ende des 2. Jahrhunderts zu datierende Fragment P.Oxy. 2949 hat die Gesprächslage verändert. Das 1972 von Coles edierte kleine Papyrusstück, das etwa zehn Zeilen umfasst und parallel mit dem Anfang des Akhmîm-Fragments läuft (EvPetr 3-5),[25] beweist, dass das EvPetr schon am Ende des 2. Jahrhunderts in Ägypten bekannt und von einigen dortigen Christen verwendet wurde. Dieter Lührmann hat zu zeigen versucht, dass darüber hinaus das ins 2. Jahrhundert zu datierende Fragment P.Oxy. 4009, das eine Parallele zu 2 Clem 5,2 bietet, als ein Teil des EvPetr zu beurteilen sei, da im Text des Fragments Petrus als Ich-Erzähler auftrete.[26] Doch ist diese Zuweisung nicht sicher, weil Petrus auch in einigen anderen bekannten Texten als Ich-Erzähler erscheint und erscheinen kann;[27] unter diesen ist aber das EvPetr eben die nächstliegende Möglichkeit. Darüber hinaus liegt noch ein 1904 veröffentlichtes kleines Ostrakon (aus dem 6. oder. 7. Jahrhundert) vor, in dem „der heilige Petrus" als „der Evangelist" (ο εὐαγελτιχ = ὁ εὐαγγελιστής) verehrt wird.[28] Diese Fundstücke sprechen für die Verbreitung des EvPetr in verschiedenen Kreisen Ägyptens. B.D. Ehrman stellte daher etwas provozierend fest, dass das apokryph gewordene EvPetr aufgrund der

---

[24] Denker, Stellung, 9-30, Zitat ibid., 30.

[25] The Oxyrhynchos Papyri, vol. XLI, ed. by G.M. Browne et al., London 1972, 15-16. Zu Rekonstruktionen von P.Oxy. 2949 vgl. D. Lührmann, POx 2949: EvPt 3-5 in einer Handschrift des 2./3. Jahrhunderts, ZNW 72, 1981, 216-226; J.C. Treat, The Two Manuscript Witnesses to the Gospel of Peter, SBL.SP 1990, 391-399; D. Lührmann, Fragmente apokryph gewordener Evangelien in griechischer und lateinischer Sprache, MThSt 59, Marburg 2000, 85 (eine neue Rekonstruktion); M. Myllykoski, POx 2949 als Fragment des Petrusevangeliums, in: Verbum et Calamus: Semitic and Related Studies in Honour of the Sixtieth Birthday of Professor Tapani Harviainen, hg. von H. Juusola et al., StOr 99, Helsinki 2004, 171-189; T.J. Kraus/T. Nicklas, Petrusevangelium. Vgl. nun auch die kritische Bewertung bei P. Foster, Are There Any Early Fragments of the So-Called Gospel of Peter?, NTS 52, 2006, 1-26.

[26] D. Lührmann/P.J. Parsons, 4009: Gospel of Peter?, The Oxyrynchus Papyri LX, London 1993, 1-5; D. Lührmann, POx 4009: Ein neues Fragment des Petrusevangeliums?, NT 35, 1993, 390-410, bes. 400-401.

[27] Kraus/Nicklas, Petrusevangelium, 63, mit Hinweis auf 1 und 2Petr; ÄthApkPetr 2; Akten des Petrus und der Zwölf 1.30-31 (NHC 5.1). Kraus und Nicklas bleiben skeptisch in Bezug auf die Möglichkeit, das Fragment einem bekannten Text zuzuordnen.

[28] P. Jouguet/G. Lefebre, Deux ostraka de Thèbes, BCH 28, 1904, 201-209. Sie haben das Ostrakon 1903 in Luxor erworben. Der Fund wurde in der Forschung des EvPetr lange Zeit übersehen. Die erste diesbezügliche Untersuchung ist D. Lührmann, Petrus als Evangelist – ein bemerkenswertes Ostrakon, NT 43, 2001, 348-367; kritisch hierzu T.J. Kraus, Petrus und das Ostrakon van Haelst 741 – einige klärende Anmerkungen, ZAC 7, 2003, 228-236. Zur Abbildung des Ostrakons, s. Lührmann, Fragmente, 94-95, und Ehrman, Christianities, 23. Vgl. auch den Beitrag von D. Lührmann im vorliegenden Band.

bekannten materialen Zeugnisse in den ersten Jahrhunderten als populärer als das kanonisch gewordene Markusevangelium betrachtet werden müsse.[29] Zu beachten ist auch, dass wir nur einen kleinen Teil des EvPetr kennen – erst ein vollständiges EvPetr-Manuskript könnte eine vollständige Grundlage für die Beurteilung seiner Rezeption bieten.

Immerhin: Die Zeugnisse für die populäre Verbreitung des EvPetr in Syrien und Ägypten sprechen dagegen, dass unser Evangelium lediglich von Doketen oder sonstigen „Häretikern" gebraucht wurde. Es scheint also nicht angemessen, das EvPetr als eine Randerscheinung im Felde der Evangelienliteratur zu beurteilen. Obwohl Serapion nicht vor seinem Besuch in Rhossus konkret mit dem EvPetr konfrontiert war, zeugt sein Brief für die weite Verbreitung der populären Evangelienliteratur in Syrien am Ende des 2. Jahrhunderts. Serapion konnte die Verlesung des EvPetr zunächst eben deshalb akzeptieren, weil die Verbreitung solcher Evangelien offensichtlich ein übliches und anerkanntes Phänomen war. Weiter kann damit gerechnet werden, dass dies nicht unbedingt die erste Begegnung des Bischof mit dem EvPetr war; er hatte von der Lektüre des EvPetr gehört, so dass der Text nicht genauer identifiziert werden musste. Wegen der angenommenen Rechtgläubigkeit der Christen von Rhossus hielt er es jedenfalls nicht für nötig, den Text genauer durchzusehen und seinen apostolischen Charakter in Frage zu stellen.

Zu (2): Die Vermutung, die Leser des EvPetr in Rhossus seien Doketen gewesen, ergibt sich aus der Darstellung des Eusebius („einige Glieder der Kirche zu Rhossus hatten sich durch die erwähnte Schrift zu falschen Lehren verleiten lassen"), nicht aus dem Brief Serapions.[30] Zur Zeit seines Besuchs schien Serapion die *ganze* Gemeinde rechtgläubig zu sein. Das galt auch für diejenigen, die ihm das so genannte Petrusevangelium gaben, um von ihm zu erfahren, ob dieser angeblich vom Apostel Petrus verfasste Text akzeptabel sei. Es ist bemerkenswert, dass die anderen Mitglieder der Gemeinde diese Leute offensichtlich nicht einer Häresie bezichtigten. Wäre dies nämlich der Fall gewesen, hätte Serapion bestimmt anders gehandelt. Es ging also nur um das Evangelium und seinen Inhalt. Nur in einer solchen Situation konnte Serapion vertrauensvoll kurz den Text durchsehen und seine Verlesung erlauben. Serapions zuversichtlicher Umgang mit der Sache lässt nicht vermuten, dass die Befürworter und Widersacher des EvPetr über den kanonischen Status dieses Evangeliums im Disput standen.[31] Der Bischof von Antiochien hat offenbar auch nicht ernsthaft gefragt, ob das Evangelium wirklich von Petrus stamme. Sein Brief, in dem er den häretischen Charakter des EvPetr diskutiert,

---

[29] Ehrman, Christianities, 22-23. Nur eine von den 30 Evangelienhandschriften, die aus dem 2. oder 3. Jahrhundert stammen, enthält das Markusevangelium. Dem gegenüber haben wir aus derselben Zeit wohl drei materielle Zeugnisse für das EvPetr: POx 2949, POx 4009 und den Brief Serapions.

[30] Mit Junod, Eusèbe, 8.

[31] Gegen Vaganay, Évangile, 7.

weist darauf hin, dass er beim ersten Blick die Herkunft des Evangeliums aus dem Wirkungskreis des Apostels ruhig annehmen konnte. Die Frage war für Serapion demnach zunächst praktischer Natur.

Der Brief Serapions gibt also nicht zu verstehen, dass die Befürworter des EvPetr in den Augen ihrer Brüder und Schwestern in Rhossus Doketen oder andere „Häretiker" gewesen wären.[32] Es ist erheblich einfacher zu vermuten, dass sie dieses Evangelium irgendwo in die Hände bekommen hatten und dass selbst die Vermittler des Petrus-Textes keine Doketen waren. Auf jeden Fall war das EvPetr dem kleinen Kreis in Rhossus lieb geworden, und man hatte es *bona fide* verwendet. Das EvPetr war also offensichtlich nicht nur ein Evangelium der Häretiker, sondern auch eine im volkstümlichen Christentum verbreitete Schrift. So ist es gut vorstellbar, dass diese Gemeindemitglieder das EvPetr in Form eines Codex besaßen.[33] Ein solcher Codex muss keine Luxusware und nicht allzu teuer gewesen sein.[34]

Wie gesagt, das Verhalten Serapions bei seinem Besuch weist gerade nicht darauf hin, dass solche Evangelien oder andere pseudepigraphische Schriften damals Seltenheit gewesen wären. Begegnungen mit solchen Schriften scheinen unserem Bischof nicht etwas Fremdes oder Neues gewesen zu sein. Sein Umgang mit dem EvPetr folgt einem leicht erkennbaren Muster. Pseudepigraphische Schriften wurden in den Gemeinden des 2. Jahrhunderts mit regem Interesse gelesen, weil die Christen fasziniert waren von alten, sich für Wunder interessierende und geheime Traditionen. Erst wenn behauptet wurde, dass eine solche Schrift falsche Lehren bzw. Einstellungen förderte und/oder von Häretikern gelesen wurde, gab es einen besonderen Grund, sie genauer zu untersuchen und sie unter Umständen als schädlich und unecht abzulehnen.[35]

Erst aufgrund von Ereignissen nach seinem Besuch schickte Serapion den von Eusebius zitierten Brief an die Gemeinde von Rhossus. Um seine Autorität zu wahren, versichert er zuerst, und zwar im Widerspruch zu seinem eigenen Verfahren in Rhossus, dass er „erfahren genug" sei, solche Schriften zurückzuweisen, die fälschlich unter den Namen der Apostel in Umlauf seien. Es ist aber nicht ganz klar, wie er zu den Bedenken gegen das so genannte Petrusevangelium gekommen ist. Etwas kryptisch behauptet er über die Leser des EvPetr, dass er „vom Hörensagen" wisse, „dass ihr Sinn in einer Häresie

---

[32] Mit Junod, Eusèbe, 8, der betont, dass Serapion letzten Endes nicht weiß, ob die Leser des EvPetr in Rhossus heterodox sind oder nicht.

[33] Stellen wir uns vor, dass das EvPetr etwa gleich lang wie das Matthäusevangelium (ein wenig mehr als 110.000 Buchstaben) war, so können wir vermuten, dass Serapion bei seinem genannten Besuch zu Rhossus flüchtig in einem kleinen Codex von etwa 160-170 Seiten (ungefähr 25 Zeilen pro Seite x 27 Buchstaben pro Zeile = 675 Buchstaben pro Seite) geblättert hat. Zur Länge der Evangelien in Codices vgl. auch H.Y. Gamble, Books and Readers in the Early Church: A History of Early Christian Texts, New Haven-London 1995, 66-67.

[34] Gamble, Books, 231-232.

[35] Vgl. die immer noch gültigen Überlegungen von N. Brox, Falsche Verfasserangaben. Zur Erklärung der frühchristlichen Pseudepigraphie, SBS 79, Stuttgart 1975, 64-65.

einnistete". Die Sache scheint dermaßen „heiß" zu sein, dass Serapion sich beeilen will, die Gemeinde wieder zu besuchen. Die meisten Ausleger nehmen an, dass Serapion jetzt besser über den Leserkreis des EvPetr in Rhossus informiert war: Er hat entweder über eine Gesandtschaft aus Rhossus oder von Vertrauten in Antiochien über die christologische Irrlehre dieser Leute erfahren.[36] Anhand der Beschreibung, die Serapion von seinem Besuch gibt, ist Letzteres nicht sehr wahrscheinlich. Hätten Serapions Vertraute in Antiochien gewusst, dass gewisse Christen in Rhossus Doketen waren bzw. Kontakte zu den Doketen hatten, hätten sie den Bischof doch rechtzeitig *vor* seinem Besuch gewarnt. Die indirekte und vage Formulierung Serapions („dass ihr Sinn in einer Häresie einnistete") hängt meines Erachtens damit zusammen, dass weder die Mitglieder der Gemeinde noch er selbst diese Befürworter des Evangeliums bei seinem Besuch als Häretiker abstempeln konnte; äußerlich war ja alles in Ordnung. Serapion sagt auch nicht, dass diese Leute ihr wahres Gesicht trügerisch verheimlicht hätten. Irgendwie seien sie trotzdem in eine Häresie verwickelt, und das weiß Serapion allein „vom Hörensagen" (ἐκ τῶν λεχθέντων μοι). Ich halte die Vermutung für sinnvoll, dass dieses Hörensagen genau das EvPetr betrifft. Es ist letzten Endes oder eigentlich nur dieses Evangelium, das sie mit einer Häresie in Verbindung bringt. So erhält Serapion ein Exemplar des EvPetr von den antiochenischen Doketen, untersucht es genau und stellt fest, dass es doketische Lehren enthält. Dann versucht er – nicht mehr und nicht weniger – den Schaden, den die häretischen Stellen dieses Evangeliums verursacht haben, wieder gut zu machen.

Nichts weist darauf hin, dass der von Serapion genannte Marcian ein Mitglied der Gemeinde von Rhossus oder ein Wanderprediger gewesen wäre, der unter der Gemeinde seine Lehre verbreitete.[37] Serapion verbindet ihn nur sehr locker mit der aktuellen Streitfrage in Rhossus. Es ist nahe liegender, dass Marcian ein berüchtigter Irrlehrer war, den auch die Leute in Rhossus namentlich kannten. Serapion weist darauf hin, dass die Gemeinde schon über diesen Mann[38] und seine innerlich widersprüchliche Lehre informiert ist. Das Verhältnis zwischen Marcian, dem EvPetr und den Doketen dagegen wird in Serapions Brief nicht deutlich. Möglicherweise erwähnt Serapion ihn nur, um das Vertrauen der Christen in Rhossus zu erwecken. Wie die Häresie des Marcian offen gelegt wurde, so ist jetzt auch die hinter dem EvPetr stehende Häresie klar geworden.

Was genau Serapion aber mit „Doketen" und „Doketismus" meint, bleibt dunkel. Die Schlüsselfigur der doketischen Gnosis in Syrien war Satornil, der

36 Junod, Eusèbe, 10 n. 19. Laut Vaganay, Évangile, 7, hat Serapion nach seiner Rückkehr in Antiochien die Sache untersucht und bemerkt, dass die Doketisten das EvPetr gebrauchen.
37 Gegen Vaganay, Évangile, 5.
38 Die armenische Fassung des Eusebius-Textes hatte J.A. Robinson, Gospel, 14-15, vermuten lassen, dass der Urtext nicht auf Marcian, sondern auf Marcion hingewiesen hatte. Junod, Eusèbe, 10 n. 20, weist meines Erachtens mit Recht diese Vermutung zurück, weil eine Verbindung zwischen Marcion und dem EvPetr unwahrscheinlich ist. Es kann nicht ausgeschlossen werden, dass das EvPetr unter den Judenchristen beliebt war.

um 120-130 gewirkt haben dürfte. Laut Irenäus von Lyon war seine Christologie durchgehend doketisch. Er „machte zur Grundlage, dass der Erlöser ungeboren, unkörperlich und gestaltlos sei, scheinbar nur als Mensch erschienen" (*adv. haer.* 1,24,2). Es ist nicht einfach, diese Form von Doketismus mit dem Text des EvPetr zu kombinieren. Clemens von Alexandrien bezeichnet die „Doketen" als eine häretische Gruppe (*str.* 7,108,1-2) und nennt Julios Kassianos, einen leib- und ehefeindlichen Dualisten, als den „Stifter der doketischen Lehre" (*str.* 3,91-95), vermittelt aber keinerlei Information über die Christologie dieser Gruppe. Erst Hieronymus identifiziert Julios Kassianos mit einem christologischen Doketismus (*comm. in Gal.* 6,8). Die von Hippolyt beschriebenen Doketen wiederum lehrten über die Taufe Jesu, dass dieser dabei mit einer andersartigen, dauerhaften Leiblichkeit versehen wurde, um „nicht nackt zu sein", wenn er am Kreuz den fleischlichen Körper aufgab (*haer.* 8,10,7).[39] Solche Doketen konnten ihre Ansichten im EvPetr gespiegelt finden. Für Serapion sind „Doketen" eine separate häretische Bewegung mit einer von der Orthodoxie abweichenden Identität. Offensichtlich bildeten diese Christen in Antiochien eine eigene Gemeinde, die Serapion nicht als ihren Bischof anerkannte.

Die Logik Serapions lässt sich also folgendermaßen beschreiben: Das EvPetr ist ein verdächtiges Buch, da es von den Doketen verwendet wird.[40] Serapion missbilligt die Doketen und mit ihnen auch das EvPetr, aber sein Urteil über das pseudopetrinische Werk ist relativ mild. Er sagt, dass im EvPetr „das meiste mit der wahren Lehre unseres Erlösers übereinstimmt, manches aber auch davon abweicht, was wir unten für euch anfügten." Diese Anfügungen, die Eusebius uns nicht bewahrt hat, sollen den heterodoxen Charakter des EvPetr beweisen und deutlich machen, weshalb es nicht mehr gelesen werden darf. Diese Schlussfolgerung hat unser Bischof schon aufgrund des Gebrauchs des EvPetr unter den Doketen gezogen und erst dann nach genauerer Durchsicht des Evangeliums verifizieren können. Diese Gesichtspunkte aber lassen die Vermutung, die Leserschaft des EvPetr in Syrien (und Ägypten) sei in der Regel doketisch orientiert gewesen, als sehr fraglich erscheinen.

Zu (3): Die allgemeine Verbreitung apokrypher Evangelien und sonstiger Sammlungen über Worte und Taten Jesu macht es nicht besonders verwunderlich, dass Serapion das EvPetr nicht kannte oder wenigstens nicht mit einem ihm schon oberflächlich bekannten Text identifizieren konnte. Wenn die Grenze zwischen den als apostolisch anerkannten und pseudepigraphischen Schriften so klar gewesen wäre, wie Serapion glauben machen möchte, muss ernsthaft gefragt werden, warum er das EvPetr nicht sofort als eine Fälschung abstempelte. Es ist auch bemerkenswert, dass er nicht mit einer

---

[39] Zum Problem siehe auch N. Brox, „Doketismus" – eine Problemanzeige, ZKG 95, 1984, 301-314, bes. 304.

[40] Siehe auch Junod, Eusèbe, 13-14: Wenn jemand unter Verdacht der Heterodoxie steht, so sind auch die von ihm verwendeten Bücher als pseudepigraphisch zu verurteilen.

Sammlung der als apostolisch anerkannten Evangelien argumentiert. Daher muss nicht angenommen werden, dass das EvPetr in Syrien das Stigma der Häresie getragen hätte und nur in marginalen und heterodoxen Kreisen verbreitet gewesen wäre. Wegen seiner inhaltlichen Nähe zu den kanonischen Evangelien konnte man das EvPetr dagegen problemlos in verschiedenen Gemeinden lesen.

Viele Autoren haben dennoch den unterschiedlichen Rang der kanonisch gewordenen Evangelien und des apokryphen EvPetr betont. Tatians Diatessaron (ca. 170) zeige deutlich, dass zu dieser Zeit die Vierevangeliensammlung in Syrien weitgehend anerkannt war. Es ist trotzdem wichtig zu bemerken, dass das Diatessaron nicht einen Vierevangelien*kanon*, sondern die Sammlung der vier Evangelien belegt.[41] Die von den vier Evangelien abweichenden Episoden und Einzelzüge des Diatessarons sprechen sogar dafür, dass die Harmonie dieser autorisierten Evangelien auch mit Hilfe populärer Evangelientraditionen und unter Umständen auch anderer Evangelien unterstützt werden konnte.[42] Zumindest im populären Gebrauch scheinen Texte wie das EvPetr noch Ende des 2. Jahrhunderts die kanonisch werdenden Evangelien im Prinzip problemlos ergänzt zu haben.

Zu (4): Immer wieder wurde auch die These von Zahn und Vaganay aufgegriffen und behauptet, Serapion habe bei seinem Besuch lediglich den privaten Gebrauch des EvPetr erlaubt. Das Argument lautet dann wie folgt: Die Verlesung des EvPetr im Gottesdienst habe der Bischof nicht einer Gruppe der Gemeindemitglieder, sondern nur der Leitung der Gemeinde erteilen können.[43] Dies setzt eine fortgeschrittene Gemeindehierarchie in Rhossus voraus, in der auch Gottesdienst scharf von privaten Versammlungen differenziert werden konnte. Entsprechend müsste man sich dann auch die antiochenische Kirchenzucht als besonders streng vorstellen.[44] Bemerkenswert ist, dass die Lesung des EvPetr zu einem grundlegenden Problem wird und zwar in einer Weise, dass Serapion in seinem Brief die besondere Eile der Sache betont („werde ich mich beeilen, wieder zu euch zu kommen"). Aber selbst

---

[41] So mit Recht T.K. Heckel, Vom Evangelium des Markus zum viergestaltigen Evangelium, WUNT 120, Tübingen 1999, 336. Siehe auch die Erwägungen von T. Nicklas, „Ein neutestamentliches Apokryphon"? Zum umstrittenen Kanonbezug des sog. „Petrusevangeliums", VigChr 56, 2002, 260-272, bes. 266-267.

[42] W.L. Petersen, Tatian's Diatessaron. Its Creation, Dissemination, Significance, and History in Scholarship, VigChr.S 25, Leiden 1994, 414-420. In einem programmatischen Artikel betont Petersen, dass selbst der Text der kanonisch gewordenen Evangelien im 2. Jahrhundert noch im Schwanken war: The Genesis of the Gospels, in: New Testament Textual Criticism and Exegesis. FS J. Delobel, ed. by A. Denaux, BEThL 161, Leuven 2002, 33-65 (über Tatian ibid., 41-43). Zur Frage, inwieweit das Diatessaron als Zeugnis eines „Vierevangelienkanons" dienen kann, vgl. nun (mit guten Gründen ablehnend) idem, Canonicité, autorité ecclésiastique et Diatessaron de Tatien, in: Le canon du Nouveau Testament. Regards nouveaux sur l'histoire de sa formation, hg. von G. Aragione/E. Junod/E. Norelli, MoBi 54, Genève 2005, 87-116.

[43] Baum, Echtheit, 105. Seine These übernimmt Bockmuehl, Memories, 128-129.

[44] Zutreffend fragt Hilgenfeld, Petrus-Evangelium, 453, in seiner Argumentation gegen Zahn: „War man schon um 200 so weit gekommen, dass niemand auch nur zu Hause etwas lesen durfte ohne bischöfliche Erlaubnis?"

jetzt richtet der Bischof seine Worte nicht gesondert an eine Gemeindeleitung, sondern an „Brüder" (ἀδελφοῖς); ob er damit die Gemeindeleitung (die Ältesten oder ähnliche), die ganze Gemeinde oder die rechtgläubige Gruppe allein anspricht, wissen wir nicht.[45] Dabei muss aber der besondere Charakter seines Briefes berücksichtigt werden. Eusebius sagt, dass sein Zitat des *Briefs* Serapions aus dessen *Arbeit* „Über das so genannte Petrusevangelium" stammt. Es ist gut möglich, dass unser Kirchenhistoriker so aus einem Brief einen λόγος gemacht hat.[46] Möglich ist aber auch, dass Serapion seinen Brief in den von Eusebius nicht zitierten Punkten zu einer kurzen Abhandlung vertieft hat. Die Abwesenheit der Gemeindeleitung in dieser dogmatisch orientierten Kommunikation ist jedenfalls Indiz dafür, dass Serapion selbst – wenigstens in dieser Situation – keine scharfe Grenze zwischen der Leitung und den Mitgliedern der Gemeinde in Rhossus zog.

Über die Verlesung von Schriften bei den Versammlungen oder Gottesdiensten der kleinen Gemeinden am Ende des 2. Jahrhunderts können wiederum nur gelehrte Vermutungen angestellt werden.[47] Das Amt des Lektors ist aus den Schriften Tertullians (*praescr.* 41) und Hippolyts (*trad. ap.* 1,12) bekannt. In Syrien zeugt hiervon die *Didascalia Apostolorum* (Mitte des 3. Jahrhunderts). Der von der syrischen Übersetzung bestätigte griechische Urtext (*Const. App.* 2,28,5) zeugt von verschiedenen Amtspersonen der Gemeinde, die Anteil an Opfergaben erhalten sollen; auch ein Vorleser, „wenn vorhanden", soll seinen Anteil mit den Presbytern empfangen. So kann gut angenommen werden, dass kleine syrische Gemeinden wie Rhossus am Ende des 2. Jahrhunderts das Amt des Vorlesers noch gar nicht kannten. Trotzdem lässt sich vermuten, dass auch sie einen oder mehrere verdiente Männer hatten, der/die die prophetischen und als apostolisch anerkannten Schriften laut, klar und einfühlsam vorgelesen hat/haben. Nach Justins Zeugnis wurden die Erinnerungen der Apostel und Schriften der Propheten gelesen, „soweit die Zeit reicht" (*1. apol.* 67,3-4). Nach der Lesung folgten die Ermahnung des Vorstehenden und die Abendmahlsfeier. Dionysius, Bischof von Korinth um 170, erwähnt, dass in den Versammlungen der korinthischen Gemeinde der Brief des Clemens gelesen wurde (Eusebius, *h. e.* 4,23,11). Beide Zeugnisse setzen einen recht offenen und freien Gebrauch der Schriften voraus. Das *Fragmentum Muratori* dagegen zeugt für Grenzen, die verschiedene Gruppen im Hinblick auf die öffentliche Lesung gewisser Schriften ziehen wollten. Nach seinem Zeugnis wollten z.B. einige Mitglieder der römischen Gemeinde die *Apokalypse des Petrus* „nicht in der Kirche lesen lassen".[48]

---

[45] Junod, Eusèbe, 9 n. 13, erwägt zwei Alternativen: Entweder schreibt Serapion an die ganze Gemeinde oder an die rechtgläubige Gruppe. Er neigt zur letztgenannten Hypothese.

[46] So Junod, Eusèbe, 5-7.

[47] Zur Geschichte des Vorleseramtes vgl. Gamble, Books, 218-224.

[48] Eine Übersetzung des *Fragmentum Muratori* ist gedruckt in A. Ritter, Alte Kirche. Bd. 1: Kirchen- und Theologiegeschichte in Quellen, hg. v. H.A. Oberman, Neukirchen-Vluyn 1977, 58-60.

Serapion macht in seinem Brief keinen Unterschied zwischen gottesdienstlicher und privater Lesung verschiedener Schriften. Bei seinem Besuch in Rhossus hatte er eine ganz einfache Streitfrage zu lösen: Darf man das von einigen Gemeindemitgliedern bevorzugte, „den Namen Petri führende Evangelium" lesen oder nicht? Da Serapion meinte, dass *alle* Christen in Rhossus den „rechten Glauben" haben, konnte er die Lesung erlauben. Die Frage ist nun, ob ein solcher Ausgangspunkt eine ausschließlich private Lesung implizieren kann. Wenn alle Mitglieder der Gemeinde den rechten Glauben haben, können sie auch ihre Schriften gemeinsam benutzen. Daher ist es nicht besonders glaubwürdig, eine Grenze zwischen öffentlichem und privatem Gebrauch der Schriften zu ziehen. Was privat gebraucht wird, kommt auch in der Öffentlichkeit zum Ausdruck.[49] Die Gemeinde scheint als Kollektiv den Gebrauch der Schriften bei den Versammlungen kontrolliert zu haben. Falls es zu Streitfragen kam, konnte sie sich an ihren Bischof wenden.

Wenn angenommen wird, dass die Christen von Rhossus in ihren Gottesdiensten noch keine maßgebliche Sammlung der vier Evangelien verwendeten, ist es keineswegs verwunderlich, dass das EvPetr aufgrund der Initiative einiger Gemeindemitglieder als Ergänzung der mehr oder weniger etablierten Evangelien gelesen wurde. Seine „Lehre" war ja selbst laut der späteren kritischen Beurteilung durch Serapion weitgehend unanstößig. Der Streit um das EvPetr scheint also aus einer offenen Praxis gottesdienstlicher Schriftlesung erwachsen zu sein.

Weder Scheinmensch noch Märtyrer: Spuren adoptianistischer Christologie im Petrusevangelium

Im Streit um die Christologie des EvPetr wurden schon einige Monate nach der Veröffentlichung des Akhmîm-Fragments folgende Stellen des EvPetr von vielen Forschern als doketisch identifiziert:

EvPetr 10

αὐτός δὲ ἐσιώπα ὡς μηδένα πόνον ἔχων.

EvPetr 19

καὶ ὁ κύριος ἀνεβόησεν λέγων· ἡ δύναμις μου, ἡ δύναμις, κατέλειψάς με. καὶ εἰπὼν ἀνελήφθη.

Diese hoheitlichen Züge des EvPetr haben deutlich etwas damit zu tun, dass der Evangelist Jesus — gegen den Sprachgebrauch der kanonischen Evangelien — nirgends als Ἰησοῦς oder als Χριστός, sondern durchgehend als ὁ κύριος und ὁ υἱὸς τοῦ θεοῦ bezeichnet. Von den übrigen christologischen Titeln verwendet er nur einmal ὁ σωτήρ (13; im Munde des reuigen Übeltäters) und ὁ βασιλεὺς τοῦ Ἰσραήλ (7 und 11, durch die jüdische Volksmenge).

---

49   So auch Junod, Eusèbe 10 n. 18.

Es war aber schon den ersten Interpreten des Akhmîm-Fragments klar, dass die Christologie des EvPetr keineswegs durchgängig als doketisch gekennzeichnet werden kann.[50] Ebenso deutlich war, dass die Kirchenväter in unterschiedlichen Zusammenhängen von verschiedenen „Doketen" geschrieben hatten. Dieser Terminus konnte als ein Sammelbegriff für solche Häretiker verwendet werden, die die Inkarnation und das volle Menschsein Christi bestritten. Als Doketen im engeren Sinne seien dagegen nur solche Lehrer des 2. Jahrhunderts zu bezeichnen, die nur von einer scheinbaren menschlichen Gestalt und einem Scheinleiden Jesu ausgingen. Der „Herr" des EvPetr ist bestimmt keine solche Scheingestalt – zu eindeutig und konkret spricht der Evangelist vom Leib des Herrn in den Episoden vor und nach seinem Tod. Kein konsequenter Doket hätte beschrieben, wie die Nägel aus den Händen des toten Jesus gezogen werden (EvPetr 21).[51]

Trotzdem gab es schon 1893 profilierte Versuche, die Christologie des EvPetr im Lichte doketisch genannter Texte zu verstehen. Besonders H.B. Swete sah in einigen Stücken der valentinianischen Fragmente des Clemens von Alexandrien deutliche Parallelen zu den christologischen Vorstellungen des EvPetr. In *exc. Thdot.* 4 wird der Herr als im Fleisch erschienenes „Licht" beschrieben und als „Kraft des Vaters" bezeichnet. Laut *exc. Thdot.* 18 hatte er nach seiner Auferstehung den Gerechten unter den Entschlafenen das Evangelium verkündigt, während in Kap. 42 das Kreuz als ein kosmisches Zeichen bezeichnet wird. Das vierte Zitat, *exc. Thdot.* 61-62, wurde zur Schüsselparallele für EvPetr 19: Beide Texte sollen laut Swete eine ähnliche doketische Christologie widerspiegeln. In diesem Passus wird erklärt, dass Jesus sterben musste, weil das Pneuma, das bei der Taufe im Jordan auf ihn herabgestiegen war, von ihm geschieden war. Nicht der *Sotēr*, sondern nur der psychische Jesus starb am Kreuz, nachdem die *Zoē* ihn verlassen hatte. Der *Sotēr* aber vernichtete den Tod, der den psychischen Leib Jesu in seiner Macht hatte, und ließ ihn auferstehen. Swete nimmt daher vorsichtig an, dass das EvPetr von der valentinianischen Schule beeinflusst war.[52]

---

[50] McCant, Gospel, 259 fasst meines Erachtens die Theorien der älteren Forschung zum Doketismus in zu einfacher Weise zusammen. Ihm zufolge war Doketismus „an explicit effort to protect the person of Jesus from involvement in matter and suffering", „its main tenet being the non-corporeality of the Lord."

[51] Robinson, Gospel, 21 n. 4: „We must distinguish these early Docetae from the later heretics, who denied the reality of Christ's body ..." Lods, Évangile, 53-54, kennzeichnet Doketismus als „maladie commune" des katholischen und gnostischen Christentums im 2. Jahrhundert. Ihm zufolge ist der Doketismus des EvPetr inkonsequent: Trotz seines naiven Doketismus interessiert sich der Verfasser des Evangeliums für die historischen und materiellen Züge der Ereignisse (ibid., 57-59).

[52] Swete, ΕΥΑΓΓΕΛΙΟΝ, xli, sieht in EvPetr 19; 39-42 und *exc. Thdot.* 4; 18; 42; 61-62 „the same distinction between the Impassible Christ and the Passible; in both the Power from above leaves the Lord at His death; in both there is a Resurrection effectuated by an external agency and apparently not extending to the natural body. Both again are characterized by the prominence which is given to the Cross and to the Preaching to the Dead, although neither of these particulars is worked out by the two writers. On the whole, while the evidence does not justify us in regarding the Petrine writer as a Valentinian, there is reason to suppose that he has

Theodor Zahn akzeptierte dieselben Paralleltexte wie Swete, wollte aber darüber hinaus die Auswirkung der valentinianischen Schule in Antiochien nachweisen. Nach seiner Deutung ist die δύναμις eine im Herrn wohnende höhere Kraft, der obere Christus, der vom Kreuz in den Himmel fährt. Der untere Christus dagegen bleibt am Kreuz, wird auferstehen und in der Hölle das Evangelium verkündigen.[53] Laut Zahn ist das EvPetr „einige Zeit vor Entstehung der wahrscheinlich von Cassian um 170 gestifteten Sekte der Doketen, etwa um 140 oder 150, in Antiochien in einem Kreise entstanden, welcher mit der orientalischen Schule Valentins entweder identisch oder innig verwandt war." Diese Doketen schrieben ihr Evangelium Petrus zu, dem ersten Bischof in Antiochien, und wollten damit der Alleinherrschaft der vier Evangelien entgegentreten, diese trotzdem aber nicht verdrängen.[54] Hans von Schubert dagegen rechnete mit einem Einfluss der von Hippolyt beschriebenen Doketen (*haer.* 8,8-11) auf das EvPetr. Diese Lehrer stellten sich die Göttlichkeit des Herrn als eine δύναμις vor und spekulierten damit, dass Jesus zwei Körper hatte, einen menschlichen und einen geistlichen (*haer.* 8,10,6-8). Der Doketismus des EvPetr sei von diesem Hintergrund her als „eine gesteigerte Veräußerlichung des Wunderglaubens" zu verstehen, in dem der geschichtliche Jesus letzten Endes völlig in den κύριος übergangen ist.[55]

Diese und andere doketische Parallelen wurden schon 1893 von einigen Autoren zurückgewiesen.[56] Vor allem aber hat Léon Vaganay in seinem Kommentar aus dem Jahr 1930 eine zusammenfassende Argumentation gegen die doketischen Theorien vorgelegt.[57] Ihm zufolge ist das EvPetr keine doketische Schrift, seine Tendenz ist vielmehr apologetisch und von kindlichem Mirakelglauben gefärbt. Daher muss das EvPetr als ein Produkt des volkstümlichen Christentums betrachtet werden.[58] In ihrer Kommentierung zum EvPetr folgt Maria Grazia Mara (1972 und 2002) weitgehend der Interpretation Vaganays, setzt aber die Theologie des Pseudo-Petrus in einen weiteren Rahmen. Ihr zufolge ist der Verfasser des EvPetr kein Fälscher der historischen Wahrheit, sondern ein einfacher und trotzdem tiefsinniger Apologet und Lehrer, dessen Interpretation der Evangelientradition und des AT in den Grenzen großkirchlicher Theologie bleibt.[59] Gewisse doketische Züge im EvPetr seien jedoch nicht auszuschließen. Mara interpretiert EvPetr 10 im Lichte der messianischen Prophetie und der apologetischen Tendenz, die

---

felt the influence of the Valentinian school." Mara, Évangile, 137-138; eadem, Vangelo, 73-74, findet den Parallelismus mit *exc. Thdot.* 61,6-7 zutreffend, betont aber, dass in EvPetr 19 der Evangelist den Tod des Herrn als seine Verherrlichung beschreibt.

[53] Zahn, Evangelium, 174-177.
[54] Zahn, Evangelium, 218. Vgl. auch Hilgenfeld, Petrus-Evangelium, 447-448.
[55] Schubert, Composition 46-47. 170-172.
[56] P. Semeria, L'Évangile de Pierre, RB 3, 1894, 522-560, bes. 524; J. MacPherson, The Gospel of Peter, ET 5, 1893/4, 556-561, bes. 560.
[57] Vaganay, Évangile, 112-118.
[58] Vaganay, Évangile, 118-122.
[59] Mara, Évangile, 28-33; eadem, Vangelo, 15.

Schmerzunempfindlichkeit des Christus als ein Element seiner Göttlichkeit darzustellen. Das Wort ἀνελήφθη in EvPetr 19 beschreibe nicht den Tod des Herrn, sondern präsentiere durch die Himmelfahrt der δύναμις die Erhöhung des Herrn in seiner Erniedrigung.[60]

In seiner gründlichen Studie zur theologiegeschichtlichen Stellung des EvPetr platziert Jürgen Denker unser Evangelium in die Frühgeschichte des Doketismus. Die Christologie des EvPetr müsse in ihrem Gesamt gedeutet werden, und in diesem Rahmen erweise sich das EvPetr als ein judenchristliches Dokument. Der *Descensus ad inferos* sei ein judenchristliches und kein gnostisches Thema. Mit der Hadesfahrt und Hadespredigt zeige der Evangelist ein besonderes Interesse am Schicksal der Entschlafenen. Laut Denker gehe sowohl die Vorstellung vom übernatürlichen Kreuz Christi als auch von den riesigen Engeln und dem riesigen Christus auf das Judenchristentum zurück. In einigen Kreisen habe diese judenchristliche, angelomorphe Christologie die Konsequenz des Doketismus nach sich gezogen. Das EvPetr könne in die Frühgeschichte des Doketismus eingeordnet werden, seine Christologie aber habe nichts mit Gnostizismus zu tun.[61] Obwohl Denker eine doketische Deutung von EvPetr 19 ablehnt, hält er es trotzdem für notwendig anzunehmen, der Verfasser des Evangeliums lasse an dieser Stelle in irgendeiner Weise die Einheit des Herrn zerbrechen. Vielleicht meine er damit nur, dass die Lebenskraft den Herrn im Augenblick des Todes verlasse. Letzten Endes sei das Wort ἀνελήφθη aber ein euphemistischer Ausdruck für den Tod Jesu.[62]

Viele neuere Studien dagegen widersprechen entschlossen der Annahme einer doketischen Christologie im EvPetr. Laut Jerry McCant wird die Leidensempfindlichkeit Jesu in EvPetr 10 nicht verneint, während in EvPetr 19 δύναμις nur als Umschreibung des Gottesnamens zu verstehen ist. Weiter sei der Ausdruck ἀνελήφθη ein keineswegs doketisch zu deutender Euphemismus für den Tod „des Herrn". Der Gebrauch des Kyriostitels, besonders in EvPetr 21, sei dagegen eher antidoketisch zu verstehen.[63] John D. Crossan und Peter M. Head argumentieren ähnlich wie McCant und gehen noch ein Stück weiter. In EvPetr 10 schweige Jesus *trotz* seines Leidens,[64] und EvPetr 19 sei reiner Euphemismus für den Tod Jesu.[65]

Das Problem scheint also erledigt. Das EvPetr enthält keine Spur doketischer Christologie, wurde später aber wohl in gewissen doketischen Kreisen verwendet. Besonders Jürgen Denker hat überzeugend aufgezeigt,

---

[60] Mara, Évangile, 105-111. 132-140. 218-219; eadem, Vangelo, 55-59. 70-75. Der nächst liegende doketische Paralleltext ist *exc. Thdot.* 61,6-7.

[61] Denker, Stellung, 93-96. 96-99. 102-106. 111-118.

[62] Denker, Stellung, 119-120.

[63] McCant, Gospel, 259-268.

[64] Crossan, Cross, 180; Head, Christology, 211-213.

[65] Crossan, Cross 220-223, bes. 223: „In any case, as with Power, so also with taken up, we are dealing with simple euphemisms …"; Head, Christology, 213-215, bes. 215: „… there is no clear indication that it [ἀνελήφθη] could refer to an ascension."

dass unser Evangelium keineswegs gnostisch, sondern eher vom juden-christlichen Hintergrund her zu verstehen ist. Der Körper Jesu wird im EvPetr sowohl mit realistisch-menschlichen als auch mit übernatürlichen Zügen versehen.

Zu EvPetr 10: Der Streit um die angemessene Interpretation dieses Verses kreiste seit 1892 um zwei Übersetzungsmöglichkeiten. Für einige Autoren ist der „Herr" des Petrusevangeliums eine doketische Gestalt, die am Kreuz schweigt, weil sie keine Schmerzen hat.[66] In ihrer Übersetzung des Verses wiesen andere einen solchen Doketismus vollkommen zurück: Der Herr schwieg, *als hätte er keine Schmerzen*. So weist das Wörtchen ὡς auf die asketische Dulderkraft des Herrn.[67] Wo die Abhängigkeit des EvPetr von den kanonisch gewordenen Evangelien angenommen wird, wird gefolgert, dass das Schweigemotiv aus der Verhörszene (Mk 14,61 par. Mt 26,63) entwickelt ist, aus der es in martyriologischem Sinn auf die Kreuzigung Jesu übertragen wurde.[68] Diese Vermutung ist aber nicht unproblematisch, weil das Schweigemotiv in Jes 53,7 und 50,7 gerade im Zusammenhang des Leidens begegnet.[69] In EvPetr 10 geht es zweifellos um die Erfüllung der Prophetie, und zur martyriologischen Deutung des Verses gibt es eine Parallele im *Martyrium des Polykarp* 8,3. Polykarp, der sich hartnäckig weigert, dem Kaiser zu opfern, wird nach dem letzten, gescheiterten Überredungsversuch gestoßen, so dass er beim Absteigen vom Wagen sein Schienbein verletzt. Er aber geht in das Stadion, als wäre ihm nichts widerfahren (ὡς οὐδὲν πεπονθώς).[70] Diese Parallele ist aber nicht ganz zutreffend. Etwas zugespitzt kann gesagt werden, dass das EvPetr „gar nicht an einer martyriologischen Darstellung des Geschicks und Todes Jesu interessiert" ist.[71] Bei der Misshandlung (EvPetr 6-9) und Kreuzigung (EvPetr 10-22) geht es eher um einen grellen Kontrast zwischen dem Herrn und seinen Mördern.[72] In der Kreuzigungsgeschichte des EvPetr geht die antijüdische Darstellung Hand in Hand mit dem christologischen Motiv. In EvPetr 5 übergibt Herodes den Herrn dem Volk (τῷ λαῷ), also der jüdischen Volksmenge, die ihn misshandelt, verspottet (EvPetr 6-9) und kreuzigt (EvPetr 10). Als ein Mitgekreuzigter die Unschuld Jesu verkündigt (EvPetr 13), lässt das Volk seine Schenkel ungebrochen, damit er unter Qualen

---

[66] So z.B. Hilgenfeld, Petrus-Evangelium, 447.
[67] So z.B. Robinson, Gospel, 19; Harnack, Bruchstücke, 20. 64.
[68] Brown, Death, 2:951.
[69] Laut Crossan, Cross, 174-187, ist das Schweigemotiv in EvPetr 10 – wie in 1Petr 2,22-24 – konform mit dem ursprünglichen Gebrauch der Prophetie – anders als die synoptischen Darstellungen, die das Schweigen Jesu als Reaktion auf die Anklage im Verhör schildern.
[70] So besonders McCant, Gospel, 261-262; Crossan, Cross, 180-181; Head, Christology, 212-213; Brown, Death, 2:1338.
[71] Denker, Stellung, 120.
[72] Denker, Stellung, 120, setzt seine Analyse weniger überzeugend fort: „Es [das EvPetr] stellt Christus nicht als einen heroischen Dulder dar, eher vielmehr als einen, der bereits tot ist, vgl z.B. die vorgezogene Bitte des Joseph." Das geht zu weit. Gegen Denker betont McCant, Gospel, 261, richtig, dass beispielsweise EvPetr 13 einen deutlichen Unterschied zwischen der gerechten Strafe der Mitgekreuzigten und der ungerechten Tötung des Herrn macht.

stirbt (EvPetr 14).[73] Schließlich versuchen „die Juden", den „Herrn" zu
vergiften (EvPetr 15-16),[74] erfüllen so alles „und machen das Maß der Sünden
über ihrem Haupt voll" (EvPetr 17). Es ist sehr schwierig, diesen aus
traditionellen Elementen eigenartig gestalteten Erzählfaden anders als höchst
antijüdisch zu deuten.[75] Gegen diesen Hintergrund ist Jesus als κύριος, als
„göttlicher Mensch" dargestellt. Die menschlichen Züge Jesu in der Darstellung kommen aus der Passionstradition, und unser Evangelist hat sie als
den Ausgangspunkt seiner Darstellung genommen. Das Schweigemotiv
unterstreicht an dieser Stelle, wie unberührt der Herr von seinen geistlich
blinden und besessenen Mördern bleibt. Er schweigt, aber die göttlichen
Zeichen, die Finsternis (EvPetr 15), das Zerreißen des Tempelvorhangs (EvPetr
20) und das Erdbeben (EvPetr 21) beweisen die Verstockung des Volkes und
das Gericht, das ihm vorgesehen ist. In EvPetr 25 wird nicht die
Reuebereitschaft des Volkes und seiner Führer beschrieben, sondern
ausgedrückt, wie sie alle zu spät ihr ungeheures Verbrechen zur Kenntnis
nehmen. Sie sehen jetzt, dass Jerusalem wegen ihrer Sünde zerstört werden
wird.[76]

In seinem Zusammenhang gibt EvPetr 10 keine Antwort auf die Frage, ob
der Herr Schmerz *empfunden* hat oder nicht. Eher wird klar, dass das
mordsüchtige Volk an seinem Gesicht keine Spur von den unmenschlichen
Schmerzen eines Gekreuzigten sehen konnte. Selbst wenn das Wort ὡς in
EvPetr 10 kausal zu übersetzen ist, muss der Satz nicht unbedingt doketisch
interpretiert werden. Umgekehrt ist es problematisch anzunehmen, dass unser
Evangelist den „Herrn" hier als Märtyrer darstellen will. Vielmehr wird dieser
gerade als auf übernatürliche Weise Herr der Situation beschrieben. Eigentlich
müsste er vor seinen Folterern und Mördern aus Pein und Verzweiflung
schreien, er aber schweigt. Genau das zeigt seine göttliche Macht. Wenn er in

---

[73] Obwohl die zornige Reaktion des Volkes auf die Worte des reuigen Mitgekreuzigten folgt, ist
es natürlicher zu vermuten, dass der Verfasser den Herrn meint, wenn er sagt, dass seine
„Schenkel nicht gebrochen wurden, damit er unter Qualen sterbe." So auch z.B. Harnack,
Bruchstücke, 20, und Mara, Évangile, 120. Laut Vaganay, Évangile, 242, und Crossan, Cross,
172, weisen diese Worte auf den reuigen Mitgekreuzigten hin.

[74] Eine einleuchtende Funktion hat die Tränkung Jesu in diesem Zusammenhang nicht. Das
Volk will den Tod Jesu beschleunigen, weil es wegen der Finsternis unruhig geworden ist:
„Denn es steht ihnen geschrieben, die Sonne dürfe nicht über einem Getöteten untergehen."
Das EvPetr ist in dieser Deutung näher am Sinn von Ps 69,21 als Mk 15,35 und Mt 27,48.
Hierzu auch McCant, Gospel, 264-265.

[75] Laut Denker, Stellung, 81-82, ist die Darstellung des Evangelisten eher apologetisch orientiert.
In EvPetr 25 macht der Evangelist einen Unterschied zwischen dem Volk und seinen Führern
und hofft noch auf Reue und Umkehr einzelner Juden.

[76] In EvPetr 23 freuen sich die Juden, weil der Leib Jesu trotzdem vor dem Sonnenuntergang
begraben werden kann. Die fromme Tat Josefs hilft ihnen, ihre „abergläubische"
Gesetzespraxis aufrecht zu erhalten. Für Ps-Petrus können die Juden erst nach dem Vollzug
der schon in EvPetr 3-5 vorangekündigten Grablegung Jesu ihre schreckliche Tat und deren
dramatische Folgen erkennen. Wichtig ist, dass dies allzu spät passiert; daher erscheint der
Erzählfaden in EvPetr so schwerfällig.

EvPetr 19 nicht mehr schweigt, ruft er nicht aus Verzweiflung, sondern stellt nur fest, dass seine Kraft ihn verlassen hat.[77]

Zu EvPetr 19: EvPetr gehört zur selben Szene wie EvPetr 10. Der Evangelist beschreibt hier den Tod des Herrn und lässt das Zerreißen des Tempelvorhangs als göttliches Zeichen für die künftige Zerstörung des Tempels unmittelbar danach folgen. Der Tod selbst wird auf jeden Fall euphemistisch beschrieben. Der eigenartige Ausruf Jesu basiert auf einer umschreibenden Deutung des Psalmzitats: statt אלי von Mk 15,34 par. Mt 27,46 steht hinter dem Ruf Jesu in EvPetr 19 der Ausdruck טלי, ähnlich wie in der Übersetzung des Aquila ἰσχυρέ μου, ἰσχυρέ μου (Eusebius, d. e. 10,8,9). Dahinter steckt eine Exegese, die die Worte von Ps 22,2 als prophetisch anerkennen will, nicht aber so, wie Markus und Matthäus sie überliefert haben. Gegen die doketische Deutung von EvPetr 19 haben heutzutage einige Autoren angenommen, das Wort δύναμις umschreibe lediglich den Gottesnamen; mehr habe auch der Evangelist nicht andeuten wollen.[78]

Aber wollte der Verfasser des EvPetr das harte Wort über die Gottverlassenheit in EvPetr 19 wirklich mit einer derartigen Umschreibung des Gottesnamens abmildern? In der einzigen christlichen Parallele, die irgendwie für diese These sprechen würde, Mk 14,62 par. Mt 26,64, gebraucht Jesus die Umschreibung des Gottesnamens in einem Satz, der vor dem Synhedrium seine künftige Erhöhung ankündigt und so zur Anklage wegen Gotteslästerung führt. Für EvPetr 19 dagegen scheint es einleuchtender anzunehmen, dass der Evangelist – oder schon die ihm bekannte Tradition – die gesamte Idee der Gottverlassenheit „des Herrn" zurückgewiesen hat.[79] Ihm zufolge hat König David ursprünglich vorausgesagt, dass die dem Herrn innewohnende übernatürliche Kraft ihn am Kreuz verlassen werde; als „Lebenskraft" lässt sich δύναμις in der Evangelientradition nirgends verstehen. Unser Evangelist hätte – wie Lukas und Johannes – das anstößige alte christliche Schriftzeugnis einfach beseitigen können; stattdessen wollte er darstellen, wie das Zeugnis ursprünglich gelautet habe. Wie das Werfen des Loses über den Kleidern (EvPetr 12; Ps 22,19) und vielleicht auch das Ziehen der Nägel aus den Händen Jesu (EvPetr 21; Ps 22,17) beweist, hat der Evangelist Ps 22 durchaus als Prophetie über das Leiden des Messias akzeptiert.[80]

---

77 Harnack, Bruchstücke, 66, interpretiert den Ausruf Jesu als eine Frage, da im syrischen Ohr *lema* einfach als Einführung zur Frage verstanden wurde. Laut Harnack hat die griechische Vorlage des EvPetr die Worte *„eli eli lema sabaktani"* ohne griechische Übersetzung bieten können.

78 Denker, Stellung, 74 („eine apologetische Aussage über den Herrn"); McCant, Gospel, 263-265; Crossan, Cross, 220-222 („a simple euphemism"); Head, Christology, 214.

79 Mit Harnack, Bruchstücke, 65: „… er [der Evangelist] hat, um das Odium der Gottverlassenheit Jesu zu tilgen, das ἠλεί mit Bewusstsein missverstanden."

80 Bei den Gnostikern und ihren orthodoxen Gegnern war die Deutung von Ps 22,2 mit etwas andersartigen Problemen verbunden. Die Rezeption von Mk 15,34 par. Mt 27,46 hat den orthodoxen Lehrern des 2. Jahrhunderts Schwierigkeiten bereitet. Codex Bezae und die ihm folgenden Handschriften (samt Porphyrius, *C. Chr. Fr.* 15; A. von Harnack, Porphyrius. Gegen

Falls der Ausruf des Herrn in EvPetr 19 als Euphemismus der Gottverlassenheit gedeutet wird, muss der zweite Satz des Verses als Euphemismus seines Todes bzw. als Hingabe seiner Lebenskraft interpretiert werden.[81] Auch diese Annahme ist problematisch. Nirgends in der klassischen griechischen Literatur bedeutet ἀναλαμβάνομαι „sterben" oder ἀνάλημψις „Tod".[82] In jüdischen und christlichen Texten gibt es eigentlich nur zwei Stellen, in denen diese Übersetzung plausibel erscheint. In den *Psalmen Salomos* 4,18 beschreibt der Ausdruck εἰς ἀνάλημψιν den Tod, kann aber kaum als Euphemismus gedeutet werden, da dieses Stück das Geschick eines Gottlosen als seine *Wegnahme* durch den Tod beschreibt. Weiter wird in den pseudoklementinischen Homilien festgestellt, dass das Gesetz μετὰ τὴν Μωυσέως ἀνάλημψιν nicht von Moses selbst, sondern von einem anderen geschrieben wurde (*Hom. Clem.* 3,47,1). Obwohl hier vom Tode des Moses die Rede sein kann,[83] kann der Ausdruck ebenso gut auf die Wegnahme, das heißt die Himmelfahrt des Moses hinweisen. Als Begründung der Feststellung (3,47,2) wird Dtn 34,5-6 zitiert: Moses starb und wurde begraben, und „niemand kennt sein Grab bis auf diesen Tag." Falls unser Evangelist in EvPetr 19 den Tod Jesu euphemistisch umschreiben wollte, ist es nicht erklärbar, warum er keinen der traditionellen Begriffe, dies auszudrücken, verwendete: ἐξέπνευσεν (Mk 15,37; ein geläufiger Ausdruck); ἀφῆκεν τὸ πνεῦμα (Mt 27,50; vgl. Gen 35,18; 1Esr 4,21); Πάτερ, εἰς χεῖρα σου παρατίθεμαι τὸ πνεῦμά μου. τοῦτο δὲ εἰπὼν ἐξέπνευσεν (Lk 23,46; vgl. Ps 31,6; Apg 7,59); κλίνα τὴν κεφαλὴν παρέδωκεν τὸ πνεῦμα (Joh 19,30). In der mirakelfreudigen Beschreibung der pseudopetrinischen Passionsgeschichte macht EvPetr 19 gerade keinen „euphemistischen" Eindruck. Warum gerade diese Verbindung von δύναμις und ἀναλήφθη statt eines klaren und unmissverständlichen Euphemismus? Andererseits ist die Beschreibung des Todes Jesu in EvPetr 19 zu knapp, um entwickelte Christologie

---

die Christen, Berlin 1916) haben hier den Text ὁ θεός μου ὁ θεός μού εἰς τί ὠνείδισάς με. Dieses Problem wird von B.D. Ehrman eingehend behandelt. Vgl. idem, The Orthodox Corruption of Scripture: The Effect of Early Christological Controversies on the Text of the New Testament, New York-Oxford 1993, 143-145. Laut Ehrman konnten die Gnostiker die Gottverlassenheit des irdischen Jesus zugunsten ihrer Separationschristologie interpretieren. Dagegen fühlten sich einige orthodoxe Lehrer gedrängt, den Psalmvers umzuschreiben. Das würde auch im Kontext einen mehr erträglichen Sinn haben: Wenn Jesus von seinen Feinden beschimpft wurde, wurde er auch von Gott beschimpft. Ähnlich ist auch der Vorschlag von Brown, Death, 2:1055: „My God, My God, why have you (allowed their having) mocked me?"

81   Crossan, Cross, 222-223 („a simple euphemism"), und Head, Christology, 215. Head räumt ein, dass in einigen Betrachtungsweisen Himmelfahrt und Euphemismus für den Tod vermischt sein können. Denker, Stellung, 74 („euphemistischer Ausdruck"). 119-120. McCant, Gospel, 265-267, rechnet mit einer undoketischen Himmelfahrt, obwohl nicht ganz deutlich wird, was er damit meint (266): „It should be noted, that ἀναλαμβάνειν may mean ascension without a denial of death ... Certainly the ascension is not necessarily a docetic conception and does not preclude death." McCant hält auch "Cerinthianism" in EvPetr 19 für ausgeschlossen (ibid., 267).

82   Dagegen bedeutet ἀνάληψις u.a. Genesung, z.B. bei Hippokrates, *Aph.* 4.27 und Platon, *Tim.* 83e.

83   W. Bauer, Griechisch-deutsches Wörterbuch zu den Schriften des Neuen Testaments und der frühchristlichen Literatur, bearb. von K. und B. Aland, Berlin-New York ⁶1988, 112.

widerzuspiegeln. Es lässt sich fragen, ob der Verfasser wirklich ausdrücken wollte, dass die Jesus innewohnende übernatürliche Kraft ihn verlässt und in den Himmel aufgenommen wird. Einige Forscher haben die doketische Theorie abgelehnt, aber die in EvPetr 19 von den Herrn ausgehende δύναμις im Rahmen volkstümlicher christlicher Vorstellungen interpretiert.[84] Trotzdem wird nicht klar, was das im EvPetr konkret bedeutet und welche Funktion eine solche „Himmelfahrt" im Akhmîm-Fragment letzten Endes haben könnte. Die Möglichkeiten und Grenzen dieser Theorie sollen zunächst geprüft werden.

Während die Umschreibung des Gottesnamens im Urchristentum dünn belegt ist, wird mehrmals von der in Jesus innewohnenden Kraft gesprochen. Nach den Evangelisten Markus und Lukas stammt die Wundertätigkeit Jesu aus solcher Kraft,[85] obwohl Jesus auch im Heiligen Geist Wunder wirken kann.[86] Sowohl die Gnostiker als auch die proto-orthodoxen Lehrer des 2. Jahrhunderts haben viel Gewicht auf die Aussage gelegt, dass die Jungfrau Maria bei der Empfängnis Jesu von der Kraft des Höchsten überschattet wurde (Lk 1,35).[87] Die Kraft ist dabei als identisch mit dem Heiligen Geist verstanden.

In der LXX beschreibt das Verb ἀναλαμβάνω die Aufnahme des Elias (2Kön 2,9-11; Sir 48,9) und Henochs (Sir 49,14) in den Himmel. In der christlichen Literatur des 1. und 2. Jahrhunderts wird das Verb in verschiedenen Schriften zur Beschreibung der Himmelfahrt Jesu verwendet,[88] und Lukas bezeichnet die Himmelfahrt als ἀνάλημψις (Lk 9,51).[89] Diese Parallelen helfen aber nicht, EvPetr 19 zu verstehen, da eine Vorstellung der Himmelfahrt Jesu vom Kreuz in den frühesten Traditionen nicht belegbar ist.[90]

Eine Lehre, nach der die Seelen der Christen in der Stunde des Todes in den Himmel aufgenommen werden, wird von Justin (*dial.* 80,4) und Irenäus

---

84 So besonders Vaganay, Évangile, 256.

85 Mk 5,30 par.; Lk 8,46; 5,17; 6,19; vgl. Lk 4,14; 4,36; 9,1.

86 Mt 12,28; Lk 4,18-19; vgl. Lk 4,1.14.

87 Justin, *dial.* 100,5; Irenäus, *adv. haer.* 1,15,3 (über Markus Magos); 3,21,4; 5,1,3 (gegen die Ebioniten); Clemens von Alexandrien, *exc. Thdot.* 60. Zur antignostischen Erweiterung von Lk 1,35 mit ἐκ σου („das Kind, das *von dir* geboren wird") vgl. Ehrman, Corruption, 139-140.

88 Apg 1,2.11.22; Mk 16,19; 1Tim 3,16; Ignatius, *Trall.* 9,4; Ignatius, *Smyrn.* 3,5; *Acta Johannis* 102; Justin, *dial.* 32,3; Irenäus, *adv. haer.* 2,32,3; 3,10,6; 4,34,3.

89 Irenäus, *adv. haer.* 1,10,1.

90 In diesem Zusammenhang interessant ist der Versuch von G. Bertram, Die Himmelfahrt Jesu vom Kreuz und der Glaube an seine Auferstehung, FS A. Deissmann, Tübingen 1927, 187-217. Er plädiert dafür, dass Jesu Auferstehung vom Kreuz für die älteste Form des Auferstehungsglaubens zu halten ist. Er sieht in Mk 2,20 par. Lk 5,35 einen Hinweis auf den Anfang des Fastens unmittelbar nach dem Tode Jesu. Das kommt auch im Hebräerevangelium zum Ausdruck, wenn der fastende Jakobus dem auferstandenen Herrn begegnet. Bei Paulus sprechen für die Auferstehung vom Kreuz Phil 2,5-11 und Röm 5,10. In Mk 14,8 und 1Kor 15,3-7 hebt die Betonung des Begräbnisses hervor, dass Jesus wirklich gestorben ist. Laut Bertram (198) haben wir schon hier „eine der Wurzel dafür, daß in der Kirche allmählich neben dem Glauben an den Erhöhten sich mehr und mehr der Glaube an den Auferstandenen durchsetzte." In EvPetr werden zwei unterschiedliche Vorstellungen kombiniert (203-204): Jesu Erhöhung vom Kreuz und – als sekundäre, apologetische Legende – seine Himmelfahrt vom Grabe. Vaganay, Évangile, 257, weist die Vermutung des primitiven Elements von EvPetr 19 zurück.

(*adv. haer.* 5,31,1) mit strengen Worten zurückgewiesen. In seinen Zeugnissen über gnostische Lehrer bietet Irenäus etliche Beispiele adoptianistischer (bzw. possessionistischer) Christologie, der zufolge Christus bei der Taufe auf Jesus herabgestiegen sei und seinen Körper vor dem Tode am Kreuz wieder verlassen habe. Laut Irenäus hätten die Valentinianer gelehrt, dass bei der Taufe „der vom Pleroma des Alls abstammende Heiland" in Gestalt einer Taube auf den seelischen Jesus hinabgestiegen sei (*adv. haer.* 1,7,2). Weiter habe eine ungenannte gnostische Gruppe ihre adoptianistische Christologie damit begründet, dass Jesus weder vor seiner Taufe noch nach seiner Auferstehung von den Toten etwas Besonderes getan habe (1,30,14). Besonders interessant in unserem Zusammenhang sind aber Karpokrates (1,25), Kerinth (1,26,1) und die Ebioniten (1,26,2), die Irenäus etwas eigenartig als Vorgänger der Valentinianer darstellt. Nach Karpokrates hatte Jesus, der von Josef gezeugt und den Menschen gleich war, eine starke und reine Seele. Deshalb habe der oberste Gott ihr eine Kraft von oben herab gesandt, damit er vor dem Schöpfer der Welt fliehen könne. Nachdem diese Kraft durch das All gegangen und von allem befreit befreit worden sei, sei sie zum obersten Gott hinaufgestiegen. Durch Kräfte, die er empfangen hatte, habe Jesus auch seine Leidenschaften vernichtet (1,25,1). Kerinth dagegen, der die Jungfrauengeburt ablehnte, habe gelehrt, dass Jesus in Gerechtigkeit, Klugheit und Weisheit allen anderen Menschen überlegen war und dass Christus nach der Taufe in Gestalt einer Taube auf ihn herabgestiegen sei. Beim Tod habe der pneumatische und leidensunfähige Christus Jesus verlassen, und Jesus sei später auferstanden.[91]

An anderer Stelle habe ich dafür plädiert, dass Kerinth ursprünglich kein Gnostiker war.[92] Erstens stellten sowohl Irenäus als auch die von ihm verwendete Tradition die meisten so genannten Häretiker als Gnostiker dar. Wie die oben genannten Beispiele zeigen, konnten die gnostischen Lehrer das Grundschema der adoptianistischen Christologie unterschiedlich in ihre eigenen Spekulationen integrieren. Zweitens steht Kerinth, der zur Zeit Trajans in Asia gewirkt haben soll, allzu vereinzelt und früh da, um ein überzeugender Bahnbrecher demiurgistischer Theologie gewesen zu sein. Drittens spricht eine starke Tradition dafür, dass Kerinth Chiliast war[93] – ein wenig glaubwürdiger Zug in der Lehre eines Gnostikers.

---

[91] In seiner Würdigung der doketischen Parallelen zu EvPetr 19 wies Swete, ΕΥΑΓΓΕΛΙΟΝ, xxxix, die Texte über Kapokrates und Kerinth zurück, da das EvPetr dieselben Ideen in einer späteren, komplizierteren und entwickelteren Form repräsentiere. Bei Karpokrates und Kerinth ist Jesus mehr menschlich – Swete spricht vom „humanitarianism" dieser Lehrer – als im EvPetr. Darüber hinaus zeigen die judaisierenden Zügen bei Kerinth, dass er keinen direkten Einfluss auf EvPetr gehabt haben kann.

[92] Zu den folgenden Argumenten siehe M. Myllykoski, Cerinthus, in: A Companion to Second-Century Christian Heretics, ed. by A. Marjanen/P. Luomanen, VigChr.S 76, Leiden 2005, 213-246.

[93] Eusebius vermittelt die Zeugnisse des römischen Gaius vom Ende des 2. Jahrhunderts (*h. e.* 3,28,1-2) und des Dionysius, der um 247-264 als Bischof Alexandriens in der Mitte des 3. Jahrhunderts tätig war (3,28,3-4; vgl. 7,25).

In der Darstellung des Irenäus wird die Lehre der Ebioniten über Christus als ähnlich der des Karpokrates und des Kerinth bezeichnet. Die ursprüngliche Version findet sich allerdings nicht in der lateinischen Fassung des Irenäus-Werkes, die hier auf einer Fehlinterpretation beruht (*adv. haer.* 1,26,2: *Dominum non non similiter ut Cerinthus et Carpocrates opinantur*), sondern der griechische Urtext des Hippolyt, der den Satz bei Irenäus exakt vermittelt (*haer.* 7,34: τὰ δὲ περὶ τὸν Χριστὸν ὁμοίως τῷ Κηρίνθῳ καὶ Καρποκράτει μυθεύουσιν). Es ist mehr als eine Vermutung, dass diese Bemerkung nicht nur auf das reine Menschsein Jesu, sondern auch auf die adoptianistische Christologie hinweist – und zwar ohne den demiurgistischen Rahmen der Tradition über Kerinth. Das Ebionäerevangelium zeigt, dass die Ebioniten nicht den Christus, sondern den Geist als das herabkommende und heraufsteigende Element verstanden haben (Epiphanius, *haer.* 30,13,7).[94]

Von der Aufnahme von Jesu Geist vom Kreuz in den Himmel ist selten die Rede, obwohl die Ebioniten wahrscheinlich diese Vorstellung in die letzten Worten Jesu in Mt 27,50 (ἀφῆκεν τὸ πνεῦμα) hineingelesen haben.[95] Diese Idee taucht in der Tat zweimal auf, in der syrischen Übersetzung von Mt 27,50 („und es stieg hinauf sein Geist") und im späten Matthäus-Kommentar des Origenes (140: *Oravit Patrem, et exauditus est, et statim ut clamavit ad Patrem, receptus est aut sicut qui potestatem habebat ponendi animam suam, posuit eam quando voluit ipse ... Miraculum enim erat quoniam post tres horas receptus est*). Es ist verlockend zu vermuten, dass diese oder entsprechende Worte schon im Ebionäerevangelium gestanden haben. Diese Belege weisen auf jeden Fall darauf hin, dass die Idee syrischer Herkunft ist; und EvPetr 19 kommt als ihr ältestes Zeugnis in Frage. Das zu vermutende Entschwinden der Kraft Jesu und ihre Aufnahme in den Himmel muss also keineswegs notwendig eine gnostische bzw. doketische Christologie voraussetzen. Die Vorstellung hinter EvPetr 19 kann vielmehr auch auf eine judenchristliche adoptianistische Christologie zurückgeführt werden.

Ein interessanter Text stammt von Justin, der den Logos[96] und das Wort Jesu[97] als die Kraft Gottes darstellt und sowohl dem Kreuz[98] als auch dem Blut Christi[99] göttliche Kraft zuspricht. Das Gespräch des Justin mit Tryphon über die Taufe Jesu (*dial.* 87-88) öffnet aber eine Frage, die in diesem

---

[94] Zur ebionitischen Christologie vgl. M. Goulder, A Tale of Two Missions, London 1994, 107-113, bes. 110-112.

[95] Goulder, Tale, 112.

[96] *1. apol.* 23,2; 32,9; *dial.* 61,1-3; 105,1; 125,3; 128,2-3; vgl. dazu andere zeitgenössische Schriften, in denen Christus als eine Macht dargestellt wird: Buch des Elchasai (Epiphanius, *haer.* 19,4,1); *Philippus-Akten* 13; *Martyrium des Philippus* 26; *Thomas-Akten* 10,2-3; 27,2.

[97] *1. apol.* 14,5; vgl. *dial.* 69,6. In *dial.* 102,5 beschreibt Justin das Schweigen Jesu vor Pilatus im Lichte von Ps 21,16 (LXX): Die gewaltige Kraft Jesu war wie das Wasser einer kräftigen Quelle in seinem Mund eingedämmt.

[98] *1. apol.* 35,2; 60,5; „Geheimnis der Kraft Gottes": *dial.* 91,1. Daher ist es das größte Symbol der Kraft und Macht Christi (*1. apol.* 55,2,6), und die Kraft Gottes ist im gekreuzigten Christus verborgen (*dial.* 49,8).

[99] *dial.* 54,2.

Zusammenhang wichtig ist. Tryphon fragt (87,2): Wie kann Christus
präexistent gewesen sein, wenn er mit den von Jesaja (Jes 11,1-3) aufgezählten
Kräften des Heiligen Geistes gefüllt wurde? Hat er diese Kräfte nicht schon
vorher gehabt? Justin antwortet: Die Kräfte sind auf Jesus gekommen, nicht
weil er sie nicht schon gehabt hätte, sondern damit sie auf ihm ruhen und an
ihren Endpunkt gelangen würden, denn mit Jesus hat die Prophetie in Israel
aufgehört (*dial.* 87,3). Justin betont, dass Jesus seine Kraft von Geburt an hatte
(88,2; vgl. auch *1. apol.* 33,6). Er geht aber weiter und nimmt auf die Taufe Jesu
sogar zweimal Bezug, in *dial.* 88,3-4 und 88,8, obwohl die Frage Tryphons dies
gar nicht erfordert. Trotz seines Geistbesitzes habe Jesus dreißig Jahre
gewartet, bis Johannes der Täufer als Verkündiger seiner Ankunft aufgetreten
ist. In 88,3-4 hebt Justin zwei mit der Taufe verbundene Elemente hervor: das
Licht im Jordan und das Herabkommen des Geistes auf Jesus. Trotzdem betont
er, dass Jesus die Taufe nicht brauchte. In 88,8 – wie in 103,6 und 122,6 –
tradiert er die Stimme des Vaters durchgehend nach Ps 2,7 in einer Fassung,
die in Lk 3,22 (D) und bei anderen westlichen christlichen Schriftstellern des 2.
Jahrhunderts belegt ist: υἱός μου εἶ· σὺ ἐγὼ σήμερον γεγέννηκά σε. Ohne besonderen Anlass von Seiten Tryphons her und ohne Anspielungen auf gnostische
Lehrer will Justin die Idee abwehren, Jesus habe den Geist erst bei seiner Taufe
erhalten.

Eine andere Frage ist, inwieweit die judenchristliche adoptianistische
Christologie die Erzähllogik des EvPetr strukturiert. In EvPetr 19 wird das
Entschwinden und die Aufnahme der Kraft Jesu vor allem als Erklärung zum
prophetischen Wort in Ps 22,2 gegeben. Für das EvPetr hat Gott den Herrn
nicht verlassen. Nur die übernatürliche Kraft ist von ihm bei seinem Tod
geschieden und in den Himmel aufgenommen worden. Diese Auffassung setzt
eine traditionelle adoptianistische Christologie voraus. Die knappe Formulierung der Szene aber und ihre lose Stellung in dem antijüdisch orientierten
Kreuzigungsbericht sprechen dagegen, dass die adoptianistische Christologie
im EvPetr eine besonders wichtige Rolle gespielt hat. Dass die Taufszenen in
Mk 1,10 und im Ebionäerevangelium vom Herabsteigen des *Geistes* in Jesus
berichten, lässt vermuten, dass das EvPetr in diesem Zusammenhang vom
Herabsteigen der *Kraft* erzählt hat. Möglicherweise hat das ursprüngliche
EvPetr aber auch eine Geschichte über die Empfängnis Marias erzählt (oder
vorausgesetzt), in der „die Kraft des Höchsten" die Jungfrau überschattete (Lk
1,35).

Hinter der Aufnahme in den Himmel in EvPetr 19 schließlich steckt
vielleicht ein sehr einfaches Motiv. Die Kraft oder der Geist Jesu mit ihrem
übernatürlichen Ursprung soll nicht in einer Leiche wohnen, sondern in der
Stunde des Todes in den Himmel zurückkehren.[100] Gegen die Theorie vom
Entschwinden der göttlichen Kraft Jesu in EvPetr 19 ist angeführt worden, dass

---

[100] Vgl. *exc. Thdot.* 61,6: Ἀπέθανεν δὲ ἀποστάντος τοῦ καταβάντος ἐπ᾽ αὐτῷ ἐπὶ τῷ Ἰορδάνῃ Πνεύματος
οὐκ ἴδια γενομένου ἀλλὰ συσταλέντος ἵνα καὶ ἐνεργήσῃ ὁ θάνατος ἐπεὶ πῶς τῆς ζωῆς παρούσης ἐν
αὐτῷ ἀπέθανεν τὸ σῶμα οὕτω γὰρ ἂν καὶ αὐτοῦ τοῦ Σωτῆρος ὁ θάνατος ἐκράτησεν ἂν ὅπερ ἄτοπον.

dem Evangelisten zufolge der Leib Jesu nicht einmal nach dem Tod seinen übernatürlichen Charakter verloren hat.[101] Zuerst schließt unser Evangelist sich an die synoptischen Evangelien an, in denen vom Zerreißen des Vorhangs des Tempels berichtet wird, verbindet aber dann das Erdbeben (Mt 27,51) mit der Kreuzesabnahme: Die ganze Erde erbebt, wenn die Juden den Leib Jesu auf die Erde legen (EvPetr 21). Der Handlungsablauf ist von übernatürlichen Ereignissen bestimmt. Dabei ist aber kaum gemeint, dass der Leib Jesu das Erdbeben verursacht. Das Erdbeben ist ein schreckliches Zeichen der göttlichen Strafe, die noch auf das jüdische Volk kommen wird. Natürlich besteht eine Kontinuität zwischen dem toten Leib und dem Auferstehungsleib Jesu, und der irdische Jesus bleibt κύριος auch nach seinem Tod (EvPetr 21; 24). Die Auferstehung des Herrn vom Grab als kosmische Gestalt rekurriert auf jüdische und judenchristliche Spekulation.[102] Offensichtlich hat die Darstellung dieses vollkommen übernatürlichen Auferstehungsleibes unseren Evangelisten nicht daran gehindert, die Erscheinung des Auferstandenen am See Galiläas zu beschreiben (EvPetr 58-60). Falls diese verlorene Szene ähnlich gelautet hat wie ihre Parallele in Joh 21, hat der Herr seine Jünger zur Mahlzeit eingeladen und mit ihnen gegessen. Weniger doketisch könnte das EvPetr kaum enden.

Zusammenfassende Bemerkungen

Der Brief des Bischofs Serapion an die Gemeinde von Rhossus, zitiert von Eusebius in *h. e.* 6,12, hat eine Vielzahl von Schwierigkeiten für das Verständnis des so genannten Doketismus verursacht. Die Zustimmung, die Serapion bei seinem Besuch für die Verlesung des EvPetr gegeben hatte, spricht dafür, dass die Grenze zwischen „apostolischen" und „pseudepigraphischen" Schriften in der Praxis überhaupt nicht so scharf war, wie Serapion selbst in seinem späteren Brief und Eusebius in seiner Beschreibung des Falles verstehen lassen wollten. Serapion verurteilte das EvPetr erst nach seinem Besuch als Pseudepigraphon, und zwar weil es durch Doketen verwendet wurde. Die Tatsache aber, dass er die Verlesung dieses Evangeliums zunächst offensichtlich problemlos akzeptierte, spricht dafür, dass in Syrien zu seiner Zeit unterschiedliche Evangelien weit verbreitet waren. Serapion begegnete dem EvPetr in Rhossus nicht unbedingt zum ersten Mal. Erst nach seinem Besuch allerdings untersuchte er es genauer – eben weil die Rechtgläubigkeit *seines Inhalts* eine Streitfrage geworden war. Die Rechtgläubigkeit der Christen in Rhossus hatte Serapion gar nicht bezweifelt, in seinem Brief kritisiert er die Leser des EvPetr nur mild, dieses enthalte nur einige Stellen, die zu verwerfen seien. Die Leser des EvPetr in Rhossus sollten daher nicht einfach für Doketen gehalten werden. In Rhossus wurde das EvPetr offensichtlich als Ergänzung zu

---

[101] Brown, Death, 2:1338.
[102] Zu einer angelomorphischen Christologie in EvPetr 39-42 vgl. Denker, Stellung, 102-106.

den allgemein verbreiteten (vier?) Evangelien gelesen. Um einen Vierevangelien*kanon* wird es sich dabei trotzdem kaum gehandelt haben. Aus dem
Brief Serapions lässt sich zudem nicht entnehmen, dass die Christen in Rhossus
um die private Verlesung des EvPetr gestritten hätten. Ich halte es für
wahrscheinlicher, dass das EvPetr bis zum ablehnenden Urteil Serapions *in
ihren Gottesdiensten* gelesen wurde.

Die neuere Forschung hat die alte Theorie vom Doketismus des EvPetr als
verfehlt erwiesen. Das EvPetr ist nicht doketisch, weil der Evangelist beim
„Herrn" keine Leidensunfähigkeit oder Schmerzunempfindlichkeit voraussetzt. Der „Herr" des Akhmîm-Fragments ist aber auch nicht als Märtyrer
gezeichnet. Er ist eher ein Mensch, dem eine übernatürliche Kraft innewohnt
und dessen Tod am Kreuz von übernatürlichen Zeichen begleitet wird. Diese
Zeichen sagen die göttliche Strafe gegen das jüdische Volk und seine Führung
voraus. Das Schweigen „des Herrn" in EvPetr zeugt nicht für seine besondere
Schmerzunempfindlichkeit oder heroische Duldungskraft, sondern für seine
souveräne Macht gegenüber seinen Mördern, deren Wahn keine Wirkung auf
ihn hat. In EvPetr 19 stellt der Herr fest, dass seine Kraft ihn verlassen hat, und
er wird „aufgenommen". Das Wort δύναμις ist keine euphemistische
Umschreibung des Gottesnamens, sondern vor allem eine positive Deutung
der problematischen Gottverlassenheit in der messianischen Prophetie von Ps
22,2. Der Ausdruck ἀνελήφθη ist kein Euphemismus für den Tod des Herrn,
sondern drückt aus, dass seine Kraft in den Himmel gestiegen ist. Die nächst
liegenden Parallelen zu dieser Vorstellung finden sich in der adoptianistischen
Christologie der Ebionäer. Das Ebionäerevangelium berichtet, wie der Geist in
Jesus herabsteigt (Epiphanius, *haer.* 30,13,7) und Irenäus bekräftigt, dass die
Ebionäer über Christus ähnlich wie Kerinth gelehrt haben (*adv. haer.* 1,26,2).
Die „Himmelfahrt" der *Kraft* in EvPetr spricht trotzdem dafür, dass es sich
auch dabei nur um eine entfernte Parallele handelt. Anlehnung an die
adoptianistische Christologie ist nur eines der Mittel, mit denen unser
Evangelist die übernatürlichen Züge des „Herrn" unterstreicht.

Die Pilatusgestalt im Petrusevangelium

Eine erzählanalytische Annäherung

von

HEIKE OMERZU

1. Von Pontius zu Pilatus

Von „Pontius zu Pilatus laufen" oder „geschickt werden" – mit dieser Rede-wendung drückt man umgangssprachlich aus, dass man in einer Angele-genheit – oft bei Behörden – viele, meist erfolglose Wege gehen muss, dass man von einer Stelle zur nächsten verwiesen wird, weil sich niemand zuständig fühlt, um sich dann doch wieder unverrichteter Dinge bei der ersten Instanz einzufinden.[1] Der Ausdruck hat seinen Ursprung in der Passions-überlieferung: Lk 23,1-12 berichtet, wie Jesus vom Präfekten Pontius Pilatus zum Verhör an Herodes Antipas geschickt wird. Dieser verspottet Jesus zwar gemeinsam mit seinen Soldaten, erkennt aber ebenso wenig eine Schuld an ihm wie der römische Statthalter (vgl. Lk 23,14-15), an den er ihn bald darauf zurückschickt.[2]

Während Markus und Matthäus nichts von einer Beteiligung des Herodes Antipas am Prozess Jesu zu wissen scheinen,[3] setzt der einzige Zeuge des apokryphen Petrusevangeliums (EvPetr), der einen längeren zusam-menhängenden Text enthält, P.Cair. 10759,[4] mit der Zusammenarbeit von Pilatus und Herodes ein. Dass in diesem so genannten Akhmîm-Codex nur ein

---

[1] Die weit verbreitete Redensart ist im Deutschen literarisch erstmals 1704 belegt, und zwar im „Fasten-Bancket der Christlichen Seelen" des steirischen Predigers P. Amandus (vgl. L. Röhrich, Art. Pilatus, Lexikon der sprichwörtlichen Redensarten, Freiburg et al. ⁵1991, Bd. 4, 1182-1184).

[2] In manchen Regionen findet sich auch die Wendung „von Herodes zu Pilatus laufen", welche offensichtlich nur auf den zweiten Teil der lukanischen Erzählung rekurriert; vgl. Röhrich, Pilatus, 1183.

[3] Vgl. dazu meine Ausführungen: Das traditionsgeschichtliche Verhältnis der Begegnungen von Jesus mit Herodes Antipas und Paulus mit Agrippa II., SNTU.A 28, 2003, 121-145.

[4] Zum Text vgl. T. Nicklas/T.J. Kraus, Das Petrusevangelium und die Petrusapokalypse. Die griechischen Fragmente mit deutscher und englischer Übersetzung, GCS.NF 11, Neutesta-mentliche Apokryphen 1, Berlin-New York 2004, 32-53; diese kritische Ausgabe wird der vorliegenden Untersuchung zugrunde gelegt, sofern nicht anders vermerkt.

Ausschnitt aus einer ursprünglich umfangreicheren Erzählung vorliegt, zeigt unter anderem der abrupte Anfang mitten im Satz.[5] Entscheidend ist jedoch, dass anders als in der lukanischen Darstellung Jesus im Petrusevangelium von Herodes *nicht* zurück zu Pilatus gesandt wird. Stattdessen gibt er sogar den Exekutions- bzw. Auslieferungsbefehl (EvPetr 2 und 5), für den nach den kanonischen Evangelien übereinstimmend der Statthalter verantwortlich ist (vgl. Mk 15,15; Mt 27,26; Lk 23,25; Joh 19,16). Pilatus wiederum erscheint gegenüber Herodes als Bittsteller für ein ordentliches Begräbnis Jesu (EvPetr 3-4).

Ausgehend von der Beobachtung, dass Jesus im Petrusevangelium also gerade nicht von „Pontius zu Pilatus" geschickt wird, sondern Herodes das Urteil in eigener Verantwortung fällt, stellt sich die Frage nach der Rolle des römischen Statthalters und seiner Gefolgsleute im Petrusevangelium, die im Folgenden näher analysiert werden soll. Da die Verantwortung der *historischen* Gestalt Pontius Pilatus für die Verurteilung und Hinrichtung Jesu auf Grund der Vielzahl unabhängiger, auch nicht christlicher Quellen sowie aus rechtshistorischen Gründen unstrittig und beides gut aufgearbeitet ist[6] und aus den gleichen Gründen weder die kanonischen Evangelien noch das Petrusevangelium als „objektive" Berichte des Prozesses Jesu angesehen werden wollen oder können, soll vor allem die narrative Darstellung und erzählerische Funktion des Pilatus bzw. der ihm zugeordneten Römer untersucht werden.

Zwar findet sich in der Literatur immer wieder der pauschale Hinweis, die apokryphe Überlieferung habe gegenüber der kanonischen die Tendenz, die Römer zu Ungunsten der Juden zu entlasten,[7] doch wurde dies bislang nicht

---

5   Das adversative δέ zu Beginn von EvPetr 1, die zweifache Erwähnung, dass die Juden ihre Hände nicht reinigten bzw. reinigen wollten (τ[ῶν] δὲ Ἰουδαίων οὐδεὶς ἐνίψατο τὰς χεῖρας καὶ μὴ βουληθέντων νίψασθαι), sowie der Umstand, dass das Aufstehen des Pilatus als Konsequenz dieser Verweigerung erscheint (καὶ μὴ βουληθέντων νίψασθαι ἀνέστη Πειλᾶτος), machen wahrscheinlich, dass in der vollständigen Fassung des Petrusevangeliums (P.Cair. 10759 ist hier nicht defektiv; vgl. Nicklas/Kraus, Petrusevangelium, 27) unmittelbar zuvor von der Handwaschung des Statthalters berichtet worden sein dürfte. Eine entsprechende Tradition findet sich auch in Mt 27,24. Vgl. dazu unten S. 335. Auch der Schluss des Petrusevangeliums ist unvollständig, es bricht nach VV. 59-60 abrupt ab.

6   Vgl. zu seiner Person E. von Dobschütz, Art. Pilatus, RE[3] 15, 1904, 397-401; E. Fascher, Art. Pilatus, PRE 20, 1950, 1322-1323; E. Bammel, Art. Pilatus, RGG[3] 5, 1961, 383-384; J.-P. Lémonon, Pilate et le Gouvernement de la Judée. Textes et Monuments, Paris 1981; D.R. Schwartz, Art. Pontius Pilate (Person), ABD 5, 1992, 395-401; idem, Art. Pontius Pilatus, RGG[4] 6, 2003, 1489-1490; H.K. Bond, Pontius Pilate in History and Interpretation, MSSNTS 100, Cambridge et al. 1998; A. Demandt, Hände in Unschuld. Pontius Pilatus in der Geschichte, Köln et al. 1999; A. Scheidgen, Die Gestalt des Pontius Pilatus in Legende, Bibelauslegung und Geschichtsdichtung vom Mittelalter bis in die frühe Neuzeit. Literaturgeschichte einer umstrittenen Persönlichkeit, Frankfurt/Main et al. 2002; vgl. zu rechtsgeschichtlichen Aspekten des Prozesses Jesu unten Anm. 33.

7   Vgl. z.B. F.F. Bruce, Außerbiblische Zeugnisse über Jesus und das frühe Christentum, hg. von E. Güting, Gießen-Basel 1991 (englisches Original: Jesus and Christian Origins Outside the New Testament, London 1974), hier: 83: „[D]er bemerkenswerteste Zug dieser Geschichte [ist], daß sie Pilatus vollständig von jeglicher Verantwortung für die Kreuzigung Jesu freispricht.

differenziert am Text des Petrusevangeliums selbst aufgewiesen.[8] Der Fokus der vorliegenden Studie soll dabei nicht auf der Frage nach dem literarischen Verhältnis zwischen der apokryphen Schrift und den kanonischen Evangelien liegen. Diese literar- bzw. traditionskritische Diskussion bewegt sich derzeit zwischen den Extremen einer sehr optimistischen Einschätzung des Alters und der Zuverlässigkeit des Petrusevangeliums als Quelle für die Rückfrage nach dem historischen Jesus[9] und der Annahme seiner Abhängigkeit von allen oder zumindest einigen der kanonischen Evangelien.[10] Nicht zuletzt angesichts dieser Aporien ist in jüngerer Zeit verstärkt die Tendenz wahrzunehmen, die neutestamentlichen Apokryphen nicht nur auf ihr Alter bzw. ihre Verwertbarkeit als historische Quelle zu untersuchen, sondern sie als eigenständige literarische und theologische Werke in den Blick zu nehmen.[11] Dies impliziert nicht notwendig eine ahistorische Sicht- und Herangehensweise, wesentlich ist vielmehr, dass die diachrone Perspektive nicht mehr die allein bestimmende ist.

(…) Er zieht sich nach dem Waschen der Hände aus dem Prozeß zurück; Herodes Antipas übernimmt von ihm den Vorsitz und damit die Verantwortung, die anzunehmen er sich in der Passionsgeschichte des Lukas weigerte. Die römischen Soldaten spielen keine Rolle, bis sie auf die Forderung der jüdischen Autoritäten hin von Pilatus geschickt werden, um die Wache am Grabe Jesu zu stellen. In der gesamten Geschichte sind ‚die Juden' die Schurken – insbesondere die führenden Priester und Schriftgelehrten. Sie sind diejenigen, die Jesus zum Tod verurteilen und beschimpfen; sie kreuzigen ihn und teilen seine Kleider unter sich." Vgl. auch G. Theißen/A. Merz, Der historische Jesus. Ein Lehrbuch, Göttingen 1996, 61; C. Bussmann, „Josef, der Freund des Pilatus und des Herrn" (Petrus-Evangelium 2). Ein Blick auf das Verhältnis Ecclesia-Imperium in den sogenannten Apokryphen zum Neuen Testament, in: Rom und das himmlische Jerusalem. Die frühen Christen zwischen Anpassung und Ablehnung, hg. von R. von Haehling, Darmstadt 2000, 85-96, bes. 90-91; P. Vielhauer, Geschichte der urchristlichen Literatur. Einleitung in das Neue Testament, die Apokryphen und die Apostolischen Väter, Berlin-New York 1975, 648.

8   Ähnliches gilt für die Darstellung der Juden im Petrusevangelium; vgl. jedoch T. Nicklas, Die „Juden" im Petrusevangelium (PCair 10759): Ein Testfall, NTS 47, 2001, 206-221.

9   So besonders J.D. Crossan, Four Other Gospels: Shadows on the Contours of the Canon, Minneapolis et al. 1985; idem, The Cross that Spoke: The Origins of the Passion Narrative, San Francisco et al. 1988; idem, The Gospel of Peter and the Canonical Gospels. Independence, Dependence, or Both?, FORUM 1/1, 1998, 7-51, sowie Crossans Beitrag im vorliegenden Band. Vgl. auch bereits H. Köster, Apocryphal and Canonical Gospels, HThR 73, 1980, 105-130, sowie die Übersicht bei R.E. Brown, The Death of the Messiah. From Gethsemane to the Grave: A Commentary on the Passion Narratives in the Four Gospels 2, New York et al. 1994, 1317-1349, hier: 1332 n. 22.

10   Vgl. z.B. M. Dibelius, Die alttestamentlichen Motive in der Leidensgeschichte des Petrus- und Johannesevangeliums, in: idem, Botschaft und Geschichte 1: Zur Evangelienforschung, Tübingen 1953, 221-247; Vielhauer, Geschichte, 644-648; vgl. für weitere Vertreter Brown, Death, 1332 n. 21. Brown selbst nimmt an, dass dem Verfasser des Petrusevangeliums die kanonischen Evangelien – besonders Mt – bekannt waren, sie ihm aber wohl nicht schriftlich vorlagen; vgl. ibid., 1332-1333; idem, The Gospel of Peter and Canonical Gospel Priority, NTS 33, 1987, 321-343; vgl. auch J.H. Charlesworth, Research on New Testament Apocrypha and Pseudepigrapha, ANRW II 25.5, 1986, 3919-3968. Zum Problem vgl. auch den Beitrag von A. Kirk im vorliegenden Band.

11   Vgl. Nicklas, Juden, 206-209; T.J. Kraus, Ad fontes: Gewinn durch die Konsultation von Originalhandschriften am Beispiel von P.Vindob. G 31974, Bib. 82, 2001, 1-16, bes. 1-3.

Daher soll im Folgenden die Pilatusgestalt im Petrusevangelium vorrangig mit Methoden des so genannten *narrative* oder *literary criticism* analysiert werden. Während literaturkritische bzw. erzählanalytische Ansätze in der angloamerikanischen[12] und frankophonen[13] Exegese bereits seit den 70er Jahren breit rezipiert worden sind, reagierte die deutschsprachige Forschung auf diese Impulse lange Zeit verhalten. Inzwischen mehrt sich jedoch im Bereich der Evangelienforschung auch im deutschen Sprachraum die Zahl exegetischer Untersuchungen, die sich Methoden des *narrative criticism* bedienen.[14] Diese Arbeiten zeichnen sich zumeist durch eine erfreuliche Distanzierung von einem exklusiv synchronen Zugang aus und sind vielmehr der Verbindung von neueren literaturkritischen mit älteren historisch-kritischen Elementen verpflichtet.[15] Für das Gebiet der apokryphen Evangelien ist eine solche Herangehensweise jedoch nach wie vor eher die Ausnahme,[16] was unter anderem mit ihrer oft fragmentarischen Textüberlieferung zusammenhängen dürfte. Daher wird in der vorliegenden Studie auch keine ganzheitliche[17] narrativ-kritische Analyse des Petrusevangeliums angestrebt, sondern es erfolgt eine Beschränkung auf die Pilatussequenzen im Akhmîm-Codex (P.Cair. 10759). Dabei werden die kanonischen Evangelien lediglich als Referenztexte herangezogen, um den Blick für die Darstellungs- und Erzählweise des Petrusevangeliums zu schärfen. Erst wenn auf diese Weise das spezifische Bild und die Funktion des Pilatus bzw. der Römer im Petrusevangelium erhoben worden sind (3.), kann versucht werden, auf Grund dieser Ergebnisse Rückschlüsse auf die Stellung des Petrusevangeliums innerhalb seines kulturellen Umfelds zu ziehen (4.). Zuvor soll jedoch die zugrunde gelegte erzählanalytische Methodik noch näher begründet und erläutert werden (2.).

---

[12] Vgl. G. Schunack, Neuere literaturkritische Interpretationsverfahren in der anglo-amerikanischen Exegese, VuF 41, 1996, 28-55.

[13] Vgl. J. Zumstein, Narrative Analyse und neutestamentliche Exegese in der frankophonen Welt, VuF 41, 1996, 5-27.

[14] Wegweisend waren hier insbesondere Arbeiten zum Markusevangelium; vgl. zuletzt den Überblick bei G. Guttenberger, Die Gottesvorstellung im Markusevangelium, BZNW 123, Berlin-New York 2004, 35 n. 190.

[15] Vgl. Guttenberger, Gottesvorstellung, 33-35.

[16] Vgl. aber Nicklas, Juden; idem, Erzähler und Charakter zugleich. Zur literarischen Funktion des „Petrus" in dem nach ihm benannten Evangelienfragment, VigChr 55, 2001, 318-326, passim.

[17] Vgl. hingegen P. Merenlahti/R. Hakola, Reconceiving Narrative Criticism, in: Characterization in the Gospels. Reconceiving Narrative Criticism, ed. by D. Rhoads/K. Syreeni, JSNT.S 184, Sheffield 1999, 13-48, hier: 14-15: „Narrative critics investigate the poetic function of the Gospels (...) from a holistic point of view, which means that narrative critics focus on the narrative of each Gospel as a whole and try to come up with an integrated interpretation of all the elements of the narrative."

2. Methodische Vorbemerkungen

In Anlehnung an das inzwischen zum erzähltheoretischen „Klassiker"
avancierte gleichnamige Werk von Seymor Chatman soll im Folgenden
zwischen *story* (Erzählhandlung) und *discourse* (Erzählstruktur/-form) des
Petrusevangeliums unterschieden werden.[18] Dabei rekurriert das Konzept der
story auf die inhaltliche Ebene der Erzählung. Ihr Gegenstand wird bestimmt
durch die Abfolge verschiedener Ereignisse (*events*) bzw. durch Hand-
lungsstränge (*plots*).[19] Wesentlich für die Konstituierung der *story* sind
außerdem die in die Ereignisse verwickelten Charaktere (*characters/actors*)[20]
und der räumliche sowie zeitliche Rahmen der Handlung (*setting*)[21]. Von dem
Was der Erzählung lässt sich unterscheiden, *wie* eine *story* entfaltet wird. Diese
Ausdrucks- oder Kommunikationsebene ist wesentlich durch die Perspektive[22]

---

[18] Vgl. S. Chatman, Story and Discourse. Narrative Structure in Fiction and Film, Ithaca-London
      1978. Diese Zweiteilung geht bereits auf Boris Tomaševskij zurück; vgl. dazu U. Eisen, Das
      Markusevangelium erzählt. Literary Criticism und Evangelienauslegung, in: Exegese und
      Methodendiskussion, hg. von S. Alkier/R. Brucker, TANZ 23, Tübingen 1998, 135-153, bes. 137.
      Von diesen beiden Text- bzw. Erzählebenen ist als dritte der (reale oder fiktive) Akt des
      Erzählens zu unterscheiden. Vgl. dazu G. Genette, Die Erzählung, aus dem Franz. von
      A. Knop, mit einem Nachwort hg. von J. Vogt, München ²1998 (franz. Original: Discours du
      récit. Essai de méthode, in: idem, Figures III, Paris 1972, 65-222), 16, der vorschlägt „das
      Signifikat oder den narrativen Inhalt *Geschichte* [franz.: *histoire*; H.O.]" zu nennen (...), „den
      Signifikanten, die Aussage, den narrativen Text oder Diskurs *Erzählung* [franz.: *récit*; H.O.] im
      eigentlichen Sinne, während *Narration* [franz.: *narration*; H.O.] dem produzierenden narrativen
      Akt (...) vorbehalten sein soll." Auch wenn diese Ebenen freilich stets aufeinander bezogen
      sind, konzentriert sich Genette vornehmlich auf die zweite, den *discours* bzw. *récit*. Vgl. in
      Anlehnung an Genette auch S. Rimmon-Kenan, Narrative Fiction. Contemporary Poetics,
      London-New York ²2002, 3, die zwischen *story* als „narrated events", *text* als deren „verbal
      representation" und *narration* als „act or process of production" unterscheidet. Zwar hebt auch
      Mieke Bal drei narrative Ebenen voneinander ab, allerdings mit abweichender Terminologie
      und Abgrenzung: text – words, story – aspects, fabula – elements. Unter einem *narrative text*
      versteht sie einen „text in which an agent relates (‚tells') a story in a particular medium". Diese
      story „is a fabula that is presented in a certain manner", eine *fabula* wiederum „a series of
      logically and chronologically related events that are caused or experienced by actors" (M. Bal,
      Narratology. Introduction to the Theory of Narrative, Toronto et al. ²1999, 5).
[19] Vgl. Chatman, Story, 43-95; Rhimmon-Kenan, Fiction, 6-28; Bal, Narratology, 182-195; M.A.
      Powell, What is Narrative Criticism? A New Approach to the Bible, Guides to Biblical
      Scholarship: New Testament Series, Minneapolis 1990, 35-50.
[20] Vgl. Chatman, Story, 107-138; Rhimmon-Kenan, Fiction, 29-42; Bal, Narratology, 195-208. Bal
      unterscheidet terminologisch zwischen dem abstrakten Begriff *actor* (auf der Ebene der *fabula*)
      und dem spezifischeren Begriff *character* (auf der Ebene der *story*), worunter sie einen „actor
      provided with distinctive characteristics" (Narratology, 114) versteht. In der Regel wird
      stattdessen lediglich zwischen Charakter und Charakterisierung unterschieden, so z.B.
      Rhimmon-Kenan, Fiction, 59: „Character, as one construct within the abstracted story, can be
      described in terms of a network of character-traits (...) that I seek to define under the heading
      of ‚characterization'."
[21] Chatman, Story, 138-145; Bal, Narratology, 208-217; Powell, Narrative Criticism, 69-83.
[22] Die Begriffe der Perspektive oder des Blickwinkels wurden in der neueren Forschung
      problematisiert, da sie z.B. nicht zwischen Erzähler und Charakteren als verschiedenen
      Subjekten des Sehens bzw. zwischen ihnen und den Objekten des Sehens differenzieren (vgl.
      S. Chatman, Coming to Terms. The Rhetoric of Narrative in Fiction and Film, Ithaca-London

des Erzählers (*narrator*)[23] und der einzelnen Charaktere der *story* auf die
erzählte Welt (*point of view/focalization*)[24], aber auch durch zeitliche Aspekte wie
Anordnung, Dauer oder Frequenz der erzählten Ereignisse[25] sowie die
Charakterisierung[26] der Akteure bestimmt, die auf vielfältige Weise – und oft
in Verbindung mit bereits aufgeführten Aspekten wie etwa der Erzähl-
perspektive – erfolgen kann. Eine grundsätzliche Unterscheidung lässt sich
zwischen direkter Zuschreibung (durch den Erzähler, andere Charaktere oder
den Akteur selbst) und indirekter Repräsentation von Charakterzügen
treffen.[27] Letztere können z.B. durch (einmaliges oder habituelles) Verhalten
einer Figur, durch ihre Sprache bzw. Aussagen (Sprechakte), aber auch durch
die Beziehungen zu anderen Akteuren bzw. den Vergleich oder die

---

1990, 139-160). An ihre Seite oder Stelle ist vielfach der Begriff der Fokalisierung getreten, der
seinerseits durchaus unterschiedlich bestimmt wird und daher – wenn er etwa nicht exklusiv
auf die Charaktere bezogen ist – diese Differenzierung zwar auch nicht notwendigerweise
leistet, aber doch für die Problematik sensibilisiert; vgl. etwa Genette, Erzählung, 134-138. 241-
244 (vgl. insgesamt zur Perspektive 115-149 und 219-244); Rhimmon-Kenan, Fiction, 72-86; Bal,
Narratology, 142-161; eadem, Kulturanalyse, hg. und mit einem Nachwort versehen von
T. Fechner-Smarsly, Frankfurt/Main 2002, 16. 119.

23 Der Erzähler ist vom impliziten wie vom realen Autor zu unterscheiden; er lässt sich auch als
„Erzählstimme" fassen. Vgl. grundsätzlich Chatman, Story, 147-151; idem, Terms, 74-123;
Powell, Narrative Criticism, 19-21.

24 B. Uspenskij, Poetik der Komposition. Struktur des künstlerischen Textes und Typologie der
Kompositionsform, hg. und nach einer rev. Fassung des Orig. bearb. von K. Eimermacher. Aus
dem Russ. übers. von G. Mayer, Frankfurt/Main 1975 (russ. Original: 1970), bes. 17-116,
unterscheidet vier Ebenen, auf der die Perspektive zu erfassen ist: Ideologie (Bewertung der
dargestellten Welt), Phraseologie (Autoren- oder Figurenrede), Raum-Zeit-Charakteristik,
Psychologie (Innen-/Außenperspektive bzw. Subjektivität/Objektivität). Vgl. außer den in
Anm. 22 genannten grundlegenden Titeln speziell zu biblischen Erzähltexten A. Berlin, Poetics
and Interpretation of Biblical Narrative, Bible and Literature Series 9, Sheffield 1983, 43-82;
M. Sternberg, The Poetics of Biblical Narrative. Ideological Literature and the Drama of
Reading, Indiana Literary Biblical Series, Bloomington 1985, 129-185; Powell, Narrative
Criticism, 23-25. 53-54.

25 Vgl. Genette, Erzählung, 21-114. 205-218; Chatman, Story, 63-84; Rhimmon-Kenan, Fiction, 43-
58; Bal, Narratology, 80-114.

26 Vgl. allgemein R. Scholes/R. Kellog, The Nature of Narrative, Oxford 1966, bes. 160-206;
Chatman, Story, 107-138; B. Hochman, Character in Literature, Ithaca 1985, bes. 86-140;
Rhimmon-Kenan, Fiction, 59-71; Bal, Narratology, 114-132; vgl. zur exegetischen Diskussion
Sternberg, Poetics, 321-364; Powell, Narrative Criticism, 51-67; D. Rhoads/J. Dewey/D. Michie,
Mark as Story. An Introduction to the Narrative of a Gospel, Minneapolis ²1999, 98-136;
E.S. Malbon, Narrative Criticism: How Does the Story Mean?, in: Mark and Method: New
Approaches in Biblical Studies, ed. by J.C. Anderson/S.D. Moore, Minneapolis 1992, 23-49, hier:
28-30; E.S. Malbon/A. Berlin, Characterization in Biblical Literature, Sem. 63, 1993;
D. Rhoads/K. Syreeni, ed., Characterization in the Gospels. Reconceiving Narrative Criticism,
JSNT.S 184, Sheffield 1999, passim.

27 Vgl. die prägnante Unterscheidung von „telling" and „showing" durch W. Booth, The Rhetoric
of Fiction, Chicago ²1983, 3-20. Eine weitere Klassifizierung ist die in „flat" und „round
characters", die von E.M. Forster, Aspects of the Novel, New York 1927, bes. 103-118, in die
Diskussion eingeführt wurde. Ein *flat character* weist nur wenige Charakterzüge und
Wandlungsfähigkeit auf, wohingegen ein *round character* komplexer angelegt ist und im
Verlauf der Handlung eine Entwicklung vollzieht. Vgl. zur Kritik an dieser Schematisierung
Rhimmon-Kenan, Fiction, 40-42.

Kontrastierung mit ihnen gezeichnet werden. In der folgenden Untersuchung sollen anhand solcher Textbeobachtungen vor allem der Charakter und die Charakterisierung des Pilatus im Petrusevangelium profiliert werden, wobei das Hauptaugenmerk auf Merkmalen indirekter Charakterisierung liegen wird, da es im an Einzelpersonen ohnehin wenig interessierten Petrus-evangelium kaum direkte Attribuierungen gibt.[28]

3. Pontius Pilatus als Charakter der erzählten Welt des Petrusevangeliums

3.1 Die Verhandlung vor Herodes (EvPetr 1-5)

Auch wenn P.Cair. 10759 sicher nicht den ursprünglichen Anfang des Petrusevangeliums oder auch nur der Einzelszene bietet,[29] reicht doch der überlieferte Text aus, um den der Erzählung zugrunde liegenden Handlungsgang (*story*) zu rekonstruieren: Jesus, der in dieser Szene weder mit Namen genannt wird[30] noch aktiv am Geschehen beteiligt ist, steht vor dem Gericht des jüdischen Königs (!) Herodes. Dieser bestätigt sein früheres Todesurteil (vgl. V. 2: ὅσα ἐκέλευσα ὑμῖν ποιῆσαι αὐτῷ, ποιήσατε) und liefert Jesus dem Volk aus (V. 5). Die Rolle des Pilatus im Prozessverlauf lässt sich anhand des vorliegenden Textes nicht exakt bestimmen. Die Opposition zu den Juden, „von denen sich keiner die Hände reinigte" (V. 1), macht lediglich wahr-scheinlich, dass der ursprüngliche Text davon berichtete, dass er seine Hände gewaschen hat. Ob und wie er an der Urteilsfindung beteiligt war, ist nicht mehr zu ergründen. Auf die Initiative seines Freundes Josef bittet Pilatus Herodes noch vor der Kreuzigung um ein ordentliches Begräbnis Jesu (VV. 3-5). Herodes erklärt diese Bitte für hinfällig, da man den Delinquenten gemäß den Forderungen des Gesetzes in jedem Fall bestattet hätte (V. 5).

Die kurze Textpassage lässt sich auf der Erzählebene (*discourse*) nochmals untergliedern in die VV. 1-2, die vom endgültigen Urteil über Jesus berichten, und in die VV. 3-5, welche die Frage seines Begräbnisses thematisieren. Dabei markiert V. 3 auf Grund der unbestimmten Ortsangabe ἐκεῖ sowie der Einführung einer neuen Person einen Einschnitt. Das Gespräch zwischen Josef und Pilatus ist an einem anderen Ort als die vorangehende Verurteilung Jesu vorgestellt, da Pilatus in V. 4 zu Herodes schicken lässt.[31] V. 5c knüpft mit der Auslieferung Jesu wieder an V. 2 an und schließt so die Gesamtszene ab.

---

28 Vgl. ähnlich J. Denker, Die theologiegeschichtliche Stellung des Petrusevangeliums. Ein Beitrag zur Frühgeschichte des Doketismus, EHS XXIII.36, Frankfurt/Main 1975, 61. 159 n. 23.
29 Vgl. oben Anm. 5.
30 Dies gilt für das gesamte Petrusevangelium; vgl. aber VV. 2-3: κύριος.
31 Offensichtlich ist dann das ἀνέστη in V. 1 als ein Weggehen aufzufassen; vgl. Nicklas, Juden, 212 n. 21.

In beiden Textpassagen stehen sich Pilatus und Herodes als Haupt-
handlungsträger gegenüber, wobei die Kontrastierung ihrer Aktionen und
Aussagen ein wesentliches Mittel ihrer Charakterisierung ist.[32] Während in den
kanonischen Passionsberichten die jüdische Seite – vertreten durch den Hohen
Rat bzw. die Hohenpriester und Ältesten (Mk 14,53-65 parr.) sowie allein bei
Lk außerdem durch Herodes Antipas (Lk 23,6-12) – zwar an der Verurteilung
Jesu beteiligt ist, bezeugen diese doch einmütig, dass das letzte Urteil in der
Eigenverantwortung des römischen Statthalters liegt.[33] Demgegenüber
erscheint in EvPetr 1-5 Herodes als derjenige, der die Befehle erteilt (vgl. V. 2:
κελεύω [bis]), dem die Macht zukommt, über die endgültige Verurteilung Jesu
(VV. 2.5) ebenso wie über die Frage seiner Bestattung zu befinden (V. 5).
Pilatus hingegen scheint keinen Einfluss auf diese Entscheidung zu haben, sein
demonstrativer Protest bleibt ohne Wirkung, ja er muss Herodes sogar um die
Herausgabe des Leichnams bitten (VV. 4.5: αἰτέω). Dieser defensiven Haltung
des Pilatus entspricht, dass allein die Verfügungen des Herodes in direkter
Rede wiedergegeben werden. Der Eindruck dieses Machtgefälles wird dadurch
verstärkt, dass Herodes als βασιλεύς[34] und sein Gefolge als Richter (κριταί)

---

[32] Vgl. ähnlich Nicklas, Juden, 213.

[33] Dies dürfte im Kern die historischen Umstände des Prozesses Jesu widerspiegeln. Den Juden
kam unter der römischen Vorherrschaft in Judäa allenfalls ein Mitspracherecht, jedoch keine
eigene Gerichtsbarkeit in Kapitalprozessen zu. Dieses Machtverhältnis spiegelt sich auch im
Petrusevangelium insofern wider, als Jesus der *römischen* Kreuzesstrafe unterliegt. Vgl. zu den
juristischen Hintergründen des Prozesses Jesu bes. P. Winter, On the Trial of Jesus, Berlin 1961;
A.N. Sherwin-White, Roman Society and Roman Law in the New Testament, Oxford 1963, 24-
47; J. Blinzler, Der Prozeß Jesu, Regensburg ⁴1969; A. Strobel, Die Stunde der Wahrheit.
Untersuchungen zum Strafverfahren gegen Jesus, Tübingen 1980; O. Betz, Probleme des
Prozesses Jesu, ANRW 25.1, 1982, 565-647; K. Kertelge, Hg., Der Prozeß gegen Jesus.
Historische Rückfrage und theologische Deutung, QD 112, Freiburg et al. 1988; Brown, Death,
passim; P. Egger, „Crucifixus sub Pontio Pilato". Das „Crimen" Jesu von Nazareth im
Spannungsfeld römischer und jüdischer Verwaltungs- und Rechtsstrukturen, NTA NF 32,
Münster 1997; A. Oppenheimer, Jewish Penal Authority in Roman Judaea, in: The Jews in a
Graeco-Roman World, ed. by M. Goodman, Oxford 1998, 181-191; M. Miglietta, Römisches
Strafrecht, in: Neues Testament und Antike Kultur 1: Prolegomena – Quellen – Geschichte, hg.
von K. Erlemann et al., Neukirchen-Vluyn 2004, 239-246, hier: 242-246 (Lit!).

[34] Freilich trug der historische Herodes Antipas nicht den Titel eines Königs, denn zum *rex socius
et amicus populi Romani* ernannten die Römer außer Herodes den Großen später nur noch
dessen Enkel Herodes Agrippa I. (vgl. E. Schürer, The History of the Jewish People in the Age
of Jesus Christ [175 B.C.-A.D. 135]. A New English Version, rev. and ed. by G. Vermes/
F. Millar/M. Black, Vol. 1, Edinburgh 1973, 316 Anm. 104. 451; D.R. Schwartz, Agrippa I. The
Last King of Judaea, TSAJ 239, Tübingen 1990. Antipas wurde nach dem Tod seines Vaters die
Herrschaft über Galiläa und Peräa in der Funktion eines Tetrarchen übertragen. Mit diesem
Titel ist er auch in Mt 14,1; Lk 3,1.19; 9,7; Apg 13,1 bezeugt, während in Mk 6,14; Mt 14,9 –
wie im Petrusevangelium – fälschlicherweise als βασιλεύς bezeichnet wird. Diese Ungenauigkeit
könnte durch Unkenntnis aufgrund des zeitlichen Abstands zu den historischen Ereignissen
bedingt sein, vielleicht auch (zusätzlich) von der Rolle Herodes des Großen in den
Kindheitserzählungen Jesu überlagert. Im Erzählzusammenhang des Petrusevangeliums zeigt
der Titel βασιλεύς jedenfalls eindeutig die Machtstellung des Herodes Antipas an. Vgl. zu seiner
Person Blinzler, Prozeß, 284-300; H.W. Hoehner, Herod Antipas, MSSNTS 17, Cambridge 1972;
Schürer, History I, 340-353; R.D. Sullivan, The Dynasty of Judaea in the First Century,

bezeichnet werden (V. 2).[35] Dagegen erscheint Pilatus ohne offiziellen Titel,[36] er wird aber von Herodes als Bruder angesprochen (V. 5). Diese Anrede begegnet auch sonst im Munde von Königen gegenüber hochgestellten Persönlichkeiten.[37] Hier zeigt sich, dass sich Herodes gegenüber Pilatus überlegen fühlt, sie hat sogar fast eine herablassende Note.[38]

Die Kontrastierung der beiden Hauptakteure wird durch die Darstellung und Aktionen der Nebenfiguren noch unterstützt. In V. 1 stehen die Juden mit ihrer Weigerung, sich die Hände zu waschen, Pilatus geschlossen (vgl. τῶν δὲ Ἰουδαίων οὐδείς)[39] gegenüber, der diese Reinigung wohl schon zuvor vollzogen hat (vgl. Mt 27,24). Als einziger Nichtjude unter den Anwesenden hat er somit durch einen jüdischen Ritus seine Unschuld bekannt.[40] Zwar erfolgt die Erklärung dieser Symbolhandlung im Petrusevangelium – anders als in Mt 27,24 – erst im Kontext der Erzählung von der Grabwache (EvPetr 46), doch ist die Bedeutung des Gestus bereits hier durch den Zusammenhang einsichtig. Das Verhalten des Pilatus ist durch die wiederholte Erwähnung der Nichtreinigung der Juden – beim zweiten Mal sogar betont als *bewusste* Verweigerung dargestellt (vgl. V. 1b: μὴ βουληθέντων νίψασθαι) – zusätzlich positiv konnotiert. Er ist derjenige, der seine Unschuld (und Reue?) öffentlich sichtbar bekennt und eine entsprechende Haltung wohl auch von den Juden erwartet. Die sachliche Distanzierung von ihrem abweisenden Verhalten wird durch die Reaktion des Pilatus unterstrichen: er steht auf[41] und geht[42]. Damit wird auch äußerlich erkennbar, dass Herodes bzw. die Juden für das Todesurteil über Jesus verantwortlich sind. Pilatus hat die Bühne verlassen, die Juden bleiben allein zurück. Konsequenterweise spricht dann auch Herodes das Urteil aus (V. 2) bzw. ist er – entgegen der kanonischen Evangelien-

---

ANRW II/8, 1977, 296-354, bes. 306-308; M. Tilly, Der Fuchs auf dem Herrscherthron. Herodes Antipas, Tetrarch von Galiläa und Peräa, WUB 24, 2002, 15-20.

[35] Für die Gegenüberstellung von Herodes und Pilatus ist es unerheblich, worauf das Pronomen αὐτοῦ hier verweist. Denn ungeachtet, ob sich auf Jesus oder Herodes rückbezieht, sind in jedem Fall die Juden die Richter Jesu, nicht der Römer.

[36] Freilich kann ein solcher in dem fehlenden Anfangsteil der Szene gebraucht sein.

[37] So z.B. OGIS 138,3; 168,26.36; Josephus, *ant.* 13,45.126; vgl. W. Bauer, Griechisch-deutsches Wörterbuch zu den Schriften des Neuen Testaments und der frühchristlichen Literatur, hg. v. K. Aland/B. Aland, Berlin-New York ⁶1988, 29.

[38] Vgl. Lk 23,12: προϋπῆρχον γὰρ ἐν ἔχθρα ὄντες πρὸς αὐτούς.

[39] Diese Geschlossenheit besteht unabhängig von der genauen Bedeutung von οὐδέ. Entweder sind Herodes und die Richter bereits eingeschlossen oder sie kommen noch hinzu.

[40] Während in Dtn 21,1-9 (vgl. 11Q19 LXIII 1-8) der ursprüngliche Zusammenhang der rituellen Entlastung Unschuldiger (da der Täter unbekannt ist) von einer Blutschuld deutlich ist, liegt in Ps 26,6; 73,13 eine übertragene Bedeutung vor. Vgl. auch die entsprechenden Deutungen in Philo, *Mos.* II 138; *Arist.* 306. Ob an dieser Stelle eine Abhängigkeit des Petrusevangeliums von Mt besteht, lässt sich nicht sicher sagen, da der Text sich ganz offensichtlich an der Septuaginta orientiert; vgl. Denker, Stellung, 58-61.

[41] Vermutlich spielt diese demonstrative Geste auf den Kontext der Handwaschung in Ps 26 (25),6 an, wonach der Beter nicht mit einem Rat der Nichtigkeit (V. 4: μετὰ συνεδρίου ματαιότητος) bzw. mit Gottlosen (V. 5: μετὰ ἀσεβῶν) zusammensitzen will (vgl. Ps 21,17 LXX). Vgl. Denker, Stellung, 58.

[42] Vgl. oben Anm. 31.

tradition (vgl. Mk 15,15 parr.: Pilatus) – derjenige, der Jesus an das Volk ausliefert (V. 5).

Die positive Zeichnung des Pilatus setzt sich im zweiten Abschnitt der Gerichtsszene fort, diesmal nicht im Gegenüber zu den Nebenpersonen, sondern in der Zuordnung zu ihnen. Indem Josef als Freund des Pilatus[43] und Jesu eingeführt wird (V. 3), tritt er als Bindeglied zwischen beide, die damit indirekt gleichfalls als freundschaftlich verbunden erscheinen. Dieser Eindruck wird durch die umgehende Reaktion[44] des Pilatus auf die Bitte des Josef bestätigt, den Leichnam Jesu zum Begräbnis freizugeben. Da Pilatus nach EvPetr 2 keine richterliche Verantwortung für die Kreuzigung und damit auch Bestattung Jesu zukommt, liegt es in der Konsequenz der Erzählung, dass er das Gesuch an Herodes weiterleitet (V. 4). Dessen Hinweis auf den νόμος ist folgerichtig auf das jüdische, nicht das römische Gesetz bezogen (V. 5: γέγραπται γὰρ ἐν τῷ νόμῳ ἥλιον μὴ δῦναι ἐπὶ πεφονευμένῳ). Inhaltlich spielt Herodes dabei auf das Verbot an, einen Gekreuzigten über Nacht hängen zu lassen (Dtn 21,22-23; vgl. auch EvPetr 15; 23 sowie Joh 19,31; Apg 5,30; 10,39). Trotz seines Bekenntnisses zur Gesetzestreue wird Herodes hier im Verhältnis zu Pilatus abermals in ein schlechtes Licht gerückt, da die Szene mit der Erwartungshaltung (des Josef wie auch des Pilatus) spielt, dass die Vorschrift im Fall Jesu missachtet werden wird.[45] Dagegen muss sich Herodes nun rechtfertigen und gerät so gegenüber dem römischen Statthalter als Übermittler des Anliegens in die Defensive.

Dass sich Josef – ebenso wie in der kanonischen Passionstradition (vgl. Mk 15,42-43.45 parr. Mt 27,57-58; Lk 23,50-52; vgl. Joh 19,31) – an Pilatus statt direkt an Herodes wendet, ist darüber hinaus ein wesentliches Mittel seiner Charakterisierung, denn abgesehen von der Nachricht, dass er der Freund des Pilatus und Jesu ist, wird er an dieser Stelle nicht näher gekennzeichnet. Aus dem Namen lässt sich zwar erschließen, dass er Jude ist. Anders als etwa Mk 15,43; Lk 23,50 steht er aber (explizit) in keiner Verbindung zu den jüdischen Amtsträgern, die in den Prozess Jesu involviert sind.[46] In EvPetr 23b wird seine Motivation nachgetragen: ἐπειδὴ θεασάμενος ἦν ὅσα ἀγαθὰ ἐποίησεν. Damit wird die Freundschaft zu Jesus noch deutlicher als Anhängerschaft qualifiziert (vgl. Mt 27,57; Lk 23,50). Josef wird auf die Seite Christi bzw. „der Christen" gerückt und vom Handeln „der Juden" abgesetzt. Dem korrespondiert, dass Josef nicht in direkten Kontakt mit der negativ besetzten Figur des Herodes tritt, sondern sein „Freund", der Römer Pilatus, zwischen ihnen vermittelt.

---

[43] Josef tritt damit also quasi an die Stelle des Herodes in Lk 23,12, wo Herodes und Pilatus, die einander zuvor feindlich gesinnt waren, im Zuge des Prozesses Jesu Freunde werden.

[44] Vgl. hingegen die erzählerische Verzögerung in Mk 15,44-45.

[45] Daher muss nicht notwendigerweise angenommen werden, dass diese alttestamentliche Stelle in der Theologie des Petrusevangeliums eine wichtige Rolle spielt, wie Denker, Stellung, 60, meint.

[46] Auch die Herkunft aus Arimathia erwähnt das Petrusevangelium nicht; vgl. dagegen Mk 15,43; Mt 27,57; Lk 23,51; Joh 19,38.

Pilatus wird somit in dieser Eingangsszene trotz seiner gegenüber Herodes untergeordneten Stellung nicht als machtlos oder ohnmächtig dargestellt. Er zeigt seine Position klar an und versucht, auf diplomatischem Weg Einfluss auf Herodes zu nehmen.

3.2 Begräbnis durch Josef (EvPetr 23-24)

Wie für die Verurteilung sind im Petrusevangelium auch für die Verspottung und Hinrichtung Jesu allein die Juden verantwortlich, auch wenn dies lediglich in den Rahmenversen EvPetr 5 und 23 ausdrücklich erwähnt wird. Doch bezieht sich οἱ δὲ λαβόντες τὸν κύριον in EvPetr 6 klar auf das vorangehende καὶ παρέδωκεν αὐτὸν τῷ λαῷ in EvPetr 5b.[47] In EvPetr 23 ist dann nicht mehr vom Volk, sondern von den Ἰουδαῖοι die Rede (im Gegenüber zu Josef!). Die Römer bzw. Pilatus kommen hingegen erst wieder im Zusammenhang des Begräbnisses Jesu in den Blick, zunächst indirekt über die Wiederaufnahme des zuvor mit Pilatus verbundenen Josef (EvPetr 23-24), dann direkt im Zusammenhang der Grabwache (EvPetr 28-48).

Die Erwähnung des Josef in EvPetr 23 knüpft insofern an EvPetr 3-5 an, als er jetzt für das dort erzählerisch vorbereitete ordentliche Begräbnis Jesu sorgt. Da er die Erlaubnis bereits vor der Kreuzigung eingeholt hat (diff. Mk 15,43 parr.), müssen hier weder Pilatus noch Herodes in Erscheinung treten. Die Juden übergeben Josef den Leichnam Jesu, den er wäscht[48] und in Leinen hüllt, um ihn dann in seinem eigenen Grab zu bestatten (VV. 23-24). Das Grab selbst wird nicht direkt beschrieben, aber als Κῆπον Ἰωσήφ bezeichnet (vgl. Joh 19,41). Aus EvPetr 32; 37; 53-54 und öfter lässt sich schließen, dass es sich um ein Felsen- bzw. Rollsteingrab handelt (vgl. Mk 15,46; 16,3-4 parr.). Josef wird hier nochmals ganz zentral in den Fokus der Erzählung gerückt – in V. 24 ist er alleiniger Handlungsträger –, erscheint danach hingegen nicht mehr. Nach einem kurzen Einschub, in dem über die Reue der Juden (EvPetr 25) und die Trauer der Jünger (EvPetr 26-27) berichtet wird, treten Pilatus und die Römer wieder auf.

3.3 Bewachung des Grabes (EvPetr 28-48)

Mit EvPetr 28 ändert sich die bisherige Darstellung der Juden als relative Einheit mit ihren Führern als öffentlichen Vertretern des Volkes.[49] In EvPetr 25

---

47 Es tritt eine Reihe inhaltlicher Beobachtungen hinzu, etwa die Rede von „ihrem" Fest in V. 5c oder der Titel „König Israels" in V. 7; vgl. dazu Nicklas, Juden, 215, der außerdem herausstellt, dass das Petrusevangelium „zumindest in dieser Stufe der Passionserzählung nicht prinzipiell zwischen jüdischen Führern und dem Volk unterscheidet".

48 Während Josef auch nach dem Zeugnis der kanonischen Evangelien Jesus in Leinen hüllt (vgl. Mk 15,46 parr. Mt 27,59; Lk 23,53; vgl. Joh 19,40 [gemeinsam mit Nikodemus]), berichtet nur das Petrusevangelium von seiner Waschung. Vgl. dazu Denker, Stellung, 81.

49 Vgl. zum Folgenden auch Nicklas, Juden, 219.

wird zwar zunächst noch von der Reue und Wehklage[50] der Juden sowie der Ältesten und Priester wegen des Todes Jesu berichtet, doch unterscheidet V. 28 dann zwischen den Reaktionen der Schriftgelehrten, Pharisäer und Ältesten auf der einen Seite und denen des Volkes auf der anderen. Dessen Murren und Klagen angesichts der himmlischen Zeichen beim Tod Jesu und der daraus folgenden Erkenntnis seiner Bedeutung löst bei den jüdischen Führern die weiter gehende Befürchtung aus, ein etwaiger Raub des Leichnams werde vom Volk als Auferstehung Jesu gedeutet, so dass es ihnen Übles antue (VV. 29-30). Diese Furcht begründet die sich nun anschließende Szene der Grabwache mit Hilfe römischer Soldaten und rahmt sie zugleich, insofern das Motiv an ihrem Ende, in V. 48, nochmals aufgegriffen und konkretisiert wird: Die jüdischen Führer fürchten die Steinigung.[51] Innerhalb dieses Abschnitts tritt das Volk nicht mehr in Erscheinung,[52] vielmehr liegt der Fokus in Bezug auf die Juden allein auf dem Agieren ihrer Führer. Während die Opposition zum Volk in V. 28 aber noch aus Schriftgelehrten, Pharisäern und Ältesten besteht, sind es im eigentlichen Bericht von der Bewachung des Grabes vor allem die Ältesten, die mit den Römern kooperieren.[53] Sie stehen dabei mit allen hierarchischen Ebenen in Kontakt, wie ein kurzer Überblick über die *story* aufzeigt.

Die Ältesten bitten Pilatus um die Abordnung von Soldaten zur Bewachung des Grabes Jesu (VV. 29-30). Dieser reagiert unverzüglich und ohne Nachfragen und überlässt ihnen den Centurio Petronius mit weiteren Soldaten, die mit ihnen zum Grab gehen (V. 31), das sie dann gemeinsam verschließen und versiegeln. Sie schlagen ein Zelt auf, um Wache zu halten (VV. 32-33). Bei Anbruch des Herrentages hören die wachhabenden Soldaten eine Stimme vom Himmel und sehen zwei Jünglinge herabkommen und in das Grab gehen, dessen Eingang sich zuvor von selbst geöffnet hat (VV. 35-37). Die Soldaten wecken den Hauptmann und die Ältesten und alle sehen drei Männer gefolgt von einem Kreuz aus dem Grab kommen und hören erneut eine Stimme aus den Himmeln (VV. 38-42). Als sie noch darüber beraten, Pilatus Bericht zu erstatten, öffnen sich erneut die Himmel; ein Mensch steigt herab und geht in das Grab (VV. 43-44). Daraufhin eilen die Leute des Centurio zu Pilatus. Sie berichten ihm, was sie gesehen haben, und bekennen sich zur Gottessohnschaft des Auferstandenen (V. 45). Pilatus beteuert zwar nochmals seine Unschuld am Tod Jesu, doch auf die Bitte der Juden hin verpflichtet er

---

[50] Vgl. zum traditionsgeschichtlichen Hintergrund dieses „Sinneswandels" Nicklas, Juden, 218-219.

[51] Diese Wiederaufnahme zeigt auch, dass ποιήσωσιν in V. 30 als *constructio ad sensum* auf das Subjekt λαός zu beziehen ist, nicht etwa auf die weiter vorn im Satz genannten μαθηταί. Entgegen der korrekten Erläuterung im Apparat ist in der Übersetzung von Nicklas/Kraus, Petrusevangelium, 41, auf Grund eines fehlenden Kommas nach „sei" das Verb auf Jesus bezogen.

[52] Wer zum ὄχλος in V. 34 gehört, wird nicht näher bestimmt, da dieser erzählerisch allein die Funktion hat, die korrekte Versiegelung zu bestätigen.

[53] So in VV. 29.31.38; nur in V. 31 treten daneben auch die Schriftgelehrten. Erst das unbestimmte πάντες in V. 47 dürfte hingegen wieder auf die in V. 28 anvisierte größere Gruppe abzielen, was die Inklusion verstärken würde, die durch das Furchtmotiv gebildet wird.

den Hauptmann und die Soldaten, nichts von den Ereignissen zu erzählen (VV. 46-49).

Auf Seiten der Römer treten also neben Pilatus der ihm unterstellte Centurio Petronius sowie weitere, nicht namentlich erwähnte Soldaten auf, die diesem offensichtlich untergeordnet sind.[54] Auf Grund der Konstellation der verschiedenen Charaktere zueinander lässt sich die Erzählung weiter unterteilen. Dabei bilden die Szenen, in denen Pilatus direkt beteiligt ist (VV. 29-31; 45-49), einen Rahmen um die Binnenerzählung von der eigentlichen Bewachung des Grabes (V. 32-44), in der die jüdischen Führer mit den subalternen Römern zusammenarbeiten. Pilatus wird dabei in V. 43 als derjenige in Erinnerung gerufen, dem man Rechenschaft zu geben hat. Dem entspricht, dass auch in den Rahmenpassagen die Handlung auf Pilatus fokussiert ist: Die Juden kommen zu ihm (vgl. V. 29 ἦλθον πρὸς Πειλᾶτον; V. 45 ἔσπευσαν πρὸς Πειλᾶτον; V. 47: προσελθόντες πάντες) und bitten um seine Unterstützung (vgl. V. 29: δεόμενοι αὐτοῦ; V. 47: ἐδέοντο αὐτοῦ καὶ περακάλουν). Er übt die Befehlsgewalt über seine Soldaten aus (vgl. V. 31: παραδέδωκεν; V. 47: κελεῦσαι; V. 49: ἐκέλευσεν), was allerdings stets nur knapp konstatiert wird.[55] Demgegenüber wird sofort in der einleitenden Rahmenpassage EvPetr 29-31 die Bitte und Motivation der Ältesten in V. 29 in direkter Rede ausgedrückt (vgl. bereits V. 28). Die Formulierung entspricht in weiten Teilen Mt 27,64.[56] Allerdings wird bei Mt von den Juden nur allgemein eine Sicherung des Grabes gefordert (κέλευσον οὖν ἀσφαλισθῆναι τὸν τάφον), wohingegen sie im Petrusevangelium ausdrücklich Soldaten zur Bewachung verlangen. Als στρατιῶται werden die Wächter bei Mt erst im Zusammenhang des Betruges in 28,12 bezeichnet, während zuvor allgemein von einer κουστωδία[57] die Rede ist (vgl. Mt 27,65-66; 28,11; vgl. 28,4: οἱ τηροῦντες). Durch die wiederholte Bezeichnung der Wachen als στρατιῶται (vgl. EvPetr 30-32; 35; 38; 47; 49) kommt Pilatus in dieser Szene durchweg in seiner Funktion als (militärischer) Befehlshaber in den Blick,[58] was noch dadurch verstärkt wird, dass er den Juden über ihre Anfrage hinausgehend einen Centurio[59] zur Seite stellt (vgl. V. 31: παραδέδωκεν αὐτοῖς Πετρώνιον τὸν κεντυρίωνα μετὰ στρατιωτῶν

---

[54] Die Soldaten könnten zwar theoretisch auch Herodes unterstellt sein, dürften aber wohl dem römischen Heer angehören; vgl. ebenso Nicklas, Juden, 215.

[55] Lediglich sein Unschuldsbekenntnis in V. 46 wird in direkter Rede wiedergegeben, wodurch es besondere Betonung erhält.

[56] In Mt 27,63 wird der Bewachungszeitraum von drei Tagen mit Hinweis auf ein entsprechendes Jesuswort begründet (vgl. Mt 12,40; 26,61).

[57] Dass es sich auch im matthäischen Sinn um eine Wache von Römern handelt, zeigt das lateinische Lehnwort κουστωδία an. Vgl. U. Luz, Das Evangelium nach Matthäus (Mt 26-28), EKK I/4, Düsseldorf et al. 2002, 393 n. 26.

[58] Wahrscheinlich ist auch ἔχετε κουστωδίαν in Mt 27,65 als Konzession dieser Bitte aufzufassen, nicht als Hinweis auf die Nichtzuständigkeit des Pilatus; so aber – wie auch die westliche Auslegungstradition (vgl. Luz, Matthäus, 393 n. 27) – Denker, Stellung, 79.

[59] Wie Mk 15,39 steht hier das Lehnwort κεντυρίων, nicht das griechische Äquivalent ἑκατοντάρχης (so aber Mt 27,54; Lk 23,47); vgl. zum synonymen Gebrauch beider Termini H.J. Mason, Greek Terms for Roman Institutions. A Lexicon and Analysis, ASP 13, Toronto 1974, 5. 163.

φυλάσσειν τὸν τάφον). Dass Petronius – anders als der Hauptmann am Kreuz in
Mk 15,39 – namentlich eingeführt wird, ist zwar im ansonsten mit Einzel-
figuren spärlich ausgestatteten Petrusevangelium bemerkenswert, allerdings
ist die Erzählung nicht eigentlich an seiner Person interessiert, sondern seine
Erwähnung zeigt vor allem die Bedeutung an, die Pilatus der Aktion beimisst.
Schließlich liegt die betonte Einführung der römischen Wachen auch in der
Konsequenz der strikten Distanzierung der Römer von der vorangehenden
Verspottung und Kreuzigung Jesu in EvPetr 6-24. Für die Hinrichtung sind
allein die Juden und ihr Apparat verantwortlich. Die Römer treten erst jetzt
nach dem Tod Jesu wieder auf (wohingegen Herodes nicht mehr als
Entscheidungsträger erscheint) – und werden zu Zeugen der Auferstehung
Jesu!

Auf dieses Geschehen ist die Binnenerzählung von der Grabwache (VV. 32-
44) zugespitzt. So wird z.B. die Kommunikation zwischen den jüdischen
Ältesten und den römischen Wachen lediglich erwähnt, aber nicht ausgeführt
(vgl. V. 39: ἐξηγουμένων αὐτῶν ἃ εἶδον; VV. 43-44: Συνεσκέπτοντο οὖν ἀλλήλοις
ἐκεῖνοι ἀπελθεῖν καὶ ἐνφανίσαι ταῦτα τῷ Πειλάτῳ καὶ ἔτι διανοουμένων αὐτῶν).
Allein der Inhalt der Stimmen vom Himmel und vom Kreuz wird in wörtlicher
Rede wiedergegeben und so prononciert (VV. 41-42: ἐκήρυξας τοῖς κοιμωμένοις
... ναί). Die Rede wird jeweils als Wahrnehmung der Wachen dargestellt (V. 41:
καὶ φωνῆς ἤκουον; vgl. V. 42: καὶ ὑπακοὴ ἠκούετο; sowie bereits V. 35: μεγάλη φωνὴ
ἐγένετο), was ebenso für die visuellen Momente der Offenbarung gilt (V. 36:
εἶδον; V. 38: ἰδόντες; V. 39: ἃ εἶδον; πάλιν ὁρῶσιν; V. 44: φαίνονται πάλιν). Ihre
Erfahrung bildet somit nicht nur die Grundlage des späteren Berichts an
Pilatus, sondern bestimmt auch die Sichtweise der Leserinnen und Leser, die
so gleichsam in die Ereignisse hineingenommen werden. Die Zuverlässigkeit
des Zeugnisses wird dadurch bekräftigt, dass die Soldaten als gehorsame und
gewissenhafte Befehlsempfänger gezeichnet werden. Sie sichern gemeinsam
mit den Juden das Grab (VV. 32-33; vgl. die Bestätigung in V. 34), halten auch
nachts Wache (V. 35), und zwar zu zweit (V. 35), und sie unterrichten
umgehend ihre Vorgesetzten von den Ereignissen (V. 38 Petronius; VV. 43 und
45: Pilatus). Der Centurio wird so schließlich selbst Zeuge der Auferstehung,
wohingegen Pilatus nur mittelbar über den Rapport seiner Soldaten (V. 45)
davon erfährt. Doch gerade dieses Wissen bildet den wesentlichen Unterschied
zur Fortsetzung der Erzählung von der Grabwache bei Mt. Denn Mt 28,11-15
entfaltet das Bemühen der jüdischen Führer, die Auferstehung vor dem
Statthalter zu verheimlichen. Im Petrusevangelium ist er nicht nur informiert,
sondern unterstützt die Juden sogar in ihrem Streben nach Geheimhaltung der
Ereignisse. Aufgrund dieser anderen Darstellung ist die Schlusssequenz der
Graberzählung (VV. 45-49) für das Pilatusbild des Petrusevangeliums
besonders aufschlussreich. Pilatus wird hier sowohl durch sein Verhalten
gegenüber den anderen Akteuren als auch durch wörtliche Rede charakterisiert. V. 46 enthält nicht nur die einzigen Worte des Statthalters im ganzen
P.Cair. 10759, er gliedert zudem die Episode, insofern sich in V. 45 zunächst

nur οἱ περὶ τὸν κεντυρίωνα an ihn wenden und in V. 48 dann πάντες zu ihm treten, wobei deren genaue Identität im Folgenden noch zu klären sein wird.

In VV. 35-44 wird die Wahrnehmung der Angelophanie durch die Soldaten ausführlich beschrieben, in V. 45 hingegen nur noch summarisch mit der Wendung καὶ ἐξηγήσαντο πάντα ἅπερ εἶδον darauf verwiesen (da die Ereignisse den Lesern und Leserinnen ja anders als Pilatus bereits bekannt sind), aber darüber hinausgehend ihre Reaktion auf die Ereignisse beschrieben. Welche Bedeutung die Wachen dem Erlebten beimessen, zeigt sich zunächst daran, dass sie unverzüglich Meldung machen, also noch *in der Nacht* (νυκτός) zu Pilatus *eilen* (ἔσπευσαν πρὸς Πειλᾶτον). Ihren Bericht tragen sie dann mit großer Bewegung vor (ἀγωνιῶντες μεγάλως). Den Höhepunkt bildet schließlich die (für die Soldaten ebenfalls zum einzigen Mal) in wörtlicher Rede wiedergegebene Deutung des Geschehens in Form des Bekenntnisses: ἀληθῶς υἱὸς ἦν θεοῦ (vgl. Mk 15,39 par. Mt 27,54). Der Gottessohn-Titel wurde zuvor im Petrusevangelium nur im Kontext der Verspottung durch die Juden verwendet (VV. 6.9), an der die Römer nicht beteiligt waren. Hier erscheint er nun völlig frei von Ironie oder Spott und damit in deutlicher Distanz zur jüdischen Haltung. Auch wenn die Erzählung an dieser Stelle eine Leerstelle[60] aufweist, ist aus dem Kontext deutlich, dass die Soldaten das wahre Wesen Jesu aufgrund der Epiphanie erkannt haben.[61] Pilatus hegt nicht die geringsten Zweifel an ihrem Zeugnis. Er stellt keinerlei Rückfragen und setzt die Gewissenhaftigkeit der Bewachung als gegeben voraus. Er sieht sich offensichtlich durch das Bekenntnis vielmehr in seiner früheren Haltung bestätigt, da er – ohne weitere Erklärung – den Titel Sohn Gottes in seiner Unschuldserklärung in V. 46 aufgreift: ἐγὼ καθαρεύω τοῦ αἵματος τοῦ υἱοῦ τοῦ θεοῦ, ὑμῖν δὲ τοῦτο ἔδοξεν. Damit wird zugleich der Bogen zurück zur Gerichtsverhandlung unter Herodes (EvPetr 1) geschlagen, insofern Pilatus nun explizit ausspricht, was er zuvor bereits symbolisch durch die Handwaschung angezeigt hat: Er weist jede Schuld am Tod Jesu von sich.[62] Den traditionsgeschichtlichen Hintergrund der programmatischen Erklärung dürfte abermals Ps 26,6 bilden, auch wenn dies sprachlich weniger deutlich ist als in V. 1.[63] Neben dem feierlichen, in

---

60 Vgl. zu diesem erzählerischen Mittel Sternberg, Poetics, 186-229.

61 Das Bekenntnis eines Römers zur Gottessohnschaft Jesu hat in der synoptischen Tradition seinen traditionsgeschichtlichen Ort am Kreuz (vgl. Mk 15,39 und bes. Mt 27,54). Da die Römer im Petrusevangelium jedoch nicht an der Hinrichtung Jesu beteiligt sind, ist es konsequent, es mit der Grabes- bzw. Auferstehungssequenz zu verbinden. Damit ist allerdings noch keine Entscheidung über die Ursprünglichkeit der einen oder der anderen Tradition getroffen.

62 Gegen Denker, Stellung, 59, der meint, die Beteuerung des Pilatus diene vielmehr dazu, „Jesus als Sohn Gottes zu erweisen, denn das Bekenntnis des Pilatus ist die stilgerechte Antwort auf die Epiphanie, von der die Soldaten erzählen. Hinter diesen Skopus tritt der andere, die Unschuld des Pilatus zu erweisen, zurück."

63 Vgl. Ps 25,6 LXX: νίψομαι ἐν ἀθῴοις τὰς χεῖράς μου (vgl. entsprechend Mt 27,24: ἀθῷός εἰμι ἀπὸ τοῦ αἵματος τούτου). Das Verb καθαρεύω („rein sein") findet sich weder in der Septuaginta noch im Neuen Testament, es ist aber in profaner sowie in der nicht kanonischen Literatur des antiken Judentums gut bezeugt; vgl. Bauer, Wörterbuch, 785. In Ps 23,4 LXX werden ἀθῷος (mit χείρ!) und καθαρός in Form eines *parallelismus membrorum* zusammengestellt (ἀθῷος χερσὶν καὶ

alttestamentlich-jüdischem Duktus vorgetragenen Bekenntnis zur Gottessohnschaft Jesu im Munde des Römers ist vor allem die scharfe Gegenüberstellung
von ἐγώ und ὑμεῖς[64] zu beachten.[65] Auf diese Weise werden die Juden
sukzessive wieder in das erzählerische Geschehen hineingenommen. Die
Redeeinleitung in V. 46, ἀποκτιθεὶς ὁ Πειλᾶτος ἔφη, lässt zwar erwarten, Pilatus
wende sich an seine Soldaten, zumal sie die einzigen sind, die nach V. 45 zu
ihm kommen, doch haben sie zuvor nichts beschlossen, so dass ὑμῖν δὲ τοῦτο
ἔδοξεν nicht an ihre Adresse gerichtet sein kann, sondern auf die Juden bezogen
sein muss. Dies bestätigt auch der Anschluss in V. 47, insofern εἶτα formal die
Reaktion auf die Pilatusrede markiert, sich die Forderung der πάντες nach
Geheimhaltung der Ereignisse am Grab inhaltlich aber gerade auf den
Centurio und die Soldaten bezieht, die somit nicht Subjekt des Satzes sein
können. Die Identifikation der πάντες mit der jüdischen Führung[66] wird
zusätzlich durch die Begründung ihrer Bitte in V. 48 bestätigt, wo die Angst
vor dem Volk aus V. 30 wieder aufgenommen wird.

Mit ihrem Zeugnis haben die Soldaten ihre Funktion für die Erzählung
erfüllt und zum Ende der Szene stehen sich wieder Pilatus und die Juden allein
gegenüber. Diese Konstellation erinnert zunächst an die Eingangsszene, in der
gleichfalls ein Kontrast zwischen Juden und Römern aufgebaut wurde. Im
Gegensatz zur emphatischen Unschuldserklärung des Pilatus – die von ihnen
ebenso unkommentiert bleibt wie ihre eigene Beschuldigung –, laden die Juden
mit ihrer Bitte um Geheimhaltung sogar bewusst weitere Schuld auf sich (vgl.
V. 48: ἡμῖν ὀφλῆσαι μεγίστην ἁμαρτίαν ἔμπροθεν τοῦ θεοῦ), um so der Rache des
Volkes zu entgehen. Durch ihr Schuldeingeständnis bestätigen sie zugleich das
Zeugnis der Soldaten.[67] Daher ist die Wendung, welche die Szene dann nimmt,

---

καθαρὸς τῇ καρδίᾳ). Die Verbindung des Stamms καθ- mit αἷμα findet sich auch in Sus 46 Θ
(καθαρὸς ἐγὼ ἀπὸ τοῦ αἵματος ταύτης) sowie in Apg 20,46 (καθαρός εἰμι ἀπὸ τοῦ αἵματος πάντων),
ἀθῷος und αἷμα auch in 2 Sam 3,28 (ἀθῷός εἰμι ἐγὼ καὶ ἡ βασιλεία μου ἀπὸ κυρίου ἕως αἰῶνος ἀπὸ
τῶν αἱμάτων Αβεννηρ υἱοῦ Νηρ) sowie in Mt 27,4 (ἥμαρτον παραδοὺς αἷμα ἀθῷον). Symmachus
liest in Ps 25,6 statt ἐν ἀθῷοις ἐν καθαρότητι (vgl. Denker, Stellung, 59).

[64] Zwar bietet das Manuskript von P.Cair. 10759 hier ἡμῖν, doch ist an dieser Stelle der
      Entscheidung von Nicklas/Kraus, Petrusevangelium, 44-45, für die Konjektur ὑμῖν zu folgen;
      vgl. ebenso M.G. Mara, Évangile de Pierre, SC 201, Paris 1973, 60; D. Lührmann, Fragmente
      apokryph gewordener Evangelien in griechischer und lateinischer Sprache, MThSt 59,
      Marburg 2000, 91.

[65] Diese Kontrastierung findet sich ähnlich in Mt 27,24 (ἀθῷός εἰμι ἀπὸ τοῦ αἵματος τούτου· ὑμεῖς
      ὄψεσθε), im Petrusevangelium ist die Schuldzuweisung an die Juden freilich im Aorist
      formuliert (vgl. aber Mt 26,66: τί ὑμῖν δοκεῖ;), da das Urteil nicht nur schon gefällt, sondern
      sogar schon vollstreckt ist.

[66] Vermutlich ist hier wieder ein größerer Kreis als nur die Ältesten anvisiert, welcher der in V. 28
      genannten Gruppe entsprechen dürfte. Ab V. 50 werden die Juden wieder undifferenziert
      genannt; vgl. VV. 50.52.

[67] Da sich auch die Ältesten an der Grabwache beteiligt haben, werden sie gleichfalls zu Zeugen
      der Auferstehung, so dass deren Leugnung, die darauf abzielte, das Volk nicht aufzubringen
      (VV. 47-48), schwerer wiegt als in der synoptischen Entsprechung Mt 28,11. Zwar könnte auch
      Mt 27,65-66 eine Beteiligung der Juden suggerieren, doch sind in 28,4.11 nur die Wachen bzw.
      Soldaten erwähnt. Somit könnte die Unterdrückung des (fremden) Zeugnisses der Wache auch

im Blick auf die Charakterisierung des Pilatus um so überraschender, denn er geht ohne weitere Diskussion oder Begründung auf ihre Forderung ein und verpflichtet seine Leute zum Stillschweigen (V. 49: ἐκέλευσεν οὖν ὁ Πειλᾶτος τῷ κεντυρίωνι καὶ τοῖς στρατιώταις μηδὲν εἰπεῖν). Da Pilatus – anders als bei Mt, wo sich nur die Wachen durch ihr Schweigen am Betrug beteiligen – durch seine Leute um die Auferstehung Jesu weiß und mit seinem Gottessohnbekenntnis zeigt, dass er ihrem Zeugnis unbedingtes Vertrauen schenkt, wird er durch diese Einwilligung zum Mittäter. Er handelt – wie die Ältesten – wider besseres Wissen und stellt sich damit faktisch aus Machtkalkül auf die Seite der Juden.

Damit wird Pilatus in dieser Szene deutlich ambivalenter gezeichnet als in der Eröffnungssequenz und das Zugeständnis an die Juden ist zugleich der letzte Eindruck, den die Leser und Leserinnen von ihm erhalten. Seine einzigen Worte in P.Cair. 10759 – ein klares Bekenntnis der Gottessohnschaft Jesu und seiner eigenen Unschuld an dessen Tod – stehen in völligem Kontrast zu seinem Handeln – der Einwilligung in die Bitte der Juden. In der Binnenlogik des Petrusevangeliums ist das Bemühen um Geheimhaltung der Auferstehung ironischer Weise freilich sinnlos, da die Frauen um Maria Magdalena in EvPetr 50-57 Zeuginnen des leeren Grabes werden und somit gesichert ist, dass die Botschaft weiter getragen wird. Pilatus schlägt sich also völlig überflüssig auf die Seite der Juden, die Botschaft der Auferstehung lässt sich durch solche Intrigen nicht aufhalten.

4. Ergebnisse

4.1 Charakterisierung des Pilatus

Die vorangehende erzähltechnische Analyse hat den Blick auf die Gestalt des Pilatus geschärft. Mangels direkter Beschreibungen gehören zu den wichtigsten Mitteln seiner Charakterisierung die – aus Perspektive eines auktorialen Erzählers vorgetragenen – Begegnungen mit und Beziehungen zu anderen Akteuren der erzählten Welt, also Herodes bzw. den Juden und ihren Führern, seinem „Freund" Josef sowie den römischen Soldaten. Sie alle sind Pilatus in unterschiedlicher Weise zugeordnet, so dass durch seinen Umgang mit diesen Figuren sowie reziprok auch durch deren Verhalten und Aussagen ein differenziertes Bild seines Charakters gezeichnet wird. Gegenüber Herodes und den Juden verhält er sich trotz sachlicher Differenzen nicht nur förmlich korrekt, sondern sogar kooperativ. Josef begegnet er hilfsbereit und

---

als Zeichen der Ungläubigkeit aufgefasst werden, wohingegen die Juden im Petrusevangelium wider ihre eigene Erfahrung handeln.

verbindlich. Das Verhältnis zu seinen Soldaten ist erzählerisch durch die
Struktur von Befehl und Ausführung geprägt und seiner Position entsprechend klar militärisch-hierarchisch geordnet. Dabei wird zugleich betont,
dass Pilatus unbedingt auf ihre Kompetenz und ihr Urteil vertraut. Dennoch
bleiben die Soldaten anonyme, typisierte Figuren,[68] deren Hauptfunktion in
der Augenzeugenschaft der Auferstehung und im Bekenntnis der Gottessohnschaft Jesu besteht. Sobald sie diese Aufgabe erfüllt haben, geht der Fokus
wieder ganz auf Pilatus und die Führer der Juden über.

Die Kommunikation zwischen den einzelnen Akteuren wird in den
Pilatusszenen meistens nur erzählt oder vorausgesetzt (z.B. V. 4: ᾔτησεν αὐτοῦ
τὸ σῶμα; V. 43: συνεσκέπτοντο οὖν ἀλλήλοις), aber nur selten in direkter Rede
wiedergegeben; eigentliche Dialoge fehlen ganz.[69] Dadurch erhalten die
wenigen wörtlichen Aussagen besonderes Gewicht, das zusätzlich durch
intertextuelle Bezüge auf die alttestamentlich-jüdische Tradition verstärkt
wird. Herodes beruft sich direkt, Pilatus indirekt auf die Tora, um die
Rechtmäßigkeit ihres Handelns zu bekunden, was insbesondere bei dem
Römer nicht einer gewissen Ironie entbehrt. Zudem ist ihr Verhalten
komplementär: Zwar übernimmt Herodes die volle Verantwortung für die
Verurteilung Jesu, besteht aber auf einem ordentlichen Begräbnis. Pilatus weist
hingegen jede Schuld am Tod Jesu von sich, ist jedoch bereit, hinsichtlich
dessen Grab mit den Juden gemeinsame Sache zu machen, insofern er zunächst
ihr Ansinnen um Grabwache unterstützt und ihnen dann hilft, die Wahrheit
um die Geschehnisse am Grab zu unterdrücken. Auf diese Weise wird er in die
Schuld der Juden, die in V. 48 nochmals sehr deutlich benannt wird, mit
hineingezogen.

4.1 Der „Charakter" Pilatus und das kulturelle Umfeld des Petrusevangeliums

Das Pilatusbild des Petrusevangeliums lässt sich nicht einheitlich bestimmen.
Pilatus erscheint als eine widersprüchliche und damit durchaus „menschliche"
Gestalt, deren Handeln nicht notwendig seinen Worten entspricht, vielmehr im
Widerspruch dazu steht. Dabei wird der „apokryphe" Pilatus teilweise vorteil-
hafter dargestellt als in der neutestamentlichen Tradition, etwa was seine
Distanzierung von der Verurteilung und Hinrichtung Jesu angeht, teilweise
aber auch negativer gezeichnet, so vor allem in der Grabwachenerzählung, da
er anders als im matthäischen Bericht um das „leere Grab" weiß. Auch wenn er

---

[68] Dies gilt auch für den Centurio, dessen Namen wir zwar erfahren, von dem wir aber darüber
      hinaus nicht mehr erfahren als von den Übrigen.

[69] Dies betrifft auch die ausgeführte Rede des Pilatus in V. 46, da er sich mit seiner Antwort, wie
      gezeigt, an die Juden und nicht mehr an die Soldaten wendet. Eine Ausnahme, die aber die
      Charakterisierung des Pilatus nur mittelbar betrifft, bildet das Gespräch zwischen der Stimme
      aus dem Himmel und dem Kreuz in VV. 41-42, die dann auch das Zentrum der gesamten
      Szene markiert.

im Petrusevangelium von der Schuld am Tod Jesu entlastet wird, ist er doch
bereit, das Zeugnis der Auferstehung zu verhindern. Daher ist das Urteil Claus
Bussmanns zu pauschal, das Petrusevangelium ziehe durch seine Belastung
der Juden und die Entlastung des Pilatus am Tod Jesu einen „Trend aus (…),
der schon in der Entwicklung der kanonischen Evangelien angelegt ist"[70], was
den Rückschluss erlaube, hinter dem Petrusevangelium stehe eine Gruppe,
„die sich in ‚mentaler Annäherung' an das *imperium Romanum*"[71] befinde.
Vielmehr ist Denker zuzustimmen, dass im Petrusevangelium „eine
philorömische, die Römer entlastende Tendenz (…) nicht konsequent zum
Tragen"[72] kommt.

Lässt sich aber aufgrund dieses ambivalenten Befundes überhaupt auf eine
Intention des Petrusevangeliums bzw. seine Stellung gegenüber dem *Imperium
Romanum* schließen? Zunächst ist festzuhalten, dass uns Pilatus – wie etwa
auch im Neuen Testament oder bei Josephus – hier als eine literarische Gestalt,
nicht als unmittelbar fassbare historische Größe gegenübertritt. Während seine
Verantwortung für das Todesurteil Jesu historisch unstrittig ist, spielt das
Petrusevangelium diesen Zusammenhang herunter. Es stellt aber gleichzeitig
deutlich heraus, dass seine Taten nicht notwendig seinen Worten entsprechen
müssen. Pilatus ist schwach und unzuverlässig bzw. unberechenbar, wenn es
um politisches Kalkül geht. Die recht nüchterne Charakterzeichnung des

---

[70] Bussmann, Verhältnis, 90. Dieses Urteil greift im Übrigen bereits für das Neue Testament zu
kurz, weshalb Bond, Pilate, 206, zu Recht betont: „[T]here is no evidence of a linear progression
throughout the gospels in which Pilate becomes progressively friendlier towards Christianity."
Vgl. etwa das kritische Pilatusbild, das Warren Carter für das Matthäusevangelium entwirft:
„In rejecting a rigid separation of political and theological concerns, I will argue that Pilate's
responsibility is not minimized, that the political nature of Jesus' death is not disguised, that
the scene [sc. Mt 27,11-26; H.O.] does not condemn or exclude Jewish people for rejecting Jesus,
and that the scene is very interested in relations with Rome which it construes as dangerous
and threatening but certainly not ultimative since they are subject to God's purpose."
(W. Carter, Matthew *and* Empire. Initial Explorations, Harrisburg/PA 2001, 145-168, hier: 147).
Vor allem ist auch das Ausmaß der *politischen* Apologetik des Lukas in der jüngeren Forschung
strittig; vgl. etwa R.J. Cassidy, Jesus, Politics, and Society. A Study of Luke's Gospel, Maryknoll
1978, bes. 63-76; W. Stegemann, Zwischen Synagoge und Obrigkeit. Zur historischen Situation
der lukanischen Christen, FRLANT 152, Göttingen 1991, bes. 30-33. M. Wolter, Die Juden und
die Obrigkeit bei Lukas, in: Ja und Nein. Christliche Theologie im Angesicht Israels. FS
Wolfgang Schrage, hg. von K. Wengst/G. Saß, Neukirchen-Vluyn 1998, 277-290, betont, dass
der Konflikt in Lk 23,1-25 auf einer „dreiseitigen Interaktion (jüdische Ankläger – Jesus –
Pilatus) basiert" (288); vgl. ähnlich Bond, Pilate, 160: „Although he [i.e. Lukas; H.O.] clearly
wants to lay the bulk of the blame on the Jewish chief priests, Pilate's lack of interest and
weakness inevitably lead him to a place in this evil alliance. The Roman governor has not been
whitewashed." Vgl. ibid., 206: „Pilate plays an important role as the representative of Roman
law who declares Jesus innocent. Yet, like the governors before whom Christians are made to
stand trail in Acts, he is of a rather dubious character." Auch C. Burfeind, Paulus *muß* nach
Rom. Zur politischen Dimension der Apostelgeschichte, NTS 46, 2000, 75-91, erkennt in der
„Theologie des Lukas eine Rom-kritische Pointe" (75).

[71] Bussmann, Verhältnis, 91.

[72] Denker, Stellung, 79, der jedoch seinerseits zu einseitig die Apologetik gegenüber den Juden
betont, das heißt das Bemühen, sich mit jüdischen Einwänden gegen das Christentum
auseinander zu setzen (vgl. ibid., 78-87).

Pilatus im Petrusevangelium lässt weder eine besondere Sympathie noch Antipathie des Erzählers für ihn erkennen. Doch gerade diese Offenheit ist es, die seinen Adressaten eine Haltung des gesunden Misstrauens gegenüber den Römern zu empfehlen scheint. Diese Beobachtung kann freilich kaum als Indiz für die konkreten Entstehungsbedingungen des Petrusevangeliums ausgewertet werden. Auszuschließen sind allenfalls Zeiten und Gegenden schwerer Verfolgung und Repression. Die Darstellung dürfte von vielfältigen Erfahrungen des Alltags getragen sein, etwa von Situationen, in denen Vertreter des Imperiums gegen ihre Einsicht – z.B. in die politische Unbedenklichkeit des Christentums – handeln, oder in denen man sich zumindest nicht auf ihr Wort verlassen kann. Entscheidend ist dabei aber, dass das Petrusevangelium nicht bei diesem Argwohn verharrt, sondern der Fortgang der Erzählung mit der Angelophanie der Frauen am Grab seine Trägergruppe vergewissert, dass die Unzuverlässigkeit und Unberechenbarkeit der Römer die Ausbreitung des Christentums so wie in der Vergangenheit auch in der Zukunft nicht aufzuhalten vermag.

Die Darstellung des Pilatus im Petrusevangelium erklärt darüber hinaus, mehr noch als die kanonische Tradition, den völlig gegenläufigen Weg seiner weiteren Wirkungsgeschichte.[73] Auf der einen Seite findet sich eine äußerst positive Rezeption, in deren Verlauf Pilatus mehr und mehr von der Schuld am Tod Jesu rehabilitiert wird, dabei zunächst heimlicher, dann offener Christ und letztlich Märtyrer wird, ja in der koptischen und äthiopischen Kirche sogar als Heiliger verehrt wird. Auf der anderen Seite hat er – nachdem er längst Eingang in die großen christlichen Bekenntnisse, das Apostolicum und das Nicänum, gefunden hat[74] – eine, die westlichen Kirchen seit dem Mittelalter bestimmende negative Auslegungsgeschichte durchlaufen. Sie erkennt im Waschen der Hände lediglich einen äußeren Ritus, aber keine Befreiung von Schuld. Pilatus erfährt in diesem Überlieferungsstrang seine wohlverdiente Strafe, meist durch Freitod. Beide Traditionslinien sind im Petrusevangelium anzutreffen und stehen ohne Widerspruch nebeneinander. Pilatus bekennt Jesus als Sohn Gottes, womit seine weitere Rezeption als Christ ermöglicht ist. Aber dennoch leugnet er seine Auferstehung, was der negativen Deutungslinie entspricht. Da die Grabwache letztlich in seinen Zuständigkeitsbereich fällt,

---

[73] Vgl. zum Folgenden Demandt, Hände, 214-230; Luz, Matthäus, 283-285; Scheidgen, Gestalt, passim.

[74] R. Staats, Pontius Pilatus im Bekenntnis der frühen Kirche, ZThK 84, 1987, 493-513, hier: 510, erklärt die (positive bzw. neutrale) Rezeption des Pilatus in den frühchristlichen Symbola von der Tradition der Fürbitte der Märtyrerkirche für die antichristliche Obrigkeit her. Vgl. kritisch dazu B.J. Diebner, „Pontius Pilatus" in der postkanonischen Literatur. Ein Beitrag zur Funktion und Rezeption der seit 2000 Jahren meisterwähnten Figur der Geschichte, in: Jüdische Schriften in ihrem antik-jüdischen und urchristlichen Kontext, hg. von H. Lichtenberger/G.S. Oegema, JSHRZ-St 1, Gütersloh 2002, 429-448, hier: 432-433. Diebner betont die soteriologische Bedeutung des Pilatus für die Bekenntnisbildung: „Pilatus *konnte* (nicht real-historisch, sondern im Rahmen der literarischen Konzeptionen in der frühchristlichen Literatur) Jesus gar nicht vor dem Kreuzestode bewahren, weil sonst das gesamte Heilswerk nicht funktionieren könnte" (441).

kommt die Redewendung „von Pontius zu Pilatus laufen" somit trotz der Betonung der Rolle des Herodes noch zu ihrem Recht. Schließlich ist nämlich Pilatus derjenige, der als letzter offizieller Verantwortlicher in Erscheinung tritt und die Ausbreitung des Christentums zu verhindern sucht – freilich erfolglos.

Bodies and the Technology of Power
Reading the Gospel of Peter under Empire

by

TODD PENNER and CAROLINE VANDER STICHELE

The Performative Function of the Passion

In his seminal and substantive study of the Gospel passion narratives, Raymond Brown revisits a particular quandary he dealt with several years earlier: the relationship of the fragmentary, so-designated *Gospel of Peter* (*GP*) and the canonical gospel traditions.[1] Sparked in part by John Dominic Crossan's controversial study, *The Cross that Spoke: The Origins of the Passion Narrative*,[2] Brown

---

1   R.E. Brown, The Death of the Messiah: From Gethsemane to the Grave, ABRL, 2 vols., New York 1994, 2:1317-49; cf. his earlier The *Gospel of Peter* and Canonical Priority, NTS 33, 1987, 321-343.

2   J.D. Crossan, The Cross that Spoke: The Origins of the Passion Narrative, San Francisco 1988. In this study, Crossan makes an extended case for viewing the *GP* passion narrative as providing an earlier version of the death-resurrection scheme than the rendition contained in the canonical gospels. Crossan embeds the *GP* account – at least its earliest stage – thoroughly in Jewish (particularly court-accusation/wisdom) traditions (cf. J. Daniélou, The Theology of Jewish Christianity [trans. J.A. Baker, London 1964], 20-21, who makes the connection between *GP* and the apocalyptic traditions of later Judaism; as well as P.M. Head, On the Christology of the Gospel of Peter, VigChr 46, 1992, 209-224; and D.F. Wright, Apologetic and Apocalyptic: The Miraculous in the Gospel of Peter, in: The Miracles of Jesus, ed. by D. Wenham/G. Blomberg, Gospel Perspectives 6, Sheffield 1986, 401-418). In Crossan's framework, three strata can be distinguished in *GP*. The oldest stratum is that of the "Cross Gospel," a pre-canonical passion narrative dated to the forties of the first century CE and located in Sepphoris. The second layer can be traced to the canonical gospels, and consists of additions based on the canonical versions in circulation at that time. This stratum is dated to the second half of the second century. The third stratum is the redactional layer, connecting the first two strata, and came into existence during the process of scribal combination (for a summary of the details, see the appendix in Crossan, Who Killed Jesus? Exposing the Roots of Anti-Semitism in the Gospel Story of the Death of Jesus, San Francisco 1995, 223-227). In The Death of the Messiah, Brown argues for the "utter implausibility" of Crossan's suggestion (2:1342 n. 45). Brown himself rather considers *GP* to be a (relatively late) "free harmonization of canonical Gospel memories and traditions" (2:1334 n. 28). For a moderating position between the two, see H. Koester, Ancient Christian Gospels. Their History and Development, Philadelphia-London 1990, 220-240, who concludes that *GP* is "on the whole" independent of the canonical gospel narratives, and that they use common traditions in divergent ways (240).

seeks to entrench the position detailed nearly seventy years earlier by Léon
Vaganay in his commentary on this "apocryphal" text[3]: the canonical gospels
are the primary historical sources for the passion of Jesus, while *GP* is derivative and secondary, adding nothing of significant historical value to the New
Testament traditions. In an attempt to illustrate how, in his understanding, *GP*
can be understood to have been loosely based on the canonical accounts,
Brown offers the following observation:

> Let me suppose that we selected in our own century some Christians who had read
> or studied Matt[hew] in Sunday school or church education classes years ago but in
> the interim had not been reading their [New Testament]. Yet they had heard the ca-
> nonical passion narratives read in church liturgies. Also they had seen a passion
> play or dramatization in the cinema, on TV, or on the stage, or heard one on the ra-
> dio; and they had attended a church service where preachers were using imagina-
> tion to fill in [Passion Narrative] lacunae ... If we asked this select group of Chris-
> tians to recount the passion, I am certain they would have an idea of the general
> outline, but not necessarily be able to preserve the *proper sequence* of any particular
> Gospel ... In other words, we would get from our test group of Christians modern
> parallels to [*GP*] ... not produced at a desk by someone with written sources
> propped up before him but by someone with a memory of what he had read and
> heard (canonical and noncanonical) to which he contributed imagination and a
> sense of drama.[4]

Brown, of course, does not intend to reflect long and hard on the mechanics of
modern passion performance. He rather seeks to illustrate that it is precisely
the performative and commemorative function of the passion narrative material that explains the secondary and popularizing nature of the *GP* account.
Moreover, his detailed arguments for the priority of the canonical passion narrative tradition stand in continuity with a long line of work dedicated to using
GP as a major link in an argument about the *origins* of Christian traditions or
even the main contours of incipient Christianity itself. As Edward Said has
aptly noted, underlying a formal quest [for beginnings] is

> an imaginative and emotional need for unity, a need to apprehend an otherwise
> dispersed number of circumstances and to put them in some sort of telling order,
> sequential, moral, or logical. Very frequently, especially when the search for a be-
> ginning is pursued within a moral and imaginative framework, the beginning im-
> plies the end – or, rather, implicates it ...[5]

Overall, then, scholars have often failed to note the (per)formative role of the
passion narrative that is operative in both modern and ancient constructions
(in the process also failing to note the critical connection that exists between the
two). Indeed, regardless of where one falls on matters of priority and dating,
more often than not specific ideological concerns dominate the agenda. Thus,
for Crossan, considering *GP* to be an early text offers an "alternative" proto-

---

3   L. Vaganay, L'Évangile de Pierre, ÉtB, Paris ²1930. Vaganay considered the text to be a docetic
     and derivative tradition arising from within popular forms of Christianity (112-122).
4   Brown, Death of the Messiah, 2:1335-1336 (our emphasis).
5   E.W. Said, Beginnings: Intention and Method, New York 1985, 41.

passion narrative to the canonical versions – the earliest recoverable Christology. For Brown, just the opposite is true: a late dating serves to protect the
legitimacy and authority of the canonical accounts. Notwithstanding the differences in opinion between Crossan and Brown, there are some remarkable
similarities in their approaches. First, both scholars approach *GP* in terms of its
relevance for the canonical gospels. Second, both are interested in the question
of their dependence, and, third, both take the next logical step to focus on the
question of chronological priority. In the end, a theological disagreement is
thus played out over the positioning of *GP* in early Christianity.

Moreover, this modern scholarly dynamic, with its overt focus on dependence issues, results in something quite important being missed in the study of
GP as a result. First, *GP* is not studied as a unity in itself, but solely in light of
the intra-canonical gospel tradition. Second, in focusing on similarities and
differences with the canonical material, the inner logic and coherence of *GP* is
not taken seriously and alternative interpretations than the ones offered by the
canonical gospels are often not taken into consideration. This situation is further complicated by the difficulties inherent in attempting to contextualize *GP*
in its own right (in fact, the canonical dependence issues may have taken on a
greater significance precisely for this reason). In general, traditional historical
approaches to ancient texts have always placed a high priority on situating and
localizing the text in question. Texts are presumed to reveal their true meaning
if they can be read within a framework of a particular geographical region or
city (its archaeology, its history and culture) or a particular type of theology or
religious practice (e.g., apocalyptic, docetic). Yet, *GP* is notoriously difficult to
date and locate (let alone to reconstruct as a *whole* text).[6] In fact, we really do
not know how early or how late *GP* is – it could be a first, or a second, or possibly even a third or fourth century tradition/text.[7] Thus, precisely because of

---

[6]   Indeed, making matters even more complex, the very designation of the text as the "Gospel of
      Peter" already represents an effort to classify an otherwise free-floating text. The name comes
      from ancient references to a "Gospel of Peter." Given the presumed role of Peter as narrator,
      GP has often been equated with that text cited in Eusebius (cf. Koester, Ancient Christian
      Gospels, 217, for the easy elision of *GP* with the gospel mentioned by Eusebius in *h.e.* 6,12,1-6,
      where it is designated as such by Serapion of Antioch). We have no way of knowing, however,
      that our *GP* is that text as opposed to any other (Petrine) text (on the various ancient
      references to Petrine gospel[s], see T.J. Kraus/T. Nicklas, ed., Das Petrusevangelium und die
      Petrusapokalypse: Die griechischen Fragmente mit deutscher und englischer Übersetzung,
      GCS.NF 11; Neutestamentliche Apokryphen 1, Berlin-New York 2004, 11-23). Rather, the
      practice of situating and localizing texts in order to interpret them has largely led scholars to
      assume the correlation. Given the extensive production of Petrine traditions in early
      Christianity (cf. T.V. Smith, Petrine Controversies in Early Christianity: Attitudes toward Peter
      in Christian Writings of the First Two Centuries, WUNT 2.15, Tübingen 1985) – and the fact
      that we have today, in our possession, only a fragmentary remnant of the textual production
      of the first three centuries of Christianity – we are in a relative bind with respect to
      identifying, naming, and classifying *GP*.
[7]   Moreover, given the on-going debate regarding the relationship of P.Oxy. 2949 to the Akhmîm
      text (the full[est?] extant version of *GP*), it is entirely possible that the text we call the Gospel
      of Peter is in fact a sixth- or seventh-century rewriting of an earlier narrative. See the

GP's resistance to being localized, and aside from the issues related to canonical dependence, there has in fact been relatively little done on this text other than comparing it with ancient traditions more generally (a means of classification through correlation) or seeking to uncover its particular theological themes in order to position it within the ambient sphere of emergent Christian traditions.[8]

Yet *GP*, along with other early Christian so-called "apocrypha," serve as critical components in the construction of the *self* in early Christian communities.[9] Therefore, the usual, contemporary focus on the logic of progression and derivation misses this point entirely, as it neglects the very reason why *GP* was written, read, recited, and performed in the first place. Indeed, those elements that can be recovered – the socio-rhetorical performance embedded in *GP's* rhetoric – may well provide the most valuable information on early Christianity a text like *GP* can yield. Then, as now, passion stories provide windows into the cultural and social ideologies of particular individuals and communities, and it is precisely this facet that deserves more serious attention in scholarship.[10] One of the critical issues facing modern scholarship of *GP* and texts like it, therefore, is the need to develop models and approaches that move us beyond the traditional questions that by necessity produce conventional answers. By way of moving the discussion in a divergent direction and in order to develop a conceptual framework that allows us to explore the discursive structure of a text like *GP*, our aim is to broaden the discussion by moving into the sphere of body representation in ancient texts. Focusing, in particular, on the role of ancient spectacle in terms of relating the individual to empire and vice-versa, the strategies for domination and control that emerge on a corporate level may prove helpful for assessing literary representations of and responses

---

discussion in D.F. Wright, Apocryphal Gospels: The "Unknown Gospel" (Pap. Egerton 2) and the Gospel of Peter, in: The Jesus Tradition Outside of the Gospels, ed. by D. Wenham, Gospel Perspectives 5, Sheffield 1984, 207-232, esp. 221-223; cf. D. Lührmann, P.Oxy. 2949: EvPt 3-5 in einer Handschrift des 2./3. Jahrhunderts, ZNW 72, 1981, 216-226. In Koester's treatment, one can perceive the fairly easy manner in which the late Akhmîm fragment is readily identified with P.Oxy. 2949 (Ancient Christian Gospels, 216-217; although, immediately after making this association, Koester then prompts for caution in assuming a direct correlation between the fragment and the longer text in an attempt to undermine Crossan's redactional thesis [219]).

[8]   For the apocalyptic connections, see the studies listed in n. 2 above. For an extensive treatment of *GP* as a docetic text, see J. Denker, Die theologiegeschichtliche Stellung des Petrus-evangeliums. Ein Beitrag zur Frühgeschichte des Doketismus, EHS XXIII.36, Frankfurt-Bern 1975. See the most recent assessment by P. Foster, Are There Any Fragments of the So-Called Gospel of Peter?, NTS 52, 2006, 1-28, whose analysis of the textual data and ancient evidence supports our more open and ambivalent conclusions here and in n. 6 above.

[9]   For the notion of the self used here, see M. Foucault, The Care of the Self, The History of Sexuality 3, trans. by R. Huxley, New York 1988, 39-68, esp. 64-67. See also J. Perkins, The Suffering Self: Pain and Narrative Representation in the Early Christian Era, London 1995, 6-7.

[10]   Most recently E.B. Aitken has traced out the origin of the non-gospel New Testament passion materials within the ritualistic cultic setting of early Christianity, demonstrating the utility of connecting textual analysis with broader cultural performances. See her Jesus' Death in Early Christian Memory. The Poetics of the Passion, NTOA/StUNT 53, Göttingen-Fribourg 2004.

to pain and suffering, such as one finds in *GP*. While any number of aspects of the text could have been selected for this study, body representation is particularly useful for moving into new analytical terrain because, as Willi Braun notes,

> [b]odies … are a modality by which ideology becomes material and body-being is both *representational* and *generative* of subjectivity in social *situ* … bodies … *are* ideological constructs, and body-selves and body practices both express and affect beliefs and compliance with those beliefs.[11]

At one level, helpful for pushing this analysis further is Michel Foucault's exploration of the ways in which individuals interact with others through the construction and domination of the *self*. Foucault focused particularly on the household as the locus for this activity, and moved away from an emphasis on the domination over others by the Roman imperial state apparatus.[12] His discussion of Christianity is of particular interest here, as he delves into the distinctive characteristics of early Christian self-disciplining. Here the discursive practice of *exhomologēsis* comes into view – the "recognition of fact" or the public identification and affirmation of the "truth" of their faith, a confession of being Christian,[13] which highlights the *theatrical* nature of this construction of the self. Moreover, a ready connection also emerges between the penitent's disposition and discourses related to death, torture, and martyrdom, which, as the most public and resolute forms of Christian self-disclosure in this ancient context, helped shape a perception that "the way the martyr faces death is the model for the penitent."[14] While Foucault in some sense failed to connect these patterns related to the self to broader patterns of control and domination in early Christian groups (and beyond that to imperial dominion), his focus on self-mastery as an individual activity helps us to see the ways in which the early Christian self took on particular contours of meaning and formation in terms of specific patterns of discourse that arose within these communities. Indeed, precisely here we see how the body represented in action embodies fully the ideology of a particular socio-cultural *situ*, while at the same time, in its public recognition, becoming a form of authority for those that encounter the representation.

---

11 W. Braun, Physiotherapy of Femininity in the Acts of Thecla, in: Text and Artifact in the Religions of Mediterranean Antiquity. Essays in Honour of Peter Richardson, ed. by S.G. Wilson/M. Desjardins, ESCJ 9, Waterloo/Ont. 2000, 220.

12 This theme is developed in detail in his famous lecture of 1980, now published in M. Foucault, Technologies of the Self, in: The Essential Foucault: Selections from the Essential Works of Foucault, 1954-1984, ed. by P. Rabinow/N. Rose, New York 2003, 145-169. See the brief but constructive summary of Foucault's argument, and criticisms of it, in C.A. Frilingos, Spectacles of Empire: Monsters, Martyrs, and the Book of Revelation, Divinations: Rereading Late Ancient Religion, Philadelphia 2004, 65-66.

13 Foucault, Technologies of the Self, 162.

14 Ibid., 163-164. In this vein, Tertullian's mandate for the Christian to "publish himself" (*publicatio sui*) reflects the affected state of the self as being subject to sin and undergoing "death" in order to gain life.

From this brief entrée into self-formation and control in early Christianity, we would highlight two particular features for our purposes here. First, particular discursive structures in early Christianity help shape individual and group identities, often in interaction with and mutual dependence on each other (in Foucault's emphasis, through the very negation of self in service of faith publicly displayed). Second, the exhibited body has a powerful effect in structuring the social and cultural ideologies of particular communities, in the process generating symbolic and ritualistic discourses of power and control. Foucault is focusing here in particular on the "technologies of the self," an expression he uses to designate the constructive interaction between private self-comportment and the publicly recognized self, thus pushing his discursive historical analysis deeper into self-identity as a form of self-domination and self-discipline. Such technologies for individual control, however, rather easily become constructive possibilities for the control of others. Moreover, at the heart of such technologies lies the use of the body as a theatrical representation in the ancient world – a spectacle that was seamlessly integrated into the socio-cultural fabric of ancient life and thought.

Spectacle and Body in the Ancient World

Along the lines developed above, we begin with a rather interesting story related to Tarquinius Priscus, the legendary fifth Roman king, which provides some insights into the theatricality of bodies in the ancient world (Pliny the Elder 35,24,106-108). In his account of the building of Roman channels, Pliny notes that the day laborers were growing weary of the work and were thus killing themselves in order to avoid further toil. He recounts:

> Since the citizens were seeking to escape from their exhaustion by committing suicide wholesale, the king devised a strange remedy that was never contrived except on that one occasion. He crucified the bodies of all who had died by their own hands, leaving them to be gazed at by their fellow-citizens and also torn to pieces by beasts and birds of prey. Consequently, the sense of shame, which is so characteristic of the Romans as a nation … then too came to their aid; but this it imposed upon them at the very moment when they blushed for their honour, since they felt ashamed while alive under the illusion that they would feel equally ashamed when dead.

In Pliny's mind, this event represents a *memorabilis exemplum*. Precisely here one observes the operative cultural-ideology. Not the idea of suicide but the humiliating public display of the body arrests the attention of the laborers. Such "memorable examples" reinforce the close relationship that exists between the cultural construction of the body and the colonizing force's use, abuse, and co-option of theatrics for the production of imperial imagery and ideology. Crucifixion is, of course, a particularly good locus for this form of bodily representation in the ancient world as the aim of this form of punishment was the visible display of the body for purposes of deterrence.[15]

In his panegyric for Trajan, Pliny the Younger equally demonstrates the rather apt connection between public spectacle and empire:

> Next came a public entertainment (*spectaculum*) – nothing lax or dissolute to weaken and destroy the manly spirit (*animos virorum molliret*), but one to inspire them to face honourable wounds and look scorn on death, by exhibiting love of glory and desire for victory, even in the persons of criminals and slaves (*Paneg.* 33.1).

Here even the lowliest bodies of the empire are able to signify the glory of public display, inspiring, in Pliny's valorization, duty and honor in the citizen. In this instance, one catches a glimpse of what Alison Futrell has labeled "idealized violence,"[16] which is violence that supports the order of the Roman empire and reinforces in the body of the subject the structures of imperial ideologies.[17] Moreover, the display of the body before the throngs of supportive spectators institutes and institutionalizes truth – the truth of the state – in and through the body bruised and bloodied, leading to a "ritual dramatization of the state's coercive power."[18] The connection between theater and the spectacle of the public arena becomes blurred precisely at this juncture, as it was not uncommon, especially in the early Empire, to provide reenactments of founding mythologies in public death. Kathleen M. Coleman has labeled this phenomenon "fatal charades,"[19] and it aptly captures the wide scope of ancient spectacle, wherein the world was in many respects a forum for identity performance – the performative dimension of the theater was as real in the arena as it was on the stage. Adding to this staged life-arena were visual representations, which

---

[15] See further D.G. Kyle, Spectacles of Death in Ancient Rome, New York 1998, 169; and K.M. Coleman, 'The Contagion of the Throng': Absorbing Violence in the Roman World, Hermathena 164, 1998, 65-88, esp. 69.

[16] A. Futrell, Blood in the Arena: The Spectacle of Roman Power, Austin/Texas 1997, 31. Cf. Perkins, Suffering Self, 115-117.

[17] E. Gunderson's contribution to this subject has been most helpful in this respect, as he seeks to establish the Roman arena as a "social organ of sight" for sustaining societal and cultural hierarchies in the empire. Using L. Althusser's concept of a "state Apparatus" for the political control of citizens, Gunderson explores the manifold ways in which the spectacle of death in the arena reinforces the cultural and political hegemony of the ruling classes. See E. Gunderson, The Ideology of the Arena, CA 15, 1996, 113-151; cf. idem, The Flavian Amphitheatre: All the World as Stage, in: Flavian Rome – Culture, Image, Text, ed. by A.J. Boyle/W.J. Dominik, Leiden 2003, 637-658; D. Fredrick, Mapping Penetrability in Late Republican and Early Imperial Rome, in his: The Roman Gaze. Vision, Power, and the Body, Baltimore 2002, 236-264, esp. 243-253; J. Walters, Making a Spectacle: Deviant Men, Invective, and Pleasure, Arethusa 31, 1998, 335-367; and Frilingos, Spectacles of Empire, 27-38.

[18] See further M.W. Gleason, Truth Contests and Talking Corpses, in: Constructions of the Classical Body, ed. by J.I. Porter, The Body in Theory, Ann Arbor 1999, 287-313, esp. 298-300. Cf. K.M. Coleman, 'Informers' on Parade, in: The Art of Ancient Spectacle, ed. by B. Bergmann/C. Kondoleon, Studies in the History of Art 56, New Haven 1999, 231-245.

[19] K.M. Coleman, Fatal Charades: Roman Executions Staged as Mythological Enactments, JRS 80, 1990, 44-73. Cf. Kyle, Spectacles of Death, 53-55.

were replete throughout the Empire and which served to reinscribe political and social power relations in larger than life images.[20] Moreover, literary texts also offered a form of spectacle for the reader, so that even in the reading of the "event," it was visualized palpably before the spectator.[21]

From the imperial(ized) margins of Empire, the spectacular gaze was both embraced but also resisted (sometimes in simultaneous movements). Lucian of Samosata, for instance, in several of his texts, offers a sardonic view of Rome as a city of spectacles, where (Greek) philosophy in particular is theatricalized and, in his view, loses its substance as a result.[22] Such resistance to the imperial gaze could also be found in a wide array of ancient texts. If "being, for a Roman, was being seen,"[23] the gaze could just as easily be reconfigured to look back on Rome – where Rome was laid bare by the "under side" of empire.[24] Reading early Christian literature within such a context of resistance to and redeployment of the imperial Roman gaze – the spectacle of power – offers a promising avenue of pursuit, not least because Christians on the edge (both socially and geographically) of empire also experienced the spectacle of violence up close, being grabbed by the throat as it were, through torture, martyrdom, and death.

Martyrdom is particularly noteworthy in this respect, as it was one of the most heightened forms of spectacle in the ancient Roman world,[25] and early Christian texts evidence extensive engagement of the visuality, visibility, and theatrics of this highly staged event.[26] In her recent book *Martyrdom and Mem-*

---

[20] Cf. J.R. Clarke, Art in the Lives of Ordinary Romans: Visual Representations of Non-Elite Viewers in Italy, 100 B.C.-A.D. 315, Berkeley 2003, 130-159; Frilingos, Spectacles of Empire, 16-21; and A. Kuttner, Hellenistic Images of Spectacle, from Alexander to Augustus, in: Art of Ancient Spectacle, 97-123; and P. Zanker, The Power of Images in the Age of Augustus, trans. by A. Shapiro, Ann Arbor 1988.

[21] For this phenomenon in Livy, see especially A. Feldherr, Spectacle and Society in Livy's History, Berkeley 1998. See further the development of this theme with respect to Acts in C. Vander Stichele/T. Penner, 'All the World's a Stage': The Rhetoric of Gender in Acts, in: Luke and His Readers: Festschrift A. Denaux, ed. by R. Bieringer/G. Van Belle/J. Verheyden, BEThL 182, Leuven 2005, 373-396, esp. 388-395.

[22] See the treatment of Nigrinus by T. Whitmarsh, Greek Literature and the Roman Empire: The Politics of Imitation, New York 2001, 254-279.

[23] C. Barton, Being in the Eyes: Shame and Sight in Ancient Rome, in: Roman Gaze, 216-235, esp. 220.

[24] See the excellent discussion of Tertullian, Achilles Tatius, and Lucian by S. Goldhill, The Erotic Eye: Visual Stimulation and Cultural Conflict, in: Being Greek under Rome: Cultural Identity, the Second Sophistic and the Development of Empire, Cambridge 2001, 154-194.

[25] See the treatment in D. Potter, Martyrdom as Spectacle, in: Theater and Society in the Classical World, ed. by R. Scodel, Ann Arbor 1993, 53-88.

[26] On this element of early Christian martyrdom narratives, see T. Penner/C. Vander Stichele, The Tyranny of the Martyr: Violence and Victimisation in Martyrdom Discourse and the Movies of Lars von Trier, in: Sanctified Aggression. Vocabularies of Violence in Bibles and Cultures, ed. by Y. Sherwood/J. Bekkenkamp, JSOT.S 400; BTFCS 3, Sheffield 2004, 175-192, esp. 176-184.

ory, Elizabeth Castelli has developed this particular theme in detail, demonstrating the variety of ways in which

> the narrative elements of performance, theatricality, and stage-managing that emerge out of various martyrological texts invite readers to understand the contest that is staged to have multiple layers of resonance and signification – and to begin to see the performative as itself a source of Christian commemorative counter-scripts.[27]

Castelli goes on to develop readings of martyrdom accounts that visualize the attempt by early Christians

> to wrest control of the spectacle from the hands of the producers and to put it in the hands either of the performers, the narrators, or the Christian audience ex post facto.[28]

As "counternarrative," these Christian accounts of spectacle in reverse seek to take the control of the body away from the perpetrators – and do so in a counter-spectacle every bit as worthy as any the imperial apparatus could contrive. Borrowing Jane Gallop's terminology, Simon Goldhill has designated this ancient counter-narrativizing strategy as "writing through the visual."[29] Herein, with respect to death and torture, the body is retrieved and restored – the spectacle of violence is reversed through the embrace of death and stoic self-acceptance of one's fate in an effort to make pain and suffering meaningful. It is true, of course, that much of the countering of spectacle was operative in *narrative* – a strategy employed by those who lack the necessary power to do so in practice. Still, much of early Christian narrative dynamics takes on more meaning if read in this context, as the political and social dimensions of the narrative become more readily open to view. Indeed, precisely at this juncture one is near, as noted above, the very center of the public performance of Christians in empire, as the technologies for the construction of the Christian self intersect with the machinery of power. Moving one step further than Foucault, one might even suggest that the very discursive structure of Christian self-identity is intricately connected to the spectacle of empire – replicating in the process its mechanisms for control and dominance.

All of these images of construction and performance are, moreover, related to perceptions of gender in the ancient world. Self-publication in this context was to be "published" as a male – exhibited before others as the ideal representation of human (and divine) performance. Depending on a variety of circumstances, there were different avenues for this exhibition of "manhood" in antiquity. As a constructed ideal identity performance, such experiences were not limited to males, of course. Select (and superior) females could also take this

---

27   E.A. Castelli, Martyrdom and Memory: Early Christian Culture Making, Gender, Theory, and Religion, New York 2004, 121.
28   Ibid., 122.
29   Goldhill, Erotic Eye, 194.

path of *manly* identity.[30] For early Christians, then, images of suffering could provide particularly potent discursive structures for argumentation and community formation, insofar as identities could be reconfigured through the use of such images. The role of body in all of this cannot be overstressed – it was precisely the centrality of the body, both as object of pain and suffering and as subject of manly display and comportment, that gave meaning to the spectacle of death by the machinery of state oppression and that also allowed such (exhibited) bodies to subvert the structures of power and dominance. Through all of this the Christian body was slowly being molded in its public display through an ongoing engagement with Jesus' bruised and bloodied flesh – the *passion* of the exemplary Christian body.

Exploring this ambient sphere of early Christian identification and reaction in more depth may help us read *and* see the *GP* in a new light. The gendered relationship of body to spectacle is, in our view, critical here to understanding the narrative logic and cultural rhetoric of this text, with the bodies on display forming a critical component of shaping *readerly* identities as a result. Bodies, both in their ideal state and in their deviant display, are thus important elements of narrative construction, and *GP* provides an intriguing forum for the examination of precisely this body matter in early Christianity.

Spectacle and Body in the Gospel of Peter

In his *Satyricon*, one of Petronius's characters, Eumolpus, tells a story about a soldier who was instructed to guard the body of a crucified man, in order to keep it from being taken down by relatives or friends (*Satyr.* 110-113). The story need not be repeated here in its entirety, but the upshot is that the soldier becomes obsessed with a woman, whose husband has died, and he tries to woo her away from her husband's dead body (which she is dutifully mourning). He succeeds, but in the course of doing so he lets down his guard and the body he is supposed to be watching is taken down off the cross. Realizing that his dereliction of duty may well cost him his life, the soldier goes into a panic, but the woman saves the day when she offers the body of her dead husband as a replacement for the one that the soldier "lost" on the cross. In its context, this story is intended to illustrate the fickleness of women, illustrating how quickly their devotion can change.

There are many features of this story that could be highlighted for a reading of *GP*, not least the issue of the dead body that disappears, and the trouble that this causes for those placed in charge of preventing such "theft." But what we want to highlight in particular here is the role that bodies play in Petro-

---

[30]   See further, Penner/Vander Stichele, Tyranny of the Martyr, 177-178 n. 11; and C. Vander Stichele/T. Penner, Paul and the Rhetoric of Gender, in their: Her Master's Tools? Feminist and Post-Colonial Engagements of Historical-Critical Discourse, Global Perspectives on the Bible 9, Atlanta 2005, 299 n. 32.

nius's story. First of all, dead bodies perform a pivotal role: *both* the one "sto-len" from the cross (which indicates the neglect of the soldier) and the one that is used to replace it – the body of the dead husband (representing the devotion of the wife). The soldier lures the woman away from the body of her husband, and the final "insult" is that the woman desacralizes the body of her beloved husband by having him hung on a cross (symbolizing, as noted in the story of Pliny the Elder above, a most horrific mode of post-mortem display). Second, in this story the bodies of the living are driven and defined by love and desire – the woman is devoted to her dead husband's body and the soldier desires the woman. Their respective actions in the narrative are understood to be the outward display and embodiment of these inner drives. Pivotal in this respect is the shift of the woman from devout widow to dedicated lover, a performative change that signals a capriciousness of character. The placement and comportment of the body thus forms a critical component for establishing the argumentative aim of the narrative. Both what is done to bodies and what is not done create the boundaries of cultural-ideology and it is evident that the body as a site of meaning – especially a "dead body" (which has attached to it all kinds of associations with rituals of honor and purity) – bears a potent argumentative force in antiquity.

In the *GP*, the body seems to function in a similar way. In this instance the crucified body of Jesus is used argumentatively to establish a powerful claim about the cultural superiority and authority of the Christian movement/faith. As we will suggest, *GP* can be read like a staged drama or play.[31] For our purposes, we are especially interested in the intersection of narrative logic, sociocultural rhetoric, and the spectacle of bodily representation in *GP*. In order to facilitate this analysis we will use the following division of the text into scenes based on narrative clues such as indications and changes of time and place and the introduction of new characters or changes of character.[32]

---

[31] It is not impossible in fact that the text may have served such a use, regardless of whether it was intended to be performed or not. The role of the theater in late antiquity is an oft neglected feature in the study of early Christianity. *GP* would have taken shape and been recited in a world inundated with theater performances and images. For the role of the theater in late antiquity, see esp. B. Leyerle, Theatrical Shows and Ascetic Lives: John Chrysostom's Attack on Spiritual Marriage, Berkeley-Los Angeles 2001, 13-41. It is quite plausible, in fact, that some Christian literary forms took their shape based on theatrical productions, perhaps deliberately being constructed with the possibility of the actual stage in view. – Seneca's tragedies, for instance, while they may not have been staged, certainly could have been in terms of the placement of the dramatic action. See W. Stroh, 'Give Us Your Applause!' The World of the Theatre, in: Gladiators and Caesars. The Power of Spectacle in Ancient Rome, ed. by E. Köhne/C. Ewigleben/R. Jackson, Berkeley-Los Angeles 2000, 119.

[32] A more detailed, if slightly different division of the text, can be found in C. Vander Stichele, Het Petrusevangelie: docetisch of polemisch? in: Het andere Christendom: De gnosis en haar geestverwanten, ed. by R. Roukema, Zoetermeer 2000, 47-64.

PART I: Execution and Death

Scene 1: End of trial and delivery to the people (vv. 1-5)
Scene 2: Execution (vv. 6-14)
Scene 3: Death (vv. 15-22)
Scene 4: Burial (vv. 23-24)

PART II: Guarding of the Tomb and Miraculous Events

Scene 1: Reactions to the death of the Lord (vv. 25-27)
Scene 2: Guarding of the Tomb (vv. 28-49)
     A. Installation of the Guard (vv. 28-33)
     B. Visit of the Crowd (v. 34)
     C. Miraculous Events (vv. 35-42)
     D. Report to Pilate (vv. 43-49)
Scene 3: Visit of the Women (vv. 50-57)
Scene 4: Return from the Feast (vv. 58-60)

Staging The Gospel of Peter

The place to begin the analysis is with a brief outline of the characters and titles that set the stage for the unfolding narrative because they already reveal something pivotal about the power dynamics at play in the text. In the first scene of the *GP* text fragment, near the end of the trial and delivery of Jesus to the people (vv. 1-5), both Herod and Pilate are presented as *rulers*. This portrayal is highlighted repeatedly in a variety of ways, most notable being that other people come to them to ask them for particular favors. Herod, moreover, is called "king" and he orders his minions to lead "the lord" away (v. 2). Although the name of "the lord" is never specified in the fragment, from a narrative standpoint it is evident that the title refers to Jesus. Indeed, this title becomes significant as it sets up the context for a "show-down" over the issue of authority. Indeed, as we will argue below, a fundamental battle for cultural identity is thereby waged and staged in the text.

In the execution scene (vv. 6-14) the same emphasis on authority continues, but here the focus shifts to the "lord." Once again the language is key, as three times specific titles are used in relatively quick succession: v. 6: "Let us drag away the *Son of God*, because we have got power over him"; v. 7: "Judge righteously, *King of Israel*"; and v. 9: "With this honour let us honour the *Son of God*." The titles thus clustered together specify the status of this lord in comparison with Herod and Pilate in the previous scene. Moreover, calling him king contrasts him more explicitly with Herod, who was identified as a king earlier. This juxtaposition of titles continues as the scene unfolds. When the lord is crucified between two malefactors, on his cross is written: "this is the *King of Israel*" (v. 11). One of the criminals reproaches the anonymous executors: "We are suffering for the evil, which we have committed. But this man, who has become the *saviour* (σοτήρ) *of men*, what wrong has he done to you" (v. 13)? To the titles "Son of God" and "King," both mentioned twice so far, the title "saviour of men" is now added, thus enhancing the importance of "the lord."[33]

The narrative soon turns from titular designations to palpable displays of power. When Jesus dies on the cross (vv. 15-22), he utters the only words he speaks in this text: "My power, power, you have forsaken me" (v. 19). Having said this, he is "taken up," at which moment the veil of the temple is torn in two. A similar effect is described in the next verse, where his body is taken from the cross and placed on the ground, which then begins to quake. Here one perceives what will become a central tenet in the following portion of the text: Jesus' death brings about climatic events that cause fear, a display of "power" patently evident everywhere. Jesus may have said that the power (δύναμις) has left him, but his body is no less potent for that.

The second part of the text (vv. 25-60) continues this line of development. The opening scene (vv. 25-27) describes the reactions to the death of the lord and situates the characters in terms of their specific responses. New characters, the elders and priests, are also introduced at this point. First, the reaction of the Jews and their religious authorities are mentioned. They begin to lament: "Woe on our sins! Judgment has come close and the end of Jerusalem" (v. 25). In vv. 26-27, the reaction of a second group is described, which provides an intriguing counterpoint to the reaction of the Jewish religious authorities. Given the consistent use of the third person in the preceding context, the sudden use of the first person here comes as a surprise. The first part of v. 26 is formulated in the singular: "But I mourned with my companions"; vv. 26b-27, however, proceed in the plural: "… and with disturbed senses we concealed ourselves. For we were being sought after by them as malefactors (cf. v. 13), and as persons who wanted to set fire to the temple" (v. 26b). The identity of the "I" and "we," as well as the identity of their persecutors, is not disclosed. Only in the last verse of this fragment, in v. 60, is the first person used again and now the identities of the speaker and his companions are revealed as Simon Peter and the other disciples. Apart from thus authorizing the embedded experience of the male disciples, this segment also sounds highly apologetic, as it justifies their earlier behavior. In other words, their absence receives a certain legitimacy, but their absence is duly noted nonetheless, and it offsets the public and involved pres-

---

[33] The imperial connotations of σοτήρ should not go unnoticed in this context; see further G. Gilbert, Roman Propaganda and Christian Identity in the Worldview of Luke-Acts, in: Contextualizing Acts: Lukan Narrative and Greco-Roman Discourse, ed. by T. Penner/ C. Vander Stichele, SBLSymS 20, Atlanta-Leiden 2003, 237-242; and T. Penner, Res Gestae Divi Christi: Miracles, Early Christian Heroes, and the Discourse of Power in Acts, in: The Role of Miracle Discourse in the Argumentation of the New Testament, ed. by D.F. Watson, SBLSymS, Atlanta-Leiden [forthcoming].

ence of the Jewish authorities in the events that are unfolding. This explicit
sense of who is present and who is absent becomes a critical aspect for setting
up the central scene of the *GP* narrative.

All events in the much longer second scene (vv. 28-49) largely take place
around the tomb, with a movement back and forth between the tomb and Pilate, whose location is not specified in the text. Again, space and place define
the relationship between the appointed Roman representatives and the now
"dead body" of the lord. The action begins with Pilate and in some sense ends
there too, but the beginning and ending point are radically redefined as a result
of the miraculous scene in between.

In the first subsection of this scene (vv. 28-33), at the request of the elders of
the Jews (vv. 29-30), Pilate orders a centurion named Petronius and his soldiers
to guard the tomb. As a result of their fear and out of worry that "his disciples
[might] come and steal him away, and the people suppose that he is risen from
the dead, and they do us evil" (v. 30), they are determined to secure the place
of burial. Scribes and elders accompany the soldiers (vv. 31-32) and all partici-
pate in rolling a large stone before the entrance, which is further secured with
seven seals. In the transitory v. 34 the visit of a crowd is noted, which inspects
the sealed tomb and thus serves as external witness to the security of the en-
tombment. Much like a modern day "magic" or "illusion" show, where the
magician asks specific members of his audience to check out the apparatus
used in the "trick" in order to ensure the integrity of event, so here the actions
serve the purpose of creating the "illusion" that this tomb is impenetrable – no
one can get in, no one can get out. Various representatives of socio-cultural and
political authorities, both Jewish and Roman, are present to ensure this im-
penetrability, as are members of the "audience" itself. While apologetic motives may also lurk behind such narrative constructions (e.g., the authorities
really did seal Jesus up in the tomb, so the disciples could not steal his body!),
the broader narrative rhetorical effect serves to heighten the potency of the
miracle that is about to unfold before the eyes of the spectators.

In the next subsection, the miracle itself is described. The events take place
"in the night in which the Lord's day dawned" (v. 35).[34] The soldiers who stand
guard hear a great voice/sound in heaven, then they see the heavens opened
and two men (δύο ἄνδρας) descend (v. 36). On its own accord, the stone before
the entrance starts to roll and the two men enter the tomb (v. 37). The soldiers
awaken the centurion and the elders (v. 38), so that all of the representative
authorities at the tomb are able to watch the unfolding spectacle. Then they see
how three men (τρεῖς ἄνδρας) come out of the tomb, two of them supporting the
third one and a cross following them (v. 39). Verse 40 further specifies that "the
head of the two reach[ed] to heaven, but that of the one who was led by them

---

[34]   The expression "Lord's day" forms a revealing type of Christian cultural intertexture, since
the "Lord's day" only takes on significance on the basis of the event just now being described
in the narrative. This kind of not so subtle infusion of Christian ritual into the narrative seems
to assume that a Christian audience is reading this text.

overpass[ed] the heavens." The onlookers also hear a voice coming from heaven, saying: "Have you preached to those who sleep?" (v. 41). To which from the cross comes the answer: "yes" (v. 42). Herein the central and unique contribution of *GP* appears: the dramatic spectacle of the resurrection. In a "procession" of sorts, and one might think here particularly of a "victory procession," the principle characters exit the tomb before the spectators. While they are still deliberating, they see the heavens open again and a human being (ἄνθρωπος) descends and enters the tomb (v. 44). They (unspecified) now hurry to Pilate to tell him what they have seen, declaring: "In truth he was the Son of God" (v. 45), urging him to commend the centurion and soldiers to keep silent (v. 47). This juxtaposition is essential, as the spectacular display of power – here literally manifested in the huge bodies of the three men – is now expressly contrasted with the fear of the rulers who put Jesus to death and are now forced to acknowledge (and cower in the face of) his superior power.[35] If the movement of the earthly powers is back and forth from the tomb to Pilate, by contrast, the movement of the heavenly powers is, as one would expect, between heaven and earth. The power nexus lies precisely at this junction of the two defining realms, securing this potent display as clearly that of an otherworldly power.

The next scene stands in stark contrast to the spectacle that has just unfolded before the narrative viewing audience, as it describes the visit of a number of women to the tomb (vv. 50-58).[36] It is all the stranger given the earlier noted absence of any disciples at the events taking place. Mary Magdalene is

---

[35] It is true, of course, that the third figure – presumably the lord – is being supported by the other two, who are evidently also spectacularly large. But one could hardly construct the unfolding event as a sign of weakness, since the narrative is clear that the spectators watch the unfolding events in awe. The imagery is much closer to images associated with the return from "battle" – a war has been waged, and the question to the cross more or less explicitly affirms this: the mission has been accomplished, the battle is over, Jesus has won (through his body), and now they emerge victorious. The unusual reference to the speaking cross is a notable feature of the *GP*. In the reading developed here, and depending on when the text is dated, the cross could also be viewed in light of the Constantinian standard. See further C. Ando, Imperial Ideology and Provincial Loyalty in the Roman Empire, Classics and Contemporary Thought 6, Berkeley-Los Angeles 2000, 259-269; and S.G. MacCormack, Art and Ceremony in Late Antiquity, Transformations of the Classical Heritage 1, Berkeley-Los Angeles 1981, 84-86. G.F. Snyder has argued that, along with most early Christian symbols in iconography, the cross, although it arises late as a symbol, nonetheless stresses victory rather than suffering. See his Ante Pacem: Archaeological Evidence of Church Life before Constantine, Macon 1985, 26-29. Thus it could quite easily elide in figurative value with the victory standard of the Roman army. By the time of John Chrysostom, the cross is clearly read as the Christian victory standard (cf. *laud. Paul.* 7) – and one can at least argue that the *GP* narrative could already have carried these associations for readers in other locales and times, if not for its initial audience/author (although the cross is a perennial feature of the passion narrative itself, so one cannot rule out that it simply plays a role in *GP* based on the narrative details).

[36] For a more detailed analysis of this passage, see C. Vander Stichele, Das Petrusevangelium: Eine Jüngerin des Herrn und ihre Freundinnen, in: Kompendium Feministische Bibelauslegung, ed. by L. Schottroff/M.-T. Wacker; Gütersloh 1998, 789-794.

explicitly introduced and described here as a "disciple of the Lord" (μαθήτρια), who goes to the tomb with her friends in order to do there "what women are accustomed to do for their dead loved ones" (v. 51). In an interesting parallel to the Jewish authority figures in the previous unit, fear is what drives the actions of these women. And if earlier the Jewish authorities and the male disciples were mourning and lamenting, it is now time for the female followers of Jesus to do so as well. But when they arrive at the tomb, they find it open and see a young man (νεανίσκος) sitting in the middle, who tells them that the one cruci-fied is risen and gone (v. 56). The response of the women to this news is fear and they flee (v. 57).

The final verses of the *GP* narrative, as we have it, once again turn to the first person (vv. 59-60). Explicit reference is now made to the twelve disciples (οἱ δώδεκα μαθηταὶ τοῦ κυρίου), who, apparently unaware of the events just de-scribed, now return home in mourning (v. 59),[37] as they do not yet know what the "outsiders" and readers know. In v. 60, the last verse of the text fragment, the identity of the "I" mentioned earlier (v. 26) is finally disclosed as Simon Peter.

Important for our analysis is that the disciples (male and female) only ap-pear at the beginning (scene 1) and end (scene 3-4) of the second part of the text and are thus clearly absent when the central events in the pivotal scene 2 take place. Their role can be perceived as marginal because their actions do not really contribute to the development of the narrative plot. This marginality, however, provides a critical lynchpin in the structure of the text: the focus thus rests squarely on the spectacle of the heavenly bodies, reaching to the heavens, witnessed by a cast of outsiders, both Jewish and Roman. Another point worth mentioning in this respect is the public character of this event, which upon closer inspection is dominated by male characters. It is the appearance of the women in the following scene which explicitly introduces the element of gen-der into the narrative, as their (lack of) initiative is explained in gender specific terms: they "had not done at the sepulcher of the Lord what women are accus-tomed to do for their dead loved ones" (v. 50). If the female disciple(s) are thus "authorized" to appear on the public forum, even if in secret, the hiding in private of the male disciples is all the more striking as a result.

Coming back, then, to the opening discussion of the crucified body in Petronius's story, it is critical to observe that the body plays a similar role in the *GP* narrative. That is, not only does the body express the socio-cultural ideol-ogy, the relationship of people to the body in question is essential for the rhe-torical argument that unfolds. Thus, the wife is depicted as fickle through her transition from one (dead) body to another (live) body, and her final act of desecration of her husband's body is understood to be a true act of treachery. Similarly, the *GP* narrative structure is overtly concerned to portray the dy-

---

37   Cf. the earlier description of their emotional response in vv. 26-27: they are grieving (ἐλυπούμην) and feel hurt (τετρωμένοι κατὰ διάνοιαν), they are mourning (πενθοῦντες) and weeping (κλαίοντες). Their actions are described as consisting of fasting, sitting and hiding.

namics of the relation to the body of the lord. Those in power have a critical role to play in terms of their public pre- and post-mortem roles in the death of Jesus. And their presence in Jesus' death and at his tomb is notably off set by the absence of Jesus' followers. The stage managing in *GP* is quite purposeful in this regard, as it brings Jesus into a direct show-down with his persecutors. Moreover, the action then becomes centered, as a result, on the pivotal scene of triumph, as the resurrection takes center stage. At this juncture, the role of the body takes on even greater significance, as the dead body of Jesus has been transformed – in quite opposite fashion to the story in Petronius, where the dead body is desecrated, here the vivified body is on spectacular and glorious theatrical display.

Heavenly Power and Male Bodies

Returning to the central event in *GP*, then, we can see how the spectacular resurrection scene is framed by two different categories of people. At stake here is a show-down of sorts between male power brokers, with the rhetorical focus being on the interplay between the two loci of power. Here titles, "confessions," and spectacular displays of power weave throughout the text, affirming the central tenet that Jesus' body – alive or dead – is a potent force to be reckoned with and that this body, and ultimately this one alone, is the ruling body. Indeed, in line with other ancient portrayals of post-mortem resurrection, the heroic paradigm frames the action in the narrative.[38] Further, the fact that the "third person" has a body that rises to the heavens – towering over those below – palpably creates the impression that this body is unique, literally and metaphorically towering above all others.[39] Although not an ascension proper (the focus of the narrative turns to the *reaction*, so we are not told of what happens to the procession issuing forth from the tomb), it would be hard not to see here some traces of apotheotic imagery in this text, especially in an ancient culture familiar with the emperor cult and *his* post-death transposition to the heavens. As Mary Beard and John Henderson aptly note, "apotheosis intrinsically turns on cinematography,"[40] the *movement* between earth and heaven being a critical component of the imagery of ascension writ large in imperial

---

[38] On resurrection as a motif in heroic portrayal, see J.P. Hershbell, Philostratus's Heroikos and Early Christianity: Heroes, Saints, and Martyrs, in: Philostratus's Heroikos: Religion and Cultural Identity in the Third Century C.E., ed. by E. Bradshaw Aitken/J.K. Berenson MacLeon, SBLWGRW 6, Atlanta 2004, 173-176.

[39] In this context, the numismatic image of Emperor Constantine standing between two sons is intriguing. In this particular coin, Constantine appears decidedly taller than the two sons who flank him, indicating his stature as the greatest one, from whom the other two descend. See MacCormack, Art and Ceremony in Late Antiquity, 189. Plate 45.

[40] M. Beard/J. Henderson, The Emperor's New Body: Ascension from Rome, in: Parchments of Gender: Deciphering Bodies in Antiquity, ed. by M. Wyke, Oxford 1998, 202.

iconography.[41] Looking at the earlier noted spatial dimensions between tomb and court-room (Pilate/Herod), we now see that the spatial dimension has shifted. The spectators still run back to Pilate to reveal what they have seen, but the axis now runs along heaven and earth. There is, however, no actual transposition from earth to heaven in this imagery. Rather than taking off in a chariot (like Julius Caesar or Marcus Aurelius), the lord is every bit as present on earth as he is in heaven. The apotheosis of this ruler does not entail a *departure* – it rather implies his *arrival*.[42] Unlike the departed *numen* of the emperor, here the body of the lord – transformed, made large in space and time – is what remains. This is truly a spectacle of absolute power, and the body is used to communicate the extremity and extent of this authority.

Furthermore, Beard and Henderson also note that these body manifestations, transformations, and movements are by necessity gendered images.[43] The show-down between the two spheres of power is a battle waged between males. As a gladiator returning from the fight in the arena, the resurrected Lord appears triumphant, supported here by the two white-robed men.[44] Quite rightly from the narrator's perspective, such a demonstration should/and does inspire awe.[45] An analysis of the narrative framing helps firm up this rhetorical dimension of the text.

The role of Joseph of Arimethia in this connection is perhaps most intriguing. He is introduced in v. 3 and called a friend (φίλος) of both Pilate and the Lord. Since he realizes that the lord is about to be crucified, he goes to Pilate and asks him for his body in order to bury it. Pilate in turn addresses Herod with the same question, to which Herod replies in v. 4: "Brother Pilate, even if no one had asked for him, we would have buried him since the Sabbath draws on. For it is written in the law that the sun should not set on one that had been put to death." Verses 23-24, describing the funeral of the body, bring this first

---

[41] Ibid., 203-204.

[42] On the ascension of the emperor, see Gilbert, Roman Propaganda and Christian Identity, 242-247. The imperial imagery that depicts Augustus as the one who unites heaven and earth – holding the power over both realms and controlling the flow of that power on earth – is abundant in the Empire. *GP* seems to draw on such enthronement imagery in its presentation of Christ as ruler of the universe. In the Sarcophagus of Junius Bassus, for instance, the enthroned Christ has "cosmos" under his feet and is flanked by two representatives. *GP* may here be combining the imagery of enthronement and the kingly adventus, where the newly arrived monarch enters the city. Cf. E. Struthers Malbon, The Iconography of the Sarcophagus of Junius Bassus, Princeton 1990, 49-53, as well as MacCormack, Art and Ceremony in Late Antiquity, 127-132. MacCormack emphasizes that the adventus has the main focus on "presence" rather than arrival (55-57), with the accent falling on the ability of the "superhuman" power to protect his subjects from harm (23).

[43] Beard/Henderson, Emperor's New Body, 204.

[44] Cf. C. Jones, Processional Colors, in: Art of Ancient Spectacle, 251-252, who notes that in a procession white is normally worn by groups and purple by individuals.

[45] G.B. Ladner draws attention to the cosmic significance of the cross (given its four-point representational nature) in late antique Christianity, which thus potentially enhances the cosmic symbolism here in *GP*. See his: God, Cosmos, and Humankind. The World of Early Christian Symbolism, trans. by T. Dunlap, Berkeley-Los Angeles 1995, 99-101.

part of the text to an end. Here, as in the first verses, the Jews and Joseph are again mentioned. The Jews are said to rejoice and to hand over the body to Joseph, who puts it in his own tomb, called the Garden of Joseph. The most interesting feature about this framing story is this: from the beginning, the rulers who put Jesus to death *do not really control his body*, although in their arrogance they may think they do so. Although there are clearly multiple ways in which this segment functions, the semiotics of the body are manifestly operative. In the Petronius and Pliny citations discussed above, the crucified body was to remain on the cross – that was where the spectacle of crucifixion received its powerfully horrific imaging. It is the exposure of the body – to the elements, to the animals, but most of all to the spectators – that made crucifixion the drama, the staged cruelty, the ancient spectacle it was. Such display of the body ultimately served the power of those who damage, desecrate, and destroy this body. Imperial power could reach out and dominate the body in this way – batter it, bloody it, torture it, expose it, kill it. The body thus bore in itself the witness to this power. *But*, in *GP*, the perpetrators – the imperial representatives – right from the beginning lose their control over this body. There is no suggestion that because of their laxity Jesus *can* therefore return; this is no mere signifier of cause and effect. Rather, it is about what bodies communicate – what control of bodies signals in this cultural ideology. From the perspective of the narrators and readers of *GP*, there never was a chance that Jesus' body could be so dominated and destroyed. Still, that recognition and "confession" does not derail the "reality" that these rulers cannot dominate and control Jesus' body with proper authority.

Joseph, a minor character (not even a disciple), is the one who has control of the body, and shows proper respect in burying it. This positioning vis-à-vis the body signals what is at stake for the diverse cast of characters. For "outsiders" it is their loss of control and the instillation of fear that results. The behavior by the "insiders" (although represented somewhat more implicitly) replicates the response of outsiders: they grieve and lament over a body they do not "control" or have in their "possession." The reasons for this portrayal of insiders deserve further exploration, as the negative stereotyping may simply function apologetically, serving to remove the disciples from the scene. But even that is noteworthy, as it signals the centrality of the body in defining the action of the narrative. In the end, then, the body of the crucified lord possesses multiple significance, ultimately functioning to characterize those who come into contact with it. Unlike in the story of Petronius noted above, however, the body of the Lord cannot be exposed or destroyed – it is invincible. As such, it represents the male body in all its *divine* glory. Moreover, given the absence of "insiders" from the resurrection scene, the grand finale is now undoubtedly a fully *public* event, wherein this male body is manifested on the public stage for all the powers that be to see.

(En)Countering Narrative

When one reads *GP* in this way, it becomes evident that the meaning of this somewhat enigmatic, fragmentary story becomes all the more complex. Above all, in this essay, we have argued for a repositioning of the body as the central trope through which to examine the rhetorical configuration of argumentation in the text. Perhaps one can perceive here traces of a cultural-ideological battle, between (vestiges of?) Roman imperial control and that of a burgeoning group of Christians in empire. One can also observe a deeply rooted commitment to offering a counter-narrative of the body in Christian discourse. This counter-narrative offers a body (of a crucified man) that is invincible, manly, with the body of the lord emerging in victory and conquest over Sin and Death, but also over Empire. Herein one perceives how narrative resistance and reversal also run the very real risk of reinscribing the mechanisms of power and domination that are being subverted. Further, more complex interplays can be observed between the body of the lord, spanning heaven and earth, ruling the *oikoumene* as the new *sotēr*, and the development of the rituals associated with the body of Christ in the Christian community. The body of Christ is *that* body with which early Christians are to identify – the one they are to mimic through self-discipline and control. At the center of these images rests a body that is thoroughly "male," which is a critically important point for consideration, as the male body is precisely the body through and in which the Christian is to "self-publish" him/herself on the public stage.

A further point to be made in this light is that, at its core, Christian reflection on the passion, at least in *GP*, is a male-centered enterprise. Here an intricate relationship takes shape between the ancient gendered dynamics and the modern academic "publication" of the self. In view of this emergent dynamic, the discussion at the outset regarding the reading of the passion in *GP* in contemporary scholarship gains added significance, as the marks of that textual male body bear a strong imprint on the scholarship that surfaces in interaction and reflection on that body. The passion as performed – from the male center – in *GP* is re-constituted in each historical reconstruction, and a reinscription of hegemonic discourse occurs as a result. True, *GP* as counter-narrative in modern scholarship replaces the passion as counter-narrative in *GP*, but the central semiotic meaning of the flesh prevails – and, as a result of failing to pay careful attention to these ancient and modern cultural dynamics, the accent on unitary origins and linear transmissions may further occlude our own complicity in the replication and dissemination of the body of/in this text.

Register

1. Stellenregister

Altes Testament

Neues Testament

Jüdische Schriften der hellenistisch-römischen Zeit

Christliche Apokryphen

Petrusevangelium

Papyri und Ostraka

2. Moderne Autoren

3. Sachregister